A METHODICAL SYSTEM OF UNIVERSAL LAW:
OR, THE LAWS OF NATURE AND NATIONS,
WITH SUPPLEMENTS AND A DISCOURSE
BY GEORGE TURNBULL

NATURAL LAW AND
ENLIGHTENMENT CLASSICS

Knud Haakonssen
General Editor

Johann Gottlieb Heineccius

NATURAL LAW AND
ENLIGHTENMENT CLASSICS

A Methodical System of Universal Law:

Or, the Laws of Nature and
Nations, with Supplements
and a Discourse
by George Turnbull

Johann Gottlieb Heineccius

Translated from the Latin by George Turnbull

Edited and with an Introduction by
Thomas Ahnert and Peter Schröder

LIBERTY FUND

Indianapolis

This book is published by Liberty Fund, Inc., a foundation established to encourage study of the ideal of a society of free and responsible individuals.

𒂼𒄄

The cuneiform inscription that serves as our logo and as the design motif for our endpapers is the earliest-known written appearance of the word "freedom" (*amagi*), or "liberty." It is taken from a clay document written about 2300 B.C. in the Sumerian city-state of Lagash.

Introduction, annotations, bibliography, index © 2008 by Liberty Fund, Inc.

C 1 2 3 4 5 6 7 8 9 10
P 1 2 3 4 5 6 7 8 9 10

Frontispiece: Copper engraving of Johann Gottlieb Heineccius by Martin Berningeroth (1732). Reproduced courtesy of Universitäts- und Landesbibliothek Sachsen-Anhalt in Halle (Saale).

Library of Congress Cataloging-in-Publication Data
Heineccius, Johann Gottlieb, 1681–1741.
A methodical system of universal law: or, The laws of nature and nations: with supplements and a discourse/by Johann Gottlieb Heineccius, George Turnbull; translated from the Latin by George Turnbull; edited and with an introduction by Thomas Ahnert and Peter Schröder.
v. cm.—(Natural law and enlightenment classics)
Originally published: London, Printed for G. Keith [etc.], 1763.
Includes bibliographical references and index.
Contents: v. 1. Of the law of nature—v. 2. Of the law of nations.
ISBN-13: 978-0-86597-478-4 (hb: alk. paper)   ISBN-13: 0-86597-479-1 (pbk.: alk. paper)
1. Natural law—Early works to 1800. 2. Natural law. 3. International law.
I. Turnbull, George, 1698–1748. II. Ahnert, Thomas. III. Schröder, Peter.
IV. Title. V. Title: Methodical system of universal law.
VI. Title: Law of nature and nations.
KZ2314.A3H45   2008
340′.112—dc22   2007031757

LIBERTY FUND, INC.
8335 Allison Pointe Trail, Suite 300
Indianapolis, Indiana 46250-1684

CONTENTS

INTRODUCTION

The development of early modern natural law theories is an integral part of the Enlightenment,[1] and the writings of Johann Gottlieb Heineccius (1681–1741) are an important example of this close relationship. Heineccius wrote when the modern European natural law tradition was already long established, especially through the important works of Hugo Grotius (1583–1645), Samuel Pufendorf (1632–94), and Christian Thomasius (1655–1728). Notably the works of Grotius and Pufendorf had gained significant influence throughout Europe, assisted by congenial translations and annotations from the Huguenot refugee Jean Barbeyrac (1674–1744).[2]

Heineccius drew on the works of these theorists and responded to them, but his *Methodical System of Universal Law: Or, the Laws of Nature and Nations* was far more than a synthesis and a commentary on the salient writings of the previous generations. It was a distinctive system of natural jurisprudence, which, together with his writings on Roman law, helped to secure Heineccius a certain international fame already in his lifetime. In the Netherlands, where he taught for several years, he enjoyed a considerable academic reputation, which was reinforced by his personal acquaintance with the house of Orange. He held prestigious positions at two leading German universities of the early Enlightenment, Frankfurt an der Oder and Halle. In England and Scotland,

---

1. This link is best accounted for in Hochstrasser, *Natural Law Theories in the Early Enlightenment*. See also Tuck, *Natural Rights Theories,* especially p. 174. This view is restated in Tuck's *The Rights of War and Peace.*

2. On Jean Barbeyrac, see Rathlef, *Geschichte jetzlebender Gelehrten, Johan Barbeirak,* 1–65; Othmer, *Berlin und die Verbreitung des Naturrechts in Europa;* and Hochstrasser, "Conscience and Reason," pp. 289–308.

George Turnbull's translation of Heineccius's *System* was issued twice, in 1741 and 1763, making Heineccius's natural jurisprudence more accessible to English-speaking audiences. Turnbull expressed great admiration for Heineccius in the preface to his translation, saying that "[t]he author of this system of the law of nature and nations is so well known, and in so high esteem in the republic of letters, that it would be arrogance in me to say any thing in recommendation of his works. Nor need I make any apology for translating into our language so excellent a book upon a subject of such universal importance."[3] As late as 1799 the Scottish lawyer Sir James Mackintosh paid Heineccius a slightly backhanded compliment by describing him as "the best writer of elementary books with whom I am acquainted on any subject."[4] Heineccius even played an important and lasting role in the Spanish, South American, and Italian academic worlds, where purified editions (*editiones castigatae*) suppressed those quotations and statements that could be seen as challenging the Catholic Church but where his divine voluntarism was welcome.[5]

Heineccius's Life

Heineccius began his academic career by studying theology in Leipzig and then law in Halle, where he became a pupil of the controversial jurist and philosopher Christian Thomasius. The University of Halle was newly founded (1694) and one of the most important centers of the early Enlightenment in Germany. It was an intellectually thriving institution, which Heineccius took advantage of by attending lectures on a variety of subjects, including philosophy and rhetoric, taught by Samuel Stryck (1640–1710) and Johannes Franz Budde (1667–1729). His intellectual curiosity clearly was stimulated, as was his talent for free oration and

---

3. Turnbull, preface, p. 5.
4. Quoted in Haakonssen, *Natural Law and Moral Philosophy,* p. 88.
5. There were no fewer than five editions of the collected works: 18 volumes, Venice 1743, 2nd edition 1761; 8 volumes, Geneva 1744–48, 2nd edition 1768–71; 12 volumes, Naples 1759. See Luig, "Gli elementa iuris civilis di J. G. Heineccius," pp. 259–74.

lecturing, which his son later praised in a laudatory biography. In 1723 Heineccius accepted a professorship at the Frisian University of Fra-neker. From this small but distinguished university Heineccius's repu-tation quickly spread to most of Europe, especially because of his text-books on Roman law, which was his main area of research and teaching at Franeker. Despite all attempts to keep him in Franeker, Heineccius changed to a professorship at the University of Frankfurt an der Oder in 1727.[6]

Two years later he declined a position at the University of Utrecht, but a royal order forced him to return to Halle in 1733 because the Brandenburg-Prussian government hoped to reestablish the reputation of this university. Halle had suffered severely from the disputes between theologians at the university and the philosopher Christian Wolff (1679–1754), who had been forced to leave Halle in 1723 after he had been ac-cused of denying the existence of free will. Heineccius spent the rest of his career in Halle and developed an impressive range of lectures. One of the products of these was his *System,* which was first published in 1738 as *Elementa iuris naturae et gentium* and which saw at least four further editions.

Heineccius's Natural Jurisprudence

In the original preface, which Turnbull did not translate, Heineccius modestly explained that he wanted to provide a short commentary on the law of nature and nations for his students and pupils. In fact, Hei-neccius in the *System* developed a distinctive theory of natural law. He disagreed, for example, with the view of the state of nature which had been put forward by Samuel Pufendorf, whose *De officio hominis et civis*

---

6. All biographical accounts rely on the information provided by Heineccius's son, J. C. G. Heineccius, in *De vita, fatis et scriptis Jo. Gottlieb Heineccii iurisconsulti.* The most recent biographical account of Heineccius with detailed information about the dissemination of his writings is to be found in Bergfeld, "Johann Gottlieb Heineccius und die Grundlagen seines Natur- und Völkerrechts." On Heineccius's critique of Grotius see Reibstein, "Johann Gottlieb Heineccius als Kritiker des grotianischen Systems."

(1673) had become *the* textbook on natural law throughout much of northern Europe.[7] Humans, Heineccius wrote, were subject to natural law in the state of nature. It was not enough to say, as Pufendorf did, that the law of nature was derived from the obligation to cultivate sociality, to which men were compelled by necessity. The law of nature included duties of humans toward themselves and toward God—duties which would be applicable even to a solitary human being.[8] Heineccius's tripartite division of the duties of humans into those toward self, others, and God had its roots in a long intellectual tradition, and it is likely that Heineccius encountered it in the writings and lectures of his teacher Christian Thomasius in Halle.[9] Heineccius's definition of the morally good as "whatever tends to preserve and perfect man" and of a "good action" as that "which contributes to human preservation and perfection"[10] is also very similar to Thomasius's definition of the morally good in his second work on natural law, the *Foundations of the Law of Nature and Nations* of 1705: "Do that which makes human life as long-lasting and happy as possible, and avoid that which makes life unhappy and hastens death";[11] so is Heineccius's definition of love as the central principle of natural law: "Love in us is the desire of good, joined with delight in its perfection and happiness."[12] There are only three possible objects

7. Hutcheson suggested that "the learned will at once discern how much of this compend [his *Philosophiae moralis institutio compendiaria*] is taken from the writings of others, from Cicero and Aristotle, and to name no other moderns, from Puffendorf's smaller work, de officio hominis et civis" (p. i of the 1747 translation, *A Short Introduction to Moral Philosophy*). For Hutcheson's "struggle with the Pufendorfian legacy" as Haakonssen puts it on p. 90 of his *Natural Law and Moral Philosophy,* see also Schröder, "Natural Law and Enlightenment in Comparative Perspective." For the widespread influence of Pufendorf throughout the eighteenth century, see Luig, "Zur Verbreitung des Naturrechts in Europa," and Dufour, "Die ecole romande du droit naturel—ihre deutschen Wurzeln."

8. Heineccius, *System*, p. 327.

9. See, for example, Thomasius's *Institutiones jurisprudentiae divinae,* bk. II, chaps. 1–3.

10. Heineccius, *System,* p. 11.

11. "Facienda esse, quae vitam hominum reddunt & maxime diuturnam & felicissimam: & evitanda, quae vitam reddunt infelicem & mortem accelerant" (Thomasius, *Fundamenta juris naturae et gentium,* p. 21.

12. Heineccius, *System,* p. 68.

of the offices of love, which correspond to the tripartite division of duties: "God, the creator of all things; ourselves, who are certainly the nearest to ourselves; and other men, whom we plainly perceive to be by nature equal to us."[13]

Love, as a motive, created an "internal" obligation to perform moral actions, which, Heineccius is suggesting, are generally also to the advantage of the agent. But this internal obligation was insufficient, because mankind was often mistaken about the nature of moral goods and, like Ixion in ancient mythology, who tried to seduce a cloud in the shape of the goddess Juno, often embraced false goods. Immorality could be a reflection of mistaken beliefs, rather than vicious intentions. Heineccius thereby modified the ideas of Christian Thomasius, who had argued that the desire for the true good was prior to any beliefs in the intellect. Once the desire for good, which Thomasius identified with the love for God, had established itself in human nature, true beliefs about the nature of the morally good followed spontaneously.[14] Heineccius, however, argued that the general desire for what was morally good was not enough. It was necessary to have a prior rule or standard, which defined what was to be considered morally good and which directed the abstract desire for morality toward the right ends. This rule constituted the external obligation arising from the will of some "Being whose authority we are obliged to acknowledge."[15] In the case of the law of nature this Being was God: "The law of nature, or the natural rule of rectitude, is a system of laws promulgated by the eternal God to the whole human race by reason."[16] Heineccius's notion of a "rule of rectitude" may well have been motivated by the desire to correct the radical anti-intellectualism of Christian Thomasius's moral theory. Thomasius's emphasis on the pre-intellectual guidance of the heart, rather than the understanding, in moral actions was a position many contemporaries

13. Ibid., p. 68.
14. Thomas Ahnert, *Religion and the Origins of the German Enlightenment*, chap. 7.
15. Heineccius, *System*, pp. 16–17.
16. Ibid., p. 19.

associated with "enthusiasm," a label Heineccius would have been keen to avoid.[17]

Turnbull's Life and His Response to Heineccius

George Turnbull (1698–1748) was one of the key figures of the Scottish Enlightenment who was familiar with contemporary developments in European theories of natural law. His education and intellectual formation took place in Edinburgh, where he graduated from the university there in 1721.[18] In 1721 he became a regent at Marischal College, Aberdeen, where Thomas Reid was among his students.[19] Leaving the university in 1727, he traveled as tutor of young aristocrats in Europe. After joining the Anglican Church (bachelor of civil law, Oxford University, 1733) he was ordained in 1739, became chaplain to the Prince of Wales, and, finally, served as a minister in County Derry. During this period he started to draw his experiences together in a wide range of different writings, including his translation of Heineccius.[20] His extensive notes surveyed modern natural law and introduced his readers to significant authors, such as Johann Franz Budde, who were barely known in Britain. At the same time, Turnbull's notes added substantially to the ideas he found in Heineccius's work. Often Turnbull developed Heineccius's theory to his own liking, telling the reader what the latter really should have said.

17. On enthusiasm and the Enlightenment see Pocock, "Enthusiasm: The Anti-Self of Enlightenment," pp. 7–28; Ahnert, "Enthusiasm and Enlightenment"; and Ahnert, *Religion and the Origins of the German Enlightenment,* especially chap. 2.

18. On Turnbull's biography and intellectual development see Norton, "George Turnbull and the Furniture of the Mind," and Stewart, "George Turnbull and Educational Reform."

19. See the introduction by Knud Haakonssen in Reid, *Practical Ethics,* especially pp. 7ff.

20. Apart from the work we are concerned with, the most important writings by Turnbull include *A Treatise on Ancient Painting* (1740), in part in *Education for Life,* edited by Stewart and Wood; *Principles of Moral Philosophy* (1740) and *Christian Philosophy* (1740), which were joined to become *The Principles of Moral and Christian Philosophy* (1740), new edition by Broadie; and *Observations upon Liberal Education* (1742), new edition by Moore.

Turnbull accepted Heineccius's definition of love, for example, as the central ethical principle of natural law, but criticized his distinction between internal and external obligation, a distinction which he regarded as artificial and unnecessary. There was no need for an external obligation in the sense of a rule imposed by a superior. The obligation of natural law was reinforced externally by the natural connection between virtue and temporal happiness or prosperity. There were exceptions, but on the whole "the far greater part of the evils and miseries complained of in human life, are the effects and consequences of vicious passions, and their pursuits. Whence else is it that honesty is so universally pronounced the best policy, and dishonesty folly?"[21] Punishments for immorality and rewards for morally good actions were part of the natural order created by God, not imposed in individual cases by particular acts of the divine will. There was no need to add another, "external" obligation, a "rule of rectitude," to this,[22] because the existing, natural connection between morality and happiness was already a sufficient indication of God's providential will for humanity. Moral philosophy, therefore, involved the study of natural causes and effects, in the same way as natural philosophy.[23] The consequence of this natural connection or tendency in human affairs was that the actual distribution of goods, such as happiness or wealth in this world, on the whole reflected the virtue and merit of those who owned or enjoyed them. It is important to note, however, that although morality was also advantageous, of course not every self-interested action was automatically virtuous. Turnbull distinguished the advantages of morality from vulgar notions of self-interest, which were attributed to Epicureans and the followers of Mandeville and which implied that actions were morally justified because they were self-interested. Turnbull's emphasis on the advantageousness of morality was intended to prove the existence of a theodicy, in a loose sense, a belief that tem-

21. Turnbull, *Principles,* ed. Broadie, p. 383. See also Ahnert, "Pleasure, Pain, and Punishment in the Early Enlightenment."

22. See Heineccius, *System,* Turnbull's comments following bk. I, chap. III (pp. 71–74).

23. Turnbull, *Principles,* vol. I, "Preface."

poral affairs reflected the benevolent influence of a divine justice and providence.

The rewards for virtue in this life included property. Although the truly virtuous person knew how to be happy without material goods, only he or she could "have true happiness from them."[24] It was "a fact too evident to be called into question" that "man is made to purchase every thing by industry, and industry only, every good, internal or external."[25] The actual distribution of property, in general, reflected the merit of its owners, for if "we own a blind fortuitous dispensation of goods, and much more, if we own a malignant dispensation of them, or a dispensation of them more in favour of vice than of virtue, we deny a providence, or assert bad administration."[26] In fact, however, "the universe is governed by excellent general laws, among which this is one, 'That industry shall be the purchaser of goods, and shall be generally successful.'"

This "general law of industry"[27] had important implications for Turnbull's political theory. Turnbull believed that political society was essential for humans to reach the highest degree of happiness possible for them in this life.[28] As Turnbull explained in another work, "many of the goods of life are by our social constitution dependent upon the right government of society," that is, on "a good politic constitution, and the impartial execution of good laws."[29] Constitutional structures and the distribution of property were closely related because "a greater share of external goods, or of property, naturally begets power. And hence it will and must always hold as a general law, That dominion will follow property or that changes in property will beget certain proportional changes in government."[30] It is this belief in the close connection between gov-

---

24. Turnbull, *Principles,* vol. I, part II, chap. iii, p. 390.
25. Turnbull's remarks on Heineccius, *System,* bk. I, chap. IX, p. 200.
26. Ibid.
27. Ibid.
28. "[T]here is a perfection and happiness attainable by a rightly constituted civil state, to which mankind can no otherwise attain" (Turnbull's remarks on bk. II, chap. VI, p. 425).
29. Turnbull, *Principles,* vol. I, part II, chap. III, p. 392.
30. Ibid.

ernment and property ownership which helps to explain Turnbull's strong interest in the political theory of James Harrington (1611–77), whom he often quotes at length in his comments on Heineccius's text.

Harrington's central aim had been to solve the same problem as his contemporary Thomas Hobbes (1588–1679), the threat of anarchy following from constitutional collapse. However, Turnbull's interest in Harrington was more the Englishman's view of the relationship between property and political power. Harrington, he said, "reasons from natural causes in these matters, as natural philosophers do about phenomena commonly called natural ones."[31] Like Harrington, Turnbull argued that the ownership of property, especially of landed property, was the natural basis of power. If one man owns far more land than all others taken together, then the constitution will be that of an absolute monarchy. If a small group of people holds the greatest proportion of land, this leads either to aristocracy or a regulated monarchy. Popular government emerges when "neither one nor the few over-balance the whole people."[32] This connection between political power and property meant that Turnbull made his theory of government into a part of his theory of divine providence and justice. Any form of government which did not reflect the prevailing balance of property in a society was unnatural and had to be based on violence. It was possible for humans to influence the distribution of property, but "wherever, thro' causes unforeseen by human prudence, the balance comes to be intirely changed, it is the more immediately to be attributed to divine providence: And since God cannot will the cause, but he must also will the necessary effect or consequence, what government soever is in the necessary direction of the balance, the same is of divine right."[33] Ultimately, the providential distribution of material goods determined the balance of power within the state.

Thomas Ahnert
Peter Schröder

---

31. Turnbull's remarks on bk. II, chap. VI, p. 438.
32. Ibid., p. 430.
33. Ibid., pp. 432.

A NOTE ON THE TEXT

The present edition is based on the text of the 1741 London edition, which was a translation of the first edition, published in Latin, in Halle, in 1738.

Heineccius's and Turnbull's notes are indicated by asterisks, daggers, and single square brackets; editorial notes within original notes are contained within double square brackets. All other new editorial notes and references are indicated by arabic numerals. The "Remarks" sections at the end of some chapters are by Turnbull.

The original references by Johann Gottlieb Heineccius and George Turnbull are often incomplete or inaccurate. We have therefore provided the full title when a work is first mentioned by Heineccius or Turnbull, though it is not always possible to determine the precise editions they used. In the case of classical authors we refer to modern editions, unless indicated otherwise in the notes. Full publication details for works cited in the notes are provided in the bibliography to the extent that this has been possible. The exact sources of quotations and paraphrases are identified whenever possible. References to Roman civil law and the Bible are not explained in the footnotes, unless there are specific reasons for doing so. The archaic spelling of the 1741 text has been retained, though printer's errors have been silently corrected. Page breaks in the original text are indicated by the use of angle brackets. For example, page 112 begins after <112>.

A general note on references to Roman law: Roman civil law, the *Corpus Iuris Civilis,* includes the *Digest,* the *Code of Justinian,* and the *Institutes.* In references these texts are abbreviated as "D.," "C.," and "Inst.," respectively. The rest of the reference is to the relevant book and title of a law—"1. 24. D. de ritu nupt.," for example, refers to the laws on the rites of marriage ("de ritu nuptiarum") in book 24 of the *Digest.*

ACKNOWLEDGMENTS

We are very grateful to Knud Haakonssen for his invitation to contribute this volume to the Natural Law and Enlightenment Classics series and for his advice and support. We are also much indebted to a number of friends and colleagues for their help and encouragement and should like to thank Antony Hatzistavrou and Jenny Gibbon, in particular, for their help in identifying the sources of some Greek quotations.

BOOK I
OF THE LAW OF NATURE

A METHODICAL SYSTEM

OF

Universal Law:

OR, THE

LAWS *of* NATURE *and* NATIONS
DEDUCED
From CERTAIN PRINCIPLES, and applied
to PROPER CASES.

Written in *Latin* by the CELEBRATED

JO. GOT. HEINECCIUS,

Counsellor of State to the King of Prussia,
and Professor of PHILOSOPHY at *Hall.*

Translated, and illustrated with Notes and Supplements,

By *GEORGE TURNBULL,* LL. D.

To which is added,
A DISCOURSE upon the Nature and Origine of MORAL and CIVIL
LAWS; in which they are deduced, by an Analysis of the Human Mind in
the experimental Way, from our internal Principles and Dispositions.

Natura enim juris ab hominis repetenda natura est.[1] CIC.

VOL. I.

LONDON:
Printed for J. NOON, at the *White-Hart,* near *Mercer's Chapel, Cheapside.* MDCCXLI.

1. The nature of law has to be derived from human nature.

TO

His ROYAL HIGHNESS,

WILLIAM

Duke of *Cumberland,*

This TRANSLATION of

A System of the Law of NATURE and NATIONS, Written in *Latin* by the celebrated *Jo. Got. Heineccius,* Counsellor of State to the late King of *Prussia,* and Professor of Philosophy at *Hall:* With the Supplements and Discourses added to it,

Is most humbly dedicated,

In Veneration of His ROYAL HIGHNESS's many great and amiable Qualities, so becoming His high Birth and exalted Rank, the suitable Care bestowed upon His Education, and the Royal Example He has daily before His Eyes, of true Greatness, and the best Use of Power,

By His ROYAL HIGHNESS's

most devoted and

most obedient Servant,

GEORGE TURNBULL.

PREFACE

The author of this system of the law of nature and nations is so well known, and in so high esteem in the republic of letters, that it would be arrogance in me to say any thing in recommendation of his works. Nor need I make any apology for translating into our language so excellent a book upon a subject of such universal importance. For the knowledge of justice and equity must be owned to be necessary in some degree to every one; but to those, in a particular manner, whose birth and fortunes afford them time and means, and call upon them to qualify themselves for the higher stations in civil society. Man, and the rights and duties of man, are certainly the most proper objects of human study in general. And surely Socrates had reason to say, "That if no man can be fit to undertake a trade, how mean and mechanical soever, without having been educated to it, and bestowed some considerable time upon the learning of it, it must be absurd to think one can be qualified for discharging public trusts and duties, without having taken great pains to instruct themselves in the principles of equity, the ends and interests of civil society, and the nature, spirit, and intention of laws." I shall only add, that every science hath its elements; and this treatise at least well deserves to be called an excellent introduction to the science of laws. As for the notes and supplements I have added, how far they are necessary, I must leave it to the reader to judge. The greater part of them relates to one question, viz. The origine of civil government, which hath not been set in its true light by any other writer besides him from whom the illustration of this point is here borrowed. The discourse upon the origine and nature of laws, is an attempt to introduce the experimental way of reasoning into morals, or to deduce human duties from internal principles and dispositions in the human mind. And hence certainly must the virtues belonging to man be deduced: hence certainly must the laws relating to the human nature and state be inferred, as Cicero in his excellent treatise of laws, has long ago told us.—Quid sit homini tributum natura, quantam vim rerum optimarum contineat; cujus muneris colendi, efficiendique causa nati, & in lucem editi simus, quae sit conjunctio hominum, & quae naturalis societas inter ipsos;— his enim explicatis fons legum & juris inveniri potest. *i.e.* *"'Tis by discovering the qualities and powers with which men are endued by nature; and the best ends within human reach; the purposes or offices for which we are fitted and made; and the various bonds by which mankind are knit and united together, and thus prompted to, and formed for society.—'Tis only by discovering and unfolding these important matters, that the source of human rights and duties can be laid open." I have not translated our author's preface; because it is principally designed to shew that the Roman law can now have no other authority in deciding controversies between independent nations or states, than as it is founded upon principles of natural equity; and it is filled up with an enumeration of the titles in the civil law, some have vainly thought sufficient to determine all questions of this kind, which it would have been of very little use to have attempted to english.*

OCTOBER 28.
1740.

CONTENTS[1]

---

1. In the Contents, the page numbers given in the chapter descriptions are those
from the 1741 edition. The bracketed page numbers in the margin are those from the
Liberty Fund edition.

BOOK II

Of the LAW *of* NATIONS.

BOOK I

Of the LAW *of* NATURE

ひ CHAPTER I ひ

Concerning the origine and foundation of the LAW *of* NATURE *and* NATIONS.

SECTION I

Whatever tends to preserve and perfect man is called *good* with respect to man: whatever hath a contrary tendency is called *ill* with regard to him:* every action therefore which contributes to human preservation and perfection is a *good action;* and every action is *evil* which tends to hurt and destroy man, or to hinder his advancement to the perfection of which his nature is capable.

What constitutes a good, and what a bad action?

---

* This is the true idea of perfection according to *Simplicius,* who upon *Epictetus Enchir.* cap. 34. observes, to have not only a beginning and a middle, but likewise an end, is the characteristick of *perfection.* [[Simplicius, *On Epictetus' Handbook* (*Commentarius in Enchiridion Epicteti*).]] So *Aristotle* likewise, in Meta. c. 4. 16. where having examined the meaning of several different terms, he reduces them all to the same idea. [[Aristotle, *The Metaphysics.*]]

SECTION II

What preservation and perfection mean, and what destruction and imperfection? Whatever conduces in any manner or degree towards our duration, or the continuance of our present state, is said to be *preservative* of man: whatever promotes and augments those properties, which belonging to human nature, and constituting our state and rank, admits of degrees, is called *perfective* of man.* Whence it is easy to under-<2>stand what may be said to hurt, wrong, or degrade us.

SECTION III

Men have power to act well or ill. Such being the nature of human will, that it always desires *good,* and abhors *ill;*† it cannot but like those actions which tend to our *preservation and perfection,* and it cannot but dislike those actions which tend to our *hurt and imperfection:* But because *good and ill* may be really what they appear to be, and on the other hand, a seeming *good* may be a real *evil,* and a seeming *evil* may be a real *good;*† it very often happens, that like *Ixion* in the fable, we embrace an empty cloud instead of *Juno;*[1] *i.e.* we are deceived by appearances, and mistake seeming for solid good, and a false semblance of *ill* for real *ill;* and thus we may make a bad or a good choice, be right or wrong in our elections, and consequently in our actions.†

* [[See note on previous page.]]

† This is observed by *Simplicius* upon *Epictet.* Enchir. cap. 34. where he greatly exalts human liberty, and defines it to be that free constitution of the human mind, in consequence of which it voluntarily, and without any constraint, sometimes pursues true, and sometimes imaginary good.

1. Ixion was invited to a banquet by Jupiter but planned to seduce Jupiter's wife, Juno. Jupiter, however, deceived him by shaping an image of Juno out of a cloud. When Ixion embraced the cloud, he was caught by Jupiter and punished.

SECTION IV

Now the power of preferring one or other of two possibles, and by consequence of acting well or ill, is called *liberty:* this power we experience; wherefore it cannot be denied that there are, with regard to us, free actions which are good, and free actions which are bad. But since all things, which may be <3> rightly directed or perverted, stand in need of a rule by which they may be rightly directed, it follows that our free actions ought to be directed by some rule.*

Wherefore men stand in need of some rule by which they may direct their actions.

SECTION V

By a rule here we understand an evident *criterion* by which *good and ill* may be certainly distinguished. And in order to answer that end, a rule must be true, right or just, clear, certain and constant. For suppose the rule not to be just, and that which is ruled by it will not be just or right. Suppose it not to be clear and certain, and it cannot be a sure *criterion* of good and evil. Finally, if we suppose it to be uncertain and variable, an action regulated by it will sometimes be good and sometimes be bad: and therefore in none of these cases would it deserve the name of a rule.†

And this rule must be right or just, sure and immutable.

---

* Thus *Epictetus* reasons in *Arrian,* l. 2. c. xi. Do you think all things are right which appear to be such to any one? but how can things, which are directly repugnant to one another, be both right? it is not therefore enough to make a thing right that it appears to some one to be such, since in weighing or measuring things we do not trust to appearances, but apply a standard. For shall there be a certain measure with regard to these things, and none other with respect to our actions besides fancy or appearance? How can it be that there should be no rule, or none which can be ascertained with respect to human conduct, than which nothing is so necessary? [[Arrian (ca. 95–180), Greek historian. See Epictetus, *The Discourses . . . , the Manual, and Fragments,* vol. 1, bk. II, chap. xi, 287.]]

† So true is that of *Lucret. de rerum nat. l. 4. v.* 515.

> *Si prava est regula prima,*
> *Normaque si fallax rectis regionibus exit,*
> *Et libella aliqua si ex parte claudicat hilum:*
> *Omnia mendose fieri atque obstipa, necessum est,*
> *Prava, cubantia, prona, supina atque absona tecta,*
> *Jam ruere ut quaedam videantur velle, ruantque,*
> *Prodita judiciis fallacibus omnia primis.*

SECTION VI

It must
likewise be
obligatory.

Further, a rule of action would be but of little advantage to mankind, if it were not of such a kind, <4> that it carried with it some *motive* (as it is called) by which human will might be impelled to make use of it, and apply it. Because man never acts without something present to his mind, by which he is excited or impelled to act; he will therefore not apply a rule, or at least he will be very indifferent whether he applies it or no, unless he be stimulated by some motive to apply it. But since we call the connection between a motive and a free action *obligation,* that a rule for the direction of human actions may answer its end, it must be *obligatory.*

SECTION VII

What is obli-
gation, and
how many
kinds of it
are there?

Obligation is a connection between motives and free actions, (§6) and motives must consist either in the intrinsic goodness and pravity of actions themselves, or arise from the will of some Being whose authority we acknowledge, commanding and forbidding certain actions under a penalty. And therefore the former species of *obligation* is called *internal;* the latter is called *external.** The first excites to *good actions,* the other

---

[[Lucretius, *De rerum natura* 4.513–19: "Lastly, as in a building, if the original rule is warped, if the square is faulty and deviates from straight lines, if the level is a trifle wrong in any part, the whole will necessarily be made in a faulty fashion and be falling over, warped, sloping, leaning forward, leaning back, all out of proportion, so that some parts seem about to collapse on the instant, and some do collapse, all betrayed by false principles at the beginning."]]

* We don't deny that the internal is the nobler species of obligation, being that which influences all wise and good men, according to the noted maxim:

Oderunt peccare boni virtutis amore.

[[Horace, *Epistles* 1.16.52, in *Satires, Epistles, and Ars Poetica:* "The good hate vice because they love virtue."]]

It is true the ancients praise the primitive race of mankind in the early ages of the world chiefly on this account, that they acted well, and did good and right, without any law compelling them to such conduct, from a virtuous disposition, and with free

to *just actions.* But right is the correlate (as it is called in the schools) to both. For if one person be under an *obligation,* some other person hath a right or title to exact something from him.

SECTION VIII

Hence it is manifest, that a rule which carries only an *internal obligation* with it, is not sufficient with respect to mankind: for since this obligation solely arises from the goodness of the action, (§7), and therefore only excites a person to act by this motive, *viz.* that his action may be good; but man is so framed by nature, that he often embraces a false appearance of good for what is really such:* (§3). Such a rule must be uncertain, and for that reason it is not deserving of being called a rule (§5). <5>

Internal obligation is not sufficient.

SECTION IX

But if a *rule* only carrying an *internal obligation* with it, would be uncertain, there is need of one which may produce an *external obligation* arising from the will of some Being whose authority we acknowledge. Since therefore that Being may oblige us to the practice of virtue and honesty, either without co-action, or may command and forbid certain

An external obligation either perfect or imperfect is therefore wanting.

---

choice. (*Seneca, Ep.* 90. "The first of mankind, and their progeny, followed the dictates of pure uncorrupted nature as their law and guide." [[Seneca (the Younger), *Ad Lucilium epistulae morales,* vol. 2, 397.]] So *Ovid* likewise, Metam. l. 1. v. 90. [[Ovid, *Metamorphoses,* vol. 1, 1.90: "Golden was the first age, which, with no one to compel, without a law, of its own will, kept faith and did the right."]] So *Tacitus* Ann. 3. 26. [[Tacitus, *The Annals of Tacitus,* vol. 1, bk. 3, chap. 26]] and *Salust.* Catil. cap. 9. [["The War with Catiline," chap. 9, in *Sallust*]]). But we deny it to be sufficient to constitute a rule, because we are enquiring after one founded in nature, and common to the good and bad, wise and foolish, in such a manner, that when reason is not able to keep them to their duty, an external obligation, or which comes to the same thing, the fear of suffering may restrain them.

Ne vaga prosiliat fraenis natura remotis.
    Horat. l. 2. Serm. sat. 7. v. 74.

[[Horace, *Satires II,* 7.74: "Lest, when the reins are removed, nature should break out and [go] wandering."]]

* [[See preceding note.]]

actions with penalties and rewards, the former species of external obligation is properly denominated *imperfect,* and the latter *perfect.* Now the will of a superior commanding and forbidding under penalty is called a *law:* and therefore a rule for the direction of our free actions, to conform to which we are under *perfect obligation,* must consist of *laws,* and a system of such is termed by way of eminence *law.** <6>

SECTION X

Of this law there can be no other author but God.

Now, since that Being may be justly denominated our superior, upon whom our being and happiness absolutely depend, and whose authority we are obliged to acknowledge, because he has a just title to exact obedience from us, and hath power to propose penalties to us in case of our refusing to obey him; and, it appears by many most evident arguments, that he never hath renounced, nor never can renounce his authority to rule and command us:† That superior Being whose authority we are

---

* (*Jus*) *Law,* when it is used to signify a rule of human action, is a system of all the laws of one and the same kind. (Elem. Inst. §33.) [[Heineccius, *Elementa iuris civilis secundum ordinem institutionum*]] (*Jus*) *Law* therefore, 'tis plain from the origine of the word itself, cannot be conceived, without referring it to the will of a superior, and supposing an external obligation. For it is not derived from Δέον, as *Menage* would have it, Amoen. Juris. cap. 39. p. 295 [[Ménage, *Iuris civilis amoenitates*]]; nor from *Jove,* as *Scipio,* Gent. Orig. p. 270 [[Gentili, *Originum ad Pandectas liber singularis*]] has asserted, and after him *Grotius,* Proleg. Jur. belli & pacis, §12 [[Grotius, *De iure belli ac pacis,* Prolegomena, §12]]; but from the Word *jubendo.* For instead of *Jura,* the ancients used *jusa* or *jussa.* Festus, jusa, jura. [[Festus, *De verborum significatu.*]] So Hieron. Magii, var. lect. 4. 1. [[Magius, *Variarum lectionum.*]] In like manner, the German word *Recht* is shewn by Jo. Geo. Wachter. Gloss. p. 1251 [[Wachter, *Glossarium Germanicum*]], to include in it *the idea of* law, or the will of a superior directing human actions.

† Not only is the *perfection and goodness* of a Being a just title to exact obedience, as is affirmed by *Mos. Amyraldus* Disser. de jure Dei in res creatas [[Amyraldus, *De jure dei in creaturas dissertatio*]], agreeably to that well known saying of Democritus: φύσει τὸ ἄρχειν οἰκήϊον πῷ δ' κρείσσονι. Authority falls by nature to the share of what is best. Stob. Serm. 37. [[Democritus (ca. 460–370 B.C.), Greek philosopher. The saying quoted by Heineccius was included in the *Sermones,* an anthology of excerpts from poets and prose writers compiled by Joannes Stobaeus (fl. fifth century A.D.) and intended for the instruction of his son. The standard modern critical edition is Stobaeus, *Anthologium.*]] But *dependence* is also such. For who will deny that he hath

obliged to acknowledge, can be no other than the most great and good God; and he therefore is the sole author of that law, which ought, as we have said, to be the rule of action to all mankind. <7>

---

a just claim to our obedience to whom we owe our existence and preservation? God therefore hath a right to command our submission and obedience: *He in whom we live, move, and have our being,* Acts 17. 28. Besides, that he can inflict punishments on the disobedient and rebellious, his omnipotence and justice leave no room to doubt. (Elem. phil. mor. §185 & seq.) Finally, if he had, or should ever renounce his authority over men, and all created beings, that would be unworthy of his wisdom and goodness; because, being infinitely wise, he must know that we would be most miserable without his government and rule, and being infinitely good, he cannot abandon his creature, which cannot guide itself, and so expose it to the greatest misery. But what is repugnant to his wisdom and goodness, that he can neither will nor do, it is allowed. Wherefore, he neither will nor can renounce his supreme jurisdiction over men and all creatures. It is proper to observe this in opposition to the celebrated Leibnitz [[Gottfried Wilhelm Leibniz (1646–1716), German philosopher and mathematician]], who, the illustrious Sam. a Cocceis [[Samuel Freiherr von Cocceji (1679–1755), Prussian jurist]], Disser. de principio juris naturalis unico vero adaequato, published at Francf. 1699, having by solid arguments demonstrated that there can be no other principle of natural law but the will of God, in the 1700, Ephemeridibus Hanoveranis for the month of July, objected against that hypothesis, among other things, "That according to it, if we suppose a creature to have so much power, that being once produced by its creator, it could not be compelled by him; such a creature must be considered as manumitted by its creator, in the same manner as children, when they come to such a degree of power, that they cannot be compelled by their parents." For to suppose such a case, is the wildest extravagance, since it implies a manifest contradiction, to imagine a finite Creature arrived to such power that it can no longer be compelled by its Creator, an infinitely powerful Being. And no less absurd are all the other fictions he puts, in order to invalidate that learned man's doctrine, as this for instance, "That if we suppose an evil genius to have supreme uncontroulable power, such an evil genius would not, because irresistible, cease to be wicked, unjust and tyranical." For we cannot suppose an evil genius to have supreme power, if we believe the divine existence. And if we deny the existence of God, it is absurd to suppose an evil genius, or indeed any created thing to exist. It is a strong argument of truth, when a proposition cannot be overturned but by suppositions which include a manifest contradiction.

SECTION XI

This law is made known to mankind in no other way but by reason.

Because we are enquiring, as appears from what hath been said, for no other rule of right but what <8> God hath given to the whole human race for the rule of their conduct, (§10) hence it follows that this rule must be intelligible to all mankind. But since what is intelligible to, or may be known by all mankind, must be discovered to them either by a divine revelation, which all men acknowledge and receive as such, or must be discoverable by the use of natural reason; because such a revelation as hath been mentioned never existed: it is obvious that the law of nature must mean laws within the discovery of all mankind by the use of reason common to all mankind, and which therefore are by nature promulgated to all mankind.*

---

* Hence Cicero in his oration for Milo, c. 4. calls it Jus non scriptum sed natum. "Law, or a rule of rectitude not written but cogenial; a rule which we have not learned, read, received by tradition, but which nature itself hath impressed upon us, and which we imbibe and draw from it; to the knowledge of which we are not formed and trained by education or example, but we are originally tinctured and stamped with it." [[See Cicero, *Pro Annio Milone,* in *The Speeches,* trans. Watts.]] So the apostle likewise says, "The Gentiles, which have not the law, are a law unto themselves, which shew the works of the law written in their hearts" [[a reference to Romans 2:14]]. This cannot be otherwise than by reasoning; and therefore by the right use of reason: this is the unanimous doctrine of all, who have, as it were, by compact, placed the law of nature in the *dictates of right reason;* a few only excepted, who have maintained there is nothing just or right by nature, as *Archelaus* in *Laertius,* 2. 16. [[Diogenes Laertius, *Lives of Eminent Philosophers*]] Aristippus, according to the same writer, 2. 93. *Carneades* in *Lactantius,* Instit. divin. c. 14. & 19. [[Lactantius, *The Divine Institutes*]] Pyrrho in *Sextus Empyricus,* Hypot. 3. 24. [[Sextus Empiricus, *Outlines of Scepticism* (*Pyrroneioi hypotyposeis*)]] and to those *Aristotle* may be added, who, as Menage has proved at the 7. 128. p. 311. of Laertius [[a reference to the comments by Gilles Ménage on an edition of Diogenes Laertius's *Lives,* the *De vitis et dogmatis et Apophtegmatis eorum qui in philosophia claruerunt*]], was not far from that opinion.

SECTION XII

The law of nature, or the natural rule of rectitude, is a system of laws promulgated by the eternal God to the whole human race by reason. But if you would rather consider it as a science, na-<9>tural morality will be rightly defined the practical habit of discovering the will of the supreme legislator by reason, and of applying it as a rule to every particular case that occurs. Now, because it consists in deducing and applying a rule coming from God, it may be justly called *divine jurisprudence*.

A definition of the law of nature and of jurisprudence, natural or divine.

SECTION XIII

Since the law of nature is a system of laws (§12) whatever properly belongs to laws may be ascribed to the law of nature, as to prohibit, permit, punish.* It may be divided as a body of laws is by the *Roman* lawyers into the permissive part, which obliges all men not to disturb any person in the use and exercise of his right and liberty; and the preceptive, which obliges all men to do good actions, and to abstain from bad ones; and it is also evident, that with respect to the preceptive part, there is no liberty left to mankind; whereas, with regard to the permissive, any one may renounce his right to what is permitted to him.* <10>

The law of nature may be divided into preceptive and permissive.

---

* The permissive part of the law of nature constitutes therefore a rule: The preceptive makes an exception. For God leaves all to human liberty, which he hath neither commanded nor forbid. Thus, *e.g.* God having only prohibited our first parents the tree of knowledge of good and evil, they had good reason to infer that they were permitted to eat of all the other fruits, Gen. iii. 2, 3. Where no obligation of law takes place, there liberty is entire. But hence it must not be concluded, that a permissive law carries no obligation with it. For it obliges all mankind not to disturb any one in the use of his liberty. Thus, *e.g.* because God has permitted every one to appropriate to his use whatever is not yet appropriated by any person, or belongs to none, and thus to constitute dominion and property, theft, rapine, fraud, depredation, *&c.* cannot but be unlawful and unjust.

SECTION XIV

Whether would there be a law of nature if there were no God?

Now seeing the law of nature comes from God (§12) as the supreme legislator, it follows by consequence, that tho' a person may do a good action, without any regard to the law of nature as such, being excited to it by the internal goodness or obligation of the action, and by his good disposition; tho' even an atheist, who hath no sense of religion, may do a good action thro' the influence and guidance of his reason, because he knows it to be good in itself, and advantageous to him; yet such a person cannot on that account be said to act *justly, i.e.* conformably to the law of nature considered as such; much less then can it be said, that there would still be a law of nature,* tho' it should be granted, which cannot be done without impiety, that there were no God, or that God did not take any care of human affairs. See *Grotius* proleg. jur. belli & pacis, §xi.

SECTION XV

Why it is said to be inscribed on our hearts.

Since the rule of rectitude we are now speaking of signifies laws promulgated by right reason, <11> (§12) and reason is nothing else but the faculty of reasoning, or of inferring one truth from others by necessary

---

* They cut the nerves, so to speak, of the law of nature, who conceive or define it independently of all regard to God, and thus feign a law to themselves without a lawgiver. All who have philosophized about it with accuracy as well as religiously, have acknowledged, that it proceeds from God as its founder and author, and that if the divine existence be denied, there remains no difference between just and unjust. God, in order to incite Abraham to the love and practice of justice, says to him, "I am the Almighty God, walk before me, and be thou perfect," *Gen.* xvii. 1. And the Apostle, *Heb.* xi. 6. says, "He that cometh to God must believe that he is, and that he is a rewarder of them that diligently seek him." Yea Cicero, de Nat. Deorum, l. 2. says, "I don't know whether piety towards God being removed, all sociality and fidelity among men, and justice, the most excellent of virtues, would not likewise be destroyed." [[Cicero, *De natura deorum* 1.2, in Cicero, *De natura deorum, Academica.*]]

consequence,* it is therefore plain why the apostle affirms that the knowledge of this rule is *engraved on our hearts,* Rom. ii. 15. For he attributes to man the power or faculty of reasoning concerning just and unjust; which power, since it does not necessarily include in it actual exercise, why some should ascribe even to infants a certain innate sense of just and unjust, is not difficult to be comprehended.

SECTION XVI

Hence it follows that the law of nature is not derived from the sacred writings, nor from any divine positive laws, such as the seven precepts given to *Noah,* of which the *Jews* boast so much;† tho' at the same time we readily grant, that the author of reason and revelation being the same, not only many things which reason dictates are to be found in the sacred

Whether the knowledge of it is derived from the sacred writings or tradition?

---

* Grotius insists much on the emphasis of this phrase, Grot. upon the Epistle to the *Romans,* ii. 15. and Joan. Clericus Art. Crit. part. 2. sect. 1. cap. 4. §10. [[Jean le Clerc (Johannes Clericus) (1657–1736) was born in Geneva but lived most of his life in Amsterdam. He was a central figure in the republic of letters with close connections to England, including Locke and Addison, and a biblical scholar who became professor of ecclesiastical history in the Remonstrant seminary. The work referred to here is his *Ars critica* of 1697. A German edition appeared in three volumes in Leipzig in 1713.]] who maintain that it means no more than that the law of nature may be easily discovered and retained without the assistance of a teacher, and they have accumulated several passages of ancient authors in which ἐγγράφειν [[ἐγγράφειν: to write, to inscribe]] signifies nothing else. But this subject has been fully treated by Jo. Franc. Bud. Inst. Theo. mor. part. 2. c. 2. §5. where he has also examined Mr. Locke's opinion with great accuracy. [[Johann Franz Budde (1667–1729), German theologian and philosopher; professor of moral philosophy at the newly founded University of Halle, where he taught Heineccius. He professed an eclecticism which rested on a broad historical foundation and was very critical of the "atheist" Spinoza. The work referred to here is Budde's *Institutiones theologiae moralis.*]]

† How the Hebrews derive the law of nature and nations from the seven precepts given to Noah, is shewn by Jo. Selden, de jure nat. & gent. secundum discipl. Hebraeorum. [[John Selden (1584–1654), lawyer, politician, humanist scholar. The reference is to *De jure naturali et gentium juxta disciplinam Ebraeorum.*]] But tho' the learned Budaeus Introd. ad philosoph. Heb. p. 14. and 15 [[Budde, *Introductio ad historiam philosophiae ebraeorum*]], thinks that tradition concerning the seven precepts given to Noah, does not want some foundation; yet it cannot be now proved, that ever any such precepts were given to Noah, and tho' some things that were commanded or forbidden by these precepts be now known to the posterity of Noah; they

writings, but there is every where a perfect harmony between them; nor can there indeed be any thing forbidden or commanded in the sacred oracles which is repugnant to the rule of right discoverable by reason. <12>

SECTION XVII

The law of
nature is
immutable.
Further, from the same principle it is evident that the law of nature is no less immutable than right reason it self, which cannot but remain unchangeably the same: and therefore God, who cannot do any thing contrary to his will, cannot give any indulgence repugnant to that eternal law in any respect; and much less can any among mortals arrogate to himself any power over that law.*

SECTION XVIII

The difference
between the
law of nature
and civil law.
Nor will it now be difficult to find out the difference between the law of nature and civil law. For the former is discovered by right reason, the latter is promulgated and made known either *viva voce* or by writing. The former extends as far as right reason: the other is the law of a particular state: The former hath for its object all actions internal as well as external, which are by nature good or evil: The other respects indifferent and ex-<13>ternal actions, so far only as the good of any people or state requires their regulation and adjustment.†

---

are known to them not by tradition but by reason, and therefore they are not positive laws, but laws promulgated by right reason.

* *Cicero* says elegantly, The law of nature cannot be altered, nothing can be derogated from it, much less can it be totally abrogated. We cannot be discharged from it by the senate or by the people; neither are we to look out for any explainer or interpreter of this law, besides reason itself. There is not one law of equity for *Rome,* another for *Athens;* one for former and another for present times, but the same law binds all nations at all times. All men have one common universal Lord, Ruler, and Lawgiver, God the founder, the establisher of reason, and the judge of all reasonable Beings. [[Cicero, *De re publica* 3.22, in Cicero, *De re publica, De legibus.*]] To this *Ulpian* consents as we have shewn elsewhere. *L.* 6. *pr. D. de just. & jure.* [[Domitius Ulpianus (ca. 160–228), Roman jurist.]]

† *Cicero de Invent. l.* 38. "All laws ought to be referred to the publick interest of the state, and to be interpreted not according to the letter, but as the end of laws,

SECTION XIX

But notwithstanding this difference, it is beyond all doubt, that the knowledge of the law of nature must be of the greatest use to all who apply themselves to the study of the civil law; because many of its precepts are adopted by civil law, and by it are fortified with additional penalties;* several conclusions are drawn from the law of nature by civil law;

The knowledge of it is of great utility with respect to civil law.

---

publick good, requires. Such was the wisdom and virtue of our ancestors, that they proposed no other end to themselves in making laws but the safety and happiness of the state: they either never enacted into laws what was hurtful, or if they happened to do so, such a law was no sooner known to be hurtful than it was abolished. No person desires the observation of laws for their own sake, but for the good of the republick." [[Cicero, *De inventione* 1.38, 112–13, in Cicero, *De inventione, De optimo genere oratorum, Topica.*]] They are therefore much mistaken who will have what they call *natural law* to be founded merely on interest, according to that saying of *Epicurus,*

> *Nec natura potest justo secernere iniquum,*
> *Sola est utilitas justi prope mater & aequi.*
> Hor. Ser. l. 3.

> [[Horace, *Satires I* 3.113: "Nature cannot distinguish between the just and the unjust [right and wrong]; utility is almost the only mother of what is just and right."]]

It is true God being infinitely wise and good commands nothing by the law of nature, but what is useful; but he does not command it because it is useful, but because it is agreeable to his nature and will. An action is not just because it is advantageous, but it is advantageous because it is just. For, as was nobly said by *Mar. Ant. Imp. l.7.74.* "Every action agreeable to nature is advantage or interest." [[Marcus Aurelius, *Meditations,* vol. 1, 144–45.]] But this error hath been sufficiently refuted by *Grotius, Proleg. jur. bell. & pac.* §16. *Puffendorff de jur. nat. & gent. L.* 2, 3, 10, 11. and the illustrious *Sam. de Coccei, de princip. jur. nat. & gent.* §2, 9.

* This is observed by *Hesiod* in that celebrated passage of his book, *Oper. & Dier.* v. 274. Τόνδε γαρ, &c. [[Hesiod, *Works and Days,* lines 276ff.]] The meaning of which is, Brute animals devour one another, because they have no idea of justice, but to men nature hath given a sense of justice, which far exalts them above the brute creation. *Jac. Cujacius* hath not removed the difficulty in his notes *ad Inst. p.8. tom.* 1. by saying, "What the brutes do by a natural impulse, if men do the same by reason, they act according to the law of nations." [[A reference to the notes on Justinian's *Institutes* by the French humanist jurist Jacques Cujas, or Jacobus Cujacius (1522–90), which are included in vol. 1 of his collected works (Cujas, *Opera omnia*).]] For thus an action will not be agreeable to the law of nature and nations merely because brute animals do the same, but because it is acting by the direction of right reason.

and natural equity must never be severed from civil law, lest according to the ancient saying, *Strict law become severe injustice.* Summum jus summa injuria. <14>

SECTION XX

The brutes are not governed by the law of nature.

Moreover from the same principle it is visible, that no other creatures besides men are subject to this law; since God hath dignified man alone with the prerogative of reason; and therefore that definition of *Ulpian* is false. Natural law is a law which nature hath taught all animals. *L.* 1. §3. *Dig. de just. & jure.* *

SECTION XXI

What is called the law of nations?

Further, since the law of nature comprehends all the laws promulgated to mankind by right reason; and men may be considered either as particulars singly, or as they are united in certain political bodies or societies; we call that *law,* by which the actions of particulars ought to be governed, *the law of nature,* and we call that *the law of nations,* which determines what is just and unjust in society or between societies. And therefore the precepts, the laws of both are the same; nay, the *law of nations* is the law of nature it self, respecting or applied to social life and the affairs of societies and independent states.† <15>

---

* [[See preceding note.]]

† The law of nature is therefore of a larger extent than the law of nations; for there is nothing dictated or prescribed by right reason, to which every particular is not obliged in some manner to conform himself. But there are certain parts of the law of nature, which cannot so properly be applied to whole societies, *e.g.* The laws and rights belonging to matrimony, paternal power, &c.

SECTION XXII

Hence we may infer, that the law of nature doth not differ from the law of nations, neither in respect of its foundation and first principles, nor of its rules, but solely with regard to its object. Wherefore their opinion is groundless, who speak of, I know not what, law of nations distinct from the law of nature. The positive or secondary law of nations devised by certain ancients, does not properly belong to that law of nations we are now to treat of, because it is neither established by God, nor promulgated by right reason; it is neither common to all mankind nor unchangeable.*

Whether it be different from the law of nature?

SECTION XXIII

It will not therefore be an useless attempt to treat of both these laws, which have the same foundation <16> in the same work, in such a manner however, as carefully to distinguish the one from the other, since they differ from one another in respect of their objects and application. We shall therefore handle them separately in this order; in the first book, we

This work divided into two parts.

---

* Many things which are referred to the positive law of nations, arise either from the law of nature itself, or from customs, or from some certain law common to many nations. Thus the rights of ambassadors, for the greater part, are deducible from the law of nature. Many things were observed among the *Greeks,* which barbarous nations payed no regard to, *v.g.* giving a truce to the vanquished to carry off their killed. The manners and customs of the *Germans* became afterwards common almost to all nations, as *Grotius* has observed, *de jure belli & pacis,* 2. 8. 1. 2. In fine, even among christian customs, some have so far fallen into desuetude, that there is no remaining vestige of them. *Leibnitz, praefat. Cod. jure gent. dipl. p.* 8. who observes, that many things established by the pope of *Rome* as head of the christian state, are held for the common law of christian nations. [[See Leibniz, *Codex iuris gentium diplomaticus,* vol. 1, Praefatio ad Lectorem, 9.]] This *Hertius & Puffend. de jure nat. & gentium, l.* 2. *c.* 3. §23. illustrates by an example, from the use of cross-bows against christians. [[Heineccius's reference is to the notes by the German jurist Johann Nikolaus Hertius (1651–1710) on Samuel Pufendorf, *Acht Bücher vom Natur- und Völkerrecht.* A philosopher, jurist, and historian, Pufendorf (1632–94) was one of the most influential theorists of natural law in the early European Enlightenment. This work is a German translation of his seminal *De jure naturae et gentium* of 1672.]]

shall enquire into the law of nature; and in the second, into the law of nations.

Remarks on This Chapter

Tho' our Author proceeds more distinctly and methodically than most other writers on the law of nature and nations, yet some steps of the reasoning of this chapter do not intirely satisfy me. For §8. he reasons thus, "A rule carrying along with it no more than *internal obligation* would be uncertain, and so would not deserve the name of a rule; because internal obligation only means the intrinsic goodness of an action, but man is so framed that he may mistake seeming for real good."—Whence he concludes §9. "That no rule can be certain, and thus sufficient for our direction, but that which carries along with it an external obligation, *i.e.* according to his definition, the command of a superior invested with sufficient power to enforce his commands." Now it is plain, that the command of God to do, or to forbear an action can only be inferred from the intrinsic goodness or pravity of that action, *i.e.* in our author's language, the external obligation of an action can only be inferred from its internal obligation. Our author acknowledges this §5, and afterwards §60, and §77, & *seq.* But this being true, it evidently follows, That we cannot be more certain about the external obligation of an action, than we are about its internal obligation: whatever uncertainty our apprehensions of the latter are liable to, our apprehensions of the former must be liable to the same uncertainty. It appears to me very odd reasoning to say, That considering how obnoxious men are to mistakes about good and evil, there must be a more certain rule for human conduct than the intrinsic goodness of actions, even the divine will; when at the same time we are told, that we cannot come at the knowledge of the divine will with respect to our conduct, otherwise than by first knowing what an action is in itself; or that we can only infer the divine will concerning an action from its intrinsic nature, its intrinsic goodness or pravity. In order to cut off many verbal disputes, with which the moral science hath been hitherto perplexed in its very first steps, it ought in my opinion to set out in this manner. 1. If there be such a thing as good or evil belonging to, or arising from actions, there is an internal obligation or a sufficient reason to choose the one and to abhor the other. But that some actions are good and others evil, must be true if preservation and destruction, pain <17> and pleasure, happiness and misery, perfection and imperfection, be not words without meaning, which will not be said. This is the substance of what our author says in his first section, and thus the better antients deduced and explained the essential differences of actions, or the natural difference betwixt virtue and vice. See my *Principles of moral and christian philosophy,* T. 1. c. 5. t. 2. §3. introduction. In other words, if there be any such thing as natural good and evil, there must be moral good and evil; for actions tending to good must be good, and actions tending to evil must be evil; or if there be any such thing as perfection and imperfection with respect to any quality, any being, as a vine, a horse, *&c.* there must likewise be such a thing as perfection and imperfection with respect to moral powers and moral agents and their acts or exertions. 2. If there be a God, he must will that we should regulate our actions by, and act conformably to the internal obligation of actions. But that there is a God is the universal plain language of nature. 3. Wherefore wherever there is internal obligation to act in such or such a manner, there is likewise an external obligation to act in the same manner, *i.e.* there is an extrinsic reason for acting so, arising from the will of God, who is infinitely perfect, and upon whom all our interests here and hereafter absolutely depend. 4. Whatever therefore in respect of its internal obligation may be called a proper rule of conduct, is at the same time a *law,* in the proper and strict sense of the word, *i.e.* it is the will, the command of a superior who hath right to command, and power to enforce the obedience of his commands, being the will of God the creator. 5. A system of rules or of directions for our conduct, having internal obligation, may be properly called a system of laws, of natural laws, of divine laws, because it is a system of precepts discoverable from their natural fitness, or internal obligation to be the will or laws of God concerning our conduct. And therefore the whole enquiry into rules of moral conduct, may be called an enquiry into the natural laws of God concerning our conduct.

It is not properly the business of such an enquiry to prove the being of a God, and that where there is internal obligation to an action, there must also be external obligation to it. It supposes that done, and proceeds to enquire into internal obligations; or to unfold the goodness and pravity of actions, and from hence to deduce general rules or laws of conduct. Now if the preceding propositions be attended to, and the difference between a rule and a law, or between internal and external obligation, according to our author's definition, be kept in mind; it may be asserted without any ambiguity, that abstractly from all consideration of the will of the supreme Being, there is no law for our conduct; there is a rule, but that rule is not a law, in the strict sense of that word. It would have prevented much jangling about the foundations of morality, if writers had carefully distinguished, with a late excellent writer, *Dr. Sykes*,[2] in his <18> *Essay on the Connexion of Natural with Revealed Religion,* between the law and the sanction of the law. cap. 2.

Our author's reasoning will proceed very clearly, if we understand the meaning of his 8 § to be to this purpose. "A rule of conduct while it is merely apprehended under the notion of reasonable, will not be sufficient to influence men; in order to have due influence upon them, it must be considered as having external, as well as internal obligation, arising from the will of God which never changes." See how Puffendorf reasons, b. 2. of the law of nature and nations, ch. 3. §20. "But to make these dictates of reason obtain the dignity and power of laws, it is necessary to call into our consideration a much higher principle, &c."

With respect to what is said, §22. of the law of nations, 'tis well worth while to add an excellent remark of the author of the *Persian Letters,* 94 and 95.[3] "As the law of nature and nations is commonly doctored, one would imagine there were two sorts of justice; one to regulate the affairs of private persons, which prevails in the civil law; the other to compose the differences that arise between people and people, which plays the tyrant in the law of nations: as if the law of nations were not itself a civil law, not indeed of a particular country, but of the world. The magistrate ought to do justice between citizen and citizen; every nation ought to do the same between themselves and another nation. This second distribution of justice, requires no maxims but what are used in the first. Between nation and nation, there is seldom

2. Arthur Ashley Sykes (1684–1756) was an Anglican clergyman and latitudinarian controversialist who wrote *The Principles and Connexion of Natural and Revealed Religion Distinctly Considered.*

3. Montesquieu, *Persian Letters,* letters 94 and 95.

any want of a third to be umpire; because the grounds of dispute are almost always clear and easy to be determined. The interests of two nations are generally so far separated, that it requires nothing but to be a lover of justice to find it out: it is not the same with regard to the differences that arise between private persons as they live in society, their interests are so mingled and confounded, and there are so many different sorts of them, that it is necessary for a third person to untangle what the covetousness of the parties strives to tie knots in, &c."

ジジ CHAPTER II ジジ

Concerning the nature and distinguishing qualities or characteristics of human actions.

SECTION XXIV

Transition to treat of human actions.

From what hath been said of the foundation and origine of the law of nature and nations, it is obvious, that it hath for its object and <19> scope the direction of human conduct; and therefore order makes it necessary to enquire accurately into the qualities and characteristics of human actions.

SECTION XXV

What is meant by action and what by passion? What by external and what by internal action?

Experience, the fountain of all knowledge, teaches us, that various motions and changes happen in the human mind; but since no motion can be produced or conceived without a sufficient moving cause, the motions which happen in the mind of man must have some sufficient cause, which must either be *within* or *without* man. And therefore motions, the sufficient cause of which is in man himself, are called *actions;* and those the cause of which must be sought after without man, are termed *passions.* But because the motion called *action,* either produces nothing without the mind, but rests there, or produces by will some effect in the body, the former are denominated *internal,* the latter *external actions.*

30

SECTION XXVI

Passions not proceeding from us, but from some external cause, are so far without our power, and therefore are not unfrequently excited in us against our will or inclination; yet they may sometimes be as it were repulsed and prevented, if we are provided with sufficient force to resist the external exciting cause; and on the other hand, in certain circumstances we can assist the external mover, so as that the motion it tends to produce may be more easily excited in us. Whence it follows that some passions are within our power, and others are not.* <20>

Passions of what kinds are they?

SECTION XXVII

Because the law of nature hath only free actions for its object, (§4) it cannot have for its object, in order to be directed by it, passions which are not within our power. Tho' it may lay down some rules relative to our passions, so far as they are in our power, yet, properly speaking, these rules are not directions to our passions, but to those free actions, by which we can resist or assist these passions, shewing what we ought to do with regard to hindering or forwarding them.†

Whether they are subject to our direction or not?

---

* All this may be illustrated by clear examples. To be warmed is a passion; sometimes we cannot avoid it, as when we are making a journey in very warm air: sometimes we can, as when in winter we remove farther from the fire: and sometimes we can as it were assist the cause, as by drawing nearer to a fire that we may become warmer. To be warmed is therefore sometimes in our power, and sometimes without our power.

† Thus laws cannot be prescribed to the passion of anger, but reason can give rules to our free actions, and directs us not to give loose reins to anger, but to resist its first motions, lest it should become impetuous and ungovernable, and to forbear acting while the mind is in too great a ferment and perturbation, &c. Who will deny that he acts contrary to the law of reason who does not observe these rules? Nothing can be more true than what Cicero says, Tusc. qu. l. 3. "All the diseases and disturbances of the mind proceed from the neglect or despight of reason, i.e. from not observing those prescriptions which reason dictates to us for hindering the mind from being overpowered by violent commotions." [[Cicero, *Tusculanae disputationes* (*Tusculan Disputations*), bk. 4, xiii.31.]]

SECTION XXVIII

Whether the law of nature extends to them?

The law of nature therefore only extends to our actions; but let it be observed, that tho' the sufficient cause of all these be in man himself, (§25) yet experience teaches us, that of some actions we are conscious and are absolute masters; others are of such a nature that they proceed from some mechanical disposition, in such a manner that we are not always conscious of them, nor have them not wholly in our power.* <21>

SECTION XXIX

Actions are either human or natural. Whether the latter are the object of the law of nature?

Actions of which we are conscious, and which are within our power, and subject to our direction, are properly termed *human* or *moral* actions; those of which we are not conscious, or not masters, are called *physical* or *natural* actions; whence it is plain, that the former are *free,* the latter *necessary;* and therefore that *human* or *moral* actions alone can be directed by the law of nature (§4), and not natural ones, except so far as it is in our power to assist and promote, or contrariwise to avoid and prevent them.† <22>

---

* Thus it is in our power to sit, stand, or walk; to be silent or speak, to give or not give, &c. as we will. And of all these actions we are conscious when we perform them; but, on the other hand, the playing of the lungs, the peristaltic motion of the intestines, the circulation of the blood, &c. do not depend on us; they are motions which we often neither feel nor know to be performed in us. The Stoicks use that distinction somewhat differently when they assert that some things are τὰ ἐφ' ἡμῖν, within our power; and others are τὰ οὐκ ἐφ' ἡμῖν, without our power. To the former class they refer opinion, appetite, desire, aversion, in one word, all our actions; to the other they refer bodily goods, possessions, glory, power, and whatever in fine is not our own acquisition or work. Epict. Enchirid. c. 1. [[Epictetus, "Manual," chap. 1, in *Discourses and Manual,* vol. 2.]] Their division is therefore a distribution of things, and not of actions only.

† Tho', as we have just now observed, we have no command over the circulation of our blood, the motion of the heart, &c. yet it is plain from experience that we can assist those motions by temperance and medicines; and that we can disturb them by intemperance, or put a period to them by poison, the sword, and other methods. Who therefore can doubt, but the law of nature may prohibit whatever tends to disturb or destroy these natural motions, and with them life itself? The ancient philosophers have agreed to this truth. For tho' some have commended self-murder as

SECTION XXX

Human or moral actions being free or within our power, and every thing being in our power which is directed by our will; it follows that human or moral actions are actions which may be directed by our will. But because the will never determines itself, unless it be excited to desire or reject by the understanding;* hence it is justly concluded, that the understanding likewise concurs in the exertion of free human actions; and therefore there are two principles of free human or moral actions; the *understanding* and the *will*.

The understanding and will are the principles of human actions.

SECTION XXXI

Understanding is the faculty by which the mind perceives, judges, and reasons. When this faculty takes the name of *imagination,* we have sufficiently shewn in another treatise, (*in the elements of rational philosophy*).

What the understanding is?

SECTION XXXII

But since the will cannot exert itself, unless it be excited by the understanding, (§30) it follows <23> that it cannot prefer a just action as such, nor abhor an unjust one as such, unless the understanding hath first distinctly perceived the action to be just or unjust, by comparing it with

Without its concurrence an action is not moral.

---

noble and heroic; yet *Democritus* elegantly says in *Plutarch de sanitate tuenda,* p. 135. "If the body should bring an action of damage against the soul, for an injury done to it, it could not escape condemnation." [[Plutarch, "De tuenda sanitate precepta" ("Advice about Keeping Well"), in Plutarch, *Moralia,* vol. 2, 213–93.]]

* The will hath good or evil for its object, and therefore it always tends towards good, and flies from evil. Whence it is plain, it cannot choose but what is represented to it by the understanding, under the appearance of good, just, or advantageous; nor reject but what is exhibited to it under the semblance of evil, unjust, or hurtful. So Simplicius upon Epictetus, cap. 1. "But it is certain that the acts of the willing power, are preceded by some judgment or opinion. If an object be represented to the mind as good or evil, propensity or aversion are excited, and appetite or desire succeeds, For before we desire any agreeable object and embrace it, or fly from any thing contrary to what is desirable, the mind must necessarily be previously prone or averse towards it." [[Simplicius, *On Epictetus' Handbook,* vol. 1, 41.]]

the rule of action, i.e. by reasoning. And therefore moral actions presuppose the capacity of perceiving a rule of action, and of comparing actions with the ideas of just and unjust.*

SECTION XXXIII

Hence conscience.

That faculty by which we reason about the goodness or pravity of our actions is called *conscience,* concerning which we have discoursed at large in another treatise. Here however it is necessary to repeat, or rather add some observations upon conscience.

SECTION XXXIV

Which is reasoning.

Because conscience reasons concerning the goodness and pravity of actions; (§33) but actions are called just, in respect of an external obligation arising from a law; conscience must therefore compare the one with the other, the law and the fact; that is, form two propositions, and from them deduce a third; which, since it cannot be done but by syllogism, it follows that every reasoning of <24> conscience is a syllogism, consisting of three propositions, the law, the action, and the conclusion.†

---

* Hence it is manifest that the law of nature does not extend to infants incapable of discerning good from evil; much less to the actions of mad persons, changelings, or such as are disordered in their judgments by any disease; because such cannot reason about just and unjust. Aristotle therefore justly observes, Ethic. c. 34. "With respect to things of which ignorance is the cause, man is not unjust. For in the case of inevitable ignorance, one is as an infant that beats its father without knowing what it does. On account of this natural ignorance children are not reckoned unjust. Whenever ignorance is the cause of acting, and one is not the cause of his ignorance, men are not to be deemed culpable or unjust." [[This is presumably from Aristotle's *Nicomachean Ethics,* though the reference is not clear.]]

† Such was that reasoning of Judas's conscience, Mat. xxvii. 4. "I have sinned in that I betrayed innocent blood." In which the first proposition expresses a law, the second Judas's action, and the last the conclusion or sentence of his conscience. Nor does any thing else pass in our mind when conscience reasons within us. It is therefore most wickedly misrepresented by Toland [[John Toland (1670–1722); Heineccius presumably refers to Toland's controversial *Christianity Not Mysterious* of 1696]] and others, as an empty name, made a bug-bear by priests.

SECTION XXXV

Since conscience in its reasonings always terminates in a sentence which it draws (§34): but every sentence either condemns or absolves according as the action is found to be conformable or disagreable to the law. Conscience, when it absolves, is called *good,* and when it condemns, it is called *evil;* the former is attended with tranquillity and confidence; the latter with suspiciousness and dread.*

It is divided into good and evil conscience.

SECTION XXXVI

We may reason either about past or future actions, and therefore conscience reasoning about actions not yet performed, is called *antecedent conscience,* and when it reasons about actions already done, it is called *consequent conscience.*

It is likewise divided into antecedent and consequent.

SECTION XXXVII

In both cases conscience compares the action with the law. But because the good and upright man, <25> who hath a due sense of virtue and duty alone sets himself to conform his future actions to the divine law; such only exercise antecedent conscience. The consequent exerts itself even in the breasts of the most profligate.†

In some persons both are found.

* Hence St. Paul, *Rom.* ii. 15. calls the acts of conscience λογισμοὺς, &c. thoughts excusing or accusing; and St. John, 1 Ep. iii. 21. says, if our hearts condemn us not, then have we confidence towards God, *&c.* So speak the Poets likewise,

> *Prima haec est ultio, quod, se*
> *Judice, nemo nocens absolvitur: improba quamvis*
> *Gratia fallaci Praetoris vicerit urna.*
> Juv. Sat. 13.

[[Juvenal, *Satires,* 13.2–4, in *Juvenal and Persius:* "This is the first vengeance: no one who is guilty is acquitted by his own verdict, even though the praetor's corrupt favor may have won the case with a rigged vote."]]

† Virtue is always united with an earnest indefatigable care to understand the divine law. The greater progress one has made in virtue, the more ardent is this desire in his breast. And hence it is, that rightly disposed minds are strict inspectors into

SECTION XXXVIII

Conscience either excites, admonishes, or reclaims.

Further, as often as we compare a future action with the law, we find it either to be commanded, forbidden, or permitted. In the first case conscience excites us to perform the action. In the second it restrains us from it. In the third, having wisely examined all its circumstances, it advises what ought to be done. Conscience is therefore divided into exciting, restraining, and admonishing.* <26>

SECTION XXXIX

Conscience is either right or erroneous.

Moreover, because conscience is a reasoning, the same things agree to it which are true of a syllogism; wherefore as reasoning, so conscience may be either *right* or *erroneous;* and as every reasoning is either faulty in the *form* or in the *matter,* so conscience errs, either because the law, or because the action is not rightly represented; or because the rules of just reasoning are not observed.†

---

the nature even of those actions which appear trivial and indifferent to others; for which reason, their conscience is said to be tender and delicate. Plutarch says elegantly, de profectu virt. sent. p. 85. "Let this likewise be added, if you please, as a mark of no small moment, that he who is making proficiency in virtue, looks upon no sin as venial, but carefully shuns and avoids every appearance of evil." [[Plutarch, "How a Man May Become Aware of His Progress in Virtue," in vol. 1 of Plutarch, *Moralia: in Fourteen Volumes,* p. 455.]]

* Thus conscience excited Moses and Zippora to circumcise their son, recalling to their mind the divine precept about circumcision, *Exod.* iv. 24. Conscience restrained David from perpetrating his intended murder of Nabal, setting before him the divine command, "Thou shalt not kill." 1 *Sam.* xxv. 32. Finally, conscience admonished St. Paul not to eat meat which he knew had been consecrated to idols, and to give the same counsel to the Corinthians. For tho' he knew that christians could not be defiled by meats and drinks; yet his conscience advised him to act prudently, lest he should give offence to any one, 1 *Cor.* x. 28. and hence his golden maxim: "All things are lawful to me, but all things are not expedient: all things are lawful, but all things edify not."

† To illustrate this by examples. The Jews erred in the *matter,* when they thought they could without sin with-hold from their parents what was due to them, provided they devoted it to God. For the *major,* in their reasoning, set forth a *false law.* "But ye say, whosoever shall say to his father or his mother, it is a gift by whatsoever thou

SECTION XL

Again, as in other reasonings, so likewise in those of conscience chiefly, it happens that an argument is sometimes taken from a certain principle, and sometimes from an hypothesis, a probable proposition, but yet merely hypothetical. Hence conscience is called *certain,* when it argues upon an indisputable law; and *probable,* when it founds upon the probable opinion of others.* Now, because there are various degrees of probability, conscience must sometimes be more, and sometimes less probable. <27>

It is either certain or probable.

SECTION XLI

Because what is probable may be true, or may be false (§40): therefore it happens that probable arguments present themselves to us on both sides of the question; now in this case we think more deliberation is required, the affair being dubious; and conscience is then said to be

What doubtful and scrupulous conscience mean?

---

mightest be profited by me." *Mat.* xv. 5. So likewise Abimelech, when he imagined he could innocently take Sarah into his bed. For he made a false state of the fact, imagining he was to lie with an unmarried woman, *Gen.* xx. 2. To conclude, the Pharisees erred in the *form,* when they inferred from the law relative to the sabbath, this false conclusion, that no work of necessity and mercy was to be done on it. *Mat.* xii. 10.

* Probable conscience must not therefore be opposed to right conscience, because probable conscience may be right. But it may be false; for as in reasoning we may be deceived by a specious shew of certainty, and mistake a *paralogism* for a demonstration; so we are much more liable to have a false appearance of probability put upon us by *sophisms:* whence we see the slipperiness of that doctrine maintained by certain modern casuists concerning the sufficiency of *probable conscience,* to exculpate from sin, of which see Lud. Montalt. Litt. ad provincial. Ep. 5. and Sam. Rachel. Disser. de *probabilismo.* [[Pascal, *Ludovicii Montaltii litterae provinciales de morali & politia Jesuitarum disciplina.* The 1664 Helmstedt edition includes the dissertation by Rachel to which Heineccius refers.]] For unless we admit a rule which is a mere *proteus* to be a good one: We cannot possibly imagine we have done our duty, if we take probable conscience for our guide, which is neither always right, nor certain, nor constant (§5): especially, since these doctors measure probability by the opinions of others; whereas the apostle forbids us to trust to the judgment of others in matters of so great moment. "Let every man be fully persuaded in his own mind." *Rom.* xiv. 5.

doubtful; but if the perplexity we are in, and cannot get totally rid of, be of smaller consequence, it is then called *scrupulous.** <28>

SECTION XLII

What free and less free conscience mean?

Besides, it may happen that the mind, precipitated into vice by impetuous appetites, and as it were enslaved by evil habits, is not able to reason freely about actions; but is strongly biassed towards the side of its passions; in which servile state conscience is not a free and impartial reasoner. But the mind which hath delivered itself from such miserable bondage into a state of liberty is free. This distinction is accurately explained by *Wolfius's Ethic.* §84.†¹

---

* That doubting of the mind, which suspends it between two opinions, is not improperly called by the learned Wolfius *Scrupulus:* [[Christian Wolff (1679–1754) was professor of mathematics and then of philosophy at the University of Halle and one of the key figures of the German Enlightenment. Wolff had to leave Halle in 1723 because of controversies with the Lutheran Pietists and went to the University of Marburg, returning to Halle in 1740 as a protégé of Frederick the Great.]] But our definition seems more agreeable to the primitive meaning of the word. For *Scrupulus* signifies a very small pebble, which yet getting into the shoe creates no small pain. So Servius explains it, ad Aen. 6. v. 236. [[Servius (fourth century A.D.) was the author of a commentary on Virgil's *Aeneid* (*Servii Grammatici qui feruntur in Vergilii carmina commentarii*).]] Apuleius opposes (scrupulum) to a more perplexing anxiety which he commonly calls *lancea.* See Scip. Gent. ad Apuleii Apolog. p. 150. [[Presumably Scipione Gentili, *In L. Apuleii Philosophi & Advocati Romani Apologiam.* This appeared in an edition in Hanau in 1607, though it is not certain whether this is the edition Heineccius used.]]

1. Wolff, *Philosophia moralis sive ethica,* vol. 1.

† Hence that paradox of the Stoics: "Every wise man only is free: and every fool is a slave." Cicero. Parad. 5. [[Cicero, *Paradoxa Stoicorum,* "Paradox V," 285.]] He whose virtue hath rescued him from slavery to vice, into a state of freedom, despises and tramples upon every disorderly passion, and says with great magnanimity: "I will not receive arbitrary commands: I will not put my neck under a yoke: I must know what is greatest and noblest; what requires most strength of mind: the vigour of the soul must not be relaxed: If I yield to pleasure, I must succumb to pain, to toil, to poverty. Nay, ambition and anger will claim the same power over me," Seneca. Ep. 51. [[Seneca, *Ad Lucilium epistulae morales,* vol. 1, 341.]] Upon which place Lipsius ad Philos. Stoic. l. 3. Disser. 12. [[Justus Lipsius (1547–1606), Flemish humanist scholar; the work referred to is his *Manuductio ad stoicam philosophiam libri tres,* first published in Antwerp in 1604]] discourses to this purpose: "Mark, says he, how many

SECTION XLIII

We know by experience that men are sometimes lulled so fast asleep by
their vices, that they have no feeling of their misery, and never think
upon duty, or right and wrong. Now, as we then say, conscience is in a
deep *lethargy;* or if it is, by a long habit of vice, become quite obdurate
and <29> callous, we say it is *seared* as with a burning iron.* So conscience seems as it were to *awake,* when a person rouzed by calamity, or
a sense of danger, begins to examine and ponder his actions with some
attention, and to reflect and reason about their goodness or depravity.

What sleeping,
awakened and
seared con-
science mean?

SECTION XLIV

We have already remarked that every one's conscience condemns or absolves him (§35): but because absolution must be accompanied with the
highest satisfaction of mind, and condemnation with the bitterest uneasiness and disquiet; hence it follows, that a good conscience, acting
upon certain evidence, is for the most part quiet and easy; an evil conscience is disturbed by racking remorse; (which torment the antients
compared to the burning torches of the furies): and a dubious one is very
anxious and restless, to such a degree, that it knows not to what hand to
turn itself. These affections however belong more properly to the effects

What is meant
by quiet,
disturbed,
anxious,
disquieted
conscience and
remorse?

---

masters he had already rid himself of? Add to these, lust, avarice, and other vicious
passions, and you will have a multitude of what may properly be called tyrants. How
wretched is the slave who is in subjection to them! How free and great is he who hath
put them under his feet? What liberty can we say remains to a conscience which so
many vitious disorderly appetites and passions have fettered and enshackled?"

* *Cauterio usta,* an emphatical way of speaking by St. Paul, 1 Tim. iv. 2. For as
the finger, or any member of the body burnt with a hot iron loses all sensibility; so
the mind inured to a vitious course, does not feel its misery which others behold with
horror: the same apostle, Ephes. iv. 19. calls such persons *past feeling.* See Beza's commentary on the place. [[Theodor Beza (1519–1605), Calvinist theologian; his commentary on the New Testament first appeared in 1565.]]

of conscience than to conscience itself, as every one will immediately perceive.* <30>

SECTION XLV

Whether con-
science be the
rule of human
actions?

Whence we see what judgment we are to form of the opinion of those who assert that conscience is to be held for the internal rule of human actions. For if a rule cannot answer the end of a rule unless it be right, certain, and invariable (§5); who will admit conscience to be a rule which is sometimes erroneous (§39); sometimes only probable (§40); sometimes doubtful and wavering; (§41) and frequently overpowered by perverse appetites (§42); wherefore, tho' he be guilty who acts contrary to conscience, whether certain or probable; yet he cannot for that reason be said to act rightly and justly, who contends that he has acted according to his conscience.† <31>

---

* So Cicero pro Sex. Rosc. Amer. cap. 24. [[Cicero, *Pro Roscio Amerino,* chap. 24, in Cicero, *Defence Speeches.*]] Now these remorses of conscience are an irrefragable argument against those who absurdly maintain, that the uneasiness of conscience arises wholly from the fear of civil punishment, to which criminals are obnoxious. For in the first place, 'tis not private persons only who are harrassed day and night by these terrible furies; but even those whom birth and grandeur have set above all liableness to punishment in this world, such as a Nero, according to Sueton. cap. 34 [[Suetonius (ca. 69–ca. 140), author of several biographies of Roman emperors (Suetonius, *Suetonius,* vol. 2, 171)]]. And secondly, if any should rather imagine he feared the just resentment of the people, there are not wanting examples of persons who in their dying moments, when they could have nothing to fear from men, have been inexpressibly tortured by a secret consciousness of crimes unknown to the world: as Chilo Lacedemonius, who in Aulus Gell. Noct. Att. l. 3. thus speaks, "I surely," said he, "at this moment do not deceive myself, when I think I have committed no crime the remembrance of which can create me any uneasiness, one only excepted," *&c.* [[Aulus Gellius, *Noctes Atticae* (*Attic Nights*), vol. 1, bk. I, chap. iii, 3.]] And Sueton relates a saying of the emperor Titus to the same purport. Tit. cap. 10.

† Conscience is not the rule, but it applies the rule to facts and cases which occur; wherefore, it is safer to omit an action concerning the pravity of which we reckon ourselves fully convinced, than it is to do an action which conscience esteems just and good, without being certain of the law. He then who follows an erroneous conscience sins on this very account, that he follows it rather than the will of the legislator: tho' he be more excusable than one who acts directly against conscience, yet he is guilty. For which reason, I cannot go along with the opinion of Limborch, who in

SECTION XLVI

Hence we may conclude, that while conscience is uncertain, and fluc-
tuates between contrary opinions, action ought to be suspended. This
we assert in opposition to Ger. Gottl. Titus,[2] in his observations on Puffendorf de off. hom. & civ. l. 1. C. 1. §6. And for one to do any thing
with such an obstinate obdurate mind, as to be very little concerned
about knowing the divine will, and determined to do the same, even tho'
he should find it to be prohibited by God, is the heighth of perverse-
ness.*

Why action ought to be suspended while conscience doubts?

SECTION XLVII

From what hath been laid down, it is plain that *ignorance* and *error* are
the great hinderances to conscience in the application of a law to a fact.
By the former is understood the mere want of knowledge; by the other
is meant the disagreement of an idea, a judgment, or a reasoning to truth,
or the nature of the thing. One therefore is said to be ignorant who hath
no idea before his mind; and one is said to err, who hath either a false
idea of the object, that is, an idea not conformable to it; an obscure,
confused, or unadequate idea. For an error in the idea must of necessity

The weak-nesses or defects of the understanding, ignorance and error.

---

his Christian Theol. l. 5. c. 2. §8. maintains, that even an erroneous conscience must
be obeyed. [[Philipp Limborch (1633–1712), Dutch Arminian theologian and friend
of John Locke. His *Theologia Christiana* first appeared in 1686 in Amsterdam.]]

   * To this purpose it is well said by Cicero de Off. l. 9. "For this reason it is a good
precept which forbids us to do any thing, of the goodness or iniquity of which we
are in doubt. For honesty quickly would shew itself by its own native brightness: and
the doubting about it is a plain intimation that at least we suspect some injustice in
it." *i.e.* He who ventures to do what he doubts whether it be honest or dishonest, by
so doing bewrays a propension to do an injury. Hence the apostle says, *Rom.* xiv. 23.
"And he that doubteth is damned if he eat, because he eateth not of faith, and whatsoever is not of faith is sin."

   2. Gottlieb Gerhard Titius (1661–1714) was professor of law at the University of
Leipzig. He developed Pufendorf's and Thomasius's natural law theories and advo-
cated the reform of criminal law. Heineccius refers to Titius's *Observationes in Samuelis L. B. de Pufendorfii De officio hominis et civis juxta legem naturalem libros duos.*

infuse itself into the judgment made concerning an object, and from thence into all the reasonings about it. <32>

SECTION XLVIII

Whether igno-
rance and error
of all sorts be
culpable?

But because all men are not under an obligation to find out the more abstruse truths which may be said to lie at the bottom of a deep well; and in reality the ignorance of some things is rather attended with advantage than detriment;* (yea, as Terence observes, Hecyra.[3] the ignorant and illiterate often do more good in one day, than ever the learned and knowing do;) hence it may be inferred, that ignorance and error of every kind is not evil and blameable.

SECTION XLIX

What kind of
ignorance and
what kind
of error is
culpable?

Yet since the will makes no election unless it be excited to it by the understanding; and therefore the understanding concurs in producing moral actions (§30), the consequence from this is, that they are not blameless who are grosly ignorant of those truths relative to good and ill, just and unjust, which it was in their power easily to understand, or who err with regard to these matters, when error might have been avoided by due care and attention to acquire right and true knowledge.

---

* An example of this might be brought from the ignorance of certain crimes, which ought not so much as to be named; for there the maxim holds, *ignotorum nulla cupido;* what is unknown is undesired. Who would not wish many were in a state of ignorance, which would effectually shut out and render the mind quite inaccessible to certain vile concupiscences? Justin. Hist. 2. 2. says, "the Scythians were better through their ignorance of several vices than the Greeks were by their knowledge of virtue." [[Marcus Junianus Justinus's *History,* bk. 2, at the end of chap. 2 (*Justini Historiae Philipicae*).]] Nor does Quintilian seem to have less admired the ancient Germans, when speaking of a most enormous vice, he says "they were totally ignorant of it: their manner of living was more pure, &c." [[Marcus Fabius Quintilianus (ca. 35–ca. 100), Roman rhetorician and author of the *Institutio oratoria* (Education of an Orator).]]

3. Terence, *The Mother-in-Law,* lines 879–80, in vol. 2 of *Terence.*

SECTION L

Hence arise various divisions or classes of ignorance and error, so far as it is or is not in our power <33> to escape ignorance, it is *vincible* or *invincible.* * So far as one is or is not the cause of it himself, it is *voluntary* or *involuntary.* Finally, if one does any thing he would not have done had his mind not been obscured by ignorance, such ignorance is called *efficacious* or *effectual.* But if he would have done the same action tho' he had not been in the state of ignorance in which he did it, it is called *concomitant.* Repentance is the mark of the former; but the latter discovers itself by the approbation given to the action done in a state of ignorance, when that ignorance no longer takes place. Now all this is equally applicable to error.

Ignorance is either vincible or invincible, voluntary or involuntary, efficacious or concomitant.

SECTION LI

We proceed now to consider the other principle of human or moral free actions, *viz.* the *will*, (§30) which <34> is that faculty of our mind by which we choose and refuse. Hence it is justly said, that truth and fals-

What will is?

---

* Ignorance and error are said to be invincible, either in regard of their cause or in themselves; or in both respects at the same time. Thus the ignorance of a drunken person is in itself invincible, so long as his madness continues; but not in respect of its cause, because it was in his power not to have contracted that madness. On the other hand, the hurtful actions of mad men proceed from ignorance, which is invincible, both in itself and in regard of its cause, since they not only do not know what they are doing, but it was not in their power to have escaped their madness. All this is true, and hath its use in the doctrine of *imputation:* But the first cannot so properly be called invincible, since it might and would have been avoided, had not the mind been very regardless of duty. The matter is admirably explained by Aristotle in his books to Nicomachus, 3. 7. where speaking of that law of Pittacus which inflicted a double punishment upon the crimes committed by drunken persons, he immediately adds: "A double punishment is appointed for the crimes of drunken persons; because these actions are in their source from them. It was in their power not to get drunk. But drunkenness was the cause of their ignorance." Concerning this law of Pittacus see Diogenes Laertius, 1. 76. [[Diogenes Laertius, *Lives of Eminent Philosophers*, vol. 1, 79]] and Plutarch in Conviv. sept. sap. p. 155 [[Plutarch, "Septem Sapientum Convivium" (Dinner of the Seven Wise Men), in Plutarch, *Moralia*, vol. 2, 403]].

hood are the objects of the understanding; but that the will is conversant about good and ill. For the will only desires truth as it is good, and is averse to falshood only as it is ill.*

SECTION LII

Its nature and acts.

From this definition we may conclude that the will cannot choose any thing but what is exhibited to it by the understanding under the shew of good, nor turn aside from any thing but what appears to it to be ill. The greater good or ill there seems to be in any thing, the stronger in proportion is our inclination or aversion; and therefore the desire of a lesser good or a lesser evil may be overpowered by the representation of a greater good or evil. Aversion does not consist in a mere absence of desire, but hath something positive in it, which is called by Koehler, exerc. jur. nat. §167.[4] *noluntas* vel *reclinatio, refusing* or *aversion.*† <35>

SECTION LIII

Its spontanity and liberty.

From the same definition it is clear that man, with regard to his will, acts not only *spontaneously* but *freely.* For *spontaneity* being the faculty of

* Thus no wise man desires to know his future calamities, because it would only serve to anticipate his suffering. And therefore, however true his foreknowledge might be, it would not be good. Children, on the other hand, are very fond of fables, even tho' they know they are feigned, because they perceive them to be fit lessons for their instruction; or at least very entertaining: and on these accounts, they look upon them as good.

† As the Civilians accurately distinguish between *non nolle & velle,* l. 3. D. de reg. Juris; so we ought to distinguish between *not willing,* and *not desiring* and *refusing,* or *having an aversion.* There are many things which a wise man does not choose or will, tho' he does not abhor them. Thus he does not desire immortality on earth, because nature hath not granted it; nor empire, because fortune hath not allotted it to his birth: But he has no aversion to these things, but on the contrary pronounces them great and noble goods. He does not desire what his rank puts beyond his power to attain, but he would not dislike it if he could obtain it. Thus *Abdolominus,* intent upon his daily employment, dressing and weeding his little garden, had no thoughts of royalty: he did not desire it, yet he did not refuse and despise it, when he was saluted king, and presented with the royal robes and ensigns. Cur. de gest. Alex. 4. 1. [[Curtius Rufus, *De gestis Alexandri Magni (History of Alexander,* Rolfe, vol. 1, 167).]]

4. Koehler, *Exercitationes juris naturalis.*

directing one's aim to a certain end, but liberty being the power of choosing either of two possibles one pleases; it is plain from experience, that both these faculties belong to our minds. The servile subjection one is under to his perverse appetites and affections till virtue makes him free, is not inconsistent with these properties. For these obstacles are of such a kind, as hath been observed, that they may be removed and overpowered by the representation of a greater good or evil to the understanding (§52).* <36>

SECTION LIV

Hence it is evident, that bodily constitution, (which philosophers call *temperament*) does not infringe upon the liberty of human will. For tho' the mind be variously affected by the body, so as to be rendered by it more propense to certain vices; yet that propensity hath no more of compulsion or force in it than there is in the inducement to walk out when fine weather invites one to it. But who can deny that the will is left intire, and not hindered or prevented from choosing either to walk out or not as it shall appear most reasonable, when inticed by all the charms of spring?

Do temperament or bodily constitution affect it?

---

* Thus, whatever propension a thief may have to steal, yet he would not yield to that wicked cupidity, could he set before his eyes the dismal effects of his crimes, the horrors of a dungeon and shackles, and the ignominy of a gibbet. And those who are most highly charmed with indolence and voluptuousness, would quickly be inflamed with the love of a nobler life and more honourable pursuits, if, calling in reason to advise them, they could fully perceive the excellence of wisdom, its agreeableness and manifold advantages on the one hand, and on the other side the irreparable ignominy and detriment which are inseparable from sloth and ignorance. Epictetus dispatches the whole matter with great brevity. Arrian. l. 17. "Can any thing overcome an appetite? Another appetite can. Can any thing get the ascendant of an inclination or propensity? Yes really another can." And he illustrates it by the same example of a thief we have just now made use of. [[Epictetus, *The Discourses as Reported by Arrian, the Manual, and Fragments*, vol. 1, 1.17.24.]]

SECTION LV

Whether affections and habits encroach upon it?

The same is true concerning all the affections and motions excited in the mind by the appearances of good and ill. For tho' the mind, with respect to the first impression, be passive, every thing else is however intirely in its power; to resist the first impulse, not to approve it, nor to suffer it to gain too much force. And it likewise holds with regard to habits, *i.e.* propensions confirmed by long use and practice. For tho' these gradually become so natural, that tho' expelled with never so much force, they recoil, Hor. ep. 1. 10. v. 24. (*si expellas furca, tamen usque recurret*)[5] yet they are not incorrigible, but may be amended, if one will but exert his liberty.* <37>

SECTION LVI

What may be said of external force.

External violence is so far from taking away the liberty of the human mind, that it affords a strong proof of our liberty. For tho' one may be hindered by force from doing what he chooses to do; yet no force can

---

* Habits are affections and propensities become strong by daily repetition or custom. Now what has been contracted by practice may by disuse be abolished and erazed, if we will but give as great pains to destroy it as we did to establish it into strength. There is an elegant passage to this effect in Aristophanes in Vespis. thus translated into Latin.

> *Usus quo fueris diu,*
> *Mutare ingenium, grave est.*
> *Multos invenias tamen,*
> *Qui mores moniti suos*
> *Mutarunt melioribus.*

[[Aristophanes, *Wasps* (*Vespae*), 1457ff.; trans. (though not exactly) into Latin. Aristophanes, *Wasps,* ed. MacDowell: "It is a serious matter to change the nature of a habit which you've had for a long time. However, you would find that many people who have taken advice and changed their ways have done so for the better."]]

5. Horace, *Epistles* 1.10.24, in *Satires, Epistles, and Ars Poetica:* "You may drive out Nature with a pitch-fork, yet she will ever hurry back."

make one will what he does not will, or not choose what he chooses.* If the understanding represents the good attending an action as greater than the imminent evil, no external violence can force one to quit his resolution, he will remain unshaken by all the menaces of power or cruelty.

> Nec civium ardor prava jubentium
> Nec vultus instantis tyranni
> Mente quatiet solida.[6]

SECTION LVII

Hence we see that the distinction between *antecedent* and *consequent will* ought not to be rejected; the former of which decides without a view of all the circumstances which may happen at the time of acting; the other suits itself to the circumstances which appear at that instant. The one therefore is not opposite to the other, tho' they be very different. Thus it is true that God loves peace, and yet that in certain circumstances he does not disapprove war. <38>

The will is divided into consequent and antecedent.

SECTION LVIII

Further, it is equally plain that those actions are *spontaneous* which are performed by a mind determining itself to a certain known proposed end; these are not spontaneous which do not proceed from such a determination of the mind, but are done without intention. Again, even spontaneous actions are *voluntary*, to perform which no external neces-

Actions are spontaneous, forced, voluntary, and mixed.

---

* This is likewise observed by Epictetus in Arrian, l. 1. 17. After he had asserted, that an appetite can only be overcome by another appetite, he adds: "But it may be said, he who threatens me with death forces me. Truly the cause is not that which is threatened, but it is owing to your thinking it better to do the action than to run the risk of dying: it is therefore your opinion which forces you, *i.e.* one appetite overcomes another."

6. Horace, *Odes* 3.3.2–4 in *Odes and Epodes:* "The man of integrity who holds fast to his purpose is not shaken from his firm resolve by hot-headed citizens urging him to do wrong, or by the frown of an oppressive despot."

sity compels; and such are *forced,* to which one is necessitated by some external urgent circumstances. We need not add *mixed,* because actions called such, being performed under some external necessity urging to it, coincide with those which are called forced actions.*

SECTION LIX

Actions not spontaneous are involuntary. Forced actions are voluntary.

Hence it is obvious that no action which is not spontaneous is voluntary (§58); but forced actions may be voluntary. For tho' we would rather not act were not a very great evil set before us, yet it is the will which determines to act; whence it follows, that the antient lawyers were in the right when they affirmed, that one who is forced, wills. D. l. 21. §5. *quod met. causa,* "coactum etiam velle." <39>

REMARKS on This Chapter

Our Author doth not enter at all into the dispute about necessity and free agency. It would have been a digression from his subject. The question is most accurately handled by Mr. Locke in the chapter of Power, in his Essay on human understanding. See likewise what I have said of it in my Introduction to the principles of moral philosophy; and in the Christian philosophy, sect. 3. prop. 4. But I think the whole matter may

---

* Those are called by some mixed actions, which one does under an urgent necessity, so as that he would rather not do them. Such as that case described by Lucretius de rer. nat. l. 2. v. 277.

> *Jamne vides igitur, quamquam vis extima multas*
> *Pellit, & invitos cogit procedere saepe,*
> *Praecipitesque rapit, tamen esse in pectore nostro*
> *Quiddam, quod contra pugnare obstareque possit?*

[[Lucretius, *De rerum natura* 2.77–80: "In this case do you see then that, although an external force propels many men and forces them often to move against their will and to be hurried headlong, yet there is in our breast something strong enough to fight against it and to resist?"]]

The same happens in every forced action. For no external violence can force us to will or not to will (§56) and therefore there is no use for the distinction between compelled or forced and mixed actions.

be dispatched in a few words. It is as much a matter of experience as
any other whatever. That several things depend upon our will as to their
existence or non-existence; as to sit, or stand, or walk; to write or not
write: to think or leave off thinking on this or the other subject, &c.
But so far as it depends in this manner on our will, or pleasure to do,
or not to do, we are free, we have power, dominion, agency; or we are
not passive but active beings. To say we are not free, but necessary, must
be to assert either that we are not conscious, which is contrary to experience; or that we never will, which is also contrary to experience; or
that our will never is effective, which is equally so, since many things
depend on our will: For necessity must mean one or other of these
three, or all of them together. There is no other property included in
the idea of a free agent; there is no other conceivable property belonging to action or agency, besides willing with power to effect what is
willed. To say that the will is not free, because it must desire good and
hate ill as such, is to say freedom or activity cannot belong to a mind
endued with the power of willing; since willing means complacency in
good, or preferring it, and aversion to evil, or desire to avoid it, *i.e.* it
is to say freedom means some property that can't exist, because it implies a contradiction, *viz.* willing without willing. Freedom is the very
idea of agency: it is that which constitutes an agent; and it signifies
having a certain degree or extent of power, efficiency, or dominion by
our will. And that we have a certain degree or extent of power, efficiency, or dominion by our will, is as manifest to experience as that we
think: nor can a proof of it be demanded, unless at the same time a
proof of thinking and consciousness be demanded.

As for what our Author says about erroneous conscience, it will be
better understood by what is said in the fourth chapter about imputation, and our remark added to that chapter. Mean time we may observe, 1. That if to acquire knowledge for the direction of our actions
be not among our τὰ ἐφ' ἡμὶν, or within our power, the direction of
our actions cannot be in our power, that is, we are not agents. If we are
not accountable for our not having knowledge sufficient to direct our
actions rightly, we cannot be accountable for our actions. 2. Our views,
our judgments of things must be our rule; we can have no other: yet
ultimately, the nature of things is the rule, because the natures of things
are stubborn, and will not yield to our misapprehensions <40> of

them. It is the same here as with regard to mechanicks, where no difficulty is started. The nature of mechanical powers and properties will not submit to our notions; yet we must work in mechanical arts according to our apprehensions of mechanical laws and properties. Our ideas and judgments are our immediate guide; but the natural qualities and relations of things are the ultimate standard. The former may vary, but the latter are unchangeable. The ultimate measure of opinions, which is truth or nature, is constant, immutable.

Of the rule of human actions, and the true principle of the law of nature.

SECTION LX

Such, we have already seen, is the nature of our free actions, that they must have a rule to direct them (§4); there we likewise shewed that a rule could not serve the purposes of a rule, if it be not streight or right, certain, evident, and invariable, and have external as well as internal obligation. Let us now enquire a little more accurately what this rule is which hath all these properties essential to a rule for human, free, moral actions.* <41>

Of what nature or kind the rule of human action must be.

---

* Let us not confound the rule of human actions with the principle of natural law. The former is what philosophers call the (principium essendi) because it constitutes the principle or source of obligation to us. By the latter we understand principium cognoscendi, *i.e.* the principle, the truth or proposition from which our obligation to any action appears or may be deduced. These are different, even with regard to civil states. For the source or principle of the obligation under which all the members of any state whatsoever lie, is the will of the supreme authority in that state, and that is also the rule to which every member of a state is obliged to conform himself. But if it is asked whence or how that supreme will may be known, in every state you will be referred to its laws; and therefore, these are likewise in every state the sole and adequate principle or source of knowledge with respect to civil duties and obligations.

SECTION LXI

The rule of human actions is not to be found in us, but without us.

The rule of human actions must either be within us or without us. If it be within us, it can be none other but either our own will, or our understanding and conscience. But neither of these faculties is always right, neither of them is always certain, neither of them is always the same and invariable; wherefore neither any of them, nor both of them together, can be the rule of human actions; whence it follows that the rule of human actions is not to be found in ourselves; but if there be any such, it must be without us.

SECTION LXII

It is to be found in the will of God.

Now without us exist other created beings, and likewise a *God,* the author of all things which exist. But since we are enquiring after a rule of human actions, carrying with it an external obligation (§9) and made known or promulgated to all mankind by right reason (§11); and since external obligation consists in the will of some being, whose authority we acknowledge (§9), there being no other whose authority we are obliged more strictly to acknowledge than the infinitely perfect and blessed *God* (§10); and seeing he alone can promulgate any thing to us by right reason, of which he is the author, it follows, by necessary consequence, that the *will of God* must be the rule of human actions, and the principle or source of all natural obligation, and of all virtue.* <42>

SECTION LXIII

The will of God is a right, certain, and constant rule.

That this rule is *right* cannot be doubted, since an infinitely perfect Being cannot will what is not perfectly good and right: it must be a *certain* rule, since reason discovers it to all men; and it must be *unvariable,* because the will of God can no more change, or be changed, than God himself,

---

* We therefore fall in with the opinion of the celebrated Sam. a Cocceis, who in his dissertations already cited (§10) has demonstrated this truth by solid arguments, and likewise defended it against objections and censures with great judgment and

or right reason, by which it is discoverable. Finally, it must be *obligatory,* since God hath the justest claim and title to our obedience; and men have no reason or right to decline his authority, and cannot indeed if they would. Hence at the same time it is evident, that every will of God is not the rule of human actions, but his obligatory will only.*

SECTION LXIV

Since therefore the *obligatory will of God,* which we have shewn to be the only rule of human actions, is his will with respect to the actions of his rational creatures, as to acting or forbearing to act (§63); it is evident, that this rule, considered with relation to man, may properly be called *a divine law,* because it is the will of the supreme Being, commanding or forbidding certain actions with rewards and penalties (§9). But because there are other laws of <43> God to mankind which are made known by revelation, and are therefore called *positive,* those which are known to man by natural reason, are justly denominated *natural;* and according as they either command, prohibit, or permit, they are with good reason divided into *affirmative, negative,* or *permissive.*

This rule may be called a law with regard to mankind.

---

erudition, Dissert. 1. qu. 2. §6. & seq. where he has gathered together very many passages from ancient authors to prove this to have been the more general opinion of ancient moralists, the chief of whom are Xenophon, Sophocles and Cicero.

* The will of God is of a large extent, and its various divisions are fully explained in treatises of natural theology; by none more accurately than by Ruardus Andala, Theolog. nat. part. 2. c. 8. §6. & seq. [[Ruardus Andala (1665–1727), Dutch Cartesian philosopher and theologician; *Syntagma theologico-physico-metaphysicum, complectens Compendium theologiae naturalis*]] and Wolfius Theolog. nat. part. 1. c. 3. [[Wolff, *Theologia naturalis*]]. It is sufficient for us to observe, that God himself being the primary object of his will, as he loves, approves, and delights in his own perfections, and the whole universe, to which he gives being by his will, is upheld, governed and moved according to certain laws chosen and approved of by him, and is therefore the object of his will; wherefore here we understand by the divine will, the will of God relative to the actions of his intelligent creatures, either with respect to doing, or not doing: and this will we call *moral* or *obligatory.*

SECTION LXV

The explica-
tion of the
divine justice
may be
deduced from
the divine will.

Now since this divine will, or divine natural law, is the source and principle of all justice (§63), it follows that every action, not only human,
but divine, which is conformable to this divine will, is *just;* and therefore
it is objected, without any reason, against this doctrine, that there could
not be any such thing as divine justice, were there no other principle or
source of the law besides the *divine will.** <44>

* The author of the Observat. Hanover. ob. 8. objects against this doctrine of
Sam. de Cocceis in this manner: "Other dangerous consequences would likewise follow from this position, such as have indeed been thrown out by some most rashly
and unwarily; as for instance, that there is no such thing as divine justice. For if justice
only means the command of the Creator, or of one who hath power to enforce his
will; it is manifest that justice cannot belong or be ascribed to God, since he cannot
be forced or compelled; and therefore he may without any injustice damn an innocent
person, and make the greatest scelerate immortally happy. Upon which hypothesis,
the fear of God will indeed remain, but the love of him cannot take place." [[The
author is probably Gottfried Wilhelm Leibniz, though it is not clear which work
Heineccius is referring to here.]] But since God wills nothing but what is right and
just, why may not the divine justice be explained from the consideration of his will?
There is indeed, with respect to God, no command, no co-action, and therefore no
external obligation: but the same holds true with regard to supreme authority in states,
in relation to the laws constituted by it. For tho' a prince who has supreme absolute
power be not strictly speaking bound by his own laws; yet we call him just, when he
renders to every one conformably to his own laws. Why then may we not call God
just, because he renders to every man what is due to him, according to his own will
and law? Man therefore is denominated just, when he gives obedience to the will of
God promulgated as a law. But God is just, because he renders to every one his due
without law, without co-action or external obligation. God cannot damn an innocent
person, or make an abandoned scelerate happy. Because by so doing, he would act
not according to his own will, by which he wills nothing but what is just, equitable,
and suitable to his own perfection.

SECTION LXVI

Herein chiefly lies the difference between *divine* and *human* justice, that with regard to the former there is no law or co-action; whereas the latter includes in it a respect to a law, and external obligation or co-action (§65 & §64). Wherefore the divine will, as it is a rule of action to men, carries with it a commination of some evil or punishment to transgressors; tho' that punishment be not, as in human laws, defined and ascertained, but be, for the greater part, indefinite, and reserved to God himself, to be inflicted according to his wisdom and justice.* <45>

The difference between the rule of divine and the rule of human justice, in what does it consist?

SECTION LXVII

But since it cannot be doubted that there is no other rule of human actions but the will or law of God (§63), it is to be enquired how we may come to the certain knowledge of this law. But since it is universally acknowledged to be promulgated to all men by right reason (§11), and since right reason is our faculty of reasoning, by which we deduce truths from other truths by a chain of consequences (§15), it is obvious that there must be some truth or proposition, from which what is agreeable to the will of God, and therefore just, may be ascertained by necessary

That we may apply this rule, there must be some principle or criterion by which it may be known or ascertained.

---

* Those who call every suffering or evil which attends a bad action, or is connected with it, *punishment,* rightly divide *punishment* into *natural* and *positive.* So the learned Koehler. exercitat. jur. nat. §362, & seq. But if by *punishment* be understood the suffering or evil which the law itself threatens against offenders, it is *positive punishment* only which properly falls under the name of *legal* or *authorative punishment. Natural punishment* is acknowledged even by atheists. *Positive punishment* those only can acknowledge who believe the divine Being, and providence: Now, tho' particular *positive punishments* be not defined; yet right reason sufficiently proves that God cannot but render to mankind according to their actions, whether they be good or bad, suitable rewards and punishments. For that plainly and directly follows from the idea of the divine justice, and is admitted by all who do not call divine providence into doubt. Xenophon Memorab. Socrat. l. 4, 16. "Do you think the Gods would have impressed human minds with an opinion that they can inflict punishments and bestow rewards upon them, if they really could not do it; and if men being for ever deceived never felt any such thing?" [[Xenophon, *Memorabilia* (Xenophon, *Memorabilia and Oeconomicus*, 1.4.16).]]

consequence. There must then be some universal principle of science with regard to the law of nature.*

<h2 style="text-align:center">SECTION LXVIII</h2>

This principle must be true, evident, and adequate.

Every principle of science must be *true, evident,* and *adequate;* wherefore the principle of science, with respect to natural law, must be *true;* lest being false or fictitious, the conclusions inferred from it be such likewise: it must be *evident,* and that not only in this sense, that it is intelligible to the literate; but universally, to the unlearned as well as the learned, all being equally under obligation to <46> conform themselves to the law of nature. In fine, it must be *adequate,* or of such an extent, as to include in it all the duties of men and citizens, not Christians only, but those also who have not the benefit of divine revelation.†

---

* How that differs from the rule itself, hath been already explained (§60). Tho' the celebrated Sam. de Cocceiis hath taken the term *principle* in a larger acceptation, yet what is objected to him by Jac. Frid. Ludovici is a mere logomachy. [[Presumably this is Ludovici's *Delineatio historiae juris divini naturalis et positivi unversalis.*]] For how the will of God may be discovered by us, he shews Disser. 1. qu. 3. and he has there clearly distinguished between the *will of God,* as a rule and principle *essendi, i.e.* of moral obligation, and the means of science, or the proofs by which the will of God may be ascertained to us, which are the principles of science with respect to the law of nature.

† In like manner therefore, as the more subtile demonstrations of the divine existence are suspected, because that truth must be capable of an evidence that may be understood by the most ordinary understanding (and therefore the apostle says, "God may be found out by searching, and is not far from any of us," Acts xvii. 27). So a too subtle principle of natural law is suspicious, since all are, ἀναπολόγητοι, without excuse, even the illiterate, and those who are strangers to subtle refined philosophy, if they offend against the law of nature.

SECTION LXIX

Therefore we must not expect to find this principle of the law of nature in the conformity of our actions to the sanctity of God: for tho' the proposition should be granted to be true, yet it is not evident enough, nor of such a nature, as that all the duties of men and citizens can be inferred and proved from it.*

Whence this principle is not to be found in the sanctity of God.

SECTION LXX

Nor is this a sufficient principle, "that what is in its own nature just is to be done, and what is in its own nature unjust is not to be done." For tho' we have already admitted, that certain actions are <47> in their own nature good, and others evil, and that man is therefore obliged to perform the one, and to avoid the other, by an intrinsic obligation (§8); yet an action antecedently to, or independently of a law, is not just (§7); not to add that this principle is not evident enough, nor that all human offices are not deducible from it.†

Nor in the justice and injustice of actions considered in themselves.

* How obscure the idea of the divine sanctity is, whether in a theological or juridical sense, hath been already proved by Sam. Puffendorf. Specim. controvers. 4. 4. and Thomas. fundam. juris. nat. & gent. [[Pufendorf, *Specimen controversiarum circa jus naturali ipsi nuper motarum.* Christian Thomasius (1655–1728), German philosopher and foundational figure in the German Enlightenment, professor at Halle. The work referred to is his *Fundamenta juris naturae et gentium.*]] And because there are many human duties, of which there is no archetype in God, as for instance, gratitude towards our benefactors, reverence toward our superiors, paying debt, and such like: For these reasons it is not the principle of moral knowledge.

† To just actions we are impelled by an external obligation (§7). External obligation consists in the will of an acknowledged superior, commanding under penalty (§9): such a will is a law (§9). Wherefore, no action can be just or unjust but in reference to a law: and hence every sin is called ἀνομία, *i.e.* a transgression of a law. 1 Ep. *John* iii. 4.

SECTION LXXI

Nor in the consent of all nations.

None, I think, will rashly go into the opinion of those learned men, who held the consent of all nations, or of all the more civilized nations, to be the principle of natural law. For it is not *true,* that what all nations agree in, is also conformable to the divine will;* nor is this universal consent *evident* to all, since it must be collected from various testimonies of authors, antient and modern; nor is it sufficiently *adequate* to point out all duties.* <48>

SECTION LXXII

Nor in the seven precepts of *Noah.*

But as those who endeavour to establish the law of nature and nations from the consent of nations, not only lay down a false, unevident, and unadequate principle; but likewise go out of the question into one of another kind, while they derive the law of nature not from nature itself,

---

* Thus Cicero thought the voluntary law of nations, as it is called, must be established, Tusc. quest. disp. 1. 13. "The agreement of all nations in a thing is to be held a law of nature." Grotius lays great stress on this principle de jure belli & pacis, proleg. §11. where speaking of the way of establishing the laws of nature and nations, he says, "I have made use of the testimonies of Philosophers, Historians, Poets, and in the last place Orators; not that we are rashly and implicitly to give credit to whatever they say (for it is usual with them to accommodate themselves to the prejudices of their sect, the nature of their subject, and the interest of their cause): But that when many men of different times and places unanimously affirm the same thing for truth, this ought to be ascribed to an universal cause; which, in the questions treated of by us, can be no other than either a just conclusion drawn from the principles of nature, or an universal consent. The former points out the law of nature, the other the law of nations." But we find a wonderful consent almost of all nations in many things which none will assert to be of the law of nature or nations; as in polytheism, idolatry, sacrifices, robbery committed in a foreign territory. Besides this agreement of nations is not easily shewn, as Grotius himself confesses, l. 1. 1. 15. "But the more extensive is the law of nations, which derives its authority from the will of all, or at least, of many nations. I say, of many, because there is scarce any right found, except that of nature, which is also called the right of nations, common to all nations. Nay, that which is reputed the right or law of nations in one part of the world, is not so in another, as we shall shew hereafter, where we come to treat of *prisoners of war* and *postliminy,* or the *right of returning.*" How many duties therefore cannot be deduced from the consent of nations?

but from the traditions or opinions of nations: so the opinion of those who have attempted to deduce the law of nature and nations from the precepts given to Noah, labours under the same defects, as hath been sufficiently proved (§16).

SECTION LXXIII

What shall we then say of the whole philosophy of Hobbes[1] in his books de Cive, or his Leviathan? when he asserts the right of every man in a state of nature to all things, he affirms a proposition which is neither *true*, nor *evident*, nor *adequate*, since the duties of men to God and themselves cannot be deduced from that principle; yea, while he goes about in <49> that manner, pretending to establish the law of nature, he really subverts it, as Hen. Cocei.[2] def. de jure omnium in omnia, has shewn. Hence it is plain what we are to think of this other principle, viz. "that external peace is to be sought and studied if it can be obtained, and if not, force and war must be called to our aid." For here likewise Hobbes lurks behind a curtain.*

Nor in the right of all to all things, or in the study of external peace.

---

* First of all, this principle is far from being evident. For what means this limitation, *if it can be had?* How liable is it, however it may be explained, to be abused by litigious persons, who will complain that they cannot enjoy peace, if others will not suffer them? like the wolf in the fable, who pled that the lamb had troubled his water. Phaed. Fab. 1. 1. Some poet has justly said,

> *Sic nocet innocuo nocuus, caussamque nocendi*
> *Invenit. Heu regnant qualibet arte lupi.*

[["Some poet": this is Aesop's story, "The Wolf and the Lamb." Phaedrus's version (*Fabulae* 1.1) is somewhat different. This version has been attributed to Walter of England (though with *hi* rather than *heu* in the last line): "Thus the harmful harms the harmless and finds a reason for harming him. Alas wolves rule by whatever means they like."]]

This defect in this principle hath been already observed by Thomas. in Fundam. Jur. nat. & gent. 1. 6. 18.

1. Thomas Hobbes (1588–1679). See *On the Citizen* (*De cive*), 1.10, and *Leviathan*, chap. 13.

2. Heinrich Freiherr von Cocceji (1644–1719), father of Samuel Freiherr von Cocceji (see note p. 17). Heinrich von Cocceji promoted a natural law theory based on an extreme theocratic voluntarism.

SECTION LXXIV

Nor in the state of integrity.

That principle laid down by Val. Alberti[3] professor of divinity and philosophy at Leipsic, hath a specious shew of truth and piety, viz. a state of *integrity.* But Puffend. Specim. controv. 4. 12. and Thomas. jurisp. divin. 4. 40 & seq. have proved it to be false. And granting it to be true, that whatever is agreeable to a state of *primitive integrity,* is truly of the law of nature; yet how unevident this principle must be, not only to Pagans, but even to Christians, is manifest. Further, since the laws of citizenship, of war, of contracts, and many others, for which there was not place in that most happy state, cannot be deduced from the idea of it, who can call this principle *adequate?** <50>

SECTION LXXV

Nor in sociability.

Grotius, Puffendorf, and several antients, were wonderfully pleased with the principle of *sociability;* nor can it be denied, as we have afterwards expressly proved, that men are so framed that they must live *socially:* but that this is not the *true, evident,* and *adequate* principle of the law of nature, hath been already demonstrated by the learned and worthy Sam.

---

* How few things are told us in the sacred records that can give us an image of that state of integrity? About what is revealed to us in scripture concerning that state, Christians are divided into various sects and very differing opinions. What then shall we say of the Heathens, ancient and modern? They have a fable among them about a golden age, which some imagine to have taken its rise from a tradition concerning the paradise-state. They have other fictions with which they are highly delighted, which have some resemblance to the Christian doctrine concerning God, of which Pet. Dan. Huet. Quaest. Alnet. p. 172. hath treated in the learned manner so peculiar to him. [[Pierre-Daniel Huet (1630–1721), *Alnetanae quaestiones.*]] But so dissonant and widely differing are all these things, that no Christian will ever be able to persuade a Pagan, nor no Pagan a Christian, that this or the other thing is of the law of nature, which the one derives from his traditions and the other from his revelation, with relation to a state of integrity. We must therefore find out some principle common to Jews, Christians and Pagans, which can be no other but that right reason which is common to all mankind.

3. Valentin Alberti (1635–97), an orthodox Lutheran theologian at the University of Leipzig, who strongly opposed the natural law theories of Hugo Grotius, Samuel Pufendorf, and Christian Thomasius. Heineccius sides clearly with the last.

de Coccius de principio juris nat. diss. 1. qu. 2. §9.[4] I shall only add this one thing, that many of our duties to God, and to ourselves, would take place, even tho' man lived solitary, and without *society* in the world.* <51>

SECTION LXXVI

Other principles of natural law are highly boasted of by others; such as the order of nature, which the Creator intends in his works; the interest of mankind; a moral Theocracy, and other such like principles.† But it is agreed to by all, that these principles are not evident or adequate; and some of them indeed cannot be admitted without some cautions and restrictions.

Nor in the order of nature, and such like hypotheses.

* Cicero de legibus 1. 5. de off. 1. 16. & seq. Seneca de Benef. 4. 18. Iamblichus in Protrept. cap. 20 [[*Protrepticus*]], and several others, have considered the preservation of society as the true fountain of justice, and the foundation of natural law: many authors of this sentiment are accumulated by Puffendorf de jure nat. & gent. 2. 3. 15. and Jo. Hen. Boecler. in Grotii proleg. p. 48. [[Johann Heinrich Boecler (1611–72), professor of law at Strasbourg and author of a commentary on Grotius's *Law of War and Peace* (*In Hugonis Grotii Ius Belli et Pacis . . . Commentario*).]] But however many, formerly or at present, may have concurred in this opinion, we cannot however choose but observe there is a great difference amongst them in their account of the reason by which men are obliged to sociability: Some assert we are instigated to it by nature; some that we are bound to it by the will of God: others again maintain, that necessity alone compels men to a social life.

† After Sfort. Palavicinus [[Sforza Pallavicini, cardinal (1606–67)]], Hen. Bodinus in Disser. de jure mundi, maintained the order of nature to be the first principle of natural law. But the latter hath been refuted by Thomasius de fundam. definiendi causs. matr. hact. recept. insufficient. §18. The utility of mankind hath been asserted to be the first principle by the famous Leibnitz and others, who with Thomasius have set up this proposition as fundamental, "That all things are to be done which tend to make human life more happy and more lasting, and that all things are to be avoided which tend to render it unhappy, or to accelerate death," Thom. fund. jur. nat. & gent. 1. 6. 21. A moral theocracy was asserted to be the first principle in a dissertation to that effect, by Jo. Shute an Englishman; from which ingenious dissertation, several observations are excerpted by the often cited Sam. de Cocceis de princip. juris nat. & gent. diss. 1. qu. 3. §8. [[Bodinus (*praeses*), Becker (*respondens*), *Jus mundi seu vindiciae juris naturae;* Thomasius (*praeses*), Buhle (respondens), *Dissertatio juridica de fundamentorum definiendi causas matrimoniales hactenus receptorum insufficientia;* John Shute, first Viscount Barrington (1678–1734), was an English politician and Christian apologist.]]

4. Heinrich von Cocceji and Samuel von Cocceji, *Dissertatio de principio iuris naturae.*

SECTION LXXVII

The will of
God intends
our happiness.
But to give the opinion, which, upon a mature examination of this sub-ject, appears to me the most solid, first of all I would observe, that God being infinitely wise and good, cannot will any thing else with relation to mankind but their happiness. For being perfect, he stands in no need of any thing; and therefore men, who of all the beings within our cog-nizance, alone are capable of felicity, were not created by him <52> for his own advantage, but that he might render them capable of true happiness.*

SECTION LXXVIII

To this the
will of God
obliges us.
This being the will of God, that man should aim at and pursue true happiness, and his will being the rule of human free actions, and there-fore the source of the law of nature and justice (§62); by consequence whereas, human legislators being themselves indigent in several respects, have their own advantage no less in view than that of their subjects in making laws, God, on the contrary, must have made laws to men solely for their own benefit, and have intended nothing by them but their at-tainment to true happiness, by conforming themselves to them.† <53>

---

* We do not exclude the primary end, which is the glory of the Creator, and the manifestation of his perfections, which so clearly appear in his works. But this end is universal, and extends to the whole universe. Wolf. von den Absichten der Dinge. cap. 1. §2. cap. 2. §1. [[Wolff, *Von den Absichten der natürlichen Dinge* (1726).]] The particular end for which God created man, must be inferred from the essential parts and properties of which man consists or is composed. Since therefore, he is endued with *understanding,* by which he may come to the knowledge of God and of true good; with *will,* by which he is capable of enjoying God and true good; and he hath a *body,* by means of which he can produce various actions, which tend to acquire and preserve his true happiness; hence it is manifest that God made man that he might be a partaker of true felicity.

† Therefore utility cannot be said, with Carneades and others, to be the sole source of justice and equity (§76). [[Carneades (ca. 214–ca. 129 B.C.), Greek philosopher who presided over the New Academy at Athens.]] For the law of nature would thus not be obligatory, but might be renounced by any one at his pleasure, or by all man-kind, as Sam. de Cocceiis has proved, Diss. 1. qu. 2. §9. But whatever we do for the

SECTION LXXIX

If therefore God intend the happiness of mankind, and the law of nature be directed towards it as its end (§78), and true happiness consist in the enjoyment of good, and the absence of evil; the consequence must be, that by the law of nature God must intend that we may attain to the enjoyment of true good, and avoid evil. But since we can only enjoy good by love, hence we infer that God obliges us to love, and that love is the principle of natural law, and, as it were, a compend of it.*

That happiness consists in the fruition of good by love; and therefore love is the principle of the law of nature.

SECTION LXXX

Love in us is the desire of good, joined with delight in its perfection and happiness. *Hatred* is <54> aversion from evil, joined with satisfaction in its unhappiness; wherefore what we *love,* we receive pleasure from its perfection and happiness, and we are disposed to promote that perfec-

What is love and hatred?

---

sake of our true happiness, according to the law of nature, we do it agreeably to the divine will and command, and therefore, according to obligation not merely internal, but likewise extrinsical: and for that reason, so far is any one from having a right to renounce his happiness, that on the contrary, any one would no less deserve punishment by violating a natural law constituted for his good, than any one who in a common-wealth should offend against a law established for the public good.

* Here we see a wonderful harmony and consent, between the natural and revealed law or will of God. Our Saviour gives us a summary of revealed law in these few words: "Thou shalt love God with all thine heart, and with all thy soul, with all thy mind, and with all thy strength: and thou shalt love thy neighbour as thy self." *Matt.* xxxii. 37. *Luke* x. 27. and he adds, "upon these hang the law and the prophets." Agreeably to this doctrine of our Saviour, the apostles call love sometimes ἀνακεφαλαίωσιν του νόμου, the sum of the law; sometimes πλήρωμα νόμου, the fulfilment of the law; at other times, συνδεσμον τῆς τελειότητος, the bond of perfectness; and sometimes, τὸ τέλος τῆς παραγγελίας, the end of the commandment, *Rom.* xiii. 9. *Coloss.* iii. 14. 1 *Tim.* i. 5. But right reason teaches the same truth, and inculcates no other principle of natural law but *love,* as the sole mean by which we can come to the enjoyment of that happiness or true good, which is the intention of God and of his law; whence Leibnitz also, Praef. t. 1. cod. juris gentium diplom. defines justice to be, *the love of a wise man.* [[Leibniz, *Codex iuris gentium diplomaticus,* Praefatio ad lectorem, vol. 1, 6.]]

tion and happiness to the utmost of our power. What, on the contrary, we *hate,* we rather desire its misery than its happiness.

SECTION LXXXI

Love does
not give
uneasiness.

Since we receive satisfaction from the excellence and happiness of what we *love* (§80) it is obvious that the lover does not will to give uneasiness to what he loves; nay, he rather suffers pain if any other should attempt any such thing. For because he who gives uneasiness to one, or suffers it to be done without feeling any pain, takes pleasure in another's unhappiness; but to take delight in the suffering of any one, is the same as to hate (§80); and to love and hate the same object at one and the same time is a contradiction; the consequence is, that it is inconsistent or impossible at the same time to love one, and to hurt him; or to bear his being hurted by another without disturbance and pain.

SECTION LXXXII

Hence the first
degree of love,
which we call
the love of
justice.

One may be hurt two ways, either by doing something which makes him more unhappy than he is by nature, or by depriving him of some happiness he is already possessed of. But seeing to do something which conduces to render one more unhappy than he is, is to *hurt* one; and to dispossess one of something he hath justly acquired, and which contributes to his happiness, is to *deny* one, *or to take from him something that belongs to him;* hence it follows, that he violates the law of love in the highest manner who hurts one, and disturbs his possession, or takes it away, and hinders his enjoyment of it; and, on the other hand, the lowest degree of love is to hurt no person, but to render to every one <55> what is due to him, or leave him in the undisturbed possession and enjoyment of what he hath; which degree of love we call the *love of justice.* *

---

* This is observed by Seneca in his Ep. 95. where he says, how small a thing is it *not to hurt* him whom we ought to profit! [[Seneca, *Epistulae morales,* ep. 95, 51: "[Q]uantulum est ei non nocere cui debeas prodesse." (Seneca, *Ad Lucilium epistulae morales,* vol. 3).]] He who does not hurt any one is only not a scelerate: he has not

SECTION LXXXIII

But because a lover receives pleasure from the happiness of him whom he loves (§80), it follows that he renders to him whom he loves chearfully, even that which is not strictly due to him, or his right, if he perceives it to be conducive to his happiness: and this is a more sublime degree of love, which we call *love of humanity, or beneficence.* * But because we call the capacity of discerning things which are contributive to our own happiness and that of others, *prudence* or *wisdom;* it is obvious that this love of humanity or beneficence must have wisdom for its guide and director.* <56>

From which there is another very differing degree, which we call the love of humanity and beneficence.

SECTION LXXXIV

Moreover, whereas he who does not observe the love of justice, who hath it not, or does not act conformably to it, is a profligate person; he, on the other hand, who hath not the love of humanity and beneficence,

The difference between them in respect of obligation.

---

yet attained to that kind of justice which the law of love requires, even to do good to others to the utmost of our abilities, and therefore he hath no virtue to glory in. Whence Leibnitz, in Praef. cod. dip. distinguishes three gradations in the law of nature. *Strict justice,* which is to do no hurt; *equity* or *love,* which is to render to every one what is due to him; and *piety,* which disposes to observe all the rules of virtue; but we must differ from him with regard to his second gradation, because he likewise gives to another his due or his own, who renders what is due to him in strict justice, and therefore *rendering to every one his own,* is not to be referred solely to distributive justice.

* Humanity and beneficence differ in this, that by the former we render to others whatever we can do, without any detriment to ourselves, for their advantage: the latter makes us not spare our own goods in order to benefit others, but disposes us to do kind offices to them to our own prejudice. Of the former Cicero speaks de off. 1. 16. "All these things seem to be common to all men, which are of the kind described by Ennius in one instance. He that directs the wandering traveller, doth, as it were, light another's torch by his own, which gives never the less light, for that it gave another." By this single example he clearly points out to us, that we ought to render even to strangers, whatever good offices may be done to them without prejudicing ourselves. Whence these following, and others of the same nature, are called common benefits, "To suffer any one to take from our fire to kindle his: To give good and faithful advice to one who is deliberating: And all things, in one word, which are beneficial to the receiver, and nowise hurtful to the giver." [[Cicero, *De officiis,* 1.16.]] Of the latter Seneca has wrote a book which is entitled *De beneficiis,* concerning benefits.

can only be said not to perform the nobler and greater virtues (§82). Now none may be forced to do virtuous actions, but all acts of wickedness may be restrained by punishments (§9). Whence it is plain, that men may be compelled to acts of justice, but not to acts of humanity and beneficence. But when obligation is joined with coaction, it is *perfect;* when it is not, it is *imperfect* (§9). We are therefore *perfectly* obliged to the love of justice, and *but imperfectly* to the love of humanity and beneficence.* <57>

SECTION LXXXV

Love, how distinguished in respect of its object.
Since *love* always tends towards good (§80). But whatever we embrace with affection as good, must either be a more perfect being than our selves, equal, or inferior to us, and less excellent. Love of the first kind, we call *love of devotion* or *obedience;* love of the second kind, we call *love of friendship;* and love of the third sort, we call *benevolence.*

SECTION LXXXVI

What love of devotion is; what love of friendship; and what benevolence?
Love of devotion or *obedience,* is love towards a more excellent and perfect being, with whose excellence and happiness we are so delighted, that we look upon such a being, as to be honoured and obeyed with the highest complacency and veneration. The *love of friendship* is the love of our equal, or satisfaction and delight in his happiness, equal to what we per-

---

* Those who fulfil their imperfect obligations are said by Seneca to be good men according to the letter of the law; but elsewhere he shews it to be a very small attainment to be good in that sense only; and that in order to merit the character of a wise and virtuous man much more is required, even the love of beneficence, to which one knows he is not strictly obliged. "Many good offices," says he, "are not commanded by law, and do not found an action, which however the circumstances and condition of human life, more powerful than all law, render fit or lay a foundation for. No human law forbids us to discover our friend's secrets; no human law commands us to keep faith with our enemy. What law obliges us to fulfil our promise to any one? Yet I will complain of him, and quarrel with him, who hath not kept the secret entrusted to him, and will look upon him with indignation who does not keep his pledged faith." Seneca de beneficiis, v. 21.

ceive in our own. The *love of benevolence,* is the love of an inferior and more imperfect being, which disposes us seriously to promote its happiness, as much as the nature of the being permits.

SECTION LXXXVII

From these definitions it follows, that we cannot have love of devotion or obedience towards a being, unless we be persuaded of its superiority and greater perfection; nor can this love take place, unless such a being be of such a character and temper as to desire to be loved by us. And this love ought <58> always to be joined with veneration and obedience suitable to the perfections of such a being.*

The nature of the love of devotion and obedience.

SECTION LXXXVIII

Further it is plain that the love of friendship arises from equality. Now equality is either an equality of *nature,* or an equality of *perfections.* Wherefore, where the former takes place, equal offices of love are reciprocally due; and for that reason, amongst all who are by nature equal, these incomparable rules ought to obtain. "Whatever you would not have done to yourself, do it not to other." And, "Whatever you would have another do to you do unto them." Matt. vii. 12. Luke vi. 31. Tob. iv. 16. The first of which is the foundation of the love of justice; the other, of the love of beneficence and humanity. But because, however equal the being beloved, and the being loving may be by nature, yet the one may be either more perfect, or more imperfect than the other; it may happen that we may be obliged to have at the same time a love of friendship towards a man, as equal to us by nature, and a love of devotion and

The love of friendship its nature.

---

* For veneration or honour is a just esteem of the perfections belonging to a being; obedience is a disposition to perform with readiness, whatever another as superior hath a title to exact from us, and to with-hold from doing what he forbids. But since there may be various degrees of perfection and superiority, there will also be as many various degrees of veneration and obedience; and the more sublime the perfection of a being is, the greater veneration and obedience are due to that being.

obedience, or of benevolence towards him as being more perfect or more imperfect.* <59>

SECTION LXXXIX

The love of benevolence.

Finally, since benevolence seeks the enlargement and promotion of the happiness of a more imperfect being, as much as its nature is capable of happiness (§86). Hence it follows, that we ought not to hurt such a being, or refuse to it what is its right and due; but that we ought to do good to it, to the utmost of our power, with prudence however; and therefore whatever kindness is not agreeable to reason, or conducted by prudence, is not benevolence and liberality, but profusion, or any thing else you please to call it.

SECTION XC

What are the objects of this love?

Now if we consider accurately the beings with which we are surrounded, we shall find there are three only, to which we are under obligation to render the offices of love: God, the creator of all things; ourselves, who are certainly the nearest to ourselves; and other men, whom we plainly perceive to be by nature equal to us. For as to spirits, such as angels, we know not their nature, nor have we such commerce with them, as to be under the obligation of certain duties towards them. And between men and brutes there is no communion of right, and therefore no duty is properly owing to them; but we owe this to God not perversely to abuse any of his creatures.† Puffend. de jure nat. & gent. 4. 3. 6. <60>

---

* Thus, tho' a prince as superior hath a right to our veneration and obedience, that does not hinder but that he is obliged to render to us the good offices founded upon equality of nature: as for instance, not to do us any injury; not to fix ignominy upon what does not deserve it; and in one word, to do what Pliny commends in Trajan, i.e. "to remember no less that he is a man, than that he is set over other men to rule them." [[Pliny, "Panegyricus," 2.4 in Pliny, *Letters and Panegyricus.*]]

† For such a communion of right must, as we shall shew afterwards, arise from compact. But brutes are not susceptible whether of active or passive obligation arising from compact. We cannot therefore assent to the Pythagoreans, Porphyry, in his books, περὶ ἀποχῆς, who not only ascribe sense and memory, but a rational mind to

SECTION XCI

Since we cannot conceive otherwise of God than as a most excellent, most perfect, and infinitely good Being, upon whom depends absolutely our existence and felicity, of whose superiority we are absolutely persuaded, as well as of his will and desire to be loved by us (§87), it follows, that we owe to him a love of devotion and obedience, which that it may be worthy or suitable to a most perfect Being, this rule or maxim immediately occurs, "That God, upon whom we absolutely depend, ought to be adored by us with all the vigour of our mind; and that to him ought to be rendered the most perfect and sincere obedience."*

The first axiom of love to God.

SECTION XCII

Our love to ourselves must consist in satisfaction and delight in our own perfection and happiness (§80). Hence therefore we are obliged to pursue <61> the preservation and augmentation of our perfection and happiness with all our might. But since the more perfect a being is, the more honour and obedience we owe to it (§87); we must take care that we do not love ourselves more than God, least our self-love should thus degenerate into immoderate and unproportioned selfishness. Whence flows this other maxim, "That man is obliged to omit nothing, that may

A second axiom concerning love to ourselves.

---

brutes. However so far as men perceive any affection in brutes, so far do they render a love of benevolence toward them; so as not to abuse their power of killing them, but to take pleasure in rendering their life more commodious to them, as we see in the instance of domestic dogs. Plutarch elegantly observes in Caton. major. "But we see benignity hath a much larger field than justice; we sometimes extend beneficence to brute animals thro' the largeness of bounty; for a merciful man looks upon himself as obliged to take care of horses which work for him, and not only of young animals but of old ones." [[Plutarch, "Cato Major" (Cato the Elder), in Plutarch, *Plutarch's Lives*, vol. 2, 301–85.]]

* For since the veneration we pay to a superior Being ought to be suitable to it (§87); we cannot but hence infer that the highest veneration is due to the most perfect Being. And because God knows most perfectly, not only our external actions, but likewise all the inward motions of our mind; we owe to him, not merely external signs of veneration, but inward reverence and piety. And this is that worship and love which the sacred writings require of us.

conduce to preserve, promote, or augment his perfection and happiness, which is consistent with his love of God."*

SECTION XCIII

A third axiom concerning love to others.

Since moreover all men are by nature equal, and that natural equality requires a reciprocal obligation to equal love (§88); the consequence of this is, that we are obliged to delight in the happiness of others, not less, but not more than in our own; and therefore to love others as ourselves; but ourselves not less than our neighbour. Whence flows a third maxim, "That man is obliged to love his fellow-creature no less than himself, and consequently not to do to any other, what he would not have him do to him; but, on the other hand, to do to others all those offices of kindness which he can reasonably desire them to render to him."

SECTION XCIV

This principle is true, evident and adequate.

In fine, upon a due consideration of the pre-requisites to a principle of moral science which have <62> been explained, we will find that this is the most genuine principle of moral science. Nothing can be more *certain,* it necessarily flows from the divine will and the nature of man; and, which is very satisfactory to me, it is authorised by the sacred writings. Nothing can be more *evident,* since it is such as may be easily conceived by the unassisted reason of every man, even among Pagans. Nothing can be more *adequate,* for in fact we shall soon see, that there is no duty of a man as such, or of a citizen, which may not be easily and clearly deduced from this first principle.

---

* For God obliges man to seek after the enjoyment of good (§79), and therefore to promote and preserve his own happiness; because therefore sometimes goods are presented to him, of which one is greater than the other; and that lesser good which deprives us of a greater one, ought to be esteemed an evil, it is obvious that God obliges us to choose that which of many goods is the greatest.

REMARKS on This Chapter

I can't help thinking that our excellent author is not so distinct in this chapter as he ought to have been, and withal too tedious. It was indeed necessary to distinguish between the *principle which constitutes external or legal obligation,* and the *principle which is the medium of knowledge with regard to it; or the mean by which it may be known and demonstrated.* Now it is the will of God which constitutes external or legal obligation. But what is the medium by which the divine will may be known? Our author had already often said, that right reason is the faculty by which it may be known. But hence it follows, that conformity to reason, is the mean by which agreeableness to the divine will may be known and demonstrated. Why then does he dispute against those who say conformity to Reason, or which comes to the same thing, to our rational nature, is the principle or mean of moral knowledge? Or why does he not immediately proceed to enquire what is, and what is not agreeable to reason or our rational nature? Why does he dispute against those who in their reasonings about the laws of nature, infer them from the divine sanctity or moral rectitude, which must mean reason, or our rational nature compared with the rational nature of the supreme Being? For if the law of nature be discoverable by reason, conformity to reason, to the reason of God, and the reason of man, must be the *principle* of knowledge with regard to the law of nature. Nor can the divine sanctity or divine moral rectitude be an obscure idea, unless conformity to reason, or to a reasonable nature, be an obscure idea. Our author seems to have forgot what he said (§1), when he says (§86), that the happiness and perfection of mankind is not a principle from which the law of nature can be inferred; and what he here refutes, he afterwards (§77) returns to, as a necessary first principle in demonstrating the law of nature, *viz.* "That God intends the happiness and perfection of mankind." For if his reasoning, <63> (§77) be just, the business of the moral science is to enquire what tends to the perfection and happiness of man, and what is necessary to it; and these will be good moral reasonings, which shew an action to be conducive to human happiness and perfection, or contrariwise: For thus they shew what the divine will commands, and what it forbids: nay, according to his reasoning in that section, we can not advance one step in morals, without first determining what our happiness and perfection requires, and what is repugnant to it. He seems likewise (§70) where he says, "That the intrinsic pravity or goodness of actions, is not a sufficient principle for deducing and establishing the moral laws of nature," to have forgot what he had said in the former chapter, and frequently repeats in succeeding ones, of the *priority* in *nature* or *idea* of *internal* to *external* obligation. And indeed, to say that the laws of nature concerning human conduct, cannot be deduced from the consideration of the internal nature of actions, is in other words to say, that they cannot be deduced by reason; for it is to say, that they cannot be deduced from the conformity or disconformity of actions to reason. All I would infer from this is, 1. That it is impossible to make one step in moral reasonings, without owning a difference between conformity and disagreeableness to reason, and using that general expression, or some one equivalent to it; for the will of God cannot be inferred but from conformity to reason, or something equivalent to it, i.e. from some principle, which however it may be expressed, ultimately signifies conformity to the nature of things, or to reason. 2. That conformity to reason, to a reasonable nature, to moral rectitude, to the divine nature, and conduciveness to the perfection and happiness of a rational being, or conduciveness to the perfection and happiness of man, as such, and several other such phrases used by moralists, have and must all have the same meaning, or terminate in the same thing. 3. That to ask why a reasonable being ought to act agreeably to reason, is to ask why it is reasonable to act reasonably; or why reasonable is reasonable. This must be the meaning of that question, as it is distinguished from this other, "Is there good ground to think, that the supreme Being, the maker and governor of the universe, wills that his reasonable creatures should act reasonably, and will proportion their happiness according to their behaviour?" which question does likewise amount in other terms, to asking whether it is agreeable to supream reason, to approve acting according to reason? There is therefore no necessity of dwelling long upon either of these questions in moral philosophy; but it is its business to enquire what rules of conduct, what methods of action are agreeable, and what are disagreeable to reason, to the nature of things, to the qualities of reasonable beings, to the perfection and happiness of mankind as such; all which phrases, as hath been said, must have the same meaning, and may therefore be promiscuously used: And indeed about them there can be no dispute, unless <64> one has a mind to make a particular favourite of some one of them in opposition to all the rest; in which case, the dispute, 'tis evident, will be merely about a phrase; as in fact, most disputes in the moral science realy are, for that very reason, viz. through a particular liking to some favourite words.

Our author's method of reasoning is, when he brings it out, plain and just enough. It amounts to this, "If we own the being of a God, and have a clear and just idea of his perfection, we must own that he wills the perfection and happiness of all his creatures, his moral creatures in particular: man therefore being a moral creature, God must will the happiness and perfection of man. He must then for that reason, will that man pursue his own perfection and happiness. But such is the nature of man, and so are things relating to him constituted and connected, that the pursuit of his perfection and happiness consists in what may properly be expressed in one word, *Love,* the love of his Creator, the love of his fellow creatures, those of his own kind in particular, and the love of himself." Now according to this way of reasoning what our author hath to prove, is the latter proposition; and accordingly he goes on in the succeeding chapters to prove it.

In other words, our author's manner of deducing human duties amounts to this, "Every *obligation* which man can be under as a rational agent, *external* or *internal,* may be expressed by one word, *Love.* For we can owe nothing to any being but love: all our obligations must therefore be reducible to these three; the love of our Creator, the love of our fellow-creatures, of those of our own kind, or with whom we are more nearly and immediately connected in particular; and the love of ourselves." And accordingly our author proceeds to explain the duties belonging to these three classes. The principle upon which he founds may justly be called clear, certain, and adequate. For if there be any such thing as obligation upon a rational agent, external or internal, it can be nothing else, but obligation to love: internal obligation can belong to nothing else but the dictates and offices of reasonable love; and therefore external obligation can belong to nothing else. Wherefore love is justly said in the sacred writings, to be the fulfillment of the law; of the law of nature, of the law of reason, of the law of God. But let me observe, that this method of our author's, is the same in other words with some of them he refutes. For is it not evidently the same thing as to say "that duty, obligation, or what is reasonable with regard to human conduct, must be inferred from the human nature, and the constitution of things relative to man. But according to the frame of man and the constitution of things, the chief happiness and perfection of every man arises from the love and the pursuit of order within and without him; or from the observation of the prevalency of wisdom and good order, and consequently of greater happiness in the administration of the universe; and from such an orderly discipline of his < 65 > affections as tend to produce universal happiness, order, and perfection, as far as his affections, and the actions they lead to, have any influence?" According to which state of the question, the remaining enquiry will be what the love of good order and general happiness requires.

Of the application of this rule to actions, and the differences of actions proceeding from thence.

SECTION XCV

Having considered the nature of human free actions, and the rule according to which they ought to be regulated; the next thing to be considered, is the application of this rule to free actions. The application of a law to a fact is called *imputation,* and therefore we shall in this chapter treat of it.

The connexion.

SECTION XCVI

Imputation being the application of a law to a fact (§95), which cannot be done otherwise than by comparing a law and a fact, i.e. by two propositions compared together, and with a third by a syllogism; the consequence is, that *imputation* is a syllogism or reasoning, the major proposition of which signifies a *law;* the minor a certain *action:* and the conclusion is the *sentence,* with regard to the agreement or disagreement of the action with the law.* <66>

Imputation is made by comparing a law with a fact; and therefore by reasoning.

---

* To *impute,* properly signifies to place something to the account or charge of another person. Sen. epist. 8. "Hoc non imputo in solutum de tuo tibi." [[Accurately: "Hoc non imputo in solutum; dedi de tuo tibi" ("I shall not charge this to the expense account, because I have given it to you from your own stock"). Seneca, *Ad Lucilium*

SECTION XCVII

Wherein it differs from conscience.

Having said much the same thing above concerning *conscience* (§94), which however is not the same with *imputation,* let us observe wherein the difference between them consists; and it lies in this: Whereas conscience is a reasoning about the justice and injustice of one's own actions: imputation is a reasoning about the agreement or disagreement with law of another's actions. In the first case, every one is his own judge: in the other, another person judges of our actions, and compares them with the law.* <67>

---

epistulae morales, vol. 3, 42.]] Now as that can't be done without ballancing accounts with one, hence it came about, that this term seemed proper to express that application of a law to facts, which is done in like manner by a similar comparison. Thus when, as the story is told by Livy, Horatius had killed his sister, and a question arose, whether the law against murder, ordaining that the person guilty of it should have his hands tied, and his head veiled, and be whipped either within or without the walls, and then be hanged upon a tree, ought to be applied to that action? The Duumviri legally appointed by Tullius Hostilius the king, to judge of the matter, were of opinion, that the law extended to the fact, upon which one of them pronounced this sentence: "I find you, Publius Horatius, guilty of murder. Go, lictor, bind his hands." But Horatius appealing, and the father himself appearing for him, the people absolved him. The Duumviri therefore reasoned in this manner, "He who knowingly with evil design kills a person, is as a murderer to be punished so and so. This is the law. Publius Horatius by running his sister through with his sword, has willingly and with evil intention killed a person. This is the fact. He is therefore to be punished so and so. Here is the sentence." But the people computed or stated the account in another manner thus: "He who kills an enemy to his country, is not to be punished as a murderer. Here is the law. Publius Horatius in killing his sister, killed an enemy of her country. Here is the fact. Therefore he ought not to be punished as a *murderer.* Here is the sentence, and it is a sentence of absolution." [[Livy, *The Early History of Rome,* 1.26, pp. 61–62.]] The Duumviri therefore imputed the fault to Publius Horatius, but the people did not impute it.

* But because it does not belong to every one to judge of the actions of others, and yet such is the weakness of human nature, that most persons are very indulgent to their own faults, and not very severe in searching their own consciences, and yet are very quick-sighted and rigid with regard to the failings and blemishes of others; it is no wonder that judging others is reprehended as unjust and wicked, not only by our Saviour, Matt. vii. 1. Luke vi. 37. and by his apostle, Rom. ii. 1. xiv. 4. 1 Cor. iv. 5. but likewise by profane writers, who had only right reason to guide them in their determinations. Hence the pleasant witty fable of the two budgets, one of which filled with his own faults a man carried on his back, the other filled with the faults

SECTION XCVIII

Every application of law to fact is called *imputation* (§9), whether an action be compared with the divine law or with a human law; and in like manner, whether God himself, or men, whose office it is, apply law to a fact. The former, however, moralists are accustomed to call imputation *in foro divino;* the latter in *foro humano.* But there is this very considerable difference between the two, that in the latter none suffers punishment for thoughts, l. 18. D. de poenis; but God being omniscient, and requiring internal obedience (§91), he justly imputes to us even thoughts which are disagreeable to his law.* <68>

An action is imputed either by God or by human judges.

SECTION XCIX

Further, whereas the law which is applied to human actions is enforced by a sanction (§64), hence it follows, that *to impute* is the same as to declare, that the effect which a certain law assigns to an action, agrees to such a particular action. This effect is called in general *merit; punishment,*

And then man is declared to have merited either punishment or reward.

---

of others he carried on his breast: To which Phaedrus subjoins this moral, fab. 4. 9. v. 4.

> *Hac re videre nostra mala non possumus:*
> *Alii simul delinquunt, censores sumus.*

> [[Phaedrus, *Fabulae* 4.10: "For this reason we are unable to see our own vices; but as soon as others commit errors we become their critics."]]

Several parallel passages of ancient authors are collected by Is. Casaubon, ad Pers. p. 340. [[probably a reference to Casaubon, *Auli Persii Flacci Satirarum liber*]] and by learned men upon this fable, whose coffers we will not pillage.

* The ancient philosophers were not ignorant of this truth, and have asserted that God seeth not only all our outward acts, but likewise our most secret thoughts. So Thales Milesius, Socrates, Plato and his followers, Pythagoras and his disciples, and all in general who entertained juster and sublimer conceptions concerning God. Testimonies to this purpose are collected by Huet. in qu. Alnet. ii. 2. 16. Hence we see, how reasonable the interpretation of the Mosaic law is, which our Saviour gave, Matt. v. 22, 28.

if the effect of an action exhibited by the law be evil; and *reward,* if the effect be good.*

SECTION C

The definition of imputation and axioms relative to it. *Imputation* therefore is a reasoning by which an action of another person, being, in all its circumstances, compared with a law, whether divine or human, is declared to merit, or not merit a certain effect proposed by a law. From which definition it is manifest, that we cannot certainly pronounce whether an action be imputable or not, unless we have a distinct comprehension both of the law and of the action in all its circumstances: and that one circumstance often alters the whole state of the case.

SECTION CI

It supposes the knowledge and interpretation of the law. Since the *law* must be known to him who would form a right judgment of the imputability of actions, the consequence is, that he ought to be sure there is a certain law, and ought rightly to under-<69>stand the whole of that law, and therefore to *interpret* it rightly, if it be conceived in concise or obscure terms; *i.e.* he ought distinctly to comprehend the mind of the law-giver declared by words, or by whatever other signs.†

---

* But since a legislator is not obliged to propose rewards, hence it is manifest that even actions in themselves just are not meritorious. To this purpose belongs that remarkable saying of Christ: "So likewise ye, when ye shall have done all these things which are commanded you, say, we are unprofitable servants: we have done that which was our duty to do," *Luke* xvii. 10. But if a law-giver promises rewards, as God has done, who has enacted his laws, not for his own sake, but for the advantage of mankind, because he wills their perfect happiness (§78); rewards may be said to be merited, not in respect of the law-giver, who of free-goodness proposed them, but in respect of imputation.

† Interpretation therefore does not properly belong to the law of nature, but only to positive laws, whether divine or human. For since legal interpretation is a distinct representation of the law-giver's mind, declared by words or other signs (§101): and the law of nature is not conceived in words, but is promulgated by right reason (§11): it follows, that the mind of the supreme law-giver cannot be collected from words or other signs; and therefore this law does not admit of interpretation. Reason suf-

SECTION CII

Seeing an *interpreter* represents distinctly the law-giver's meaning, de- clared by words or other signs; it follows, that in interpreting laws, great attention must be given both to the proper and the metaphorical signification of words; to their connection with what precedes and what follows, and to the nature and character of the subject itself; and yet more especially to the scope and intention of the law-giver, which induced him to enact the law; wherefore they judge well, and we agree with them who assert the reason of the law to be its spirit or soul. See our preface ad Elem. Pandect.*[1] <70>

Its foundation.

SECTION CIII

Further, since the reason of a law is as it were its soul, hence it must follow, that the law ceases when the sole reason of it wholly and absolutely ceases: that if it do not agree to a certain case, that case cannot fall under the law on account of the very reason of the law; and this is the foundation of what is called *restrictive interpretation;* to which may be rightly referred *equity, i.e.* a power of correcting the law in respect of

Its various sorts.

---

ficiently understands itself without an interpreter. Arrian. Diss. Epict. 1. "The reasoning faculty being conscious to itself, clearly perceives what it is, and what it can do, and of what price and value it is, if it applies itself to the direction of our other faculties." [[Epictetus, "Discourses," 1.17 in *The Discourses as Reported by Arrian.*]]

* We have a remarkable example of the utility of this rule in our Saviour's explication of the law about the sabbath, when he was censured by the Jewish doctors for teaching, that works of charity and mercy ought not to be intermitted on the sabbathday. He on that occasion shews the source whence the interpretation of that law must be brought. He says, "The sabbath was made for man, and not man for the sabbath," *Mar.* ii. 27. From which reason of the law it clearly follows, that all works which tend to disturb the tranquillity and piety of mankind were forbidden to be done on that day; but not such as conduce to human preservation and happiness. But take away this sole and adequate reason of that law, and it is most certain that in the words of the law themselves, there is nothing from which one would have inferred our Saviour's doctrine.

1. Heineccius, *Elementa iuris civilis secundum ordinem Pandectarum.*

universality: Grot. de Aequit. indulg. & facilit. c. 1. n. 3.[2] that if the words of a law do not quadrate with a certain case, and yet the reason of the law be applicable to it, then there is place for what is called *extensive interpretation:* Finally, that when the words and reason of the law keep as it were pace together, then there is only room for *declarative interpretation.** <71>

SECTION CIV

The difference between authentic, customary, and doctrinal interpretation.

Besides, because the law is interpreted either by the legislator or judge, or some other, to whose office it belongs to apply the law to facts, or by a lawyer, interpretation on these accounts is therefore called *authentic, customary,* or *doctrinal;* the foundation of the first is the will of the legislator; of the second, practice in courts of justice; and of the last, the application of the rules of interpretation abovementioned.†

---

* For example, our Saviour interprets the law of the sabbath restrictively; the laws concerning adultery and homicide extensively, *Mat.* v. which not being done by the Pharisees, they reasoned ill concerning the imputation of actions. Hence it was, that they accused the apostles of impiety for plucking ears of corn on the sabbath; and our Saviour himself for healing the sick on the sabbath; and that they reputed those righteous who fulfilled the traditions of the Rabbins, and washed, *e.g.* their cups carefully, paid tithes, gave alms to the poor, fasted frequently, though they did all this thro' vain-glory, neglected the weightier matters of the law, and committed gross crimes.

† We have examples of all these three in the sacred writings: Thus, after God, *Numb.* xxvii. 7. had given this law: "If a man die and have no son, then ye shall cause his inheritance to pass unto his daughter," the supreme legislator himself adds this interpretative clause, *Numb.* xxxvi. 5, 6. "So shall not the inheritance of Israel move from tribe to tribe." This is an example of *authentic* interpretation, which is frequently the same as a new law. We have an instance of *customary* interpretation, *Ruth* iv. 7. where the plucking off and casting the shoe, which was originally restricted to a particular case, *Deut.* xxv. 7. is by judicial interpretation extended to rejection of inheritance; with relation to which custom we have a curious disquisition by An. Bynaeus de Calc. Heb. l. 2. c. 7. [[Bynaeus, *De calceis Hebraeorum libri duo.*]] Finally, there is an instance of *doctrinal* interpretation, *Nehemiah* viii. 13.

2. Grotius, *De aequitate, indulgentia, et facilitate liber singularis.*

SECTION CV

Because he who would interpret a law aright, ought to know all the cir- An action is
cumstances of the fact, (§108), and the principal circumstance is the per- imputed to its
son acting; hence we conclude, that an action is to be imputed to him cause.
who is the author or cause of it; and, on the contrary, imputation ceases
if any thing be done, of which the doer is neither the cause nor the
author, tho' we sometimes impute the merits of one to others; which
imputation is commonly called *imputation by favour,* in contradistinction to that which is *of debt* or *merit,* strictly so called. Puffend. de jur.
nat. & gent. 1. 9. 2.* <72>

SECTION CVI

If therefore an action be imputed to none, unless he be the cause or What actions
author of it (§105); but a person cannot be called the author of any action are not
which is not *human; i.e.* which is not done by the will, under the direc- imputable.
tion of the understanding (§30); hence it is obvious, that neither passions, nor natural actions, nor events wholly providential, nor things
done in a fit of madness, nor natural imperfections either of body or
mind, nor things done in sleep or drunkenness can be imputed to any
person, but so far as it depended upon the agent to prevent them (§26,
29, 49).† <73>

---

* And this is the origine of hereditary nobility; yea, sometimes of hereditary kingdoms. Thus among the Germans, the distinguishing nobleness, or the eminent services of fathers, gave dignity even to striplings, Tacitus, de moribus Germ. c. 13. And
of hereditary kingdoms, Polyb. Hist. 6. 5. "This is the origine of hereditary sovereignty: hence it is, subjects obey for a long time, not only kings but their Offspring,
through a persuasion that being descended from them, and educated by them, they
will be like to them in temper and disposition." [[Tacitus, *Germania,* 82; Polybius,
The Histories, vol. 6, bk. 6, chap. 7 (not 5), p. 283.]]

† Thus impudence is imputed to one, if he neglect the decorum with regard to
natural actions. Thus shipwreck is imputed to the commander of the ship, if by his
fault the ship was lost; whereas in other cases, what can be more true than what Tacitus
says, Ann. 14. 3. "Who is so unjust as to make a crime of what the winds and waves
have done?" [[Tacitus, *The Annals of Tacitus,* vol. 2.]] Thus deformity is imputable

SECTION CVII

Whether actions done thro' igno-rance or error be imputable. As for what relates to ignorance and error, since both these imperfections of the understanding are either *culpable* or *inculpable* (§48, 49), *vincible* or *invincible, voluntary* or *unvoluntary* (§50), it follows from the same principles, that inculpable, invincible, involuntary ignorance cannot justly be imputed to a person; but that an action done thro' culpable, vincible, and voluntary ignorance is justly imputable: and the same holds

---

to one who has sacrificed his nose to Venus [[that is, been deformed as a result of venereal disease]], whereas in other cases Phaedrus justly pronounces, Fab. 3.

> *Sed quid fortunae, stulte, delictum arguis?*
> *Id demum est homini turpe, quod meruit pati.*

> [[Phaedrus, *Fabulae* 3.11, the Eunuch to a wicked man: "But why, fool, do you bring as a charge against me that which is the fault of Fortune? What is really disgracful is what he has *deserved* to suffer."]]

Much more reasonably still is ignorance imputed as a fault to a man who had op-portunity of a good education in his youth, which is not reckoned criminal in the vulgar; yea, dreams are imputed, which are occasioned by waking thoughts and ac-tions throughout the day; of which kind of dreams called by the antients ἐνύπνια, according to Macrobius in Somn. Scip. 1. 13. [[Macrobius, *Commentary on the Dream of Scipio*, bk. 1, 13.]] Claudian justly asserts,

> *Omnia, quae sensu voluuntur vota diurno,*
> *Pectore sopito, reddit amica quies.*
> *Furto gaudet amans, permutat navita merces,*
> *Et vigil clapsas quaerit avarus opes.*
> Hon. Aug. Praef. v. 1.

> [[Claudian, *Panegyric on the Sixth Consulship of Honorius Augustus* (*Pane-gyricus de sexto consulatu Honorii Augusti*), Preface, 1–2 and 7–8: "All the de-sires that are turned over in our senses during the day are brought back to us by the friendly quiet of the night when our breasts are stilled. The lover rejoices in secret activity, the sailor exchanges his merchandise and the miser searches for the wealth he has lost while awake."]]

To which Gasp. Barth. in his notes, p. 714. has added more examples. [[Caspar Barth (1587–1658), German poet who produced a commentary on Claudian, which was published in several editions. The edition used here appears to be the 1650 *Claudii Claudiani poetae praegloriosissimo quae exstant.*]] In fine, wilful drunkenness, and the actions perpetrated in that condition, are imputed for a reason that needs not be mentioned, it is so obvious.

with regard to error: much less can ignorance or error be any excuse to one, if the action itself be unlawful, or be done in an unlawful place, time, or manner; because, in such cases, it not only was in the agent's power not to be ignorant or not to err, but he was absolutely obliged to omit the action.* <74>

SECTION CVIII

Further, one may err either in point of *fact* or in point of *law.* To the former belong the rules already laid down (§107), because a circumstance in a fact may escape the most prudent persons, and therefore his error, in point of fact, may be *inculpable, invincible, involuntary.* But error, in point of law, with relation to the law of nature, does not excuse, because right reason promulgates this law to every one, unless, perhaps, when age, stupidity, and the more subtle nature of a particular law dictate a milder sentence. But as for civil law, ignorance of it is so far imputable, as it is so framed and promulgated that the person might know it.† <75>

Of error in fact and in law.

---

* Judah, when he went into Thamar his Daughter-in-law, could not plead ignorance, because the action was in itself unlawful, *Gen.* xxxviii. 15, 16. Nor is he excusable, who sporting with darts in an unlawful time and place, ignorantly wounds a man, because an action done in a place and time in which it ought not, is in itself unlawful, §4. Inst. de lege Aquilia. Nor is an injury done to one who was pruning a tree near the highway, if he be charged with killing a man, whom he might have saved by calling out to him, §5. instit. eodem. Those who were thus employed among the Romans used to cry aloud *cave,* take care: among the Athenians φύλαξαι [[Φύλαξαι: "Watch out!" / "Be on your guard!"]], as Theod. Marcil. ad §5. instit. eod. shews. [[Justinian, *Imp. Caes. Iustiniani P. P. Augusti institutionum quatuor.*]] Wherefore the sentence of the Areopagites mentioned by Aristot. mag. mor. 1. 17. [[Aristotle, *Magna moralia,* in *The Works of Aristotle,* vol. 9]] absolving a woman who killed a young man by a love-charm which she gave him, because it was not done designedly, having given him the draught out of love, and missed her aim, was blameable, since it proceeded upon a supposition that it was not unlawful to give such love-making medicines. How much more justly does the Roman lawyer Paullus, l. 38. §5. D. de poenis, condemn such practices, as giving medicines to create love or abortion: Qui abortionis aut amatorium poculum dant, etsi dolo non faciant, tamen quia mali exempli res est, &c. [["They who give a drink that causes either miscarriage or another person to fall in love, and do so without deceit, yet, because it sets a bad example, etc." (trans. Eds.)]]

† For who would rigidly exact an accurate knowledge of the law of nature from infants, or those hardly arrived beyond the infant state, from deaf and dumb persons,

SECTION CIX

Whether undersigned and forced actions are imputable.

Since the free will of man must concur to render an action such of which one can be called the author and cause (§30); but unintended actions are such, that they do not proceed from the determination of the mind (§58); hence it follows, that an action which one does against his will, or without intention, cannot be imputed to him; on the contrary, whatever is done spontaneously, is imputable, and much more whatever is done of one's own free accord: yea, what one is forced to do is imputable to him, if he who forced him had a right to force him; but not, if he who forces him was not in the exercise of his right, or if the person forced was, previously to the force used, under no obligation of doing it.* <76>

---

from changelings, or from stupid persons brought up among the brutes? Besides, tho' the law of nature be as it were written or engraved on the minds of men, yet it cannot be otherwise known than by reasoning about just and unjust (§15): now, because some precepts of the law of nature flow immediately from clear principles of reason, others are derived from principles of reason by many intermediate steps, and a long chain of reasoning, none can doubt that precepts of the first sort may be known by every person who is not quite stupid; whereas those of the latter sort are more difficultly understood, and require a more improved and perfect understanding. Hence by the Roman law, tho' it reckoned incest forbidden by the law of nations, l. 38. §2. D. ad L. Jul. de adult. c. 68. D. de rit. nupt. yet the punishment was sometimes mitigated, both with respect to men and women; as, for instance, if a son-in-law should after divorce lie with his mother-in-law, l. 38. §5. D. ad L. Jul. de adulterio: of which no other reason can be given but because the unlawfulness of incest cannot be inferred immediately, or without a long train of reasoning from the principles of natural law.

* Because, tho' a person compelled or forced wills (§58), yet *right* and *obligation* are correlates, which mutually found or destroy one the other (§7); and therefore, when *right* ceases, *obligation* must also cease: the consequence from which is, that if the one hath no right to compel, the other can be under no obligation to do what he was unjustly compelled to. Hence it is, that the promise of a stubborn debtor, extorted by the magistrate by threatning execution is valid, because the magistrate is in the exercise of his right when he forces stubborn debtors to pay: But if a robber forces a traveller to promise him a certain sum of money, because the robber hath no right to force him, the traveller can be brought under no obligation to perform what he was thus compelled to promise. To this effect is that famous Epigram of Martial.

> Quid si me tonsor, dum curva novacula supra est,
>   Tunc libertatem divitiasque roget?
> Promittam, nec enim rogat illo tempore tonsor,
>   Latro rogat: res est imperiosa timor.

SECTION CX

But seeing neither temperament, affections, propensions, habits, nor external force, hinder the free exercise of the will (§54 & seq.) it is abundantly manifest, that neither bodily constitution, which hath so great an influence commonly on the affections of the mind, nor passions, however impetuous and vehement, nor habit, tho' become a second nature, can hinder the imputation of an action; tho' sometimes, in human courts, he be reckoned an object of just commiseration, who was transported into a bad action by the violence of just grief, or any afflictive passion.*

Whether bodily constitution, habit, &c.

SECTION CXI

Hence it is easy to see whether one be in any degree excusable, who being overpowered by fear, to which the bravest mind may succumb, commits <77> any action contrary to law. For if the fact be such that there is no room to plead necessity, in vain is it pretended. But in what

Whether actions extorted by some are imputable?

Sed fuerit curva quum tuta novacula theca:
Frangam tonsori crura, manusque simul.
Epig. ii. v. 5.

[[Martial, *Epigrams* ii.58.5–10: "What if the barber, while the curved/drawn [*stricta* in original rather than *curva*] blade is over me, should at that moment ask for freedom and riches? I should promise, for at that moment it's a robber asking, not a barber, and fear is an imperious thing. But when his razor is safe in its curved sheath, I shall break the barber's legs, and his hands too."]]

* It is easier, as Aristotle has observed, to resist lust, or any voluptuous appetite, than the afflictive passions. See Nicomach. 3, 12. 3, 15. 7, 7. Mag. moral. 2. 6. The same is observed by Marcus Antoninus, ἐις ἑαυτόν, 2. 10. [[Εἰς ἑαυτόν (To himself), that is, Marcus Aurelius's *Meditations.*]] So that one cannot but wonder to find Aristotle, as if he had forgot himself, asserting, ad Nicom. cap. 2. "That it is more difficult to resist the impulses of pleasure than of anger," since to be deprived of pleasure is only a privative evil, and that only for the greater part but apparent, not real; whereas to feel pain is a positive, and very frequently a real ill. Who does not think parricide more to be imputed to Nero, who was not excited to that wickedness by any afflictive passion, but by mere cruelty and wickedness, than to Orestes, who giving the reason why he killed Clytemnestra, says, *Now is she who betrayed my father's bed killed.* Eurip. Orest. v. 937. [[Euripides, *Orestes.*]]

cases necessity cannot be pleaded, we shall enquire more accurately afterwards.*

<h2 style="text-align:center">SECTION CXII</h2>

When and
how an action
is imputed to
the moral
cause?

Whensoever the understanding and will, and the physical motion of the body concur to an action, then he who does it is called *the physical cause of the action;* but if the mind alone acts without any corporeal motion, he is called *the moral cause.* Since therefore understanding and will are the only principles of human actions (§30), hence it follows, that an action is no less imputable to the *moral cause* than to the *physical cause,* if the concurrence of the will and understanding in both be equal; more imputable to the *moral* than to the *physical cause,* if one induces another, who is under obligation to obey him, to act, by commanding or compelling him; less imputable to the *moral* than to the *physical cause,* if one concurs with the action by advice or approbation only.† <78>

* Truly, if any thing be commanded contrary to piety and justice, that then no pain or force ought to be yielded to, both the scriptures and reason teach. This is acknowledged by several Pagan writers. So Juvenal, §8. v. 80. [[The following verse is quoted slightly inaccurately.]]

> *Ambiguae si quando citabere testis,*
> *Incertaeque rei: Phalaris licet imperat, ut sis*
> *Falsus, & admoto dictet perjuria tauro,*
> *Summum crede nefas, animam praeferre dolori,*
> *Et propter vitam vivendi perdere caussas.*

[[Juvenal, *Satires* 8.80–84, in *Juvenal and Persius:* "If you're summoned as a witness in some tricky, murky case, even if Phalaris commands you to commit perjury and dictates his lies with his Torture-bull close by, think it to be the worst evil to put survival ahead of honour and for the sake of life to lose the reasons for living." Phalaris was a tyrant of Agrigentum who slow-roasted his victims in a bronze bull.]]

† Hence that distinction of Hen. Koehlerus, in his Exercit. juris natur. §108. & seq. between *efficacious will,* when the effort is sufficient to produce or suspend the action, and *inefficacious will,* when the effort alone is not sufficient, is to be admitted as of great use: wherefore, if the will of the moral cause be *efficacious,* the action is justly imputed to him; and in proportion as the will is more or less such, the action is more or less imputable to one. For who doubts, for instance, that if a father command his son to steal, the theft is more imputable to him than to a stranger, either commanding or persuading to do it?

SECTION CXIII

To the circumstances of the person to whom an action is imputable (§105), belong his dignity, rank, and quality; and therefore it is indisputable, that when many persons concur in the same action, if the action be just it is less imputable, and if the action be unjust, it is more imputable to him whom relation, prudence, duty, age, dignity, ought to influence to good conduct, and restrain from bad, than to a stranger, an ignorant, stupid person, one under no particular tie, a boy, a stripling, or, in fine, a person of no rank or dignity.* <79>

Whether the condition of the agent contributes any thing toward imputability.

SECTION CXIV

Since, in the imputation of actions, regard ought to be had not only to the person of the agent, but to all the other circumstances; but that concurrence of circumstances in the object, of time and place, together with sufficient abilities, without which an action cannot be done, is called *occasion* or *opportunity;* it follows necessarily, that he is not excusable

Occasion being wanting, the action is not imputed.

---

* Thus, whatever good service was done to a relative, the ancients called *a good office,* what was done to a stranger they called *a benefit.* Seneca de Benef. 3. 18. The latter is more imputable than the former. On the other hand, an injury done to a father by a son, whom filial duty ought to have restrained from such a crime, is more imputable than one done by a stranger is to him. And who does not blame the faults committed by a prudent person well instructed in the thing, more than those done by a stupid ignorant person: those committed by a person of age and experience, or even by a man arrived at the years of discretion, than those done by a youth: those committed by a theologue skilled in sacred matters, than those done by an illiterate person: those, in fine, committed by a person of distinction, or placed in any honourable station, more than those done by a vulgar person of lower life? So Hieronymus in Ezech. 2. Salvianus de gubern. Dei, p. 118. [[Hieronymus, *Commentarius in Ezechielem et Danielem, Homiliae in Jeremiam,* in Hieronymus, *Opera,* vol. 5; Salvianus, *De gubernatione Dei*]] and so likewise Juvenal in these well known lines.

> *Omne animi vitium tanto conspectius in se*
> *Crimen habet, quanto, qui peccat, major habetur.*
> Sat. 8. v. 140.

[[Juvenal, *Satires* 8.140 in *Juvenal and Persius:* "[T]he higher the wrongdoer's status, the more glaring the criticism."]]

whom occasion tempts to commit any crime; nor he who loses the opportunity of doing a good action thro' indolence or negligence; but an omission of an action is not to be imputed to one who had no opportunity of doing it.*

SECTION CXV

Whether the omission of things impossible can be imputed, or how and when?

Much less then can the omission of these actions be imputed to one, which are either impossible in the nature of things, or contrary to laws and good manners, or at least which he had not sufficient ability to perform, except so far as one had weakened the abilities with which he was endowed by his own fault, or had rashly, with bad intention, promised what he might have foreseen to be impossible for him to perform.† <80>

SECTION CXVI

What actions are good, and what are evil?

Moreover, actions compared in this manner with a rule of action, take different names. If they, in all their circumstances, be agreeable to right reason, not obliging by external obligation, or to internal obligation merely (§7), they are *good;* but if in one or more circumstances they

---

* For the occasion of committing a fault or temptation to it, ought to be avoided; and one ought to resist the allurements of vice. He who does it not is blameable, if he yields to sinful appetites or passions. He is therefore the author and cause of that action; and it ought to be imputed to him. It is therefore a wretched excuse Chaereas offers for himself in Terence: "Should I lose so desirable, a so much longed for, so favourable an opportunity?" [[Terence, *The Eunuch,* lines 604–6, in vol. 1 of *Terence.*]] For he suffered himself to be tempted to sin. On the other hand, how blameable the not taking hold of an opportunity of doing well is, Christ elegantly sets forth to us in the parable of the servants, *Matt.* xxv. 14.

† Hence it is plain, why a debtor who had squandered his estate is still liable, and is not excusable on account of his indigence, because he reduced himself by his own fault: and why an alchymist, who had promised mountains of gold, when he was found to have deceived, was as justly condemned of fraud, as one who had knowingly, and with evil intention promised a treasure. See an example in Tacitus, Annal. 16. 1. in the story of Cesellius Bassus. [[Tacitus, *Annals* 16.1, tells the story of a Carthaginian (said to be a madman) who convinced Nero that he had discovered, through a dream, Dido's treasure buried in a cave.]]

deviate from right reason to whatever side, they are *bad*. From which definitions it follows, that an action must be both materially and formally good (as the schools speak) in order not to be classed with bad actions.*

SECTION CXVII

Again, if we compare actions with a law, those which are in all things agreeable to law are *just;* those which are, in any one circumstance, disagreeable to law, are *unjust,* and are therefore called *sins.* Whence we may learn why St. *John* places all sin in ἀνομία, *i.e.* a transgression of a law.

What actions are just, and what are unjust?

SECTION CXVIII

Finally, since the divine law or will obliges us to *love* (§79), and love is either love of *justice,* or love of *beneficence* (§82), an action agreeing in <81> all circumstances with the love of justice, is a *just action,* and one ever so little repugnant to it, is an *unjust action;* but those which proceed from the love of humanity and beneficence, are called *honest,* and those which are not agreeable to that love, are called *dishonest, base, inhumane;* and hence it is easy to understand wherein the difference lies between *expletive* and *attributive justice.*

The difference between just and honest actions, and between unjust and dishonest actions.

REMARKS on This Chapter

Our Author's positions concerning the interpretation of laws, and the imputation of actions *in foro humano,* are very clear and just. But it

---

* Hence the largesses, the fastings, and all the austerity of the Pharisees were not good actions, tho' *materially* conformable to right reason, because not done from a good motive, but from ostentation and vain-glory. We ought not only to do good things, but we ought to do them in a right manner. The just man is rightly described by Philemon in Stobaeus, Serm. 9. thus: "Not he who does good things in whatever manner he does them, but he who sincerely desires not merely to be thought, but really to be upright in all his conduct, is good."

may not be improper to add the following observations concerning the effects of ignorance and error *in foro divino, i.e.* with respect to the good and bad consequences of actions occasioned by ignorance or error, according to the laws of God in his government of the world.

1. It must be as true in morals as it is confessed to be in mechanics, that deviation from truth will lead into a wrong manner of acting; and all action must be liable to all the consequences of the laws of nature, *i.e.* to all the consequences connected with it in the regular and wise constitution of things, according to which every cause operates, means are proper and effectual, and different operations have different effects. And in fact we know no mistakes in action through ignorance, rash judgments, or whatever way it happens, which do not produce hurtful consequences; insomuch that there is good reason to conclude, that more of the misery of mankind is owing to wrong methods of action which are the effects of ignorance or error, than to any other cause. It must be true in general, that in a world governed by general laws; or in which connexions are invariably established, every deviation from truth, every mistake about the connexions of things in it, must be in some degree hurtful.

But, 2. Since all the interests of intelligent agents require government by general laws, or fixed connexions which operate invariably, the government of the world will be perfectly good, if the connexions or general laws which constitute it are the best adapted that may be, to promote the greater good of rational agents in the sum of things. Now, that it is so, must be certain, if the being and providence of an infinitely good God can be proved *à priori.* And there is sufficient reason to conclude that it is so *à posteriori,* because the more examples we find by enquiring into the government of the world, of such good general laws, the greater is the presumption that the whole is governed by the best general laws. But the further we enquire, the further we search, the more and clearer instances do we find <82> of good, of perfect government. See my *Principles of Moral and Christian Philosophy.*

3. Our great business therefore is to endeavour to acquire just notions of the connexions of things; or of the good and bad consequences of actions, in order to act agreeably to them. If getting knowledge to direct our conduct were not in our power, directing our conduct could not be in our power: wherefore, if ignorance, want of knowledge, error,

false notions or judgments be not imputable to us, wrong actions are not imputable to us. So that ultimately, whether we speak of the imputation of actions in the juridical stile, or in other words, as we have now spoken of it, (both of which must mean the same thing) it is ignorance or error in judgment that is imputed, when action is imputed; it is ignorance or error that brings evil upon us, when wrong action does it; because every action is directed by our present opinion and judgment, and the affection corresponding to it. And for that reason, our chief business, interest and duty, must be to have just or true ideas of the nature and consequences of actions; or of the connexions of things, according to which our actions ought to be regulated, since it is according to them that actions have certain effects or consequences.

4. False judgments, which tend to direct into a wrong course of action, or to introduce a wrong temper into the mind, must, (as hath been said) be hurtful. But, on the one hand, it is as sure as that there is a God, and that the world is governed by good laws, for the greater general good of the whole, that a virtuous reasonable temper, and virtuous reasonable conduct, are, upon the whole of things, the most advantageous course of acting. It is so in fact in the present life considered by itself without any regard to futurity; and it must be so in a special manner in a future state. And, on the other hand, it is as sure as that there is a God, that no opinions, tho' false, which do not tend to corrupt the temper, or to lead into a wrong course of action, can render us obnoxious to the divine displeasure, can be provoking to him, as such, if the bent of the heart be sincerely towards truth and right; or can as such involve in any hurtful consequences appointed to be punishments of false opinions, not tending to corrupt the temper, nor to lead to vitious behaviour; and not proceeding from want of love to truth and right in any degree, or from want of impartial, honest diligence, as far as that is in our power, to find out truth and avoid error.

How moral conscience, or our sense of right and wrong may be, and only can be impaired, corrupted, or overpowered, is explained at great length in the *Enquiry concerning virtue,* Characteristicks, T. 2. p. 40, *&c.*[3] And to improve it, and preserve it pure and untainted, must

3. Anthony Ashley Cooper, Third Earl of Shaftesbury (1671–1713), *An Enquiry Concerning Virtue or Merit* (1699), in Shaftesbury, *Characteristics of Men, Manners,*

be our chief duty and interest. Enquiries therefore into right and wrong conduct are of the utmost importance. They are enquiries into the natures and consequences of things, and are in that sense *philosophy.* But which is more, they are enquiries into the natures and consequences of <83> things which ought to direct our conduct; and therefore they are *moral philosophy,* or compose the science of life, the science of right conduct, the science and art of living suitably to our nature and rank, suitably to our dignity; agreeably to the will of our Creator, manifested by the connexions of things established by him; and agreeably to our own best interest. For this must be certain, that it is the established connexions of things which constitute our best interest. And if the established connexions of things be according to the best order, acting according to virtue or the best order, must be in the sum of things our best interest. And why should we doubt that it is really so in a future state, and for ever, since it is really so at present, even while virtue is but in its first state of education, culture and discipline; since the compleat natural effect of highly improved virtue cannot take place till virtue be brought to a great pitch of perfection by gradual culture, because the effect cannot precede the cause. But that virtue is our best interest, as well as acting according to the best order, and easily discoverable to be such, will appear as our author proceeds in his deduction and demonstration of particular duties or virtues. I thought it proper to add this remark, as well on account of those who speak vaguely and loosely about the imputability of ignorance and error, as of those who maintain opinions which result in asserting, That sincere love of truth, and impartial diligence to discover it, is not the best temper, the best part we can act, nay, all the good within our power, with regard to knowledge, speculative or practical. And if this be not the temper and conduct which leads to happiness, according to the constitution of things, what a terrible, what a wretched constitution of things must it be!

Opinions, Times, 163–230. This is one of the rare references by Turnbull to Shaftesbury.

Of the duties of man to God.

SECTION CXIX

Hitherto we have but premised some of the first principles of the beau- A Transition
tiful moral science; let us now proceed to consider the *offices* or *duties* to the doctrine
which the *law of nature* prescribes to mankind; to all and every one of of duties.
the human race. What the Greek philosophers called τὸ Δέον, and the
Stoics τὸ καθῆκον, Tully afterwards, in explaining this part of philosophy in the Roman language, called <84> *officium,* not without deliberating about the matter a long time, and consulting his friends.*

---

* That the Stoics called it τὸ καθῆκον, and held the doctrine of *duties* as the chief
part of moral philosophy, we are assured by Diogenes Laertius, who has not only
briefly and clearly explained the chief precepts of the Stoics with relation to human
duties, but has likewise commended their treatises on the subject, as that of Zeno, l.
7. 4. of Cleanthes, cap. 7. of Sphaerus ibidem, &c. Plutarch mentions a book of
morals by Chrysippus de repugn. Stoic. [[Plutarch, "On Stoic Self-contradiction"
(De Stoicorum repugnantiis), in Plutarch, *Moralia: in Seventeen Volumes,* vol. 13, pt.
2, 412–602. Plutarch refers to a number of works by Chrysippus in the text.]] Cicero
mentions one of Panaetius upon duties (de off. 3. 2.) and in his letters to Atticus, 16.
11. he speaks of one by Posidonius. When, after their example, Cicero had wrote a
treatise of the same kind in Latin, after long deliberation what title to give it, all things
duly considered, he could not find a more proper word to express the τὸ καθῆκον of
the Stoics than the Latin word *officium.* So he writes to Atticus, 16. 6. "Quod de
inscriptione quaeris, non dubito, quin καθῆκον officium sit, nisi quid tu aliud. Sed
inscriptio plenior *de officiis.*" [[Cicero, *Epistulae ad Atticum* 16.6: "As to what you
enquire about my writing, I do not doubt that καθῆκον is to be translated *officium*
(duty). But there will be a fuller writing '*de officiis*' ('On Duties')."]]

SECTION CXX

Office or duty defined.

By *office* or *duty* I understand an action conformable to the laws, whether of perfect or imperfect obligation. Nor can I entirely approve the definition given by the Stoics, who say, it is an action, for the doing which a probable reason can be given; or, in other words, an action which reason persuades to do.* Diog. Laert. 7. 107. 108. Cicero de finibus, l. 3. 17.[1] <85>

SECTION CXXI

The nature of duty.

But since office or duty means an action conformable to law, it is plain that duty cannot be conceived without a law; that he does not perform a duty, who imposes upon himself what no law commands; that an action ceases to be duty, when the law, or the reason of the law enjoining it ceases; and that when a law extends to certain persons only, of two persons who do the same action, the one performs his duty, and the other acts contrary to his duty.†

* For since nothing is done even rashly, for which a probable reason may not be given, whatever is done, not only by men, but by brutes, may be called *officium, office* or *duty.* And thus the Stoics understood the word, of whom Laertius says, l. 7. 107. "They extended the word to plants and animals, for with regard to these there are offices." [[Diogenes Laertius, *Lives,* 7.107.]] It is true, an office ought to be founded upon a reason, but it ought to be a reason which is proper to determine men to act or forbear acting, and not brutes, i.e. an obligatory reason.

† It is proper to illustrate these propositions by examples. None will say that Origen did a duty when he emasculated himself, whether by an instrument, as Hieronym. [[St. Jerome (ca. 342–420), one of the four Latin doctors of the church]] relates, ep. 65. or, as others have narrated, by medicines. Epiph. Haer. 64. [[Epiphanius, *The Panarion of St. Epiphanius,* 215.]] For there is no divine precept commanding it, insomuch that Origen himself afterwards acknowledged he had misunderstood that passage in St. Mat. xix. 12. See Huet. Origeniana I. 1. 13. p. 8. [[Huet, *Origeniana.*]] None will deny that a christian would act contrary to his duty, if he should not submit to the law of circumcision, or offer sacrifice to God, tho' formerly both were duties, Gal. iii. 23, 25. iv. 3, 4, 5. 2 Col. ii. 20. Heb. ix. 9, 10. Finally, if a priest usurps the office of a judge, he acts contrary to his duty, and is guilty of intrusion into a charge not committed to him; whereas a judge doing the same action, does his duty, 1 Peter iv. 15.

1. Cicero, *De finibus bonorum et malorum.*

SECTION CXXII

The obligation binding one to do his duty being either perfect or imperfect (§120), *duty* must likewise be divided into *perfect* and *imperfect;* the former being done in obedience to perfect obligation, or a law; the other being performed in consequence of imperfect obligation, or from virtue.* <86>

Duty divided into perfect and imperfect.

SECTION CXXIII

Further, law being the rule of duties (§121), because law is either *divine* or *human,* and divine law is either *natural* or *positive,* there are so many corresponding divisions of duties. Those which are commanded by the divine natural law, are called *natural duties.* Those commanded by the divine positive law, are called *christian duties;* and those, in fine, which are enjoined by human laws, are called *civil offices* or *duties.* †

Into natural and christian.

SECTION CXXIV

But the principal division of duties is taken from their object. For as there are three objects to whom we owe certain duties, GOD, *ourselves,* and *other men* (§90), so there are duties of three kinds; *duties to God, duties to ourselves,* and *duties to other men;* of all which we are to treat in order.

Into duties to God, to ourselves, and to others.

---

* Accordingly, to do hurt to no person, to fulfil contracts, to repair damage done by us, and such like duties, are perfect. To relieve the indigent, give alms, shew those who are gone out of their way the right road, give counsel to those who are in doubt, and such like duties, are imperfect. See Cicero de off. 3. 12. & seq.

† To worship God with religious reverence, to honour our parents, to defend ourselves against injuries, are *natural duties,* l. 2. l. 3. Dig. de just. & jure: To deny ourselves, take up our cross, and follow Christ, are *christian duties:* to pay civil taxes, to observe particular forms and times in law-suits, and such like, are *civil duties.*

SECTION CXXV

The founda-
tion of our
duties towards
God.
As to our *duties towards God* we have already observed, that they must be inferred from the consideration of the divine perfections (§87); and hence we concluded, that God ought to be loved with a love of *devotion and obedience,* and therefore ought to be worshipped with all the powers of our soul, as the most perfect of Beings, upon whom we wholly depend, and to be obeyed with the most sincere and perfect obedience (§91). <87>

SECTION CXXVI

Our obligation
to know God.
Since the duties we owe to *God* must be deduced from his infinite perfections (§125), it follows, by necessary consequence, that man is obliged not only to acquire the most lively knowledge of God, and of his perfections, but daily to encrease this knowledge, and advance in it, that he may attain daily to greater and greater certainty and perfection in it; which, since it cannot be done but by daily meditation upon those truths which reason is able to discover concerning God, by the careful and serious contemplation of his works of creation and providence, so full of evident marks of his infinite wisdom and goodness; hence it is manifest that we are obliged to these exercises, and that those who neglect these means of coming to the knowledge of God, which are in every one's power who has a sound mind, are in a state of inexcusable ignorance; and those who ascribe any imperfection to God, are in a state of inexcusable error (§107).* <88>

---

* Hence the apostle says what may be known of God is manifest to the Heathens, because the invisible perfections of God from the beginning of the world are clearly discovered by his wonderful works, and therefore they are without excuse who know him not, Rom. i. 20. And whence else indeed that universal consent in the acknowledgment of his being and perfections urged by Cicero, Qu. Tusc. 1. 13. de nat. deorum, 2. 2. Maxim. Tyr. diss. 38. Aelian. Var. hist. 2. 31. Sen. ep. 117? [[Maximus of Tyre, *Dissertationes,* 303–12; Aelian, *Varia historia* (*Historical Miscellany*).]] For tho' this universal consent be not a demonstrative argument of the Being of God (§71), yet hence it is manifest, that as the apostle says, "What may be known of God is easily discoverable." For which reason, Cicero de nat. deorum, 2. 2. affirms, "If any one

SECTION CXXVII

Hence it likewise follows, that we are obliged, or that it is our duty to have just apprehensions of the divine perfections, and to know and believe that he is the Creator and Governor of all things, that all things are made by him, and are under his providence and government, human affairs principally; and that he is one *pure, eternal, independent, omnipotent, incomprehensible, intelligent, wise, omniscient, free, active, good, true, just,* and most *excellent Being.* *

And to have just apprehensions of his perfections.

SECTION CXXVIII

He who obstinately denies the being, or any of the perfections of God, is *impious:* he who ascribes imperfections to God, repugnant to his nature, is called a *blasphemer:* since therefore they, who do not know the perfections of God, are inexcusably ignorant, and they, who attribute any imperfection to him, inexcusably err; it is incontrovertible that all *blaspheming* and *impiety* are inexcusable. But they are therefore *impious,* and without excuse, who, with a hardened mind, deny the divine existence or providence; and they are *blasphemers,* who, with *Homer,* and other poets, assert a plura-<89>lity of Gods, and represent them as contending and quarrelling one with another; as adulterers, incestuous, or deformed, lame, in pain, and groaning in an effeminate manner; and who have not only professed in words such absurd opinions of the Gods,

All impiety and blasphemy are inexcusable.

---

doubt whether there is a God, I cannot comprehend why the same person may not as well doubt whether there be a sun or not." [[Cicero, *De natura deorum.*]]

* Epictetus Enchirid. c. 38. tells us, "The chief thing in religion is to have just ideas of the immortal powers, and of their infinitely wise and good administration." [[Epictetus, *Enchiridion,* but chap. 31, rather than 38 (Epictetus, *The Discourses and Manual,* vol. 2:226).]] And they are in a great error indeed, who think that the whole of our duty consists in probity and integrity, of life, and that it is a matter of indifference what one thinks of God, or what notions he entertains of divine things. For since our duties to God can only be inferred from his perfections (§125), how can one render to God the homage and reverence due to him, or that sincere and universal obedience to which he is justly entitled, if he be ignorant of his perfections, or has imbibed false and corrupt notions of them?

but have not hesitated to set them forth to the eyes of men under horrible images, and by wicked and vile ceremonies.*

SECTION CXXIX

Our obligation to promote the glory of God.

He who has a just and lively notion of any perfections, cannot but be highly delighted with the contemplation of them, and will spare no pains to persuade others to pay the same regard to the Being possessed of them; it is therefore our duty to endeavour to bring others to the knowledge of the divine perfections, and to restore those who err to a right appre-

* The ancient writers of apologies for the christian religion have severely reproached the Pagans for this impiety and blasphemy, as Justin Martyr, Athenagoras, Theophilus Antiochenus, Tatianus, Hermias, Tertullian, Cyprian, Minucius Faelix, Arnobius, Lactantius, Eusebius, Julius Firmicus Maternus, and others. But which is more surprizing, some Pagan authors have likewise reproved this madness of their contemporary countrymen. Not to quote several passages of Lucian and other Heathen writers to this effect, I shall satisfy my self with mentioning one of Sophocles preserved to us by Justin Martyr Paraenes. ad Graec. p. 17. and de monarchia Dei, p. 104, and by Eusebius, Praep. Evang. p. 348, and some others. "In truth, there is one God who made heaven and the spacious earth, the ebbing and flowing sea, and the mighty winds. But many of us having lost our understanding, for a consolation in our calamities, make to ourselves Gods, and endeavour to propitiate lifeless images by sacrifices to them: we celebrate festivals foolishly, imagining ourselves pious in so doing." Is it not truly wonderful to find Sophocles reproaching his fellow Pagans for the same impiety the apostle charges them with, Rom. i. 21, 22, 23. [[For the references to Sophocles in the *Paraenesis* (or *Cohortatio*) *ad Graecos* and *De monarchia dei*, see Pseudo-Iustinus, *Cohortatio ad Graecos, De Monarchia, Oratio ad Graecos,* 48 and 88. The same passage, with very small alterations, is attributed to Sophocles by Eusebius in his *Praeparatio evangelica,* 680b (Eusebius, *Praeparationis evangelicae libri XV*). The passage by Sophocles is as follows:

There is in truth One God, and One alone,
Who made the lofty heavens, and wide-spread earth,
The sea's blue wave, and might of warring winds.
But we poor mortals with deceived heart,
Seeking some solace for our many woes,
Raised images of gods in stone or bronze,
Or figures wrought of gold or ivory,
And when we crowned their sacrifice, and held
High festival, we thought this piety.
(Trans. E. H. Gifford)]]

hension of them; and, as much as in us lies, to convince the impious, by solid and per-<90>suasive reasoning with them, of their absurdity and wickedness, and bring them to render due reverence to God: and they who do so, are said to exert themselves *to promote the glory of God.* *

SECTION CXXX

Because he who has a just conception of the divine perfections, cannot but highly delight in them (§129), and the desire of good to an object, with delight arising from the consideration of its perfection and happiness, is *love* (§8), the consequence is, that God must be loved. And because of the more excellent and sublime a nature a Being is, the more love and veneration is due to it (§87): God ought to be loved with the most perfect love; *i.e.* as the scripture expresses it, "with all our heart, with all our soul, and with all our strength," Mat. xxii. 37. Luke x. 27. Because goodness is one of the divine perfections (§127); God is in himself, and with regard to mankind, infinitely good: he is therefore to be loved for both these reasons.† <91>

And to the love of God.

---

* I have said by solid and persuasive arguments, not menaces and penalties. For since ignorance and error are vices not of the will, but of the understanding, there is no other remedy for them, but to convince persons of the truth, and to excite them by proper arguments to embrace it; and hence it is evident, that those can never be serviceable to the ignorant or erring, who are for employing fire and gibbets against atheists, especially since it hath never been an uncommon practice to brand with that name (to use the words of Clemens Alex. in Protrept.) "men living regularly and modestly, who were quicker-sighted in discerning impostures about the Gods than the generality of mankind." [[Clement of Alexandria, "Protreptikos pros Hellenas" (The Exhortation of the Greeks), in *Clement of Alexandria*, 3–263.]] Of this many examples are brought by the learned. See Aelian. Var. Hist. 2. 31.

† What the Epicurean philosophers and the Sadduceans in ancient times said of the pure love of God, is well known to the learned: And in our own times, some mystick divines have renewed that doctrine, the chief of whom is Franc. Saignac de Fenelon, Archbishop of Cambray, whose treatise entitled, "The maxims of the saints," gave rise to a controversy, of which I have elsewhere given a short history (Elem. Philos. moral. §198). [[Heineccius, *Elementa philosophiae rationalis et moralis.*]] [[François de Salignac de La Mothe-Fénelon (1651–1715) was archbishop of Cambrai and tutor of Louis Duke de Bourgogne, grandson and heir to Louis XIV. He is best known for his *Les aventures de Télémaque* (1699) [*Telemachus, Son of Ulysses,*

SECTION CXXXI

And likewise obedience and fear.

Among the divine perfections are omnipotence and omniscience (§127); but none can keep these perfections in view without being excited to the diligent, unintermitted study of doing whatever may be pleasing to God, and of avoiding whatever may be disagreeable to him; which study and endeavour we call *obedience* to God. And since none can represent God to himself as a most just Being, without being seriously concerned not to offend him; not to do or say any thing that is dishonourable to him, or tends to create his displeasure; it must be our duty to *fear* him: for this concern not to incur his anger is *fear,* and when united with the love of him above described (§130), it is properly called *filial fear.* *

SECTION CXXXII

As also to avoid superstition.

He who fears God with a servile fear, separates the love of God from the fear of him (§131); but because love of God consists in delight in the consideration of the divine perfections (§130); he therefore who fears God without any knowledge of his perfections, is called *superstitious;* and hence it follows, that a good man ought carefully to avoid <92> all superstition, because it proceeds from ignorant servile fear.†

1994]. Heineccius refers here to Fénelon's *Explication des maximes des saints sur la vie intérieure* (1698), which was condemned by the pope.]] But who can conceive God otherwise than as good to all his creatures? How idle then is the question about the pure love of God? nay, how dangerous? This hath been shewn by Leibnitz, in Praef. prodrom. & mantissae codicis juris gentium, by Wolfius and others.

   * *Filial fear,* is therefore attended with love, and *servile fear* with hatred: it excludes love. But since it is our duty not only to fear God, but likewise to love him (§130), the consequence is, that the law of nature requires *filial* not *servile fear* of God, the latter of which wicked men and evil spirits cannot shake off.

   † *Superstition* is fear of God, which results not from the contemplation of the divine perfections, but from false conceptions of God. This is Theophrastus's meaning, Charact. p. 47, where he defines superstition, "Δειλίαν πρὸς τὸ δαιμόνιον, a trembling dread of the Divinity." [[Theophrastus, *Theophrastus: Characters,* 97.]] By Δειλίαν, Casaubon in his notes understands fear different from that which becomes good men who have just ideas of the Deity; and by τὸ δαιμόνιον, the Gods and Demons, and whatever in times of ancient ignorance was thought to have any share

SECTION CXXXIII

All superstition, internal and external, being inconsistent with just ap-   Its effects.
prehension of the divine perfections (§132), one who has just notions
of them, will keep himself carefully from all slavish fear of created beings, and from those absurd errors, whereby God is represented as avar-
itious and placable by gifts; and likewise from magical arts and divina-
tions, from idol-worship; and, in fine, from this absurd opinion, that
God may be propitiated by mere external worship, tho' not accompanied
either with internal fear or love.* <93>

---

of Divinity. This absurd dread, as it is in the mind, is called *internal superstition,* and
as it discovers itself in outward acts, it is called *superstitious worship.*

* These are the principal branches of *superstition,* to which all its other effects may
be reduced. See Budd. de Super. & Atheismo, cap. 7 & 8. [[Buddeus, *Theses theologicae de atheismo et superstitione variis observationibus illustratae.*]] Hence it appears
how idle the comparison between *superstition* and *atheism* is, both being equally repugnant to true piety, as the same learned writer has proved against Bayle, cap. 4. §5.
None however will deny, that very many great evils proceed from *superstition,* insomuch that there is reason to cry out with the Poet,

   Quantum religio possit suasisse malorum.

   [["So potent was superstition in persuading to evil deeds!" (See Lucretius, *De
   rerum natura* 1.101.)]]

If by *religio* be meant the *dread of God,* disjoined from *love,* i.e. *superstition.* Upon
this subject Juvenal's fifteenth satyr is well worth our reading. For it often happens,
that as the Poet there says,

   Inter finitimos vetus atque antiqua simultas,
   Immortale odium, & nunquam sanabile vulnus
   Ardet adhuc Ombos & Tentyra. Summus utrimque
   Inde furor vulgo, quod numina vicinorum
   Odit uterque locus, quum solos credat habendos
   Esse Deos, quos ipse colit.

   [[Juvenal, *Satires* 15.33, in *Juvenal and Persius:* "Between the neighbours
   Ombi and Tentyra there still blazes a lasting and ancient feud, an undying
   hatred, a wound that can never be healed. On each side the height of mob
   fury arises because each place detests the gods of their neighbours. They think
   that only the gods they themselves worship should be counted as gods."]]

SECTION CXXXIV

And to repose our trust in God.

Further, since none can represent the divine perfections to himself without presenting to his mind the ideas of perfect wisdom, power and goodness; such a person cannot but place his confidence and trust in God, and be satisfied in his mind with the divine administration; and thus be disposed to submit to whatever may happen to him in the course of divine providence with a firm and cheerful soul; nor will he be stumbled because evils fall upon the good, and good things fall to the share of the wicked, but be persuaded that all things shall co-operate to the good of the virtuous, to good in the whole.

SECTION CXXXV

Of internal and external worship.

In these and the like offices does that *internal worship* of God consist, by which we understand the love, fear and trust, with which we embrace God in our pure minds. But man being so framed, that his affections naturally exert themselves in certain external actions, his internal love of God could not be thought sincere unless it exerted itself in *external love; i.e.* in such external acts as express love, fear, and resignation towards God.* <94>

---

* Some have denied that the necessity of external worship can be proved from principles of reason, partly, because God does not stand in need of it; (as the philosopher Demonax in Lucian, in Demonacte, tom. 1. p. 861, asserts, when being accused of impiety, for not offering sacrifice to Minerva, he answered, "I did not think she stood in need of sacrifice"). [[A reference to a life of the philosopher Demonax by the Greek satirist Lucian (A.D. ca. 117–80), republished in several editions in the early modern period (see, for example, *Demonactis philosophi vita ex Lutiano latine conversa a Christophoro Hegendorphino*).]] Partly because human society, and the tranquillity of human life, is not hurt by the omission of external worship: (See Thomasius, Jurisprud. divin. 2. 1. 11. and his introd. in Ethic. 3. 37. & seq.) [[Thomasius, *Einleitung zur Sittenlehre.*]] But neither does God stand in need of internal worship, which none will deny to be a duty. And the other argument falls to the ground, when that fundamental error is refuted, which asserts that nothing is of the law of nature but what can be inferred from sociability (§75). See Hochstet. Colleg. Pufend. Exercit. 3. 38. [[Hochstetter, *Collegium Pufendorfianum.*]]

SECTION CXXXVI

Since therefore the external worship of God consists in actions flowing from love, fear, and resignation towards God (§135), but love must naturally exert itself in praising the Being in whose perfection and happiness we highly delight, it must be our duty always to speak honourably of God, and with due reverence, and to excite others by our actions to love him, to sing praises to him, and not to dishonour his name by rash swearing, by perjury, or by whatever irreverent discourse.

External worship ought to flow from the love of God.

SECTION CXXXVII

From the fear and obedience we owe to God as the most perfect of Beings, we may justly conclude that all our actions ought to be conformed to his precepts, and that we ought always to have in mind his omnipresence and omniscience, by which he discerns our most secret thoughts; whence it follows, that all hypocrisy and dissimulation ought to be avoided, as being necessarily accompanied with injurious and contemptible apprehensions of God.* <95>

As also from the fear of God.

SECTION CXXXVIII

In fine, he who places his trust in God (§134), will never cease to send up pure devout prayers to him, and will cheerfully embrace every occasion of speaking well of and with God privately and publicly. For this is what right reason prescribes concerning the external worship of God. As for the external rites, it is likewise obvious, that public worship cannot

Confidence ought to be placed in God.

---

* Thales Milesius, acknowledged this sublime truth, when being asked, "whether God saw unjust actions," he answered, "yea and unjust thoughts likewise," Clemens Alexand. Strom. 5. p. 594. [[Clement of Alexandria, *Les Stromates* (*Stromateis*), *Stromate V*, vol. 1, chap. 14, 96.4, p. 113.]] But who can choose but fear an omnipotent God, who knoweth and seeth all things? Epictetus says elegantly in Arrian, "Wherefore, doors and windows being shut, or when you are in darkness, say not you are alone; for you are not. And you certainly are not, because God is present." [[Epictetus, *The Discourses as Reported by Arrian*, bk. 1, 14.13–14.]] We are therefore under the strongest obligation to sincere piety, since we are always in the sight of God.

be performed unless certain times and places be devoted to it; and a duty of such importance ought to be done with all decency; but as to the rites or ceremonies themselves, reason can lay down no other rule about them, but in general, that they ought to be in every respect such as are proper to recal to our minds those sentiments in which divine worship consists.

REMARKS on This Chapter

I have but little to add to what our Author hath said of Religion. Our Harrington justly lays down the following truths relative to religion as aphorisms. "Nature is of God: some part in every religion is natural; an universal effect demonstrates an universal cause; an universal cause is not so much natural, as it is nature itself; but every man has either to his terror or his consolation, some sense of religion: man may therefore be rather defined a religious than a rational creature; in regard that other creatures have something of reason, but there is nothing of religion."[2] So we frequently find ancient philosophers reasoning about human nature and religion, as I have shewn from several authorities in the 7th chapter of my *Principles of Moral Philosophy,* the whole of which treatise is designed to be a demonstration *à posteriori, i.e.* from the wisdom and goodness of providence, that the whole world is made and governed by an infinitely perfect mind, in the contemplation, adoration and imitation of whom the chief happiness of man consists, according to his make and frame. The arguments, *à priori,* for the proof of a God, are shewn in the conclusion of that essay not to be so abstruse as is said by some; and they are more fully explained in my *Christian Philosophy.* The end, the happiness, the duty of a Being (all which ways of speaking must mean the same thing) can only be inferred from its frame and constitution, its make and situation. But nothing can be more evident than, "That man is made to love order, to delight in the idea of its universal prevalence throughout nature, and to have joy and satisfaction from the <96> consciousness of order within his own breast, and in the conduct of his actions." All the joys of which man is susceptible, which never nauseate or cloy, but are equally remote from

2. Harrington, "Political Aphorisms," nos. 30–35 in Harrington, *Political Works,* pp. 765–66.

grossness and disgust, or remorse, may be reduced to the love of order and harmony: nothing else can give him any pleasure in contemplation or in practice, but good order; the belief of good administration in the government of the world; the regular exercises of those generous affections which tend to public good; the consciousness of inward harmony; and the prevalence of good order and publick happiness in society, through regular and good government: to these classes are the principal pleasures for which man is framed by nature, reducible, as might be shewn, even from an analysis of the pleasures belonging to refined imagination or good taste in the polite arts: but whence such a constitution? Does it not necessarily lead us to acknowledge an infinitely perfect author of all things; an universal mind, the former and governor of the universe, which is itself perfect order and harmony, perfect goodness, perfect virtue? Whence could we have such a make? whence could we have understanding, reason, the capacity of forming ideas of general order and good, and of delighting so highly in it, but from such a Being? Thus the ancients reasoned. Thus the sacred writers often reason. And this argument is obvious to every understanding. It is natural to the mind of man. It is no sooner presented to it than it cleaves to it, takes hold of it with supreme satisfaction, and triumphs in it. And what part of nature does not lead us naturally to this conception, if we ever exercise our understanding, or if we do not wilfully shut our eyes? But having fully enlarged upon this and several other arguments for the Being of a God in my *Principles of Moral Philosophy;* I shall here only remark, 1. That Polybius, Cicero, and almost all the ancients, have acknowledged that a public sense of religion is necessary to the well-being and support of society: society can hardly subsist without it: or at least, it is the most powerful mean for restraining from vice, and promoting and upholding those virtues by which society subsists, and without which every thing that is great and comely in society, must soon perish and go to ruin. 2. That with regard to private persons, he who does not often employ his mind in reviewing the perfections of the Deity, and in consoling and strengthening his mind by the comfortable and mind-greatning reflexions to which meditation upon the universal providence of an all-perfect mind, naturally, and as it were necessarily lead, deprives himself of the greatest joy, the noblest exercise and entertainment the human mind is capable of; and whatever obligations there may be to virtue independent of, or abstract from such a perswasion, he cannot make such progress in virtue, he cannot be so firm, steady and unshaken in his adherence to it, as he who being persuaded of the truth just mentioned, is daily drawing virtuous strength and comfort from it. This is fully proved by an excellent writer on morals, who, not-<97>withstanding hath been often most injuriously reproached for aiming at a scheme of virtue without religion.[3] This author hath fully proved that the perfection and heighth of virtue must be owing to the belief of a God; since, where the latter is wanting, there can neither be the same benignity, firmness or constancy; the same good composure of the affections, or uniformity of mind, Characteristics, T. 2. p. 56, &c. 3. I would remark, that the being and providence of an universal, all-perfect mind, being once established, it plainly follows from hence, by necessary consequence, that all the duties of rational creatures may be reduced to this one, with several antient moralists, *viz.* "to act as becomes an intelligent active part of a good whole, and conformably to the temper and character of the all-governing mind." This is acting agreeably to nature; to the nature of an intelligent creature endued with active powers, a sense of public good and order; agreeably to the nature of the Supreme Governor of all things, and to the order of his creation and government. All our duties may be reduced to, or comprehended under that one general article of acting as becomes an intelligent part of a good whole: for to do so, we must delight in the author of the world, and resign to his will cheerfully the management of all things independent of our will; and by our will cheerfully cooperate with him in the pursuit of publick good, as far as we are active and have power, or as things are made by him dependent upon our will and conduct. He who is incapable of receiving pleasure from the belief of a God, and the contemplation of general order and harmony, must be a very imperfect creature: for he wants the noblest of senses or faculties. And he who can delight in the contrary persuasion, *i.e.* in the idea of a fatherless world and blind chance, or, which is yet more horrible, malignant administration, must have a very perverted mind, if perversion has any meaning: he must be as properly a monster, in respect of a moral frame, as any deformity is monstrous in regard to bodily texture.

3. That is, the Earl of Shaftesbury.

CHAPTER VI

Of the duties of man to himself.

SECTION CXXXIX

Nothing is nearer to man, besides the ever-blessed God, than he is to himself; nature having inlaid into his frame such a sensibility to his interests, and so tender a love of himself, that we justly look upon him to be out of his senses and distracted, who <98> hates and wishes ill to himself. Nor is this *self-love* unjust, while it does not disturb good order. For it is that love with which one delights in his own perfections and happiness, and is concerned to procure and augment these goods. But since God hath created us, and adorned us with many excellent perfections, and given us the means of improving in perfection and happiness, he must be concluded to will that we should endeavour to promote our happiness and perfection, and be delighted with it; *i.e.* that we should love our selves (§92).

Man is obliged to love himself.

SECTION CXL

From which we have already inferred (§92), that man is bound to pursue, promote, and preserve his own perfection and happiness, as far as is consistent with the love of the supreme Being.*

What this love is.

* Therefore, we do not perform these duties to ourselves that we may be happy (for we have shewn above, that this tenet is false, that utility is the only source or rule of just and unjust) but because God wills that we study to promote our happiness and perfection: and therefore to promote our perfection and happiness is itself our duty; and is not the cause which impels or obliges us to it.

SECTION CXLI

What are its objects.

Since man is obliged, by the will of God, to all and every thing which tends to promote, preserve, and enlarge his happiness and perfection (§140); and man consists, not only of mind, but of body likewise, in such a manner, that he is a compound of *body* and *mind;* the consequence is, that man is obliged to promote the perfection of both his constituent parts; and because the faculties of the mind are two, *understanding* and *will,* he is obliged to study the perfection of both; wherefore the duties of man, with respect to himself, are relative partly to the *whole man,* partly to the *understanding,* partly to the *will,* and partly to his *body* and *external state.* * <99>

SECTION CXLII

These duties ought not to be severed.

Whence we conclude, that these duties ought not to be severed from one another; and therefore, that neither the mind nor the body ought totally to be neglected: but if it should happen that the duties due to both cannot be performed, we ought, of many perfections and goods, which cannot be obtained at one and the same time, to choose the most excellent and necessary (§94). And therefore the mind being more excellent than

---

* It is proper to observe this, in opposition to the doctrine of Socrates and others, who maintained that the body is not a part of man, but his instrument only, and that external things do not properly appertain to man, or in the least concern him. So Simplicius, in his preface to his commentary on Epictetus, "If a man commands his body, and the body doth not so much as command itself, then man is not body, and for the same reason, he is not both mind and body, but wholly mind." [[Simplicius, *Commentarius in Enchiridion Epicteti* (*On Epictetus' Handbook,* Introduction, 37– 40).]] Whence he a little after reasons thus: "He who bestows his care upon the body, bestows it upon things which belong not to man, but his instrument: But he, whose study and cares are set upon riches, and such like external things, bestows his care neither upon man, nor his instrument, but upon things subservient to that instrument." Many other such foolish boasts we find in some ancient writers, which are equally false and hurtful.

the body, we ought to be more diligent about the perfecting of our minds than our bodies, yet so as not to neglect the latter.* <100>

SECTION CXLIII

As for what relates to the *whole man,* as consisting of soul and body, his felicity and perfection as such, consists in this, that the union of his mind and body be safe, because these parts being separated, tho' the mind, being immortal, survive, yet the man no longer subsists. Man therefore is obliged to take care to preserve his life, and to avoid the dissolution of the union between his body and mind, which is death, unless the mind be persuaded of a greater good to be obtained by death: in which case one ought not indeed voluntarily to choose death, but to suffer the menaces of it and itself with a brave and intrepid magnanimity.†

Man is obliged to preserve his life and eschew death.

---

* They therefore act contrary to their duty, who are so taken up about the body that they suffer their mind, as it were, to brutalize. But, on the other hand, they do not fulfil the whole of their duty, who impair their bodies by their too sedulous uninterrupted application to the culture of their minds in knowledge and wisdom. Neither of these duties is to be neglected.

† There is reason therefore to pronounce Hegesias πειθιθάνατος, to have been mad, who thought man obliged to put an end to his life, and went about urging men to destroy themselves, by so many arguments that his hearers threw themselves in great numbers into the sea. Cic. Tusc. 1. 34. Valer. Max. 8. 9. [[Valerius Maximus, *Memorable Doings and Sayings,* vol. 2, 249.]] For if it be true, that one must be distracted and out of his senses to hate himself (§139), we must say of Hegesias's doctrine and conduct with a poet on another occasion,

Non sani esse hominis, non sanus juret Orestes;

[[Persius, *Satires* 3.118: "which the mad Orestes himself would swear were the acts of a madman."]]

especially, since he reduced all human obligations to pleasure, and admitted not of a future existence, from which any consolation could be drawn to make death more desirable than an afflicted life. On the other hand, the apostle's desire was not contrary to his duty, when he *longed to be dissolved:* nor are the martyrs to be blamed, who, supported by the hopes of immortal glory after death, feared no tortures; because an evil which delivers us from a greater one, and procures us a very great good, is rather to be accounted good than ill.

SECTION CXLIV

And therefore self-murder is unlawful.

Hence moreover we infer, that he acts contrary to his duty who lays violent hands on himself. And this may be proved from other considerations, as, that this action is repugnant to the nature of <101> love, and to a right disposition of mind, and therefore involves an absurdity or contradiction in it; that it is inconsistent with that trust and resignation which are due to God, and that acquiescence in the divine will, which we have already shewn to be commanded by the law of nature (§134). But it will be sufficient to add this one argument. Man is obliged to love man as himself; and therefore himself as others (§93). But the love of justice does not permit us to kill a man, therefore self-love does not permit us to destroy ourselves.*

SECTION CXLV

So is the neglect of life and health.

From the same principles laid down (§143), it is evident that they act no less contrary to their duty who hasten their death by immoderate labour, or by luxury and lasciviousness, or who do not take proper care of their health; and who, when neither duty calls, nor necessity urges, voluntarily expose themselves to danger, and bring themselves into peril or pain by their own fault.† <102>

---

* Thus we ought to reason with those who are capable of reasoning; as for those who are furious and out of themselves, the fatal action is not to be imputed to them (§106). Nothing can excuse self-murder but madness: not a guilty conscience, since there are means of quieting it, *viz.* by reformation: nor the greatest distress and pain; for tho' it be true, that of two evils the least ought to be chosen; yet voluntary self-murder is not a physical but a moral evil, which cannot be chosen; and no calamity or pain is so great, but it may be alleviated by resignation to the divine will: let me add, that it is not the least species of madness to die for fear of dying. See Wolf. Philosoph. Moral. §340 & seq. [[Wolff, *Philosophia moralis sive ethica,* vol. i.]]

† For whoever is the author or cause of an action, to him that action is justly imputable (§105). But who will call it into question, that he is the cause of his death who destroys and tortures himself by excessive toil? he who wears out and wastes the strength of his body by riotous living? He who takes no care of his health, but exposes himself unnecessarily to manifest dangers? Since therefore, even *in foro humano,* by the *Lex Cornelia,* not only he is guilty of murder, who with premeditated evil inten-

SECTION CXLVI

The perfection of human *understanding* certainly consists in the knowledge of truth and good; to acquire, enlarge, and preserve which man
being obliged (§140), the consequence is, that every one is bound to exert
himself to strengthen and cultivate his understanding, or to improve his
faculty of discerning truth from falshood, and good from evil; and to
let no opportunity pass neglected, whether of instruction from others,
from books, or from experience, of learning useful truths, and wholesome precepts and maxims concerning good and evil,* that thus he may
attain to all the useful knowledge within his reach; and if he be in that
condition of life that does not allow him to learn all that it is useful to
know, he may at least be master of what it is most necessary and advantageous for him to understand, and have that at his command as ready
coin, so to speak.

The duties of man with regard to his understanding.

SECTION CXLVII

From which last proposition (§146), it follows, that whereas all persons
are equally obliged to the <103> duties hitherto mentioned; every one
is for himself in particular obliged to that special culture of his understanding, which is suitable to his particular talents and genius, and to
his rank and condition in life; and therefore every one ought to know
his force and genius, and one is hardly excusable if he chooses a way of

Of the particular culture to which particulars are obliged.

----

tion directly kills a man, but even he who was the cause of his death; (I. 16. §8. Dig.
de poenis, I. 1. D. ad L. Corneliani de Sicar.) who can doubt but he must be guilty
of self-murder *in foro divino,* who was the cause of his own death?

* This knowledge is equally necessary to all men, partly because the will cannot
pursue but what the understanding represents to it as good, nor decline but what the
understanding hath discerned to be evil (§30); and partly because even actions done
through ignorance are imputed, so far as the law might, and ought to have been
understood (§108). Sophocles therefore says with good reason in his Antig. v. 1321.
"To have wisdom is the principal thing with regard to happiness." [[Sophocles, *Antigone,* line 1348, in *Sophocles,* ed. and trans. Lloyd-Jones.]]

life to himself for which he is not qualified, or if he forces any in his power,* under his authority, or committed to his direction, so to do.

SECTION CXLVIII

Duties relative to the will.

The perfection of the *will* consists in the desire and fruition of good. But since we cannot pursue good, unless we have first conceived a just notion of its excellence, nor avoid evil, unless we know it to be such (§30); hence it is manifest, that we ought not to acquiesce in any knowledge of good and evil whatsoever, but exert ourselves with all our power to have a true and lively conception of them; that not every good is to be chosen, but of <104> many goods that which is best and most necessary: yea, that evil ought not to be avoided, if it be necessary to our attaining to a greater good: and finally, that our chief good ought to be desired and pursued above all things; and that we ought to bear the want of other goods with a patient and satisfied mind, if we cannot attain it without being deprived of them.†

* The culture therefore of our understanding, to which we are obliged, is either general, to which all men are equally bound, of which §146; or special, of which in this section. The foundation of this distinction is, that all men have reason in common; but every particular person has his particular cast and genius, his particular talents; understanding, memory and judgment not being common to all in the same degree. All men are therefore obliged to cultivate their reason, but all men are not equally well qualified for the same way of life, the same profession and business. Whence we may, moreover, conclude, that an *internal special call* (if we set aside divine inspiration) is nothing else but the will of God concerning the particular kind of life one ought to choose, manifested to one by the gifts and talents with which he is endued, of which Perseus speaks, Sat. 3. v. 71.

> *Quem te Deus esse*
> *Fussit, & humana qua parte locatus es in re,*
> *Disce.* ——

[[Persius, *Satires* 3.71: "Learn what god has ordered you to be and in what part of the human condition you have been placed."]]

† They are therefore mistaken, as we have already observed, who place our chief happiness, which we ought to pursue in this life, in the enjoyment of all goods; as Plato in Cicero. Qu. Acad. l. 6. [[Cicero, "Academica Libri," I.19–21 in Cicero, *On Academic Scepticism*.]] For because such enjoyment is above human power, and the

SECTION CXLIX

Further, since he who is obliged to the end, is likewise obliged to the means, it follows, that none of these means ought to be neglected which right reason shews to be necessary or proper for attaining to our greatest happiness; but that we ought to apply ourselves with uninterrupted care daily to amend and perfect our minds, to obtain the right government of our affections, and to rescue ourselves from every vitious appetite and passion.* <105>

The amendment of the will is chiefly necessary.

SECTION CL

It now remains to speak of our *body*, the perfection of which consists in the fitness of all its parts to perform their necessary functions; and it is plain that we are obliged to take care of our health, and therefore to direct our eating and drinking, labour, exercise, and every thing to that end; to the preservation of our health, and the increase of our strength and

Our obligation to preserve and perfect our body.

---

condition of this life, the consequence is, that we should apply our endeavours to attain to our best and greatest good, what our Saviour elegantly calls, "τὴν ἀγαθὴν μερίδα, the good part," Luke x. 42.

* For these often so mislead a man, that he falls short of his end; is deprived of true happiness, and makes a sad shipwreck of it. Besides, in general none can perform his duty aright who is not master of his passions and appetites, because these so distort and pervert the judgment, that nothing can be done in order, or according to the right rule. Hence that excellent advice of the poet,

> *Ne fraenos animo permitte calenti:*
> *Da spacium, tenuemque moram, male cuncta ministrat*
> *Impetus.* Pap. Stat. Theb. l. 10. 626.

[[Statius, *Thebaid,* vol. 2, bk. 10, 703–5 (not 626).]]

The case is this: "Reason, to which the reins are committed, is strong, while it is undisturbed by the affections: but if these mix with it they darken and pollute it; it cannot govern or keep within due bounds what it cannot restrain or withdraw: the mind, when it is shaken and agitated by any passion, is a slave to it, and driven by it at its pleasure." Seneca de Ira, v. 7. [[Seneca, *De ira,* 1.7, in *Moral Essays,* vol. 1, 125.]]

agility;* and, on the other hand, to avoid, as much as lies in our power, whatever tends to maim, hurt, or destroy our bodies, or any of its members, in any degree.

SECTION CLI

How far one is obliged to seek riches.

But all this is enjoined in vain, if one be so distressed by poverty, that he has it not in his power either to live in a wholesome manner, nor to regu-<106>late his labour as his health requires; and therefore it is obvious, that a person must have a right to seek after the things that are necessary to subsistence and decent living. When the provision of these things is abundant, it is called *wealth* or *riches;* and every one is obliged to acquire as large a share of them as he can by just means, and to preserve and use prudently what he hath justly acquired.†

* But in this every one ought to have regard to his rank and station in life. For one degree and kind of vigour, agility and dexterity is requisite in one station, and another in another; one, *e.g.* to a wrestler, another to an artist, another to a soldier, and another to a man of letters. Whence it follows, that the same kind of exercise is not proper to every person; and therefore that prudence ought to have its end before its eyes, and to choose means suited to it. Regard ought also to be had to different ages of life. "An old man, if he be wise, does not desire the strength of a young man, no more than a young man does that of a bull or elephant," says Cicero, Cato major. c. 9. [[Cicero, *Cato maior de senectute* 9.27, p. 66.]] And for this reason, one kind of exercise is proper to old men, and another to young. "As we ought to fight against diseases," says he, "so ought we likewise against old age. We ought to take care of our health, to use moderate exercise, and to eat and drink so as to refresh, not oppress our bodies."

† We do not by saying so approve of *avarice,* the basest and most pernicious of vices. For an avaricious person desires riches for riches sake; but a person who is wisely selfish, only desires them for the sake of living decently. To the former, no gain, nor no means of increasing wealth appear base and sordid; nay, so much as unjust; but this is the constant language of his heart,

> O cives, cives, quaerenda pecunia primum:
> Virtus post nummos.

[[Horace, *Epistles* 1.1.53, in *Satires, Epistles, and Ars Poetica:* "O citizens, citizens, money you first must seek; virtue after pelf."]]

The other does not scrape riches, but takes hold of every allowable opportunity of gaining them. In fine, whereas the miser is insatiable, and yet does not enjoy his

SECTION CLII

But because the end cannot be acquired without the means, and there is **And therefore** no other mean of acquiring what is necessary to supply our necessities but **to industry.** labour and industry, it is manifest that every one is bound to go through with the labours of the business <107> in life he hath chosen with a cheerful mind, and to give all diligence to get a comfortable subsistence; and therefore he acts contrary to duty who lives in idleness, and thus brings poverty and misery upon himself; for such distress is ignominious; whereas poverty is not criminal or shameful, when one, who does all in his power, is overwhelmed by some private or public calamity; or when one, without his own fault, can find no occasion of doing for himself.*

---

possessions, the other manages his affairs quite otherwise; and this is the genuine language of his soul,

> *Haud paravero,*
> *Quod aut avarus ut Chremes terra premam,*
> *Discinctus aut perdam ut nepos.*

[[Horace, *Epodes* 1.32, in *Odes and Epodes:* "I do not mean to amass something simply to bury it in the ground like that miser Chremes, or to squander it like a slovenly wastrel."]]

He manages his estate with prudent oeconomy, that he may not be forced to live at the expence of others, or shamefully to spunge them; that he may not be a burden or a shame to his friends; that he may not be continually harassed by dunning creditors or squeezing usurers; that he may have wherewithal to relieve the indigent, and assist his friends, and that his children may have no cause to reproach him after his death for their distress. And who will deny that these duties are incumbent upon every good man?

* Both therefore belong to the duty of a good man, not to let any occasion slip of bettering his fortune without profiting by it, and to bear honest poverty with an equal mind. Job did both. And Horace joins both these duties together, who thus complains, in his elegant way, of the instability of fortune:

> *Laudo manentem. Si celeres quatit*
> *Pennas: resigno, quae dedit, & mea*
> *Virtute me involvo, probamque*
> *Pauperiem sine dote quaero.*
>   Carm. l. 3. 29. v. 53.

[[Horace, *Odes* 3.29.53, in *Odes and Epodes:* "I praise her [Fortune] while she

SECTION CLIII

And likewise
to preserve and
increase our
good name.

Since a person ought not to neglect any of those things which are nec-essary to increase or preserve his happiness (§140); and none can doubt but a *good name,* which consists in the favourable opinion of others with regard to our virtue and accomplishments, is necessary to preserve and increase our happiness. [For one, of whose virtue and accomplishments all think well, all think worthy of happiness, and all are therefore sollic-itous to promote his happiness.] For these reasons, every one is obliged to take care of his *reputation,* as a mean of his happiness; and therefore to act in every affair, private or public, as reason directs, and not only to preserve his good name by worthy actions, but, as much as lies in his power, to increase it.* <108>

SECTION CLIV

And to refute
aspersions.

But if it be one's duty to take care to preserve his good name unblem-ished (§153); since *calumnies,* i.e. *false reports,* may blacken it; the con-

---

stays, but if she shakes her swift wings, I return her presents, wrap myself in my virtue, and go in search of honest Poverty, though she brings no dowry."]]

* But if this be the interest and duty, even of those who have never diminished or sullied their reputation by any base action, how much more are those, whose youth is not free from blemishes, obliged to endeavour to wipe them off, and procure a good reputation by virtuous deeds? Themistocles is an example to us of this, of whom Cornelius Nepos, c. 1. says, "This reproach did not break but erect his spirit. For perceiving it could not be overcome but by the greatest virtue, he devoted himself wholly and zealously to the service of the public and of his friends, by which means he soon became illustrious." [[Cornelius Nepos, "Themistocles," 23, in *Cornelius Ne-pos,* trans. Rolfe.]] Sueton observes of Titus, "That he was recovered from the vices into which his mind had strayed in his youth, by shame and the fear of ignominy," Tit. c. 7. [[This appears to be a—not entirely accurate—paraphrase of, rather than a quotation from, a passage in Suetonius's life of Titus (Suetonius, *Suetonius,* vol. 2, 330–31).]] Other Examples are to be found in Valerius Maximus, c. 9. and Macrobius, Saturn. 2. 9. [[Valerius Maximus, *Memorable Doings and Sayings,* vol. 1, bk. II, chap. 9; Macrobius, *Saturnalia,* though the reference to bk. 2, chap. 9, appears to be in-correct, and it is not clear which passage Heineccius has in mind here.]]

sequence is, that we ought to omit nothing that is necessary to wipe off aspersions cast injuriously upon us, unless they be so groundless and malicious, or the author of them so contemptible, that it is better to overlook them with generous contempt.* <109>

SECTION CLV

Tho' so far the love of ourselves be most just and lawful; yet, no doubt, it becomes vitious, so soon as it exceeds its due bounds, and gets the ascendant over our love to GOD, the most perfect of Beings (§92); and hence we concluded above, (§140), that all our duties to ourselves keep their due rank and place, if they are performed in proper subordination to the love of God, or do not encroach upon it; whence it is manifest, that the common maxim, *"That necessity has no law,"* is not universally true.†

Whether in case of necessity our duties to ourselves ought to be prefered before those to God.

---

* Those are called *manifest calumnies,* which it is not worth while to give one's self the trouble of confuting. These no more disturb a good man than the barking of little dogs. And he who shamefully spits out such against one, does not hurt another's reputation, but wholly destroys his own. So Simplicius upon Epictetus, c. 64. teaches us: "As, if it be day, the sun is above the earth, and he who denies it does hurt only to himself, and not to the truth. So he who injures you, or throws false calumnies upon you, wrongs himself, he does not hurt you, or do you any mischief." [[Simplicius, *On Epictetus' Handbook,* vol. 2, p. 110.]] The case is different if the calumny be *specious, i.e.* attended with some probability, which may not only deceive the unwary, but even the most prudent and cautious. For he who does not take proper methods to refute such reproaches and clear himself, must appear diffident of his cause, and therefore he falls short of the care he is obliged to, with respect to maintaining his good character and name entire and unblamed. For that ought to be as dear to one as life.

† This aphorism is in every one's mouth, and produced on every occasion as an oracle, as if there were nothing so base and criminal but necessity would render it excusable. Euripides, in a fragment of Hippolyt. obtect. says,

> Quoties periclum est, ex mea sententia
> Necessitati debet & lex cedere.

"In my opinion, in cases of imminent danger, even law ought to give way to necessity." [[Euripides, *Hippolytus* (translated into Latin).]] And if this maxim were absolutely true, the martyrs must have sinned, who paying no regard to the indulgence

SECTION CLVI

Upon what it is founded.

But seeing this rule is not always true; and yet in some cases it ought to be admitted (§155); different cases must be distinguished: now, because in <110> an action imposed upon us by sovereign necessity, no other circumstance can vary the case, but either *necessity* itself, the nature of the *law,* or the nature of the *duty* to be omitted, these circumstances ought therefore to be a little more accurately and distinctly considered, in order to be able to determine how far necessity has the power of a law, and when it has not.

SECTION CLVII

Necessity what it is, and of what kinds.

By *necessity* we understand such a situation of a person, in which he cannot obey a law without incurring danger. This danger, as often as it extends to life itself, is *extreme;* and when it does not, it ought to be measured by the greatness of the impendent evil. Again, necessity is *absolute,* when it cannot be avoided by any means but by violating a law; and it is *relative,* when another might avoid it, but not the person now in the circumstances.*

---

necessity affords, could not be induced to offer the smallest quantity of incense to false deities, to escape the severest tortures: nor did Joseph act less foolishly, who chose rather to expose his life and liberty to the greatest danger than satisfy the lust of his mistress: Nor would any wise man blame a soldier for deserting his station, when attacked by an enemy whom he was not able to resist. And I might add more examples, but these are sufficient to shew, that this maxim about necessity cannot be absolutely true in every case.

* The martyrs were in the case of *extreme necessity,* being obliged to renounce Christ, or to undergo the most violent tortures. But it was not extreme necessity which forced the Christians to apostacy, when *Julian* excluded them from all opportunities of liberal education, from civil honours, and from military service. [[Julian ("the Apostate") was Roman emperor from 355 to 363. He reversed the religious policies of his Christian predecessors and restored pagan religion.]] Daniel was in the case of *absolute necessity,* when he was to be exposed to savage beasts, unless he gave over praying to God. The necessity with which David struggled when he must have perished by hunger, or have eat the shew-bread, was *relative.* For another who had undertaken a journey without flying precipitantly, would certainly have found other bread to satisfy his hunger.

SECTION CLVIII

Now every one may easily perceive, that not only *extreme necessity,* but even necessity in which life is not in danger, comes here into the account. For because some calamities are bitterer than death, who can doubt but such may strike terror into the most <111> intrepid breast; such as being deprived of one's eyes, and other such like distresses. Besides, since of two physical evils the least is to be chosen, the consequence must be, that not only absolute necessity deserves favour, but even relative necessity, if one had no hand in bringing himself into the strait.*

Where necessity merits favour.

SECTION CLIX

Law being either *divine* or *human,* and both being either *affirmative* or *negative* (§64); because even a sovereign cannot oblige one to suffer death without a fault, the consequence is, that all *human laws* ought regularly to be understood, with the exception of necessity. And the same is true of *divine affirmative laws,* because the omission of an action cannot be imputed to one, if the occasion for performing it was wanting (§114), unless the omission be of such a nature and kind, that it tends directly to reflect dishonour on God; in <112> which case, the negative law, for-

Affirmative laws, divine and human, admit the exception of necessity.

* If one unnecessarily exposes himself to danger, he is the cause of the necessity he is brought under, and therefore the event ought to be imputed to him (§105). And for this reason, the necessity into which one threw himself, who having torn an edict against the Christians into pieces, was most terribly tortured, scarcely merited favour. Lactant. de mort. persequut. cap. 13. [[Lactantius, *De mortibus persecutorum,* 21.]] But if one should commit any thing contrary to probity and justice, even to escape death and tortures, who will deny that he does ill? Quintus, mentioned by the church of Smyrna, in a letter concerning the martyrdom of Polycarpus, is an example of this, who having voluntarily offered himself to martyrdom, and persuaded others to do the same, so soon as he saw the beasts, swore by the genius of Caesar, and defiled himself by offering an idolatrous sacrifice: upon which occasion the Smyrneans thus express themselves, "We do not approve, say they, our brethren who unnecessarily or imprudently expose and betray themselves, since it is otherwise commanded in the gospel." And we find the like admonitions in Origen upon John xi. [[Origen (ca. 185–ca. 254): early Greek Father of the Church and author of a commentary on the Gospel according to John.]]

bidding all such actions likewise concurs (§131). And to this case belongs the action of Daniel, Dan. vi. 10.*

SECTION CLX

But not divine negative laws relative to our duties to God or ourselves.

Divine *negative* laws bind us either to duties towards *God,* towards *ourselves,* or towards *other men* (§90 & 124). Those which respect our duties towards God are of such a nature, that they cannot be intermitted without dishonouring God. But we are strictly bound to avoid whatever tends to dishonour God; the consequence of which is, that no necessity can excuse the violation of the negative laws relating to our duties towards God.† On the other hand, in a collision of two duties respecting

---

* All this is clear. Men when they submit themselves to civil government, transfer to the magistrate all power, without which the end of government cannot be obtained. They therefore transfer to him the power of life and death, not promiscuously, because that is contrary to the end of government, but only so far as the public safety requires it. Therefore the supreme magistrate cannot oblige his subjects to suffer death without a reason, but then only when the public safety or good requires it; and therefore, his laws are regularly to be understood, with the exception of necessity. Hence Grotius says elegantly, de jure belli & pacis, 1. 4. 7. 2. "Laws ought to be, and commonly are made by men with a sense of human weakness."

† Hence it is plain, that there is no excuse for him, who suffers himself to be tempted by any necessity he may be under to blaspheme God, sacrifice to idols, or contaminate himself by perjury. This the Pagan writers have acknowledged. So Juvenal,

> *Ambiguae si quando citabere testis*
> *Incertaeque rei, Phalaris licet imperet, ut sis*
> *Falsus, & admoto dictet perjuria tauro,*
> *Summum crede nefas, animam praeferre pudori*
> *Et propter vitam vivendi perdere caussas.*
> Sat. 8.

[[Juvenal, *Satires* 8.80–84, in *Juvenal and Persius:* "If you're summoned as a witness in some tricky, murky case, even if Phalaris commands you to commit perjury and dictates his lies with his Torture-bull close by, think it to be the worst evil to put survival ahead of honour and for the sake of life to lose the reasons for living."]]

But tho' those who succumb under such a direful necessity are not excusable, yet the sense of human weakness obliges us to pity their lot who were shaken by such a cruel necessity, since we know that Peter found pardon for having denied Christ, after he had repented, Matt. xxvi. 75.

ourselves, the safest course is to choose the least of two physical evils.
<113>

SECTION CLXI

As to our duties towards other men, affirmative laws, 'tis certain, admit
of favour in the case of necessity; partly because an omission cannot be
imputed when the occasion of performing a duty was wanting (§114);
partly because the law of benevolence does not oblige us to delight in
the happiness of others more than our own, or to love others better than
ourselves (§94); and so far the maxim holds just, "Every one is nearest
to himself."*

Divine affirmative laws respecting our duties to others admit of favour in the case of necessity.

SECTION CLXII

Moreover *negative laws,* relative to our social duties, in the case of providential necessity, interfere either with the duty of self-preservation, or
with the duty of defending and increasing our perfection and happiness.
Now in the former situation, since we are not obliged to love others more
than ourselves, (§94), without doubt, in the case of necessity, every way
of preserving ourselves is allowable, when a man hath not fallen under
that necessity by his own neglect or default; or if the condition of the
persons be equal; for equality leaves no room to <114> favour or privilege.
In the latter case, it is better for us to want some perfection, or some
particular kind or degree of happiness, than that another should perish
that we may have it.†

What is the case with regard to negative laws.

---

* Thus, *e.g.* the divine law does not oblige one to ruin himself to save another, or
to give to another the small morsel of bread that remains to himself, when he is
starving. That, the most holy and strict law of love inculcated by the Christian religion
does not require, 2 Cor. viii. 13. Wherefore Seneca says rightly, de benefic. 2. 15. "I
will give to the needy, but so that I may not want myself: I will relieve him who is
ready to perish, but so that I may not perish myself." [[Seneca, "On Benefits," in
Seneca, *Moral Essays,* vol. 3.]] And this was the meaning of the scholastic doctors,
when they pronounced this rule, "Well ordered charity begins at home."

  † For to want any perfection is a physical evil, if it be not our fault that we have
it not. But to make another perish is a moral evil, which is always to be reckoned

SECTION CLXIII

What if the necessity proceeds from human malice? All this holds true, if the necessity we are under be merely providential (§142); but if it proceeds from the malice of men, they do it either that we may perish, or that they may lay us under the necessity of acting wrong. And in the former case, since we are not bound to love any other better than ourselves, much less a bad person (§94); he is justly excusable who suffers another to perish rather than himself. In the latter case, the cruelest things ought to be submitted to, rather than do any thing dishonourable to God (§131).* <115>

SECTION CLXIV

An admonition with regard to the application of these rules to particular cases. Having mentioned these rules, most of which have been fully explained by others,† it will not be difficult to determine the cases proposed by Pufendorff and others. Indeed, if we attend narrowly to the matter, we will find that many proposed on this subject are such as very rarely happen, and many others are of such a nature, that all is transacted in an instant, so that there is hardly time or room for calling in reason to give

---

greater than any physical one. But since the least of two physical evils ought to be chosen, and therefore a physical evil is to be undergone rather than any moral one is to be acted, he certainly doth no evil, who in such a case chooses to save another person with some detriment to himself; wherefore, tho' he is not to be blamed who in a shipwreck catching hold of a plank which will not hold two, hinders another from getting upon it, yet he is altogether inexcusable, who by the hopes of greater happiness to himself, is induced to betray his friend against all honour and conscience.

* Thus, for example, if we should fall into the ambuscades or hands of robbers, every way of extricating ourselves out of this danger is allowable, because no reason binds us to prefer the safety of a robber to our own. But Joseph would have acted ill, if he had feared a prison, and chains more than adultery, to which Potiphar's wife endeavoured to seduce him.

† Most of the preceding rules have been already treated of by Thomasius, Jurisp. divin. 2. 2. 143. & seq. but not upon the same principles we have here laid down. But the same author afterwards is for sequestrating them from the law of nature, and for recalling this one rule, "That all laws include a tacite exception of necessity": but we can see no ground for omitting or sequestrating exceptions, which, what hath been said, fully proves to be founded upon, and to flow from right reason itself.

its judgment of the justice, or injustice of an action; to which cases, we may not improperly apply what Terence says,

Facile omnes, quum valemus, recta consilia aegrotis damus,
Tu, si hic esses, aliter sentires. Andr. 1. 1. v. 9.[1]

For which reason, it is better to leave many of these cases to the mercy of God, than to enter into too severe a discussion of them.

SECTION CLXV

Thus none can doubt but necessity will excuse a person who must let a member be cut off to prevent his perishing; or that the other parts may not be endangered by it. For tho' we owe both these duties to ourselves, *viz.* to preserve our life, and to preserve every member intire, yet the least of two physical evils is to be chosen (§160); and it is certainly a lesser evil to be deprived of a member than to lose life. It is therefore a lawful <116> mean of saving life to do it by the loss of a member.*

Whether it be lawful to cut off a member.

* But it is a more difficult question, whether it be a preceptive law of nature, and whether he does contrary to his duty, who being in the direful necessity above mentioned, chooses rather to die than to bear pain, to which he feels himself unequal; especially when it is not certain what may be the event of the amputation, seeing not fewer who have undergone the torment with great constancy have perished than have been saved. Old age, bodily infirmity, the dangerous nature of the disease, the difference in opinion among the physicians, the unskilfulness or want of experience in the surgeon, all these considerations may easily determine one to think the cure more uneligible than death itself, and to judge it better to die without suffering such exquisite pain, than run the risk of undergoing it without success. Wherefore, I would have us to remember the admonition given above, and to leave such cases to the divine judgment and mercy, rather than to pronounce hardily and rashly about them.

1. "We can all readily give good advice to the sick when we're well. If you were in my place, you would feel differently." (*The Woman of Andros*, lines 309–10, in vol. 1 of Terence, *Terence*.)

SECTION CLXVI

Whether it be lawful to eat human flesh in extreme necessity?

There is no doubt but that they are excusable, who in extreme hunger and want have recourse to any food, even to the flesh of dead men: for since here there is a contest between two duties towards ourselves; of two physical evils, death and detestable food, the least ought to be chosen (§160). But he is by no means excusable who kills another, that he may prolong a little his own miserable life by eating his flesh; for however direful and imperious the necessity of long hunger may be, it does not give us a right to another's life that we ourselves may be saved, because here the condition and necessity* of both persons are equal (§162). <117>

SECTION CLXVII

Whether in shipwreck?

The case is not the same, when one in shipwreck, having got upon a plank only sufficient to save himself, keeps others from it with all his force; or with those who leaping first into a boat, will not allow others, whom it cannot contain with safety, to come into it, but precipitate them into the sea; because in these cases, he who first seized the plank, or they who first got into the boat, are in possession, and therefore others have no right to deprive them of it, tho' they be in the same danger. And who will not own, that it is a less evil that a few, than that all should perish, or a greater good that a few, than that none should be saved?† <118>

---

* But what if all the persons being under the same fatal necessity should by consent commit it to lot to determine which of them should be sacrificed to the preservation of the rest, (as in the case of the seven Britons, quoted by Ziegler upon Grotius de jure belli & pacis, 2. 1. 3. [[Caspar Ziegler (1621–90), German jurist, professor at Wittenberg. He published *In Hugonis Grotii De jure belli ac pacis libros.*]] from the observations of Tulpius, Obser. medic. 1. 43.) [[Tulp, *Observationes medicae.*]] Here I affirm the same thing. For none hath a right to take away another's life. And he who consents to his own murder is as guilty as he who kills himself or another. Ziegler justly asserts, ibidem p. 189. "That none ought so far to despise his own life, as to throw it away to satisfy another's hunger, nor ought others to attack their neighbour's life to quell their own cravings." To which Pufendorff hath not given an answer altogether satisfactory, de jure nat. & gent. 2. 6. 3.

† Upon the same principle may the case be decided of soldiers flying into a fortified camp or city, who shut the gates against those who arrive a little later, lest the

SECTION CLXVIII

I can by no means think an executioner, or any other, excusable, who being commanded to put an innocent person to death, thinks he ought to obey, and that his own danger is sufficient to exculpate him. For this necessity proceeds from the wickedness of men; and in such a case every one ought to bear every thing, rather than do any thing tending to dishonour God (§163).*

Whether necessity excuses an executioner commanded to put an innocent person to death.

SECTION CLXIX

But an innocent person, to save his life, may, in flying from his enemy, push out of his way, or throw down any person who stops or hinders his flight, even tho' he may have reason to suspect the person may thereby be hurted. For if one stops the person who flies with a bad intention, this necessity proceeds from human malice, and such a person really does what he can to make the person flying perish. And if one be in his way, without any intention to hurt him, this necessity is providential in re-

Whether it be lawful to throw down one who is in our way when we fly.

---

enemy should get in at the same time with them. Such was the deed of Pandarus, described by Virgil, Aen. 9. v. 722. & seq. [[Virgil, *Aeneid,* bk. 9, l. 722 (*Virgil,* trans. Fairclough, vol. 2, 163)]] and of others, of which cases, see Freinsh. ad Curt. 4. 16. 8. [[This refers to a commentary by Johann Frenshemius on Quintus Curtius Rufus's history of Alexander the Great (*Alexander magnus*), which was reprinted in several editions in the seventeenth century.]] But in all these, we are carefully to consider whether the necessity be extreme and absolute (158), or the danger be more remote, and such as might otherwise be avoided. Hence the humanity of Darius, flying from Alexander, is very commendable, who, when he was pressed to cut the bridge over the Lycus, answered, "That he would much rather leave a passage to the pursuers, than cut it off from the flyers," Curt. 4. 16.

* Besides, nothing ought to be done in opposition to the certainty of conscience (§45): but here the executioner is supposed to know certainly the person whom he is commanded to put to death to be innocent: who then can absolve him from guilt? Nor does Pufendorff's distinction alter the case: "For tho' he says, that when an executioner merely executes the command of another, the action can no more be imputed to him than to the hatchet or sword," jur. nat. & gent. 1. 5. 9. 8. 1. 5. 6. yet certainly there is a wide difference between a sword or a hatchet, mere inanimate things, and a man endued with reason, whose conscience tells him the sentence he is to execute is unjust.

spect of the flyer. But in both cases, every way of saving one's self is allowable (§163).* <119>

SECTION CLXX

Whether in case of necessity we may lawfully seize upon another's goods? — The same must be said of those cases in which one is necessitated by hunger or cold to lay hold of the goods belonging to others;† or when, in the danger of shipwreck, the goods of others must be thrown over board. For, in the first case, the necessity arises from the malice of men in suffering any to be in imminent danger from hunger or cold, (§163); and, in the last case, of two physical evils the least is chosen, when, in the danger of shipwreck, men perceiving that they must either perish themselves together with the goods, or make reparation to others for their goods which are cast in this necessity into the sea (§160),‡ throw them over board. <120>

SECTION CLXXI

The conclusion of this chapter. — But numberless such cases may happen, or at least may be put, some of which are truly perplexed and dubious; and therefore let us not forget

---

* We need not stay to refute the contrary opinion of Albertus. Comp. jur. nat. orthod. conform. cap. 3. §17. [[Alberti, *Compendium juris naturae, orthodoxae theologiae.*]] For his argument taken from the unlawfulness of killing an innocent person in the state of integrity, is nothing to the purpose; because neither is the principle of natural law to be deduced from that state (§74); nor in that state can any danger be conceived that must be avoided by such an unhappy flight.

† Those who differ from us in this matter call these actions *theft,* which they pronounce so great a crime that it can never be committed without guilt, even in circumstances of the most urgent necessity. But if killing a man, even according to the principles those very authors go upon, cannot be imputed to one as a crime, in the case of unblameable self-defence, why should theft be reckoned criminal by them, in the case of self-preservation? Besides, who imagines theft to be a crime when done without any malicious intention, nay without so much as any design to make profit by it? Finally, since persons in the meanest circumstances may easily, after they have extricated themselves out of their pinching straits, make reparation for the very small matter necessity can force them to take from another, who can make a crime of choosing to take a little from its lawful owner, that may be estimated and repaid, with a serious design to make reparation, so soon as it possibly can be done, rather than to perish? Add chap. 3. 10. of *theft.*

‡ [[See preceding note.]]

the admonition already mentioned (§164). We shall add no more upon the subject, leaving other questions to those who assume to themselves the province of commanding or guiding mens consciences.

REMARKS on This Chapter

The principles our author hath laid down in this chapter, are most exact, and proper to decide all questions which can be proposed concerning the right, the privilege, the favour, the leave, or whatever we call it, that arises from necessity. It is however well worth while to look into what the learned Barbeyrac[2] hath said upon this difficult subject in his notes upon Pufendorff's sixth chapter, book second, of the law of nature and nations. Pufendorff, in the beginning of that chapter, quotes an excellent passage of Cicero with regard to necessity, in which the general rule is very clearly stated. It is towards the end of his second book of *invention;* too long indeed to be inserted here, but deserving of attentive consideration. The chief design of our Author's *scholia* being to refer his readers to passages in ancient authors, where moral duties are rightly explained and urged by proper arguments, in order to shew that the duties of the law of nature are discoverable by reason, and were actually known in all ages to thinking persons, at least, he might very properly have on this occasion referred us to that place in Cicero. For this is no doubt the most perplexed subject in morals, *The right and priviledge of necessity.* And upon it we find Cicero reasoning with great accuracy and solidity: insomuch, that if we compare with this passage the 25th chapter of his second book of offices, where he treats of comparing things profitable one with another; and the 3, 4, 5, and following chapters in the third book, where he considers competition between *honesty* and *interest,* or *profit,* we will find full satisfaction upon this head. In the 4th chapter of the 3d book he hath this remarkable passage.—"What is it that requires consideration on this subject? I suppose it is this, that it sometimes happens men are not so very certain, *whether the action deliberated upon be honest or not honest.*" For that which is usually counted a piece of villainy is frequently

2. The Huguenot refugee Jean Barbeyrac (1674–1744) gave Grotius's and Pufendorf's works considerable circulation throughout Europe by his heavily annotated translations from Latin into French.

changed by the times or circumstances, and is found to be the contrary. To lay down one instance, which may serve to give some light to a great many others: pray what greater wickedness can there be upon earth (if we speak in general) than for any one to murder not only a man, but a familiar <121> friend? And shall we therefore affirm that he is chargeable with a crime who has murdered a tyrant, tho' he were his familiar? The people of Rome, I am sure, will not say so, by whom this is counted among the greatest and most glorious actions in the world. You will say then, *Does not interest carry it against honesty?* No, but rather honesty voluntarily follows interest. If therefore, we would upon all emergencies be sure to determine ourselves aright, when that which we call our advantage or interest seems to be repugnant to that which is honest, we must lay down some general rule or measure, which, if we will make use of in judging about things, we shall never be mistaken as to point of duty. Now this measure I would have to be conformable to the doctrine and principles of the Stoics, which I principally follow throughout this work. For tho' I confess, that the ancient Academics and your Peripatetics, which were formerly the same, make honesty far preferable to that which seems one's interest: yet those who assert, that whatever is honest must be also profitable, and nothing is profitable but what is honest, talk much more bravely and heroically upon this subject than those who allow, that there are some things honest which are not profitable, and some things profitable which are not honest. The principle of the Stoics he explains more fully a little after, where he asserts with them, "Certainly greatness and elevation of soul, as also the virtues of justice and liberality, are much more agreeable to nature and right reason than pleasure, than riches, than even life itself: to despise all which, and regard them as just nothing, when they come to be compared with the public interest, is the duty of a brave and exalted spirit: whereas to rob another for one's own advantage, is more contrary to nature than death, than pain, or any other evil whatever of that kind." This question concerning the interferings which may happen between duty and private interest, or self-preservation, will clear up, as we go on with our Author in the enquiry into our duties to others, and into the rights and bounds of self-defence; I shall only add to what our author asserts, in opposition to Pufendorff, about executioners, that if we consult the apology of Socrates by Plato, and that by Xenophon, we will find several fine passages, which shew that we ought never to obey our superiors to the prejudice of our duty; but very far from it; and unless we are in an entire incapacity to resist them, we ought to exert ourselves to the utmost of our power, and endeavour to hinder those who would oppress the innocent from doing them any mischief. See Grotius, l. 2. c. 26. §4. 9. as also Sidney's discourse upon government, ch. 3. §20,[3] and Mr. Barbeyrac's notes on Pufendorff, of the law of nature and nations, b. 8. c. 1. §6. I beg leave to subjoin, that I know nothing that can better serve to prepare one for wading through all the subtleties, with which morality in general, and this particular question about the contrariety or competition that may happen between self-love and benevolence in cer-<122>tain cases, are perplexed, than a careful attention to two discourses upon the love of our neighbour, by Dr. Butler (Bishop of Bristol) in his excellent sermons,[4] to copy which would take up too much room in these notes, and to abridge them without injuring them is hardly possible, with such conciseness and equal perspicuity are they wrote. These sermons make the best introduction to the doctrine of morals I have seen; and the principles laid down in them being well understood, no question in morals will afterwards be found very difficult. It is owing to not defining terms, or not using terms in a determinate fixed sense, (the terms *self-love, private interest, interested* and *disinterested,* and other such like, more particularly) that there hath been so much jangling about the foundations of morality. They who say, that no creature can possibly act but merely from self-love; and that every affection and action is to be resolved up into this one principle, say true in a certain sense of the term *self-love.* But in another sense, (in the proper and strict sense of *self-love,*) how much soever is to be allowed to it, it cannot be allowed to be the whole of our inward constitution; but there are many other parts and principles which come into it. Now, if we ought to reason with regard to a moral constitution, as we do with respect to a bodily frame, we must not reason concerning it from the consideration of one part singly or separately from the rest with which it is united; but from all the parts taken together, as they are united, and by that union constitute a particular frame or consti-

3. Algernon Sidney (1623–83), *Discourses Concerning Government.*
4. Joseph Butler (1692–1752), *Fifteen Sermons Preached at the Rolls Chapel.*

tution. The final cause of a constitution can only be inferred from such a complex view of it. And the final cause of a constitution is but another way of expressing what may properly be called the end for which it was so framed, or the intention of its Author in so constituting it. The end of our frame therefore, and by consequence the will of our Maker with regard to our conduct, can only be inferred from the nature of our frame, or the end to which it is adapted: But if we are to infer our end from our frame, no part of this frame ought to be left out in the consideration. Wherefore, tho' self-love ought to be taken into the account, yet several particular affections must also be taken into the account; benevolence must likewise be taken into the account, if it really belongs to our nature; a sense of right and wrong, and reason must also be taken into the account; and whatever is taken into the account must be taken into it as it really is, *i.e.* affections must be considered as subjects of government, and reason must be considered as a governing principle, for such they are in their natures. But of this more afterwards, in the remark upon the duties reducible to benevolence. <123>

CHAPTER VII

Concerning our absolute and perfect duties towards (others in general), and of not hurting or injuring others (in particular).

SECTION CLXXII

Let us now proceed to consider *our duties towards others,* the foundation of which lies, as was observed above, in this, that man is by nature *equal* to man, and therefore every man is obliged to love every other with a love of friendship (§85 & 88). And because equality of nature requires equality of offices, hence we concluded, *that every man is obliged to love every man no less than himself* (§93).

The foundation of our duties towards others.

SECTION CLXXIII

We have also shewn that there are two degrees of this love, one of which we called *love of justice,* and the other *love of humanity and beneficence* (§82 & seq.) But because the former consists in doing nothing that may render one more unhappy, and therefore in not hurting any person, and in giving to every one his own, or what is due to him; and the latter consists in endeavouring, to the utmost of our ability, to increase and promote another's perfection and happiness, and in rendering to him even what we do not owe to him by strict and perfect obligation; the consequence of this is, that of the duties we owe to others, some are duties of justice, which are of *perfect* obligation, and others are duties of humanity and beneficence, which are of *imperfect* obligation. <124>

They are either perfect or imperfect.

131

SECTION CLXXIV

These duties
defined.

Therefore those are *perfect duties,* to which one is bound by such perfect obligation, that he may be forced to perform them; such as to injure no person, and to render to every one what is due to him: those are *imperfect,* to which we cannot be forced, but are only bound by the intrinsic goodness of the actions themselves; such as, to study to promote the perfection and happiness of others to the utmost of our power (§84).*

SECTION CLXXV

They are
divided into
absolute and
hypothetical.

Since *perfect duties* may be reduced to *not injuring any one, and rendering to every one his due* (§174); but to injure, is to render one more unhappy than he is by nature, or would otherwise be (§82); and one may call that his *due,* or *his own,* which he hath justly acquired (§82); it follows, that obligation not to injure any one is *natural;* and obligation to render to every one his due is *acquired;* whence the former is called *absolute,* and the latter we call *hypothetical.* † <125>

---

* *Perfect duties* therefore lay us under a necessity of not rendering any one more imperfect or more unhappy: *imperfect duties* shew us, that we then only arrive to the glory of being truly good and virtuous, when we delight in promoting the perfection and happiness of others, as much as in us lies. These duties were accurately distinguished by ancient lawyers, when with Paullus they said, some were rather of good will and virtue than of necessity (voluntatis & officii magis quam necessitatis) l. 17. §3. D. commodati. Add to this a passage of Seneca quoted above in the scholium upon §84.

† *Absolute duty* is what one man has a right to exact from another, without any right acquired to himself by any previous deed: hypothetical duty is what one can exact from another, in consequence of a right acquired by some deed. Thus a man has a right, to exact from every other that he should not take away his life, which is not acquired by any particular deed: But no person hath a right to complain, that things are taken from him by another unjustly, unless he hath acquired a right or property in them by some deed: therefore, not to kill any one is a duty of an absolute nature: but not to steal, is a duty of a hypothetical kind. If Salmasius had attended to this distinction (Salmasius de usur. cap. 9.) [[Claude Saumaise (Claudius Salmasius), *De usuris liber*]] he would easily have understood why the lawyers said that theft is forbidden by natural law (furtum admittere jure naturali prohibitum esse) l. 1. §3. D. de furt. §1. Inst. de oblig. quae ex delict.

SECTION CLXXVI

Further, since the right we acquire to any thing arises either from *dominion,* or from *compact* or *convention,* it follows that all *hypothetical* duties spring either from *compact* or from *dominion;* and therefore this will be the properest order we can follow, to begin first with considering *perfect absolute* duties, and then to treat of *imperfect* ones; next to speak of those *hypothetical* duties, which arise from *dominion* or *property;* and lastly, to handle those which arise from *compact.* But *imperfect* ones ought to be considered before we come to the *hypothetical* ones, because after *dominion* and *compacts* were introduced into the world, humanity becoming very cold and languid, men have sadly degenerated into selfishness.

In what order these duties ought to be treated.

SECTION CLXXVII

First of all, it ought to be laid down as a maxim, that men are by nature equal (§172), being composed of the same essential parts; and because tho' one man may share perfections, as it were by his good lot, above others, yet different degrees of perfection do not alter the essence of man, but all men are equally men: whence it follows, that every one ought to treat every other as equally a man with himself, and not to arrogate to himself any privilege in things belonging to many by perfect right, without a just cause; and therefore not to do to <126> any other what he would not have done to himself (§88).*

Every man ought to treat every other as his equal.

---

* This rule is so agreeable and so manifest to right reason, that it was known to the Pagans. Lampridius [[Aelius Lampridius was the alleged author of several emperors' biographies (see, for example, Boxhorn, ed., *Historiae Augustae scriptores Latini minores.*)]] tells us, that Alexander Severus delighted in this maxim. cap. 1. "He had this sentence," says he, "frequently in his mouth, which he had learned from Jews or Christians: 'Do not to others what you would not have done to yourself.' And he ordered it to be proclaimed aloud by a public crier, when he was to correct or animadvert upon any person. He was so charmed with it, that he ordered it to be inscribed every where in his palace, and on all public works." It is not improbable, as Lampridius observes, that Alexander had learned this maxim from Christians: For we find it in the affirmative sense, Mat. vii. 12. and Luke vi. 31. But it does not follow

SECTION CLXXVIII

And then no
person ought
to be injured.

Since therefore we ought not to do to any one what we would not have done to ourselves (§177); but none of us would like to be deprived by any other of our perfection and happiness which we have by nature, or have justly acquired; *i.e.* to be injured or hurt (§82); the consequence is, that we ought not to render any one more imperfect or unhappy, *i.e.* injure any one. And because to what constitutes our felicity and perfection, belongs not only our *body,* but more especially our *mind,* this precept must extend to both these parts, and an injury to our mind must be as much greater than an injury to our bodily part, as the mind is more excellent than the body.* <127>

SECTION CLXXIX

No person
may be killed,
no injury may
be done to
one's body,
health, &c.

The perfection and happiness of man consists in *life, i.e.* in the union of his soul and body (§143), which is of all he hath received from nature the most excellent gift, and is indeed the basis or foundation of all the rest: since therefore it is unlawful to deprive any one of the perfection and happiness he hath received from nature, and we would not choose to have our life taken away by another, (§178), it is self-evident, that it is our duty not to kill any person; not to do the least detriment to his health; not to give any occasion to his sickness, pain, or death, or not to

---

from hence, that reason could not have discovered this truth. We find similar precepts and maxims in Simplicius upon Epictetus Enchirid. cap. 37.

* Hence Epictetus severely reproaches those who look upon that only as an injury by which their body or their outward possessions are impaired, and not that by which their mind is rendered worse. "When we have received any damage in what belongs to our bodies or estates, we immediately think we have suffered a great loss. But when any detriment happens to us with respect to our will or temper, we think we have suffered no damage, for as much as he who corrupts or is corrupted by another, hath neither an aking head, stomach, eye or side, nor hath not lost his estate; and we look no farther than to these outward things. But with us it admits no dispute, whether it be better to have a pure and honest will, or an impure and dishonest one, &c." Arrian. Diss. Epict. 2. 10.

expose him to any danger, without having a right to do it, or with an intention to have him killed.*

SECTION CLXXX

Yet since none is obliged to love another more than himself (§94), and it may often hap-<128>pen that either one's self or another must perish; the consequence is, that in case any one attack us, in this doubtful state of danger, every way of saving one's self is lawful (§163); and therefore we may even kill an aggressor, provided we do not exceed the limits of just self-defence.

Unless necessity obliges to lawful self-defence.

SECTION CLXXXI

But what are the limits of just self-defence none will be at a loss to understand, who calls to mind, that absolute or inevitable necessity merits favour, (§158): For hence it follows, That blameless self-defence takes place, if one be in absolute necessity, or even in relative necessity, provided he be so, not by his own fault (§158): That all danger being past, there is no further any right of defence: That when danger can be avoided without hurting the aggressor, or by a lesser evil, there is no right to kill him;† because of two evils the least ought always to be chosen.

Its limits.

---

* For he who exposes a person, over whom he hath no authority, to danger, is no less guilty than he who, abusing his right and power to command, exposes one whose death he desires, to danger, purposely that he may get rid of him. There are examples of this in Polybius, 1. 9. Diod. Sic. Bibl. 14. 73. 19. 48. Justin. Hist. 12. 5. Curt. 7. 2. [[Polybius, *The Histories;* Diodorus Siculus, *Bibliotheca historica;* Justinus, *Justini Historiae Philipicae;* Curtius, *History of Alexander*]] and likewise in the sacred writings, 2 Sam. xi. 15. and xii. 9. where Nathan accuses David of murder for having placed Uriah in a most dangerous situation, with intention that he might perish. See Pufend. de jure nat. & gent. 8. 2. 4.

† Man is always bound to choose that which is best, (§92); but that is best which is the safest and easiest mean for obtaining our end. We are therefore obliged to take the safest and least hurtful mean of saving ourselves, and therefore to avoid killing a person, if there be any other way of delivering ourselves from danger. Theocritus says rightly, "It is fit to remove a great contention by a small evil." [[Theocritus (ca. 310–250 B.C.), Greek pastoral poet.]]

SECTION CLXXXII

Against whom we may use it.

These evident principles being attended to, nothing can be more easy than to answer all the questions which are commonly proposed with relation to due moderation in self-defence. For if it be asked against whom it is allowable, you will answer rightly, if you say, against all by whom we are brought into danger without any fault of our own (§81); and therefore even against mad persons, persons disordered in their senses, and even against those <129> who attack you by mistake, when they are intending to assault another. For as Grotius of the rights of war and peace, 2. 1. 3. has well observed, the right of self-defence in such cases does not proceed from his injustice or fault, by whom the danger is occasioned, but from our own right of repelling all danger by any means, and of not preferring in such circumstances the life or safety of another to our own.*

SECTION CLXXXIII

The extent of it in a state of natural liberty.

Nor will it be less easy to determine how long this right of defence against an aggressor continues. For here doctors justly distinguish between those living in a state of nature, and subject to no magistrate, by whom they may be defended and protected, and those who live in a civil state, and under magistracy. For since, in a state of natural liberty, there is none to protect us against injuries, our right of self-defence cannot but begin the moment our danger commences, and cannot but continue while it lasts, or till we are absolutely secure, (§181). But our danger begins the moment

---

* And to this belongs the fable of Oedipus, who having unknowingly killed his father, who attacked him, in his own defence, thus excuses himself in Sophocles, in Oedip. v. 1032. [[Sophocles, *Oedipus at Colonus,* lines 991–99, in *Sophocles.*]] "Answer me one thing. If any one should attack you, even a just person, to kill you, would you ask whether it was your father, or would you not immediately defend yourself? I think, if you loved your life, you would defend yourself against the aggressor, and not stay to consider what was just. I fell into such a misfortune by fate, as my father, could he revive, would himself acknowledge."

one shews a hostile disposition against us, and while that continues, our right of self-defence lasts.* <130>

SECTION CLXXXIV

On the other hand, in a civil state, one who shews enmity against an-   And in a
other, trapps, or lays snares for him, may be coerced by the civil mag-   civil state.
istrate; the consequence of which is, that a member of a civil state, hath not a right, by his own force and arms, to resist another member who attacks him, or lays snares for him; nor, when the danger is over, to take that revenge at his own hand which he might expect from the magistrate. And therefore, the space or time of just self-defence is confined within much narrower limits in that state; it begins with the danger, and lasts no longer than the danger itself lasts.†

SECTION CLXXXV

Moreover, from these principles (§181), you may easily see that self-   The measure
defence to the point of killing the aggressor is not lawful; if one was   of violent
forewarned of the assault, or foreseeing it in time, could have kept at   self-defence.
home, or retired into a safer place, or could, by wounding or maiming the injurious person, disable him:‡ tho' no person, when he is assaulted,

---

* And this is the foundation of the whole rights of war, *viz.* that we may carry on acts of hostility against any person who hath clearly shown his hostile disposition against us, and refuses obstinately all equal terms of peace, till having laid aside his enmity, he is become our friend: of which afterwards in its own place.

† And therefore the lawyers rightly permit violent self-defence, only in the moment of assault. Ulpian, l. 3. §9. D. de vi & armis. "We may repel him by force who assaults us with arms, but in the moment, and not some time after." And Paullus more expressly in another place, where he says, "That one who throws a stone against one rushing upon him, when he could not otherwise defend himself," was not guilty by the Lex Aqu. l. 45. §4. D. ad leg. Aquil.

‡ Much less then can one with right have recourse to force and killing, after the aggressor desists, and shews he is reconciled to his adversary. Whence Aristides in Leuctric. 1. justly observes, "That the Thebans being disposed to all that was equal, and the Lacedemonians being obstinate, the goodness of the cause was transferred from the latter to the former." [[Publius Aelius Aristides (117–after 181), sophist and

be absolutely obliged to betake himself to flight, because of the danger or uncertainty of it, unless there be near at hand a place of most secure refuge, <131> (Pufendorff of the law of nature and nations, 2. 5. 13.). But upon this head it is proper to observe, that under civil governments, the time of making an unblameable self-defence being confined within very narrow bounds, and indeed almost reduced to a point or instant, since, in such a perturbation of mind, one cannot think of all the ways of escaping; therefore, with good reason, such cases ought not to be too rigidly exacted, but great allowances ought to be made.

SECTION CLXXXVI

For what things it is lawful.

Hence we may likewise perceive for what things one may proceed to self-defence by force and violence: for since some calamities are bitterer to man than death, and not only extreme necessity, but even that which may be undergone with safety to our life, merits favour (§158); the consequence is, that what is allowable for the sake of life, is permitted likewise in defence of health, the soundness of our bodies, and even our chastity;* and likewise in defence of magistrates, parents, children, friends, and all others whom we find in danger. <132>

---

man of letters. His Leuctrian orations are historical declamations, which consider the arguments for and against an alliance of Athens with either Sparta or Thebes. See Aristides, *The Complete Works,* vol. 1.]] See Grotius, 2. 1. 18. and Pufendorff, 2. 5. 19.

* But here many differ from us, as Augustinus de libero arbitrio, 1. 5. [[Augustine, *On Free Choice of the Will* (*De libero arbitrio*)]] Thomasius, Jurisp. 2. 2. 114. Buddeus Theolog. mor. part. 2. c. 3. §3. [[Budde, *Institutiones theologiae moralis*]] because chastity being a virtue of the mind, cannot be forced or extorted from us. But tho' the chastity of the mind be secure enough, yet no injury is more attrocious to a chaste virgin or matron than a rape. Wherefore, Quintilian says justly, Declam. 349. "You have brought an injury upon the girl, than which war hath nothing more terrible." [[Quintilian, *Declamatio* 349, in Quintilian, *Declamationes quae supersunt CXLV,* p. 347.]] Who then will blame an honest woman for defending herself against so high an injury, even at the expence of the ravisher's life?

SECTION CLXXXVII

The question, whether one is excusable for killing another in defence of his honour and reputation, *e.g.* for a box on the ear, or some more slight injury, is more difficult. But tho' nothing be more valuable, life only excepted, than honour; and therefore some think, that in this case violent self-defence is not unlawful; (see Grotius of the rights of war and peace, 2. 1. 10.) yet because the danger of losing life, or other things upon an equal footing with life, alone give us the right to blameless self-defence (§186); and because honour and reputation are not lost by an injury done to us; and there are not wanting in civil governments lawful means of revenging an injury; we cannot choose but assent to their opinion, who prudently affirm, that the right of violent self-defence ceases in these cases.

Whether it be allowable in defence of our honour and reputation?

SECTION CLXXXVIII

Again, the absolute duty of not hurting any person extends no less to the *mind* than to the body (§178), and the faculties of the mind are *will* and *understanding:* as to the first therefore, none can deny that he greatly injures a person, who seduces into error a young person, or any one of less acute parts than himself by falsehood and specious sophistry; or who prepossesses any one with false opinions, or he who, even by a tedious disagreeable method of teaching, or affected severity, begets, in any one committed to his charge, an aversion to truth and the study of wisdom.*

No person ought to be injured with regard to his understanding.

<133>

* Thus Petrus did a very great injury to Maximilian I. Emp. of whom Cuspinianus relates, p. 602. "Maximilian when he was of a proper age for being instructed in letters, was put under the care of Petrus, where he learned Latin for some time with other fellow scholars of quality. But his teacher employed all his time in inculcating upon him certain logical subtleties, for which he had no disposition or capacity; and being often whipped on that account by one who better deserved to be whipt himself, seeing such usage is for slaves and not free-men, he at last conceived an utter disgust at all learning, instead of being in love with it." [[Probably Cuspinianus, *De Caesaribus atque imperatoribus Romanorum . . . opus.*]] He never forgot what a detriment that was to him. The same Cuspinianus tells us, that he often complained very heartily

SECTION CLXXXIX

Nor with respect to the will.
Now because that injury done to the *will,* which is called *corruption,* is no less detrimental to one; the consequence is, that they act contrary to their duty who corrupt any person, by alluring him to pursue unlawful pleasures, or to commit any vice, and either by vitious discourse or example, debauch his mind; or when they have it in their power, and ought to restrain one from a vitious action, and reclaim him into the right course of life, either do it not, or set not about it with that serious concern which becomes them; but, on the contrary, do all that lies in them to forward him in his vitious carrier.* <134>

---

of his fate, and sometimes said at dinner, while many were present, "If my preceptor Petrus were alive, tho' we owe much to our teachers, I would make him repent his having had the care of my institution," Add. Ger. a Roo. l. 8. p. 288. [[Probably Gerardus de Roo (d. 1589), *Annales rerum belli domique ab Austriacis Habsburgicae gentis principibus.*]]

* How great an injury this is, Dionysius the Sicilian tyrant well knew, who being desirous to give pain to Dion, who he heard was levying an army, and preparing to make war against him, ordered his son "to be educated in such a manner, that by indulgence he might be corrupted with the vilest passions: for which effect, while he was yet a beardless boy, whores were brought to him, and he was not allowed to be sober one minute, but was kept for ever carousing, reveling and feasting. He afterwards, when he returned to his father, could not bear a change of life, and guardians being set over him to reform him from this wicked way of living he had been inured to and bred up in, he threw himself from the top of the house, and so perished." Corn. Nep. Dion. cap. 4. [[Cornelius Nepos, "Dion" in *Cornelius Nepos.*]] This art was not unknown to the Romans. Examples of treating their enemies, or their suspected friends in this manner, are to be found in Tacitus Hist. 4. 64. and Agricola's life, 21. 1. [[Tacitus, *The Histories;* Tacitus, *Tacitus,* vol. 1: *Agricola, Germania, Dialogus.*]] This secret tyranny is taken notice of by Forstner upon Tacitus's annals, l. 1. [[Christoph Forstner (1598–1667) produced an annotated edition of Tacitus's *Annals.*]] I wish then, that from such examples, youth easily corrupted into a vitious taste and temper, and averse to admonitions, would learn this profitable lesson, to look upon those as their worst enemies who endeavour to seduce them from the paths of virtue into luxury and softness, and to consider them as tyrants to whom they are really in bondage, who set themselves to deprave their morals.

SECTION CXC

Since it is not more allowable to hurt one's *body* than his mind (§178), it is certainly unlawful to beat, strike, hurt, injure, wound any one in any manner or degree, or to maim any member or part of his body; to torment him by starving, pinching, shackling him, or in any other way; or by taking from him, or diminishing any of the things he stands in need of in order to live agreeably and comfortably; or, in one word, to do any thing to any one by which his body, which he received from nature sound and intire, can, by the malice or fault of another, suffer any wrong or detriment. Because since we ourselves certainly are so abhorrent of all these things, that death itself does not appear less cruel to us than such injuries do; surely what we would not have done to ourselves by others, we ought not to do to them, and we must, for that very reason, or by that very feeling, know that we ought not to do so to them.* <135>

Nor with respect to the body.

SECTION CXCI

As to the state or condition of man, to this article chiefly belongs *reputation,* not only a simple good name, or being looked upon not as a bad person, but likewise the superior reputation one deserves by his superior merits above others; (for of wealth and possessions, which cannot be conceived without dominion or property, we are afterwards to speak). Now, seeing one's fame cannot but be hurt by *calumnies* (§154), or deeds and words tending to disgrace one, which we call *injuries;* it is as clear

Nor in respect of fame and reputation.

---

* And hence it seems to be, that by many ancient laws, retaliation was proposed against those who broke or hurt any member of another person. See Exod. xxi. 23. Lev. xxiv. 50. Aulus Gellius, Noct. Attic. xx. 1. Diod. Sicul. xii. 17. For tho' it be not probable, that either among the Hebrews or the Romans, this law of retaliation took place (κατὰ τὸ ῥητὸν) strictly: (Joseph. antiq. Jud. 4. 7. [[Flavius Josephus, *Antiquitates Judaicae* (*Judean antiquities 1–4,* trans. Feldman)]] Gellius 20. 1.) yet by this it appears, that the best law-givers acknowledged it to be most just, that one should not do to another what he would not have done to himself.

and certain that we ought to abstain from all these, as it is, that we ourselves take them in very ill part.*

SECTION CXCII

Nor in respect of chastity. Besides, the condition of a person may be wronged in respect of *chastity,* because being thus corrupted by violence, or by flattery, one's good name suffers, and the tranquillity of families is disturbed, (§178); whence it is plain, that we ought not to lay snares against one's chastity, and that all uncleanness, whether violently forced, or voluntary; and much more, adultery, and other such abominable, cruel injuries, are absolutely contrary to the law of nature.† <136>

* Therefore Simplicius upon Epictetus Enchirid. cap. 38. p. 247. calls contumelies and such injuries, evils contrary to nature, nay diseases, spots in the soul. But what is contrary to the nature of the mind is certainly an evil, and what is such, cannot but be contrary to the law of nature, which obliges us to do good.

† For tho' when both the parties consent, the maxim, "Do not to another what you would not have done to yourself," ceases; yet, first of all, in general, none desires any thing to be done to him that would render him less happy. But he is more unhappy, who is allured by temptations to pleasure, or to any vice. His will is hurt or injured (§189). Again, others very often are wronged, such as parents, husbands, relations, and at least, with regard to them, the debaucher violates the maxim, "Do not to another what you would not have done to you." Finally, he who seduces a woman into lewdness, corrupts her. But since, if we are wise, we would not choose to be corrupted ourselves by guileful arts, neither ought we to have any hand in corrupting any person. So far is seduction of a woman by flattery into unchastity from being excusable, that some lawyers have thought it deserving of severer punishment than force, "Because those who use force, they thought, must be hated by them to whom the injury is offered; whereas those who by flattering insinuations endeavour to persuade into the crime, so pervert the minds of those they endeavour to debauch, that they often render wives more loving and attached to them than to their husbands, and thus are masters of the whole house, and make it uncertain whether the children be the husband's or the adulterer's." Lysias, Orat. 1. [[Lysias, "On the Murder of Eratosthenes," chap. 33 in *Lysias.*]]

SECTION CXCIII

From what hath been said, it is plain enough that a person may be wronged even by internal actions; *i.e.* by *thoughts* intended to one's prejudice, as well as by external actions, as *gestures, words,* and *deeds* (§18); whence it follows, that even hatred, contempt, envy, and other such vices of the mind, are repugnant to the law of nature. And that we ought to abstain from all gestures shewing hatred, contempt, or envy, and what may give the least disturbance to the mind of any person. But that hurt, which consists in words and deeds, is accounted greatest (in *foro humano*) in human courts of judicature.* <137>

One may be injured by thoughts, gestures, words, and deeds.

SECTION CXCIV

Because a person may be hurt by *words* or *discourse* (§193), it is worth while to enquire a little more accurately into our duties with relation to *speech.* For such is the bounty of the kind author of nature towards us, that he hath not only given us minds to perceive, judge and reason, and to pursue good, but likewise the faculty of communicating our sentiments to others, that they may know our thoughts and inclinations. For tho' the brutes, we see, can express, by neighing, hissing, grunting, bel-

The faculty of speech distinguishes man above the brute creation.

---

* Because the author of the law of nature is καρδιογνώστης, *a discerner of hearts,* he undoubtedly no less violates his will, who indulges any thought contrary to his commands, than he who transgresses them by words or deeds: and for that reason we have observed above, that the law of nature extends to internal as well as external actions (§18). Besides, love being the genuine principle or foundation of the law of nature (§79), which does not consist principally in the external action, but in the desire of good to the object beloved, and delight in its happiness and perfection (§80), it must needs be contrary to the law of nature to hate any person, and to delight in his unhappiness and imperfection: or to have an aversion to his happiness and perfection, though it should consist merely in thought and internal motion, must be repugnant to that law. Hence our Saviour, the best interpreter of divine law, natural or positive, condemns even thoughts and internal actions repugnant to the law of nature, Matt. v. 22. 28. And this we thought proper to oppose to those who assert, that the law of nature extends to external actions only.

lowing, and other obscure ways, their feelings,* yet to man is given the superior faculty of distinctly signifying his thoughts by words, and thus making his mind certainly known to others. <138>

SECTION CXCV

What discourse is.

Seeing what peculiarly distinguishes us from the brutes, with relation to speech, consists in our being able clearly to communicate our thoughts to others, (§193), which experience tells us we do by articulate sounds;† *i.e.* by sounds so diversified by our organs of speech as to form different words, by which all things, and all their affections and properties or modes may be expressed; therefore discourse is articulated sound, by which we impart the thoughts of our minds to others distinctly and clearly. <139>

* Thus a dog expresses anger by one sound, grief by another, love to mankind by another, and other affections by other sounds: but he does not distinctly or clearly express his particular thought, nor can he do it, tho' dogs and many other animals have almost the same organs of speech with which man is furnished. The more imperfect an animal is, the less capable is it of uttering any sound whereby it can give any indication of its sensations, as fishes, oisters, for instance, and other shell-fish. And therefore Pythagoras really affronted men's understandings when he pretended to understand the language of brute animals, and to have had conversation with them, and by this shewed either a very fantastical turn of mind, or a design to impose upon others. See Iamblichus's life of Pythagoras, cap. 13. [[Iamblichus, *Iamblichus on the Mysteries . . . and Life of Pythagoras.*]]

† Human genius hath not rested in finding certain and determinate names for all things, but hath invented other signs to be used in place of discourse, when there is no opportunity for it. Thus we have found out the way of communicating our minds to distant persons by the figures of letters so distinctly, that they do not hear but see our words: which is so surprising an invention, that some have ascribed it to God. There is also a method of speaking, as it were by the fingers, invented in Turkey by the dumb, and very familiar to the nobles in that country, as Ricaut tells us in his description of the Ottoman empire, cap. 7. 12 [[see Ricaut, *The History of the Present State of the Ottoman Empire*]]: Not to mention speaking with the eyes and the feet, upon which there are curious dissertations by Mollerus Altorffensis. [[Daniel Wilhelm Moller (1642–1712) was *praeses* of a number of dissertations at the university of Altdorf. It is not evident here to which one Heineccius is referring.]] Tho' all these do not deserve to be called *speech,* yet they supply the place of it; and therefore, whatever is just or obligatory with regard to speech, holds equally with regard to them.

SECTION CXCVI

From this definition it is obvious enough, that the faculty of speech is given us, not for the sake of God, nor of brutes, but for our own advantage, and that of our kind; and therefore, that God wills that by it we should communicate our thoughts to others agreeably to the love he requires of us: for which reason, he wills that we should not injure any one by our discourse, but employ it, as far as is in our power, to our own benefit, and the advantage of others.*

How it ought to be employed.

SECTION CXCVII

The design of discourse being to communicate our sentiments to others (§196), which is done by articulate sounds, denominating things, and their affections, modes, qualities, and properties (§195); it follows, that being to speak to others, we ought not to affix any meaning to words but what they are intended and used to signify in common discourse; <140> or if we make use of uncommon words, or employ them in a less ordinary acceptation, we ought accurately to explain our mind. But no person has reason to be displeased, if we use words in a sense they have been taken in by those acquainted with languages, or which is received at the present time, if the construction of words and other circumstances admit of it.

We ought to use words in their received signification.

---

* We say rightly, that the faculty of speech was not given us for the sake of God, since God without that assistance intimately knows our most secret motions and thoughts: nor for the sake of the brutes, who do not understand our discourse as such, or any otherwise than they do other signs to which they are accustomed. And therefore it remains, that it can be given us for no other reason but for the sake of ourselves and other men. But it cannot be given us for our own sake, in order to our communicating our thoughts to ourselves, of which we are immediately conscious; but that we may inform others what we would have done to us, and in what they may be useful to us. And for the sake of others it is given to us, that we may signify to them what it is their interest to know, or what may be of use to them. Since therefore we ought to love others equally as ourselves, and what we would not have others to do to us, we ought not to do to others; the plain consequence is, that we are obliged not to hurt any one by our discourse, but to endeavour to be as useful as we can to others by it.

SECTION CXCVIII

No person ought to be wronged by discourse.

And since God wills that we communicate the sentiments of our mind to others by speech, agreeably to the love of others he requires of us by his law (§196); which love does not permit us to hurt any person by our discourse: but it is to injure a person, to detract any thing from his perfection or felicity (§82): hence it follows, that we ought, not to hide from any one any thing, the knowledge of which he hath either a perfect or imperfect right* to exact from us; not to speak falsehood in that case: not to mislead any person into error, or do him any detriment by our discourse. <141>

SECTION CXCIX

We may hurt another by dissimulation, by lying, by deception.

He who conceals what another has a perfect or imperfect right to demand certain and true information of from him, *dissembles.* He who in that case speaks what is false, in order to hurt another, *lies.* Finally, he who misleads any one to whom he bears ill-will into an error, *deceives* him. Now, by these definitions, compared with the preceding paragraph,

---

* *Perfect right* is the correlate to perfect obligation, *imperfect right* to imperfect obligation. The former requires that we should not wrong any person, but render to every one his own (§174): And therefore every one can as often demand from us by perfect right the truth, as he would be hurt by our dissimulation, by our speaking falsely, or by our disguising and adulterating the truth: or as often as by compact, or by the nature of the business itself which we have with another, we owe it to him to speak the truth. And since the latter obliges us by internal obligation, or regard to virtue, to promote the perfection and happiness of others to the utmost of our power, it is very manifest that we are obliged to speak the truth openly, and without dissimulation, as often as another's happiness or perfection may be advanced by our discourse. He therefore offends against the perfect right of another, who knowing snares to be laid for him by an assassin, conceals it, or persuades him that the assassin only comes to him to pay his compliments; as likewise does he, who having undertaken the custody of another's goods, knowingly hides the breaking in of thieves, or endeavours to make them pass for travellers come to lodge with him. He acts contrary to the imperfect right of another, who when one is out of his way, denies he knows the right road, tho' he know it, or directly puts him into the wrong one.

it is abundantly plain, that dissimulation, as we have defined it, and all lying and deception, are contrary to the law of nature and nations.

SECTION CC

But since we are bound to love others, not with greater love than our-selves, but with equal love, (§94); the consequence is, that it is lawful to be silent, if our speaking, instead of being advantageous to any person, would be detrimental to ourselves or to others: and that it is not unlawful to speak falsly or ambiguously, if another have no right to exact the truth from us (§198); or if by open discourse to him, whom, in decency, we cannot but answer, no advantage would redound to him, and great dis-advantage would accrue from it to ourselves or others; or when, by such discourse with one, he himself not only suffers no hurt, but receives great advantage.* <142>

When it is allowable to be silent, to speak falsly or ambiguously.

SECTION CCI

Hence we may infer, that all *dissimulation* is unjust (§199), but not all *silence:* (by which we mean, not speaking out that to another which we are neither perfectly nor imperfectly obliged to discover to him (§200); that all *lying* is unjust (§199), but not all *false speaking* (§200); that all

What is meant by taciturnity, what by false speech, and what by fiction.

---

* Thus, none will blame a merchant, if being asked by some over curious person how rich he might be, he should not make any answer, or should turn the conversation some other way. Nor ought a General more to be blamed who deceives the enemy by false reports or ambiguous rumours, because an enemy, as such, hath no right, perfect or imperfect, to demand the truth from an enemy as such. Moreover, the prudence of Athanasius is rather commendable than blameable, who detained those who were pursuing him with such ambiguous conversation, that they knew not it was Athanasius with whom they were conversing, Theodoret. Hist. Eccl. 3. 8. [[Theo-doretus (393–458), *Ecclesiasticae historiae libri quinque.*]] For he could not remain silent without danger, and plain discourse would not have been of any advantage to his pursuers, and of great hurt to himself. Finally, none can doubt but a teacher may lawfully employ fables, fictions, parables, symbols, riddles, in order to suit himself to the capacity of his hearers, and insinuate truth into their minds through these channels, since these methods of instruction are far from being hurtful to any persons, and are very profitable to his hearers.

deception is unjust (§199); but not all *ingenious* or *feigned discourse* (§200). And therefore all these must be carefully distinguished, if we would not deceive ourselves, and make a false judgment concerning them.* <143>

SECTION CCII

What truth and veracity mean.

The same holds with respect to *truth* and *veracity*. For since one is said to be a person of *veracity*, who speaks the truth without dissimulation, whenever one has a perfect or imperfect right to know the truth from us; the consequence is, that *veracity* always means a commendable quality. On the other hand, speaking *truth* may be good, bad, or indifferent; because it consists in the agreement of words and external signs with our thoughts, and one does not always do his duty who lays open his thoughts.†

* Amongst the Greeks the word ψεῦδος was somewhat ambiguous, signifying both *a lie* and *false speech*. Demosthenes [[Demosthenes (384–322 B.C.), considered the greatest Athenian orator of classical antiquity]] takes it in the first sense in that saying so familiar to him, "That there is nothing by which we can hurt others more than by (ἡ ψεύδη λέγων) lies." Chariclea understands by it false speech, in that famous apophthegm of his, "That false speaking (τὸ ψεῦδος) is sometimes good, *viz.* when it is in such a manner advantageous to the speaker as to hurt no other body." Heliod. Aethiop. l. 1. c. 3. p. 52. [[Heliodorus, *Aethiopica* (*An Ethiopian Romance*, trans. Hadas). Charicles is one of the main characters in Heliodorus's story.]] But the word *lie* is not one of these ambiguous words, but being always used to signify a base and detestable vice, ought to be distinguished from false speaking, and the other words we have above mentioned.

† It is a known apophthegm of Syracides. (*sapienti os in corde, stulto cor in ore esse*, a wise man's mouth is in his heart, and a fool's heart is in his mouth). A rich person who discovers his treasures to thieves tells truth, but none will on that account commend his virtue and veracity: whereas, on the other hand, he would not be reproached with making a lie who kept silent to a thief, or turned the discourse another way (§200). Hence the saying of Simonides, "That he had often repented of speaking, but never of silence." And that of Thales, "That few words are a mark of a prudent man." To which many such like aphorisms might be added.

SECTION CCIII

Words, by which we seriously assert that we are speaking truth, and not falsly, are called *asseverations*. An asseveration made by invoking God as our judge, is called an *oath*. Words by which we wish good things to a person, or pray to God for his prosperity, are called *benedictions*. Words by which we, in the heat of our wrath, wish ill to our neighbour, are commonly called *malediction* or *cursing*. When we imprecate calamities upon our own heads, it is called *execration*. <144>

SECTION CCIV

From the definition of an asseveration (§203), it is plain that no good man will use it rashly or unnecessarily, but then only, when a person, without any cause, calls what he says into doubt, and he cannot otherwise convince him of the truth whose interest it is to believe it; whence we may conclude, that he acts greatly against duty, who employs asseverations to hurt and deceive any one.*

SECTION CCV

Since we desire happiness no less to those we love, and in whose felicity we delight, than to ourselves, it cannot be evil to wish well to another, and pray for all blessings upon him, provided it be done seriously and from love, and not customarily and in mere compliment.† But all mal-

---

* For since to circumvent and deceive a person, is itself base and unjust (§199), what can be more abominable or unjust, than to deceive by asseverations? And hence that form used among the Romans, "As among good men there ought to be fair dealing," "That I may not be taken in and deceived by putting trust in you, and on your account." Cicero, de off. l. 3. 16. For it is base to cheat and defraud any one; and it is much more base to cheat and defraud by means of one's credit with another. See Franc. Car. Conradi de pacto fiduc. exerc. 2. §4. [[Conradi, *De pacto fiduciae.*]]

† And therefore many congratulatory acclamations, which on various occasions are addressed to illustrious persons and men in power, degenerate into flatteries: nay, sometimes they are poison covered over with honey, because at the very time these fair speeches are made, the person's ruin is desired, if snares be not actually laid for

edictions breathe hatred, and are therefore unjust, unless when one with commiseration only represents to wicked persons the curses God hath already threatened against their practices. Finally, execrations, being contrary to the love we owe to ourselves, and the effects of immoderate anger and despair, are never excusable; but here, while we are examining matters by reason, certain heroic examples do not come into the consideration, they belong to another chair. <145>

SECTION CCVI

What is the use of an oath?

As to an *oath,* which is an asseveration by which God is invoked as a witness or avenger (§203), since we ought not to use a simple asseveration rashly or unnecessarily (§204); much less certainly ought we to have recourse rashly or unnecessarily to an oath; but then only when it is required by a superior as judge; or by a private person, in a case where love obliges us to satisfy one fully of the truth, and to remove all suspicion and fear of deception and falsity. And this takes place with regard to every oath, and therefore there is no need of so many divisions of oaths into *promissory* and *affirmatory,* and the latter into an oath for bearing *witness,* and an oath decisive of a *controversy:* for the same rules and conditions obtain with respect to them all.* <146>

---

him. Since all this proceeds not from love but hatred, who can doubt of their being repugnant to the law of nature, which is the law of love?

* Besides, if we carefully examine the matter, we shall find that every oath is *promissory.* For whoever swears, whether the oath be imposed by a judge, or by an adversary, he promises to speak the truth sincerely and honestly. And the distinctions between oaths about contracts past or future, the former of which is called *an oath of confirmation,* and the other *a promissory oath;* an oath about the deed of another, and an oath about our own deed, the former of which is called *an oath of testimony,* the other *a decisory oath,* which again, if it be tendered by the judge is called *judicial,* if by the party, without judgment, *voluntary:* these and other decisions belong rather to Roman law than to Natural law, as is plain from their not being in use in several other nations, as the Greeks and Hebrews. See Cod. Talmud. tom. 4. edit. Surenhus. [[Probably Willem Surenhuys (1666–1729), *Mischna sive totius Hebraeorum juris, rituum, antiquitatum, ac legum systema.*]] Maimonides de jurejurando, edit. Diethmar. Leiden 1706. [[Maimonides, *Constitutiones de jurejurando.*]] Selden de Synedr. Heb. xi. 11. [[Selden, *De synedriis & praefecturis juridicis veterum Ebraeorum.*]] Jac. Lydius

SECTION CCVII

Since by those who swear God is invoked as a witness and avenger (§203), Who and how. the consequence is, that atheists must make light of an oath, and that it is no small crime to tender an oath to such persons; that an oath ought to be suited to the forms and rites of every one's religion;* and therefore asseverations by things not reckoned sacred, cannot be called oaths; that he is justly punished for perjury, who perjures himself by invoking false gods; nay, that even an atheist is justly punished for perjury, who concealing or dissembling his atheistical opinions, swears falsely by God, seeing he thereby deceives others.

SECTION CCVIII

Moreover, since one ought not to swear rashly, or without being called to it (§206); hence it follows, that an oath is made for the sake, not of the swearer, but of him who puts it to the swearer; and therefore it ought to be understood and explained by his mind and intention, and not according to that of the person sworn; for which reason <147> all those equivocations and mental reservations, as they are called, by which wicked men endeavour to elude the obligation of an oath, are most absurd. Those interpretations of oaths are likewise absurd, which require

How an oath ought to be administred.

---

de juramento. [[Lydius, *Dissertatio philologico-theologica de juramento.*]] To which may be added what Petit [[Pierre Petit (1617–87), French physician]] and other writers on antiquities say of the use of an oath among the Greeks.

* Provided the form doth not tend to dishonour the true God, because such actions are not excusable even by extreme necessity (§160). Hence it is plain, that an oath tendered to a Jew may be suited to his religion, because such a form contains nothing which tends to the dishonour of the true God. But I doubt whether it be lawful for a Christian judge to order a Mahometan to swear before him by Mahomet, as the greatest prophet of the one God, especially since the nature of the Mahometan religion is not such, that an oath by the true God, the Creator of heaven and earth, does not equally bind them to truth, as if they at the same time made mention of that impostor.

base or unreasonable things of one, who of his own accord had sworn
to another not to refuse him any thing he should ask of him.*

SECTION CCIX

The obligation
and effects of
an oath.

Again, an oath being an invocation of God, (§203), it follows that it
ought to be religiously fulfilled; that it cannot be eluded by quibles and
equivocations, but that the obligation of an oath must yield to that of
law: and therefore that it can produce no obligation, if one swears to do
any thing that is base and forbidden by law; tho' if it be not directly
contrary to law, it be absolutely binding, provided it was neither extorted
by unjust violence, nor obtained by deceit (§107 & 109): whence is manifest what ought to be said of the maxim of the *canonists,* "That every
oath ought <148> to be performed which can be so without any detriment to our eternal happiness."†

---

* Tho' he be guilty in many respects, who takes such an oath, because he does it
of himself, unnecessarily and without being called to it (§206); and because he thus
swears before hand not to refuse, without knowing what the person may demand,
and so exposes himself either to the danger of perjury, or of a rash oath: yet by such
an oath no person is bound to fulfil what he promised by his oath, if the other, taking
advantage of it, requires any thing of him that is impossible, unjust or base. For since
he swore voluntarily, and of his free accord, his oath ought without doubt to be
interpreted according to his own mind and intention. But no man in his senses can
be supposed to mean, to bind himself to any thing which cannot be done, either
through physical impossibility, or on account of legal prohibition. Herod therefore
sinned, Mat. xiv. in promising to his daughter by a rash oath to grant her whatever
she should demand of him; but he was yet more guilty in yielding to her when she
desired John the Baptist's head.

† It comes under the definition of *evasion, cavillatio,* if one satisfies the words,
but not the mind and intention of the imposer: the impiety of which is evident. He
who thinks of satisfying an oath by evasion or equivocation, deceives another. But
to deceive any person is in itself unjust (§199): it must be therefore much more unjust
to deceive one by invoking God to witness, and as judge and avenger. An oath then
excludes all cavils. Hence it is plain that Hatto archbishop of Mentz was guilty of
perjury, when, having promised to Albertus, that he would bring him back safe to
his castle, pretending hunger, he brought him back to breakfast, thinking that he had
thus satisfied his oath. [[Hatto (ca. 850–913), archbishop of Mainz, who was allegedly
implicated in a treacherous capture of Duke Adalbert of Badenberg.]] Otto Frising.
Chron. 6. 15. [[The work to which Heineccius refers is Otto of Freising's (1112–58)

SECTION CCX

We have sufficiently proved that it is unlawful to hurt any one by word or deed, nay even in thought. Now, since whosoever renders another more unhappy, injures him; but he renders one most unhappy, who, having injured him, does not repair the damage; the consequence is, that he who does a person any injury, is obliged to make reparation to him; and that he who refuses to do it, does a fresh injury, and may be truly said to hurt him again; and that if many persons have a share <149> in the injury, the same rule ought to be observed with regard to making satisfaction and reparation, which we laid down concerning the imputation of an action in which several persons concur (§112 & seq.).*

He who does an injury, is obliged to make reparation.

SECTION CCXI

By *satisfaction* we here understand doing that which the law requires of one who has done an injury. Now, every perfect law requires two things,

What is satisfaction?

Rerum ab origine mundi ad ipsius usque tempora gestarum libri octo, also known as *Chronica.*]] Marian. Scot. ad ann. 908. [[Marianus Scotus, *Chronicorum libri tres.*]] Ditmarus Merseb. l. 1. [[Dietmar von Merseburg, *Chronicon* (see Thietmar von Merseburg, *Ottonian Germany*)]] at the beginning, wonders at this subtlety of the archbishop, and he had reason, since even the Romans would not have suffered a captive to escape without some mark of ignominy who had by such guile deceived an enemy, Gell. Noct. Att. 7. 18. Of such fraud Cicero says justly in his third book of offices, cap. 32. "He thought it a sufficient performance of his oath: but certainly he was mistaken: for cunning is so far from excusing a perjury, that it rather aggravates it, and makes it the more criminal. This therefore was no more than a foolish piece of craftiness, impudently pretending to pass for prudence: whereupon the senate took care to order, that my crafty gentleman should be sent back in fetters again to Hannibal."

* Aristotle Ethic. ad Nicom. 5. 2. derives the obligation to make reparation from an involuntary contract: Pufendorff of the law of nature and nations, 3. 1. 2. deduces it from this consideration, that the law against doing damage would be in vain, unless the law-giver be likewise supposed to will that reparation should be made. But we infer this duty from the very idea of wrong or hurt. For he does not render us more imperfect or unhappy who robs us of any thing belonging to us, than he who having robbed us, does not make restitution or satisfaction. If therefore injury be unlawful, reparation or satisfaction must be duty.

1. That the injury be repaired,* because a person is hurt or wronged.
2. That the injurious person should suffer for having transgressed the law by doing an injury, because the legislator is leased by his disobedience or transgression. And for this reason satisfaction comprehends both reparation and punishment, (Grotius of the rights of war and peace, 2. 17. 22. & 120.). The one doth not take off the other, because the guilt of the action for which punishment is inflicted, and the damage that is to be repaired, are conjunct in every delinquency. But of punishment in another place. <150>

SECTION CCXII

How it is to be made. *Damage* done, is either of such a nature that every thing may be restored into its former state, or that this cannot be done. In the former case, the nature of the thing requires that every thing should be restored into its first state, and, at the same time, that the loss should be repaired which the injured person suffered by being deprived of the thing, and by the expences he was obliged to in order to recover it. In the latter case, the nature of the thing requires, that the person wronged should be indemnified by as equal a valuation of his loss as can be made; in which regard is to be had not only to the real value, but to the price of fancy or affection. Pufendorff hath illustrated this doctrine by examples in murder, in maiming, in wounding, in adultery, in rapes, in theft, and other crimes. Puf. of the law of nature and nations, B. 3. c. 1.

REMARKS on This Chapter

We shall have occasion afterwards to consider a little more fully with our Author, that natural equality of mankind upon which he founds our natural obligation to mutual love. Let me only observe here, that

---

* If damage be done by the action of no person, no person is obliged to satisfaction; for what happens solely by divine providence, cannot be imputed to any mortal (§106). And hence it follows, that when a proprietor suffers any damage in this way, he is obliged to bear it. For what is imputable to no person we must suffer with patience.

it is at least an improper way of speaking among moralists to say, "That all men are naturally equal in this respect, that antecedently to any deed or compact amongst them, no one hath power over another, but each is master of his own actions and abilities; and that none are subjected to others by nature." For we ought, as in physics, so in morals, to reason from the real state, frame, constitution, or circumstances of things. And with regard to mankind, abstractly from all consideration of inequality occasioned by civil society, this is the true state of the case: 1. "That men are born naturally and necessarily subject to the power and will of their parents; or dependent upon them for their sustenance and education. The author of nature hath thus subjected us. 2. Men are made to acquire prudence by experience and culture; and therefore naturally and necessarily those of less experience and less prudence, are subjected to those of greater experience and prudence. There is naturally this dependence among mankind. Nay, 3. which is more, the Author of nature (as <151> Mr. Harrington says in his Oceana) hath diffused a natural aristocracy over mankind, or a natural inequality with respect to the goods of the mind. And superiority in parts will always produce authority, and create dependence, or *hanging by the lips*,[1] as the same author calls it. Such superiority and inferiority always did universally prevail over the world; and the dependence or subjection which this superiority and inferiority in parts or virtues creates, is natural. 4. Industry, to which, as the same excellent author says, *nature or God sells every thing*, acquires property; and every consequence of property made by industry is natural, or the intention of nature. But superiority in

---

1. See Harrington, *The Commonwealth of Oceana* (1656), in *The Political Works of James Harrington*, 172–73: "Twenty men, if they be not all idiots—perhaps if they be—can never come together, but there will be such difference in them that about a third will be wiser, or at least less foolish, than all the rest. These upon acquaintance, though it be but small, will be discovered, and (as stags that have the largest heads) lead the herd; for while the six, discoursing and arguing one with another, show the eminence of their parts, the fourteen discover things that they had never thought on, or are cleared in divers truths which had formerly perplexed them; wherefore in matters of common concernment, difficulty or danger, they hang upon their lips as children upon their fathers, and the influence thus acquired by the six, the eminence of whose parts is found to be a stay and comfort to the fourteen, is *auctoritas partum*, the authority of the fathers." Harrington distinguishes authority from power, which is based on material dependence ("hanging by the teeth": see note 9, p. 202).

property purchased by industry, will make dependence, *hanging,* as that author calls it, *by the teeth.* Here is therefore another dependence or subjection amongst mankind, which is the natural and necessary result of our being left by nature each to his own industry." All these inequalities, or superiorities and dependencies, are natural to mankind, in consequence of our frame and condition of life. Now the only question with regard to these superiorities, and the right or power they give, must be either, 1. "Was it right, was it just and good to create mankind in such circumstances, that such inequalities must necessarily happen among them?" To which question, because it does not belong immediately to our present point, it is sufficient to answer, "That we cannot conceive mankind made for society, and the exercise of the social virtues without mutual dependence; and mutual dependence necessarily involves in its very idea inequalities, or superiorities and inferiorities: and that as we cannot conceive a better general law, than that the goods of the mind, as well as of the body, should be the purchase of application and industry; so the advantages arising from superiority in the goods of the mind, or from superiority in external purchases by ingenuity and industry, *i.e.* the authority the one gives, and the power the other gives, are natural and proper rewards of superior prudence, virtue and industry." 2. Or the question must mean, "Does it appear from our constitution, to be the intention of our Author, that man should exercise his natural or acquired parts and goods for the benefit of his kind, in a benevolent manner, or contrariwise?" To which I answer, "That as it plainly appears from our constitution to be the intention of our Author, that we should exercise our natural abilities to the best purpose, for our own advancement in the goods of the mind and of the body; and that we should improve in both, and reap many advantages by improvement in both, the chief of which is superiority over those who have not made equal advances either in internal or external goods: so it as plainly appears from our constitution, to be the will and intention of our Author, that we should love one another, act benevolently towards one another, and never exercise our power to do hurt, but on the contrary, always exercise it or increase it, in order to do good." If this appears to be the will of our Maker, from the consideration of <152> our constitution and condition of life, then to act and behave so is right; and to act or behave otherwise is wrong, in every sense of these words, *i.e.* it is contrary to the end of our make; and consequently repugnant to the will and intention of our Maker. Now, that we are made for benevolence; and are under obligation by the will of our Maker, to promote the good of others to the utmost of our power, will be fully proved, if it can be made out, that we are under obligation by the will of our Maker, appearing from our make and constitution, to forgive injuries, to do good even to our enemies, and in one word, to overcome evil by good. If the greater can be proved, the lesser involved in it, is certainly proved. And therefore, if it can be made appear, that by the law of nature, (in the sense we have defined these words) we are obliged to benevolence, even towards our enemies, all that our Author hath said about not injuring one by word or deed, or even by thought; and about the caution and tenderness that ought to be used in necessary self-defence, will be indisputable. Now, that it appears to be the will of our Author, from our make, that we should be benevolent even to the injurious and ungrateful, must be owned by any one who considers, that resentment in us is indignation against injustice or injury; is not, or cannot be otherwise excited in us; and therefore is not in the least a kin to malice; and that as resentment is natural to us, so likewise is compassion. For if both these passions be in us, and we have Reason to guide them, as we plainly have, it is clear, that they must be intended to operate conjointly in us, or to mix together in their operations. Now what is resentment against injury, allayed or tempered by compassion, under the direction of reason, but such resentment as the suppression of injustice requires, moderated by tenderness to the unjust person. And what is compassion, allayed, mixed or moderated by resentment against injustice, but such tenderness towards the injurious person himself, as the preservation of justice, and consequently of social commerce and public good, permits? This argument is fully illustrated in my *Christian Philosophy*, p. 395, *&c*. And therefore I shall not here insist any longer upon it. The same thing may be proved, and hath been fully proved by moralists from other considerations. But I choose to reason in this manner, that we may see how reasonings about duties may proceed in the same manner as physical reasonings about the uses of parts in any bodily frame, or the final cause of any particular bodily whole. For if it be good reasoning to say, any member in a certain bodily organization is intended for such an end in that composition, it must be equally good reasoning to say, a moral constitution, in which there is a social and benevolent principle, compassion, and many public affections, and no hatred or aversion or resentment, but against injustice, together with reason capable of discerning public good, and delighting in it, is intended by its Author for the exercises of social affections; for justice; nay, for benevolence, and for commiserating <153> even the injurious, as far as public good admits that tenderness to take place.

Having mentioned the necessity of reasoning from the frame of mankind, and our condition, in order to infer the will of our Creator concerning our conduct, it may not be improper to add, that there is no difficulty in determining the will of our Creator, even with respect to our conduct towards inferior animals, if we state the case as it really is in fact, which is, "That such is the condition of mankind by the will of our Maker, that our happiness cannot at all be procured without employing certain inferior animals in labouring for us; nor even the happiness of the inferior animals themselves, in a great measure." For that being the case, tho' we can never have a right to employ inferior animals for our service by compact, they being incapable of it, yet we have a natural right to it, a right arising from the circumstances of things, as they are constituted by the Author of nature. But the right which arises from these circumstances, is not a right to torment them unnecessarily, because not only our happiness does not require that, but we really are framed by nature even to compassionate suffering brutes. But we shall have occasion afterwards to shew more fully, that a right may arise from the nature and circumstances of things, previous to compact or consent; or where there cannot be any compact or consent. Whoever would see the true meaning of the precept, *to love our neighbours as ourselves,* fully and clearly laid open, may consult Dr. Butler's sermon already quoted upon the love of our neighbour. That the precept, *Do as you would be done by,* is not peculiar to Christianity, but is a precept of the law of nature, and was known and inculcated by Confucius, Zoroaster, Socrates, and almost all ancient moralists, Pufendorff hath shewn, and Mr. Barbeyrac in his history of the moral science, prefixed to his notes on Pufendorff's system: so likewise our Author in the following chapter.

Concerning our imperfect duties towards others.

SECTION CCXIII

We think our obligation not to hurt any person, and the nature of injury have been sufficiently cleared and demonstrated. The next thing would be to explain with equal care our obligation to render to every one his own, and the nature of that duty (§175); were not the nature of our hypothetical duties such, that they could not be explained <154> without having first considered the nature of our imperfect absolute duties. But this being the case, it is proper to begin with them; and this premonition is sufficient to skreen us against being charged with the crime reckoned so capital among the critics of this age (ne ὕστερον πρότερον) transgressing order designedly, and with evil intention.

The order and connexion.

SECTION CCXIV

The source of all these duties is *love of humanity* or *beneficence* (§84), by which we cheerfully render him whom we love, not merely what we owe him by strict and perfect right, but whatever we think may conduce to his happiness. But because *humanity* commands us to be as good to others as we can be without detriment to ourselves; and *beneficence* commands us to do good to others even with detriment to ourselves (§83); therefore our *imperfect duties* are of two kinds, and may be divided into those of *humanity,* or *unhurt utility,* and those of *beneficence* or *gener-*

The foundation and division of imperfect duties.

osity. Both are, for many reasons, or on the account of many wants, so necessary, that it is impossible for men to live agreeably or conveniently without them.

SECTION CCXV

Axioms con-
cerning them. Since there can be no other measure with respect to these duties but the love of ourselves, and therefore we are obliged to love others as ourselves, (§93); the consequence is, that whatever we would have others to do to us, we ought to do the same to them (§88); whence above, in premising a certain principle to which all our duties to others might be reduced, we laid down this rule, *Man is obliged to love man no less than himself, and not to do to any other what he would think inexcusable if done to himself,* (from which principle we have deduced our perfect duties); *but, on the contrary, to do to others what he would desire others to do to him* (§93). Now <155> hence we shall see that all our imperfect duties may be clearly inferred.

SECTION CCXVI

Our obligation
to the duties
which may
be done to
others without
detriment to
ourselves. First of all, none would have those things denied to him by others which they can render to him without hurting themselves; wherefore every one is obliged liberally to render such good offices to another; and consequently it is justly reckoned most inhuman for one, when it is in his power, not to assist another by his prudence, his counsel and aid; or not to do all in his power to save his neighbour's goods; not to direct a wanderer into the right road; to refuse running water to the thirsty; fire to the cold; shade to those who languish with excessive heat; or to exact any thing from another to his detriment, which can more easily, either without hurting ourselves or any other, be procured some other way. This kind of benignity is so small and trivial, that either by law or custom, the duties of this class have passed almost every where into duties of perfect obligation.*

---

* Thus, among the Athenians, it was reckoned a most attrocious crime not to

SECTION CCXVII

It belongs to the same class of unhurt utility to communicate such things to others as we can, <156> (such is our abundance), spare them without any loss or hurt to ourselves; and to dispense among others things which would otherwise be lost and perish with us; insomuch, that they are very inhuman who suffer things to corrupt and spoil, who destroy in the fire, throw into the sea, or bury under ground things on purpose that no other may be the better for them.*

It extends to those things with which we abound.

---

direct one who wandered, into his right road. Hence that saying of Diphilus, "Don't you know that it is amongst the most execrable things, not to shew one his way." So by the Roman laws, one could by an action compel another, who was neither bound to him by any compact, nor by delinquency, to exhibit a thing. Latona in Ovid. Metamorp. 6. v. 349. appeals to custom,

> Quid prohibetis aquas? usus communis aquorum est.

> [[Ovid, *Metamorphoses,* bk. 6, l. 349: "Why do you deny me water? The enjoyment of water is a common right." (trans. Miller)]]

And Seneca, Controv. 1. says, "It is barbarous not to stretch out our arms to one who is falling, this is the common right of mankind," (*commune jus*) that is, a common right or duty by the consent of all nations. [["Iniquum est conlapsis manum non porrigere: commune hoc ius generis humani est." Seneca (the Elder), *Controversiae* 1.1.14, in *Declamations.*]]

  * This is also a very common sort of humanity, or another very low degree of it. As therefore, they are very cruel and inhuman, who refuse such good offices to others, so they are very unequal prizers of their actions, who expect very great thanks on account of any such good deeds. Terent. And. 2. 1. v. 31. says well, "It is not a mark of a liberal cast of mind, to desire thanks when one hath merited none." [[Terence, *The Woman of Andros,* lines 330–31, in vol. 1 of *Terence.*]] But who thinks the Calabrian did any considerable favour to his guest? to which Horace alludes. Ep. 1. 7. v. 14.

> Non quo more piris vesci Calaber jubet hospes.
> Tu mefecisti locupletem. Vescere sodes.
> Jam satis est. At tu quantumvis toile. Benigne:
> Non invisa feres pueris munuscula parvis.
> Tam teneor dono, quam si dimittor onustus.
> Ut libet: haec porcis hodie comedenda relinques.
> Prodigus & stultus donat, quae spernit & odit.

> [[Horace, *Epistles* 1.7.14–19, in *Satires, Epistles, and Ars Poetica:* " 'Twas not in the way a Calabrian host invites you to eat his pears that you have made

SECTION CCXVIII

What if our humanity would be hurtful to ourselves?

But since we are bound to render such good offices to others from the love we are obliged to entertain towards others by the law of an infinitely good and merciful God (§215), and yet none is obliged to love another more than himself (§93); the consequence is, that we may deny these good offices to others, if we foresee the doing them may be detrimental to ourselves or our friends; which, since <157> it may easily happen in a state of nature, where there is no common magistracy to protect and secure us, if we readily render these good offices even to our manifest enemies; there is therefore a plain reason why the good offices, even of *harmless use,* may be refused to an enemy in that state, as being ill disposed towards us; whereas in a civil state to deny them rashly to others under that pretext, would be very blameable.*

---

me rich. 'Eat some, pray.' 'I've had enough.' 'Well, take all you please.' 'No thanks.' 'Your tiny tots will love the little gifts you take them.' 'I'm as much obliged for your offer as if you sent me away loaded down.' 'As you please; you'll be leaving them for the swine to gobble up today.' The foolish prodigal gives away what he despises and dislikes."]]

He is inhuman who can deny such things to those who stand in need of them: and he is more than inhuman, who when he gives them, appears to himself so wonderfully beneficent, that he would have a person think himself under perpetual and unpayable obligation to him on that account.

* Thus in war we deny our enemies the benefit of watering, and have even a right to corrupt provisions, that they may be of no advantage to our invaders. But all these things we have only a right to do as they are enemies. For otherwise, when they cannot hurt us, it is humanity that deserves praise to assist enemies, e.g. when they are in captivity or in sickness. And seeing in a civil state, an enemy cannot easily hurt us, whom at least the magistrate cannot reduce into order, he is most inhuman who refuses to an enemy, to a scelerate, the offices of innocent profit or unhurt utility, since he is an object of commiseration: *"If not the manners, yet the man, or if not the man, at least humanity,"* according to that excellent saying of Aristotle in Diogenes Laert. v. 21. For which reason, the inhumanity of the Athenians is scarcely excusable, "who had such an aversion to the accusers of Socrates, that they would neither lend them fire, nor so much as answer them when they spoke, nor bath in the same water which they had used, but would order their servant to pour it away as polluted and defiled, till impatient of such a miserable state of reproach, the wretches became their own executioners." Plutarch. de invid. & odio. p. 538. [[Plutarch, *De invidia et odio* ("On Envy and Hate"), in *Moralia: in Fifteen Volumes,* vol. 7, p. 107.]]

SECTION CCXIX

Yea rather, since the love which is the source of all these duties, is due, not for the merits of others, but on account of the equality of nature (§88), it is very evident, that even to enemies those things in which we abound, and which we can give them without any hurt to ourselves, ought to be given. And this humanity is so much the more splendid <158> and noble, the less hope there is of our ever returning into great friendship with the enemy to whom such services are rendered.*

Humanity is due to enemies.

SECTION CCXX

But because this love of humanity, from which these duties flow as their fountain or source, ought to have prudence for its director, which is that faculty by which things conducive to our own happiness and that of others is discerned; hence it is conspicuous, that regard ought to be had not only to persons, but to the necessities they labour under; and therefore in like circumstances, if it be not in our power to satisfy all, greater humanity is due to a good man than to a scelerate; more is owing to a friend than to an enemy; more to a kinsman and relative than to a stranger; and more to him who is in greater, than to him who is in less in-

The degrees of relation and affinity ought to be considered.

---

* We know this is inculcated upon Christians, Mat. v. 45. Luke vi. 35; and before their eyes the example of our heavenly Father is set, "Who maketh the sun to arise, and his rain to fall upon the just and the unjust." But that right reason, from the consideration of the equality of human nature, may discover this truth, is plain from hence, that Socrates set himself expressly to refute this vulgar maxim, "That we are to do good to our friends, and hurt to our enemies." So Themistius tells us, Orat. ad Valent. de bello victis. [[A speech addressed by Themistius to the emperor Valens (in Themistius, *Orationes quae supersunt*).]] And what could have been wrote by one unacquainted with the sacred books, more excellent than this passage of Hierocles on the golden verses of Pythagoras, p. 69. "Whence it is justly said, that a good man hates no person, but is all love and benignity. For he loves the good, and does not regard the evil as his enemies. If he seeks out for a virtuous man, in order to associate with him, and loves an honest man above all things, yet in his love and goodness he imitates God himself, who hates no person, tho' he delights in the good, and embraces them with a peculiar affection." [[Hierocles of Alexandria (fl. A.D. 430), author of *Commentary on the Golden Verses of the Pythagoreans*.]]

digence of our assistance; and therefore so far the illustrious Leibnitz defines very justly, justice to be *the love of a wise man.* * <159>

SECTION CCXXI

Our obligation
to beneficence.

That degree of love, which we called above *love of beneficence* (§214), is of a sublimer kind, because it excites us to exert ourselves to the utmost, and even with detriment to ourselves, to promote the good of others. Now, since what we would desire to be done to us by others we are obliged to do to them (§88), and many cases happen in which we ourselves would be very unhappy unless others should liberally bestow upon us what we want, and there is none who does not desire that others should so treat him; the consequence is, that we are obliged, in such cases, to supply others liberally with what they stand in need of, even with some detriment to ourselves.† <160>

---

* Hence it is that Pythagoras has distinguished certain degrees of love in his golden verses, v. 4. &c. which are excellently interpreted by Hierocles, p. 46.

Inde parentis honos sequitur: tum sanguinis ordo:
Post alii sunto, virtus ut maxima, amici, &c.

[[Hierocles, interpreting Pythagoras, *Elements of Ethics* (*Fragmenta philosophorum Graecorum* 1.408): "Then the honour of the father follows, then the blood-line; after, let there be other friends, as their virtue is the greatest."]]

† We are said to give liberally, not what we lend, or give for hire, but what we bestow on others, without hope of restitution or retribution. If I give that I may receive, such an action is a kind of contract. But if I give without any desire of, or eye to retribution or restitution, this is bounty or liberality. Seneca of benefits, c. 14. says, "I will entirely pass those whose good services are mercenary, which, when one does, he does not consider to whom, but for how much he is to do them, and which therefore terminate wholly in self. If one sells me corn when I cannot live without buying, I do not owe my life to him, Because I bought it. I do not consider so much the necessity of the thing to my life, as the gratuity of the deed, and in such a case I would not have got, had I not bought; and the merchant did not think of the service it would do me, but of his own profit: what I buy I do not owe." [[Seneca, "On Benefits," 6. 14, in vol. 3 of Seneca, *Moral Essays.*]] But tho' benefits ought not to be done with selfish views, yet none does good to another, without desiring to bind the person he obliges to him by mutual love; and therefore the receiver by receiving tacitely obliges himself to mutual love.

SECTION CCXXII

A *benefit* is a service rendered to one without hope of restitution or retribution; and therefore readiness to render such services we call *beneficence;* as readiness to do good offices, to lay on obligation of restoring or compensating by services to one's self is called *officiousness* by Sidon. Apollin. 23. v. 478.[1] But tho' such services be not properly called *benefits;* yet they ought to be highly valued, and gratefully received, if they are greater than to admit of payment, or are rendered to us by one whom the nature of the good office did not oblige to do it.*

What is meant by beneficent, and what by officious.

SECTION CCXXIII

Since therefore beneficence is readiness to render such offices to others as we have reason to think will be serviceable to them (§222), every one must <161> see that they have no title to the praise of beneficence, who, as the servant in Terence, Hecyr. 5. 4. v. 39. "do more good ignorantly and imprudently, than ever they did knowingly, and with design (§48)," or who do good with an intention to hurt; or who do good only, because they think the benefit will turn more to their own advantage than to that of the receiver. From all which it is manifest, that in judging of benefits

Beneficence ought to proceed from inclination to be useful to others.

---

* This likewise is observed by Seneca, c. 15. "According to this way, one may say he owes nothing to his physician but his petty fee: nor to his preceptor, because he gave him money. But among us, both these are greatly reverenced and loved. To this it is answered, some things are of greater value than what is paid for them. Do you buy from your physician life and health, which are above all price; or from your instructor in useful arts and sciences, wisdom, and a well cultivated mind. Wherefore, to them is paid not the value of the thing, but of their labour and their attendance on us; they receive the reward, not of their merit, but of their profession." Afterwards he gives another reason why we owe gratitude to those who render us such good offices, cap. 16. "What then? why do I still owe something to my physician and preceptor, after I have given them a fee; why have I not then fully acquitted my self? because from being my physician and preceptor, they become my friend: and they oblige us not by their art, which they sell, but by their generous and friendly disposition." [[Seneca, "On Benefits," 6. 15–16, in vol. 3 of Seneca, *Moral Essays.*]]

1. Apollinaris Sidonius, *Poems and Letters,* vol. 1, p. 314.

the mind and intention of the benefactor are more to be considered than the act or effect itself.*

SECTION CCXXIV

Benefits ought to be dispensed with prudence.

Since benefits flow from love, which is always joined with prudence (§83), it is plain that whatever is not agreeable to reason is profusion, and any thing rather than liberality: nor are those offices deserving of the name of benefits, which proceed from ambition and vain-glory, more than from love, and are bestowed upon the more opulent, and not the indi-<162>gent;† upon unworthy persons preferably to men of merit;

* To illustrate these conclusions by examples; none will say, that a person is benefited by one, who not knowing any thing of the matter, delivers him letters with agreeable news; or by one who praises him merely to get him out of his place, that he may be lord of the hall; or by one who planted trees for his own pleasure, when he enjoys the shade of them, without or contrary to his intention. To such cases belongs the elegant fable in Phaedrus, I. 22. of the weasel, who being catched by a man, when it urged him to spare its life, because it had cleared his house from troublesome mice, had this answer:

> Faceres, si caussa mei:
> Gratum esset, & dedissem veniam supplici:
> Nunc quia laboras, ut fruaris reliquiis,
> Quae sint rosuri, simul & ipsos devores,
> Noli imputare vanum beneficium mihi.

[[Phaedrus, *Fabulae* 1.22 ("The Man and the Weasel"): "If you were doing this for my sake, it would be something to thank you for, and I should have granted you the pardon for which you ask. But as it is, since you do the job to profit by the scraps that the mice would have nibbled, as well as to feed on the mice themselves, don't set me down as your debtor for imaginary services."]]

For this fable, according to the interpretation of Phaedrus himself, ought to be applied to them who serve their own ends, and then make a vain boast to the unthinking of their merit.

† For besides, that such benefits are snatched from the indigent, they are likewise not unfrequently baits to catch; and for that reason likewise they do not merit to be called benefits, Mat. v. 46, 47. Luke vi. 32. Besides, as to the more opulent, whatever benefit is rendered to them is neither grateful, nor has it the nature of a benefit. Thus we know Alexander the Great mocked at the pretended favour, when the Corinthians offered him the right of citizenship, tho' they boasted of having never made the

or, in fine, which are done contrary to that natural order founded in natural kindred and relation, of which above (§220).

SECTION CCXXV

Besides, because benefits ought to be advantageous to persons (§222), it is evident from hence, that benefits ought to be suited to every one's condition and necessities; and therefore that those are not benefits which do no good to a person; much less such as do him great hurt, or at least are attended with considerable inconvenience to him.* <163>

Benefits ought to be proportioned to the necessity and condition of persons.

SECTION CCXXVI

Since that love of humanity and beneficence which binds to render good offices, extends even to enemies (§219), it is clear that those have a much better title to our love, who have done us all the kindnesses they had in their power; and that they are the worst of men, nay, more hard-hearted than the most savage brutes, who are not won to love by favours: they are so much the more unjust that it cannot be denied, that by accepting favours, we bind ourselves to mutual love (§221).

The degrees of kindred and connexion are to be considered.

---

compliment to any but Hercules and Alexander. Seneca of benefits, 1. 13. But the memory of benefits formerly received from one yea: the customs of the state in which we live, and other reasons, may excuse such benefits: and therefore, at Rome none could blame this liberality of clients, because the right of patronage there established, required such liberality from the clients to their patrons, Dionys. Halic. 2. p. 84. Plutarch. Romul. p. 24. [[Dionysius Halicarnassus, *Roman Antiquities;* Plutarch, "Romulus" in his *Lives,* vol. 1, 90–187]] Polyb. Hist. 6. p. 459. Nor were the Persians blameable for bringing gifts to their king, since there was a law, "That every one should make presents to the king of Persia according to his ability." Aelian. var. hist. 1. 31.

    * He is not beneficent who gives a hungry person a jewel, to a thirsty person a fine garment, to a sick person a feast. *Bessus* did not surely deserve to be called a benefactor, who put chains of gold upon *Darius,* Curt. l. 5. cap. 12. Finally, that Roman, who being saved from proscription was carried about for a shew in a ludicrous manner, had reason thus to reproach his benefactor, and to say, "He owed him no obligation for saving him, to make game and a show of him." Seneca of benefits, 2. 11.

SECTION CCXXVII

The obligation to gratitude.

Love to benefactors is called *a grateful mind* or *gratitude;* wherefore, seeing one is obliged to love him from whom he hath received favours, the consequence is, that every one is obliged to shew gratude in every respect: yet this duty is imperfect, and therefore one cannot be compelled to perform it; an ungrateful person cannot be sued for his ingratitude in human courts, unless the laws of the state have expressly allowed such an *action.* Some such thing we have an example of in Xenophon's institution of Cyrus, 1. 2. 7. p. 9. Edit. Oxon.*² <164>

SECTION CCXXVIII

The rules relating to it.

Seeing gratitude is love to a benefactor (§227), it follows, that one is obliged to delight in the perfection and happiness of his benefactor; to commend and extol his beneficence by words, and to make suitable returns to his benefits; not always indeed the same, or equal, but to the utmost of his power; but if the ability be wanting, a grateful disposition is highly laudable.

SECTION CCXXIX

The obligation to the other.

In fine, since we are obliged, even to our own detriment, and without any hope of restitution or retribution, to do good to others (§221), the

* Ingratitude is commonly distinguished into *simple,* of which he is guilty who does not do good to his benefactor to his utmost power: and *pregnant,* of which he is guilty who injures his benefactor. The former, Pufendorff of the law of nature and nations, 3. 3. 17, says, a man cannot be sued for at the civil bar; but mixed ingratitude he thinks not unworthy of civil punishment. But if we may say the truth, in this case the ungrateful person is not animadverted upon as such, but as having done an injury; and he is liable to punishment who does an injury even to a person from whom he never received any favours. However, we readily grant, that an injury is much more attrocious, when it is joined with that basest of vices, ingratitude. And therefore they are justly reckoned more wicked who are injurious to parents, instructors, patrons, than those who only wrong strangers, to whom they are under no special ties.

2. The edition used here presumably is Xenophon, *De Cyri institutione libri octo,* ed. Hutchinson.

consequence is, that we ought much less to refuse favours to any one which he desires with the promise of restitution or retribution; and therefore every one is obliged to render to another what we called above *officiousness* (§222), provided this readiness to help others be not manifestly detrimental to ourselves (§93).

REMARKS on This Chapter

It is not improper to subjoin the few following observations upon our Author's reasoning in this chapter.

1. When duty is defined to be something enjoined by the divine will under a sanction, duties cannot be distinguished into *perfect* and *imperfect* in any other sense but this: "That some precepts of God give a right to all mankind to exact certain offices or duties from every one. But other precepts do not give any such right." Thus the precept of God not to hurt any one, but to render to every one his due, gives every one a right to exact his due, and to repel injuries. But the precept to be generous and bountiful, gives no man a right to exact acts of generosity and bounty, tho' it lays every man under an obligation to be generous and bountiful, to the utmost of his power. So that he who sins against the former is more criminal, or is guilty of <165> a higher crime than he who does not act conformably to the other. This is the only sense in which duties can be called, some *perfect,* and others *imperfect,* when duty is considered, with our Author, as an obligation arising from the divine will commanding or forbidding. For all such obligation is equally perfect, equally full. The distinction takes its rise from the consideration of what crimes do, and what crimes do not admit of a civil action, consistently with the good order of society; and it is brought from the civil law into the law of nature. But it would, in my opinion, be liable to less ambiguity in treating of the law of nature, instead of dividing duties into those of *perfect* and those of *imperfect* obligation, to divide them into greater or lesser duties, *i.e.* duties, the transgression of which is a greater crime, and duties the omission of which is a lesser crime: or, in other words, duties the performance of which may be lawfully exacted, nay compelled; and duties the performance of which cannot be compelled or even exacted. But our Author's terms mean the same thing, and cannot, if his definitions be attended to, create any

ambiguity. However, we may see from his reasoning in this chapter, the necessity (as we observed in our preceeding remarks) of having recourse to internal obligation (as our Author calls it) or the intrinsic goodness and pravity of actions, in deducing and demonstrating human duties.

2. Since our Author's reasoning wholly turns upon the reasonableness of this maxim, "Do as you would be done by; and do not to another what you would not have done by any one to you in like circumstances." Perhaps some may have expected from him demonstration of the reasonableness of this maxim. Now this truth, which is indeed as self-evident as any axiom in any science, as for instance, "That two things equal to some common third thing, are equal to one another": and which therefore, it is as hard to reason about as it is to demonstrate any axiom, for the very same reason, viz. that it does not in the nature of the thing require or stand in need of any reasoning to prove it: This truth may however be illustrated several ways, in order to make one feel its evidence and reasonableness. As with Pufendorff, law of nature, &c. B. 3. cap. 2. §4.[3] thus: "It as much implies a contradiction to determine differently in my own case and another's, when they are precisely parallel, as to make contrary judgments on things really the same. Since then every man is well acquainted with his own nature, and as well, at least, as to general inclinations, with the nature of other men, it follows, that he who concludes one way as to his own right, and another way as to the same right of his neighbour, is guilty of a contradiction in the plainest matter: an argument of a mind unsound in no ordinary degree. For no good reason can be given, why what I esteem just for myself, I should reckon unjust for another in the same circumstances. Those therefore are most properly sociable creatures who grant the same privilege to others which they desire should be allowed themselves; <166> and those, on the other hand, are most unfit for society, who imagining themselves a degree above vulgar mortals, would have a particular commission to do whatever they please." He observes in another place, B. 2. c. 3. §13. "For the easy knowledge of what the law of nature dictates, *Hobbes himself commends the use of this rule* (De civ.

3. The translations here are those of Basil Kennet (see Pufendorf, *Of the Law of Nature and Nations*).

c. 3. §26.)[4] *when a man doubts whether what he is going to do to another be agreeable to the law of nature, let him suppose himself in the other's room.* For by this means, when self-love, and the other passions which weighed down one scale, are taken thence and put into the contrary scale, 'tis easy to guess which way the balance will turn." He afterwards shews us it was a precept of Confucius, and of Ynca Manco Capace, the founder of the Peruvian empire, as well as of our Saviour. And in answer to Dr. Sharrock, who is of opinion (De off. ch. 2. n. 2.)[5] "That this rule is not universal, because if so, a judge must needs absolve the criminals left to his sentence, in as much as he would certainly spare his own life, were he in their place; and I must needs give a poor petitioner what sum soever he desires, because I should wish to be thus dealt with, if I was in his condition, &c." He replies, "The rule will still remain unshaken, if we observe, that not one scale only, but both are to be observed; or that I am not only to weigh and consider what is agreeable to me, but likewise what obligation or necessity lies on the other person, and what I can demand of him without injuring either of our duties." Thus Pufendorff reasons about this principle. But both he and our Author seem to consider it not as a fundamental or primary principle of the law of nature, but rather as a Corollary of that law, which obliges us, *To hold all men equal with ourselves.* But it cannot be so properly said to be a Corollary from that principle, as to be the principle itself in other words. For what is the meaning of this rule, *To hold all men equal with ourselves,* but to hold ourselves obliged to treat all men as we think they are obliged to treat us? The equality of mankind means equality of obligation common to all mankind, with regard to their conduct one towards another. Now, if any one seeks a proof of the reasonableness of holding all men equal in this sense, that it is reasonable for us to do to others what it is reasonable for them to do, or for us to expect they should do to us in like circumstances; if any one, I say, should seek a proof of this maxim, he really seeks a proof to shew, that like judgments ought to be given of like cases, *i.e.* that like cases

4. See Hobbes, *On the Citizen* (*De cive*), 3.26: "All these natural precepts are derived from just one dictate of reason, that presses on us our own preservation and security. . . . This rule is not only easy; it has long been famous in the words: *Do not do to another what you would not have done to you.*"

5. Sharrock, Ὑπόθεσις ἐθική *de officiis secundum naturae jus.*

are like cases;—and if, owning the truth of the proposition, he asks why it ought to be a rule of action, does he not ask a reason why a reasonable rule should be admitted as a reasonable rule; or why reason is reason, as we had occasion to observe in another remark?

3. But in the third place, that we are made for benevolence because we have benevolent affections, and our principal happiness consists in the exercise of the social affections, or the social <167> virtues; and our greatest and best security for all outward enjoyments, and for having and possessing the love of others, is by being benevolent;—that upon these and many other accounts, we are made and intended for benevolence, is as evident as that a clock is made to measure time, and in consequence of the same way of reasoning, viz. the way we reason about any constitution, or any final cause. We see what sad shifts they are reduced to, who would explain away into certain selfish subtle reflexions, all that has the appearance of social, kindly and generous in our frame; and the perplexity and subtlety of such philosophy is the same argument against it, which is reckoned a very good one against complicated, perplexing hypotheses in natural philosophy, compared with more simple ones. (See some excellent observations on Hobbes's account of pity in Dr. Butler's excellent sermon on compassion, in a marginal note.)[6] Who feels not that we are naturally disposed to benevolence, and what is the way in which our natural benevolence operates, and so points us to the proper exercises of it, while Cicero thus describes it: "There is nothing," says he, "so natural, and at the same time so illustrious, and of so great compass, as the conjunction and society of men, including a mutual communication of conveniencies, and general love for mankind. This dearness begins immediately upon one's birth, when the child is most affectionately beloved by the parent; from the family, it by degrees steals abroad into affinities, friendships, neighbourhoods; then amongst members of the same state; and amongst states themselves, united in interests and confederacies; and at length stretcheth itself to the whole human race. In the exercise of all these duties, we are farther disposed to observe what every man hath most need of, and what with our help he may, what without our help he cannot attain; so that in some cases the tye of relation must yield to

6. Butler, *Fifteen Sermons,* p. 81.

the point of time; and some offices there are which we would rather pay to one relation than to another. Thus you ought sooner to help a neighbour with his harvest, than either brother or a familiar acquaintance; but, on the other side, in a suit at law, you ought to defend your brother or your friend before your neighbour, &c." Cicero de fin. l. 5. c. 23. Who feels not that this is the language of nature; that thus our affections work; that thus nature moves, prompts and points us to work? And who can consider this natural tendency or course of our affections without perceiving by his reason, the advantage, the usefulness of this their natural tendency, with regard to ourselves and others equally; and consequently the fitness of our taking care that they should always continue to operate according to this rule, according to this their natural tendency? Or who does not feel that indeed this is the true account of human happiness, the happiness nature intended for us, our best and noblest happiness? <168>

> Happier as kinder! in whate'er degree,
> And heighth of bliss but heighth of charity.
> Essay on Man, Ep. 4.[7]

But if nature points out this course, this regular course of our affections; if it is felt to be the state of mind that alone affords true happiness; and if the general happiness of mankind plainly requires this direction and course of our affections: If, in one word, nature dictates it, and reason must approve of it in every view we can take of it, in what sense can it be denied to be our natural duty and the will of our Creator? And is it any wonder, that this rule of conduct hath been known to thinking men in all ages (as we cannot look into ancient authors without clearly seeing it hath been) since every heart dictates it to itself? This rule, "Do as you would be done by,"[8] is a rule of easy application, and it is universal, or it gives an easy, ready and clear solution in all cases. This appears from our Author's preceding and following applications of it to cases: for it is from it alone he reasons

7. Pope, *Essay on Man,* epistle 4, l. 360–61.
8. This is the so-called "golden rule" to which Turnbull referred above in the quotation from Pufendorf citing Hobbes. For the golden rule see Matthew 7:12 and Luke 6:31, as well as Kant's criticism in his *Groundwork of the Metaphysics of Morals,* in I. Kant, *Practical Philosophy,* ed. Gregor, 80f.

throughout all his deductions of duties. And that it is an equal, just, or reasonable rule, cannot be denied without asserting this absurdity, That what is true and just in one case, is not always and universally true and just in all similar cases. Again, that we are made to love mankind, and to live in the exercise of love and benevolence, is plain from our make and frame, and the intention of our Maker thereby discovered to us, according to all the received rules of reasoning about final causes. And therefore the principles upon which our Author builds, are in every view of them beyond all dispute. He now proceeds to enquiries of a more complex nature; but he still continues to argue from the same self-evident truths.

Concerning our hypothetical duties towards others, and the original acquisition of dominion or property.

SECTION CCXXX

What hath hitherto been explained, belongs partly to the *love of justice,* and partly to that which we call the *love of humanity and beneficence* (§84). From the latter we have deduced our imperfect duties in the preceding chapter; from the former our perfect ones are clearly deducible, which we said, consist in not injuring any person (and <169> this we call an *absolute duty*), and in rendering to every one his due (which we call an *hypothetical duty*). Now, having treated of *absolute duty* in the seventh chapter, we are now to consider our *hypothetical duties* with the same care and accuracy. The connection.

SECTION CCXXXI

That is properly called one's *own* which is in his *dominion.* By *dominion* we mean the right or faculty of excluding all others from the use of a thing.* The actual detension of a thing, by which we exclude others from the use of it, is called *possession.* Again, we claim a right to ourselves either of excluding all others from the use of a thing, or of excluding all others, What is meant by our own, by dominion, by possession, by property, by community.

---

* That dominion consists solely in the faculty of excluding others from the use of a thing, is obvious. For all the other effects of dominion, which are usually enua few only excepted. In the former case, the thing is said to be in *property;* in the other case, it is said to be in *positive communion,* which is either *equal,* when all have an equal right to the common thing; or *unequal,* when one has more, or a greater right than another to that thing. And it again is either *perfect,* when every one has a perfect right to the common thing, or *imperfect,* when none hath a perfect right to it, as in the case of the soldiers of an army, to whom a certain reward in money is appointed by the prince. But if neither one, nor many have right or design to exclude from a thing not yet taken possession of, that thing is said to be in *negative communion;* and this communion alone is opposite to dominion, because in that case the thing is yet under the dominion of no person. <170>

SECTION CCXXXII

The right of man to created things.

Now since reason plainly discovers that men were created by God (127), it is manifest that our Creator must will that we exist. But he who wills the end, must be judged to will the means likewise. And therefore God

-----

merated in the definition of it, may be separated from it, and yet one may remain master or owner of it, or have it in his dominion. Thus, e.g. we may observe, that the right or faculty of receiving all the profits of a thing by usufruct, is separated from propriety, while the dominion remains entire: and it is known, that the faculty of disposing of a thing does not belong to minors, whom none however will deny to have dominion. Whence Seneca of benefits, 7. 12. says, "It is not a proof that a thing is not yours, that you cannot sell it, waste it, &c. For even that is yours, which is yours under certain limitations and conditions." In fine, we find the faculty taken away in certain countries from the owner, of vindicating to himself from a third possessor, a thing lent or deposited, where the law takes place, *Hand muss hand wah-ren.* Since therefore that only ought to enter into the definition of a thing, which so belongs to its essence that it cannot be absent, but the faculty of excluding others from the use of a thing being taken away, one immediately ceases to have any dominion, it cannot be doubted but this alone completes the definition of dominion. And this I take to be Arrian's definition, when he says, one who hath dominion is, "τὸν τῶν ὑπ᾽ ἄλλων σπουδαζομένων ἢ ἐκκλινομένων ἔχοντα ἐξουσίαν, He who hath those things which others desire or fly from in his power." [[See Epictetus, *The Discourses as Reported by Arrian,* vol. 1, bk. 2, chap. 2, p. 231.]]

must have willed that men should enjoy all things necessary to the preservation of their being which this earth produces. Further, God having given evident signs of his particular love to man, by having made him a most excellent creature, it cannot be doubted that he desires and delights in our perfection and happiness (§80). And by consequence he must will that we should enjoy even all things which can conduce to render our life more perfect, more satisfactory, more happy, provided we do not abuse them (§90).* <171>

* It hath been called into question by some, whether man hath a right to the use of the brutes for the preservation of his life, which cannot be killed without their feeling pain? nay some have denied it, because they thought it an injury to the brutes, and not use but abuse of them, to kill them in order to feed upon them, especially since men may sustain their lives without such bloody revelling. Others add, that eating flesh is not wholesome, and renders men cruel and savage. This argument was first urged, we know, by Pythagoras, and afterwards by Porphyry in his books περὶ ἀποχῆς. See Scheffer de Philosoph. Italica, cap. 14. [[Porphyrios (234–ca. 305), scholar and philosopher. The work Περὶ ἀποχῆς ("On abstinence") is a treatise on vegetarianism. See Scheffer, De natura et constitutione philosophiae italica.]] But in the first place, this whole hypothesis about injury done to brutes, is founded on another erroneous opinion of the transmigration of souls, or of their having souls in common with us, and therefore a common right with us (κοινῷ δικαιῷ ψυχῆς) as it is called by Pythagoras in Diogenes Laertius, 8. 13. in explaining which Empidocles says in the same author,

> Nam, memini, fueram quondam puer, atque puella,
> Plantaque, & ignitus piscis, pernixque volucris.

[[Diogenes Laertius 8.12, "Empedocles" (Lives of Eminent Philosophers): "For, I remember, I was a boy once, and a girl, and a plant, and a fiery fish, and a swift bird."]]

Add. Iamblichus's life of Pythagoras, 24. 108. and Porphyry's life of Pythagoras, p. 188. But it is false that there is any communion of right between us and the brutes (§90). And hence it is false, that an injury is done to the brutes. We are not therefore to abstain from things because we can be without them; for God not only wills that we exist, but that we live agreeably; and that use is not abuse, which is not contrary to the will of God. In fine, that unwholesomeness which they alledge, is not sufficiently proved, and most probably, it arises not from the moderate eating of flesh, but gluttony, and the abuse of created things, which we also condemn.

SECTION CCXXXIII

Originally all things were in a state of negative communion.

Since God then hath given to man for his use and enjoyment all things conducive to render his life agreeable (§232), he undoubtedly wills that none should be excluded from any use of these things; and therefore, according to the intention of God in the beginning of things, all things were in a state of negative communion, and so were in the dominion of none (§231).* <172>

SECTION CCXXXIV

But it was lawful to depart from this state, necessity so urging.

Whatever God willed, he willed for the most wise reasons, and therefore it ought not to be altered by men but in case of great necessity. But since all the divine affirmative laws, such as this is, "That all things should be in common for the common use of all mankind," admit of exception in case of necessity (§159); and by necessity here is to be understood not only extreme necessity, but even such as makes it impossible to live conveniently and agreeably (§158 & 232); the consequence is, that men might, necessity so urging them, lawfully depart from that negative communion, and introduce dominion, which is opposite (§231) to negative communion.

---

* And thus not only the sacred records, Genesis 1. 28, 29. but even the ancient poets describe the primaeval state of mankind, which they have celebrated under the name of the golden age; for then, as Virgil says, Georg. 1. v. 125.

> *Nulli subigebant arva coloni,*
> *Nec signare quidem, aut partiri limite campum*
> *Fas erat: in medium quaerebant: ipsaque tellus*
> *Omnia liberius, nullo poscente, ferebat.*

[[Virgil, *Georgics* 1.125–28, in vol. 1 of *Virgil:* "[N]o tiller subdued the land. Even to mark the field or divide it with bounds was unlawful. Men made gain for the common store, and Earth yielded all, of herself, more freely, when none begged for her gifts."]]

They deny then, that there was at that time any divisions of land into different properties marked by boundaries, but assert that all things were in common, and so left to the use of all mankind, that none could be excluded from the use of them.

SECTION CCXXXV

Now it is very evident, that if mankind had been confined to a small number, there would have been no need of any change with regard to the primeval negative community of things, because the fertility of nature would have sufficed to render the lives of all, if not agreeable, at least commodious or tolerable. But so soon as mankind was spread over the whole earth, and dispersed into innumerable families, some things began not to be sufficient to the uses of all, whereas other things <173> continuing to be, because of their vast plenty, sufficient for all; necessity itself obliged men to introduce dominion with regard to the things which were not sufficient for the uses of all (§234), leaving those things only in their original negative community which are of inexhaustible use, or which are not requisite to the preservation and agreeableness of life.*

What necessity urged men to introduce dominion.

SECTION CCXXXVI

Dominion therefore was introduced, and negative community was abolished by necessity itself. But that this institution of mankind is injurious to none is manifest, because in negative communion none has a right to exclude another from the use of things (§231); and therefore it must be

This institution is not unjust.

---

* And hence the lawyers have pronounced such things common by the law of nature, §1. Inst. de rerum divis. and that not, "as those public things which are the patrimony of a whole people, but as for those things which are originally a present of nature, and have never passed into the dominion of any person," as Neratius says, l. 14. pr. D. de adqu. rerum dom. [[Lucius Neratius Priscus was an eminent Roman jurist in the late first and early second centuries.]] The best and most beautiful of things, on account of their abundance, have always remained in the primeval negative communion. Hence Petronius Satyr. c. 6. says, "What is common, that is in its nature most excellent? The sun shines to all; the moon, attended with numberless stars, even guides the wild beasts to their food. What is more beautiful than water? and it is for common use." [[Petronius Arbiter, *Satyricon,* trans. Heseltine, in *Petronius and the Apocolocyntosis of Seneca.* The poet Petronius (d. 66) was held in high esteem by Nero. See Sullivan, *The Satyricon of Petronius.*]] Neither does any one affect dominion over flies, mice, worms, and other things, which are either hurtful, or of no benefit to mankind.

lawful to any one so to appropriate to himself any thing belonging to none, that he could not afterwards be forced by any person to yield him the use of it, but might detain it to himself, and set it aside for his own use.* <174>

SECTION CCXXXVII

After that things are either positively common or in property.

When men, obliged by necessity to it, have introduced dominion (§235), this must consist either in positive communion, or in property (§231). Wherefore, from the moment men depart from negative communion, all things are either positively common to many, or they begin to be proper to particulars; and community arises from the resolution of many to possess the same thing undivided in common, and to exclude all others from the use of it.† But property takes its rise either from immediate occupancy and possession at first of a thing belonging to none, or from an after-deed, in consequence of a division or cession of things positively common. <175>

* For what none hath a right or intention to exclude me from the use of, that belongs to none. But a thing ceases to be none's, so soon as I apply it to my uses, and I have resolved to make use of my right granted to me by God (§232); because since he hurts and injures me, who endeavours to render me more imperfect or unhappy, (§178), he certainly injures me, who endeavours to deprive me of what I have taken to myself for the sake of my preservation, and living agreeably. The same happens in this case, that Arrian. dissert. Epict. 2. 4. says of the theatre, tho' it be positively common. "Is not the theatre common to all the citizens? But if one takes a place in it, turn him out of it if you can." And Seneca of benefits, 7. 12. "I have truly a place among the Equestrian order; but when I come into the theatre, if these places be full, I have a right to a place there, because I may sit there; and I have no right to a place there, because all the places are possessed by those with whom I have my right in common."

† This, no doubt, was done at first immediately, when families and tribes began to separate and disperse into different parts of the world. For then each family took possession of some region for itself in common, and without division for a while, till necessity urging, they divided the common possession, or by compact gave the liberty to each particular of occupying as much as he wanted. The antients mention several nations which in the beginning possessed whole provinces in common without division, as the Aborigenes in Justin, 43. the Scythians and Getar. in Horace, Carm. 3. 4. the Germans in Tacitus, c. 26. the inhabitants of the island Lipara, the Panchaeans and Vaccaeans, Diodorus Siculus, Biblioth. v. 9 & 45.

SECTION CCXXXVIII

Truly, if such were the happiness of mankind, that all were equally virtuous, we would neither stand in need of dominion, nor of any compacts, because even those who had nothing in possession, would want nothing necessary to their comfortable subsistence. For in that case every man would love another as himself, and would cheerfully render to every one whatever he could reasonably desire to be done by others to him. And what use would there be for dominion among such friends having all in common? But since, in the present state of mankind, it cannot be expected that any multitude of men should be all such lovers of virtue, as to study the happiness of others as much as their own; hence it is evident, that positive communion is not suitable to the condition of mankind, as they now are, and therefore that they had very good and justifiable reasons for departing from it likewise.* <176>

Why it was necessary to depart from positive community.

---

* Whoever mentions the being of such a communion any where among mankind, represents at the same time these men as extremely virtuous. This there is reason to say of the church of Jerusalem, Acts iv. 32. Nor did the poets think what they say of the community among mankind in the golden age could have been credited, if they had not also represented them as most studious of virtue; who, as Ovid says, Metam. l. v. 90.

> *vindice nullo,*
> *Sponte sua, sine lege, fidem rectumque colebant.*

[[Ovid, *Metamorphoses* 1.90: "[The Golden Age] with no one to compel, without a law, of its own will, kept faith and did the right."]]

The Scythians beyond the Maeotis, among whom Scymnus Chius [[ancient Greek author of a description of the earth]] tells us this community obtained, are said by him to have been τους σφόδρα, ἐυσεβεστάτους, a most pious race. Iamblichus in his life of Pythagoras, §167, tells us, that Pythagoras derived his community of things from justice as its source: But virtue, justice and piety becoming rare and languid amongst men, that this communion could not take place or subsist, is manifest.

SECTION CCXXXIX

What are the
original ways
of acquiring
dominion or
property?

And hence also it is conspicuous how property was introduced, and what are the ways of acquiring property in a thing. For a thing is either still without dominion, or it is in the dominion of some person or persons. Now, in the former case we call the *original* ways of acquiring property with Grotius, those by which we acquire either the very substance of a thing yet belonging to none, or the accretions which may any how be added or accede to it. The first of which is called *occupancy;* the latter *accession.*

SECTION CCXL

What are the
derivative
ways?

But if a thing be already in any one's dominion, then it is either in the property of many, or of a particular (§231). In the first case, things in common are appropriated by *division* or *cession;* in the latter by *tradition.* Nor is there any other *derivative* way of acquiring dominion, which may not be most conveniently reduced to one or other of these sorts.

SECTION CCXLI

What occu-
pancy is, and
what a thing
belonging to
none?

Occupancy is taking possession of a thing belonging to none. A thing is said to belong to *none,* which none ever had a right to exclude others from the use of, or when the right of none to exclude others from it, is evidently certain, or when the right of excluding others from the use of it is abdicated by the possessor himself freely; in which last case, a thing is held *for derelinquished.* But seeing none has a right to exclude others from the use of things which belong to none (§231), the consequence is, that things belonging to none, fall <177> to the share and right of the first occupants. Nor can this be understood to extend to things that are lost, carried off by fraud or force, cast over board in imminent danger of shipwreck, or taken away by brute animals; for in no sense are such things belonging to none, since they had owners, and these owners never abdicated their right and dominion.*

* Therefore the fisher Gripus philosophizes very soundly in Plautus, Rud. 4. 3.

SECTION CCXLII

Occupancy being taking possession of a thing belonging to none (§241), and possession being detention of a thing, from the use of which we have determined to exclude others (§231), it is plain that occupancy is made by mind and body at once, and that intention alone is not sufficient to occupancy, if another has a mind to use his right; nor mere taking possession of a thing, without intention to exclude others from the use of it; but by the tacite consent of mankind the declaration of <178> intention to appropriate a thing to one's self, joined with certain sensible signs, is held for occupancy.*

Occupancy is made by mind and body at once.

---

v. 32. concerning the fish he himself had caught in the sea, when he pleads they were his own, because none could justly exclude him from the use of them:

> *Ecquem esse dices mari piscem meum?*
> *Quos quum capio, siquidem cepi, mei sunt: habeo pro meis:*
> *Nec manu adseruntur, neque illic partem quisquam postulat.*
> *In foro palam omnes vendo pro meis venalibus.*

[[Plautus, *The Rope*, lines 971–74, in vol. 4 of *Plautus:* "Gripus: Would you call any fish mine while it's still in the sea? When I catch them, supposing I do, then they are mine; I have them for my own, and no one lays claim to them or expects any part of them. And I sell them all in the public market as my wares."]]

But he gives a very bad reason, when he claims to himself a purse, which being lost by shipwreck, he had brought out of the sea in his net:

> *In manu non est mea,*
> *Ubi demisi rete atque hamum, quidquid haesit, extraho.*
> *Meum, quod rete atque hami nacti sunt, meum potissimum est.*

[[Ibid., lines 983–85: "It's a thing I can't control. When I let down my net and hook, I pull up whatever's stuck to 'em. Anything my net and hook gets hold of is mine, yes, sir, mine."]]

For to this Trachalio answers very right, v. 42.

> *Quid ais, impudens,*
> *Ausus etiam, comparare vidulum cum piscibus?*
> *Eadem tandem res videtur?*

[[Ibid., lines 981–83: "How's that, you cheeky rascal? So you've got the cheek to compare trunks with fish, eh? Really now, does it seem the same to you?"]]

* Thus one is reckoned to have taken possession of a field, tho' he hath not walked round every spot of it, l. 3. §1. l. 48. D. & l. 2. C. de adqu. vel amitt. possess. if he

SECTION CCXLIII

And either in the lump, or by parts.

Moreover, since every thing may be occupied which is none's possession (§241), it will therefore be the same thing whether whole tracts of land unpossessed be occupied by many in lump, or whether particular parts be occupied by particular persons. The former, Grotius of the rights of war and peace, calls occupying *per universitatem,* by the whole; and the latter, occupying by parcels, (*per fundos*). But because he who takes possession of the whole, is judged to take possession of every part, hence it follows, that when any number of men, as a people in an united body, seize on some desolate tract of land by the whole, nothing becomes proper to any particular person, but all contained in that region, if particular parts be not <179> taken possession of by particulars, belongs to the whole body, or to their sovereign.*

---

hath testified by some sign, such as cutting a branch from the tree, &c. to those present, his intention of appropriating that field to himself. But since these signs have their effect by tacite convention, they are not arbitrary; and therefore, he who threw his spear into a city deserted by its inhabitants, seems no more to be the occupant of that city than a hunter is of a wild beast, which, having flung his spear at it, he neither kills nor wounds. And hence may be decided the famous controversy between the people of Andros and Chalcis, about their right of occupancy with respect to the city of Acanthos, the former pleading that their spy seeing himself outrun by the Chalchidian spy, threw the spear which he had in his hand at the city gate, which stuck there; the other denying that cities could be occupied in this manner by throwing spears, and asserting their right to the city, because their spy had first entred into it. The story is related by Plutarch, Quaest. Graec. 30. [[See Plutarch, *The Greek Questions of Plutarch,* 139.]]

* Hence, in a tract of land, particulars may appropriate each to himself a particular part, and yet the whole territory may belong to the people, or the united body. Dio Chrysostom in Rhodiaca 31. "The territory is the state's, yet every possessor is master of his own portion." [[Dio Chrysostom (ca. A.D. 40/50–after 110), Greek orator and popular philosopher. See "The Thirty-first Discourse: To the People of Rhodes," in *Dio Chrysostom,* vol. 3, p. 51.]]

SECTION CCXLIV

None therefore can deny that *hunting, fishing, fowling,* are species of occupancy, not only in desart places unpossessed, but likewise in territories already occupied, since such is the abundance of wild beasts, fish, and winged creatures, that there is enough of them for all men (§235); yet, if there be any good or just reason* for it, a people may, without injury, claim to themselves all such animals as are not under dominion (§243) or assign them to their sovereign as his *special right;* and that being done, it becomes contrary to the law of justice for any one rashly to arrogate to himself the right of hunting already acquired by another.

Whether wild beasts, fishes, birds, be things belonging to none.

SECTION CCXLV

But wherever the right of hunting is promiscuous, reason plainly teaches that this right does not extend to tame animals, because they are in domi-<180>nion, nor to creatures tamed by the care of men, while one possesses them, or pursues them with an intention to recover them, or hath not by clear signs manifested his design to relinquish them:† nay, that it

What animals may be hunted.

* Many such reasons, tho' not very proper ones, are accumulated by Pufendorff, of the law of nature, *&c.* 4. 6. 6. The one of greatest moment is, that wild beasts, fish and fowls, are not every where in such exhaustless abundance that the destruction of the whole species may not be feared, if the right of hunting be promiscuously given to all (§235), whence we may see why men are nowhere forbid to hunt and kill savage beasts, which are hurtful to mankind; nay, in some countries, rewards are offered to those who can, by bringing their heads, skins, or talons to the magistrate, prove he hath cleared the province from such pests.

† Thus he will hardly be excusable, by a pretended right of hunting, who seizes a stag with bells about his neck, tho' wandering, if his owner be known: Nor is he to be defended, who keeps the master of a bee-hive, who is pursuing his bees, out of his court, that he may take possession of them himself; tho' that seemed not unjust to the Roman lawyers, §14. Inst. de rerum divisione. For tho' a master have the right to exclude others from the use of his own, yet he who enters our house to recover his own, does not use ours, but reclaims his own. And how can it be more just to keep a person out of our court who is pursuing his bees, than to drive a neighbour away from our house who comes to reclaim his hens which had flown into our court? Wherefore that law of Plato was much more equal, de legibus, l. 8. "If any person

does not extend to wild beasts inclosed in a park, to a fish-pond, a warren, a bee-hive, &c. but to those which, as *Caius* elegantly expresses it, l. 1. §1. de adqu. dom. *Terra, mari, caelo capiuntur,* are caught in the sea, air, or land.

SECTION CCXLVI

When animals fall to the share of those who take them.

Moreover, since besides the intention of excluding others from the use of a thing, corporal possession is required to occupancy (§242); the consequence is, that it is not enough to wound a wild beast, much less is it sufficient to have a mind to seize one that shall fall by its wound; but it is requisite either that it be taken alive or dead by the hunters dogs, nets, or other instruments; for if neither of these be done, any one has a right to seize and kill a creature, tho' wounded by another, because it is not yet made property.* <181>

SECTION CCXLVII

Whether occupancy by war be of this kind?

Another species of occupancy is called *occupancy by war,* by which it is asserted, that persons, as well as things, taken in lawful war, become the taker's by the law of nations, l. 1. §1. D. de adqu. vel amitt. poss. But because occupancy can only take place in things possessed by none (§241), and things belonging to an enemy can only be by fiction,† and

---

follows his bees, and another by moving the air invites them into his ground, let him repair the damage." [[Plato, *The Laws of Plato,* 843e.]]

* But there hath always been a great diversity of opinions about this matter; and hence it is, that the laws of countries are so different about it. See the different judgments of Trebatius and other Roman lawyers on this head, l. 5. D. de adqu. rerum dom. The Salic law, tit. 35. §4. does not permit a wild beast that was so much as but raised by another's dogs to be intercepted by any one. The Langobard law, l. 1. tit. 22. §4. & 6. adjudges to the seizer the shoulder with seven ribs, and the rest to the wounder. These, and other such like laws among the ancients are collected by Pufendorff of the law, &c. 4. 6. 10.

† Pufendorff, of the law of nature, &c. 4. 6. 14. thus explains this fiction: "By a state of war, as all other peaceful rights are interrupted, so dominion thus far loses its effect with regard to the adverse party, as that we are no longer under obligation to abstain from their possessions, than the rules of humanity and mercy advise us.

free persons cannot so much as by fiction be deemed to belong to none; it follows, that occupancy by war does not belong neither to the original ways of acquiring, nor to occupancy, but must be derived from another source, even from the right of war itself. <182>

SECTION CCXLVIII

To occupancy *finding* is properly referred, since it consists in taking hold   Of finding.
of a thing belonging to none; and there is no doubt that a thing not yet possessed, or left by its possessor, falls to the finder, who first seizes it with an intention of making it his own; wherefore the law of the Stagiritae, Biblienses and Athenians, is contrary to the law of nature: "ἃ μὴ ἔσθου, μὴ ἀνέλῃ." "What you did not place, do not take up," unless it be only understood of things lost; Aelian. Hist. Var. 3. 45. 4. 1. Diog. Laert. 1. 57. Nor do they less err, who adjudge a thing found in common to the finder, and him who saw it taken up.* But this right ought not to be extended to things which a people possess themselves of by the right

---

In war, therefore, the goods of one party, in respect of the other, are rendered, as it were, void of dominion. Not that men do by the right of war cease to be proprietors of what was before their own; but because their propriety is no bar against the enemy's claim, who may seize and carry away all for his own use." But when things are rendered void of dominion, none has a right to exclude others from the use of them (§231); now, an enemy always preserves his right of excluding an enemy from the use of his things; nor does he any injury to any one, while he fights for his own with all his might. Who then will call such things, things void of dominion? which if it be so, an enemy does not lose the things taken by his adverse party, because he has not the right of excluding an enemy, but for want of sufficient force to repel his enemy.

* It was an ancient custom to demand in common what was found, and it was done by a *formula* called, *in commune,* or among the Greeks κοινὸς Ἑρμῆς, or κοινὸν τῷ Ἑρμῇ, of which *formula* see Erasmus in adagiis [[Desiderius Erasmus (1469–1536), famous humanist scholar. Heineccius refers to Erasmus's *Proverbs,* or *Adages* II. i. 85 (Erasmus, *Adages,* vol. 33 of *Collected Works*).]]: Many things are noted with relation to it by the learned upon Phaedrus Fab. 5. 6. v. 3. See likewise Plautus Rudent. 4. 3. v. 72. But since things in the possession of none fall to the most early occupant (§241), and none has a right to exclude another from the use of such things (§231); and he, in fine, who only seized a thing with his eyes, but does not take hold of it, cannot be said to occupy (§242), it is evident that such a one has no right to demand any share of what is found, unless the civil laws of a country or custom permits it.

of occupancy made by an united body in whole, or hath ceded to their sovereign as a special privilege, which may be lawfully done, as we have already observed (§243). <183>

SECTION CCXLIX

And things abandoned, as treasures.

Nor is it less manifest that things belong to the finder which are abandoned by one of a sound mind, and master of his actions, with intention to abdicate them; and therefore scattered gifts, nay, even treasures, whose former owners cannot be certainly known, which are found by accident, unless the people or their sovereign claim them to themselves (§243). About which matter various laws of nations are quoted by Grotius of the rights of war and peace, 2. 8. 7. Pufendorff 6. 13.[1] and Hertius in his notes upon these sections; Ev. Otto upon the institutes, §29. inst. de rer. divis.[2] Yet regard ought to be had to the proprietor of the ground, as having a right to all the profits of it of every sort.* And therefore the emperor Hadrian, justly, and conformably to the laws of natural equity, adjudged one half of a thing found to the finder, and the other to the proprietor of the ground where it was found. Spartian in Hadriano,[3] c. 18. §39. inst. de rerum divisione.

---

* This is so true, that some nations thought the finder was to be preferred, as the Hebrews, Mat. xiii. 44. Selden de jure nat. & gent. See Hebr. vi. 4. the Syrians, the Greeks, and not a few among the Romans. (See Philostrat. vita Apoll. Tyan. 2. 39. de vita Sophist. 2. 2. Plautus Trinum. 1. 2. v. 141. l. 67. [[Philostratus, *Philostratorum quae supersunt omnia;* Plautus, *Three Bob Day,* lines 172–80, in vol. 5 of *Plautus.*]] Dig. de rei vind. Where a part is granted to the finder, there seems to be no distinction between one hired to dig our ground, and one not hired. For tho' hired workers acquire to us by their hired labour, yet that does not seem a just reason for a distinction, if one hires himself not to search for treasures, but to dig a pit, or for any other like work. See Corn. van Bynkersh. observ. 2. 4. [[Cornelius van Bynkershoek (1673–1743), Dutch jurist. Heineccius refers to Bynkershoek's *Observationum iuris Romani,* which first appeared in 1710.]]

1. Pufendorf, *Acht Bücher vom Natur- und Völkerrecht.*
2. Otto, *Ad fl. Iustiniani PP. aug. Institutionum commentarius.*
3. Presumably a reference to Boxhorn's *Historiae Augustae scriptores sex.*

SECTION CCL

Another original way of acquiring dominion is *accession,* by which is understood the right of claiming to ourselves whatever additions are made to a <184> substance belonging to us. Now, since substances belonging to us may be augmented either by natural growth, by our own industry, or by both conjointly; *Accession* is divided by the more accurate doctors of the law into *natural, industrious,* and *mixed.* *

What accession is.

SECTION CCLI

As to *natural* accession, what belongs to us either receives an addition we cannot certainly discover the origine and former owner of, or an addition by something known to belong to another. In the first case, since a thing, whose master cannot be certainly known, belongs to none (§241), there is no reason why such an increment may not go with the thing to which it hath acceded, and so be acquired to us. But in the other case, the thing hath an owner, who can by right exclude others from the use of it (§231); and therefore I have no more reason to think such a thing, however it be added to my goods, is acquired to me, than when a strong wind blows the linen of Titius, that were hung out in his garden, into my court.† <185>

The foundation of natural accession.

---

* Thus to nature we owe the breed of animals, increments by rivers, a new cast up island, a forsaken channel: To our own industry, a new form, any thing added to what belongs to us, mixed or interwoven with it, joined or fastened to it, by lead or iron, or any other way; writing upon our paper, painting upon our cloath or board, *&c.* And partly to nature, and partly to industry, the fruits of harvest, these being owing conjointly to the goodness of the soil, and the clemency and favourableness of the weather, and to our own skill and labour. And therefore the first sort are called *natural* increments, the second *industrious* acquirements, and the third *mixed.* For what others add under the title of *fortuitous,* is more properly referred to the occupancy of things belonging to none.

† No reason can be imagined why an owner, who is well known to be such, should lose the property of any thing belonging to him while it subsists, if he hath neither abdicated his property, nor transferred it to another by any deed: And it would be cruel to take advantage of one's misfortune or calamity to deprive him of his right. If then one continues proprietor or master of a thing, which is added by whatsoever

SECTION CCLII

Of the breed of animals in particular.

From the foregoing most evident principles, (§251), we may also conclude, that *offspring*, or a *birth*, the origine of which is not evident, (which often happens with regard to animals, and likewise to persons born out of lawful marriage) follows the dam or mother as an accessory increment, and that Ulpian, l. 24. D. de statu hominum, not without reason ascribes this effect to the law of nature. But this does not appear equal if both parents be certainly known,* unless the male be kept at common expence for procreation, as a bull often is in common to many, or when the owner lets his bull or stallion to his neighbours for a certain hire.

SECTION CCLIII

Of new islands, whether cast up, or artificial.

Nor is it less difficult to determine to whom a new *island*, that starts up in the sea, or in a river, belongs. For since it is impossible to discover with certainty to whom the different particles of earth belonged which have coalited into an island (§251), it follows, that an island must be adjudged an acces-<186>sion to the sea or river;† and therefore, if the

---

chance to our goods, he hath still the right of excluding any other from the use of that thing (§231); and therefore the dominion of it cannot be acquired against his will.

* Hence with regard to slaves, a division of children commonly takes place; so that the first belongs to the mother's owner, and the next to the father's, and thus the offspring is shared by turns between the two masters. Of this I have discoursed in my Element. jur. Germ. 1. 1. 30. [[Heineccius, *Elementa juris Germanici tum veteris tum hodierni*]] where I have quoted examples of it among the Wisigoths and others, &c. From Goldast. rerum Alam. Tom. 2. charta 2. [[Goldast and Senckenberg, *Rerum Alamannicarum scriptores aliquot vetusti*]] & Aventin. Annal. Boic. l. 7. 14, 23. p. 708. [[*Annales ducum Boiariae* (Annals of the Dukes of Bavaria) by Johannes Turmair, also known as Aventinus. See Turmair, *Johannes Turmair's genannt Aventinus Sämmtliche Werke.*]]

† There is therefore no reason why a new island should accede to the neighbouring fields upon each side, if it is formed in the middle, or to the one of them to which it is nearest; which however several lawyers have asserted, §22. Inst. de rer. div. l. 7. §3. l. 29. l. 30. §1. D. de adqu. rer. dom. For the particles of earth forming the island come from grounds in a way that it cannot be certainly determined from what pos-

sea or river belong to no person, the island likewise is without an owner, and must fall to the first occupant. But if, as often happens, either the sea or river belongs to a people or their sovereign (§243), that people or sovereign will have a just title to the island. In fine, since a thing which appertains to a known master, cannot be acquired by any person by accession (§251), an owner cannot lose his ground which is washed by a river or channel into a new island, as the Roman lawyers have acknowledged, l. 7. §4. 1. 30. §2. D. de adqu. rer. dom.

SECTION CCLIV

The same is to be determined of *alluvion,* and ground separated *by the force of a river.* For as to the former, as nothing certain can be known concerning the origine of particles gradually annexed to our ground (§251), there is no doubt but what is added to our ground in that manner is accession <187> to us; and what is thus added to a public way, or any public ground, accedes to the public.* On the other hand, when the

So likewise by alluvion, and the force of a river.

---

sessors they were carried off, and it is more probable that they were washed from more remote than from nearer fields. Besides, the river itself sometimes sweeps along with it, particles washed from the bottom, which at last collecting, form an island, according to Seneca, nat. quaest. 4. 9. This however was the opinion of Cassius Longinus, which his followers afterwards defended as by league and compact. Aggen Urbic. de limit. agr. p. 57. [[Aggenus Urbicus, *De limitibus agrorum libro duo.*]] But the Proculiani, whose leader was Labeo, have exploded it in their way, Labeo apud Paullum, l. 65. §4. D. de adqu. dom. "Si id quod in publico innatum aut aedificatum est, publicum est: insula quoque, quae in flumine publico nata est, publica esse debet." [[Marcus Antistius Labeo (jurist at the time of Augustus) in Justinian's *Digest* (1.65, 4 D. de adqu. Dom.): "If that which is natural or built in public, is public, an island also, which is born in a public river, ought to be public."]]

* And upon this foundation is built the distinction of lawyers and measurers of ground between *arcifinious grounds,* which are not bounded by any other but their natural limits, and such as are encompassed with artificial bounds, and parcelled out by a certain measure, as by the number of acres, l. 16. D. de adqu. Dom. l. 1. §6. D. de flumin. of which difference between lands, see Isidor. orig. 11. 13. [[Isidore, *Isidori Hispalensis episcopi Etymologiarum sive Originum.*]] Auctores de limitib. p. 203. edit. Guil. Goesii. [[The "auctores de limitibus" (that is, authors on the question of boundaries) are presumably those in Goes and Rigault, *Rei agrariae auctores legesque variae.*]] Jo. Fr. Gron. ad Grotium de jure belli & pacis, 2. 3. 16. 1. [[Grotius, *De jure belli ac*

master of the ground carried off is known (§251), no change can be made in this case as to dominion, unless the master abdicates and leaves what is thus taken away from his possession; which in governments is commonly inferred from the not claiming it during a certain time fixed by law, §2. Inst. de rerum divis. l. 7. §2. D. de adqu. rerum dom.

SECTION CCLV

By a river's changing its channel and inundation.

In fine, as to a river's *changing its channel,* if the channel it deserts, as far as can be known, was in the dominion of no person, it cannot accede to those who possess the adjoining lands in proportion to their grounds, as the Roman lawyers thought, l. 7. §5. D. de adqu. rer. dom. But because the property of the river of which the channel is a part, is certainly known (§251), it will, as a part of the river, be his to whom the river belonged; as, for the same reason, the new channel, if again deserted, without doubt belongs no less to the first masters, than an overflown ground, after the water retires from it.* <188>

SECTION CCLVI

Of accession by industry, first axiom.

Let us now consider *industrious* and *mixed* accession, concerning which some lawyers have treated with so much subtlety. And we think, if the things be joined by mutual consent, it cannot be doubted but each is

---

pacis.]] For what lies between artificially limited grounds and a river, it is either public, or the propriety of some private person. But in neither of these cases, does any thing accede to limited ground.

   * It is otherwise, if the inundation be perpetual, so that it *becomes now sea where Troy stood,* according to the saying; for then the ground is as it were extinct, and can be of no utility to any one. But of a non-entity, or what can be of no advantage to any person, there can be no dominion, no propriety (§235). Whence it follows, that their case is extremely hard, who are still obliged to pay tributes or taxes for lands long ago swallowed up by an inundation, unless, perhaps, they may have deserved it by their negligence in restoring the dikes, tho' even a penalty in that case seems unreasonable and cruel: For why ought things to be burdened with taxes, or imposts to be exacted, when the propriety, the usufruct, the possession or passage are lost? l. 23. de quibus modis ususfr. amit. l. 3. §17. l. 30. §3. D. de adqu. possess. l. 1. §9. D. de itin. actuque priv.

master according to his proportion, and in this case there is a positive community introduced (§231). But we are here speaking of an accession made without the other's consent. Now, seeing a master has a right to exclude all from the use of what is his (§231), he has a right certainly to hinder any thing from being joined to what is his against his will. Wherefore, since what is added to any thing of ours, either renders it useless, or at least worse, or renders it more valuable and better, because he who renders our goods worse hurts us (§178); the consequence is, that he who has rendered our goods either useless or worse by any industrial accession, is obliged, taking the spoilt goods, to repair our damage; and if he did it by deceit, and with evil intention, he is likewise liable to punishment (§211). <189>

SECTION CCLVII

But if our goods are rendered better and more valuable by any artificial accession, then there is a great difference when the two things can be separated without any considerable loss, and when they cannot. In the former case, since the master of each part hath a right to exclude all others from the use of what belongs to him (§231); but that cannot now be done otherwise than by separating the two things; the consequence is, that in this case the things are to be immediately separated, and to each is to be restored his own part. But, in the other case, the joined things ought to be adjudged to one or other of the two, the other being condemned to pay the value of what is not his to the owner who is thus deprived of it;* and if there be any knavery in the matter, punishment is deserved (§211).

Second and third axiom.

---

* For whosoever intercepts any thing from another, he stands in need of for his sustenance or agreeable living, injures him (§190); but he who injures one is bound to satisfaction (§210), which, when what is done cannot be undone, consists in making a just estimation of the thing, and paying it (§212); wherefore, he who desires to intercept any thing belonging to another person, and to appropriate it to himself, is obliged to pay its just value. Whence this law appears to be very equitable, "That none ought to become richer at the expence or detriment of another."

SECTION CCLVIII

A fourth axiom, &c.

But since in the last case, the joined things are to be adjudged to some one of the two, there (§257) ought to be some good reason why one should be preferred (§177): because therefore, there can be no other besides the superior excellence of one of the two things, which is oftner measured by rarity and affection than by utility; hence we infer, that the rule which adjudges *the accessory to its principal,* is not always equal. Justinian him-<190>self, and before him Caius, acknowledged the absurdity of it in the case of a picture, §34. In. de rer. divis. l. 9. §2. D. de adqu. dom. And therefore the joined things ought to be assigned to him whose part is of the greatest price,* either on account of its rarity, or of his affection, labour, care and keeping; and he ought to be condemned to make an equivalent to the other for what was his, if he insists upon it, and does not rather choose to make a present of it to him.

SECTION CCLIX

What is just with respect to specification.

Hence we may plainly see what ought to be determined in the case of *specification,* by which a new form is given to materials belonging to another. For since very frequently all the affection or value is put upon the form on account of the workmanship or art, and none at all is set upon the substance (§258), a new species will rightly be adjudged to him who formed it;† but so as that he shall be obliged to make a just equiv-

---

* The ancient lawyers did not found in this matter upon any certain natural reason, and therefore divided into different opinions, as is observed by Jo. Barbeyrac upon Pufendorff, of the duties of a man and a citizen. The first who attempted to reduce this affair into order, and to distinguish things that had been confounded together, was Christi. Thomasius dissertat. singulari, de pretio adfectionis in res fungibiles non cadente, Hal. 1701, where he has by the same principles most accurately examined the doctrines of the Roman lawyers concerning accession by industry. [[Thomasius (*praeses*) and Hecht (*respondens*), *Dissertatio inauguralis juridica de pretio affectionis in res fungibiles non cadente.*]]

† There is no solidity in the distinction by which Justinian proposed to clear this intricate question, §25. Inst. de rer. divis. whether the new form could be reduced without hurting the substance, or not? For there is no good reason why, in the former

alent for the price or value of the materials, and shall be liable to punishment, if there be any fraud or knavery in the case (§256). So Thomasius, in the differtation above quoted, §43. & seq. Yet for the same
reason above mentioned, the owner of the substance ought to be preferred, if it be rarer and of greater value than the form added to it by
another's labour and art: *e.g.* if one shall make a statue or vase of Co-
<191>rinthian brass, amber, or any precious matter belonging to another,
the owner of the materials shall have it, but he shall be obliged to pay
for the workmanship, provided the fashioner acted *bona fide, i.e.* without
any fraudulent design.

SECTION CCLX

Again, *adjunction* is no inconsiderable species of industrious accession,
when something belonging to another is added to our goods by inclusion, by soldering with lead, by nailing or iron-work, by writing, painting, *&c.* Now since inclosing is often of such a kind, that the things
joined may be severed without any great loss, in such cases the things
may be separated, and every one's own restored to him, and this is equal
(§257): There is certainly no reason why the gold may not be restored to
whom it belongs, when another's precious stone is set in it, and the gem
to its owner. And the same holds with regard to soldering, fastening,
inter-<192>weaving, and other such like cases, when the things can be
separated without any considerable loss: Otherwise the joiner ought to

(margin) What with regard to adjunction, inclusion, &c.

---

case, the owner of the materials, and in the latter the fashioner should be preferred,
especially, seeing the matter without the fashion is frequently of very little value. (See
Pufend. of the law of nature and nations, 4. 7. 10.) Yea sometimes the fashion, is of
a hundred times more value than the materials. Now who will say in this case, that
the form belongs to the owner of the substance, because the fashion may be destroyed,
and the substance reduced to its first state? But since the value of the planks can be
more easily paid than the value of the ship made of them, who therefore will adjudge
the ship to the owner of the planks, because the ship can be taken down. If an old
ship be repaired with another's timber, Julian follows our principle in this case, l. 61.
D. de rei vind. and yet without doubt the materials can also be reduced to their former
state, even when a new ship is built with planks belonging to another, l. 26. pr. D.
de adqu. rer. dom.

be preferred, because the substance rarely admits of any price of affection (§258).*

SECTION CCLXI

What as to
building
upon, &c.

If any one builds upon his own ground with the materials of another person, when there was no knavery in the design, and the building is of timber, there is no reason why, if the mistake be very soon discovered, the building may not be taken down, and the timber be restored to its proprietor† (§257). But if the building be of stone, or if the timber would afterwards be useless to its owner, it will then be most equal to say, that the builder should have the property of the building, but be obliged to make a just satisfaction, for the materials, and be moreover liable to punishment, if there is any knavery in the case (257 and 258). If one build with his own materials upon another's ground, if the building can be taken down without any considerable loss, it ought to be done (§257); or what admits of a price of affection ought to be adjudged to the proprietor of the ground (§258), unless the building be plainly of no use to the lord of the ground, in which case <193> the builder retaining the

---

* Besides, it would not seldom be an inconvenience to the owner of the materials, if he were obliged to retain them with the accession, and to pay the price of the thing adjoined, especially if it be what he cannot use on account of his condition, age, or other circumstances, *e.g.* if one should add to the vestment of a plebeian a *laticlave,* or much gold lace, the materials are in such a case, as to use, rendered truly worse to him, or quite useless. But whoever renders our materials worse or useless to us, is obliged to take the spoilt goods, and to repair our damage; and if there be any fraud or knavery in the case, he is also liable to punishment (§256).

† The reason why the *Decemviri* forbid timber edifices to be pulled down was, that cities might not be molested with ruins, l. 6. D. ad exhib. l. 7. §10. de adqu. rerum dom. l. 1. D. de tigno juncto, and is merely civil, and has nothing in natural reason to support it. Hence many nations, where the houses were not built of stone but of timber, not only allowed but commanded by their laws buildings in this and like cases to be pulled down. See jus. prov. Sax. 2. 53. and what I have observed on this subject in my Elements juris. Germ. 2. 3. 66. To which I now add the Lombard Constitution, 1. 27. 1. [[*Jus provinciale Saxonicum* (Saxon provincial law): this refers to the *Saxon Mirror,* which had been codified by the Saxon jurist Eike von Repgow in the early thirteenth century; see Repgow, *Saxon Mirror,* pp. 108–9. The "Lombard constitution" presumably refers to Langobard feudal law, which was often used to supplement classical Roman law.]]

building to himself, is bound to pay the worth of the ground, and if there be any bad intention, he is moreover liable to punishment.

SECTION CCLXII

There is less difficulty as to writing and painting. For since those things upon which another sets no value, are to be left to him who puts a value upon them (§258), and the value for the most part falls upon the writing and painting, and never upon the cloth or paper, the paper ought to yield to the writing, and the board or cloth to the painting, if the writer and painter will make satisfaction for them.* And if the painting and writing have no value, as if one should scrible a little upon my paper, or dawb my board with fooleries, even in this case, the writer and painter ought to take the thing, and pay the value of the paper or board by the first axiom (§256). <194>

As to writing and painting.

SECTION CCLXIII

Further, as to the *mingling* of liquids, or the *commixture* of dry substances, tho' the Roman lawyers have treated of a difference with much subtlety, l. 23. §5. D. de rei vind. yet there is none. For if things be mixed or confounded by the mutual consent of parties, the mixed substance is

With respect to confusion and mixture.

---

* It is strange that the Roman Lawyers, some of whom agreed to this principle, in the case of painting, should not admit it in the case of writing. As if it were more tolerable that the writing of a learned man should become an accession to a trifle of paper, than that the painting of Appelles or Parrhasius should become an accession to a contemptible piece of board. [[Apelles (fl. 4th/3rd century B.C.) and Parrhasius (fl. 5th century B.C.) were Greek painters.]] Besides, when the Roman lawyers compare writing with building upon one's ground, §23. Inst. de rerum divis. l. 9. D. de adqu. dom. may it not very reasonably be asked, why there should not be room for the same comparison with regard to painting? And what likeness can there be imagined between the ground upon which one builds, and the paper upon which one writes? The one we seldom or never can want without suffering very great loss: The other we do not value, provided we receive satisfaction for it, or as much paper of the same goodness. This is a poetical resemblance taken from the action of writing, upon which account the Latin writers used the phrase *exarare literas* for *scribere*. But such a similitude of things is not sufficient to found the same decision about them in law and equity.

common, and ought to be divided between them proportionably to the quantity and quality of the ingredients (§256). If it be done against the will of one of them, then the substance, which is of no use, ought to be adjudged to the mixer, and he ought to make satisfaction, and to undergo a penalty if he had any bad or fraudulent intention (§256); but yet, if one would rather have a part of the substance than the price of his materials, there is no doubt that he now approves the mixture which he at first opposed, and therefore a proportionable part of the common matter cannot be refused to him.* <195>

SECTION CCLXIV

About mixed accessions, sowing and planting.

To conclude; by the same principles may we determine concerning *sowing* and *planting*, which were above referred to the *class of mixed accessions*, (§250). For trees and plants, before they have taken root, may be severed from the soil without any great loss, and so be restored to their owners (§257); but when they have taken root, as likewise seed sown, seeing they cannot easily be separated from the soil, and yet do not admit of a price of fancy or affection, they are acquired to the proprietor of the soil, he making satisfaction for the value of the trees or seed, and the expences of culture (§258), unless, in this last case, the proprietor of the soil is willing to leave the crop to the sower for a reasonable consideration.†

---

* For subsequent approbation is consent, tho' it be less imputable than command and previous consent (§112): Wherefore, if by an accidental confusion of our metals, a matter of great value should be produced, like the Corinthian brass by the burning of Corinth; there can be no reason why we may not claim each a share of the common matter: for since it would have been common if it had been made by our consent (§256), and approbation is adjudged consent (§112), there is no reason why it should not become common by approbation, and every one have his proportionable share.

† For which the lord of the soil may have just and proper reasons: As for instance, if the ground was ill-dressed or ill-sown, so that he has no ground to expect a good crop: Then the crop would be of little use to him, and the first axiom is in his favour (§256).

SECTION CCLXV

As to a *tree* in our neighbourhood, he who plants it, consents that a part of its branches should hang over into the court of his neighbour; and the neighbour, who has a right to exclude others from his court, by not doing it, also consents to it; wherefore the accession being made with the mutual consent of both parties, the tree is common, (§256); and for this reason, while it stands in the confines, it is common in whole, and when it is pulled up, it is to be divided in common: so that in the former case the leaves and fruits are in com-<196>mon; and in the latter case the timber is to be divided between the two neighbours in proportion.*

About the fruits of trees in one's neighbourhood.

REMARKS on This Chapter

The questions in this chapter, however intricate they may appear at first sight, or as they are commonly treated by the doctors of law, are in themselves very simple and easy. Nothing more is necessary than to state them clearly, or in the simplest terms, in order to discover on which side the least hurt lies. Our Author's divisions and definitions are exceeding distinct: And all his determinations turn upon this simple principle he had in the preceeding chapters fully cleared, "That no injury ought to be done; and injuries that are done ought to be repaired." He sets out in this chapter, as good order and method require, by inquiring into the nature and origine of dominion and property. And tho' I think he hath handled this curious question, which hath been so sadly perplexed by many moralists, better than most others, yet something seems to me still wanting to compleat his way of reasoning about it. Our Locke, in his treatise on Government, book 2. c. 4.[4] as Mr. Barbeyrac hath observed in his notes on Pufendorff of the law of nature and nations, b. 4. c. 4. hath treated this question with much more perspicuity and accuracy than either Grotius or Pufendorff. The book

---

* This simplicity is preferred by our ancestors to the subtleties of the Roman law, concerning the nourishment attracted by the roots of trees, which gradually changes their substance, l. 26. §2. D. de adqu. dom. For the nations of a German extraction considered the branches of trees more than their roots, as we have shewn in our Elem. of the German law, 2. 3. 69.

4. John Locke (1632–1704), *Two Treatises of Government*, ed. by P. Laslett, 265–428.

being in every one's hands, I shall not so much as attempt to abridge
what he says on the head. The substance of it is contained in this short
sentence of Quintilian, Declam. 13. "Quod omnibus nascitur, industriae praemium est." "What is common to all by nature, is the purchase,
the reward of industry, and is justly appropriated by it."[5] Let us hear
how our Harrington expresses himself upon this subject (the original
of property) in his art of law-giving, chapter 1. at the beginning in his
works, p. 387 "The heavens, says David, even the heaven of heavens
are the Lords, but the earth has he given to the children of men: yet
says God to the father of these children, in the sweat of thy face shalt
thou eat thy bread, Dii laborantibus sua munera vendunt. This donation of the earth to man, comes to a kind of selling it for industry,
a treasure which seems to purchase of God himself. From the different
kinds and successes of this industry, whether in arms, or in other exercises of the mind or body, derives the natural equity of dominion or
property; and from the legal <197> establishment or distribution of
this property (be it more or less approaching towards the natural equity
of the same) proceeds all government."[6] Now, allow me to make some
very important observations upon this principle, which, as simple as it
appears, involves in it many truths of the last importance, in philosophy, morality and politics. 1. That man is made to purchase every thing
by industry, and industry only, every good, internal or external, of the
body or mind, is a fact too evident to be called into question. This hath
been long ago observed. When Mr. Harrington says, "Nature or God
sells all his gifts to industry," he literally translates an ancient Greek
proverb: Θεοὶ τα ἀγαθὰ τοῖς πονοῖς πολοῦνται,[7] (see Erasmi adagia) as
did the Latins in their many proverbial sentences to the same purpose,
"Labor omnia vincit": "Omnia industriae cedunt," &c. See Virg.
Georg. 1. v. 121, &c. 2.[8] But as ancient and evident as this observation
is, yet none of the ancient philosophers ever had recourse to it in the

---

5. Quintilian, *The Major Declamations*, 13.8, pp. 169–70.

6. Harrington, *Political Works*, p. 604.

7. "Θεοὶ τα ἀγαθὰ τοῖς πονοῖς πολοῦνται": "The gods sell their goods for hard
work" (see note 3, p. 571, of Turnbull's "Discourse").

8. "Labor omnia vincit": "Toil conquered the world"; see Virgil, *Georgics* 1, line
145, in vol. 1 of *Virgil*. "Omnia industriae cedunt": "Everything yields to industry";
this is from a different, unidentified source.

celebrated question, "Unde bonis mala, &c." *i.e.* about the promiscuous distribution of the goods of fortune (as they are commonly
called) in this life; tho' this fact contains a solid refutation of that objection against providence, and from it alone can a true answer be
brought to it. Mr. Pope in his *Essay on Man,* ep. 4. v. 141, &c. (as I have
taken notice in my *Principles of Moral Philosophy,* part 1. chap. 1. and
chap. 9. and part 2. chap. 3.) is the first who hath given the true resolution of this seeming difficulty from this principle, that according to
our constitution, and the frame of things, the distribution of goods
internal or external, is not promiscuous; but every purchase is the reward of industry. If we own a blind fortuitous dispensation of goods,
and much more, if we own a malignant dispensation of them, or a
dispensation of them more in favour of vice than of virtue, we deny a
providence, or assert bad administration. There is no possibility of rec-
onciling bad government with wisdom and goodness; or irregularity
and disorder with wisdom and good intelligent design, by any future
reparation. But the alledgeance is false; for in fact, the universe is
governed by excellent general laws, among which this is one, "That
industry shall be the purchaser of goods, and shall be generally successful." And that being the fact, the objection which supposes promiscuous, fortuitous, or bad government, is founded upon a falsity in
fact. In fine, there is no way of proving providence, but by proving
good government by good general laws; and where all is brought about
according to good general laws, nothing is fortuitous, promiscuous or
bad. And not to mention any of the other general laws in the government of the world, constituting the order according to which effects
are brought about; and consequently the means for obtaining ends to
intelligent active creatures; what better general law can we conceive
with regard to intelligent active beings, than the general law of industry; or can we indeed conceive intelligent agency and dominion without such a law? Are not the two <198> inseparable, or rather involved
in one another? But where that law obtains, there is no dispensation or
distribution properly speaking; for industry is the sole general purchaser, in consequence of means uniformly operative towards ends. But
having elsewhere fully insisted upon this law of industry, in order to
vindicate the ways of God to man; let me observe, 3. in the third place,
Mr. Harrington is the first who hath taken notice, or at least fully

cleared up the consequences of this general law of industry with respect to politics, that is, with respect to the natural procreation of government, and the natural source of changes in government. Every thing hangs beautifully and usefully together in nature. There must be manifold mutual dependencies among beings made for society, and for the exercise of benevolence, love and friendship; that is, there must be various superiorities and inferiorities; for all is giving and receiving. But dependence, which supposes in its notion superiority and inferiority, must either be dependence in respect of internal, or in respect of external goods; the former of which Mr. Harrington calls *hanging on the lips,* and the other *hanging on the teeth.* Now the law of industry obtaining amongst men placed in various circumstances (and all cannot be placed in the same) will naturally produce these dependencies. A greater share of wisdom and virtue will naturally procreate authority, and the dependence on the lips. [This perhaps is the meaning of that ancient saying of Democritus mentioned by Stobaeus, serm. 27. "φύσει τὸ ἄρχειν ὀικήϊον τω κρεισσονι," "Authority falls naturally to the share of the better, more excellent or superior."] And a greater share of external goods, or of property, naturally begets power, and the other dependence on the teeth. And hence it will and must always hold as a general law, That dominion will follow property, or that changes in property will beget certain proportional changes in government: and this consequently is the natural seed, principle or cause of procreation and vicissitude in government, as Mr. Harrington has demonstrated fully and accurately.[9] I only mention these things here, because we shall

---

9. Harrington's argument that "a greater share of external goods, or of property, naturally begets power" was a response to Thomas Hobbes. Harrington was interested in solving the same problem as Hobbes, the threat of anarchy resulting from constitutional collapse. However, Harrington believed that the fault in Hobbes's argument was exposed by the dissolution of the Rump Parliament in 1653, the Rump being an example of a Hobbesian sovereign, whose rule was based on conquest. According to Harrington, Hobbes had not taken into account that the sovereign's power depended on the military, so that the question of actual control over the army was critical to the sovereign's ability to maintain himself in power. The Rump Parliament did not control the army and therefore could be dissolved by it. The answer to control of the army lay in men's dependence on riches, especially land. The more land a person owned, the greater his empire. Political power thus followed landownership (see Fukuda, *Sovereignty and the Sword*).

have occasion to have recourse to them afterwards, when our Author comes to treat of government. The conclusion that more properly belongs to our present purpose is, 4. in the fourth place, It must necessarily have happened soon after the world was peopled that all was, must have been appropriated by possession and industry: and therefore, at present, our business is to determine how, things being divided and appropriated, the duties of mankind stand. But it is clear, 1. in the first place, that suppose the world just beginning to be peopled, or suppose a considerable number of men just cast ashore upon a desart country (setting aside all compacts and regulations previously agreed upon) every one will have a right to the purchase of his industry; to the fruits of his labour; to improve his mind, and to all the natural benefits and rewards of that culture; and to the fruits of his skill, ingenuity and labour, to get < 199 > riches, with all the natural benefits and rewards of them; but yet every one will be obliged, in consequence of what hath been already said of the law of love and benevolence, to exercise his abilities, and to use his purchases in a benevolent way, or with tender regard to others. This must be the case with regard to our right and obligation, previous to all compacts, conventions or regulations. 2. And where lands are already appropriated, and civil government settled, this is a true principle still, that one has a right to all the purchases of his industry, with respect either to external or internal riches, (if I may so speak) consistent with the law of benevolence, or the law of not injuring any one, but of doing all the good to every one in our power; and hence it is, that every one in formed society hath a right to his purchases by the arts of manufacture and commerce, &c. Tho' a state, to fix the balance of dominion or of government, may fix the balance of property in land, and likewise make regulations about money, (as in the Commonwealths of Israel, Lacedemon, Athens, Rome, Venice, &c. in different manners) in consequence of the natural connexion between the balance of property and the balance of dominion: Tho' this may be done in forming or mending government by consent, yet even where an Agrarian law obtains, this principle must hold true and be untouched, that every one has a right to the purchases of his industry, in the sense above limited: For otherwise, there would be no encouragement to industry, nay, all must run into endless disorder and confusion. 3. And therefore universally, whether in a state of nature, or in constituted civil governments, this must be a just, a necessary principle, that industry gives a right to its purchases, and all the benefits and rewards attending them. 4. And therefore, fourthly, it can never be true, that a person may not, as far as is consistent with benevolence, endeavour to have both power and authority. If we consider what would be the consequences of denying this principle, that is, of setting any other bounds to the purchases of industry but what the law of benevolence sets, we will soon see that this must be universally true. And if we attend to our frame, and reason from it to final causes, as we do in other cases, it is plain, that there is in our constitution naturally, together with a principle of benevolence, and a sense of public good, a love of power (of *principatus,* as Cicero calls it in the beginning of his first book of offices) without which our benevolence could not produce magnanimity and greatness of mind, as that desire of power would, without benevolence and a sense of public good, produce a tyrannical, overbearing and arrogant temper. Some moralists do not seem to attend to this noble principle in our nature, the source of all the great virtues, while others ascribe too much to it (as Hobbes), and consider it as the only principle in our nature, without taking our benevolence and sense of public good, which are as natural to us, into the account. (See what I have said on this head in my *Principles of Moral* <200> *Philosophy.*)[10] But both principles belong to our constitution; and therefore our virtue consists in benevolent desire of, and endeavour to have authority and power in order to do good. 5. It is in consequence of this principle, that it is lawful to have dependents or servants, and that it is lawful to endeavour to raise ourselves, or to exert ourselves to encrease our power and authority. The great, sweet, the natural reward of superiority in parts and of riches, and consequently the great spur to industry, is the dependence upon us it procreates and spreads. And why should this noble ambition acknowledge any other bounds but what benevolence sets to it: Any other limits but what the Author of nature intended should be set to it, or rather actually sets to it, by making the exercises of benevolence so agreeable to us, as that no other enjoyments are equal to them in the pleasure they afford, whether in immediate exercise, or

10. See Turnbull, *Principles of Moral and Christian Philosophy,* especially vol. 1, pt. 1, chap. vi, p. 208.

upon after reflection; and in making mankind so dependent every one
upon another, that without the aid and assistance of others, and consequently without doing what he can to gain the love and friendship
of mankind, none can be happy, however superior in parts or in property he may be to all about him. Every man stands in need of man; in
that sense all men are equal; all men are dependent one upon another;
or every man is subjected to every man. This observation is so much
the more necessary, that while some moral writers assert, that man has
a right to all things and persons to which his power of subjecting them
to his use can extend or be extended; others speak of our natural equality in such a manner as if nature had not designed any superiorities
among mankind, and as if all desire of, or endeavours after power or
authority were unlawful; which last must result in asserting, that all
culture of the mind, and all industry are unlawful, because the natural
consequence of the one is superiority in parts, and the natural effect
of the other is superiority in property; while the other terminates in
affirming there is no distinction between power and right, or between
power rightly and power unreasonably applied, *i.e.* no distinction between moral good and ill, *i.e.* no distinction between reasonable and
unreasonable; which difference must remain, while there is such a thing
as public good or benevolence, or such a thing as reason, as hath been
already fully proved. 6. If the preceeding principles be true, due attention to them will lead us through most of our Author's succeeding
questions about derivative acquisitions and succession. Because the effect of property, which makes it the great reward of industry, is a right
to dispose of our own in our life, or at our death, which admits no
limitations but what benevolence sets to it; in consequence of which
right and duty, succession to him who dies without making a disposition of his estate, ought to take place in the way a wise man, directed
by benevolence, must be presumed to have intended to dispose of his
own at his death, *i.e.* according to the natural course in which benevo-
<201>lence ought to operate and exert itself, already taken notice of.
For when the will of a person is not declared, his will ought to be inferred from his duty. We shall therefore for some time have but little
occasion to explain or add to our Author.

Of derivative acquisitions of dominion or property made during the life of the first proprietor.

SECTION CCLXVI

Transition to derivative acquisitions. Dominion being acquired, a change sometimes happens, so that one acquires either property or dominion in a thing, neither of which he before had; and such *acquisitions* we called above, (§240), *derivative.* Now, seeing the thing in which we acquire property was before that common: the thing in which we for the first time acquire dominion, was before that the property of some person: as often as we receive our own proper share of a common thing, there is *division;* as often as we acquire the whole thing in property, there is *cession;* * and as often as another's property passes by his will into our dominion, there is, as we called it above (§240), *tradition,* or transferring.

---

* The term *cession,* is sometimes taken in a larger acceptation, so as to signify all transferring of rights or actions from one to another. But since in that sense it may be comprehended under *tradition,* we use it here in a more limited signification, and mean by it, *the transferrence of right and dominion common to many, to one of the associates made by the consent of the rest.* Thus, *e.g.* if co-heirs transfer their whole title of inheritance to one of the co-heirs, they are said to have *ceded* their title or right to him.

SECTION CCLXVII

In all these cases, what was ours ceases to be ours any longer in whole or in part, and passes into the dominion or property of another person; and <202> this we call *alienation,* which, when it proceeds from a prior right in the acquirer, is termed *necessary;* when from a new right, with the consent of both parties, it is called *voluntary.* * But the effect of either is, that one person comes into the place of another, and therefore succeeds both to his right in a certain thing, and to all the burdens with which it is incumbered. Alienation is called *pure,* when no circumstance suspends or delays the transferrence of the dominion; and when the transferrence is suspended, it is called *conditional* alienation.

By them is made alienation necessary, voluntary, pure, or conditional.

SECTION CCLXVIII

Voluntary alienation cannot be understood or take place otherwise than by the consent of both parties: but there may be consent either for a *present* alienation, so that the dominion may be transferred from us to another in our own life, or for a *future* alienation, so that another shall obtain the possession of what is ours after our demise: and this consent to a future alienation, is either actual, or it is inferred from the design and intention of the person.† Now by the first of these is what is called

And that either for the present time, or for a time to come.

---

* Thus the alienation of a thing common to many, which is made when one of the associates demands a division, is necessary, because he who insists upon a division has already a right in the thing. In like manner, the alienation of a thing pledged to one is necessary, because it is done by virtue of the right the creditor had already acquired in that thing. On the other hand, the alienation of houses, which, one who is to change his habitation, sells, is voluntary, no person having a right in them. Thus is the division in the Roman law to be explained, l. 1. D. de fund. dot. l. 2. §1. D. de rebus eorum qui sub tut. l. 13. l. 14. D. fam. ercisc. and elsewhere frequently.

† We therefore refer to future alienation, that possession of our goods which devolves upon a person after our death. If this be done by ourselves truly willing it, such a will is called a *testament,* and succession by virtue of such a will is called *testamentary succession.* But if it be inferred from the design and intention of the defunct, that he willed his inheritance to pass to certain persons, preferably to all others, this is *succession to an intestate.* Now, against both these ways of succession it may be objected, that no person can will any thing at a time when he cannot will at all; and that alien-

testamentary succession; and by the latter is what is termed *succession to one who dies intestate.* We shall now treat of *present* alienation, and in the succeeding chapter we shall consider *future* alienation. <203>

SECTION CCLXIX

What division is, and why one may demand it.

The transition from community to property is made by *division* (§266), which is an assignation to any of the associates of his competent part of the whole in positive community. Now seeing any associate or sharer can exclude all but his fellow associates or sharers from the use of the thing common to them (§231); the consequence is, that any of the associates may demand the use of the thing according to the share belonging to him, and therefore <204> may demand a division; and the others, if they should oppose a division, are so much the less to be heard, that positive community doth very ill suit the present state of mankind (§238).*

---

ation cannot be made in this manner by a person while he lives, because he does not transfer neither right nor dominion to heirs while he lives; nor by a dead person, because, what he himself does not possess, he cannot transfer. And for these reasons, many very learned men deny that wills are of the law of nature, as Merill. obs. 6. 25. [[Mérille, *Observationum libri VIII.*]] Thomas. not. ad tit. inst. de test. ord. p. 173. [[Thomasius, *Notae ad singulos institutionum et pandectarum titulos varias juris Romani antiquitates imprimis usum eorum hodiernum in foris Germaniae ostendentes.*]] Gothofr. de Coccei. diss. de testam. princ. part. 1. §22. & seq. [[H. von Cocceji (*praeses*) and J. G. Cocceji (*respondens*), *Disputatio juridica inauguralis de testamentis principum.*]] If these arguments conclude against the foundation of wills made by the dying person's real declaration of his will, *i.e.* testaments, in the law of nature, they conclude more strongly against succession to intestates; and therefore all this doctrine we have now been inculcating concerning *future alienation* is a chimera. But as we easily allow that these arguments prove wills, as defined in the Roman law, not to proceed from the law of nature (see my dissertation de testam. jure Germ. arct. limitibus circumscripta, §3.) [[Heineccius (*praeses*) and Gunther (*respondens*), *De testamentifactione iure Germanico arctis limitibus passim circumscripta*]] so we think they do not conclude against all sorts of future alienation and succession. And what the law of nature establishes concerning them, shall be enquired in the following chapter.

  * For since such a communion can only subsist among men endowed with great virtue, and it must become inconvenient in proportion as justice and benevolence wax cold and languid (§238), how can it hold long in our times? Which of two associates does not envy the other? Who is so careful about a common thing as his own?

SECTION CCLXX

A subject is either easily *divisible* into parts, or it is *indivisible;* either because in the nature of the thing, or by laws and customs, it cannot be divided into parts. If therefore an associate demand a division of a thing in its own nature divisible, nothing is more equal than to divide it into as many parts as there are associates, and to commit the matter to the decision of lot. But if the thing be indivisible, it is either to be left to one of the associates, who can pay, and bids most for it, or to whom age or chance gives a preference, who, a valuation being made, is to satisfy the rest; or it is to be sold to the best advantage, and the price is to be divided proportionably among the sharers; or they are to have the use of it alternately, each in his turn.* <205>

How it may be done whether the subject be divisible or indivisible.

How apt is one to hinder another when he would medle with a common thing? Who does not endeavour to intercept a part of his associate's profits? Hence a thousand animosities and contentions, as Aristotle has demonstrated, in opposition to the Platonic communion, Polit. 2. 2. [[Aristotle, *Politics,* bk. 2, chap. 2.]] So that the Romans had reason to pronounce partnership and communion the mother of discord, and to give power to any associate to demand a division, l. 77. §2. D. de legat. 2.

* Thus we know the land of Palestine was divided among the Hebrews by lot, it having been separated in parts according to the number of their tribes. On the other hand, it often happens among co-heirs, that one of them, either with the consent of the rest, or by the decision of lot, buys at a certain price the whole indivisible inheritance, and gives every one of the rest his share of the price. It likewise sometimes happens, that none of the co-heirs being rich enough to be able to satisfy the rest, the inheritance is sold to a stranger upon the best terms, and the co-heirs divide the price. Finally, Diether, in contin. thesauri Besold. voce *Mutschirung,* p. 417. [[Dietherr, *Orbis novus literatorum praeprimis jurisconsultorum detectus, sive continuatio thesauri practici Besoldiani,* i.e., a continuation of Christoph Besold, *Thesaurus practicus.*]] Wehner observ. pract. ibidem, p. 370 [[probably Wehner, *Practicarum iuris observationum selectarum liber singularis*]], have observed, that the alternate use of a common thing hath sometimes been agreed to by illustrious brothers, which is in some places called *Die Mutschirung.* We have an instance of it in the family of Saxony in Muller. in Saechs. annal. p. 203. [[Müller, *Des chur- und fürstlichen Hauses Sachsen . . . Annales.*]]

SECTION CCLXXI

When equality is to be observed in division of things perfectly common.

Moreover, because with regard to a common thing all may have equal right, or some one may have more right than others (§231); it is evident that division is either *equal* or *unequal*. In the first case, all are called to equal shares, and in the second, to unequal shares. Now, since the natural equality of mankind obliges every one not to arrogate any prerogative to himself above any other without a just reason, in things belonging to many by perfect right (§177); it is manifest that division ought to be equal, and that none ought to claim any preference, unless his right to it can be clearly proved.* <206>

SECTION CCLXXII

Whether it ought likewise to be observed in the division of things imperfectly common.

These rules belong to *perfect* community. But there is likewise an *imperfect* community, as often as none of the partners hath a perfect right to the thing (§231). Now, when by the bounty of another any thing becomes thus common to many persons, it is at his option to give equal shares, or to give more or less according to merit.† And in this case it would be most unjust for any one to complain that a person of less merit

---

* Such a pre-eminence may be due to one by law, by compact, and by the last-will of the former possessor, but not on account of greater strength or power, which Hobbes however seems to admit of, as giving a just prerogative above others in division, (de cive, c. 3. 15). For if such a reason be allowed to be just, the division of the lion in the fable is most fair and equal, Phaed. fab. 1. 5. who being to divide the prey with his fellow hunters, reasoned in this manner; "I take the first share as called *lion;* the second as being stronger you will give me; the third shall follow me because I am superior to you all, and woe be to him who dares to touch the fourth. Thus did his injustice carry off the whole booty." Whoever can call this a fair and just division, and he only, will grant what Hobbes asserts concerning a natural lot (sortem naturalem) as he calls superior power.

† And this is that distributive (διανεμητική) justice which ought to attend all those virtues which pursue the interest of others; as liberality, compassion, and rectoreal prudence, (the prudence of magistrates in conferring dignities, &c.) Grotius of the rights of war and peace, 1. 18. who justly remarks, that this justice does not always observe that comparative proportion, called *geometrical proportion;* and that therefore Aristotle's doctrine on this head, is one of those things that often not always takes place, Grotius ibidem, n. 2. Nor is this opinion of Grotius overturned by Pufendorff

is put upon an equal footing with him (Mat. xx. 12, 15), or to take upon him to judge rashly of his own merit; or to think benefits conferred upon this or the other person, may be pled as precedents. <207>

SECTION CCLXXIII

When a thing in common to many is resigned by the rest to one of the sharers, this is called *cession*. Wherefore, since in this case one succeeds into the place of all the others, the consequence is, that he succeeds into all their rights to that thing, and also into all the inconveniencies and burdens attending it (§267). And hence the Roman lawyers justly inferred that the same exceptions have force against the person ceded to, which would have had force against the ceder, l. 5. c. de her. vel act. vend.

What is cession of a thing in common?

SECTION CCLXXIV

Since, whether the thing in common be divided, or whether it be ceded to one of the sharers, this seems to be the nature of the deed, that those who get the thing by division or by cession, acquire the right of excluding all others from the use of that thing; (§231) it is manifest that in both cases the associates oblige themselves, that he to whom the thing is transferred, shall not be hindered from taking possession of it; and therefore oblige themselves to warranty, and to repair all his loss, if it be evicted by another with right, and without the possessor's fault; since they have

The obligation of the partners to make good.

---

of the law, &c. 1. 7. 9. because he speaks of the distribution of things owing to many of good desert by perfect right, as by promise or pacts. Then what Arrian says is absolutely true, ep. 3. 17. "Such is the law of nature, that he who excels another is in a better condition in respect of what he excels in, than one who is worse or inferior." [[Epictetus, *The Discourses as Reported by Arrian,* vol. 2, "Discourses," bk. 3, chap. 17.]] But in matters proceeding from mere good-will, this law of nature can hardly be pled; nor could these veterans justly complain of the emperor Hadrian, whom he ordered to rub one another in the bath, tho' some days before he had made a present of servants and money to one of their companions, whom he saw rubbing himself against the marble, Spartian Had. c. 17. because benefits are not to be wrested into examples. [[See Boxhorn, *Historiae Augustae.*]]

their shares safe and entire, while the other hath got a thing with an encumbered or burdened title.* <208>

SECTION CCLXXV

What tradition or delivery is, and if necessary to the transference of dominion?

We proceed now to *tradition*, by which an owner who has the right and will to alienate, transfers dominion to another, accepting it for a just cause. I say *dominion*. For tho' the Roman law orders the thing itself and its possession to be transferred, and does scarcely allow any right in a thing to arise previously to delivery: l. 20. C. de pact. yet such subtlety cannot be of the law of nature,† as is justly observed by Grotius of the rights of war and peace, 2. 6. 1. 2. 2. 8. 25. and Pufendorff of the law of nature and nations, 4. 9. 6: and the Roman lawyers themselves acknowledge, "That nothing can be more agreeable to natural equity, than that the will of an owner willing to transfer his goods to another, should take place and be confirmed." §40. Inst. de rer. divis. l. 9. D. de adqu. rer. dom. Whence we conclude, that the will of an owner concerning transferring his dominion to another, whether expressly declared, or deducible from certain signs, is sufficient to transfer his dominion to another without delivery. <209>

---

* Thus the doctrine of eviction, which hath found place likewise in tradition or transferring, flows from natural equity, tho' many things be added to it by the civil law for clearing it, with respect to the form and effect of it, *e.g.* as when it requires that one should transfer to another in his own name; that the possessor should inform the transferrer of the suit in time; that the thing be evicted for a cause preceeding the contract; and not by violence, but by right, &c. For every one may discern at first sight, that all these conditions proceed from natural equity.

† Nor did the Romans themselves anciently require that in every case. Delivery was only necessary with respect to things (nec mancipi) of which one had not the full possession, as of provincial farms, Simplic. inter rei agrar. script. p. 76. [[Simplicius, in Goes and Rigault (eds.), *Rei agrariae auctores legesque variae.*]] Things (mancipi) of which one had the property and full possession, were alienated (per aes & librain), so that the conveyance and title being made, the dominion was immediately acquired. Varro de lingua lat. 4. [[Varro, *On the Latin Language* (*De lingua Latina*).]] Therefore, from the time that Justinian took away the distinction between *res mancipi* and *nec mancipi,* and the *dominium Quiritarum* and *bonitarium.* l. un. C. de nudo jure Quirit. toll. & l. un. C. de usucap. transform, this law again prevailed, that dominion should be transferred without delivery or putting in possession.

SECTION CCLXXVI

Since therefore the will of the owner to transfer his dominion to another, is equivalent to delivery, and is a valid transferrence of his dominion to another (§275), it follows, that it must be equal, whether one absent, by intervening letters or words, or present, by giving the thing from hand to hand, or by inducting him into it, whether by long or short hand, or by certain symbols, according to the usage of the province (§242), or in whatever way he delivers it; so that nothing hinders but that a right may be conveyed or transferred to another without delivery, or by a *quasi-delivery.* *

How it is done.

SECTION CCLXXVII

But since he only who hath dominion can transfer it or alienate (§275), it is plain that tradition can have no effect, if it be made by one, who either by law, convention, or any other cause, hath no right to alienate; much less, if it be made by one who is not himself master of the thing; for none can convey a right to another which he himself has not.† But,

Who has a right thus to transfer dominion.

* That symbolical delivery was not unknown to the Romans, appears from l. 1. § pen. D. de adqu. poss. l. 9. §6. D. de adqu. dom. l. 74. D. de contr. empt. And the nations of German origine have been more acute in this matter: For they, in delivering conveyances and investitures, made use of almost any thing, a stalk of a tree, a rod, a turf, a branch, a straw of corn, a shrub, a glove, and other such things. See my Elem. juris Germ. 2. 3. 74. & seq. to which belongs the *Scotatio* Danica, c. 2. 10. de consuet. of which Strauchius Amoenit. jur. can. ecl. 5. [[Strauchius, *Amoenitatum juris canonici semestria duo*]] and also Gundlingliana part. 7. diss. 4. [[Nicolaus Hieronimus Gundling (1671–1729), most important follower of Thomasius and from 1705 professor of philosophy at the University of Halle. Heineccius refers to Gundling's essays *Gundlingiana.*]]

† Yet such a tradition, if made to one without his knowledge that it is so, constitutes an honest possessor till the true owner claims his own. Grotius of the rights of war and peace, 2. 10. and Pufendorff of the law of nature and nations, 4. 13. 6. & seq. endeavour to shew what such a possessor is obliged to do in point of restitution, what profits he may retain, and what he ought to restore, by a multitude of rules. We shall treat of this matter afterwards in its own place expresly (§312), and shall there shew, that the whole affair is reducible into two rules, 1. An honest possessor, during the time that the true owner doth not appear, is in his place, and therefore

on the other hand, it is the same in effect, whether the master himself transfers his right immediately by his own will, or by his order and approbation. <210>

SECTION CCLXXVIII

By transference dominion is not transferred for every cause.

Because alienation ought to be made for a just cause (§275); but it is evident, from the nature of the thing, that by a just cause must be understood one sufficient for transferring dominion; therefore dominion cannot pass to another if a thing be delivered to one in loan, in trust, or letting; much less, if it be delivered to him on request and conditionally, or upon any terms revocable at the pleasure of the deliverer; yea, that no cause is sufficient, if he, to whom a thing is delivered, does not fulfil his bargain.* <211>

SECTION CCLXXIX

Nor does one always deliver with that design.

Besides, we said, in order to transfer, one must deliver with the design and intention of transferring dominion (§275). From which it is plain, that tradition cannot be made by infants, by madmen, by persons disordered in their senses, and other such persons, who are presumed not

---

has the same rights that the owner would have, were he in possession. 2. When the true owner appears, he, if the thing subsists, is obliged to restore it with its existing profits; and if the thing does not subsist, he is only obliged to make restitution, so far as he hath been made richer by enjoying it.

* For when alienation is made to a person upon condition that he shall do something, it is conditional. But because the condition suspends the transferrence of dominion, the consequence is, that if the other does not perform what he promised, the dominion is not transferred, and the tradition becomes of no effect. Hence the Romans pronounced things bought and delivered not to be acquired to the buyer till the price was paid, or other satisfaction was made to the seller, §41. Inst. de rerum divis. Hence Varro says, de re rustica, 2. 2. "A herd sold does not change its master till the money be paid." [[Varro, *On Farming,* 2.2.6.]] So Quintilian, Declam. 336. "By what right can you claim the thing which you have not paid the price of?" [[Quintilian, *Lesser Declamations,* vol. 2, p. 199.]] So Tertullian de poenitentia. "It is unreasonable to lay your hands on the goods, and not to pay the price." [[Tertullian (ca. 160–ca. 220), probably the most important Christian theologian before St. Augustine. His treatise *De poenitentia* is on ecclesiastical penance (Tertullian, *Treatises on Penance*).]]

to know what is transacted: nor is it valid, if the owner gives a thing to one with the intention of lending, depositing, pawning it; or with any such like design; as likewise, that any one may reserve or except whatever right he pleases in transferring a thing; and that in this case, so much only is transferred as the alienator intended to transfer.

SECTION CCLXXX

Whence it is easy to conceive the origine of *imperfect* or *less full dominion*. For since by that is understood nothing else but dominion, the effects of which are inequally shared between two persons; it is highly probable that its origine is owing to transferrence, with exception, or with reservation of a part of the dominion; which being done, there are two masters, one of whom acquires the right of excluding all others from reaping and using the fruits and profits of the thing, and of taking them to himself; the other has the right either of concurrence with respect to the disposal of it, or of exacting something, by which the acknowledgment of his dominion may be evidenced.* <212>

The origine of full, and of imperfect dominion.

SECTION CCLXXXI

Since the nature of the (dominium utile) or dominion with respect to the use, is such, that the superior owner reserves to himself the right of concurrence with regard to the disposal of the thing, or the right of exacting something in acknowledgment of his superior dominion (§280); the consequence is, that tho' there may be various kinds of less full dominion, yet the whole matter in these cases depends on the agree-

The various species of it.

---

* The last kind of less full dominion, the lawyers of the middle ages called *directum,* the former they called *prius utile;* not so elegantly indeed, but by terms received at the bar and in the schools, and which therefore it is not now time to discard. But the one may be called the *superior (dominus superior vel major)* the other the *inferior master (dominus minor),* after the example of the Romans, who called the *patremfamilias, herum majorem,* and the *filiosfamilias, heros minores,* Plaut. Capt. 3. 5. v. 50. Trinum 2. 2. 53. Asinar. 2. 66. [[Plautus, *Plautus,* trans. Nixon, vols. 1 and 5.]]

ment of the parties. However, if one stipulates with the possessor of the
thing delivered to him for homage and services, and that the thing be
not alienated without his consent; hence arise (*feudum*) the right of *fief*
or *fealty;* if he stipulates that an annual tribute shall be paid in acknowledgment of his superiority; hence arises (*jus emphyteuticum*) the right
of *holding in fee.* Finally, if he stipulates for a ground-rent, hence arises
(*jus superficiei*) the right of *ground-rent;** and these are the principal
kinds of dominion with regard to use in any nations. <213>

SECTION CCLXXXII

If not the thing itself, and the dominion of it, but a certain use only be
conveyed, he who receives it, acquires a *servitude* upon a thing belonging
to another; and if the use be restricted to the person and life of him who
is to have the use, it is *personal;* and if it be annexed to the estate itself,
the use of which is conveyed, it is *real.* Since therefore in all these cases
just so much right is transfered as the transferrer willed to transfer (§279),
it follows, that in these cases likewise the matter comes to be intirely an
affair of an agreement between parties; and therefore, almost all the subtleties to be found in the doctors about services are of positive law.†

---

* Of holding in fee we have an example, Gen. xlvii. 26. according to Josephus,
Antiq. 2. 7. Tho' Hertius thinks the lands of Egypt were rather made censual, or paid
a land-tax, ad Puffend. jus nat. &c. 4. 8. 3. But if he place the difference between
holding in fee and censual, in this, that in the former the possessor has only the dominion of use, and in the latter full dominion, it may be clearly proved, that the
Pharaoh's of Egypt had a part of the dominion. For the Words of the Patriarch
Joseph are, Gen. xlvii. 23. "This day I have bought you and your lands to Pharaoh."
Of the (*jus superficiarium*) or the right of ground-plots, there is a remarkable instance
in Justin. Hist. 18. 5. Concerning the origine of fiefs the learned are much divided,
tho' they be common throughout all Europe. That there are many other sorts of less
full dominion among the nations of German extract, I have shewn in my element.
juris Germ. 2. 2. 23. & seq.

† Hence the known tenets, that service consists not in doing, but in suffering or
not doing; that it is indivisible, that its cause ought to be perpetual, that because the
thing is to be used and enjoyed without hurting its substance, usufruct does not take
place, where there is nothing to be used or enjoyed: That there is a great difference
between usufruct, use, habitation, and the labour of servants; that some of these
rights are lost by change of state, and some not: All these are of such a nature that

SECTION CCLXXXIII

If a thing is delivered by the owner to his creditor, so that the deliverer continues to have the dominion, but the creditor has the possession for his security, then the thing is said to be *in pawn*. If it be delivered in these terms, that the creditor shall likewise have the fruits of it by way of interest, <214> it is called *jus antichreticum*. Finally, if the right of pawn be conveyed to a creditor without delivering the pawn, we call it *hypotheca, mortgage*. As therefore in the former cases the creditor has a right, the debt not paid, not only to retain the thing pawned, but also to dispose of it, and deduct from the price what is due to him; so, in the latter case, the creditor may prosecute his right of possession of what is pledged to him for his security, *i.e.* attach it; and then detain it until his debt be paid, or even dispose of it for his payment.*

What right of pawn and mortgage, &c.

SECTION CCLXXXIV

To conclude; we said, that by transferring, dominion passes to him who *accepts* of the transferrence (§275). But we *truly accept*, when we testify by words or deeds our consent that a thing transferred should become ours, and we are *presumed* to accept, whenever, from the nature of the thing, it cannot but be judged that we would not refuse or despise the thing one would transfer to us. In like manner, a thing may be *transferred* by the will of the transferrer, either expresly declared, or presumable

How dominion passes to the accepter.

---

right reason neither precisely commands them, nor opposes them, but they may be variously fixed and altered by pacts and conventions.

* ('Tis not improper to take notice here, that this sort of mortgage called *Antichresis* in the Roman law, is nearly the same with that which is termed *vivum vadium* in the English law; which is, when a man borrows a sum of money of another, and maketh over an estate of lands unto him, until he hath received the said sum of the issues and profits of the lands, so as in this case neither money nor land dieth, or is lost. And therefore it is called *vivum vadium,* to distinguish it from the other sort of mortgage called *mortuum vadium,* Coke 1. Instit. fol. 205. Domat's civil law, &c. by Dr. Strahan, T. 1. p. 356.) [[Coke, *The First Part of the Institutes of the Laws of England,* bk. 3, sect. 332. Jean Domat (1625–96), French jurist; see Domat, *Les loix civiles dans leur ordre naturel,* and *The Civil Law in Its Natural Order,* trans. Strahan.]]

from certain signs (§275). The most certain sign is gathered from his end and intention who hath acquired a thing, and hath bestowed care in keeping and preserving it.* <215>

SECTION CCLXXXV

Transition to succession by will, and to intestates.

Since therefore every one has a right to transfer his goods to others, and that alienation may be made upon any conditions (§267); the consequence is, that it may be made upon this condition, that another may obtain, after the alienator's death, the dominion and possession of a thing. Now, since this will may be truly declared, or can be certainly inferred from the intention of the acquirer; and since, in neither of these cases, the real and express acceptance of the other person to whom the transferrence is made, is necessary (§284); the former comes under the name of *succession to a last-will or testament;* and the latter is the genuine foundation of *succession to a person who dies intestate.*

* But the end and intention of men in acquiring and managing with great care, is always, not only that they may not want themselves, but that it may be well with theirs when they are dead and stand in need of nothing. Hence Euripides in Medea, v. 1098.

> *Sed quibus in aedibus est liberorum*
> *Dulce germen, eos video curis*
> *Confici omni tempore,*
> *Primum quidem, quo pacto bene ipsos educent.*
> *Et unde victum relinquant liberis.*

[[Euripides, *Medea,* l. 1098: "But as for those in whose houses sweet children are born, I see them worn out all the time by cares, first, as to how they can bring them up well and then from what source they can leave a livelihood to their children."]]

And in Iphigenia in Aulide. v. 917.

> *Res est vehemens parere, & adfert ingens desiderium:*
> *Communeque omnibus est, ut laborent pro liberis.*

[[Euripides, *Iphigenia in Aulis,* l. 917: "To give birth is a terrible thing and it brings a huge desire: it is common to all, to labour on behalf of children."]]

Of derivative acquisitions by succession to last-will and to intestates.

SECTION CCLXXXVI

A *Testament*, in the notion of Civilians, is a solemn declaration of one's will concerning the transition of his inheritance and all his rights to <216> another after his demise. And therefore, while the testator is alive, no right passes to his heirs; nay, not so much as any certain hopes of which they may not be frustrated; but the testator, while he lives, may alter his intention, and tearing or destroying his former will, make a new disposition, or die without a will.*

How a testament is defined by the Roman lawyers.

SECTION CCLXXXVII

But that such a testament is not known to the law of nature is evident. For tho' right reason easily admits that solemnities should be added to so serious an action, which is obnoxious to so many frauds; yet it implies a contradiction, to suppose a person to will when he cannot will, and to

Such a testament is not of the law of nature. First argument.

---

* Hence these known maxims of law, That the will of a testator is ambulatory till his death: That the last will alone is valid, being confirmed by death; or as Quintilian, Declam. 37. expresses it, "That testament alone is valid after which there can be no other," and several other such; yea, so far does this liberty with regard to testaments extend, that it is said none can deprive himself of the liberty of changing by any clause of renunciation, nor even by confirming his former testaments with an oath, l. ult. D. leg. 2. Grotius de jure belli & pacis, 2. 13. 19. Leyser. medit. ad Pand. spec. 43. n. 6. & 7. [[Augustin Leyser (1683–1752), *Meditationes ad Pandectas.*]]

desire his dominion to pass to another, then, when he himself has no longer any dominion. This is so absurd, that the Romans owned the contradiction could not be removed but by mere fictions.* <217>

SECTION CCLXXXVIII

Another argument. Add to this, that no reason can be imagined why the survivers should hold the will of the defunct for a law, especially when it very little concerns one, whatever his condition be, after death, whether Dion or Thion enjoys his goods:† yea, the last judgments of dying persons often proceed rather from hatred and envy than from true benevolence; and

---

* For since a testator neither transacts any affair with his heir when he disposes of his effects, nor the heir with the testator, when he acquires; and therefore, in neither case does any right pass from the one to the other; many things were feigned by lawyers, always very ingenious in this respect, to reconcile these inconsistencies. Hence they feigned the moment of testament-making to be the same with the very instant of dying, and the instant of death to be the same with the moment of entering upon a succession, bringing it back by fiction to the instant of death, l. 1. C. de 55. eccl. l. 54. D. de adqu. vel amitt. hered. l. 193. D. de reg. jur. Besides, they feigned the inheritance not entered upon to be no person's, but to represent the person of the deceased, §2. Inst. de hered. inst. l. 31. § ult. D. eod. l. 34. D. de adqu. rer. dom. Ant. Dadin. Alteserra de Fict. jur. tract. 4. 2. p. 143. [[Hauteserre, *De fictionibus juris tractatus quinque*]] Jo. Gottfr. a Coccei. de testam. princip. part. 1. §24.

† Hence Seneca of Benefits, 4. 11. says very elegantly "There is nothing we settle with such religious solemn care as that which nowise concerns us." As this very grave author denies that these last judgments belong to men; so in the same sense Quintilian Declam. 308, calls them a will beyond death. [[Quintilian, *Lesser Declamations*, vol. 1.]] Since therefore the Civilians do not allow even a living person to stipulate, unless it be the interest of the person stipulating, §4. Instit. de inut. stip. how, pray, can the same Roman lawyers before the validity of the wills of deceased persons, when it is not for their interest? We readily grant that the souls of men are immortal, (which we find urged by the celebrated Leibnitz, nov. method. jurisp. p. 56. [[Leibniz, *Nova methodus discendae docendaeque jurisprudentiae*]]) but hence it does not follow, that souls delivered from the chains of the body retain the dominion of things formerly belonging to them, much less that they should be affected with any concern about them.

Id cinerem & Manes credis curare sepultos?
Virg. Aen. 4. v. 92.

[[Virgil, *Aeneid* 4.34 (not 92), in vol. 1 of *Virgil:* "Thinkest thou that dust or buried shades give heed to that?"]]

in such cases, it seems rather to be the interest of the deceased that his will should not take effect, than that his survivers should religiously fulfil it. See our dissertation de testam. jure Germ. arct. limit. circumscript. §5. <218>

SECTION CCLXXXIX

Since therefore the law of nature scarcely approves of testament-making, as described by the Roman laws, *i.e.* as Ulpian elegantly defines it, tit. 20. "A declaration of our mind solemnly made to this end, that it may take place validly after our decease," (§286); the consequence is, 1. That it no more approves like customs of other nations; and therefore, 2. That testaments of the same kind among Greeks or Barbarians, are no more of the law of nature and nations than those* of the Romans; and for the same reason, 3. No nation hath accommodated their manners in this respect more to the simplicity of the law of nature than the Germans where there was no testament; (*heredes successoresque sui cuique liberi, & nullum testamentum;* Tacitus de mor. Germ. c. 20).[1] <219>

What with regard to the testaments in other nations.

---

* We find, from the time of Solon among the Athenians, a similar kind of testament, consisting in will on one side, with regard to what ought to be done after death, Plutarch. in Solone, p. 90. and among the Lacedemonians from the times of the Ephor Epitadeus. Plut. in Aegid. & Cleom. p. 797 [[Plutarch, *Plutarch's Lives,* vols. 1 ("Solon") and 10 ("Agis and Cleomenes")]], and among other Greeks, who all agreed, in this matter, in the same practice, as Isocrates tells us, in Aeginet. p. 778. [[Isocrates, "Aegineticus," in *Isocrates,* vol. 3, 298–353.]] There are likewise examples of such testaments among the Egyptians, as of Ptolomy in Caesar de bello civil. 3. 20. [[Caesar, *The Civil War*]] Hirt. de bello Alex. cap. 5. [[Hirtius, *Caii Iulii Caesaris de bellis gallico et civili Pompeiano nec non A. Hirtii aliorumque de bellis alexandrino, africano, et hispaniensi commentarii*]] Attalus King of Pergamos, in Florus, Hist. 2. 20. [[Florus, *Epitome of Roman History*]] Hiero of Sicily, of whom Livy, 24. 4. [[Livy, *History of Rome*]] and finally among the Hebrews themselves, of whose way of making wills, see Selden de success. ad leg. Heb. cap. 24. [[Selden, *Uxor Ebraica.*]] But that it was not of ancient usage among them, and that it owed its rise to the interpretations of their doctors, may be proved, amongst other arguments, by this consideration, that there is not a word in their language for a testament, and therefore they gave it a Greek name. See our Dissertation de testamentif. jure Germ. arct. limit. circumscript. §6.

1. Tacitus, *Germania* 20.5: "Yet each man has his own children as heirs, and successors and wills are unknown."

SECTION CCXC

What with regard to Grotius's definition.

This being the case, Grotius gave a new definition of a *testament,* (of the rights of war and peace, 2. 6. § ult.) he defines it thus; "Alienation to take place at the event of death, before that revocable, with retention of the right of use and possession." But as this definition does not quadrate with what we commonly call *testament,* and is faulty in several respects; (Ziegler. ad Grotium, 2. 6. Pufend. de jure nat. & gent. 4. 10. 2. and the illustrious Jo. Gottfr. de Coccei. ibid. §4. & seq.) so it does not follow that testament-making is of the law of nature, because that law does not disallow of alienation at the event of death, revocable before that event, with retention of the right of possessing and using.

SECTION CCXCI

What disposition with regard to succession after death is lawful by the law of nature.

But tho' the arguments above-mentioned plainly shew, that testament-making, according to the Roman law, is not of the law of nature, yet they are by no means repugnant to all dispositions with respect to future succession (§268).* Let us therefore enquire what these are which are approved by the law of nature. And I answer, they are nothing else but pacts, by which dying persons transfer a possession itself, with the dominion to others; or men in good health give others the right of succeeding to them at the event of their death. For since we can dispose of our own, not only for the present, but for the future (§268), we may

---

* And in the earliest ages of the world men disposed of their goods in no other way than this. So Abraham, having no children, had destined his possessions to his steward Eleasar, Gen. xv. 3. no doubt, by some successory, pact, or donation to take place at his death. The same Abraham, his wife Sarah being dead, having children by Kethura, distributed, while he was in health, part of his goods by donation, and gave the residue to Isaac, Gen. xxv. 5, 6. Thus Cyrus also at his death, in the presence of Cambyses, gave his eldest Son the kingdom, and to the younger the lordships of the Medes, the Armenians and Cadusians, Xenoph. Cyrop. 8. 7. 3. [[Xenophon, *Cyropaedia,* vol. 2, 8.7.2.]] Mention is made of a division and donation made by parents amongst their children upon the approach of death, Gen. xlviii. 22. Deut. xxi. 16, 17. 1 Kings, i. 35. Syrac. xxxiii. 24. and examples of it among the Francs are quoted by Marculf. Form. 1. 12. 2. 7. [[Marculfi Monachi, "Formularum Libri Duo," bk. I.12, cols. 381–82, in *Capitularia Regum Francorum,* vol. 2.]]

certainly make a pact for transferring to another what belongs to us, either to take place at present, or at our death.* <220>

SECTION CCXCII

Since every one therefore hath a right to transfer his goods for the present or for the future, at the event of his death (§291); the consequence is, that there is no reason why pacts about succession may not be pronounced agreeable to the law of nature.† But, on the contrary, they ought to be deemed valid by the best right, whether they be reciprocal, or obligatory on one side only; and whether they be acquisitive, preservative, or remunerative; for as to dispositive pacts, that they bind the contracters, but not him whose heritage is disposed of, is evident, because he hath made no pact about his own. <221>

What succes-
sory pacts are
valid.

SECTION CCXCIII

Besides, since such is the nature of all transfers of property, that any one may except or secure to himself any part of, or any right in his own he pleases, in which case, so much only is transmitted as the owner willed to transmit (§279); it is evident, that it is at the option of the owner to transfer the possession to his heir by pact at once; or the right only of succeeding to his estate after his death; to transfer either revocably or

How one may
dispose of his
inheritance.

---

* [[See note on previous page.]]

† The Roman law does not approve of them, but pronounces them contrary to good manners, and liable to very fatal consequences, l. ult. c. de pact. But the objections taken from the desire of one's death, that may thus be occasioned, do not lie stronger against such compacts than against donations in view of death, which are valid by the Roman law. Nor are those sad effects which Rome once suffered by legacy-hunters, an argument of any repugnancy between such pacts relative to succession after death and honesty, because neither testament nor any other human institution, is proof against the abuse of wicked men.

irrevocably;* with or without any condition; in whole or in part; so that there is no natural opposition between testate and intestate, as Pomponius seems to have imagined, l. 7. D. de reg. juris.

SECTION CCXCIV

Whether an heir be obliged to accept of the heritage destined for him.

But because a thing may be accepted, not only actually but presumptively, when from the nature of the thing it cannot but be concluded, that one will not refuse what another designs to transfer to him (§284); it must therefore be the same in effect by the law of nature, whether one be present and declares his consent, or being absent, so that he cannot accept verbally, there is no ground to apprehend that the liberality of another will be disagreeable to him;† especially, if the inheritance designed for him be very profitable. There is however this difference between these cases, that in the former the heir acquires a valid and irrevocable <222> right, unless the owner hath expresly reserved to himself the faculty of revoking; whereas in the latter, there is liberty to revoke till acceptation be made: And whereas an heir having declared his consent, cannot renounce the heritage he hath accepted, he whose consent

---

* Thus Abraham transferred an irrevocable right to his Sons by Kethura. And Telemachus in Homer's Odyss. B. 17. v. 77. transferred a revocable one to Piraeus,

> We know not yet the full event of all:
> Stabb'd in his palace, if your prince must fall,
> Us, and our house, if treason must o'erthrow,
> Better a friend possess them than a foe:
> Till then retain the gifts.

[[Lines 90 (not 77) to 96, bk. 17, in Pope's translation of the *Odyssey.*]]

† This whole matter is admirably illustrated by the chancellor of our college, my beloved collegue Jo. Petrus a Ludewig, in a dissertation wrote with great judgment and erudition, de differentiis juris Romani & Germanici in donationibus, & barbari adnexus, acceptatione. Hal. 1721 [[Ludewig (*praeses*) and Krimpff (*respondens*), *De differentiis iuris Romani & Germanici*]], where he hath shewn by impregnable examples and arguments, that neither the nature of donation, nor the Justinian, nor the Canon, nor the German law, requires acceptation made by words or other signs, and hath solidly refuted all objections.

is presumed, may enter upon or refuse the heritage transferred to him, as he thinks proper.

SECTION CCXCV

But if an owner can really and truly will that his goods may be transferred to one after his death (§291), there is no reason why as much should not be attributed to one's will, presumed from his end and intention, as to one's will expressed by words or signs (§268). Now we have already shewn, that it is not the end and intention of those who acquire any thing, and take care of their acquisitions, that they should after their death be held for things relinquished to the first occupant; but that they should be advantageous to those whom they love and wish well to (§284). But hence we may justly conclude the succession to belong to them, preferably to all others, for whose sake chiefly the defunct acquired and took care of his acquisitions with so much concern and sollicitude.*
<223>

The foundation of succession to one who dies intestate.

SECTION CCXCVI

But because this is not a duty of perfect obligation, but rather a species of humanity, which pays regard to persons and ties or connexions, and therefore prefers relatives to strangers (§220); hence we have reason to

Axioms relating to it.

---

* This is so true, that nothing ordinarily is so vexatious and tormenting to men as the thoughts of their estate's falling to men they hate, after their death, and when, as the Poet has it,

> *Stet domo capta cupidus superstes,*
> *Imminens lethi spoliis, & ipsum*
>   *Computet ignem.*

[["Let the greedy man stand, a survivor when the house is captured, hanging over the spoils of death and calculating the very fire" (Statius, *Silvae* 4.7.38–40).]]

Nothing is more certain than what Pindar says in a passage quoted by Pufendorff on this subject (of the law of nature and nations, 4. II. I.) "Riches which are to fall into the hands of a stranger, are odious to the dying person."

infer, that relatives exclude all strangers from succession, and that among relatives those of the nearer degrees are preferable; and that many of the same line and degree have equal rights to succession.* <224>

SECTION CCXCVII

The succession of children.

Since of relatives the more remote are excluded by the nearer (§296), but none can be reckoned nearer to one than children are to their parents; therefore they are justly preferred in succession to their parents before all others, and that without distinction of sex or age:† For as to the preference given in some countries to males, and to the first-born, that, because it is making an unequal division among equals, proceeds from civil

* For tho' it be not always true, that kindred are dearer to one than strangers: yea, so far is it from it, that love amongst brothers is very rare: yet since, if the defunct had been of that opinion, nothing hindered him to have disposed of his estate as he pleased, and to have left it to whom he liked best (§291); and he chose rather to die without making such a disposition; he cannot but be judged not to have envied the inheritance of his goods to his relatives, whom natural affection itself seems of choice to call to the succession. But one is nearer, not only in respect of degree, but likewise in respect of line. For Aristotle hath justly observed, that natural affection falls by nature upon the descending line, and failing that upon the ascending line, and failing both these upon the collateral, Nicomach. 8. 12. Hence Grandchildren, tho' in the second degree, are nearer than a parent, and a great grandfather, tho' in the fourth degree, is nearer than a brother, &c.

† But if the thing be indivisible, there is no doubt it may (ceteris paribus) be left to the first-born, on condition that he make satisfaction to the rest (§270). The first-born are wont to have a special prerogative, if the heritage be indivisible; especially if it be a crown or sovereignty. Cyrus in Xenophon says elegantly, "This also I must now declare to you, even to whom I leave my kingdom, lest that being left doubtful, should occasion disquiets. I love you, my sons, both with equal affection: But I order that the eldest should govern by his prudence, and do the duty of a general, when there shall be use or occasion for it, and that he should have, in a certain suitable proportion, the larger and superior use of my demesnes." [[Xenophon, *Cyropaedia* 8.7.8.]] Tho' the affections of kings be equal towards all their children; yet the nature of government itself seems to require, that sons should be preferred in succession to sovereignty to daughters, and amongst them the eldest to the younger, insomuch that it is become, as Herodotus says, a received law in all nations, l. 7. p. 242. [[Herodotus, *Histories*, Selincourt translation, bk. 7, p. 372]] and what is done against this rule, is, according to the ancients, against the law of nations. See Justin. Hist. 12. 2. 24. 3. Liv. 40. 9.

law, pact, or some other disposition; and so it is not of the law of nature (§271).

SECTION CCXCVIII

But if in succession to parents children be justly preferable to all others (§297), and this may be concluded from the presumed will of parents, (§295); the consequence is, that it ought to be <225> certainly known who is the child. But because that cannot be ascertained except in the case of lawful marriage; hence we infer, that legitimate children only, even posthumous ones, and not illegitimate ones, or bastards, succeed to a father; but that all children succeed promiscuously to a mother; tho' none will deny that a father may take care of his illegitimate children in his disposition.

Legitimate children only succeed to the father, but to the mother even illegitimate children succeed.

SECTION CCXCIX

Besides, it may be inferred from the same will of parents (§295), that the succession of descendents extends not only to children of the nearest, but of the more remote degrees; and therefore that grandsons and granddaughters are admitted to inherit, as well as sons and daughters; and that not only if there be no children of the first degree, but if they concur with them; so that the right of representation, by which children of the remoter degrees succeed into the room of their parents, and receive their portion, is most agreeable to the law of nature.* <226>

How grandchildren succeed.

* And this is the foundation of the succession of children of the first degree, *in capita,* by heads, and those of remoter degrees, *in stirpes,* by descent. That this is consonant to the law of nature appears even from hence, that if contrariwise, all should succeed *in capita,* the condition of the surviving children would be rendered worse by the death of a brother or sister, and the condition of grandchildren would be bettered by the death of their parents, and so there would be no equality among them. For if the father were worth a hundred pieces, and had four children, each would get twenty five pieces. Now suppose one of the four, contrary to the course of nature, to have died before the father, leaving seven grandchildren to him: in that case, if all succeeded *in capita,* each would get ten pieces; and thus by the brother's death, the three children of the first degree would have lost forty five pieces, and the

SECTION CCC

What if none
other exist?

From the same rule, that the nearest of many relatives are to be preferred (§296), it follows, that grandchildren are to be preferred both to the parents of the grandfather, tho' nearer in degree, and to his brothers and sisters, tho' equal in degree. For one is to be judged nearer, not only in respect of degree, but chiefly in regard to line (§296).* But whether natural equity in this case calls grandchildren to succession by heads, or by descent, may be easily understood from what hath been said in the preceding scholium.

SECTION CCCI

Succession in
the ascendent
line.

Since, failing the line of descendents the nearest is the ascendent (§296), hence it is plain, that the mournful succession to their children is due to the progenitors,† and in such a manner, that <227> the nearer in degree

---

seven grandchildren would have gained as much by the untimely death of their father. But since no reason can be assigned why the death of a brother should diminish the patrimony of the surviving brothers or sisters, and add to that of the grandchildren; no reason can be given why both should be admitted to succession equally *in capita*.

* For no reason can be brought, why the condition of one issue should be bettered and another worsted by the untimely death of parents; which must however be the case, if the grandchildren surviving their parent should be admitted by heads: Because, suppose a man worth a hundred pieces to have four sons, and to have by the first, one, by the second, two, by the third, three, and by the fourth, four grandchildren alive; if the sons had survived they would have received each twenty five pieces, and have consequently transmitted each to his children as much. But if they dying, the grandchildren be admitted to succession by heads, each would get ten pieces, and thus the one grandchild by the first son would lose fifteen pieces, the two by the second five, and the three by the third would gain five, and the four by the fourth would gain fifteen. But if this be unreasonable, it must be unreasonable to admit grandchildren in this case to succession by heads.

† This is so agreeable to right reason, that whereas the divine law established this order of inheritance, that the sons should stand first, the daughters next, then the brothers, and in the fourth place the uncles by the father's side, Num. xxvii. 8. & seq. Philo [[Philo of Alexandria, a philosopher, writer, and political figure in the first century A.D., a leading exponent of Jewish Alexandrian culture in that period. His writings on the Old Testament were strongly informed by Platonism.]] remarks, that something ought here to be supplied by right reason. "For it would be foolish (says

excludes the more remote, and those of the same degree come in equally. Nor does the law of nature in this case suggest any reason why the inheritance of children should be divided among many of the same degree according to lines; so that these, and like cases, must rather be left to the determination of civil laws.

SECTION CCCII

It follows from the same principle (§296), that failing both the ascending and descending line, the succession to intestates devolves on the collateral kindred, according to the degree of nearness in which they stand; nor is there any reason why the *right of representation* should take place among collaterals;* much less is there any reason why duplicity of ties, or the origine of the goods should <228> make any difference. In this case, many of the same degree equally divide the inheritance: nor is there any difference how far they may be removed from the defunct, seeing it

Succession of collaterals.

---

he) to imagine, that the uncle should be allowed to succeed his brother's son, as a near kinsman to the father, and yet the father himself be abridged of that privilege. But in as much as the law of nature appoints (*where by the law of nature Philo undoubtedly understands the order of nature*) that children should be heirs to their parents, and not parents to their children, Moses passed this case over in silence as ominous and unlucky, and contrary to all pious wishes and desires, lest the father and mother should seem to be gainers by the immature death of their children, who ought to be affected with most inexpressible grief: Yet by allowing the right of inheritance to the uncles, he obliquely admits the claim of the parents, both for the preservation of decency and order, and for the continuing the estate in the same family." Nor do the Talmudists reason otherwise about succession in the ascendent line. See Selden de success. in bona def. ad leges Hebr. cap. 12. where this matter is fully and accurately handled.

* For since succession belongs preferably to those for whom the defunct chiefly acquired and managed with care (§295), and experience shews us, that affection is commonly no less ardent towards the remoter than the nearer descendents: Hence it is justly concluded, that grandfathers had no inclination to take from their grandchildren what was due to their parents; and on account of this presumed inclination or will, they ought to succeed to the rights of their parents. On the other hand, the same experience teaches us, that with respect to collaterals, affection diminishes every remove, and therefore it does not follow that a brother's son, *e.g.* should come into the same place with the uncle as his brother. Hence there is no reason why a brother's son should concur with brothers in succession.

was in his power to appoint another heir, if he had no mind they should be made happy by his estate.

SECTION CCCIII

Much is here left to civil legislators.

So far does right reason acknowledge the right of succession in kindred. But because it is obvious to every one, that all these things belong rather to the permissive than to the preceptive part of the law of nature, much must here be left to civil legislature, to fix and determine by their laws, as the end and interest of their states may require (§18). And hence it is easy to give a good reason why legislators have thought the surviving wife should be taken care of; and why there is no branch of law almost in which civil laws and statutes so much differ, as with regard to succession to intestates.

SECTION CCCIV

Whether any heirs be necessary?

Seeing this whole right of succession proceeds from presumed will (§285); but he, whose consent is presumed, may enter upon an inheritance, <229> or renounce it as he pleases (§294), it must be evident to every one, that *necessary* heirs are unknown to the law of nature.* And therefore that no person is heir to an intestate by unalterable right, but becomes such by his consent, declared by words or deeds.

---

* That reason is quite a stranger to heirs necessary, voluntary and extraneous, is plain, because it knows nothing of the reason lawyers had in their view in making such distinctions. First of all, this quality and difference of heirs belongs chiefly to testamentary heirs, to which, as we have already observed, the law of nature is a stranger (§287), because to one who dies intestate, no servant succeeds as necessary heir. Again, a testament among the Romans was a sort of private law. And they thought a testator could indeed give law to his servants and children, whose duty and glory it was to obey their will, but not to strangers not subject to their power. Hence they called those *necessary* and these *voluntary* heirs, (Elem. sec. ord. Inst. §95). [[Heineccius, *Elementa iuris civilis secundum ordinem Pandectarum.*]] But since the law of nature knows nothing of all this, it cannot possibly know any thing of this difference with respect to heirs.

SECTION CCCV

Now, when one determines to succeed to another, nothing is more equal, than that he should be adjudged to succeed to all his rights and burdens (§267); whence it follows, that an heir, whether by the real disposition of the deceased, or by his presumed will, acquires all his rights, which are not extinguished by his death; and that he has no reason to complain, if he be bound to satisfy all his obligations, as far as the inheritance is sufficient.* <230>

How heirs succeed to the rights and obligations of the deceased.

---

* Not therefore, *in solidum,* in whole. For since there is no other reason why an heir is obliged to fulfil what the defunct was bound to do by buying or hiring, and to pay his debts, but because he hath acquired his goods, no reason can be imagined why he should be bound farther than the inheritance is sufficient to answer. Besides that rigour of the Roman law, by which an heir succeeded to all the obligations of the defunct, turns upon a fiction, that the heir and the defunct are the same person, l. 22. D. de usucap. l. 14. C. de usufr. Novell. 48. praef. Ant. Dadin. Alteserra de fiction. jur. tractat. 1. cap. 20. p. 48. [[Antoine Dadin de Hauteserre, *De fictionibus juris.*]] Now since the law of nature knows no such fiction, it cannot know that which follows from it alone.

∞ CHAPTER XII ∞

Concerning the rights and duties which arise from property or dominion.

SECTION CCCVI

A three-fold effect of dominion.

Dominion is the right of excluding all others from the use of something (§231). But when we exclude others from the use of a thing, we pretend to have the sole right of using it. Hence the first effect of dominion is the *free disposal* of a thing; *i.e.* the right or faculty of granting any one the use of it; nay, of abusing it, and of alienating it at his pleasure. Again, from what we can justly exclude others, that we retain to ourselves with that intention, and therefore *possession* is amongst the effects of dominion. Finally, we also exclude others from the use of a thing, when, being in another's possession, we reclaim it. But to reclaim a thing in another's possession, being to endeavour to *recover* it, it follows, that one of the noblest effects of dominion is the right of *recovering* our own from whomsoever possessing it.* <231>

* All these effects of dominion are acknowledged by the Roman law. For what is said by Caius, l. 2. D. si a par. quis man. "That it is unjust for men not to have the liberty of alienating their goods," it is to be understood of free disposal. In like manner Paullus infers, from the right of possession belonging to the lord or master only, l. 3. §5. D. de adqu. vel amitt. possess. "That many cannot possess the same thing in whole; and that it is contrary to nature that you should possess what I possess. That two can no more possess the same thing, than you should occupy the same place in which I am." All belonging to the reclaiming of a thing, which is the principal action arising from dominion, is well known. Hence it is among the paradoxical themes of dispute, "That the lord of timber cannot recover it, if it be joined," §29. Inst. de rer. divis.

SECTION CCCVII

Since therefore the owner has a right to *apply* his own to any use what-soever (§306), the consequence is, that he has a right to enjoy all the profits arising from the thing itself, and from its accessions and incre-ments, as far as these can be acquired by the proprietor (§250); and there-fore to reap all the fruits, and either to consume or share them with others, or to transfer them to others upon whatsoever account. Nay, be-cause the yearly fruits and profits of things may be increased by art and careful management, nothing hinders a master from altering the thing, and so rendering it more profitable, provided he do not by so doing deprive another of his right.*

Hence the owner has the right to use the profits.

SECTION CCCVIII

Since he hath likewise the right of abusing (§256), *i.e.* of consuming, or of destroying the thing and its fruits, Donat. ad Terent. Andr. <232> prolog. v. 5.[1] the consequence is, that the master may destroy the thing which is his own, provided he do it not with that intention that another may thereby receive detriment.† For tho' such a spoiling of our own goods, which may be beneficial to others, be repugnant to the love of

As likewise of corrupting or spoiling it.

* This right belongs to the master only, as is plain when we consider the right of usufruct, of use, of loan, of hire, all which, because they are exerced about a thing belonging to another, do not include the right of changing a thing at pleasure, tho' all of them include the right of reaping the fruits. Therefore the right of taking the profits may be common to the master with others, but the faculty of changing the thing, *i.e.* the principal or substance, is proper to the master only, nor can he who has the right of use, usufruct, loan or hire, claim it without his permission.

† For if any corrupts his own with an intention to hurt another, he does it with a design to injure another, and by doing hurt to him, really injures another. But it being the first and chief principle of natural law, not to hurt any one (§178), the consequence is, that he acts contrary to the law of nature who spoils his own goods with such an intention. And to this class belongs the wickedness of those who poison their flowers to destroy their neighbour's bees, Quinct. Declam. 13. [[Quintilian, *The Major Declamations.*]]

1. Aelius Donatus (fl. 4th century A.D.) was the author of a commentary on the works of Terence.

humanity (§217); yet he does not violate expletive justice, who, in consequence of his having dominion, abuses his own, and without any necessity urging him so to do, corrupts it.

SECTION CCCIX

As likewise of alienating them.

Because the free power or right of a master to dispose of his own comprehends likewise the right of alienation (§306), it may easily be understood, that an owner can abdicate his dominion, and transfer it to another, either now, or for a time to come, and grant any other advantage by it, or right in it, to any person; and therefore give it in use, usufruct, mortgage, pledge, as he will, provided no law, no pact, no other more valid disposition stand in his way.

SECTION CCCX

Since possession also is one of the effects of dominion (§306), it is plain that the owner can take possession of what belongs to him, and defend his possession against every one, even by force; and that it makes no difference whether one possesses by himself or by another; yea, that possession once <233> acquired, may be retained by an absent person, and by will merely, while another hath not seized it.*

SECTION CCCXI

The right also of recovering it.

Finally, the right of *recovering* a thing being among the effects of dominion (§306), it cannot but be that we may use our right against any possessor of what is ours; nor does it make any difference as to the restitution, whether one detain what is ours from us honestly or fraudu-

---

* For possession is the retention of a thing, from the use of which we have determined to exclude others (231). As long therefore as we have determined to exclude others from the use of a thing, so long we have not relinquished it (§241): Wherefore, such a thing is not without a master, and none has a right to seize it. But what none hath a right to seize, I certainly retain the possession of, even tho' at distance, by my will merely.

lently; nor whether he be known to us or a stranger; because we do not reclaim the thing on account of any deed of his; but because we have a right to it. Besides, since to reclaim and recover a thing is not the same as to redeem it; it is manifest, that when an owner recovers his own, he is not bound to restore the price; tho' equity doth not permit that one should be inriched at another's expence ($257), or that he should refuse the necessary and useful expences laid out upon a thing by the possessor.* <234>

SECTION CCCXII

Since the owner can claim to himself all the accessions and fruits of his own goods ($307), it may be enquired, whether an honest possessor be obliged to restore to the owner reclaiming his own, all the accessions, and all the fruits, nay, all the gain he hath received from another's goods? We conceive thus of the matter in a few words. He who honestly, and with a just title, possesses a thing, as long as the true owner is not known, has the right of excluding all persons from the use of what he possesses. But he who has this right is in the room of the owner ($231), and therefore enjoys all the same rights as the owner; yet, because he is not the true master who possesses a thing honestly, there is no reason why he should desire to be inriched to the loss of the true owner; as there is none, on the other hand, why the master should claim to himself the fruits not existing, which were not owing to his care and industry.† <235>

How far he may recover the accessions and fruits.

---

* To which case, without all doubt, belong the expences, without which the master himself could not have recovered his own from robbers, especially if the possessor redeemed it with intention to have it restored to its owner, Pufend. law of nature, &c. 4. 12. 13. at which paragraph Hertius in his notes has brought an excellent example from Famian. Strada's Decades de bello belgico, l. 7. ad annum 1572. "When the merchants of Antwerp had redeemed merchandize of above a hundred thousand pieces in value, from a Spanish soldier, who had plundered the city of Mechlin, for twenty thousand, the owners got them back, upon restoring that sum, because they could not have recovered the goods with less expence." [[Strada, *De bello belgico decas prima.* See also Pufendorf, *Acht Bücher.*]]

† For a natural accession to a thing, the master of which is not known ($241), belongs to none, and so goes to the first occupant. Since therefore the honest possessor has seized the fruits which he produced by his own care and industry, there is no reason why they should be taken from him. And therefore the Justinian law not ab-

SECTION CCCXIII

The accessions and the fruits belong to the master. Because neither ought to be inriched at the other's loss (§312), the consequence is, that even the accessions ought to be restored to the master reclaiming his own thing, and therefore he hath a right to demand the existing and hanging fruits,* the expences laid out upon them being deducted; because the master would be inriched to the detriment of the honest possessor, if he should take to himself the fruits upon which he had bestowed no care.

SECTION CCCXIV

The fruits gathered and consumed to the possessor. But since a natural accession to a thing, the owner of which is not known, goes to the first occupant as a thing belonging to no body, the same is to be said of the civil fruits (§212); consequently, the fruits gathered ought to be left to an honest possessor, who bestowed his labour and care about them, unless he be made richer by them (§212).† <236>

---

surdly says, "That it is agreeable to natural equity and reason, that the fruits which an honest possessor hath gathered, should be his for his care and labour." Nor is the case different with regard to civil fruits. For they, in like manner, when they are received having no certain master, and the true master of the substance producing them, having had no trouble about, belong also to an honest possessor, so long as the true master does not appear.

* This Grotius grants (of the right of war and peace, 2. 8. 23. and 2. 10. 4.) but only with respect to natural fruits. But since even the industrial fruits are accessions to the principal of an owner, who is now known, no reason can be imagined why an honest possessor should claim them to himself. But the master can by no means refuse to repay expences, because he would otherwise demand fruits which he did not produce by his care and industry (§312). Whence the Hebrews thus proverbially described a hard austere man, "One who reaps where he did not sow, and gathers where he did not straw," Mat. xxv. 24. Luke xix. 21.

† The Civilians follow this principle in demanding an inheritance, l. 25. §11. & §15. l. 36. §4. l. 40. §1. D. de hered. petit. But in reclaiming a thing, they adjudge indiscriminately the reaped fruits to an honest possessor, and make no account of the matter, whether he be enriched by them or not, l. 4. §2. D. fin. regund. l. 48. pr. D. de adqu. rer. dom. But the reason of this difference is merely civil, and not founded in natural law. For in suing for heritage, as being an universal action, the price is deemed to succeed into the room of the thing, not in singular actions. But the law

SECTION CCCXV

From the same rules, that an honest possessor is in the room of the owner, but yet cannot inrich himself at the detriment of another (§312); we infer, that he is no more obliged to make restitution to the owner, if he infraudulently consumed the thing, than if it had perished in his possession by chance; but that he is obliged, if he sell the thing he acquired without paying any price, or a small price, for a greater price, because he would be richer at another's cost, if he kept the profit to himself. On the other hand, this obligation ceases, if the owner hath already received the value of his thing from another; partly because in this case an honest possessor is indeed made richer, but not at the cost of the owner; and partly because the owner has a right not to sue for gain, but only for loss.

Whether an honest possessor be obliged to pay the value of a thing consumed, perished, or alienated.

SECTION CCCXVI

Because all this belongs to honest possessors only; and, on the other hand, because fraudulent possessors are neither in the room of the owner, nor have they the right of use, on this score, that the owner is not known to them; and therefore none of these reasons, why one may enjoy any advantage by a thing, or its fruits, takes place; hence it is plain, that they are strictly bound not only to restore what is existing, but to refund the value of things consumed or alienated; and much more, <237> of all the fruits they have, or might have reaped from them, and likewise to run all risks.*

What a fraudulent possessor is obliged to restore.

---

of nature does not make these distinctions; and therefore it is most equal that those received fruits should be indiscriminately restored to the true owner, by which one is made richer. And that this is now the practice observed in courts, is observed by Stryk. Us. hod. Digest. 6. 1. 12.

* For tho' accidents be regularly imputable to no person (§106), yet this rule does not take place if it was the agent's fault that any accident happened (§ ibidem), because then there is default as well as accident. Now, a fraudulent possessor could and ought to have restored the thing to its true owner, and if he had done it, he would have prevented its perishing in his hands. He is therefore obliged to answer for all accidents; whence the Roman lawyers have rightly determined, that a thief and robber

SECTION CCCXVII

The effects of dominion are sometimes restricted by civil laws.

Now these are the rights which arise plainly from dominion; but since it belongs to civil law to adjust indifferent actions to the interest of each people or state (§18); and it is frequently the interest of a state, that no member should make a bad use of his goods (Instit. §2. de his qui sui vel alieni juris sunt,) it is no wonder that dominion is sometimes confined within narrower limits by governors of states, and that sometimes the liberty of disposal, sometimes the right of taking possession, and sometimes the right of recovering, is either wholly taken away from owners, or not allowed to them but under certain restrictions.* <238>

SECTION CCCXVIII

Sometimes by the pacts and dispositions of the first owners.

And because an owner has the liberty of disposing of his goods in his life, or in the prospect of death (§268), and then just as much is transferred to another, as he who alienates willed to transfer, (§279), it is plain the effects of dominion may be restricted by the pact and disposition of the former owner,† and in this case the possessor can arrogate no more

---

are answerable for all chances, because they are always the cause why a thing is not in the possession of its owner, (*quia semper in mora sint*) l. 8. §1. D. de condict furt.

* Thus we find the civil law taking the free disposal of their goods from pupils, mad persons, prodigals, minors. The same law does not allow a legatee, tho' owner of the thing left to him in legacy, to take possession, and gives the heir a prohibition against him, if he goes to seize at his own hand. (Interdictum quod legatorum) tot. tit. D. quod legat. Again, it is known that he, whose timber another hath joined, tho' he be the owner of the materials, and doth not lose his dominion, yet he cannot recover the timber when joined, by the laws of the twelve tables, §29. Inst. de rerum divis. l. 7. D. de adqu. rerum dom. So that there is almost no effect of dominion which the civil laws suffer to remain always and wholly safe and entire, if the public good of the common-wealth require it should not: For this magistrates justly account the supreme law in all those matters, which belong to the permissive part of the law of nature. Because, since any one by the law of nature may renounce his permissive rights (§13), a people may also renounce them, and hath actually renounced them by submitting themselves to the laws enacted by the supreme power under whose authority they have put themselves.

† Thus sometimes the right of reaping all advantage from a thing is circumscribed within narrower limits by the disposition of the former owner, as, *e.g.* if he hath

to himself than he received from the former owner, unless he in whose favour the restriction was made, voluntarily quit his right, cease to exist, or lose his right by a just cause. <239>

SECTION CCCXIX

Hitherto we have only treated of rights arising from dominion or property. Now since right and obligation are correlates, and therefore a right being constituted an obligation is constituted (§7); the consequence is, that as many rights as dominion gives to an owner, just so many obligations does it lay others under with regard to the owner. Because therefore an owner hath the liberty of disposing (§306), they injure him who hinder him in disposing or enjoying the fruits of his own:* They also do him damage who corrupt or spoil the fruits and accessions of his property. And in general, since he who intercepts or corrupts any thing that tends to the perfection or happiness of another certainly wrongs him (§82), but none ought to be wronged (§178); hence we may justly conclude, that none ought to have his free disposition of his own disturbed or hindered; that none ought to have his goods damaged; and therefore, if any thing of that kind be done, the author of the injury is bound to make reparation, and is moreover liable to punishment.

A proprietor ought not to be hurt by any one in the use of his own.

---

given another the usufruct, any right of service, or hath pawned it (§282). Sometimes the liberty of disposing, destroying, and alienating is taken from the master, as when the dominion or right of use merely is given him (§279); or when the thing is burdened with some fiduciary bequest, &c. An usufruct being constituted, even the right of possession, which could not otherwise be refused to the owner, is restricted; as when the right of use is given to one, the direct or superior lord has neither the right of possessing the thing, nor of claiming what appertains to the right of use.

* For the Roman lawyers define *an injury* to be not only any wrong done to a person by words or deeds, but any action by which one is hindered from the use either of public things, or of what is his own, or by which one arrogates to himself any degree of liberty in disposing of what belongs to another. Thus by the leg. Cornel. he is guilty of injury who enters another's house forcibly, l. 5. pr. D. de injur. he who hinders one to fish in the sea, or to draw a drag-net, to bath in public baths, to sit on a public theatre, or to act, sit, or converse in any other place, or who does not permit us to have the use of what is our own, l. 13. §7. D. eod.

SECTION CCCXX

Nor directly nor indirectly intercept or hinder his possession.

Seeing possession belongs to the rights of property (§306), the consequence is, that it is our duty to <240> suffer every one to possess his own quietly and unmolested, and not to deprive any one of his possession against his will directly or indirectly. And that if any one can be proved to have done any such thing, he is bound as an injurious person, to repair all the damage he has done, and is moreover liable to condign punishment.

SECTION CCCXXI

It is done directly by theft, rapine and violent ejection.

One carries off another's possession directly, either by open force, or by taking it away clandestinely. The latter is called *theft.* The former, if the thing be moveable, is called *rapine;* and if it be immoveable it is called *force,* or *violent ejection. Theft* is therefore taking away another's goods in a clandestine manner, without the knowledge and against the will of the owner, to make profit of them.* *Rapine* or *robbery* is bearing off a

---

* If a thing be carried away to affront one, or by way of contumely, it is called an *injury;* if it be carried away in order to spoil it, it is called *damage.* Thus in Homer, Iliad. A. v. 214. Minerva says that Chryseis was taken from Achilles ὕβριος εἵνεκα, to rub an affront upon him. It was therefore an injury, and not theft or robbery. And he is more properly said to have damaged than to have stollen, who, as Horace says, Serm. 1. 3. v. 116.

> *Teneros caules alieni infregerit horti.*

[[Horace, *Satires I* 3.116: "has cut some young cabbages from another's garden."]]

But without doubt Cacus was guilty of theft properly so called,

> *Quatuor a stabulis praestanti corpore tauros*
> *Avertit, totidem forma superante juvencas,*
> *Atque hos, ne qua forent pedibus vestigia rectis,*
> *Cauda in speluncam tractos, versisque viarum*
> *Indiciis, raptos saxo occultabat opaco.*
>   Virg. Aeneid, 8. v. 207.

[[Virgil, *Aeneid* 8.205ff., in vol. 2 of *Virgil:* "But Cacus, his wits wild with frenzy, that naught of crime or craft might prove to be left undared or unes-

moveable thing by violence, against the owner's will, to make profit of it: And *force* is ejecting one violently out of his possession of an immoveable thing. <241>

SECTION CCCXXII

One is said to take away another's possession *indirectly,* who by fraudulent words or deeds is the cause of his losing it; and this we call *defraudation.* Now since one is likewise hurt in this manner, but none ought to do to another what he would not have done to himself (§177); it is self-evident, that they are no less guilty than thiefs and robbers, who, by insidious words, cheat one out of his goods;* or by moving boundaries, using false weights and measures, and other such knavish practices, adventure to take off any thing from one's estate.

Indirectly by defrauding.

---

sayed, drove from their stalls four bulls of surpassing form, and as many heifers of peerless beauty. And these, that there might be no tracks pointing forward, he dragged by the tail into his cavern, and, with the signs of their course thus turned backwards, he hid them in the rocky darkness."]]

Tho' the ancients thought theft might be said of immoveables (l. 38. D. de usurp. & usucap. Gell. Noct. Attic. 11. 18. Plin. Hist. nat. 2. 68. [[Pliny the Elder, *Natural History,* vol. 1, bk. 2, chap. 68]] Gronov. observ. 1. 4. p. 42. [[Gronovius, *Observationum libri III*]]) yet this application of the word is inconvenient, and therefore we do not use it in that sense.

* For all these crimes agree in one common end, this being the design of the thief, the robber and the defrauder, to bereave others of their goods. They agree also with regard to the motive or impelling cause, *viz.* knavery. They agree likewise in the effect, which is making one poorer. Nay the defrauder is sometimes worse than the thief or robber in this respect, that he circumvents one under the mask of friendship, and therefore cannot be so easily guarded against as a thief or robber. They are therefore, with good reason, joined together by that excellent teacher of morals, Euripides in Helena, v. 909. who there says, "God hates force, and commands every one to possess the purchase of his own industry, and not to live by plunder. Base and unjust riches are to be renounced with contempt." [[Euripides, *Helen,* lines 903–5, in *Euripides,* vol. 5: *Helen, Phoenician Women, Orestes.*]] To which unjust and base riches belongs more especially, as every one will readily acknowledge, whatever one knavishly cheats others of.

SECTION CCCXXIII

What is
another's
ought to be
restored
to him.

The last right which belongs to the lord of a thing, *viz. the right of re-covering it,* must found <242> an obligation *to restore what belongs to another to its owner.* But hence we conclude, that every one, into whose hands any thing belonging to another comes without his fault, is obliged to take care that it be restored to its owner;* and therefore, that it ought not to be hid or concealed, but that public notice ought to be given of it, that the owner may have it again, upon making his right to it appear, Deut. xxii. 1. l. 43. §4. D. de furt. and that the possessor ought to be much more ready to restore it, if the author claim it, or publickly advertise his having lost it. But in both cases equity requires partly that the restitution should not be made at the expence of an honest possessor, and partly that he may not be made richer at another's cost (§312). <243>

---

* But even this obligation to restitution does not always take place, because sometimes right reason dissuades from restitution, sometimes the civil laws free the possessor from all obligation to restitution. An example of the first case is a madman claiming his sword deposited by himself; of which Seneca of benefits, 4, 10. Cicero de offic. 1. 10. 3. 25. And like examples are adduced by Ambros. de offic. 1. ult. [[Ambrose, *De officiis.*]] To the last exception belong *usucapion* and *prescription.* For that these are unknown to the law of nature, seems most certain and evident; because time, which is a mere relation, can, of its own nature, neither give nor take away dominion. And, as we observed above, our dominion cannot otherwise pass to another than by tradition or transferring. Whence it is plain, that one can neither acquire dominion without some deed of the proprietor, nor can the proprietor lose it without some deed of his own. Wherefore *usucapion* and *prescription* owe their origine to civil laws, which introduced both for the public good, l. 1. D. de usurp. & usucap. partly to put a period to the trouble and danger of contests, Cicero pro Caecin. c. 26. [[Cicero, "Pro Caecina," in *Pro lege Manilia, Pro Caecina*]] partly to excite men who are indolent and neglectful, to reclaim their goods in due time, by giving them to see the advantages of vigilance above negligence; so that the observation of Isocrates is very just in Archidam. p. 234. "All are persuaded that possessions, whether private or public, are confirmed by long prescription, and justly held as patrimonial estate." [[Isocrates, *Isocrates,* vol. 1, "Archidamus," 26 (p. 361).]] But it does not follow, that whatever many are persuaded of is therefore a precept of the law of nature. And this it was proper to mention, that none may be surprized that we have taken no notice of *usucapion* and *prescription* in treating of property or dominion.

SECTION CCCXXIV

But if the true owner do not appear to claim a thing, it is understood to be no body's, and therefore it justly falls to the honest possessor* (§241). And tho' those who have assumed to themselves the direction of consciences, commonly exhort to give things to the poor when the owner of them does not appear; yet he cannot be called unjust, who, making use of his right, takes to himself a thing morally free from dominion. See Nic. Burgund. ad consu. Flandr. l. 2. n. 1.[2]

What if the true owner do not appear.

REMARKS on This Chapter

We have not had occasion for some time to add to our Author, or to make any remarks on his reasonings. And indeed the reason why I choose to translate this Author into our language, is because there is seldom any occasion to add to what he says, and almost never any ground of disputing against him, so orderly, clear, just and full, is his method of proceeding in this most useful of all sciences. But because *usucapion* and *prescription* are usually treated of at greater length by writers on the laws of nature and nations than our Author does; and because this is a proper occasion to explain a little upon the distinctions that are commonly made <244> by moralists about the dictates of the law of nature and right reason, or conformity to them, let me subjoin the following observations.

1. First of all, it is proper to observe the difference which the Roman law makes between *prescription* in general, and that kind of it which they distinguished by the name of *usucapio*. By *usucapio* they meant

* Besides, the master of a thing alone has the right of excluding others from the use of it. Since therefore the master does not appear, none has this right; and, for this reason, nothing hinders why an honest possessor may not retain it to himself. But because in many countries things free from dominion of any value may be claimed by the people or prince (§242), it is plain, that in such countries, where that custom or law prevails, an honest occupant ought to offer things, the master of which is not known, to the magistrates, and may expect from them μήνυτρον, the reward of telling (Grotius of the rights of war and peace, 2. 10. 11).

2. Bourgogne, *Ad consuetudines Flandriae aliarumque gentium tractatus controversiarum.*

the manner of acquiring the property of things by the effect of time. And prescription had also the same meaning; but it signified moreover the manner of acquiring and losing all sorts of rights and actions, by the same effect of the time regulated by law. See l. un. C. de usucap. transf. & Inst. de usucap. and Domat's civil law, in their natural order, T. 1. p. 485. But writers on the law of nature have now very seldom occasion to make use of the word *usucapio;* that of *prescription* being now common by usage, both to the manner of acquiring the property of things, and to that of acquiring and losing all sorts of rights by the effect of time. 2. The chief reasons assigned by the Roman law for the first introducing of property by prescription, are, as Pufendorff of the law of nature and nations hath observed, book 4. cap. 12. §5. "That in order to the avoiding of confusion, and cutting off disputes and quarrels, it is of great consequence to the public welfare, that the proprieties of things should be fixed and certain amongst the subjects, which would be impossible, should perpetual indulgence be allowed to the negligence of former owners, and should the new possessors be left in continual fear of losing what they held. (Ne scilicet quarundam rerum diu & fere semper incerta dominia essent, l. 1. ff. de usurp. & usucap.) Again, trade and commerce could not otherwise subsist in the world. For who would ever contract with another? who would ever make a purchase, if he could never be secured in the quiet possession of any thing conveyed to him? Nor would it be a sufficient remedy in this case, that if the thing should be thus challenged by a third party, the person from whom we receive it should be obliged to make it good; for after so long a course of time, thousands of accidents might render him incapable of giving us this satisfaction. And what grievous commotions must shake the commonwealth, if at so vast a distance of years, so many contracts were to be disannulled, so many successions were to be declared void, and so many possessors to be ejected? It was therefore judged sufficient to allow such a time, as large as in reason could be desired, during which the lawful proprietors might recover their own. But if through sloth and neglect they suffered it to slip, the *Praetor* might fairly reject their too late importunity. And tho' it might so happen, that now and then a particular person lost his advantage of recovering his goods, utterly against his will and without his fault, only because he was unable to find out the possessor, yet the damage and inconvenience arising from that general statute to some few private men, is compensated by the benefit it affords to the public." It was a judicious reflexion of Aratus of <245> Sicyon in Tully's offices, l. 2. c. 23. "He did not think that possessions of fifty years should be disturbed, because in so long time many things in inheritances, purchases and portions, might be held without an injury to any." 3. Now from the nature of property acquired by prescription, *i.e.* by the effect of time regulated by law, and the reasons upon which the utility, or rather necessity of it is founded, it is plain on the one hand, that whatever is not subject of commerce, cannot be the object of prescription, such as *liberty;* so prime, so essential a blessing; a blessing so much dearer than life, that none can ever be presumed so much as tacitely to have consented to be a slave! Liberty, a blessing, a right in the nature of things unalienable; or to renounce which is contrary to nature, and the will of the author of nature, who made all men free! *Public places, goods belonging to the public,* &c. So, on the other hand, whatever is the object of commerce may be the object of prescription, *i.e.* property in it may be acquired by the effect of time. As every man who is otherwise capable of acquiring dominion, is likewise capable of prescribing; so by this right of prescription we may acquire dominion over both sorts of things, moveable and immoveable, unless they are particularly excepted by the laws. But moveable things may pass into prescription sooner than immoveable, for this reason, that immoveables are judged a much greater loss than moveables; that they are not so frequently made the subject of commerce between man and man; that it is not so easy to acquire the possession of them, without knowing whether the party that conveys them be the true proprietor or the false; and consequently, that they are likely to occasion fewer controversies and suits. Plato's rules for the prescription of moveables are these: "If a thing of this kind be used openly in the city, let it pass into prescription in one year; if in the country in five years: if it be used privately in the city, the prescription shall not be compleated in less than three years. If it be thus held with privacy in the country, the person that lost it shall have ten years allowed him to put in his claim, de leg. l. 12."[3] As for the prescription of immoveables, the constitution of Plato's common-

3. Plato, *The Laws* 954d.

wealth was not acquainted with it. It is proper to observe here, that by the civil law prescription has not only respect to property; but it destroys other rights and actions when men are not careful to maintain them, and preserve the use of them during the time limited by the law. Thus a creditor loses his debt for having omitted to demand it within the time limited for prescription, and the debtor is discharged from it by the long silence of his creditor. Thus other rights are acquired by a long enjoyment, and are lost for want of exercising them. See Domat's civil law, &c. T. 1. book. 3. t. 7. §4. 1. and the Roman laws there quoted. And all the long reasonings in *Thomasius de perpetuitate debitorum pecuniariorum*, and in *Titius's observations on Lauterbach, obs.* 1033, and elsewhere, quoted by the very learned Barbeyrac on Pufendorff, of the law of nature <246> and nations, book 4. cap. 12. 1.[4] to shew how far prescription is of natural right, and what civil law adds to it, do not prove, that the law of nature does not permit, nay require, that a time should be limited, even for claiming rights, upon the elapsing of which, rights and actions, and what the lawyers call incorporeal things, are prescribed. No one ever pretended, that the law of nature fixed a time which gave a title by prescription with regard to things corporeal or incorporeal. But if security of property and commerce require, that such a time should be fixed, where there is property and commerce, then the law of nature or right reason requires that a time prescribing be fixed so far as security of property and commerce, and quiet possession by honest industry require it, whether with respect to corporeal or incorporeal things. Let me just add upon this head, that whereas it was said above, that things out of commerce cannot be prescribed, yet by the civil law one may acquire or lose by prescription, certain things which are not of commerce; but it is when they are connected with others, of which one may have the property. They are acquired by their connection with such other things. See Domat ibidem. Now, if here also it be said, that the law of nature knows no such distinction: the answer is, that the law of nature or right reason acknowledges every distinction which the public utility of a state requires, in order to pre-

---

4. Thomasius (*praeses*) and Hofmann (*respondens*), *Dissertatio juridica de perpetuitate*. For Titius's observations, see Schütz and Lanterbach, *Thesaurus juris civilis*.

vent confusion and quarrels, and to render honest industry secure in
the enjoyment of its just acquisitions. For, 4. whatever distinctions
moral writers have made about belonging or being reducible into the
law of nature, directly or indirectly, immediately, remotely, or abu-
sively; this is plain, that in order to determine what the law of nature
or right reason says about a case, the circumstances of the case must be
put. For in the science of the law of nature, as well as other sciences,
however general the rules or canons may be, yet in this sense they are
particular, that they only extend to such or such cases, such or such
circumstances. Now, if we apply this general position to the present
question, it will appear that prescription is of the law of nature, in the
same sense that testamentary succession, or succession to intestates is
of the law of nature, *viz.* That right reason is able to determine with
regard to prescription, in like manner as with regard to the others, some
general rules which equity and public, common security require to be
settled about them, where any number of men live in commerce, and
property is established, that industry may have due liberty and security.
Testamentary succession, and succession to intestates, as we have found
them to be regulated by right reason, may be detrimental in some cases
to the public, because in some cases, it may be more the interest of the
public that any other should succeed to an estate than the heirs according to these general rules with regard to succession, by or without
testament. But notwithstanding such detriment that may in some cases
happen to the public, general rules about succession are necessary; and
none are fitter to be such than those which most encourage in-
<247>dustry, by best securing the possessor in his right of disposing
of his own, the great motive to industry; and those which determine
succession in the way it is properest for the general good, that men's
affections should operate towards others. In like manner, whatever detriment may arise in certain cases from the general rule, that time should
give a title by prescription; yet the general rule ought to obtain, because
it is the best general rule that can be conceived, the least inconvenient,
or rather the best for the security of commerce and property, being the
best encouragement to honest industry, by giving the securest possession of its honest acquisitions. In fine, if we ask what the law of nature
says about succession, or prescription, or any thing else, we must put
a case or enumerate the circumstances; and therefore, we must either

ask what it requires about them where men are in a state of nature, or where men are under civil government. If we confine the questions of the law of nature to the former case (tho' there be distinctions to be made even in that case, as will appear afterwards) yet we limit the science too much, and render it almost useless: But if we extend it to what right reason requires under civil government, we must, in order to proceed distinctly, define the principal end of the civil constitution, and its nature, before we can answer the question; which will then be twofold. Either, 1. What that particular constitution requires, in consistency with its end and frame, with regard to prescription, for instance, or any other thing? Or, 2. Whether the end and frame of that constitution requiring such and such rules about prescription for instance, or succession, or any other thing, be a good end, and a good frame, *i.e.* whether all the parts of it, considered as making a particular constitution, do make one consonant to the great general end of all government, *public happiness?* Thus, if we attend to the necessity of thus stating the meaning of what is called determination by natural law, we will easily see that what is urged from the laws in the Jewish commonwealth against prescription, does not prove that right reason does not require that every state should make some regulation with regard to the effect of time, as to security in possession. For tho' the divine law, which prohibited perpetual alienations for several reasons, abolished by that means prescription, yet the letter of this law being no longer in force, where alienations which transfer the property for ever are allowed, the use of prescription is wholly natural in such a state and condition, and so necessary, that without this remedy every purchaser and every possessor being liable to be troubled to all eternity, there would never be any perfect assurance of a sure and peaceable possession. And even those who should chance to have the oldest possession, would have most reason to be afraid, if together with their possession they had not preserved their titles. See Domat's civil laws, *&c.* T. 1. p. 483. God, for reasons arising from the constitution of the Jewish republic, forbad the perpetual alienation of their immoveable estates (and not of their goods in general, as some objectors against prescription urge) but all their <248> laws concerning usury, conveyances, and other things, were necessarily connected together, and with their Agrarian law, (as we shall see afterwards). And therefore there is nothing in the law of Moses that condemns prescription as an unjust establishment; and we can no more infer it from hence to be such (as Barbeyrac well observes, ibidem)[5] than we may conclude that the perpetual alienation of lands is odious, and not conformable to natural right. But not to insist longer on this head, it is not only evident that the law of nature for the security of property and the encouragement of industry requires, that a time should be regulated for the effect of possession as to prescribing, in all states which admit of alienations and commerce; but that it requires that this time should be the most equal that can be fixed upon, all the circumstances of a particular state being considered, with regard to the non-disturbance of honest industry, *i.e.* the properest to prevent unjust dispossession on either side, *i.e.* either with respect to the first or the last possessor. And therefore, 5. There is no difficulty with regard to the following general maxims about it. 1. That prescription may affectually proceed, 'tis requisite that the party receiving the thing at the hands of a false proprietor, do obtain this possession by a just title; and consequently, that he act in this matter *bona fide,* with fair and honest intention. For this is necessary to just possession. "A man doth not become a just possessor of a thing barely by taking it to himself, but by holding it innocently." Detaining is otherwise, as Tacitus expresses it, *diutina licentia,* a long continued injustice. Upon this head Pufendorff observes, that according to the civil law, 'tis enough if a man had this uprightness of intention at his first entring on the possession, though he happens afterwards to discover, that the person who conveyed it to him was not the just proprietor. But the canon law requires the same integrity throughout the whole term of years, on which the prescription is built. But Barbeyrac justly takes notice in his notes, "That the maxim in the civil law is better grounded than that of the canon law. And the artifice of the clergy consists not so much in this, that the determinations of the Popes require a perpetual good intention in him that prescribes, as in this, that they will have the goods of the church look'd upon as not capable of being alienated, either absolutely, or under such conditions as will make all prescriptions void."[6] 2. Another

5. See note 1 by Jean Barbeyrac in bk. 1, xii.7, of Pufendorf's *Law of Nature and Nations.*

6. See note 5 by Jean Barbeyrac in bk. 4, xii. 3 of Pufendorf's *Of the Law of Nature and Nations.*

necessary condition is, that it be founded on constant possession, such as hath not been interrupted, either *naturally,* as if the thing hath returned in the mean while to the former owner, or hath at any time lain abandoned or forsaken: or *civilly,* as if the owner had been actually engaged at law with the possessor for the recovery of what he lost; or at least by solemn protestations hath put in a salvo to his right. 3. That the space of time during which the prime possessor holds the thing, shall be reckoned to the benefit of him that succeeds in the possession, provided that both the former and the latter first entered upon it < 249 > with honest minds, and upon a just title. For otherwise the prime possessor shall not be allowed to make over his time to the next holder, and consequently, if the former come to the possession by dishonest means, the time he passed in it shall not be computed towards the prescription of the latter, tho' he, for his own part, obtained the possession fairly and justly. See Pufendorff, ibidem. 4. Prescription does not run against minors. And if one that is major happens to have a right undivided with a minor, the prescription which could not run against the minor, will have no effect against the major. And the same reason for which prescription does not run against minors, hinders it likewise from running against those whom a long absence disables from pursuing their rights; which is to be understood not only of absence on account of public business, but also of other absences occasioned by accidents, such as captivity. See Domat's civil law, ibidem. And for the same reasons, it is highly agreeable to reason, that the time during which a country hath been the seat of war, shall not avail towards prescription. But with regard to minority, it is remarked by Pufendorff ibidem, that there may be a case in which the favour of possession shall overbalance the favour of majority. As for instance, suppose it should so happen, that when I want only a month or two of compleating my prescription, and it is morally certain that the ancient proprietor will not within that space give me any trouble about the title, and if he should then decease leaving an infant heir, it would be unreasonably hard, if after five and twenty years possession, I should be thrust out of my hold for want of those two months, especially if it be now impossible for me to recover damages of him from whom I received what is thus challenged, as I might have done, had the dispute happened before the goods devolved on the minor. See this subject more fully discussed than it can be done in a short note, by Pufendorff and Grotius. It is sufficient for our purpose to have taken notice of these few things relative to prescription; and to have observed once for all, that unless the determinations of the law of nature be confined to signify the determinations of right reason with regard to a state of nature, (a very limited sense of the law of nature, in which it is hardly ever taken by any writer) every decision of right reason concerning equity, justice, and necessity or conduciveness to the public good of society, or of men having property and carrying on commerce, is a decision of the law of nature. Whatever reason finds to be the best general rule in this case is a law of nature; and in this sense, prescription is of the law of nature, *i.e.* reason is able to settle several general rules about it in consequence of what commerce, the security of property, and the encouragement of industry make necessary. So that where reason is able to make any such decisions, it is an impropriety to say, that thing is not of the law of nature, because some forms and modes relative to it must be determined and settled by convention, or by civil constitution; as the parti-<250>cular spaces of time, for instance, with regard to prescription of moveables and immoveables, *&c.* must be. For if right reason requires, that time should have a certain effect with regard to property, then is prescription of the law of nature, which by its definition is the acquisition or addition of a property, by means of long possession. But indeed we may safely say, that the law of nature is an absolute stranger to the debates among lawyers, whether prescription should be defined with Modestinus *adjectio,* or *adeptio* with Ulpianus; for all such disputes are mere verbal wranglings, grievossly cumbersome to right reason and true science.

ᖌᖎᖍ CHAPTER XIII ᖌᖎᖍ

Concerning things belonging to commerce.

SECTION CCCXXV

How men
began to want
many things.
After men had departed from the negative communion of things, and dominion was introduced, they began to appropriate useful things to themselves in such a manner, that they could not be forced to allow any one the use of them, but might set them aside wholly for themselves, and their own use (§236). But hence it followed of necessity, that all men had not the same stock, but that some abounded in things of one kind, which others wanted; and therefore one was obliged to supply what was wanting to himself either by the labour of another, or out of his provision. Yea, because every soil does not produce every thing,* necessity

---

* To this purpose belongs that elegant observation in Virgil, georg. 1. v. 54.

> This ground with Bacchus, that with Ceres suits,
> That other loads the trees with happy fruits.
> A fourth with grass, unbidden decks the ground,
> Thus Tmolus is with yellow saffron crown'd.
> India black ebon and white ivory bears,
> And soft Iduma weeps her od'rous tears.
> Thus Pontus sends her beaver stores from far,
> And naked Spaniards temper steel for war.
> Epirus for the Elian chariot breeds,
> (In hopes of palms) a race of running steeds.
> Thus is th' original contract; these the laws
> Impos'd by nature, and by nature's cause.

To the same effect does this poet sing at greater length, georg. 2. v. 199. & seq. Compare with these passages, Varro de re rustica, 1. 23. Ovid. de arte amandi, 4. v. 578.

forced men to give to others a share of the things in which they abounded, and which they had procured by their own art and industry, and to acquire to themselves what they wanted in exchange; which when they began to do, they are said to have instituted *commerce*. <251>

SECTION CCCXXVI

Indeed if all men were virtuous, none would have reason to fear any want. For every one would then liberally give to those who wanted of what he had in abundance (§221). But since the love of mankind *hath waxed cold,* and we live in times when virtue is praised, and starves, there was a necessity of devising that kind of commerce, by which another might be obliged, not merely by humanity and beneficence, but by perfect obligation, to transfer to us the dominion of things necessary or useful to us, and to assist us by their work and labour.

The necessity of commerce.

SECTION CCCXXVII

By *commerce* therefore we understand the exchange of useful things and labour, arising not from mere benevolence, but founded on perfect obligation. But since by commerce either work is performed, or dominion and possession is transferred, which obligation ought to be extorted from none <252> without his knowledge, and against his will (§320); the consequence is, that commerce requires the consent of both parties. Now, that consent of two persons concerning the exchange of necessary work, or things which is not of mere humanity and beneficence, but of perfect obligation, is commonly called *a contract;* and therefore it is obvious, that commerce cannot be carried on without the intervention of contracts.*

That could not be done but by contracts.

---

and above all, Seneca, ep. 87. who having quoted the passage of Virgil above cited, adds, "These things are thus separated into different provinces, that commerce amongst men might be necessary, and every one might want and seek from another." [[Ovid, *Amores;* Seneca, *Ad Lucilium epistulae morales,* vol. 2, letter 87, p. 335.]] Aristotle urges the same origine and necessity of commerce, Nicomach. 5. 8. Polit. 1. 6.

* This is observed by Isocrates, except. adv. Callimach. p. 742. "There is such a

SECTION CCCXXVIII

Most of them suppose the price of labour and things fixed.

From the nature of commerce, as it hath been defined (§327), it is evident, that it will rarely happen that one will communicate his goods or labour with another gratuitously; but every one will desire something to be returned to him, which he thinks equivalent to the goods or labour he communicates. Wherefore, those who would commute things or labour one with another, must compare things together; which comparison cannot otherwise be made, than by affixing a value to things, by means of which an equality can be obtained and preserved. But a quantity, moment, or value affixed to goods and labour, by means of which they may be compared, is called *price*. And therefore most contracts cannot take place without affixing or settling *price*.* <253>

SECTION CCCXXIX

Price is either vulgar or eminent.

This comparison is instituted either between goods and work by themselves, or a common measure is applied, by which all other things are valued. In the first case, *vulgar* or *proper price* takes place, or the value

---

force in pacts, that many affairs among the Barbarians, as well as Greeks, are transacted by them. Upon the faith of them we bargain, and carry on commerce. By them we make contracts with one another; by them we put an end to private feuds or public war. This one thing all men continue to use as a common good." [[Isocrates, *Isocrates,* vol. 3, "Against Callimachus," secs. 27–28, p. 271.]]

* Hence by the Greeks not only pacts and contracts, but all kinds of commerce are called συμβολάς, σύμβολα, συμβόλαια, συμβόλαια κοινωνικά, from the verb συμβάλλειν, which signifies to bring together and compare. For those who are to interchange goods or labour, compare them together, every one assigns a certain value to his goods or work, and so demands a proportional return. Thus, *e.g.* if we fix the proportion of gold to silver to be as eleven to one, we affix to each metal a moral quantity or price; which being done, nothing is more easy than to exchange these metals, and keep equality. But we say most contracts suppose the price of things determined, not all. For some are gratuitous, and therefore contracts are rightly divided into *onerous,* when the burden on both sides is equal; *beneficent,* when one obliges himself to do any thing to another gratuitously; and *contracts of chance,* in which fortune so reigns, that one may receive what is done by another sometimes with, and sometimes without any onerous title.

we put upon goods and labour compared amongst themselves. In the latter case, there is a common measure by which we estimate all things that enter into commerce, which is called *eminent price;** such as is money amongst us. But in both cases equality is required. <254>

---

* Hence Aristotle justly defines money; "A common measure to which all things are referred, and by which all things are estimated," Nicomach. 9. 1. And hence all things which enter into commerce are said to be purchasable by money. This alone is reprehensible, that men should estimate things by money, which do not enter into commerce; such as, justice, chastity, and conscience itself. And against this venality the antient poets have severely inveighed. Horat. serm. 2. 3. v. 94.

> *Omnis enim res,*
> *Virtus, fama, decus, divina humanaque, pulchris*
> *Divitiis parent: quas qui construxerit, ille*
> *Clarus erit, fortis, justus, sapiensne etiam, & rex,*
> *Et quidquid volet.*

> [[Horace, *Satires II,* 3.94: "For everything, virtue, reputation, glory, the human and divine, obeys beautiful riches: as for the man who piles them up, he will be famous, brave, just, even wise, and a king, and whatever he may want."]]

So Propertius, 3. 10.

> *Aurea nunc vere sunt saecula, plurimus auro*
> *Venit honos, auro conciliatur amor.*
> *Auro pulsa fides, auro venalia jura,*
> *Aurum lex sequitur, mox sine lege pudor.*

> [[This passage is not from Propertius, *Elegies* 3.10, but from Ovid, *Ars amatoria* 2.277: "These truly are the golden ages, the highest honour comes to gold, love is won by gold, faith is broken by gold, oaths are on sale for gold, the law follows gold, soon shame without a law."]]

Many such like passages are to be found among the antients, as in Petronius's satyricon, c. 137. and in Menander, of whom we have this elegant saying concerning a rich man preserved;

> *Opta modo, quidquid volueris: omnia evenient:*
> *Ager, domus, medici, supellex argentea,*
> *Amici, judices, testes: dederis mado.*
> *Quin & deos ipsos ministros facile habebis.*

> [["Only choose whatever you want: everything will turn out: land, houses, doctors, silver supplicating, friends, judges, witnesses: now you will have given them. In fact you will easily have the gods themselves too as your servants" (translation by the editors). Menander (342–292 B.C.), Athenian au-

SECTION CCCXXX

How vulgar
or proper
price is fixed.

That in the earlier times of the world men knew nothing but the *proper* price of things, is plain, because eminent price could not have been instituted without the consent of many; but every one imposed vulgar price upon his own work and goods at his pleasure. But since that is done with intention, and in order to purchase by them what one wants from another (§325); it is plain, that regard ought to be had in fixing the price of goods and labour to others from whom we want certain things; and therefore they ought to be estimated at such a rate, as it is probable others will be willing to purchase them.* <255>

SECTION CCCXXXI

What circum-
stances ought
to be attended
to in fixing it.

Now, since work or things ought to be valued at such a price as it is probable others from whom we want any thing will purchase them; it is obvious, that sometimes the necessity and indigence of others will raise the price of things;† and sometimes the scarcity of the thing will raise

---

thor of comedies, the greatest part of which have only survived in fragmentary form. It is not evident from which play this particular quotation has been translated.]]

* For if we suppose the Arabians to estimate their incense and spiceries at such a price, that they would not give above one dram of them for six hundred bushels of corn, they would never get corn at that price, because none would exchange it upon so unequal terms, nor would others get their spices; and thus there would be a stop to commerce, for the sake of which price is devised. Since therefore the means ought to be as the end, the consequence is, that price ought to be fixed so that commerce can be carried on; and for this reason, in settling it regard ought to be had to others from whom we would purchase any thing.

† It is true indeed, that the most necessary things have not always the highest price, kind providence having so ordered it, that the things which we can least dispense with the want of are abundant every where; and those things only are rare and difficult to be found, which are not necessary, and which nature itself does not crave, as Vitruvius justly philosophizes, Architect. 8. praef. [[Vitruvius, *Ten Books on Architecture.*]] But if necessity be joined with scarcity, *e.g.* if there is every where a dearth of corn, the price of it rises very high, as experience tells us. And then happens, as Quintilian says, declam. 12. "In magna inopia, quidquid emi potest, vile est." "In great scarcity, what can be bought is cheap." [[Quintilian, *The Major Declamations Ascribed to Quintilian,*

it; and that regard ought likewise to be had to workmanship, the intrinsic excellence of the thing, the labour and expence bestowed upon it, the danger undergone for it; and, in fine, to the paucity or multitude of those who want the goods or labour, and various other such circumstances.

SECTION CCCXXXII

It may be objected, that men are accustomed to put an immense value upon their own goods, a much greater certainly than any one will purchase them at, whether it be that the author renders them precious, or their rarity, or some remarkable event which they recal to our memory. But since we are now treating of the duties which ought to be observed in commerce, and that kind of price is not commonly considered in commerce, but on-<256>ly in repairing damages (§212),* it is evident that this price does not destroy our rule.

What is called price of affection.

"XII: The Case of the People Who Ate Corpses," 159.]] The seven years famine in Egypt was an instance of this, Gen. xlvii. 14. & seq.

* Fancy or affection is of such a nature, that it cannot pass from one to another; and therefore it will be no motive to one to purchase a thing from me at a greater price, because it is agreeable to me on account of its serving to recal something to my memory that gives me pleasure. But this however is but generally true: for sometimes in commerce even this price is considered; as when, 1. The affection to a thing is common on account of the author or artist, or of its singular beauty and rarity. Hence the statues of Phidias, and the more finished pictures of Apelles or Parrhasius, sold at a higher than the vulgar or proper price, because they deserved the common esteem of all mankind. 2. If the purchaser has a greater affection to a thing than the possessor; *e.g.* if my possession would greatly better another's, and he therefore desire, like him in Horace, who thus speaks, serm. 2. 6.

    O si angulus ille
Proximus accedat, qui nunc denormat agellunt!

[[Horace, *Satires II,* 6.8–9: "Oh, if that nearest little corner could be added, which now disfigures the shape of my little farm!"]]

SECTION CCCXXXIII

Why eminent price was invented.

But since commerce was instituted among men that one might supply his wants out of another's stock or labour (§326), and price was devised for no other reason but that equality might be obtained in the exchange of goods or labour (§328); it could not but happen very often, that one might not have a very great abundance of what another might want, that one might despise what another would desire to exchange, and that the value of things which persons might desire to commute, might be so uncertain and variable, that some of the parties must run a risk of loss; and that the things to be exchanged might be of such a bulk, that they could not be commodiously transported to distant places, or could not be taken proper care of in the journey.—All which inconveniencies not being otherwise avoidable, necessity itself at last devised some eminent <257> price that all would receive, and the proportion of which to goods could easily be determined.*

SECTION CCCXXXIV

Its necessary qualities.

The end of money, or eminent price, requires that the matter chosen for that purpose be neither too rare, nor too common, nor useless, and in itself of no price;† that it be easily divisible into small parts, and yet not

---

* This is observed by Paullus JC. l. 1. D. de contra empt. who describes the origine of buying and selling as above. Aristotle likewise gives much the same account of the matter, ad Nicomach. §8. and Polybius 1. 6. upon which passages Perizonius hath commented with much erudition, de aere gravi §2. p. 6. & seq. [[Perizonius, *Dissertatio de aere gravi*]] as has Duaren. upon that of Paullus animad. 1. 6. [[Franciscus Duarenus (François Douaren) (1509–59), French humanist jurist.]]

† Wherefore Aristotle justly calls Money, Nicomach. 5. 8. "a surety, which if one carries along with him he may purchase any thing." Whence Pufendorff of the law of nature and nations, v. 1. 13. justly reasons thus: "As we accept a man of known credit and value, and not every common fellow for a surety, so no man would part with his goods, which perhaps he had acquired with great labour and industry, for what he might meet with any where, as a handful of dust and sand; it was necessary therefore, that money should consist of such a matter, as might be convenient for keeping, and by reason of its scarcity, should have the value of many things crowded and united with it."

too brittle; that it may be easily kept and laid up, and easily transported to any distance; because, if it was too scarce, there would not be a sufficient quantity of it to serve the uses of mankind; and if it was too common, it would be of no price or value, in which case, it would not be received by all; if it could not be easily divided into any portions, equality in commerce could not be obtained by it; and yet, if it was too brittle, it would easily wear out by use, and thus its possessors would be impoverished. In fine, if it could neither be conveniently kept, nor easily transported, the same inconvenience which rendered commerce difficult before the invention of it, would still remain (§333). <258>

SECTION CCCXXXV

But because these properties belong to no other matter but the more precious kinds of metals, as gold, silver and brass; these metals are therefore applied to this use, and hence coined money of various weights and sizes hath seemed to most civilized nations the properest substance to answer the ends of commerce. If any people hath thought fit to give an eminent price to any other matter,* it hath been done out of necessity, and for want of money, and with this intention, that the scarcity or difficulty being over, every one might receive solid money for the symbol-

Why the nobler metals are used to this purpose.

---

* Thus the Carthaginians used instead of money something I know not what, fastened to a bit of skin, and marked with some public stamp, Aeschin. dialog. de divit. c. 24. p. 78. edit. Petri Horrei. [[Aischines, *Aeschinis Socratici dialogi III.*]] The Lacedemonians an useless lump of iron, idem ibid. p. 80. Plutarch. Lycurg. p. 51. [[Plutarch, "Lycurgus," in *Plutarch's Lives,* vol. 1]] other nations used shells, Leo Afr. l. 7. [[Leo Africanus, *Africae descriptio IX libris absoluta*]] others grains of corn, kernels of fruit, berries, lumps of salt, Pufendorff. §1. 13. [[Pufendorf, *Law of Nature,* bk. 5, chap. 1.]] Examples of paper, leather, lead, and other things made use of for money in besieged towns, are to be found (not to mention instances from more modern history) in Polyaenus Stratagem. 3. 10. [[Polyaenus, *Stratagems of war*]] and there Masuic. p. 274. Seneca de beneficiis, 5. 14. But all such money used in barbarous nations, is capable of carrying on but a very small trade among themselves. And symbolical money used in public calamities, is really to be considered as tickets or bills, which the supreme magistrate obliges himself to give ready money for, when the distress is over. Thus Timotheus is said by Polyaenus to have persuaded merchants to take his seal for money, to be received upon returning it.

ical; or such money hath only been used by a nation within itself, and was not proper for carrying on commerce with foreign nations. <259>

SECTION CCCXXXVI

What price is to be put on money.

Tho' it belong to the supreme power in a state to fix the value of money (as we shall shew afterwards in the proper place); yet, as with respect to vulgar or proper price, regard ought to be had to others from whom we would have any thing in exchange (§330); so it is evident, that a value ought to be put upon money, at which it is probable other nations, with whom we are in commerce, will not refuse it; and therefore the value of it ought to be regulated according to that proportion of one metal to another, which is approved by neighbouring civilized nations, unless we would fright other nations from having any commerce with us, or be ourselves considerable losers.*<260>

* For if we put too high a value on our money, foreign nations will either not care to have commerce with us, or they will raise the price of their commodities in proportion to the intrinsic value of our money. But if we put a less value on our money than neighbouring nations, nothing is more certain, than that our good money will remove to our neighbours, and their bad money will come to us in its room, so that none will know what he is worth. Hence it follows, in the more civilized nations, the proportion of gold to silver varying according to times, and being sometimes as twelve, sometimes as eleven, sometimes as ten to one, the price of gold must be sometimes higher and sometimes lower. (See our dissertat. de reduct. monet. ad just. pret. §24.) [[Heineccius and Egelgraser, *De reductione monetae.*]] Wherefore the Arabians could not but be great losers, who, according to Diodorus Siculus, Bibliothec. 3. 45. received for brass and iron an equal weight of gold; or, as Strabo, Geogr. 16. p. 1124. [[Strabo, *Geography*]] paid for brass three times the weight of gold, for iron twice the weight, and for silver ten times the weight, partly through their ignorance of arts, and partly through their indigence of those things which they bartered for it, that were more necessary to them. See what is related of the Peruvians by Garcillass. de la Vega dans l'histoire des Yncas, 5. 4. p. 425. [[Garcilaso de la Vega (1539–1616), author of the *Commentarios reales que tratan del origen de los Incas* of 1609 (*Royal Commentaries of the Incas and General History of Peru*).]]

SECTION CCCXXXVII

That we may now come to the *contracts,* by means of which commerce is carried on (§327), it is obvious to every one, that one kind of contracts took place while the proper price of things only was known, and money or eminent price was not yet in use (§330), and that after money was invented another kind took place, and that some were known both after and before money was in use. Among those which took place before money was in use, the first and principal is *bartering.* For in the first ages of the world commerce was only carried on by exchanging or bartering commodities and labour; and therefore bartering is the most antient of contracts; and it continued still to be in use in many nations, after money was in use, as well as where no price was yet put upon gold, silver, and brass.*

The most antient of all contracts before the invention of money was bartering.

SECTION CCCXXXVIII

Bartering is giving something of our own for something belonging to another; which, because it may be done two ways, *i.e.* either with, or without estimating and putting a certain price upon the <261> things exchanged, it therefore follows, that when no estimation is made, it is called *simple bartering;* and when an estimation is made, and price fixed, it is called *estimatory bartering.* The former is somewhat like mutual donation, and the latter somewhat like buying and selling, l. 1. C. de per-

How many sorts there are of it.

---

* So it was among our ancestors the ancient Germans, Tacitus de moribus Germ. c. 5. who observes, that in his time the Germans who lay nearest to the Roman provinces, had conceived some desire of money. Justin, hist. 2. 2. relates the like of the Scythians. Pomponius Mela of the Satarchi, a People in the European Scythia, de situ orbis, 2. 1. [[Pomponius Mela (fl. 40 A.D.), Latin geographer. His *De situ orbis* was published in various editions in the first half of the eighteenth century.]] Strabo of the Spaniards, Geogr. 3. p. 233. The same is yet practised by several nations in Asia, Africa and America: And it is the less to be wondered at with respect to barbarous countries, since the Greeks and Romans, long after the invention of money, carried on commerce in no other way but by barter. We have a noted example of it among the Greeks in Homer, Iliad 7. v. 482. and among the Romans in Plin. nat. hist. 18. 3. 33. 1.

mut. l. 1. §1. D. de contr. emt. For tho' Pufendorff of the duties of a man and a citizen, 1. 15. 8. asserts that mutual donation is quite a different business from bartering, because it is not necessary that equality should be observed in it, yet there is no difference in this respect; for neither is equality observed in *simple bartering.* *

SECTION CCCXXXIX

What is just with respect to simple barter.

Because *simple barter* is somewhat like mutual donation, and it is not necessary that equality should be observed in it (§338), it is plain neither of the contracting parties can have any reason to complain of being wronged, unless the other use force or guile (§322. and 321.) nor is such a contract null on account of injury, except when he who exchanges a more precious thing for a thing of no value, has not <262> the free disposal of his goods (§317); and more especially, if the thing thrown away in such a manner, be of such a kind that it cannot be alienated without doing something base, unless the accepter himself be perchance guilty of equal baseness.†

* For in it, each of the contracting parties estimates not his own but the other's; and not at the just price others would put upon it, but according to his fancy; and so there is in such a contract no equality of goods, but of affection or fancy only. Because as often as the affection of the acquirer is greater than that of the possessor, regard is had in commerce, as we have already said (§332), to price of affection. The commerce between Glaucus and Diomedes in Homer, exchanging their arms, furnishes us with an example, Iliad 2. v. 236.

Aurea aereis, centena novenariis, &c.

[["[G]olden for brass, the worth of an hundred oxen for the value of nine." (Homer, *The Iliad,* vol. 1, 6.236)]]

Of which barter Maximus Tyrius, Dissert. Platon. 23. very elegantly observes, "Neither did he who received the gold get more than he who got the brass. But both acted nobly, the inequality of the metals being compensated by the design of the exchange." [[Maximus of Tyre, *The Philosophical Orations,* Oration 35.3, p. 277.]]

† Hence it may be doubted, whether the exchange made by Jacob and Esau, the latter of whom shamefully sold his birth-right for pottage, Gen. xxv. 29. would have been valid *in foro humano.* For tho' Esau was very blame-worthy in setting so small a value upon the prerogative God had favoured him with, and he be on that account very justly called by the apostle, Heb. xii. 6. *a profane person;* yet Jacob acted no less

SECTION CCCXL

In *estimatory* permutation or barter, since here a price is put upon the things to be exchanged, (§338), equality ought certainly to be observed, and neither ought to wrong the other; nor is the barter valid if either be circumvened, unless the injury be of so little moment that it be not worth minding.* <263>

What is just with regard to estimatory permutation.

SECTION CCCXLI

But men not only barter commodities, but likewise work for work, or work for other considerations; whence these contracts, *I give that you may do; I do that you may give, and I do that you may do;* which being of the same kind and nature with barter, or reducible to barter, *simple* or *estimatory* (§338), the same rules already laid down concerning them (§338) must, it is evident, be observed in those contracts. For either one's work is estimated with respect to another's work or goods, (which kind of negotiation is called, not unelegantly, by Ammian. Marcell. hist. 16. 10.[1] *pactum reddendae vicissitudinis*) or work for goods is done without

Of the contracts, I give that you may do: I do that you may give; I do that you may do.

---

basely in taking advantage of his brother's hunger, to defraud him of so great a privilege (§322). For what Esau could not sell without a crime, that his brother could not buy without a crime; and it was his duty to dissuade his brother from such folly, and not to abuse his weakness. But many things of this sort are admirable in their typical sense, which are scarcely defensible by the rules of right reason.

* For the vulgar or proper price of things is either legal or conventional; the former of which is fixed by law, or the will of superiors, the latter by the consent of the contracting parties. Now, seeing the former is fixed, and consists, as it were in a point, but the latter is uncertain, or admits of some latitude; in the former case one is justly thought to be wronged who does not receive the full price; in the latter case, the damage ought to be of some consideration to invalidate the contract *in foro humano.* "For," as Seneca says of benefits, 6. 15. "what's the matter what be the value of a thing, if the price be agreed upon between the buyer and the seller? The price of every thing is temporary. When you have highly praised things, they are just of so much value and no more than what they may be sold for." Hence in formed governments, we may observe that a contract is only annulled when the injury is enormous, as by the Roman law, when one of the parties was wronged above half the price, l. 2. C. de rescind. vendit.

1. Marcellinus, *Ammianus Marcellinus*, 16.12 (not 10) .26.

any estimation.* And in the former case equality ought to be observed, and damage of any considerable moment ought to be repaired; but in the latter all complaints about wrong or hurt are to no purpose. <264>

SECTION CCCXLII

Contract of loan.
There are other contracts by which commerce was carried on before the invention of money, *viz.* all gratuitous ones, by which, what before was only owing to one by imperfect right, or by mere love and benevolence, became due to him by perfect right, such as a contract of loan. For since we are obliged to what was called (§228) *officiousness,* we are likewise bound to accord to one who may want it, the use of any *commodity* belonging to us not consumable, with his obligation to restore it; *i.e.* to lend, or give in loan.† But the love of mankind becoming cold, it could

---

* Such was the promise of Agamemnon in Homer, Iliad. 10. v. 135.

> *If gifts immense his mighty soul can bow,*
> *Hear all ye Greeks, and witness what I vow:*
> *Ten weighty talents of the purest gold,*
> *And twice ten vases of refulgent mold;*
> *Seven sacred tripods, whose unsully'd frame,*
> *Yet knows no office, nor has felt the flame;*
> *Twelve steeds unmatch'd in fleetness and in force,*
> *And still victorious in the dusty course,* &c.

[[Homer, *The Iliad of Homer*, vol. 3, 10.155 (not 135)–162]]

All this to pacify Achilles.—Whence it is plain, that it was a practice for one to stipulate with one for inestimable services, and to promise him for them whatever he thought would be most agreeable, without any regard to equality.

† Loan therefore is a perfect obligation to allow another the use of something belonging to us, on condition of his restoring it to us in specie, gratis. And hence it is plain, that in natural law a loan scarcely differs from (precarium) what is granted to one upon his asking it, between which there is however some difference in civil law. Hence also may this question easily be decided, "Whether a contract of loan derives its essential obligation from the consent of the contracting parties, or from the delivery of the thing?" For tho' by the law of nature, consent alone to the use of a thing obliges (§327); yet it is not a loan till the thing be delivered; because he to whom the promise of a loan is made, before he hath received the thing thus promised, is not obliged to restore it in specie: it is only a pact or agreement about a loan. But that there is a difference between these two is plain from hence, that the borrower,

hardly be hoped that one would do this service to another spontaneously (§326), and therefore necessity forced men to invent a kind of contract, by which men might be obliged by perfect right thus to grant the use one to another of their not consumable goods. <265>

SECTION CCCXLIII

Now, because the use of a thing is granted by loan, on condition of the borrower's restoring it in species (§342),* the former is obliged not only not to apply the thing borrowed to other uses than those for which it was given, but likewise to apply it to these uses with the greatest care and concern; and therefore, when the use is over, or when the proprietor re-demands it, to restore it to him in species, and if it hath suffered any damage by his fault, to repair it; but he is not bound to make up fortuitous damages, unless he had voluntarily so charged himself (§106);* nor can he demand for any expences he may have laid out upon it, unless they exceed the hire to be paid for the letting of such a thing.

The duties of the borrower.

SECTION CCCXLIV

Again, the love of humanity obliges every one to promote the good of others to the utmost of his power (§216); but since we have only an imperfect right to demand such good offices, it is often our interest to

The contract of deposite.

---

by loan, is obliged to restore the thing, but by a compact about lending, he who promises to lend is obliged to give the thing in loan: so that different obligations arise from these two negotiations.

* Grotius of the rights of war and peace, 2. 12. 13. was the first who distinguished here, whether a thing would have perished in like manner in the hands of its proprietor or not; in the latter of which cases, at least, he thinks the loss should fall upon the borrower: And Pufendorff of the law of nature and nations, 5. 4. 6. is of the same opinion; So likewise Mornac, ad l. 1. C. commod. [[Mornac, *Observationes in 24 priores libros digestorum.*]] But since accidental or fortuitous events, arising merely from providence, are imputable to no person (§106), they certainly cannot be imputed even to a borrower. Nor is the divine law repugnant to this sentence, Exod. xxii. 14. For it cannot be understood otherwise than when the borrower is in fault. See Jo. Clerici Comment. in Exod. p. 110. [[le Clerc, *Mosis prophetae libri quatuor.*]]

stipulate with others, in order to their <266> being obliged by a perfect right to take the custody of our things deposited with them; and this is the intention of the contract of *deposite* or *charge,* by which we understand a perfect obligation upon another to keep gratis our things intrusted to his faith, and to restore them to us upon demand in species.*

SECTION CCCXLV

The duties of the trustee. It is plain from the definition of a *charge,* (§344), that the trustee is obliged to the most watchful custody of his charge, not so much as to untie it, or take it out of its cover, much less apply it to his use, without the master's consent; in which case, the contract becomes not a charge, but contract of loan or use. And that the trustee is obliged to restore the thing intrusted to his keeping to its owner whenever he calls for it, unless right reason dissuade from so doing (§323); and consequently he is not only bound to make satisfaction, but is likewise worthy of severe punishment, if knowingly and guilefully he refuses to restore it, more especially, if it was lodged in his trust in a case of distress.† <267>

* Nothing was more sacred among the ancients than this contract, because the deponent reposes the greatest trust and confidence in the trustee; and nothing can be more base than to deceive a friend under the mask of friendship (§322). Hence the religious veneration paid to such trusts, not only among the Hebrews, of which see Exod. xxii. 7. and Josephus's antiquities of the Jews, 4. 8. 38; but among the Greeks likewise, and several other Pagan nations, as we may learn from the story of Glaucus in Herodot. 6. 87. and from Juvenal, Sat. 13. v. 15. who there calls it *depositum sacrum.* Hence it is not to be wondered, that the ancients pronounced such terrible curses against those who dared to refuse to give back their charge; and looked upon them as no less infamous, and equally to be punished with thieves. See what is said on this subject by Gundlingius in Gundlingianis, part. 2. diss. 8.

† For because regard is had to all circumstances in imputation (§113), therefore such a crime is so much the more vile and odious, in proportion as he is more inhuman, who not only cheats under the cloak of friendship (§322), but cruelly adds affliction to the afflicted. This is warmly urged by Hecuba against Polymnestor, who, when Troy was destroyed, killed Polydorus, son to Priam, that he might have the gold entrusted with him to himself, Hecub. v. 1210, & seq. Euripides. [[Euripides, "Hecuba," in *Euripides,* trans. Way, vol. 1.]]

SECTION CCCXLVI

Again, the love of humanity ought to excite every one to assist another as readily as himself (§216); but because one cannot be sure of that from another, there is need of a contract, by which we may oblige one to manage our business which we have committed to him diligently, without any reward.* Now this contract we call *commission,* as when one without his knowledge, undertakes another's business, or orders and manages it for him voluntarily gratis, he is said *negotia gerere,* to take another's business upon him of his own accord. <268>

The contract of commission.

SECTION CCCXLVII

Wherefore, since a proxy undertakes another's business *committed* to his care (§346), but it depends upon the master's pleasure what, and how

The duties of a proxy.

---

* It is a true and solid remark of Noodt, in his probabilia, 1. 12. [[Gerard Noodt (1647–86), Dutch jurist, professor at Leiden. See his *Opera omnia ab ipso recognita.*]] that a mandate or commission in ancient times, had not perfect obligation, but that the proxy or person commissioned, was only bound by the laws of humanity and friendship, to the diligent and honest execution of his commission: and that the symbol used was giving the hand; whence it is not unlikely that this contract was called *Mandatum,* Isidor. orig. 4. 4. You may see examples of thus giving hand to proxies in Plautus Capt. 2. 3. 82. where the youth says,

> *Haec per dextram tuam, te dextera retinens manu,*
> *Obsecro, infidelior mihi ne fuas, quam ego sum tibi.*

[[Plautus, *The Captives,* lines 441–42, in vol. 1 of *Plautus:* "This I beseech you by this hand, this hand I hold in mine: don't be less true to me than I am to you."]]

And in Terence Heaut. 3. 1. v. 84.

> *Cedo dexteram: porro te idem oro, ut facias, Chreme.*

[[Terence, *The Self-Tormentor,* line 493, in vol. 1 of *Terence:* "Give me your hand. I beg you to continue that way, Chremes."]]

Anciently therefore, this whole business depended upon integrity, and not laws, till benevolence becoming very cool among mankind, necessity obliged them to make it a contract, that thus the proxy might be laid under a perfect obligation of executing his commission diligently. And the case is the same with regard to all the other gratuitous contracts.

far to commit; it is plain, that the person giving the commission, either gives him full power to do all as he shall judge proper, or circumscribes the person commissioned within certain limits; or at least, by way of counsel, suggests to him what he would have him do. In the second case therefore, the proxy cannot exceed the bounds of his commission. In the first, he is only obliged to answer for knavery. In the third, that he may expede his commission by doing something equivalent. But, in all these cases, the procurator or proxy is obliged to render account of his management, in consequence of the very nature of a commission.*

SECTION CCCXLVIII

As likewise of him who takes another's business upon him uncalled. He also who takes *another's business* upon him without commission, without being called to do it, <269> of his own accord, and gratis (§346), by so doing binds himself to manage it to the best advantage, and to bestow all possible care about it, and therefore to render account, and to stand to all the losses that may happen by his fault.†

---

* To this belongs that noted passage of Cicero, pro Q. Rosc. c. 38. "Why did you receive a commission, if you was either resolved to neglect it, or to make your own advantage of it? Why do you offer your service to me, and yet oppose my interest? Get away: I will transact the affair by another. You undertake the burden of an office to which you think yourself equal: an office which does not appear heavy to those who have any degree of weight or sufficiency in themselves. Here there is a base violation of two most sacred things, faith and friendship. For one does not commission another unless he have confidence in him, nor does one trust a person except he have a good opinion of his integrity. None therefore but the most abandoned villain would both violate friendship, and deceive one who could not have been hurt had he not trusted to him." [[Cicero, *Pro Quinto Roscio Comoedo,* in Cicero, *Pro Publio Quinctio.*]]

† To the cause or author of a deed are it and all its effects imputable (§105). Since therefore, he who takes upon him another's business is the author of the administration (§346), to him are all the consequences of the administration justly imputable. But the consequences of administration are giving account and repairing damages incurred by the fault of the administrator. And therefore he who takes upon him the administration of another's business is obliged to give account, and to make reparations for damages proceeding from any fault in him. So that there is no need of deriving this obligation, with the lawyers, from feigned or presumed consent, since such an administrator as hath been described, by his own deed in undertaking another's business, tacitly indeed, but truly obliges himself to all that hath been said.

SECTION CCCXLIX

These then are the contracts which took place, money or eminent price not being yet found out: and with regard to them all, we have one thing yet to observe, which is, that because in the three last, one obliges himself to give and do something gratuitously, but not to suffer any hurt on another's account, in them therefore no one ought to suffer by his good offices, and consequently he who lends is obliged to restore to the borrower expences that are not immoderate (§343), and the deponent is obliged to restore to the trustee all necessary charges; and the person giving a commission, or the person whose affair is undertaken and managed without his commission, is obliged to restore necessary or useful charges; and they are all of them bound to repair all the damages that may have been incurred for their sake, or on account of managing their af-<270>fairs by the borrower, the trustee, the proxy, or the voluntary undertaker, without their fault.*

The duties of a lender, a deponent, a person giving a proxy, and of one whose business is managed by another without commission.

SECTION CCCL

We now go on to another kind of contracts which began to take place when money was invented, the chief of which are *buying* and *selling, renting* and *hiring.* The first is a contract for delivering a certain thing for a certain price. The second is a contract for granting the use of a certain thing or labour at a certain rate or hire. But as the *price in buying*

The contracts which took place after the invention of money, buying, selling, renting, hiring.

* We say those damages ought to be repaired which a proxy hath suffered by managing another's affairs. For it is not enough that he hath incurred any accidental damage on occasion of his having undertaken another's business: because none being obliged to answer for accidents, a person giving commission to another is not. Wherefore, if a proxy, while he is expeding his commission, is robbed by highwaymen, or falls into a dangerous sickness, the loss he may thus providentially suffer is not to be imputed to his constituent. "For such accidents," says Paullus, l. 26. §6. D. mandati, "are imputable to fortune, not to commission." See Grotius of the rights of war and peace, 2. 14. 13. But it is otherwise with respect to one commissioned by a prince to do some public business in a foreign country. For he to whom the glory of obeying is the chief reward, ought to be indemnified by the public. See Hubert. Eunom. ad l. 26. D. mandati. Pufendorff of the law of nature and nations, 5. 4. and Hert. de lytro, 2. 10. [[Hertius (*praeses*) and Viselius (*respondens*), *De Lytro von Rantzion.*]]

is the value of the thing itself in money, so *hire* is the *value* of the use of a thing, or of labour in money; and therefore, from the very definitions, it is plain that buying and selling, renting and hiring, now-a-days, require payment in money, and in that are different from bartering, and the other contracts defined above; *"I give that you may give; I give that you may do; I do that you may give, and I do that you may do."** Yet they all agree in the chief points, and have almost all the same common properties or effects. <271>

SECTION CCCLI

The seller is obliged to tell the qualities, of the thing he sells to the buyer.

Since therefore this is the nature of the contract *buying* and *selling* (§351), that a thing is delivered at a certain price; the consequence is, that the buyer and seller ought equally to know the thing; and therefore the seller ought not only to point out to the buyer all its qualities, all its imperfections, faults or incumbrances, which do not strike the eyes and other senses;† but he is likewise bound to suffer him to examine it with his

---

* For tho' estimatory barter bears some affinity to buying and selling (§338), yet it really differs from it in this respect, that in selling, money intervenes, but in estimatory barter, an estimated thing is given for another thing. Whence it is very manifest, what ought to be determined concerning the ancient controversy between the Sabiniani and the Procullani, whether price in buying and selling could only consist in money, or might consist in other things. Upon which see, besides the learned commentators upon §2. de empt. vend. instit. V. C. Gottf. Mascou. de sect. Sabin. & Procul. 9. 10. 1. & seq. [[Mascovius, *Exercitatio inauguralis de sectis Sabinianorum et Proculianorum in jure civili.*]]

† There are faults and imperfections which are so glaring, that it would be needless to point them out; so that if one is deceived with respect to such faults, he deservedly suffers by his own blindness and heedlessness; to which case belongs the contest between Marius Gratidianus and C. Sergius Orata in Cicero, off. l. 3. 16. But the Roman laws, that men might be more firmly bound to do this good office one to another, ordained that all the faults should be told in selling which were known to the seller, and appointed a punishment for those who hid any, or did not discover them. "For tho' the twelve tables," says Cicero, "ordered no more than this, that the seller should be bound to make good those faults, which were expresly mentioned by word of mouth in the bargain, and which whoever denied was to pay double damages, the lawyers have appointed a punishment for those, who themselves do not discover the faults of what they sell: For they have so decreed, 'That if the seller of an estate, when he made the bargain, did not tell all the truth in particular, that he knew of it, he should afterwards be bound to make them good to the purchaser,' " de off. 3. 16. The

eyes, and by all other means; so that of things belonging to the taste, the sale is not perfect till they are tasted; and of others which stand in need of other trials, the sale is not perfect till the trial hath been made: And therefore, if what Euripides says be true with respect to any contract, it certainly holds with regard to this chargeable one, "Light is necessary to contractors." Cyclop. v. 137.[2] <272>

SECTION CCCLII

Hence it is also plain, that equality between the thing sold and the price paid, ought to be observed (§329); and therefore every injury ought to be repaired, whether it be done by guile or force, or be occasioned by a justifiable mistake.* Yet here we ought to call to mind what was before observed, that the wrong ought to be of some considerable moment, because here price does not consist as it were in a point, but admits of some latitude, and it would justly be reckoned being too sharp, and opening a door to endless suits and contentions, to rescind a contract for every small loss (§340). <273>

Neither of the parties ought to be wronged.

SECTION CCCLIII

It is disputed to whom the *loss* and *gain* belongs while the *thing sold* is not delivered; whether it immediately passes to the buyer so soon as the price is agreed upon, or whether it still belongs to the seller while the

To whom the loss and gain belong before delivery.

---

same author, c. 12. disputes, "Whether an honest merchant bringing, when corn was scarce at Rhodes, a large quantity thither from Alexandria, and withal knowing, that a great many ships, well laden with corn, were in the way thither from the same city, was bound to tell the news to the people of Rhodes, or might lawfully say nothing of it, but sell his own corn at the best rates he could?" of which question see Grotius of the rights of war and peace, 2. 12. Pufendorff of the law of nature and nations, 5. 3. 4.

* If it should be invincible, involuntary and inculpable (§107): For otherwise, if one buys any thing at a certain price, which he hath not seen nor sufficiently examined, his error ought to fall on himself, if the seller used no guile to deceive him, (which we know Laban did to Jacob in buying his wife, Genesis xxix. 23.) because he suffers justly for his mistake, who might not have mistaken, had he not been supinely negligent.

2. Euripides, *Cyclops,* in *Euripides,* vol. 1.

thing is undelivered? What the Roman law has determined in this case is well known; nor will any one expect that we should insist long upon the reasons of that decision. To us, who are now only enquiring into the determination of the law of nature, it seems incontrovertible, that the owner or master is to stand all chances (§211); nor does it appear less certain to us, that what proceeds from delay or fault, is not mere chance; and therefore he, who by any deed damages another, is obliged to repair that damage (§211). Whence it follows, that because the buyer may, by the law of nature, be master of the thing bought without delivery (§275), the risk, after the sale is compleated, immediately falls upon the buyer, unless the seller be guilty of any delay in delivering it, or some other fault.* <274>

SECTION CCCLIV

Whether the decision of the Roman law is agreeable to the law of nature? Now, because the buyer immediately becomes master or proprietor even before delivery, and therefore ought to stand to all chances (§353); the consequence is, that the doctrine of the Roman lawyers concerning the risk of a thing sold is true, but is not so consistent with their own principle, which denies that the dominion passes to the buyer without delivery; that since the proprietor hath the right of all the fruits, accessions, and other advantages of what is his own (§307), he hath also a right to all the gains of a thing sold to him; but so, that this rule shall then only

---

* Pufendorff's opinion (of the law of nature, &c. 5. 5. 3.) is much the same, but more obscurely told, where he distinguishes whether a certain day was fixed for the delivery or not, and if fixed, whether it be elapsed or not. For he thinks it most equal that the seller should run the risk till the term is elapsed; but that, the term being elapsed, if the thing perishes, it perishes to the buyer. But since the buyer is master, by the law of nature, without delivery, and the term being elapsed, it may not be always the seller that is in delay, but that may often be the fault of the buyer; we think in general the risk belongs to the buyer, in whose power it was to have received the thing immediately, upon paying down the price. But if he hath fulfilled the conditions of the contract on his side, or if he is ready to fulfil them, the seller who delays the delivery, deservedly runs the risk, whether a certain term for delivery was agreed upon or not.

take place, if the buyer hath any way satisfied the seller for the price;* because otherwise he would, at the same time, have the thing and the price, and thus he would be made richer at another's detriment (§257).

SECTION CCCLV

But since a thing justly perishes to the loss of the seller when he is guilty of delay in delivery, or of any other fault (353), it is manifest that the buyer is exempt from all risk, if the seller, when he offers him the price, refuses to give him full possession of the thing sold, or cannot do it; and likewise, if it can be proved to have been owing <275> to the seller's fault or negligence, that the thing sold perished either in whole or in part.

When the risk belongs to the seller.

SECTION CCCLVI

Buying and selling is done on purpose that a thing may be delivered for a certain price (§278). But since he who transfers dominion to another for an onerous cause, as, for a certain price, is obliged to warranty (§274), the seller must be obliged to warrant the buyer, if the thing be evicted from him upon account of any cause antecedent to the contract; but not, if, after the sale, something shall then happen, on account of which one is deprived of his property, or if it be taken from him by accident, or by superior force.†

The seller owes warranty to the buyer.

---

* But not only he seems to have given satisfaction as to the price, who hath paid the money, but he also to whom the seller trusts, having, *e.g.* stipulated to himself an annual interest. For tho' this is the most simple kind of contract, in which the price being paid down, the thing is immediately delivered, *i.e.* if men merchandize *Graeca fide,* which was the only kind of commerce Plato allowed in his commonwealth de legibus, l. II. yet that cannot always be done, and experience shews us, that commerce consists more in credit than in ready money.

† Truly, what happens by superior force happens by accident; wherefore, since when the contract of buying and selling is perfected (§353), the owner must stand all chances, even when a thing sold is carried off from the buyer by chance or superior force, he cannot seek warranty or reparation from any person. Moreover, there is no doubt, but, as other pacts added to this contract ought to be valid; so the buyer and seller may agree that there be no warranty, but that the thing may be entirely at the

SECTION CCCLVII

Other pacts
may be added
to this contract.

Moreover, because buying and selling is a contract, (§350); but a contract requires the consent of both parties (§327), it is manifest, that in buying and selling all turns upon agreement; and therefore any other pacts may be added to it by consent, provided they be not absurd, unjust, or fraudulent; as for instance, *addictio in diem,—lex commissoria,—pactum de retrovendendo,—pactum protomiseos,—pactum de evictione non praestanda,—pactum* <276> *de poena in casum poenitentiae praestanda,* and such others.*

---

buyer's risk. Such a pact was added to the selling of the girl by Sagaristio in Plautus, in Persa, 4. 4. v. 40.

> *Prius dico: hanc* Mancupio *nemo tibi dabit, jam scis?*
> Do. *Scio.*

> [[Plautus, *The Persian,* line 589, in vol. 3 of *Plautus:* "I tell you this first: nobody will give you a warrant with her. You understand now?" "I understand."]]

* The definitions of these pacts are known from the civil law. *Addictio in diem,* is a pact which gives the seller leave to accept of any better bargain that shall offer itself by such a day, which may be done two ways. First, when the bargain is compleated, but upon condition that it shall be null, if better terms offer themselves: Or, secondly, if it be only agreed, *de futuro,* that it shall be a bargain, if better offers are not made. *Lex commissoria,* makes void the bargain, if the price be not paid by such a day. We have an example of it in Cornelius Nepos in the life of Atticus, c. 8. *Pactum de retrovendendo,* is an agreement, that upon tender of the price at any time, or by such a certain day, the buyer shall be obliged to restore the goods to the seller or his heirs. Such is that sale in Livy, 31. 13. and that in Julius Capitolin. in Marco c. 17. [[See Boxhorn, *Historiae Augustae scriptores latini minores.* Vol. 2 includes writings by Julius Capitolinus.]] *Pactum protomiseos,* is the privilege of the first refusal, that is, if the buyer be hereafter disposed to part with the commodity, he must let the seller, or his heirs, have the first refusal, at the same rate he would sell it to another. The nature of the rest is obvious from the terms by which they are expressed. [*Eviction* is the loss which the buyer suffers, either of the whole thing that is sold, or of a part of it, because of the right which a third person has to it; so that *pactum de evictione non praestanda,* is an agreement between the seller and the buyer, that the former shall not be obliged to warrant the buyer against all danger of being evicted or troubled in his possession of the thing sold. Warranty being a consequence of the contract of sale, there is a first kind of natural warranty, which is called *warranty in law,* because the seller is obliged to it by law, altho' the sale make no mention of it. And

SECTION CCCLVIII

From the same principle we infer that a seller may *except* something for himself in the sale, and <277> that either party may add to the bargain any *condition* not repugnant to honesty and good manners, as likewise appoint a day, before which the thing is to be delivered, and the price paid.* Nay, that they may also agree, that the price not being paid, the property shall remain for some time with the seller, or that the buyer, retaining some part of the price in his hands, for which he is to pay interest, may be thus secured against eviction; that accessions shall go with the principal, that some fixed things may be carried off, that the thing sold shall be let at a certain rate to the seller, &c.

As likewise exceptions and conditions.

SECTION CCCLIX

Besides, we conclude from the same principle, that tho' buying and selling requires equality, (§352); yet, by the consent of both parties, a sale may be agreed upon which shall not be null on the account of any inequality whatsoever. Such are *auction*, when the price is not fixed by the seller, but by the highest of contending bidders: *emptio sub hasta*, which is nothing else but a more solemn auction, instituted by public authority: *emptio per aversionem*, when things of different value are not rated separately, but sold together: and *emptio spei*, when the purchase is no certain thing, but hope and expectation only, on which, by agreement of the parties, a price is laid. In all which contracts, since equality is not required, by consequence neither of the parties can complain of injury

Buying by cant or auction.

---

it being in our power to augment or diminish our natural engagements by covenants, there is a second kind of warranty, which is a warranty by deed or covenant, such as the seller and buyer are pleased to regulate among themselves. *Pactum de poena in casum poenitentiae praestanda,* is an agreement to pay a fine, in case of repenting and not standing to the bargain.]

* Nay the sale may be so agreed upon, as that a certain term of years agreed upon being run out, the thing sold shall then return to the seller or his heirs, and yet the buyer shall not redemand the price paid. Estates are often sold in this manner. See Pufendorff, law of nature, &c. 5. 5. 4.

in these cases, unless there be some knavery on either side, or the thing produced by the event was not thought of by the contracters.* <278>

SECTION CCCLX

Of letting and hiring.

The other contract which took place after the invention of money, is *letting* and *hiring* (§350): For tho', according to the Roman law, in letting farms a part of the fruits was paid for the rent, which was called *quanta,*†
1. 21. 6. loc. conduct. and thus this contract could take place before money was in use; yet there is no reason why it may not be referred to the contract, *"I give that you may give"*; because in this case the use of the thing is not compared with money or eminent price, but with the

---

* And hence we may decide the famous suit between the fishers and the Milesian youth, who had bought the cast of a net from them, occasioned by the fortune of the cast, the fishermen having drawn out a golden tripod in their net, each party contended this unexpected treasure was theirs, and the oracle very absurdly adjudged it to the wisest.

> *De tripode ex Phoebo quaeris, Milesia pubes?*
> *Huic tripodem addico, cui sit sapientia prima.*

Laert. 1. 28. Val. Max. 4. 1. [[Valerius Maximus, *Facta et dicta memorabilia* (*Memorable Doings and Sayings*) 4.1, ext. 7. Also cited in Diogenes Laertius, *Lives of Eminent Philosophers,* 1.28: "Are you enquiring about the tripod from Phoebus, Milesian youth? I assign the tripod to him who is of the greatest wisdom."]] But it is plain that the tripod belonged to the fishermen, if its owner was not known (§324), notwithstanding the contract, the Milesian youth having only had regard in the contract to what fish should be caught, and not to golden tripods, of which neither of the parties could have any thoughts. See l. 8. §1. D. de contr. empt. l. 11. §ult. & l. 12. D. de act. empt.

† For if the lord of the mannor stipulate to himself a certain portion for his rent, that bargain hath the nature of partnership, as will appear from the definition of these contracts, when we come to treat of them. Moreover, letting a fruitful farm for a certain share of the fruits, is not a contract of renting and hiring, as is plain from this consideration, that the latter is an onerous contract, in which equality is required (§324); but in the former it cannot obtain. For if one should stipulate to pay for the use of a farm for six years, every year so many measures of grain, it may happen that in one year of great plenty, when corn is very abundant and cheap, the rent shall be moderate, and proportioned to the use of the farm, but another year of scarcity it shall be immoderate on the account of scarcity and dearness. And therefore, we have already said, that renting and hiring requires that the price be paid in money (§350).

proper or vulgar price of the fruits; and therefore the value of fruits not being always the same, but higher or lower according to the plenty or scarcity of the season, one year the proprietor might be a loser, and another year the tenant. <279>

SECTION CCCLXI

Because *renting* and *hiring* is a contract for the use of a thing, or labour at a certain rate or hire; the consequence is, that he who lets ought to grant the use of a thing, or the labour contracted for, to the person who hires it; and therefore, if, by his fault, or by accident, it happens that he who hires cannot have the use of the thing hired, or cannot perform the labour promised, the stipulated hire justly diminishes in proportion.* Yea, sometimes the lessor may be sued to the value; and the same holds, if the landlord should expel, without a just cause, the tenant before his lease is out. <280>

The duties of the landlord.

SECTION CCCLXII

In like manner it is the tenant's duty to pay in due time the stipulated rent, to use what he hath the use of as another's, to be returned in specie, like an honest man, to make up damages owing to his fault; and not to desert the farm while his lease is yet unexpired, unless he be forced to it by just causes, as the incursion of an enemy, the fear of a plague, and other such dangers. For since the landlord is obliged to deliver him the thing safe and sound, to indemnify him, and not to turn him out before

And of the tenant.

* This equity was acknowledged by all the ancients, as by Sesostris king of Egypt, who, if any part of the land was washed away by the force of the river, ordered the rent to be proportionably diminished, Herodot. 1. 2. p. 81. edit. Steph. [[Herodotus, *Herodoti Halicarnassei historiae libri IX.*]] Nor did the Romans observe less equity in this affair, according to Polybius, hist. 6. 15. and among them Caesar, by Sueton's relation, cap. 20. But it is manifest, that here likewise ought to be understood a considerable loss, and not a very small one, seeing the barrenness of one year is often compensated, especially in farms, by the plenty of a succeeding year; and it is unreasonable that the tenant should have all the advantages, and yet refuse to bear the smallest share of loss.

his time is expired (§361); it is most equal, that what he would not have another do to him, he should not do to another; and, *vice versa,* what he would have another do to him, that he should do to another (§88); especially since in this chargeable contract equality ought in justice to be observed (§329).

SECTION CCCLXIII

Of pacts which may be added to this contract.

But this contract also depends wholly upon consent (§327); and therefore it is plain that several pacts may be annexed to it, provided they be consistent with good morals;* and therefore that it may be with, or without conditions, and for a certain time. And since tacite consent is held for real consent; hence we may infer, that *tacite re-hiring* is valid, if the first lease being elapsed, neither party renounces the contract; and that in this case it is just that the same terms should take place as in the former engagement. <281>

SECTION CCCLXIV

Of the loan of consumable commodities.

Now those are the contracts which began to take place after money was in use; we are therefore, in the next place, to consider those contracts which could have place either before or after money was found out. The chief of which is the contract of loan, *mutuum;* by which we understand granting the use of consumable things, on condition that as much shall

---

* Hence it is, that estates are often let out on such conditions that in renting and hiring very little remains of the nature of such a contract. Hence perpetual leases, hence irregular ones, by which at once the dominion, and all hazards, are devolved upon the lessee; of which we have an instance quoted from Alfenus Varus [[Alfenus Varus was a lawyer and consul in 39 B.C.]] by Corn. van Bynkershoek, observ. 8. 1. & seq. ad legem 31. D. locati. There is such a contract among the Germans, of which I have treated Element. juris Germ. 2. 14. §105, after Tabor, who has given us a dissertation on this subject. [[Possibly the *De servitutibus realibus: Dissertatio juridica* by the German jurist Johann Otto Tabor (*praeses*) and Hermann Hopfener (*respondens*).]]

be restored in kind.* For since not only money, but every consumable commodity may be credited in this manner, it is plain that this contract had place before men had acknowledged money for a common measure of things, and it is now most frequent.

SECTION CCCLXV

It is plain, from the definition of this contract, (§364), that the debitor has the power of abusing the thing credited to him; and therefore the credi-<282>tor has abdicated his right of excluding the debtor from the use of it; and thus he hath, only upon condition of receiving as much from the debtor, transferred to him all his right; but to transfer the right of excluding others from the use of a thing, is to transfer dominion (§231); wherefore this contract is an alienation, by which the dominion of the things credited passes intirely to the debtor.†

The dominion of the thing credited is transferred to the debtor.

---

* We call those consumeable things which we can number, measure or weigh. And this is the nature of them, 1. That they cannot be used without being abused or consumed. 2. That they may be returned either in kind or in species, 1. 2. §1. D. de rebus cred. *i.e.* if I owe a hundred guineas, my creditor will own himself satisfied whether I return him the same guineas I received from him, or others of the same kind. And hence it is plain what is meant by the same kind: it means the same in quantity and quality. But thence follows another property of consumeable commodities. 3. *viz.* That with respect to them as much is the same, Nor, 4. do they (as Thomasius has observed de pretio adfect. in res fung. non cad.) admit of a price of fancy, unless they be very scarce, so that as much in kind cannot easily be found. Thus, tho' at Rome Falernian wine was a consumeable commodity, yet a price of fancy fell upon Trimalchion's Opimian wine of a hundred years old, Petronius Arbit. Satyric. cap. 34.

† It is well known what a bustle Alexius a Massalia, *i.e.* Claudius Salmasius, has made about this affair, endeavouring to turn the defenders of this Thesis into ridicule. But all his weapons borrowed from the civil law, and much stronger ones, have been turned against him by Wissenbachius, Fabrottus, and other learned men, insomuch that the subject is now exhausted. [[A reference to a debate between the jurists Charles Annibal Fabrot (1580–1659), Claude Saumaise (1588–1653), and Johann Jakob Wissenbach (1607–65). Wissenbach's and Fabrot's positions were published in one volume with Saumaise's *Disquisitio de mutuo.*]] But the principles here laid down shew, that right reason is not against the Civilians in this matter, and does not favour Salmasius. It is true that the creditor does not alienate the quantity, but preserves it safe to himself, by obliging the debtor to return him the same in kind: But the dominion

SECTION CCCLXVI

The debtor's obligation.

From the same definition we infer, that the debtor is obliged to return as much, not only in quantity, but in quality; and therefore, if it be money that is lent to him, and its intrinsic value should afterwards be augmented or diminished, regard is to be had to the time when the contract was made; and accordingly so much ought to be diminished as the money has rose, or so much ought to be added as the money has fallen. Moreover, the debtor ought not to delay paying; nor is he delivered from his obligation by the perishing of the consumeable commodity he received from his creditor, nor by any accidental event.* <283>

SECTION CCCLXVII

Whether usury be allowable by the law of nature?

But tho' this contract be in its nature gratuitous, (as well as commodatum, of which above, *i.e.* loan of not consumeable things); yet the love of mankind waxing cold, it hath become customary for creditors to stipulate a reward to themselves for what they lend to their debtors; which, if it consist in paying monthly or yearly a certain proportion of the sum lent, as 3, 4, or 5 per cent. it is called *interest* or *usury*, tho' that last term is often taken in a bad sense for exorbitant interest, by which creditors reduce their debtors to the last dregs. Concerning usury, it is a celebrated question, that has been severely agitated by learned men, whether it be

---

of the species credited, and all the risks, pass undoubtedly to the debtor, as Salmasius himself, being pushed to the utmost extremity, is forced by his adversaries to own.

* For since the dominion of a consumeable commodity is transferred to the debtor (§365), but he who has the dominion must stand chances (§211), the creditor cannot be freed from his obligation, if, *e.g.* the wine lent him should turn into vinegar, or the money lent should be stoln from him, or be lost by any other accident. Much less then will poverty excuse a debtor from payment, if he has squandered away his estate, or, like an idle drone, lives at another's expence, and wantonly consumes on his pleasures the gains of another's sweat and labour. For this is a most pestiferous race, ready to engage in the vilest schemes. And they who have wasted their own substance must needs covet that of others. See Salust. Catil. cap. 20.

agreeable to the law of nature for creditors to stipulate with debtors for it.* <284>

SECTION CCCLXVIII

But since, 1. It is not unjust to communicate our goods with others, not gratuitously, but for a hire (§328). 2. Since one often makes great gain by the use of another's goods, while, in the mean time, the creditor suffers loss or inconvenience by the want of them; but none ought to inrich himself at the detriment of another (§257). 3. Besides, since he runs a great risk who lends his goods to another on these terms, that he may consume or abuse them, it is not unreasonable that the creditor should exact a hire from the debtor in proportion to the risk (§331).—From all these considerations, we think it may be justly concluded, that a pact about interest with one who may make gain of our money, is not contrary to the law of nature.† And tho' interest ought to be proportioned

What is to be affirmed here.

---

* We need not insist long upon the history of this controversy, which was revived in Holland the last century. We are saved this labour by Noodt de foenore & usuris, 1. 4. [[G. Noodt, *De foenore et usuris libri tres*]] Martinus Schook exercit. var. p. 430. [[Martin Schoock (1614–69), *Exercitationes variae, de diversis materiis*]] and Thomas. not. ad Lancellot. 4. 7. not. 275. p. 2024. [[Lancelotti, *Institutiones juris canonici,* ed. Thomasius]] the last of whom hath given us a full history of the rise of this dispute, and of the managers on both sides of the question. It must however be acknowledged, that most of the learned who have wrote upon this subject have been more taken up about the divine positive law than the law of nature; so that very little advantage is to be reaped from them by students of natural law.

† To this doctrine it is in vain objected, as, 1. "That money is a barren thing, and therefore that usury, as a kind of offspring, ought not to be required for it." For it is a barren thing in a physical sense, but not in a civil sense; for in commerce the double, and very often more, is gained by it, Mat. xxv. 16. 17. Or, 2. "That loan of inconsumeable things is gratuitous, and therefore loan of consumeable goods ought to be so too." For he who lends an unconsumeable thing suffers less inconvenience, and runs less risk than a creditor who transfers to his debtor the dominion of a consumeable thing, with the power and right of abusing it. Or, 3. "That God hath prohibited such pacts, Exod. xxii. 25. Lev. xxv. 37. Psalm xv. 5. Luke vi. 34." For God proscribed such pacts from the Israelitish common-wealth, so far only that an Israelite could not exact interest from an Israelite; they were permitted with strangers, Deut. xxiii. 19. 20. But the law of nature makes no difference between fellow citizens and strangers. See Jo. Selden de jure nat. & gent. See Heb. and Jo. Cleric. ad Exod. xxii. 25. p. 112.

to the gain which the debtor may, in all probability, make of the sum;
yet it is not iniquous that it should be augmented in proportion to the
risk, the scarcity of money, and other circumstances (§331), as the custom
of *bottomry* shews us, dig. 1. 22. tit. 2. de nautico foenore. <285>

SECTION CCCLXIX

What is meant
by pledge,
mortgage, and
antichretic
pact.

Another contract of this kind is *pawn* or *pledge,* by which we understand
an obligation to deliver something to a creditor for the security of what
he lends or credits. For if a thing, especially if it be in its nature immoveable, be not delivered, but yet the creditor hath a right constituted
to him in it, of taking possession of it, in case the debt be not cancelled,
that transaction between the creditor and debtor is called *hypotheca,
mortgage.* Again, if it be agreed that a creditor should receive the fruits
of a thing delivered to him for the security of what he hath credited, in
lieu of interest, this invention is termed *pactum antichreticum* (§283).

SECTION CCCLXX

What is just
about a pawn.

From the definition of a *pawn,* it is plain that it ought to be the debtor's
own; and therefore he deserves punishment who pawns any thing belonging to another, whether lent to him, deposited with him, or hired
by him. That the creditor ought not to use a pawn, if it may be rendered
worse by use, but to preserve it with as much care as his own goods, and
to return it to the debtor, when the debt is cleared. Finally, since the
owner regularly runs risks (§211),* the consequence is, that the risk of

---

* By the law of Germany in the middle ages, when a pawn perished by chance,
the debtor was freed from all obligation to pay his debt, jus prov. Sax. 3. 5. Sometimes
it was provided by a special pact, that the risk should belong to the creditor, as in
Pontan. hist. Dan. 1. 9. ad annum 1411. [[Pontanus, *Rerum Danicarum historia.*]] But
because that proceeded from this singular principle of the Germans, that the creditor
got the dominion of the pawn, of which see our Elem. jur. Germ. l. 2. 11. §319. the
reasons given in this section do not permit us to attribute these things to the law of
nature.

the pawn belongs to the debtor, and that perishing by accident, he is notwithstanding obliged to pay his debt. <286>

SECTION CCCLXXI

From the definition of *mortgage* (§369), we infer, that it can scarcely consist in moveables, which a debtor may easily alienate and transfer to a stranger without his creditor's knowledge; but it consists chiefly in immoveables, as houses, lands, cities and territories;* and likewise in larger stocks of moveable things, which are not easily transported from place to place, as large libraries; yea, in rights and actions likewise, if great advantage accrue from them to the possessor. But whatever is thus pledged to a creditor, his right in it continues, to whomever it may be transferred; for otherwise his *hypotheca* would be without effect. <287>

What is just about mortgage.

SECTION CCCLXXII

From the definition of the *pactum antichreticum*, (§369), it is obvious that it can only take place in pawning things which yield increase; and since the fruits are in lieu of interest, they ought not greatly to exceed that measure of interest which we have found to be most agreeable to

What is just about the pactum antichreticum.

---

* This we add on account of what Pufendorff says of the law of nature, *&c.* 5. 10. 16. "In the state of nature such mortgages are needless; for if the debtor refuses payment, the possession of the mortgage assigned in security, must be detained by force of arms. But in that state, even without such a particular assignment, it is lawful to seize on any thing that belongs to the debtor." But examples of such mortgages are not wanting even among independent nations, as Hertius has shewn in his notes upon this passage of Pufendorff, p. 738. & seq. who elegantly replies to Pufendorff's argument, that this mortgage may be of great use, if the town thus pledged should fall into a third person's hands. Moreover, we readily grant, that independent nations do not rashly satisfy themselves with such simple mortgages, but do at least stipulate the right of keeping a garison in these cautionary towns, as Elizabeth queen of England did in the 1585, when the Hollanders put several towns into her hands, Em. Meteran. Rer. Belg. l. 13. and the other Belgic annalists for that year. [[Emanuel van Meteren (1535–1612), author of a history of the Low Countries, frequently republished with additions after his death (*Historien der Nederlanden en haar naburen oorlogen tot het jaar 1612*).]]

equity. The creditor, in this case, is not liable to accidents, unless it be so agreed; and therefore if the creditor, on account of barrenness, or any public calamity, does not receive the value of the interest due to him, the debtor is obliged to make it up.

SECTION CCCLXXIII

What is common to all these conventions.

This is in common to all these contracts, that being designed for the security of the creditor, (§369), the creditor, if the debtor be tardy in his payment, has a right to alienate the pawn or mortgage, and deducting his principal and interests, is obliged only to refund the overplus to the debtor, unless there be an accessory pact, *lex commissoria;* by which it is stipulated, that the pawn, if not relieved within a certain time, shall be left to the creditor for his principal and interests. For tho' the more recent Roman laws did not allow of such a pact,* l. un. C. Theodos. de commissor. rescind. l. ult. C. de pact. pign. and that might have been justly done on account of the exorbitant avarice of creditors; yet it does not follow from hence, that the law of nature, which permits every owner to alienate his own on whatsoever conditions, does not allow of such a pact (§309), which Hertius hath shewn, by many examples, to have been in use amongst princes and independent nations, in his notes upon Pufendorff, 5. 10. 14. p. 737. <288>

---

* The more ancient laws among the Romans adhering more strictly to the simplicity of the law of nature, are not contrary to this commissory pact; yea, while the republic was yet free, it was looked upon as lawful, as appears from a passage in Cicero's epistles, epist. ad famil. 13. 56. quoted by Hertius, and before him by Jac. Gothofred. ad l. un. Theodos. de commiss. rescind. (Philotes Alabandenses ὑποθήκας Cluvio dedit: hae commissae sunt.) [[Cicero, *Epistulae ad familiares* 13.56: "Philocles of Alabanda has mortgaged some property to Culvius. The time of the mortgage has expired."]] But the terrible severity of creditors, by which debtors were unmercifully squeezed, being forced to pawn, in this manner, things of much greater value than the debt, at last obliged the emperors to proscribe this pact, as exceeding detrimental to debtors.

SECTION CCCLXXIV

The third contract which may take place before and after money is in- Of suretyship.
vented, is *suretyship; i.e.* an obligation a person comes under to pay another's debt, if he does not. For if one binds himself not merely to pay,
the other failing, but conjointly with him *in solidum* for the whole debt,
he is debtor, and the obligation of both is equal. Again, he who, with
the consent of the creditor, delivers a debtor from his obligation, and
takes it upon himself, is called *expromissor, Bail.* All these contracts, as
well as that of pawn or mortgage, are contrived for the security of creditors, and afford an ample proof of the decay of benevolence among
mankind.*

SECTION CCCLXXV

Moreover, from the definition of *suretiship,* (§374), it is plain that there For what
is no place for suretiship, which is a subsidiary security, unless the <289> things it is
debt be such that it may be as conveniently paid by another as by the surety.
principal debtor; and therefore suretiship for condemned persons, tho'
some ancient nations admitted it, is contrary to right reason.† But yet

---

* For if benevolence prevailed, as it ought to do, among mankind, a creditor
would not distrust a debtor, nor would a debtor allow one thought of defrauding his
creditor to enter into his mind; and thus there would be no occasion for pawns or
sureties. But now that men are become so suspicious and diffident, that they will not
believe unless they see, this is an argument of the decline of benevolence, and of the
prevalence of perfidy among men. This is allowed by Seneca in a most beautiful
passage (of benefits, 3. 15).

† Pufendorff, 5. 10. 12. hath brought many instances of it among the Greeks; and
Hertius in his notes on Pufendorff, ibidem, p. 735, produces statutes approving of
such sureties. But as for others who pretend to justify this kind of suretiship by examples in the sacred writings, they are easily refuted, Gen. xlii. 37. For every one may
perceive that obligation of Reuben to have been foolish, especially seeing he did not
pledge his own head, but the lives of his innocent children; and besides, it was not
for a condemned person, but for his brother Benjamin's return out of Egypt. Whence
it is not probable that the pious and prudent Jacob accepted of the offered security,
Gen. xliii. 9. Juda offers security, but not for a condemned criminal, nor does he
pledge his life. Finally, 1 Kings, xx. 39. there no person pawns his life for a guilty

there is no reason, when the crime may be expiated by a mulct, why another person may not interpose in behalf of the criminal, and oblige himself to pay the mulct, if the criminal fail.

SECTION CCCLXXVI

The obligation of sureties.

As to the obligation of sureties, it is plain, from the definition (§374), that they oblige themselves to the same which the creditor has a right to exact from his debtor, and therefore it is unjust for a creditor to stipulate more to himself from a surety than from the debtor; that the obligation of a surety is subsidiary, and therefore that by the law of nature a surety does not stand in need of the *singulari beneficio ordinis vel excussionis*,[3] as it is called in the civil law; but may then be sued, when it clearly appears that the principal debtor has not <290> wherewith to pay.* Many sureties engaged for the same persons and debts, are only bound proportionably, unless they have voluntarily and expresly bound themselves for the whole; and therefore the benefit of division is due to them by the law of nature, as being proportionably bound, unless one's fellow sureties be insolvent, and one could not but know they were so.

---

criminal, but the custody of a captive is demanded under the peril of death. So that there is nothing in the sacred writings to justify this custom among the ancients.

* A contrary opinion hath prevailed in many nations, who thought that recourse might be had to the surety before the principal debtor. Concerning the Hebrews, see Prov. xx. 16. xvii. 18. As for the Greeks, that saying of Thales is well known, "Be surety, and ruin is at your heels." The ancient Germans had likewise such a proverb. See Schilt. Exercit. 48. 21. [[Johann Schilter (1632–1705), *Exercitationes theoretico-practicae ad L libros Pandectarum.*]] The same rigour was also observed by the Romans, till Justinian introduced the beneficium ordinis vel excussionis, novella 4. But since a surety only accedes as a subsidiary security on failure of the principal, if he might be immediately sued, there would be no difference between the Surety, the Expromissor or Bail, and the Principal debtor. It is therefore agreeable to right reason, that he who is bound as a subsidiary security, should not be sued before the discussion of the principal debtor. So Cicero Epist. ad Attic. 16. 15. "Sponsores adpellare, videtur habere quamdam δυσωπίαν." [[Cicero, *Epistulae ad Atticum* 16.15: "To call upon sureties seems to have a certain shame [attached]."]]

3. "The right of bringing an action in a particular order" (that is, first against the principal debtor, then against the surety).

SECTION CCCLXXVII

When two or more become debtors of one and the same *thing* (§374), it is evident, that every one of them being obliged to the creditor for the whole debt, the creditor may exact the whole debt from either of the two he pleases;* and when any one of them pays the debt, the other is discharged from his obligation to the creditor, but not with respect to his fellow-surety; for he who paid for him (§346) did his business, and therefore ought to be indemnified by him (§349). <291>

Of the solidity among two or more debtors.

SECTION CCCLXXVIII

Again, from the definition of an *expromissor* or *bail* (374), we infer, that his obligation is the same with that of the principal debtor, insomuch that the latter, bail being accepted by the creditor, is free; and therefore neither can this kind of surety plead the discussion of the principal debtor before him; nor can the creditor, if he cannot recover his debt from this surety, any more have recourse to the principal debtor whom he hath once freed, but he must depend upon this surety alone for it, upon whose faith he had relieved his debtor.

As to an expromissor or bail.

SECTION CCCLXXIX

The next contract which may take place either where money is, or is not in use, is *partnership,* as it may plainly do, since it is nothing else but sharing among many the profit or loss that may arise from joint stock

The contract of partnership.

---

* There is therefore no place here for the division of an obligation. But because if both who are bound in solidity be solvent, and both may easily be sued, there is no just cause why the creditor should press one, and extort the whole sum from him alone; humanity does not allow one so rigorously to prosecute his right, as to press any one singly, but commands us to have recourse to both. For surely humanity doth not permit us to demand any thing from any other which we can obtain otherwise, without detriment to ourselves or any other (§216).

or labour:* for commodities and labour may be communicated either before or after money is in use. <292>

SECTION CCCLXXX

What is just with respect to partnership.

Because in *universal* partnership all things, in *general* partnership some things only are common; so that these contracts somewhat depend upon chance (§379); the consequence is, that amongst such partners the loss and gain must be common, but the contribution may be very unequal; and therefore such a partner hath no reason to complain if his fellow-partner expends more than him, when his necessities require it; yea, a partner is obliged to pay his proportion of debt contracted by his fellow-partner; for which reason, it cannot be doubted that it is highly reasonable that every one of such partners should share of the gain made by any one of them; and that he who has a right to the gains, ought to bear his share of the loss, damages, or inconveniencies.

SECTION CCCLXXXI

What in singular partnership.

But since in *singular* or particular partnership equality ought to be observed (§380), which however is not always observed in the contribution; it follows, that the equality in dividing loss and profit cannot be *arithmetical,* but must be *geometrical.* † And therefore he who hath contrib-

---

* We are therefore here treating of community in consequence of the consent of partners. But because consent may be either tacit or express, and both have the same effect (§275), the consequence is, that partnership may be contracted by tacite consent, *i.e.* by deed, Hert. diss. de societate facto contr. [[Hertius (*praeses*) and Gilfeld (*respondens*), *De societate facto contracta.*]] Now, since either all goods and labour, or a certain share only, or some particular goods and labour, may be joined, partnership may be either universal, or general, or particular. Grotius of the rights of war and peace, 2. 12. 24. hath justly remarked, that universal and general partnership have something of chance in them; but that in particular or singular partnership, equality ought to be observed.

† Some have said, that arithmetical equality ought to be observed here, as among brethren; and thus they interpret, l. 6. l. 29. l. 80. D. pro Soc. and other Roman laws, Connan. Comment. jur. civ. 7. 19. 5. Huber. Praelect. ad tit. Inst. de societate. [[Connan, *Commentariorum;* U. Huber, *Praelectionum juris civilis tomi* 3.]] But this fra-

uted more stock or labour, ought to have a proportionably greater share of profit and loss than he who contributes less. But seeing any one can grant to any other whatever advantages he pleases with regard to his own goods (§309), it is undeniable that partners may agree one with another in any manner; and may observe, in dividing loss and gain, either arithmetical equality, or any inequality, unless, by the knavery of one or other of them, the division degenerates into that of the lion in the fable, Phaed. Fab. 1. 6. <293>

SECTION CCCLXXXII

In fine, since partnership is formed by consent, and by way of convention (§379), this rule of the Roman law can hardly be deduced from the principles of the law of nature, *viz.* "That any one may quit partnership, provided he do it not fraudulently, nor at an improper time."* The whole matter rather turns upon the conditions of the agreement; and therefore, if the partnership was contracted for perpetuity, it ought to be perpetual;

Whether one partner may quit the partnership against the other's will?

---

ternity of partners is a fiction, to which the law of nature is a stranger; and besides, in this case the profit arises from joint stock and labour; wherefore, nothing can be more just than that loss and gain should be shared proportionably to stock and labour. So Aristotle rightly decides the matter, ad Nicom. 8. 16.

* This may be proved from the very reasons brought by ancient lawyers. For sometimes they give this reason, "That community is the mother of discords," l. 77. §20. D. de legat. Sometimes they say, "It is a natural vice to neglect what is in common," l. 2. C. quando & quibus quarta pars. To which some add another reason, "That respect is had in the choice of a partner to his abilities and industry; and therefore, if either partner does not answer his co-partner's hope and expectation, with regard to his honesty and diligence, the other hath a right to renounce the partnership." But buying and selling, renting and hiring often produce as much discord, in which contracts they allow no place for changing one's mind, or repenting. And houses let, are often no less neglected than houses in common to many, and yet it is not allowable to break such a contract before the time is out. Again, he who hires one to work for him, hath regard to the skill, honesty and industry of the person he hires, and yet he cannot break his contract before the time is expired. If therefore this rule takes place in other contracts, why may it not be allowed to take place likewise in partnership, l. 5. C. de obl. & art. "As every one is at liberty to contract or not contract, so none can renounce the obligation he hath once come under, without the consent of his party."

if for a time only, it is but for the time fixed; unless one of the partners be injurious to the others, and do not fulfil the articles of agreement; in which case, it is most just that the others should have the right of renouncing the partnership even before the time agreed upon in the contract. <294>

SECTION CCCLXXXIII

Of donation. Let us add *donation,* by which we understand a promise to transfer something of ours to another gratuitously. From which definition, it is plain that it may be made with or without conditions; and therefore in view of death. So that *donations* are justly divided into *donations among the living,* and *donations in prospect of death.* And a donation among the living obliges to deliver the thing promised, and leaves no room to the donor to revoke his promise. But from what was said above, it is evident, that he who receives the donation cannot demand warranty from the donor, if the thing be evicted (§274), and that he is obliged to shew gratitude to his benefactor by words and deeds on all occasions (§222).

SECTION CCCLXXXIV

Some corolaries about contracts in general. To conclude; with regard to all contracts in general, it is to be observed, that because they consist in consent (§327), they can only be formed by those who are not incapable, by nature of by law, of consenting. Again, because they were devised for the sake of commerce (§327), they must be about things which may be in commerce honestly, and with the permission of the laws; and therefore contracts about impossible or base things, or things exeemed by the laws from commerce, are null: <295> but as many things are exeemed by positive laws from commerce, which naturally are subjects of it, so positive laws may likewise permit contracts about several things which are not subjects of commerce, according to the laws and manners of other nations.*

---

* For example, with us it is base and to no purpose to pawn dead bodies. But the

Remarks on This Chapter

It seems necessary to add a little to what our Author hath said in this chapter concerning usury, to shew at one and the same time, the true state of the case with regard to the forbidding of usury in the Israelitish commonwealth, and how civil laws may confine and alter natural rights, consistently with the law of nature. And here all we have to do is to copy a little from our excellent politician Mr. Harrington, in his prerogative of popular government (p. 245).

Mr. Harrington, who hath shewn at great length, that property must have a being before empire or government, or beginning with it must still be first in order, because the cause must necessarily precede the effect, reasons thus: "Property comes to have a being before empire two ways, either by a natural or violent revolution: natural revolution happens from within, or by commerce, as when a government erected upon one balance, that for example, of a nobility or a clergy, through the decay of their estates, comes to alter to another balance; which alteration in the root of property, leaves all to confusion, or produces a new branch or government, according to the kind or nature of the root. Violent revolution happens from without, or by arms, as when upon a conquest there follows confiscation. Confiscation again is of three kinds, when the captain taking all to himself, plants his army by way of military colonies, benefices or Timars, which was the policy of Mahomet; or when the captain has some sharers, or a nobility that divides with him, which was the policy introduced by the Goths and Vandals; or when <296> the captain divides the inheritance, by lots or otherwise, to the whole people; which policy was instituted by God or Moses in the commonwealth of Israel. Now this triple distribution, whether from natural or violent revolution, returns, as to the generation of empire, to the same thing, that is, to the nature of the balance already

---

laws of the Egyptians permitted pawning of dead bodies, and denied burial to children if they neglected to relieve such pledges by paying their parents debts, Diod. Sicul. Bibl. 1. 93. On the other hand, it is unnatural and abominable to pawn wives and children, as was permitted in the kingdom of Pegu, because it must be attended with most miserable consequences. And therefore the Romans judged him worthy of banishment, who knowingly accepted in pawn a free-born child from his father, l. 5. D. quae res pign.

stated."[4] Mr. Harrington having fully proved these points, or that property is the natural cause of government, and that changes in it must make proportional changes in government, it follows from hence, that unless the balance of property be fixed, empire or government cannot be fixed, but will be continually altering as the balance of property varies; but property in land can only be fixed by an Agrarian law. Now these principles being laid down, the following truths concerning money, and the methods of regulating it in governments will be manifest, namely, "That the balance in money," as Mr. Harrington expresses it, "may be as good or better than that of land in three cases: First, where there is no property of land yet introduced, as in Greece during the time of her ancient imbecility; whence, as is noted by Thucydides, *The meaner sort, through a desire of gain, underwent the servitude of the mighty.* Secondly, in cities of small territory and great traffic, as Holland and Genoa, the land not being able to feed the people, who must live upon trade, is over-balanced by the means of that traffic, which is money. Thirdly, in a narrow country, where the lots are at a low scantling, as among the Israelites; if care be not had of money in the regulation of the same, it will eat out the balance of land. For which cause, tho' an Israelite might both have money, and put it to usury, (Thou shalt lend [upon usury] to many nations, Deut. xv. 6. and xxiii. 19.) yet might he not lend upon usury to a citizen or brother. Whence two things are manifest. First, that usury in itself is not unlawful: And next, that usury in Israel was no otherwise forbidden, than as it might come to overthrow the balance or foundation of the government. For where a lot, as to the general, amounted not perhaps to four acres, a man that should have a thousand pounds in his purse, would not have regarded such a lot in comparison of his money; and he that should have been half so much in debt, would have been quite eaten out. Usury is of such a nature, as, not forbidden in the like cases, must devour the government. The Roman people, while their territory was no bigger, and their lots, which exceeded not two acres a man, were yet scantier, were flead alive with it; and if they had not helped themselves by their tumults, and the institution of their tribunes, it had totally ruined both

4. Harrington, "The Prerogative of Popular Government," in *The Political Works of James Harrington,* bk. I, chap. III, 405–6.

them and their government. In a commonwealth whose territory is very small, the balance of the government being laid upon the land, as in Lacedemon, it will not be sufficient to forbid usury; but money itself must be forbidden. Whence Lycurgus allowed of none, or of such only as being of old or useless iron, was little better, or if you will, little worse than none. The prudence of <297> which law appeared in the neglect of it, as when Lysander, General for the Lacedemonians in the Peloponnesian war, having taken Athens, and brought home the spoil of it, occasioned the ruin of that commonwealth in her victory. The land of Canaan, compared with Spain or England, was at most but a Yorkshire, and Laconia was less than Canaan. Now, if we imagine Yorkshire divided, as was Canaan, into six hundred thousand lots, or as was Laconia into thirty thousand, a Yorkshireman having one thousand pounds in his purse, would I believe, have a better estate in money than in land: Wherefore, in this case, to make the land hold the balance, there is no way but either that of Israel, by forbidding usury, or that of Lacedemon, by forbidding money. Where a small sum may come to over-balance a man's estate in land; there, I say, usury or money, for the preservation of the balance in land, must of necessity be forbidden, or the government will rather rest upon the balance of money, than upon that of land, as in Holland and Genoa. But in a territory of such extent as Spain or England, the land being not to be overbalanced by money, there needs no forbidding of money or usury. In Lacedemon merchandize was forbidden; in Israel and Rome it was not exercised; wherefore, to these usury must have been the more destructive; but in countries where merchandize is exercised, it is so far from being destructive, that it is necessary; else that which might be of profit to the commonwealth, would rust unprofitably in private purses, there being no man that will venture his money but through hope of some gain; which, if it be so regulated, that the borrower may gain more by it than the lender, as at four in the hundred, or thereabouts, usury becomes a mighty profit to the public, and a charity to private men: In which sense, we may not be persuaded by them, that do not observe these different causes, that it is against scripture. Had usury to a brother been permitted in Israel, that government had been overthrown: But that such a territory as England or Spain cannot be over-balanced by money, whether it be a scarce or plentiful commodity, whether it be accumu-

lated by parsimony, as in the purse of Henry VII. or presented by fortune, as in the revenue of the Indies. For in general this is certain, that
if the people have clothes and money of their own, these must either
rise (for the bulk) out of property in land, or at least, out of the cultivation of the land, or the revenue of industry; which, if it be dependent, they must give such a part of their clothes and money to preserve
that dependence, out of which the rest arises, to him or them on whom
they depend, as he or they shall think fit; or parting with nothing to
this end, must lose all; that is, if they be tenants, they must pay their
rent, or turn out. So if they have clothes or money dependently, the
balance of land is in the landlord or landlords of the people. But if
they have clothes and money independently, then the balance of land
must be in the people themselves, in <298> which case they neither
would, if there were any such, nor can, because there be no such, give
their money or clothes to such as are wiser, or richer or stronger than
themselves. So it is not a man's clothes and money or riches, that oblige
him to acknowledge the title of his obedience to him that is wiser or
richer, but a man's no clothes, or money, or his poverty. Wherefore,
seeing the people cannot be said to have clothes and money of their
own, without the balance in land, and having the balance in land, will
never give their clothes or money or obedience to a single person, or a
nobility, tho' these should be richer in money, in such a territory as
England or Spain, money can never come to over-balance land. Henry
VII. tho' he missed of the Indies, in which, for my part, I think him
happy, was the richest in money of English princes. Nevertheless, this
accession of revenue did not at all preponderate on the king's part, nor
change the balance. But while making farms of a standard he increased
the yeomanry, and cutting off retainers he abased the nobility, began
that breach in the balance of land, which proceeding ruined the nobility, and in them that government. The monarchy of Spain, since the
silver of Potosi sailed up the Guadalquiver, which in English is, since
that king had the Indies, stands upon the same balance in the lands of
the nobility on which it always stood."[5] See Mr. Harrington himself.
What hath been now quoted from him is sufficient to shew in what
manner we ought to reason about the regulation of money in a state.

5. Ibid., 406–8.

There will be occasion afterwards to consider the natural causes of government more fully. But it is plain from what was said in a former remark, 1. That superior wisdom and virtue will naturally create authority. And that, 2. Property alone can give or create power, and will naturally produce it. And therefore, 3. That empire will follow the balance of property: And by consequence, 4. There is no natural mean of fixing government, but by fixing the balance upon which it depends. Wherefore, 5. That is a proper regulation of money with respect to the preservation of a government, which is necessary or proper to fix the balance upon which the nature of that government depends or turns. But, 6. Men have a natural right to form themselves into any form of civil government proper to promote their greater happiness; and consequently, to make any regulations necessary or proper to that effect. Thus the Lacedemonians had a right, for the preservation of their government, to forbid money, and the Israelites to forbid usury. And thus our government has a right to regulate the interest of money as the nature and end of our government, *i.e.* as the greater good in our government requires. If it be asked what the law of nature says about money in a state of nature, the answer is obvious; it requires that commerce be carried on with or without money, in an honest candid way; so as none may be made richer at the detriment of others; and allows bartering, buying, letting and hiring, and other contracts, all imaginable latitude or liberty <299> within the bounds of honesty, the general dictates of which, with regard to all contracts, are sufficiently explained by our Author.

Concerning pacts.

SECTION CCCLXXXV

The difference between pacts and contracts.

Tho', by the law of nature, there be no difference between *pacts* and *contracts,* both deriving their subsistence and force from consent; yet it may be said, that *contracts,* according to the antient way of speaking, related to commerce about goods and labour (§327); and *pacts* to other things and deeds, which are not matters of ordinary commerce.* Thus, *e.g.* tho' free persons of either sex are not in commerce, yet among them agreements are made about marriage, to be celebrated either immediately, or some time after; and both these agreements, the former of which is called *betrothing,* the other *full marriage,* come under the title of *pacts.* <300>

---

* Pufendorff, law of nature, *&c.* 5. 2. 4. has acknowledged this difference. And tho' the Roman writers, because they use the words in another sense, and make another distinction between contracts and pacts, do not always make use of the word *contrahere* in speaking of things in commerce, or the word *pacisci* in speaking of things out of commerce; (for they say *contrahere nuptias,* l. 22. D. de ritu nupt. and *pacisci ab aliquo numos,* Val. Max. 9. 4. 2.) yet the word *contractus* is seldom or never used by them but to signify an agreement about things in commerce. This is so true, that the civilians (contra Donell. comm. juris, 13. 18.) [[Hugo Donellus (Hugues Doneau, 1527–91), French jurist and commentator on Roman civil law (*Commentariorum juris civilis libri viginti octo*)]] deny *marriage* to be a *contract,* because it relates to persons and their inseparable union, which are not things in commerce. We may therefore admit this difference between *contracts* and *pacts.*

SECTION CCCLXXXVI

Now, since men cannot live comfortably and agreeably, except they render one to another those duties of *humanity* and *beneficence* which we have already defined (§214); and yet benevolence is become so cold and languid amongst men, that we can hardly depend upon one another's humanity and beneficence for them (§326); and besides, these are duties not of perfect, but imperfect obligation, (§122),* and therefore duties which cannot be extorted from the unwilling: for these reasons, there is no other security for our obtaining them but another's obligation to us by his consent; and therefore we ought thus to secure to ourselves the performance of those good offices by others to which we would have a perfect right. Now, this consent of two or more to give, or do any thing which could not be otherwise exacted from them by perfect right, but was due merely in consequence of the law of humanity and beneficence, is called a *pact*.

Why pacts are necessary.

SECTION CCCLXXXVII

Nor can it be questioned that such pacts ought to be faithfully fulfilled. For since he who promises any thing, declares his mind, whether by words or other signs; and words are so to be used, that the person we speak to may not be de-<301>ceived (§196); the consequence is, that all fraud, all lying, all falshood ought to be far removed from those who deliberately make covenants or pacts; and therefore that nothing ought to be held more sacred than keeping faith, or more detestable than perfidy.†

Such pacts ought to be fulfilled. A first argument to prove it.

---

* The history of Abraham and Abimelech furnishes us with an example. The law of humanity and beneficence required, commanded both of them, Abraham especially, an upright pious man, who had received many favours from Abimelech, to behave kindly and graciously towards one another: natural reason obliged Abraham to gratitude: And yet we read, Genesis xxi. 23. that they bargained or covenanted friendship the one with the other. And thus the ancients obliged one another by covenants to perform what they were previously obliged to by the law of humanity and beneficence.

† For as by pacts we in some measure supply our indigence; and we make covenants or pacts with others, that they may be obliged to render us those good offices

SECTION CCCLXXXVIII

A second
argument.

There is a second reason which every one will own to be of no less weight. And it is this, the love of justice is the source of all the duties we owe to one another (§173), and this love commands us not to do to others what we would not have done by them to ourselves (§177). But surely none would desire to be deluded by the promises and pacts of another. It is therefore our duty not to deceive any one by our pacts or promises; not to defraud one, by making him trust to our fidelity; but faithfully and conscientiously to perform what we engage to do.* <302>

SECTION CCCLXXXIX

Pacts of
several sorts.

Pacts are either *unilateral* or *bilateral.* By the former, one party only is bound to the other; by the latter, both parties mutually oblige or engage themselves one to another; and therefore this latter kind of pacts includes in them a tacite condition, that one is to perform his promise, if the other likewise fulfils the pact on his side. Both however are either *obligatory* or *liberative.* By the former, a new obligation is brought upon one

---

of humanity and beneficence, which we can hardly expect from them without such pacts; it is plain that human life, and all the interests of social commerce, depend upon fidelity in fulfilling them. Therefore Cicero says justly, pro Q. Roscio comoedo, c. 6. "To break one's faith is so much the more base and attrocious, that human life depends upon faith." Hence unlying lips have always been reckoned a noble quality, as Euripides expresses it in Iphig. in Taur. v. 1064. [[Euripides, *Iphigenia in Tauris.*]]

Καλόν τι γλωσσ᾽, ὅτῳ πίσις παρῇ.
A faithful tongue is a beautiful thing.

* We do not here use this argument, "That civil society could not subsist without faith and honesty." For tho' this argument proves the necessity of pacts, and of faithfulness amongst mankind, and Cicero hath elegantly demonstrated this necessity from this consideration, "That without some share of this justice, without faith and pacts among themselves, even those who live by villainy and wickedness could not subsist." [[Cicero, *De officiis* (On duties), 2.11.40.]] Yet we have already shewn, that the origine of moral obligation is not to be derived from this principle of sociality (§75): And therefore we have rather chosen to give these two reasons in the preceding sections derived from our first principle of *love.*

or other, or upon both. By the latter, obligations formerly constituted are taken off. Again, pacts may be of a mixed kind; such are those by which former obligations are annulled, and new ones are constituted at the will of the parties covenanting. Of this kind principally, it is evident, are *novations* and *transactions* about doubtful or uncertain affairs. But there is one rule for them all, which is, that they ought to be faithfully and religiously kept, especially if one hath not promised with an intention to lay himself under a strict obligation.* <303>

SECTION CCCXC

Hence we infer, that by the law of nature there is no difference between pact and stipulation; and therefore that Franc. Connanus, in his comment. 1. 6. is mistaken, when, to exalt the excellence of the Roman laws, he denies that by the law of nature obligation arises from promises, as

By the law of nature, naked or bare pacts oblige perfectly.

* This we add, in opposition to those who assert, that there is a perfect and an imperfect promise; the former of which they define to be a promise, wherein the promiser not only designs to be obliged, but actually transfers a right to another, to exact the thing promised from him as a debt: And the latter they define to be a promise wherein the promiser designs indeed to be obliged, but not in such a manner as that the thing promised may be exacted from him by the person to whom he promises it. To which kind they refer this way of promising, "I have purposed to give you such a thing, and I desire you may credit me." As likewise, the promises of great or complaisant men, when they promise one a vote or a recommendation, Grotius of the rights, &c. 2. 2. 2. Pufendorff of the law of nature, &c. 3. 5. 5. But, 1. Such promises are often not pacts, but words or asseverations only, which Grotius and Pufendorff themselves distinguish from pacts: Yea, sometimes, they are but preparations to pacts, or what is called treaties. 2. It is a contradiction to say, one wills to promise, and yet does not will to give a right to exact from him. It is a fiction, by which, if it be admitted, I know not what pacts and promises may not be basely eluded, after the example of the Milanese, who being reproached with perjury, answered, "We swore indeed, but we did not promise to keep our oath." Upon which answer, when Radevicus de gestis Friderici I. l. 2. c. 25. relates it, he justly says, "A suitable answer indeed, that their discourse might be of a piece with their profligate manners; and that they who lived perfidiously and infamously, might speak as wickedly as they lived, and their discourse might be as impure and villainous as their actions." [[Radevicus, *De rebus gestis Friderici I. Romanorum Imperatoris.*]] 3. Finally, tho' the promises of great men should sometimes be imperfect with respect to exaction, it does not follow from hence, that they are imperfect in respect of obligation.

long as they are simple agreements, and are not converted into contracts. His arguments have been sufficiently refuted by Grotius of the rights of war and peace, 2. 2. 1. and Pufendorff of the law of nature and nations, 3. 5. 9. We shall only add, that Connanus speaks not in so high a strain of the natural obligation of bare pacts as the Romans themselves did, who never denied their perfect obligation, tho' they did not grant an *action* upon them for particular reasons.* <304>

SECTION CCCXCI

Express and tacite pacts.

A pact being the mutual consent of two or more in the same will or desire (§386); *i.e.* an *agreement* of two or more about the same thing, the same circumstances; the consequence is, that this internal consent must be indicated by some external sign. But such signs are words either spoken or written, and deeds; the former of which make express, the latter tacite consent (§284); and therefore it is the same, whether persons make a pact by express, or by tacite consent, provided the deed be such as is held to be significative of consent by the opinion of all mankind, or of the particular nation;† nay, consent is sometimes justly inferred,

---

* According to the Romans, one was perfectly obliged by a bare pact; and they looked upon him who broke his word with no less contempt than other nations. Besides, they did not think the obligation imperfect which arose from such bare promises as were not confirmed by stipulation, when there was place for compensatio, 1. 6. D. de compens. *constituto,* l. 1. § pen. D. de pecun. const. *novatio,* l. 1. fin. D. de novat. *fideijussoribus & pignoribus,* l. 5. D. de pign. *exceptio.* l. 7. §5. l. 45. D. de pact. l. 10. l. 21. l. 28. C. eodem: Whence even what a promiser paid by mistake, could not be recovered *condictione indebiti,* l. 19. D. de cond. indeb. most of which cases are of such a nature that they can hardly be brought under the notion of imperfect obligation. The Romans only refused to grant an action upon bare pacts, because they had contrived a certain *civil* method which they ordered to be used in agreements or pacts, *viz.* stipulation. Wherefore, as in several countries the laws do not grant an action upon the pawning of immoveable things, unless the pawn be registered in the public acts, and yet these laws do not detract from the perfect obligation of pawn, which exerts itself in other ways; so neither did the Romans think that pacts did not produce a perfect obligation, because they did not grant an action upon bare pacts.

† Hence by the Roman law, a nod was reckoned consent, l. 52. § ult. D. de obl. & act. Quintilian. declam. 247. Nay, submission and silence were reckoned consent, l. 51. pr. D. locat. l. 11. §4. 7. D. de interr. in jure fac. and elsewhere, which we likewise

from the very nature of the business, if it be of such a kind, that a person cannot be imagined to dissent (§284). <305>

SECTION CCCXCII

It is plain from the definition of a pact as requiring consent (§391), that they cannot covenant who are destitute of reason, and therefore that the pacts of mad persons are null, unless they were made in an evidently lucid interval from their madness; as likewise the pacts of infants, and of all whose age cannot be supposed capable of understanding the nature of the thing; or of such persons, whose minds are disturbed by their indisposition; or of persons in liquor, even tho' their drunkenness be voluntary;* or finally, of those who promised any thing to another, or stipulated any thing from another to themselves in jest. <306>

Who can, and who cannot make pacts.

SECTION CCCXCIII

From the same principle it follows, that pacts made thro' ignorance or mistake are unvalid, if this fault of the understanding was culpable, vincible and voluntary (§107); but not, if it be of such a nature, that the most prudent person is liable to it; (§108), as, if the covenanting persons

Of pacts made by mistake or ignorance.

---

admit to be true, unless there be some probable reason why one might, tho' he did not assent, rather choose to be silent, than to testify his dissent by words or deeds, *e.g.* if a son, afraid of a cruel father, being asked by him, whether he would marry Mavia whom he hated, should be silent, he cannot be thought to have consented. For what if a son, when such a father bids him go hang himself, should say nothing, would he therefore be deemed to have consented?

* For tho' in other cases, an action done in drunkenness be imputed to one whose drunkenness was voluntary (§50), yet here another sentence must be pronounced, and the degrees of drunkenness must be distinguished. For either the promiser was quite drunk, or only a little in liquor. Now, if he was quite drunk, that could not but be perceived by the party bargaining with him; and therefore, the latter either acted knavishly, or at least he is blameable for covenanting with such a person; so that there is no reason why, when the person has recovered from his drunkenness, such a contracter should have any right to demand the fulfilment of such a promise. But if the person be not quite drunk, his promise must be obligatory, because he was not quite incapable of judging what and to whom he promised.

had different persons and objects in their view; or if either of them was mistaken about the person, or object, or any circumstances of it which could not easily be known, and which, had he known, he would not have made the pact.*

SECTION CCCXCIV

Of fraud or knavery.

Much less still is a pact valid if one be led into it by the fraud or knavery of the other; or in which one is involved, and by which one is wronged by another's cunning and deceitfulness; because he cannot be deemed to have consented, who was so blinded or deluded by another's artful misrepresentations, that he had quite a different opinion of the person or object when he covenanted, than he afterwards <307> found to be the case.† On the other hand, there is no reason why a pact should be null when a third person induces one to make it without the other's knowledge, tho' in this case it be indisputable, that the person by whose fraudulence the pact was made, is obliged to repair the damages of the persons whom he hath thus injured.

* By these rules may all the cases be resolved that are usually put upon this head. Thus, for instance, the pact will not be valid, if one promised to espouse a virgin, who is afterwards found to be pregnant, because the most prudent person might have mistaken in this case: Nor is the contract of marriage valid, if Afrania be betrothed to one in mistake, instead of Tullia whom he had in view, but did not know her name; because not having the same person in view, they did not consent to the same thing: In fine, if Tullia after betrothment is found to be Epileptical, or liable to any other hideous disease, the betrother shall not be bound in such a case, because he was ignorant of, or in an error about a circumstance which he could not easily discover, and which, if he had known, it is not probable he would have desired the marriage.

† Hence none will say, that Jacob's marriage with Lea was valid by the law of nature, since it was brought about by the fraudulence of Laban, Gen. xxix. 22. Nor was the custom of the country, by which Laban pretended to exculpate himself, sufficient to excuse him, or to oblige Jacob to submit, and suffer himself to be so maliciously deceived by his father-in-law. For that custom was not obligatory; and if it really had been received as a law, Jacob ought to have been pre-admonished of it, and Laban ought not to have promised Rachel to Jacob, but to have acquainted him, who was a stranger, that by the customs in Syria, the younger sister could not be betrothed before her elder sister. This transaction was therefore full of knavery, nor could it have been valid, had it not seemed better to Jacob, who was a stranger, to put up the injury, than to involve himself in an ambiguous suit.

SECTION CCCXCV

And since nothing can be more repugnant to consent than force and fear; nor can an action be imputed to one, if he was forced to it by one who had no right to force him (§109); hence it is clear, that one is not bound by his promise to a robber, or to any one who unjustly uses violence against him. But a pact is not invalid, if it be made with one who had a right to use violence; and much less is a pact null, if not he to whom the promise is made, but a third person, without his knowledge, used violence, or was the cause of the pact.* Nor is a pact invalid, if the person forced to it, afterwards freely consents and confirms his promise, because he then becomes obliged, not by his first <308> promise extorted from his by force and fear, but by his after voluntary consent (§109).

Of force and fear.

SECTION CCCXCVI

Moreover, since a pact consists in the consent of two or more to the same thing (§386), it is very plain that this rule must hold not only in bilateral, but likewise in unilateral pacts; and therefore a promiser is not bound, unless the other signify that the promise is agreeable to him. But this may be justly presumed, either from the condition of the person to whom the promise is made; or from the nature of the thing promised; or from antecedent request, provided, in this last case, the same thing that the other had demanded be promised.

The consent of the parties ought to be mutual.

---

* For since imputability ceases, if one be neither the cause nor doer of a thing (§105), but in this case, he to whom a promise is made, is neither the author nor cause of the violence by which the other was forced to promise, the violence cannot be imputed to him. Thus, e.g. if any person in imminent danger from robbers or pirates, should hire a convoy at a high price, it would be in vain for him to pretend to his convoy, when the hire is demanded, that he promised it in fear of robbers. So Seneca decides the matter, Controv. 4. 27. [[Seneca, *Controversiae,* in Seneca (the Elder), *Declamations.*]]

SECTION CCCXCVII

What with regard to impossible things. Again, because pacts are made about something to be performed (§386), but impossible things cannot be performed, and therefore the omission of them is imputable to none (§115); the consequence is, that pacts about things absolutely impracticable are null: no obligation arises from them, unless the thing, at the time the pact was made, was in the power of the promiser, and he shall afterwards destroy, by his own fault, his power to fulfil his promise; or unless one fraudulently promised a thing not absolutely impossible, but which he knew to be impracticable with regard to him (§115). <309>

SECTION CCCXCVIII

What with regard to immoral things. And since those things are justly reckoned among *impossibles,* which, tho' not impossible in the nature of things, yet cannot be done agreeably to the laws and to good manners (§115); hence it is evident, that pacts and promises contrary to the laws of justice and humanity, or even to decency, modesty and honour, (and which, for that reason, we ought to be judged not to be capable of doing, as Papinianus most justly and philosophically speaks, l. 15. D. de condit. instit.) are not valid. A person is not obliged to fulfil a promise by which he engaged to commit any crime; nor is he who promised to pay one a reward for perpetrating any crime bound by such a promise; and therefore all pacts about base and dishonest things, whether unilateral or bilateral, are of no effect.*

* For it is manifestly contradictory, that the law of nature should confirm pacts contrary to itself; that it should at the same time prohibit a pact, and command it to be fulfilled; or that a pact should be at one and the same time null, and yet obligatory. And therefore, a pact is departed from without perfidy, which could not be fulfilled without committing a crime. Nor does he deserve the character of faithful, who performs what he cannot do without incurring guilt. And for this reason the nurse gives an excellent answer to Dejanira, when she would have her to promise silence.

> *Praestare, fateor, posse me tacitam fidem,*
> *Si scelere careat, interim scelus est fides.*
>   Seneca in Herc. Oeteo. Act. 2. v. 480.

[[Seneca, *Hercules Oetaeus* 2.480, in Seneca (the Younger), *Tragoediae incer-*

SECTION CCCXCIX

Hence again we infer, that one is not obliged to perform promises, the fulfilment of which would manifestly be detrimental to the other, tho' this other should urge the fulfilment of the promise to his own ruin. For since we are forbid to injure any person by the law of nature (§178), and none <310> can make pacts contrary to the law of nature, (§398), no pact by which another is hurt can be valid; and he who keeps such a promise, even to one who insists upon the fulfilment of it, is no less deserving of punishment, than he who hurts one against his will, and by force.*

What with regard to detrimental promise.

SECTION CCCC

Besides, because we make pacts about those things which we desire to have a perfect right to exact from others (§386); but those things can neither be done, nor given, which are not at our disposal, but subject to the dominion of another person; we have therefore reason to deny that one can make a valid pact about things belonging to others, without commission from the owner, or even about his own things, to which any other hath already acquired some right by a prior pact. He indeed who hath engaged to use all his diligence to make another give or do, is

What with respect to pacts about the deeds and things of others.

----

torum auctorum: "I confess that I can offer silent faith, if it is free from crime, meanwhile, faith is the crime."]]

* Nor can the maxim, *volenti non fieri injuriam* [["there is no injury done to someone who is willing to suffer it"]], be opposed to this doctrine. For we have already shewn, that this maxim does not take place when it is unlawful to consent. But it is unlawful to consent to what God hath prohibited by right reason, or by his revealed will. For this reason, tho' Saul being wounded, had begged the young man to slay him, yet he was so far from escaping unpunished for consenting to this request, that David ordered him to be put to death as guilty of Regicide, 2 Sam. l. 15, &c.

obliged to fulfil that promise.* Yea, he is obliged to answer for the value of it, if he hath engaged himself to get another to give, or do a thing to any one; but he to whom a third person hath made such a promise, hath no right to exact the thing or deed, thus promised to him, from the person to whom it belongs to dispose of it. See Hertius de oblig. alium datur. facturumve.[1] <311>

SECTION CCCCI

What with regard to conditional pacts, &c.

From the same principle, that promise to give or do consists in the consent of both parties (§386), it manifestly follows, that it depends upon the parties to make a pact *with,* or *without conditions,* and any agreement with regard to *time* they please; and that these circumstances ought to be observed by the persons engaging, provided what regards the condition truly makes the effect of the pact depend upon an uncertain event; *i.e.* provided it be truly a *condition.* Whence it is plain, that what is promised under what is called *an impossible condition,* is not obligatory, since such an additional clause hardly deserves to be termed *a condition:*† and

---

* For since he hath promised no more than his help and diligence, the other hath no right to exact more from him. And in general, as often as one stipulates something to himself, which he knew, or might have known not to be in another's power; so often is the Promissor discharged from his promise, by using all his diligence. This is elegantly expressed by Seneca of benefits, 7. 13. "Some things are of such a nature, that they cannot be effectuated; and in some things it is to do them, to have done all that one could in order to effectuate them. If a physician did all in his power to cure one, he hath done his part. Even tho' a person be condemned, an advocate deserves the reward of his eloquence, if he exerted all his skill. And praise is due to a General, tho' he be vanquished, if he exerted all due prudence, diligence and courage." [[The reference to bk. 7, chap. 13 is incorrect.]]

1. Hertius (*praeses*) and Gärtner (*respondens*), *Disquisitio juridica de obligatione alium daturum facturumve.*

† For a condition is a certain circumstance expressed by the stipulating parties, by which the effect of the pact is suspended, as by an uncertain event. But seeing *impossible* does not mean an uncertain event, but an event which it is certain cannot happen, it is plain that such a circumstance does not suspend the effect of a pact, and therefore it is not a condition. Miltiades therefore cavilled, when he required the Lemnians to surrender their city according to their pact, because, coming from home he had arrived at Lemnos by a north wind, Nepos, Miltiad. c. 1. and 2. For the Lem-

those who have promised or stipulated what they foresaw could not be done, must be deemed either to have been in jest, or to have been mad: in the first of which cases, they must be judged not to have consented; and in the other of which they must be judged not to have had it in their power to have consented (§392). <312>

SECTION CCCCII

But since base and dishonest things are justly reckoned amongst impossibles (§115), and what is promised upon an impossible condition is null and void, (§401); and since in general it is unlawful to make pacts about base or dishonest things (§398); hence we may justly infer, that base and dishonest conditions render a pact null;* and that he who promised upon such a condition is not bound to fulfil his promise; but

What with regard to a base condition.

---

nians meant Athens: nor could Miltiades understand the Lemnians in any other sense, since he at that time had no home but at Athens. The condition was impossible, and therefore rendered the pact null; especially seeing the Lemnians might easily have been perceived by Miltiades to have spoken in jest and to banter him.

* For a particular reason, the Romans held conditions, whether physically or morally impossible, in testaments, as not written, not existing, §10. Inst. de her. inst. l. 1. l. 19. D. de condit. Inst. l. 8. & l. 20. D. de condit. & dem. For as it seemed absurd to indulge jesting and trifling to a testator in so serious an affair; so neither could the omission of an impossible action be deemed fraud in an heir, since he could never have consented to it (§115). And hence by the Roman law they would have got their legacies which were left to them by Eumolpus in Petron. Sat. cap. 91. tho' they had not fulfilled the condition. [[Petronius, *Satyricon*, 141, p. 321.]] "All who have legacies by my testament, except my children, shall only have them upon condition that they cut my body into pieces, and eat it up publickly." But since, in our opinion, the law of nature knows no other last-wills beside those which are done by way of pact (§291), all that hath been said of pacts is applicable to last-wills; so that the law of the Thebans was absurd, which ordered ridiculous conditions to be performed, as that one who had flattered a woman in order to be her heir, should carry her naked corps besmeared with oil upon his shoulders.

Scilicet elabi si posset mortua, credo,
Que nimium institerat viventi.
      Hor. Serm. 2. 5.

[[Horace, *Satires II,* 5.87: "Of course, I believe, if she could slip away from him when she was dead—he had pressed too hard on her while she was alive."]]

that if it be fulfilled, he is justly liable to punishment for having done a crime; as is the other party likewise, being, by making such a condition, the moral cause of that crime (§112). <313>

SECTION CCCCIII

Whether one may not promise and covenant by another?

Moreover, since one may assist another, or promote his advantage by means of a mandate, or by undertaking his business without a commission (§346), we must conclude, that it is the same whether one promise and make a pact in person, or another do it for him by his order. But since he who undertakes another's business without a commission from him, is obliged to manage it to his advantage (§348), which he does not do, who is liberal of another's goods, and gives any thing of another's away without the owner's consent (§400); the consequence is, that he who undertakes another's business without a commission, may stipulate to that person; (so that this rule in the Roman law is not agreeable to natural equity, "That none can stipulate to another, unless he be under subjection to him," §4. Inst. de inut. stip.) but he cannot promise for him without his knowledge; and such a promise does not bind the owner.

SECTION CCCCIV

What hath been said of pacts extends likewise to contracts.

Finally, because, as we observed in the beginning of this chapter, there is no distinction, by the law of nature, between pacts and contracts, both deriving all their subsistence and force from consent (385), it is evident, that all the rules which have been laid down in this chapter, do no less belong to contracts than to pacts; and that one does not proceed in a wrong method, who deduces the <314> nature of contracts from the nature of pacts, and so begins by considering the latter.

By what means obligations arising from pacts and contracts are dissolved.

SECTION CCCCV

We have already proved that pacts ought to be religiously fulfilled, and that nothing is more sacred than one's pledged *faith* (§387); but by *faith* is meant nothing else but the performance of promises and pacts; (and therefore Cicero de off. I. 6. justly, tho' not exactly according to etymological rules, says, "Fidem appellatam, quia fiat, quod dictum est").[1] Hence then we infer, that those who covenant have then attained to their end, when they have satisfied the terms of their covenant, and what was agreed upon is done. But the end (which according to the philosophers, is first in intention, and last in execution) being obtained, or being of such a nature that it cannot be obtained (§397), the obligation arising from a promise or pact must cease.* <315>

General axioms.

* The civil law distinguishes between the ways by which obligation is removed *ipso jure,* in the nature of the thing, and the ways by which it is taken off by *exception.* When the obligation is cancelled by any deed of the parties contracting, as by paying, compensation, acquittance, &c. then it expires *ipso jure* by the nature of the thing. But if it be dissolved on the account of equity, it is said to be removed by an *exception.* But tho' we do not think this distinction quite idle, or without foundation, (upon which see an excellent dissertation by Hen. Cocceius de eo quod fit ipso jure) [[H. von Cocceji (*praeses*) and Zaunschliffer (*respondens*), *Discursus juridicus inauguralis de eo quod fit ipso jure*]] yet it will easily be granted to us, not to be of the law of nature, by those who are acquainted with the judiciary affairs of the Romans, and the reason which induced them to make this distinction.

1. Cicero, *De officiis* (*On duties*), 1.7.23: " 'Good faith' is so called because what is promised is 'made good.' "

SECTION CCCCVI

Of the first way by payment.

Since an obligation arising from a pact or promise ceases when it is fulfilled, and that which was agreed upon is done (§405); the consequence is, that it ceases by payment, which is nothing else but the natural performance of the thing promised or agreed upon. But it is the same thing to him who is to be paid, by whom he be paid, provided the thing itself which was owing to him, or, (if it be a consumeable commodity) the equivalent be paid to him (§364); because thus the obligation to him is naturally discharged. So, for the same reason, it is evident, that he who is under an obligation by his pact, is not delivered from that obligation when another offers to fulfil it for him, if it be of such a nature as not to admit of being performed by another in his room.*

SECTION CCCCVII

What, and to whom payment ought to be made.

From the same principle we infer, that the species is to be restored, if the use or custody only of an inconsumeable thing was granted; and the same in kind and quantity, if the use of a consumeable thing was granted; that one thing cannot be obtruded upon a creditor for another against his will; <316> and much less can he be forced to accept of a part for the whole; or to take payment later, or in another place than was agreed upon in the contract;† because, in all these cases, the thing in

---

* This happens as often as a person's quality or virtue engaged one to make a pact with him. And therefore, if *Titia* be obliged by contract of marriage to marry *Sempronius,* she is not freed from this obligation, tho' *Sulpicia* should be ever so ready and willing to fulfil the contract in her stead, because *Sempronius* chose *Titia* for her age, her figure, her personal good qualities, and it is not the same to him whom he espouses. On the contrary, to a lender it is the same, whether he receive the book he lent from the person who borrowed it, or from another with whom he had nothing to do: And it is the same to a creditor, whether he receive his money and interest from his debtor, or from a third person unknown to him, because thus the thing in obligation is naturally performed.

† For tho' necessity may require some indulgence to a debtor, and tho' the laws of humanity may often oblige a creditor to remit a little of his rigour, we are here speaking of right; and by it pacts and contracts ought to be punctually and faithfully performed. "For," as Cicero says, Off. 2. 24. "nothing cements or holds together in

obligation is not naturally performed (§307). Further, it is plain, from the same principle, that we are to pay to no other but our creditor, provided the laws allow him to receive payment, or to him to whom he has ceded his right, or given commission to receive payment; for otherwise, tho' the thing in obligation is performed, yet it is not fulfilled to him to whom one is debtor by the contract (§406).

SECTION CCCCVIII

Again, because obligation ceases when a contract is fulfilled, and with respect to consumeable things as much is held for the same (§364); the consequence is, that obligation is removed by *compensation,* which is nothing else but balancing debt and credit, both of which have a certain value, one with another.* <317>

The second way, Compensation.

SECTION CCCCIX

From the definition of compensation it is plain, that it can only take place among those who are mutually owing one to another, and therefore that another's debt to me cannot be obtruded upon my creditor. Compensation has place with respect to consumeable things, which, since they do not regularly admit of price of fancy, have always a certain value; but species cannot be compensated by species, nor a thing of one kind by a thing of a different kind, nor personal performances by like performances, because all these things admit of a price of affection, and are of an uncertain value. In fine, compensation, even by unequal quantities, amounting to the sum, holds good, tho' it does not appear reason-

What is just with regard to it.

---

union all the parts of a society, as faith and credit, which can never be kept up, unless men are under a necessity of honestly paying what they owe one to another." [[Cicero, *De officiis* 2.24.84.]]

* There is yet another reason: For since he is paid who gets what was owing to him (§406), and he to whom a consumeable thing was owing, gets it when he gets as much (§363); it follows, that in such a case, he who any way receives as much as was owing, is paid; and therefore, compensation is but a short way of paying; and it is most reasonable that it should have the same effect as payment.

able to desire to compensate a clear debt by one not so clear or contended for.*

SECTION CCCCX

A third way, Acquittance.

Moreover, since every one can abdicate his own right (§13), an obligation may likewise be dissolved by acquittance or voluntary remission, by which we understand a creditor's voluntary renounc-<318>ing his right of exacting a debt. And since it is the same whether one manifests his will by words, or other signs (§195), it is also the same whether one renounces his right to a debt by words or by deeds, as by giving up, tearing or burning the bond, provided some other intention of the creditor be not evident, or the bond be not destroyed by the creditor, but by another without his order, or be not rather accidentally lost, destroyed or effaced, than by the will of the creditor.†

---

* Much less does he act justly, who would compensate a clear debt by this consideration, that he hath abstained from injuring his creditor by unjust violence, because in this case plainly there is no mutual obligation. It was therefore a very odd way of compensation by which Vitellius satisfied his creditors, Dion. Cass. Hist. l. 65. p. 735. "When he went into Germany he was so embroiled in debt, that his creditors would scarce dismiss his person upon any security; but a little after, when he was made Emperor, and returned to Rome, they hid themselves. And he ordering them to be brought before him, told them that he had restored them safety for their money, and demanded back the bonds and instruments of contract." [[Dio Cassius, *Dio's Roman History*, vol. 8, bk. LXIV, pp. 229–31.]] As if a robber could reckon it for credit to a traveller, that when he had it in his power to murder him, he had only robbed him, without shedding one drop of his blood.

† Thus the Romans might justly say, that their taxes and other fiscal debts were remitted to them, when Hadrian with that design burnt all their bonds and obligations, that by such a stupendous liberality he might win the affections of the people, Spartian. Had. cap. 6. [[Spartianus' life of the Emperor Hadrian, included in vol. 3 of Boxhorn, *Historiae Augustae scriptores Latini minores.*]] But a debtor would most absurdly conclude so, if his creditor should deliver him his bond in order that it might be drawn up in a new and better form, or if his bond was burnt by accidental fire. And hence we may see, why it hath always been pronounced most iniquitous in the Roman people, for one plunged in debt, *novas tabulas postulare, i.e.,* to demand a remission of his debt from the magistrates or tribunes of a turbulent genius. For thus the acquittance came not from the creditors, but from magistrates profuse of what did not belong to them, and whose office and duty it was to render justice to creditors,

SECTION CCCCXI

Moreover, since any one may resign his right, and remit a debt due to him (§410), it follows, that both parties in a bilateral contract, may by mutual agreement dissolve their contract, especially, *since nothing is more natural, than that a thing may be dissolved in the way it was formed,* l. 35. D. de reg. <319> jur. But so, that this manner of dissolving an obligation cannot have place, if the positive laws ordain a contract to be indissolveable: such as matrimony now is amongst Christians, which among the Romans, might, as is well known, be dissolved by consent.

A fourth way. Mutual disagreements.

SECTION CCCCXII

But because the obligation of a bilateral contract can only be dissolved by mutual consent (§411), the will of one of the parties does not dissolve it; and therefore the treachery of either party does not dissolve the contract, as Grotius of the rights of war and peace, 3. 19. 14. and Pufendorff of the law of nature and nations, 5. 11. 9. seem to think. For even he who does not fulfil his part, remains obliged to do it, because he cannot liberate himself by his own single will from an obligation, which can only, as hath been said, be dissolved by mutual consent, and the other has a right to compel him to fulfil his pact; tho' if the latter will not use his right,* then the obligation ceases on both sides, because it is now removed by the consent of both (§411).

Whether obligation be dissolved by treachery?

---

instead of liberating debtors against the will of creditors. This practice, of most pernicious example, was first put in use by Sylla, Liv. Ep. l. 88. And that Cataline expected the same, and that the people expected the same from Caesar is manifest, tho' men of that turbulent spirit were then disappointed, Salust. Catil. cap. 21. Caesar de bello civili, 3. 1. Sueton. Jul. cap. 42. Plutarch. Solon. p. 86.

* But either can do that, if the other will not fulfil the pact. For in every bilateral contract, this condition is supposed, that the one is obliged to perform what he promised, if the other performs his part (§379). If one therefore does not satisfy his promise, the condition fails upon which the obligation depended (§401), and therefore the obligation of both ceases.

SECTION CCCCXIII

The fifth and sixth way. The term elapsed, and the condition not fulfilled. But seeing any circumstance may be added to a pact, and these circumstances must be observed (§401), it is evident that an obligation being conceived *ex die, i.e.* so that what is promised cannot be demanded till a certain day, it cannot be demanded before that time fixed: But if it be conceived *in diem,* within the compass of a certain time, <320> then when that day comes, the obligation is dissolved *ipso jure.** And the condition upon which the effect of a pact depended not taking place, obligation is dissolved for the same reason, unless one being ready to fulfil his part of the pact, is hindered either by his party or a third person, without whom the pact could not be fulfilled.

SECTION CCCCXIV

The seventh manner. Besides, there are obligations which are contracted with an eye to a certain person, and his qualities; but these are of such a nature, that they cannot be performed by other persons (§406): And therefore it is clear, that these obligations cannot pass to heirs and successors, and that they expire with the death of the promiser. Something like this we observed with respect to the obligation of a betrother, and of one who accepteth of a commission or trust. But this way of obligation's being dissolved, does not belong to other obligations, which can be fulfilled out of the goods of the person obliged; because these, as admitting of performance in the room of the person obliged, are justly transmitted to heirs, as we have shewn in its proper place (§305).

SECTION CCCCXV

The eighth change of state. The case is the same, if we are bound to perform any thing as being in a certain state. For it is the same, as if the promise had been made upon

---

* Therefore, this rule of the Roman lawyers hath too much of subtlety in it, *viz.* ex contractu stricti juris non posse ad tempus deberi, *&c.* §3. Inst. de verb. oblig. l. 4. pr. D. de serv. l. 44. §1. D. de obl. & act.

condition this state should continue. And therefore the condition failing, the obligation likewise ceases (§413): Thus he who contracted as a manager, his administration being at an end, is no more <321> bound, the obligation being solely founded upon his state as administrator, l. ult. D. de Instit. act. l. 26. C. de adm. tut. But this is only true of obligations arising from pacts or positive law, and not of those which arise from the law of nature.*

SECTION CCCCXVI

Moreover, since the obligation ceases if the end be such as cannot be obtained (§406), he must be delivered from his obligation who promised the species itself, if it be quite lost by accident, unless he promised it for a certain value, or as it were in part of payment, and the first obligation be not removed by renovation. Besides, since impossibility is no excuse, if one be in fault or delay, it is evident that he ought to bear the loss who is in fault or delay; and therefore, all that was said above concerning the risks in buying and selling takes place and might be repeated here (§353). *The ninth.*

SECTION CCCCXVII

In fine, since one may pay by another (§407), and remit an obligation to another (§411), and parties may depart from a pact by mutual consent, and introduce a new obligation, which last kind of agreement we called above *a mixed pact* (§389), it follows, that any one may remit to another his former obligation, and accept a new one from him in its place, which is called *renewal* or *novation;* or if it be about matters subject to contention and dispute, *transaction,* and that a creditor may remit <322> a debtor, upon condition that another, whom he approves of, be substi- *The tenth, novation and delegation.*

---

* Thus the special duties owing to a city by one as consul, cease so soon as one ceases to be consul. Thus likewise the duties of a son, as far as they proceed from positive law, cease, so soon as the son is no longer under paternal power. But the duties to which the law of nature binds him, such as obedience, reverence, gratitude, remain after emancipation, nor can they be refused to parents by children no longer under paternal power.

tuted in his place, which is called *delegation,* and that novation ought to be made in express words, or by the most evident signs, and that delegation must be done with the united consent of all concerned in the affair; and, in fine, that there is a great difference between delegation and cession, by which a creditor transfers an action against his debtor to another, without his debtor's knowledge, and against his will.

Remarks on This Book

Our Author may perhaps be thought by some to have mentioned several cases; as for instance, with regard to alluvion, casting up of islands, &c. which are rather curious than useful. But let me answer to such objections against our Author, (Grotius, Pufendorff, and other writers on the law of nature), 1. That of as little use as these questions may appear to us, they were not so in other countries, such as Egypt, where, as Strabo observes, Geograph. l. 17. p. 1139. edit. Amst. "They were obliged to be particularly exact and nice in the division of their lands, because of the frequent confusion of boundaries, which the Nile, by its overflowing occasioned, taking from one part, and adding to another, changing the very form and look of places, and entirely concealing those marks that should distinguish one man's property from another's. For which reason, there was a necessity for their often making new surveys, &c."[2] And it is so still in Holland and other countries, in some measure; nay some such cases may and do happen in every country, where there are large and impetuous rivers, &c. 2. But however rarely any such cases may happen, yet as one cannot be an expert, ready natural philosopher, without having run through many possible cases, and determined how gravity, elasticity, or any other physical powers, would operate in these circumstances according to their laws of working; and therefore, such exercise is by no means useless, but highly useful: So for the same reason, one cannot be ready and expert in the moral science, so as to be able readily to determine himself, or advise others how to act upon every emergency, without having practised himself in

2. The edition used here is presumably Strabo, *Rerum geographicarum libri XVII* (Amsterdam, 1707).

resolving all, or very many possible cases, *i.e.* in determining what is requisite in such and such cases, in order to do the least harm, and render every one his due. Thus, it is evident, must one prepare himself for being able to judge readily what ought to be the general rules of justice in states with regard to different cases. Thus alone can one prepare himself for judging of cases in enacting, abrogating or mending laws. And indeed the proper way of studying the laws of any particular country, is by comparing <323> them all along with the dictates or the laws of nature concerning the same cases, in an orderly way, proceeding from simple to more and more complex cases gradually. Whence it is evident, that one well versed in the knowledge of natural law, can never be at a loss to find out what ought to be the general positive law in certain cases, and how positive law ought to be interpreted in cases, which, tho' not expresly excepted in a law, which must be general, yet are in the nature of things excepted. 3. The same thing holds with respect to the duties of societies, one towards another, for the laws by which particular persons ought to regulate their conduct in all pacts, covenants, bargains or contracts, under whatsoever denominations they are brought by the doctors of laws, are the very rules by which societies ought likewise to regulate their conduct one towards another; societies being, as we shall find our author himself observing afterwards, moral persons. Whence it follows, that the former rules or laws being determined, it cannot be difficult to fix or determine the latter. And indeed our Author having fixed the former in such a manner, that there was almost no occasion to differ from him, and but very little occasion to add to him; in following him while he deduces and fixes the other in the succeeding book, there will be very little need of our adding any remarks, except in the affair of government, that not having been distinctly enough handled by any writer of a system of the law of nature and nations, for this reason that, as we have already had occasion to observe, none of them has ever considered government in its natural procreation, or its natural causes. Nor do I know any author by whom that hath been done but our Harrington, tho', as he himself shews, the principles upon which he reasons were not unknown neither to ancient historians, nor to ancient writers on morals and politics. It will not therefore be a disadvantage to young readers, for whom this translation, with the remarks, is chiefly intended, in order to initiate them into this useful science, if we, upon proper occasions, in the following book concerning the laws of nations, add a few things to set the more important questions about government in a clear light. On this subject, we of this nation, and we only, dare write freely. For our happy constitution is the blessed effect of thinking freely on this matter: and it must last uncorrupted, unimpaired, while we continue to exercise the right to which we owe it: A right without the exercise of which men are not indeed men. For who will say that slaves, who know not the price of liberty, or who know not that they are slaves, deserve to be called men!

The end of the first book.

BOOK II
OF THE LAW OF NATIONS

A METHODICAL SYSTEM

OF

Universal Law:

OR, THE

Laws *of* Nature *and* Nations
Deduced
From Certain Principles, and applied
to Proper Cases.

Written in *Latin* by the CELEBRATED

JO. GOT. HEINECCIUS,

Counsellor of State to the King of Prussia,
and Professor of Philosophy at *Hall.*

Translated, and illustrated with Notes and Supplements,

By *GEORGE TURNBULL, LL. D.*

To which is added,
A DISCOURSE upon the Nature and Origine of Moral and Civil
Laws; in which they are deduced, by an Analysis of the human Mind in
the experimental Way, from our internal Principles and Dispositions.

Natura enim juris ab hominis repetenda natura est.[1] Cic.

VOL. II.

LONDON:
Printed for J. Noon, at the *White-Hart,* near *Mercer's Chapel, Cheapside.* MDCCXLI.

1. The nature of law has to be derived from human nature.

BOOK II

Of the LAW *of* NATIONS

ॐ CHAPTER I ॐ

Concerning the natural and social state of man.

SECTION I

Hitherto we have considered *the law of nature,* by which the actions of particulars ought to be regulated. Now, the next thing to be done in this undertaking, is to deduce *the laws of nations* from their principles, and to give a compendious view of them. This we promised (l. 1. §23). But since *the law of nations* is the law of nature, applied to social life, the affairs of societies, and of independent political bodies (l. 1. §21), we cannot treat of it distinctly, without first giving a clear notion of what we call *states* and *societies.*

The connection.

SECTION II

Of man's physical and moral state.

State in general means the quality which constitutes a particular thing, or makes it what it is; and thus the qualities constituting man are rightly said to make *his state*. Now, we may either consider man merely as consisting of certain faculties of body and mind with which he is endowed by his Creator, or we may consider him as subjected <2> to laws for the regulation of his free actions. The first way of considering man is called *considering him in his physical state.** The second is *considering him as a moral being,* or *in his moral state.* But in treating of the law of nations, the objects of which are mens free actions, it is evident, that it is not merely man's physical, but more directly his moral state, which then falls under consideration.

SECTION III

What is meant by a natural, and what by an adventitious state.

This *moral state,* by which men are so greatly distinguished, is either cogenial to them, or it depends upon some deed of ours. The first is called *natural;* the other *adventitious.* Wherefore the *natural state* of man is that quality or condition imposed upon man by nature, without any deed of his, by which our free actions are subjected to, and limited by a natural law, suitable to the nature of that state. The *adventitious state* of man, on the other hand, is a quality or condition which man brings

---

* Thus it is by regulations arising from the will of the Creator, that men are male and female, that some have well formed, and others distorted bodies; that some have a strong and robust, others a weakly and feeble constitution; that some are beautiful, and others deformed; and which is more, that some have a very quick and vigorous apprehension, an universal penetrating genius, while others are exceeding slow and dull, and have no capacity almost for any thing. All these differences, it is plain, belong to the *physical* or *natural* state of man, as it is called by the civilians. On the other hand, the free actions of man are differently limited, if he be a husband, from what they are, if he live in celibacy; differently according to the different personages or characters one bears, as of a parent, or a child, a master or a servant, &c. For which reason, all these differences are referred to the *moral state* of man, which is called by civilians his *civil state.* But let it be observed, that the moral state of man extends a little farther than what they call the civil state, to which they only refer the *state of liberty, citizenship, and a family state.*

him-<3>self into by his own deed, in consequence of which his free actions are subjected to, and limited by a natural law, suitably to the nature and exigencies of that state.*

SECTION IV

We do not then oppose *a natural state* to the state of brutes, for the difference between our nature and that of the brutes belongs rather to our physical than our moral state (§2); nor to what the Civilians call *a contra-natural state,* such as they have feigned the state of slaves to be, §2. Inst. de jure pers. but to a social and a civil state; both of which being imposed upon men by themselves, are equally adventitious. But what this state is, shall be more accurately considered, and thereby it will appear, why so great a number of men, forsaking their natural state, have put themselves into other states, attended with many and various uneasinesses.† <4>

Natural state is not opposed to the state of brutes, nor to a state contrary to nature.

---

* And in consequence of these limitations, both states give men certain rights, and oblige them to certain duties: Thus certain duties belong to those who live in a state of nature, and other duties belong to husbands and wives, others to parents and children, others to masters and servants, and others to citizens. And therefore our definition of a state comes to the same with that of Pufendorff, of the duties of a man and a citizen, 2. 1. 1. where he defines that state to be in general, "a condition in which men are understood to be placed in order to a certain course of action, and which is accompanied with certain rights."

† From this state of mankind, by which their Creator hath so far exalted them above the brute creation, Pufendorff deduces certain duties of mankind, ibidem, §3. "As that man ought to acknowledge his Creator and worship him, contemplate and admire his works, and live in quite a different manner from the brutes." Simplicius ad Epictet. c. 79. seems to have entertained much the same sentiments, when he prays to God, "to keep him in mind of the dignity given to human nature, by his distinguishing favour." [[Simplicius, *On Epictetus' Handbook,* "Epilogue," vol. 2, p. 127.]] But we are obliged to all these duties, not because we have received endowments superior to those bestowed on the brutes, but by the will of God, the sole source of all moral obligation (l. 1. §62), and consequently, we have deduced all these duties from that principle (l. 1. §126. §149).

SECTION V

It is a state of equality. We have already observed (l. 1. §88), that all men, tho' one may be more perfect than another, are however equal by nature. And who can call this into question, since all men consist of the same essential parts, body and mind? But hence it follows, that a state of nature is a state of equality; and consequently, among those who live in it, there is no superior or inferior; and therefore in it empire and subjection, and distinction of dignities, have no place; so that Ulpianus justly says, "That by the law of nature all men are equal," l. 32. D. de reg. jur. l. 4. D. de just. & jure, l. 12. §3. D. de accusat. l. 64. D. de condict. indeb.*

SECTION VI

And likewise of liberty. But there being, in a state of nature, no place for empire and subjection (§5), it must be a state of liberty;† nor can either political subjection, or

* Merillius observ. 1. 15. observes, that all this is taken from the Stoics. And indeed many such sayings are to be found in their writings. See Arrian. ad Epict. 1. 13. Seneca, ep. 47. and of benefits, 3. 22. which passages are quoted by Merillius. But this principle was rather common to all philosophers and poets, because none could choose but admit it, who had considered human nature with any attention. To this purpose is that of Euripides in Hecuba, v. 291.

> Lex enim vobis & liberis aequa
> Et de servili sanguine natis lata est.

> [["Lo the same law is stablished among you for free and bond as touching blood-shedding": Euripides, *Hecuba*, ll. 291–92 (see Euripides, *Euripides*, vol. 2, trans. Way).]]

And that fragment of Varro apud Nonium Marcell. 2. 98. "Natura in humanis omnia sunt paria." [[Marcellus, *Nonii Marcelli nova editio*, chap. 2, "De honestis at nove veterum dictis, per literas," p. 81.]] Not to mention many other testimonies of ancient authors to the same purport.

† *Liberty* is the faculty of acting according to our own will and pleasure, and for our own advantage. And it is either *political* or *civil*, when one acknowledges no superior, according to whose will, and for whose interest he is obliged to regulate his actions: Or *of the law of nations*, which they enjoy who are under the power of no master, to whose will they are bound to conform, and for whose interest they are obliged to act. To the first, which we called *political liberty*, *subjection* is opposite. To the other, which we called, *of the law of nations*, *servitude* is opposite. Thomasius has

<5> that servitude which is introduced by the law of nations, have place in it; so that in it there can be no positive laws, no magistrates, no positive punishments, nor none of those things which suppose a certain prerogative in some above the rest.

SECTION VII

Yet because magistracy, and positive laws and punishments, have no place in this state merely on account of the natural equality of mankind (§6), which reason does not at all affect that eternal law which is constituted by God himself; it is plain that the actions of men, even in a state of nature, are subject to the law of nature; and those who live in that state, are no less bound than we who have put ourselves into adventitious states, to love and obey God, to love, preserve, and perfect ourselves, and to love other men as ourselves; to do no injury to any one, but to render to every one his own, and to all the duties of humanity and beneficence.* <6>

But the law of nature must have place, and be of full force in it.

---

added a third species of liberty, *viz. natural,* which is defined, §2. Instit. de jure person. [[Thomasius, *Notae ad singulos institutionum et pandectarum titulos varias juris Romani antiquitates imprimis usum eorum hodiernum in foris Germaniae ostendentes.*]] But we shall not here take any notice of it, since it belongs rather to the physical than the moral state of mankind.

* And this is the chief argument by which we above exploded that first principle of *sociality,* laid down by Pufendorff (l. 1. §75). This learned author derives the law of nature from our obligation to sociality, to which men are compelled by necessity itself. But man would be under obligation to perform duties to God and to himself, tho' he were not united by any ties with other men, and every man lived apart and independently. With what shew of reason then can one set about to derive duties from our obligation to sociality, the greater part of which would have place, tho' there were no social state?

SECTION VIII

And therefore in this state all men had not a right over all, nor were men mere brutes. Whence it is evident, how absurdly *Hobbes*[1] derives all right from compact, and therefore attributes to every man, in a state of nature, a right to all, and over all; and thus prescribes the law of nature from this state (l. 1. §73) nor do those writers speak less unreasonably, who represent a state of nature, as a state in which men would differ very little from brutes, as being bound or cemented together by no ties, no obligations.*

SECTION IX

In a state of nature, all men have the right of making war. Now, since where magistracy, and positive laws, and punishments, do not take place, as we have <7> said, they do not in a state of nature (§6); there the oppressed can have no recourse, have no defence but in them-

* Thus a natural state is described by Cicero, pro Sext. Roscio, cap. 42. So Horace, Serm. 1. v. 99.

> *Quum processissent primis animalia terris*
> *Mutum & turpe pecus: glandem atque cubilia propter*
> *Unguibus & pugnis, dein fustibus, atque ita porro*
> *Pugnabant armis, quae post fabricaverat usus.*
> *Donec verba, quibus voces sensusque notarent,*
> *Nominaque invenere, dehinc absistere bello,*
> *Oppida coeperunt munire, & condere leges,*
> *Ne quis fur esset, neu latro, neu quis adulter.*

[[Horace, *Satires I,* 99–106: "When animals crawled forth on the first earth, a dumb and base creation, they used to fight for their acorns and places to sleep with claws and fists, then with clubs and so step by step with the weapons which need had later forged, until they found words, with which they could signify their cries and feelings, and names: from this time on they began to refrain from war and to fortify cities and to lay down laws that no-one should be a thief, nor a robber nor an adulterer."]]

Many such passages are to be found among the ancients, which are collected by Pufendorff of the law of nature, *&c.* 2. 2. 2. But all this is fiction, and highly improbable. For tho' we should grant, that in a state of nature men would be very brutal; and tho' we find that in former times, and even now, several nations are not very far removed from the brutes; (such an account is given of the Hunni by Ammian. Marcell. 31. 2.) [[Marcellinus, *Ammianus Marcellinus,* vol. 3, bk. 31, chap. 2, 381–87]] yet it does not follow from hence, that in a state of nature, the law of nature cannot at all be known, nor does at all oblige.

1. See Hobbes, *On the Citizen,* 1.10.

selves; the consequence is, that in a state of nature every one has a perfect right to repel violence and injury by force, and to extort from others by violence whatever they owe him by perfect obligation; but not to extort from any one the offices of humanity and beneficence (l. 1. §84.) unless he hath voluntarily bound himself by pact to do them (l. 1. §386), or extreme necessity forces one to seize something belonging to another, and to convert it to his own use (l. 1. §170); especially if the good offices be of such a kind, that one might perform them without any detriment to himself, were he not quite devoid of all humanity (l. 1. §216).*

SECTION X

But seeing, in a state of nature, none can be compelled to the good offices of humanity and beneficence, and therefore he who would be sure of them, must secure the performance of them to himself by pacts (§9), it follows, that all we have said about pacts, and the duties of those who make compacts or contracts, as likewise of the rights of commerce, hath place, or at least may have place in a state of nature; nay, that men <8> ought, in this state, frequently to stipulate to themselves even the performance of what is due to them by perfect right, by intervening pacts; and therefore that there is no stronger tie to hold men together in this state than the religious regard to pacts, which failing, or being contemned, all friendship and correspondence must cease.

Pacts are chiefly necessary in this state.

* Wherefore, the violence with which David menaced Nabal upon his refusing him certain offices of beneficence, would not have been excusable, even in a state of nature, 1 Sam. xxv. 21, 22. For Nabal was only obliged by the law of gratitude to supply David. But to such offices none can be forced, unless the ingratitude be pregnant, and attended with injustice (l. 1. §227). Extreme necessity would have excused force, but not such revenge as David threatened, while Nabal had not yet resisted him, but had only denied his request, which it is plain he had a right to do, especially, as he was not yet convinced of the justice of the cause.

SECTION XI

Whether the misery of this state be so great as it is commonly represented.

Now, these things being premised, it is obvious, that tho' this state be represented as most miserable by Hobbes, and even by Pufendorff, yet many things which seem to them to be wanting in it, and of which they seem so much afraid, ought not to be attributed to this state itself, so much as to the wickedness of mankind; and that some things for which they reproach this state, as solitude, poverty, weakness, barbarity, and perpetual strife, might be avoided in a state of nature, as well as in a civil state, if men would follow right reason,* and are equally unavoidable in a civil state as in a natural one, if men will not act conformably to right reason, Titius obs. ad Pufend. de offic. hom. & civ. 2. 1. 9.[2] <9>

SECTION XII

Why men have preferred the civil state.

Therefore it was not the extreme misery of a state of nature (§11), but partly the hopes of greater convenience and security, and partly the malice of men that made them form themselves into societies, as shall be

---

* For solitude can only be conceived amongst a few, and for a short space of time. Indigence, hunger and cold could not oppress men more in a state of nature, than they may do in a civil state, since nothing hinders men to possess themselves of necessaries, and carry on commerce in a state of nature as well as in civil states, that inequality of dignities which begot luxury, the mother of poverty, being unknown. Barbarity and ignorance are cured by the culture of reason. But why might not men have improved reason, as well in a state of nature as in a civil state? Nay, are not simplicity and candour often misrepresented as rudeness; and on the other hand, is not an affectation of elegancy too often set forth as politeness? Besides, since even in civil states the only remedy for the weakness of particulars, is by pacts and covenants, why may not the same be done in a state of nature? In fine, if strife and war be reckoned amongst the evils of a state of nature, a civil state will not be found to have much preeminence above it in this respect, since in consequence of the latter, whereas in ancient times, particulars tried their strength one with another to the hazard of a few, now whole nations wage war to the destruction of myriads. Let any one therefore pronounce a state of nature worse than a civil state if he can, when it is evident that the latter is liable to all the same inconveniencies as the former; and that is not subject to some to which this is obnoxious.

2. Titius, *Observationes in Samuelis L. B. Pufendorfii De officio hominis et civis juxta legem naturalem.*

shewn afterwards. But since there is no stronger tie or bond for holding men together than pacts and conventions, the consequence is, that societies were constituted by pacts and conventions; and because a few more easily consent in the same end than many, it is probable that men first formed more simple, and then more complex societies.* <10>

SECTION XIII

Here we understand by *society* the consent of two or more persons in the same end, and the same means requisite to obtain that end; wherefore, while such consent lasts, there is society. And so soon as they who had formerly consented in the same end and means, begin to propose and pursue each his own end, that society is broke and dissolved, and each begins to have his own to himself.† Whence a *state* in which men live in society is called a *social state*.

What society and a social state is.

---

* Sacred history sufficiently confirms this. For first, we find Adam and Eve in the matrimonial state, the most simple of all societies, Gen. ii. 22, 23. Then children are born to them, and thus a new society was produced, Gen. iv. 1, 2. somewhat more complex, between parents and children. None could then be born slaves, unless you say that our first parents reduced their children and grandchildren into slaves. Nay, since Noah was saved by the ark with his wife, his sons and his sons wives only, it is probable that pious men then had no slaves in their families, Gen. vi. 18. Tho', on the other hand, it is evident, from what is said of the posterity of Cain, Gen. vi. 4 that some men then oppressed others, and reduced them into servitude. Again, we have an instance of the most complex sort of society, Gen. iv. 17. So that it appears very certain, that the progress was gradually from more simple to more complex societies, and from these to the most compounded of all, which is commonly a civil state or republic.

† I would not be understood to mean, that the pact by which society is formed becomes null by the dissent of any one of the parties. This opinion I have already confuted (§382): But that such a one can no longer be considered by the rest as an associate, who does not concur with them in the same end and means, and shews that disposition by incontestible signs and evidences. For in that case, the others continue to have a right by the convention to force him to fulfil his pact, and all the terms and articles of his agreement; or if that can't be done, to repair their damage, and to make them satisfaction. But such a person can no longer be said to be an associate, because the definition of an associate no longer agrees to him from the moment he perfidiously breaks the bond of union and society.

SECTION XIV

Societies in respect of their ends are of very different kinds.

But since every society proposes or tends to a certain end (§13), but the ends may be very different; hence it follows, that if the end be *just* and *lawful,* the society formed for that end is likewise *just* and *lawful* (l. 1. §398). Wherefore societies of pyrates, robbers, and such like societies, are most base and flagitious. Societies must be judged of by their ends;* and hence means must be judged of by their ends, and the laws, rights and duties of <11> persons united in a society, must be inferred from the end of that society.

SECTION XV

Societies in respect of consent are either voluntary or forced.

But since society cannot be understood without consent (§13), which is either voluntary or extorted by force, which we call *forced consent,* and which may become valid by ratification (l. 1. §345); hence it follows, that some societies are *voluntary* and *cordial,* and others are *forced;* but that the latter ought not to be pronounced unjust, because they had a vitious or faulty origine, if those who were at first forced to enter into society do afterwards expresly or tacitly ratify their consent (l. 1. §381).† <12>

---

* This we have already seen with respect to the contract of *partnership,* the end of which is common gain (l. 1. §379). But matrimonial society has another end; a society of masters and servants has another end; and in fine, that most complex of all societies, which we call a republic, has yet another end. Therefore, as many different ends as there are, so many different kinds of society there are, and so many societies so many different ends must there be. Aristotle begins his political work with a remarkable observation to this purpose. "Because we see all communion or society is constituted for the sake of some good (for all things are done with a view to something that appears good to the agent) it is evident that all societies have some good as their proposed end." (Politic. 1. 1.)

† Thus was matrimony ratified between the Romans and the Sabines; and between the Benjamites and the daughters of Shiloh, Judg. xxi. 21. tho' its origine in both cases was unjust, being violent; because the ravished afterwards confirmed the deed by their consent, and adhered to their marriages, tho' they had been forced, Dion. Hal. antiq. Rom. l. 2. p. 110. [[Dionysius of Halicarnassus, *Roman Antiquities,* vol. 1, bk. II, chap. 30, p. 401.]] In like manner, the society between masters and their slaves taken in war, is originally forced: And yet sometimes, the mildness and hu-

SECTION XVI

Besides, consent being either express or tacite, which is inferred from some deed, of which kind is even patience (l. 1. §391), it follows, that societies may be formed either by *express* or *tacite* consent: and it is the same as if persons had consented, when they afterwards live with others in society, and pursue the same end with them by the same means; nay, seeing sometimes we judge one to have consented from the very nature of the thing, (l. 1. §391), it is plain that society may arise from presumed consent.*

They are formed either by express, tacite, or presumed consent.

SECTION XVII

Sometimes it happens, that not only individuals, but also whole societies intend the same end, and agree upon the same means for obtaining it. But such consent or agreement being society (§13), the consequence is, that not only individuals, but that whole societies may coalite into society; and therefore societies are either *simple,* such as are those formed by individuals; or they are more complex, such as those entred into by

Some societies are simple, and some are more compounded.

---

manity of masters has engaged the slaves to serve with good will, and to say seriously, what in Plautus, Capt. 2. 2. v. 21, one says with great grief,

> *Quamquam non fuit multum molesta servitus:*
> *Nec mi secus erat, quam si essem familiaris filius.*

> [[Plautus, *The Captives*, lines 272–73, in *Plautus*, vol. 1: "[B]ut being a slave hasn't bothered me much, though: I wasn't treated any differently than if I'd been a son of the house."]]

See Exod. xxi. 5.

* Such is the consent between parents and children. For so far are children from consenting directly to that society at the time they enter into it, that they are then absolutely incapable of consenting. And tho' coming afterwards to understand the nature of the thing, they might consent if they would; yet so far are all of them then from testifying this consent by words and deeds, that many more dissent and rebel. But this society is not therefore dissolved, because the education of children requires this society, and it is presumed that children cannot but consent to live with their parents in such society, without which they can neither be conveniently preserved nor educated.

simple socie-<13>ties, which are then considered as associates. In the same manner, it is evident that complex societies may become larger and more compounded; so that some societies may consist not only of many thousands, but of myriads.*

SECTION XVIII

Some are equal, and some are unequal. In fine, those who consent in the same end and means, are either equal or not equal. The former, as equals, by common consent consult about, and find out the means necessary to a common end, and thus *equal* society is formed. In the latter, the business of finding out the end and means is intrusted <14> or committed to one or more, and then society

---

* Experience confirms and illustrates all this. The most simple societies are those of persons joined in marriage, of parents and children, masters and servants. Of these societies coalited among themselves, is formed a larger society, which we call a family. Of many families are formed hamlets, villages, towns. Of many villages, &c. are formed whole states or republics; of many republics are formed systems of republics, such as were the Greek republics. See Cicero's offices, i. 17. that is, if lesser and more simple societies are not sufficient to obtain a certain end, it is necessary to form greater and more complex societies by the consociation of many little ones. Hence Justin, hist. i. i. observes, that in the beginning kingdoms were confined within the narrow bounds of particular counties. [[The reference is to Turnbull's own translation of Marcus Junianus Justinus, *Justini Historiae Philipicae,* which appeared in 1742 and in a second edition in the same year as his Heineccius translation, 1746, under the title *Justin's History of the World, Translated into English* (bk. I, chap. 1, p. 4).]] And this is plain from the examples of the Canaanites, the Phoenicians, the Greeks, the Gauls, the Germans, the Britons, whose provinces were originally split into several different states, kingdoms, or governments, Gen. xiv. 1. Jos. xii. 7. Judg. i. 7. Strabo, Geograph. 16. p. 519. and other writers. [[Strabo, *Geography,* vol. 8, bk. 16, chap. 2.14 (p. 257) and chap. 4.3 (p. 311). It is not clear who the "other writers" are.]] But by degrees, several states being oppressed by violence, coalesced with others into a larger state; and many states being in danger from their neighbours, formed a still larger system or confederacy of republics. Thus the Amphyctionian confederacy shook the power of the Medes; and the Greeks, tho' otherwise very inconsiderable, became strong merely by their union and consociation. See Jo. Henr. Boecler. de concilio Amphictyonum. [[Boecler, *Synedrion Amphyktyonikon.*]]

is *unequal,* and this society is likewise called *Rectoreal.* Now, it is plain, from the nature of the thing, and from human temper and disposition, that the larger a society is, the less practicable is it, that so great a multitude of associates should find out necessary or proper means by common consent and suffrage; and therefore the larger the society is, the more necessary it becomes that it be rectoreal and unequal.*

SECTION XIX

But of whatever kind society be, it is plain, from the description of it, that it is designed in order to obtain an end by certain means (§13). But since to consent in this manner is to will the same thing, the consequence is, that the understanding and will of every society are to be considered as one will and one understanding (l. 1. §32), and therefore every society constitutes one person, which, in contradistinction to a physical person, is called *a moral one.* † <15>

Every society is one moral person.

* Hence experience teaches us, that the more extensive empires are, the less liberty they have; and empire daily extending itself and enlarging its dominions, necessity often obliges men, otherwise great lovers of liberty, to bear subjection with patience. For in a large but free and equal society, because the greater number will overpower the better part, bad councils must often take place and be pursued; and liberty degenerating into licentiousness, must create disorders, and rend the state into factions. In which cases, there is often no other remedy but subjection to one head, as it happened in the Roman republic, when Augustus usurped the sovereign power, according to the opinion of the most prudent among them. (Tacitus. annal. 1. 9.)

† Cicero de off. 1. 17. observes, "that by every kind of union and friendship, many persons become one, and that because all think and will the same thing." [[See Cicero, *De officiis* 1.17.59.]] Add. Catilin. 4. 7. So Apuleius de habit. doctrin. Platon, l. 2. p. 25. "A state," says he, "is a conjunction of many persons, in which some govern, and others are governed, formed by concord for mutual assistance; and who being ruled by the same good laws, and having thus the same manners, constitute one body, every member of which hath the same will." [[Apuleius, "On the Philosophy of Plato," bk. 2, chap. 24, p. 288, in Apuleius, *Apuleius' Golden Ass or The Metamorphosis, and Other Philosophical Writings.*]] We may learn the nature of a moral person from Seneca likewise, Ep. 102. as also from l. 30. D. de usurp. & usucap.

SECTION XX

Therefore the laws and duties of societies, and of individuals are the same.

Now, if every society be, as it were, one person (§19), it must, by consequence, be subject to the same laws as individuals or physical persons;* and therefore all the duties which the law of nature prescribes to particular persons, ought likewise to be religiously observed by all societies greater or lesser. In like manner, the same rights which belong to particular persons, belong also to societies, and associated persons have the same common things and rights; yea, all the affections or properties of bodies and persons may justly be attributed to societies; and thus they, by very elegant metaphors, are said *to flourish,* or *to be sick;* nay, *to die and perish.* See Koehler. spec. jur. gent. 1. §20. & seq.[3] <16>

* And hence appears the truth of what was said above (l. 1. §21.), that the law of nations is nothing else but the law of nature applied to a social state, and the affairs of societies and whole political bodies. Wherefore, it is justly called by Koehler, ibidem, "Jus naturale societatum, the natural law of societies." [[Koehler, *Juris socialis et gentium ad ius naturale revocati specimina VII.*]] And hence likewise it is evident how sadly they reason, who, as it were, absolve empires and states from the obligation of natural law, and pronounce all things lawful to emperors which are for their private interest, or that of their empires. It was therefore a most accursed saying of Caesar (in Cicero de off. 3. 21.)

> *Si violandum est jus, regnandi gratia*
> *Violandum est, aliis rebus pietatem colas.*

> [[Cicero, *De officiis* 3.21.82: "If wrong may e'er be right, for a throne's sake were wrong most right—be God in all else feared!" This is a Latin translation from Euripides' play *Phoenician Women,* lines 524–25, in vol. 3 of *Euripides.*]]

Hertius has said a great deal to excellent purpose on this execrable doctrine, Polit. paed. §13. p. 22. & seq. [[It is not certain which work by Johann Nikolaus Hertius is being referred to here.]]

3. Koehler, *Juris socialis et gentium ad ius naturale revocati specimina VII.*

SECTION XXI

From the same principle we may justly conclude, that every associate, or member of a society, is obliged to adjust his actions to the common end of that society; and therefore that he injures his fellow-associates, who seeks his own advantage at their detriment, or who does any thing contrary to the end of the society of which he is a member, or hurts any one of its members. For which reason, no injustice is done to him, if he be forced, by what is called *punishment,* to repair the injuries he has done, and to behave better with regard to his society for the future, (l. 1. §211). And it is no less evident, that an associate cannot be blamed if he separates such a bad associate from himself, or if he leave a society in which no regard is paid to its common end, nor to the means requisite to that end.

The obligations of associates or members with regard to society, and of society with respect to them.

SECTION XXII

Hence likewise it is perspicuous, that society ought *to hurt no person,* but *to render to every person his own;* but is not obliged to prefer the interest of any private person, or of any other society to its own. For since every society constitutes a moral person, (§19), and hath the same rights with physical persons (§20), and no person is obliged to love another more than himself (l. 1. §94), or to perform to another the offices of humanity, which would be hurtful to himself, or to his friends, to whom he is under special obligations (l. 1. §218); hence it follows, that no society is bound to render such offices to another society, or to prefer the interest of another society to its own.* <17>

The obligations of one society with respect to the others.

---

* Therefore the consociates in a mercantile society are not inhuman when they refuse a share in their monopoly to a private person, or another society. For that would be a detriment to themselves. Nor will any one say the Cimbri, Teutones and Helvetians, who seeking a new habitation to themselves, desired, as by their right, that the Romans would turn out in their favour, and leave them certain tracts of land they possessed. For that the Romans could not grant to them without manifest detriment to their republic. For as Florus says, "Quas enim terras daret populus, agrariis legibus intra se dimicaturus?" (3. 3). [[Florus, *Epitome of Roman History,* trans. Forster, bk. I,

SECTION XXIII

With respect to larger societies.

In like manner it is demonstrable, that in more compounded societies, the interest of the lesser is not repugnant to that of the larger, but ought to submit to it; because, in this case, the lesser societies are considered as individuals (§17); but individuals ought to consent to the same end and means, (§13), and not to prefer their private interest to the common end of the society (§21); and therefore lesser societies, which have coalited into a larger, or more compounded society, can do nothing which is manifestly contrary to the interest of that larger society, without injustice.* <18>

SECTION XXIV

General axioms concerning the duties of associates.

To conclude; since the duties of the members of societies must be inferred from the end of the society (§14), it is plain that this is, as it were, the sum and substance of all the laws of societies; "That all the members of a society are bound to do every thing, without which, the end proposed by that society cannot be obtained; and therefore the happiness of society is justly said to be the supreme law of all its members."

---

chap. 38, p. 169: "But what land could the Roman people give them when they were on the eve of a struggle amongst themselves about agrarian legislation?"]] And Caesar gave a very just answer to the Tencteri and Usipetii, who demanded much the same thing, "That there were no vacant lands in Gaul which could be given, especially to such a multitude, without doing injustice" (de bello Gallico, 4. 8). [[See Caesar, *Gallic War*, bk. IV, chap. 8, p. 189.]]

* Thus, for example, it would be no small advantage to a family to be exempt from certain imposts and taxes; but because such an exemption would be detrimental to the republic; none will say its governors act unjustly, when they refuse it to a family that asks it. On the contrary, magistrates and princes would be justly blamed, if they should thus cut the nerves of a republic, in order to promote the private interest of certain families; and therefore, when Nero thought of taking off all the taxes, and making a glorious present to the people of a total immunity from them, the senate interposed, pronouncing it a dissolution of the empire to diminish the revenues by which it was to be supported, Tacit. Annal. 14. 50.

Remarks on This Chapter

I cannot see how the physical state of man, as it is defined by our Author, can be said not to belong directly to the moral science. For whence can a man's duties or obligations, which constitute his moral state, be inferred but from his physical state, from his frame, condition, rank and circumstances; from his make, and the relations he stands in, in consequence of his make and situation? Properly speaking, man's physical state lays him under moral obligations; or binds and obliges him to a certain behaviour; binds and obliges him to choose to act, in a certain manner, or according to certain rules: or, in other words, man's physical state constitutes the law of his nature, by which he is bound, whether he consents or not, being bound to consent and choose to act agreeably to that law. Man cannot be said to be under the law of nature, or subject to it by his consent in any other sense, but this, that were he not capable of discerning the law of his nature, of perceiving its reasonableness, its excellence, and of consenting to it, he would not be a moral creature; but being such by his make, he is by his nature under natural and immutable obligations to know the law of his nature, and to regulate his conduct in all instances by it. And all men are equally under or subject to the law of nature: no man is less or more subject to it: but all *men* as *men,* are equally, universally obliged to observe it as the law of their nature, the law of reason, the law of God their Creator. And in this sense all men are equal, or there is an equality of obligation, and of right belonging to all men. Whence it follows, that all men are by nature equally *subject* and equally *free;* equally subject to the same universal law, and equally free or exempt from all obligations but those which arise from the law of nature. All are equally bound by the law of nature; and for that reason, all are equally free from all obligations but those which the law of nature lays equally upon all. All are equally obliged to direct their conduct according to the law of nature; and therefore every one <19> hath a right, an unalienable right, to make the law of nature his rule of conduct; and none hath a right so much as to advise, far less to force or compel any one to act contrary to the law of nature, or to hinder any one from making the law of nature his rule, and exercing his right to judge of it, and to act according to it: nay, none hath a right to dispose of, quit or resign this natural right and obligation. For that would be a right to throw off his natural obligations, and to choose or take another rule to himself. Man is free, or master of his actions, free and master of his consent; but how far? within the bounds that the law of nature or of reason sets to him. That is, he is free to consent and to dispose of himself and his actions, in any way not contrary to the law of nature; but not in any way that is repugnant to it, or which the law of nature forbids. Now, if this be carefully attended to, it will not be difficult to determine any of the questions that are commonly put by moralists about what are called by our Author adventitious obligations, or obligations imposed upon man by himself, or some deed of his own. For, from what hath been said, it is evident that man can bring himself under no obligation contrary to the law of his nature. Such adventitious impositions upon himself are *ipso jure* null, being morally not in his power, as being contrary to the law of nature, which he cannot abrogate, rescind or dispense with. This general principle shall afterwards be applied to civil society, and the impositions or obligations men lay themselves under by a civil contract. Here, we shall only observe, that the natural inequalities which take place amongst mankind, are not inconsistent with the moral equality and freedom of mankind that hath been defined. The first distinction which subjects some persons to others, is that which is made by birth between parents and children, which distinction makes a first kind of government in families, where the children owe obedience to their parents, who are the heads of families. But of this we shall say nothing here, because our Author treats expresly of it at great length in a succeeding chapter. It will be better for us to supply here a few things not touched upon by our Author, which however it is of importance to clear up. 1. Then, there is an evident inequality amongst mankind, intended by nature in respect of the goods of the mind. And it might easily be shewn, were this the proper place for it, that, as our excellent poet most beautifully expresses it,

> *Order is heav'n's first law; and this confest,*
> *Some are, and must be greater than the rest,*
> *More rich, more wise; but who infers from hence*
> *That such are happier shocks all common sense.*
> *Heav'n to mankind impartial we confess,*
> *If all are equal in their happiness:*

But mutual wants our happiness increase,
All nature's difference keeps all nature's peace.

Essay on Man, Ep. 4.[4] <20>

But what we would observe, is in the first place the fact. "God, who does nothing in vain, (says an excellent author often quoted in our remarks) hath so differenced or divided men, that twenty men (if they be not all idiots, perhaps if they be) can never come together, but there will be such a difference in them, that about a third will be wiser, or at least less foolish than the rest, these, upon acquaintance, tho' it be but small, will be discovered, and (as stags that have the largest heads) will lead the herd: For while the six discoursing and arguing one with another, shew the eminence of their parts, the fourteen discover things that they never thought of, or are cleared in divers truths which had formerly perplexed them. Wherefore, in matter of common concernment, difficulty or danger, they hang upon their lips as children upon their fathers: And the influence thus acquired by the six, the eminence of whose parts are found to be a stay and comfort to the fourteen, is the *authority of the fathers.* Wherefore, this can be no other than a natural aristocracy diffus'd by God throughout the whole body of mankind, to this end and purpose. And therefore, such as the people have not only a natural but a positive obligation to make use of as their guide; as where *the people of Israel are commanded to take wise men and understanding, and known among their tribes, to make them rulers over them.* The six will acquire an authority with, and imprint a reverence upon the fourteen; which *action* and *passion* in the *Roman Commonwealth* were called *authoritas patrum,* and *verecundia plebis.* Nevertheless, if the few endeavour to extend the authority which they find thus acquired, to power, that is, to bring the fourteen to terms or conditions of subjection, or such as would be advantageous to the few, but prejudicial to the many; the fourteen will soon find, that consenting, they hurt not only themselves, by endamaging their own interests, but hurt the six also, who by this means come to lose their virtue, and so spoil their debate, which, while such advantages are procurable to themselves, will go no farther upon the common good, but their private

4. Pope, *Essay on Man,* epistle 4.1, lines 49–56.

benefit. Wherefore, in this case they will not consent, and not consenting, they preserve not only their own liberty, but the integrity of the six also, who perceiving that they cannot impair the common interest, have no other interest left but to improve it. And neither any conversation, nor any people, how dull soever, and subject by fits to be deluded, but will soon see thus much, which is enough, because what is thus proposed by the fourteen, or by the people, is enacted by the whole, and becomes that law, than which, tho' mankind be not infallible, there can be nothing less fallible in mankind." Art, says our Author, "is the imitation of nature; and by the observation of such lines as these in the face of nature, a politician limns his commonwealth."[5] This is the fact, God having divided mankind into the natural aristocracy and the natural democracy, hath laid in nature the foundation of social union and civil government, and thereby delineated the whole mystery of a commonwealth, which lies only in <21> *dividing* and *choosing*. "Nor has God (if his works in nature be understood) as the same Author speaks, left so much to mankind to dispute upon, as who shall divide, and who choose, but distributed them for ever into two orders, whereof the one hath the natural right of dividing, and the other of choosing."[6] 2. But this natural division of mankind gives no more than authority to the aristocracy, or the right of counselling, and not the power of commanding; it gives them ability and right to advise or counsel right, and lays an obligation upon the many to seek and follow advice and counsel: But, as it cannot give a right to the few so much as to counsel, far less to command what is contrary to reason and the law of nature; so it can lay no obligation upon the many to be led by the few to what is wrong or contrary to the law of nature. The few are under obligation to conform to the law of nature in their advices or counsels; and the many are under obligation not to be influenced by the few to act contrary to the law of nature, tho' by the nature of the thing, and by the law of nature, they be under obligation to ask and take counsel from the few. Put therefore the case, that a few being

5. The first half of this quotation is from Harrington's *Oceana* (see *The Political Works of James Harrington*, 172–73); the second (from "The six will acquire an authority . . .") is from his *Prerogative of Popular Government* of 1658, bk. I, chap. 5 (*Political Works of James Harrington*, 416–17).

6. Harrington, *Oceana*, 172, in *Political Works of James Harrington*.

discovered to be capable of leading or counselling in matters of common concernment, the many, by voluntary consent and agreement,
should put themselves under the guidance, under the command, if you
will, of the few; then, it is true, they would be under an obligation by
consent to obey; and the natural authority of the few, would be then
changed into a right to lead or command the many; but not to lead or
command contrary to the law of nature, because neither have the many
power to contract with the few for such submission and obedience,
nor have the few power (I mean moral power or right) to stipulate to
themselves such submission and obedience. 3. There is an inequality
amongst mankind intended by nature, or at least not contrary to nature, in respect of external goods or the goods of fortune, all which
may be comprehended in one word *wealth.* But as superiority in respect
of the goods of the mind begets authority; so superiority in respect of
external goods, begets power or dominion, "in regard that men (as the
same Author expresses it) are hung upon these not of choice, as upon
the other, but of necessity, and by the teeth, for as much as he who
wants bread is his servant that will feed him; and if a man thus feeds a
whole people, they are under his empire. There is a real distinction
between authority and power. Wherefore, the *leviathan,* tho' he be
right, where he says *riches are power,* is mistaken where he says, that
prudence, or the *reputation of prudence,* is power. For the learning or
prudence of a man is no more power, than the learning or prudence
of a book or Author, which is properly authority. A learned writer may
have authority, tho' he has no power; and a foolish magistrate may have
power, tho' he has otherwise no esteem or authority. The difference of
these two is observed by Livy in Evander, of whom he says that he
governed rather by the authority of others than <22> by his own power.
It is property that in proportion to it begets or gives power, or makes
necessary dependence."[7] But now what we said just now of authority,
will likewise hold here. Whatever superiority one may have over others
in dominion or empire, by the necessary dependence on him his superior property creates, yet he can never have a right to exercise that
dominion, empire, or power, contrary to the law of nature: nor can his

7. Ibid., 163. Harrington's reference is to Livy's history of Rome (see Livy, *The
Early History of Rome,* bk. I, chap. 7).

dependents come under any obligation, even by consent added to necessary dependence, to be governed by his will, contrary to the law of nature, and the essential and immutable obligations they are under to obey it. And therefore dominion exerced contrary to the law of nature, is exerced without right, nay, contrary to right and obligation: For which reason, every dependent on any superior in power, has a right to refuse submission to, and to shake off dominion exerced over him contrary to the law of nature. That must be true; or of necessity it must be said, that superiority in dominion releases from the obligations of the law of nature; and that inferiority or dependence knows no other law but the arbitrary lawless will of a superior in property, and by consequence in power: which is to say, that there is no law of nature but the law of strength or force. It is indeed absurd to say, that it is contrary to the law of nature to seek, or to have superiority in property, *i.e.* to have dominion and dependents. Whatever property is purchased by honest industry, it, with all the superiority it gives, is a lawful purchase. But it is no less absurd to say, that the law of nature does not extend to those who have power, or does not limit its exercises, and lay it under certain obligations. And yet unless there be no obligations with regard to the exercise of dominion or power by the law of nature, there must be an exercise of power that is unlawful, and to which consequently, it is unlawful to submit or obey. Now, if it is asked, what is this law of nature with regard to superiors and inferiors, we answer, with our Author, it is the law of love or benevolence. And he goes on in the succeeding chapters to shew, what that law of love and benevolence requires in all different coalitions or societies of mankind, whether natural, as that between parents and their children, or adventitious, as that between masters and servants, and subjects and magistrates, *&c.* Nor, as he observes, can we ever be difficulted in any case, to find out the duties of the members of any society towards its head and towards one another, or of any one society towards any other distinct independent society, if we remember that societies are moral persons, invested with the same rights, and lying under the same moral obligations as physical persons. For that being remembered, it must, for instance, be true, that societies are bound to justice and charity, as well as individuals; and that societies have the rights of self-defence and preservation, as well as individuals. If which two principles be granted, it will be an

easy matter to resolve any question about the rights and duties of superiors and inferiors in any society; or about the rights and <23> duties
of any distinct independent societies. Mean time it is evident, that the
natural inequalities amongst mankind, or the inequalities made necessary by the state and circumstances of mankind, and which must for
that reason be said to have been intended by the Author of nature, do
not destroy the moral equality and freedom of all mankind, essential
to man as such, *i.e.* the equal subjection of all mankind to the law of
nature, and their equal liberty and right to act agreeably to it, and to
demand from one another behaviour conformable to it. In this respect,
all men are equally bound and equally free; or all men have the same
common rights and duties.

Of the duties belonging to the
matrimonial state, or society.

SECTION XXV

Matrimony
is a lawful,
and the most
simple society.

That God wills mankind should be propagated, and that the number of those who daily pay their debt to nature should be supplied by a new race, is plain from hence, that otherwise his end in creating mankind could not be obtained (l. 1. §77.) they therefore who have this end in view, propose a good end to themselves, and are obliged to have recourse to the means for compassing that end. Since then this end cannot be accomplished, unless a man and a woman consent to copulation, the consequence is, that matrimony is a society (§13), and that it is honest and lawful, being proper to a good end, which is very agreeable to God; and because it consists of the fewest persons of different sexes that may be, it is the simplest of all societies (§17).* <24>

---

* Hence the Greeks justly called the conjugal state, *the root of all other societies,* and, as it were, *the seminary of mankind,* because without it man would be but of a single age, as Florus says of the Romans while they had not wives, Hist. 1. 1. The matter is reasoned most philosophically by Seneca the tragedian in Hippolyt. v. 466.

> *Providit ille maximus mundi parens,*
> *Quum tam rapaces cerneret fati manus,*
> *Ut damna semper sobole repararet nova.*
> *Excedat, agedum, rebus humanis Venus,*
> *Quae supplet ac restituit exhaustum genus:*
> *Orbis jacebit squallido turpis situ.*

SECTION XXVI

But the end of God, as the author of mankind, being not merely that   Its end is not
men should exist, but that they should be truly happy (l. 1. §77), it fol-   only procreation, but
lows, that mankind ought not only to be propagated, but that the off-   education.
spring should be carefully educated, that they may not be useless burdens
on earth, but may grow up into useful members of the human state.
Now, since this duty of educating offspring can be incumbent upon
none but parents, in whose minds God hath, for that effect, implanted
a most tender regard to their offspring;* hence we justly infer, that parents ought not only to have in their view, as the end of matrimony, the

---

And a little after he adds,

> *Caelibem vitam probet*
> *Sterilis juventus: hoc erit, quidquid vides,*
> *Unius aevi turba, & in semet ruet.*

[[Seneca (the Younger), *Hippolytus,* 466–67: "The almighty father of the
world provided for this when he saw that the hands of Fate were so greedy,
so that losses would always be made good by new offspring. Well then, if
Venus were to depart from human affairs, she who supplies and restores an
exhausted race; the world will lie debased in a foul state." 478–81: "Let sterile
youth approve the celibate life: this, which you see, will be the only crowd
of a single generation and it will collapse upon itself."]]

  * Men, as Justinian observes, l. un. §5. C. de rei uxor act. are strongly stimulated
by a natural impulse to the care and education of their children. Nay not only are
men thus impelled by nature, but the brutes likewise, who do not abandon their
offspring till they are capable of providing for themselves. But seeing God does nothing in vain, it is evident that God requires of man, that love and care of his offspring,
which is the only end for which this instinct could have been implanted in us by him.
Hence Euripides justly observes, in a passage already quoted in Medea, v. 1098.

> *Sed quibus in aedibus est liberorum*
> *Dulce germen, eos, video curis*
> *Confici omni tempore:*
> *Primum quidem, quo pacto illos bene educent,*
> *Et unde victum relinquant liberis.*

[[Euripides, *Medea,* 1098–1102, ed. Elliott: "But as for those in whose homes
sweet children are born, I see that they are consumed with care all the time:
first, how they are to bring them up well and from where they are to leave a
means of support for their children."]]

preservation of children, but likewise their education; and therefore preservation and convenient education are the genuine end of marriage. <25>

SECTION XXVII

Matrimony defined, and some axioms relating to it.

Matrimony therefore is a simple society between persons of different sexes formed for procreation and education. And, from this definition, it is plain, that marriage cannot be contracted without the consent of the persons of both sexes (§13); and that the united parties are bound to all, without which, procreation and convenient education cannot be obtained,* and that every thing ought to be omitted which is repugnant to this end, (§24).

SECTION XXVIII

Marriage is made by consent.

Since marriage cannot be formed without consent (§27), it is obvious, that marriage between a ravisher and a ravished person is not valid, (l. I. §109) unless the latter shall afterwards ratify it by consent† (§15); nor

---

* For certainly, it would be better not to procreate, than to give a bad education to children. It would be but a small loss to mankind if every one was not equally prolific. But mankind receive great hurt from any one who is a disgrace to the kind on account of his bad education. How unhappy was it for mankind that there was a Nero? And therefore Juvenal says with great gravity and judgment, Sat. 14. v. 70.

> Gratum est, quod patriae civem populoque dedisti,
> Si facis, ut patriae sit idoneus, utilis agris,
> Utilis & bellorum & pacis rebus agendis.
> Plurimum enim intererit, quibus artibus, & quibus hunc tu
> Moribus instituas.

[[Juvenal, *Satires,* Satire 14, lines 70–74, in *Juvenal and Persius:* "Thank you for producing a citizen for your fatherland and your people, just so long as you make him an asset to his fatherland, capable of farming, capable of action in war and peace alike. The fact is, the habits and behavior you train him in will make a huge difference."]]

See likewise Seneca of benefits, 3. 30.

† That is, if real force was used. For often in ancient times maids suffered an agreeable violence, not that they were averse to the marriage, but that they might not

is marriage more valid, if any violence was done to either party (ibid.) or if either of the parties was seduced by any knavish art into a marriage, to which, had the party not been deceived, consent would not have been <26> given (l. 1. §57). But tho' this nuptial consent of the parties be absolutely necessary, yet because there can be no society without consent to the means as well as to the end, we think mere consent to the end does not, by the law of nature, constitute marriage, but that immediate consent to conjunction of bodies is requisite.

SECTION XXIX

Hence it is evident, at the same time, that consent to marriage is more properly called, *contract to marriage,* or *betrothing,* than *marriage;* so that the distinction of the canonists between *sponsalia de praesenti & de futuro,* is too subtle for the law of nature; yet, because betrothing is a pact, and all pacts, by the law of nature, are perfectly obligatory (l. 1. §387), none can question but a contract of marriage ought to be fulfilled,* unless any of these circumstances take place, by which, we have already observed, that all other pacts are rendered null (l. 1. §382); or unless difference of tempers, or some other just reason, render it more adviseable

The difference between betrothing and marriage.

---

seem to rush into an embrace. This was an ancient custom, as is plain from Dion. Halicarn. antiq. Rom. 2. p. 100. where, to excuse the rape of the Sabines by the Romans, he says, "That this kind of rape was not an injury, but done with a view to marriage, according to a very old custom among the Greeks, which did honour to the women desired in marriage." [[Dionysius of Halicarnassus, *Roman Antiquities,* vol. 1, bk. II, chap. 30, p. 401.]] This was practised in other nations, it being judged more decent, that a virgin should be taken with an appearance of violence, than that she should give herself up to a man of her own accord. And that such force is not repugnant to consent is very manifest.

* It may seem odd, that whereas the other Latin nations allowed an action upon betrothment, *ad id quod interest,* if the pact was not fulfilled, (Gell. noct. Attic. 4.4.) the Romans left the betrothed persons at perfect liberty to renounce, l. 1. c. de sponsal. l. 2. c. de repud. But there being amongst the Romans so much liberty with respect to divorce, it is impossible that this pact could be firmer than marriage itself was among them, or that there could be less latitude with regard to it than there was with respect to divorce after marriage.

that it should be departed from, than that it should be compleated to the great misfortune of the parties. <27>

SECTION XXX

The hability of persons in respect to age.

Since the end of matrimony is procreation and convenient education (§26), and nothing ought to be done that is repugnant to this end (§27); it follows, that those who think of matrimony, ought to be of an age in which it may be expected they can be fit for both these ends; and therefore matrimony is not allowed, by the law of nature, to infants, or such young persons, as either have not vigour enough for raising up a new vigorous seed, or not the virtue and prudence requisite to provide for a wife and children, and to take care of their children's education and conduct.* <28>

SECTION XXXI

Whether aged persons may marry?

Hence likewise it is evident what ought to be said of the matrimony between aged persons. For tho', on account of the indissolubility of this society (of which afterwards) married persons, who have become old in the conjugal state, ought not to be separated; and tho' marriage between a man in the decline of life, who is yet vigorous, and a young woman, is tolerable, because the end of marriage may yet be accomplished by such matrimony; yet no person of sound judgment can approve of marriage between two aged persons, or between a young man and a decrepit

* In this respect Lycurgus excelled all other legislators. For he, as Xenophon informs us, de rep. Laced. cap. 1. §6. did not allow every one to marry when he pleased, but provided that matrimony should be contracted when persons were in the best condition for propagation. [[Xenophon, "Constitution of the Lacedaemonians," p. 139 in Xenophon, *Scripta minora.*]] This he thought necessary in order to the propagation of a wholesome vigorous race. And whereas he observed that many parents were fitter to propagate than to educate, he gave the care of education to the public; he made it a matter of public concernment; and an inspector of the youth was appointed from amongst those who had been employed in the supreme magistracy, who was called *Paedonomos.*" See Xenoph. ibid. cap. 2. §2. And this is a piece of civil prudence which ought not to be neglected in other states.

old woman, by which there can neither be consent to the end nor to the means of matrimony, without the most shameless immodesty.* <29>

SECTION XXXII

Much less is marriage to be permitted to those who have been deprived of their virility, either by accident or maliciously, or who are naturally incapable of procreation; and therefore, tho' examples of such marriages be not wanting, they are contrary to the law of nature, unless the impotence of the man, or the sterility of the woman, be unknown and uncertain, or be not beyond all hopes of cure, and the parties be satisfied to wait in hopes of a change to the better.†

Of eunuchs, &c.

---

* For what is more impudent and shameless, than for an old woman, who as Martial says, Epig. 3. 64.

> *Cum tibi trecenti consules Vetustilla*
> *Et tres capilli, quatuorque sint dentes,*
> . . . .
> *Verumque demens cineribus tuis quaeris.*

[[Martial, *Epigrams* 3.93. 1–2 and 19 (not 64): "Although, Vetustilla, you have seen three hundred consuls out, and have three hairs and four teeth . . . you madly search for a man for your burnt-out ashes [reading *virum,* not *verum*]."]]

These sort of matches are tolerated in commonwealths, tho' they do not deserve the name of marriage (since, as Quintilian expresses it, Declam. 306. quaedam & nubendi impudicitia est) [["Even marrying may involve a sort of wantonness" (Quintilian, *Lesser Declamations,* vol. 1, 306.29, p. 183)]]; but of them Pufendorff of the law of nature and nations says very justly, 6. 1. 25. "Perhaps we shall not speak improperly if we call these *honorary marriages,* as we term those offices *honorary,* in which a title only is conferred, without action or business. Nero (Sueton. cap. 35.) when he deserted his wife Octavia's bed, excused himself with saying, 'Sufficere sibi uxoria ornamenta'; he was contented with the bare ornaments and badges of marriage; in allusion to the triumphalia ornamenta, sometimes bestowed on persons without the real solemnity of a triumph."

† Such marriages therefore among the Egyptians were absurd, of which see Grotius, ad Deut. xxiii. 2. as are those likewise among the Turks, of which Ricaut, in his state of the Ottoman empire, 2. 21. And yet, even among Christians, it hath been made a question whether such marriages are not lawful. There is a little treatise on this question, entitled, de Eunuchi conjugio, reprinted Jenae, 1737. [[Hieronymus

SECTION XXXIII

Whether all habile persons be obliged, by the law of nature, to marry? Tho' we may rightly conclude, from the same principle, that those contract marriage allowably, who find themselves in proper circumstances for answering its ends and uses; yet the obligation to marriage is not of such a nature, as that he can be judged to have acted contrary to the law of nature, who prefers chast celibacy to inauspicious marriage.* For since omission of an action cannot be imputed to one who had no opportunity of doing it, (l. 1. §114); and it often happens, that many accidents disappoint one's design of marrying, and so deprive him of an occasion; surely, in such cases, celibacy cannot be blamable, since provi-<30>dence hath not offered an allowable opportunity of engaging in marriage.

SECTION XXXIV

All copulation out of a married state is unlawful. But because procreation and convenient education are the ends and uses of copulation, and every thing ought to be omitted which is repugnant to these ends, nothing can be more certain, than that they are exceedingly guilty who abuse that mean which is destined by divine appointment to these ends for the gratification of their lust; and therefore all these wicked

---

Delphinus, *Eunuchi conjugium = Capaunen-Heyrath.*]] But such things may well be reckoned amongst those prodigies of which Juvenal speaks in his time, Sat. 1. v. 22.

> *Quum tener uxorem ducat spado, Maevia Tuscum*
> *Figat aprum, & nuda teneat venabula mamma:*
> *Difficile est, satyram non scribere.*

[[Juvenal, *Satires,* Satire 1, lines 22–23 and 30, in *Juvenal and Persius:* "When a womanly eunuch takes a wife!—when Mevia shoots a Tuscan boar, holding the hunting spears with one breast bared! . . . then it is hard *not* to write satire."]]

* This was the opinion of the Jews, as Selden has shewn, jure nat. & gent. secundum discip. Hebraeorum, 5. 3. But it cannot be inferred from Gen. i. 38. for that is not a command but a blessing: And it is absurd to accuse those, who prefer celibacy for just reasons to marriage, of not consulting the interests of mankind, as if mankind could suffer great loss by the not marrying of one or a few, who are hindered from it by allowable reasons. They seem to have forgot St. Paul's precept, 1 Cor. vii. who, leaving the paths of Christians, go into this Jewish opinion.

kinds of venery, which it is better to have no idea of than to know, all adultery, all whoredom, all stolen love, (which is, over and above its being contrary to the end of copulation, likewise attended with injuriousness to others); all uncleanness and unchastity, and all the infamous trade of bawding and pimping are diametrically repugnant to right reason, and the law of nature; and, in fine, that there is no other lawful way of propagating and supplying human race, but by the conjugal society we have described.* <31>

SECTION XXXV

For the same reason, πολυανδρία,[1] that is, plurality of husbands is contrary to right reason; as likewise, that community of wives which was permitted by Plato in his republic. (See Aristotle, polit. 2. 2.) For since, in both cases, the offspring must be uncertain on the father's side, and this uncertainty will be a hindrance to the care of education, (§34); so far is reason from approving such conjunctions, that even those nations which permitted polygamy, or a plurality of wives to one husband, have given no woman right to have more than one husband at a time.†

Whether plurality of husbands be lawful?

---

* These impure conjunctions are not designed in order to propagate, but to satiate lust: And the ordinary effect of them is, that the persons who thus copulate are industrious to prevent progeny by such conjunctions. And if nature disappoints this their wicked intention, so that children are procreated and brought into the world contrary to their desire and intention, the parties are so far from having had any view to education, the other end, that they (the father chiefly) utterly neglect the offspring, leaving them to the public, as an uncertain birth; whence it happens, for the most part, that such misfortunate children become rather a disgrace and a pest to mankind, than an ornament. Now, since all these miserable consequences ought to be prevented, it is plain that magistrates do not act unjustly, when they oblige lewd persons to provide for their bastards, and force men to marry the women they had debauched under promise of marriage.

† And therefore the contrivance of Papirius Praetextatus to elude his mother, which is so well known, was very acute. See Gellius noct. Attic. 1. 23. But so far were the Romans from permitting a plurality of husbands, that the most barbarous nations never admitted of it, tho' some have allowed the promiscuous use of wives. See Pufendorff, law of nature, &c. 6. 1. 15.

1. Πολυανδρία: polyandry, plurality of husbands. This is not a classical word.

SECTION XXXVI

Arguments for polygamy.

The question about the lawfulness of *polygamy,* or *a plurality of wives,* is more difficult. For, 1. Such a conjunction does not hinder propagation. Nor, 2. Does it render offspring uncertain. Besides, 3. Many nations, even the people of God, have approved of this, and seemed to think themselves happy in having the privilege of taking home many wives. Not to mention, 4. The Turks, and <32> other eastern nations, where it is not worse in respect of procreation and education, when one has many wives, than when one has but one wife. And, 5. Sometimes the husband's vigour, sometimes the wife's intolerable humour, or her barrenness, sometimes the interest of the republic, and sometimes other reasons plead in favour of Polygamy.*

---

* Those are the principal arguments by which the defenders of polygamy support their opinions taken from reason. And as for those fetched from the sacred writings, they belong to another chair. This question has been greatly agitated by Huldericus Neobulus, of whose book on the subject see Seckendus Hist. Lutheran. 3. 79. addit. 3. litt. 10. p. 281. Bernardus Ochinus, who is expresly refuted by Beza de polygamia, and by Jo. Gerard de conjugio, §207. of which author see Bayle's dictionary sub Ochinus; by Jo. Lyserus, who under the assumed names of Theoph. Alethaeus, Vinc. Athanasius, & Gottl. Wahrmundi, has published several books on this subject, of which see Vinc. Placcius Theatr. pseudonym. n. 97. 277. 2867. Against those authors have written Jo. Brunsmannus, Jo. Musaeus, Dickmannus, Feltmannus, Gesenius (who has been injurious to Pufendorff) Jo. Meyerus and others. The defence of polygamy hath been undertaken by one whose better studies such a design ought not to have interrupted, Daphnaeus Arcuarius, not to mention the late writings of a lawyer of Dantzick, in every body's hands, which have been of very little service, if not of great hurt to the church. [[Huldricus Neobulus (i.e., Johann Lening, 1491–1566) was a German Protestant theologian who defended the second marriage of the Protestant landgrave Philip of Hessia. Seckendus (i.e., Veit Ludwig von Seckendorff, 1626–92) was a Lutheran governmental administrator and writer, "Cameralist," and author of *Commentarius historicus et apologeticus de Lutheranismo.* Bernardinus Ochinus (1487–1564) was an Italian Protestant convert from Catholicism and radical reformer. Theodor Beza was a Calvinist theologian and author of *Tractatio de polygamia* (Treatise on polygamy), which was reprinted several times in the late sixteenth and the seventeenth century and was directed against the opinions of Ochinus. Johann Gerhard (1582–1637) was a German theologian, author of the *Loci theologici* (Theological problems), which included a volume on marriage and related questions. See Pierre Bayle (1647–1706), *Dictionnaire historique et critique,* 672–79. Johann[es] Musaeus (1613–81) was a Lutheran theologian; Gerhard Feltmann (1637–96) a Ger-

SECTION XXXVII

But since it is the duty of married persons to avoid every thing repugnant to the end of a married state (§27), and all discord about the end or means is contrary to society (ibid.) and so much the more unavoidable as the society is more numerous (§18); hence we justly conclude, that polygamy is less agreeable to right reason than marriage with one woman; wherefore, since the law of nature obliges us <33> to choose the best of two goods* (l. 1. §92), we are rather obliged to monogamy than to polygamy.

It is not agreeable to right reason.

SECTION XXXVIII

Nor are the arguments brought in defence of it of such force as to oblige us to desert our cause. For grant, 1. That the procreation of children is not hindered by polygamy, yet the other end, convenient education, which ought not to be separated from the former, is hindered by it (§26 and 37). 2. Tho' progeny be certain in polygamy, yet this certainty does

An answer to the first and second argument.

---

man jurist. Johann Lyser published *Alethophili Germani discursus inter polygamum et monogamum de polygamia* (A discourse by a truth-loving German between a polygamist and a monogamist on polygamy), a response to Friedrich Gesenius's *Ad Sincerum Warenbergium Suecum Epistola seu Dissertatio super polygamia simultanea,* which had been a reaction to one of Lyser's earlier writings, the *Sinceri Wahrenbergs Kurtzes Gespräch von der Polygami.* The work by Vincenz Placcius, *Theatrum anonymorum et pseudonymorum,* is a key to authors' pseudonyms. See also Johann Brunsmann, *Monogamia victrix: sive orthodoxa ecclesiae Christianae sententia, de unis duntaxat eodem tempore concessis Christiano nuptiis, a criminationibus vindicata;* Johann Meyer, *Pyrrhonii und Orthophili Unterredung von der im nechsten Jahr unter dem Nahmen Daphnaei Arcuarii ans Liecht gekommenen Betrachtung des . . . Ehestandes.* Daphnaeus Arcuarius was the pseudonym of Lorenz Beger, who wrote *Daphnai Arcuarii Kurtze, doch unpartheyisch- und gewissenhafte Betrachtung des in dem Natur- und Göttlichen Recht gegründeten Heiligen Ehstandes.* It is not clear who the lawyer from Danzig is.]]

* This is most certain, that discord, jealousies, envy, and hatred, must arise among many wives. But in this intestine war, what place is there for harmony, or consent in the education of children of different and jarring mothers? The families of Abraham and Jacob saw such sad effects, Gen. xvi. 5. xxi. 9. xxix. 30. xxx. 1. And what may not happen when men maintain at home many wives, which instead of being virtuous and good, are furies?

not hinder but each mother may only love her own children, and prosecute the rest with terrible hatred, or at least endeavour, by novercal arts,
to render them less agreeable to the father than her own. 3. To oriental
nations, of a hotter temper, and more prone to venery, which approved
of polygamy, we may oppose examples of more civilized nations which
disapproved it. Nor is the practice of the Jews a rule, since our Saviour
teaches us, that all things in which the Jews dissented from the primitive
rule, were rather tolerated than approved by God in them; "For the hard-
ness of their hearts," Mat. xix. 8.* <34>

SECTION XXXIX

An answer
to the fourth
and fifth
arguments. Of the same nature are all the other arguments by which polygamy is
defended. For, 4. What is said of domestic quiet and peace among the
Turks and other eastern nations, is partly false, according to the annals
of these countries, and is partly obtained by means repugnant to the
matrimonial society.† And what, pray, 5. is more incredible, than that
one is not sufficient for one? Or what is more uncertain, than that when
one has an immodest or indiscreet wife, that the other he brings home
shall be more modest and discreet? or that if one be barren, the other
shall be more prolific? what if he should get two furies instead of one?

* For no reason can be given why more regard should be paid to the primitive
institution of marriage in the question about divorces, than in that about polygamy.
Nay, from what our Saviour says of divorce, we may draw an argument against the
lawfulness of polygamy. For if he who unjustly divorces his wife and marries another,
be guilty of adultery, he is certainly much more guilty of adultery, who, while his
marriage subsists, takes another wife, because the reason given by our Saviour, *viz.*
that God, when he instituted matrimony, willed that "two should become one flesh,
Mat. xix. 5." is no less an obstacle to polygamy than to divorce.

† It is known that in the eastern countries, those who have plurality of wives, keep
them in a *Seraglio,* as in a prison, and that they are no better than servants. Hence
Aristotle. Polit. 1. 2. says, That among the barbarous nations, wives and servants are
of the same rank. See a remarkable passage in Plutarch. in Themist. p. 125. "They are
confined by eunuchs; and the education of children, of the male-kind especially, is
seldom trusted to the mother, but for the most part, to some eunuch or servant. Now,
how contrary all this is to the end of the matrimonial society, is too obvious to be
insisted upon." [[This passage does not appear to be in Plutarch's life of Themistocles.
See Plutarch, *Lives,* vol. 2.]]

But all their arguments depend upon a principle we have already shewn to be false.

Sola est utilitas justi prope mater & aequi. (l. 1. §78)[2]

SECTION XL

It is a no less difficult question, whether by the law of nature reverence is to be paid to blood, and whether, for that reason, it prohibits marriage <35> within certain degrees of kindred and affinity? For since such marriages are not repugnant to the end of matrimony, they cannot be forbidden on that account. Yet, since marriages between ascendants and descendants are attended with the greatest and most hurtful confusion of different natural relations amongst persons, reason itself perceives and acknowledges their turpitude; and therefore the Civilians justly asserted these marriages to be incest by the law of nations, l. 38. §2. D. ad leg. jul. de adult. And they likewise with reason pronounced marriages between persons of the nearer degrees of kindred, to be contrary to modesty and virtue, l. 68. D. de ritu nupt.* <36>

Whether certain degrees are prohibited by the law of nature.

2. This should be "atque ipsa utilitas, iusti prope mater et aequi": "Expediency alone, we might say, is the mother of what is just and right" (Horace, *Satires I,* 3, l. 98).

* For nature cannot approve of contradictory things, but such are the obligations of wife and mother, father and brother, mother and sister: They cannot subsist in the same person without the greatest confusion. Such marriages therefore cannot be lawful which confound these relations together in one and the same person, as in the marriage of Hersilus and Marulla, according to an old epigram.

> *Hersilus hic jaceo, mecum Marulla quiescit:*
> *Quae soror, & genitrix, quae mihi sponsa fuit.*
> *Me pater e nata genuit: mihi jungitur illa:*
> *Sic soror & conjux, sic fuit illa parens.*

> [["I, Hersilus, lie here, and with me rests Marulla, who was sister and mother and wife to me. My father conceived me from his daughter; she was joined to me: so she was my sister and wife, so she was my parent."]]

Such marriages were looked upon by the Pagans as contrary to nature. See Ovid, Metam. 10. v. 9. where Myrra thus speaks:

> *Tunc soror nati, genitrixque vocabere fratris?*
> *Nec, quod confundas & jura & nomina, sentis?*

SECTION XLI

Of solem-
nities.

Since all copulation without marriage is unlawful, and there is no other lawful way of propagating mankind but by marriage (§34); the consequence is, that it is the interest of the married parties, and of the children, that the design of contracting the matrimonial society should be testified by some external sign, that thus a legal wife may be distinguished from a concubine, and legitimate children from illegitimate ones; which, since it cannot be done conveniently, unless marriage be publicly celebrated, we may easily see a good reason why almost all nations have judged some solemnities requisite to indicate nuptial consent, and have appointed some such.*

[[Ovid, *Metamorphoses* 10, line 348, vol. 2: "Will you be called the sister of your son, the mother of your brother?" and line 346, "And do you not think how many ties, how many names you are confusing!" though original text reads *"Et quot"* for *"Nec"*—"Think how many ties, . . ." etc.]]

Among collaterals, the same degree of confusion is not to be feared: Yet a certain confusion of relations cannot be avoided, if the same person be sister and wife. And therefore we think it better to assert, that such marriages are not permitted, unless absolute necessity render them excusable. And thus it is very accountable why the children of Adam married without being guilty of incest, tho' they are who now do the same. For this prohibition of certain degrees is of those laws of nature which must yield to providential necessity (l. 1. §162).

* There is no barbarous nation which hath not instituted some rites of marriage: And therefore it is not to be wondered at, if all civilized nations have; such as the Hebrews, the Greeks and Romans, *&c.* concerning which customs, antiquaries have wrote such large and learned volumes, that I need not say one word on this subject. Let me only add, that the Romans, when their ancient discipline degenerated, took little or no care in this matter; and hence it was, that it was frequently so difficult to determine whether a woman was a wife or a concubine; and it was necessary to have recourse sometimes to the articles or instruments of dowry to determine this question, l. ult. Inst. de nupt. and sometimes the thing could only be judged of from the condition or quality of the woman, l. 24. D. de ritu nupt. l. 31. pr. D. de donat. But how easily might these disputes have been avoided by performing marriage with certain rites?

SECTION XLII

The conjugal duties are obvious. For, since the nature of this society requires consent (§32), which cannot be hoped for without love and con- <37>cord, the consequence is, that husband and wife are obliged to love one another; and not only to manage their common family interest* with common care and prudence, but mutually to assist one the other, especially in the education of their children, and to have one common fortune.

Of the conjugal duties arising from the nature of the pact.

SECTION XLIII

These are the duties which arise from the very nature of consent and society. But from the end of matrimony we infer, that husband and wife are obliged to cohabit, and to allow to one another only the use of their bodies, and therefore to abstain from all adultery, whoredom, and stolen love;† to love all their children with equal affection; and that the one

Of those arising from the end of matrimony.

---

* Indeed what effect this community of goods ought to have after the decease of one of the parties, or what part of the common substance belongs to the surviver, and what to the defunct's heirs, must be determined by pacts or by civil laws. But that while marriage subsists, all ought to be in common, right reason teaches us. For since associates, by unity of will, are one person (§19), and therefore have all the things and rights belonging to their society in common (§20), it is manifest, that the same must hold with respect to persons united by marriage; and so, however it came to be afterwards, was it anciently among the Romans, according to Dionys. Halicar. Antiq. Rom. l. 2. p. 95. for by Romulus's law, there was, "Omnium bonorum & sacrorum communio." And even their later laws appointed, "Communem utrique conjugi bonorum usum." [["Common ownership of all goods and sacred things"; "common use of goods for each spouse." (See Dionysius of Halicarnassus, *Roman Antiquities,* vol. 1, bk. II, chap. 25, p. 383.)]] Whence it is evident why Modestinus retaining the old definition of marriage, and agreeably to his own time, says it is, "Conjunctio maris & foeminae, consortium omnis vitae, divinique & humani juris communicationem," l. 1. D. de ritu nupt. [["The union of a man and a woman, life-long cohabitation, sharing in divine and human law."]]

† Some think this duty belongs to the wife only, and not to the husband, because, if he neglects it, the children are not rendered uncertain. But tho' all copulation be unlawful which renders progeny uncertain, yet it does not follow, that all is lawful which does not render it uncertain (§38). See Gundlingii dissert. an major a seminis, quam a viris, castitas requiratur. [[Gundling (*praeses*) and Benz (*respondens*), *Disser-*

ought not, by any means, to disappoint or render ineffectual the other's care about their education. <38>

SECTION XLIV

Whether the husband has any superior command?

Moreover, it is manifest that this society would be very imperfect, if it were equal in such a manner that neither had the faculty of deciding in any common dispute, because it may happen, in many cases, that the two may differ in their opinions about the choice of means, and between two, in such cases, the dispute would be endless; wherefore, tho' the prudentest counsel ought to be preferred (l. 1. §92),* yet, because it would often be controvertible which of the two parties in this society was in the right, there is reason to approve the common practice in this matter,

---

tatio iuridica, qua doctrina vulgaris maiorem a feminis, quam a viris, requirens casti-tatem.]] We draw an argument from this principal rule of natural justice, "what one would not have done to him, *&c.*" But surely the husband would not have his wife to love another man more than him, or grant any other the use of her person. And therefore the husband is bound to the same duty. See Chrysostom. Homil. 19. in 1 Cor. vii. Lactantius Inst. divin. 6. 3. [[John Chrysostom, *Homilies on the Epistles of Paul to the Corinthians,* "Homily XIX," 105–11; Lactantius, *Divine Institutes, Books I–VII,* bk. VI, chap. 23 (not 3), 457–62]] Hieron. ad Ocean. & can. 20. Causs. 32. quaest. 5. But at the same time, we grant that the wife's unchastity is more repugnant to the end of marriage than the husband's.

* For since the parties are bound to all, without which the ends of the society, procreation and convenient education, cannot be accomplished (§27); they are obliged to consent to this prerogative in one of them, without which consent in the same means could not be expected. Now, because this prerogative in a society of equals is due to the more prudent, and in the conjugal society the husband for the most part is such, the wife is, for this reason, obliged to consent to the husband's prerogative.

Inferior matrona suo sit, Prisce, marito:
Non aliter fuerint femina virque pares.
    Martial. Epig. 8. 12.

[[Martial, *Epigrams* 8.12.3–4, trans. Bailey: "Let the matron be subject to her husband, Priscus: in no other way are a man and a woman equal."]]

See Plutarch's conjugal precepts, p. 139. [[Plutarch, "Advice to Bride and Groom," lines 303–9, in Plutarch, *Moralia: in Fourteen Volumes,* vol. 2.]]

and so to give a certain prerogative to the husband about affairs belonging to the common safety or advantage of the society. <39>

SECTION XLV

But since this prerogative of the husband extends only to affairs belonging to the welfare and interest of the society (§44); the consequence is, that this marital authority ought not to degenerate into such an empire of a master, as we have already observed to have taken place in some barbarous nations;* nor does it reach to a power of death and life, as it did in some nations. Gellius 10. 23. Tacit. annal. 13. 32. Caesar, de bello Gallico, 6. 19. Tacit. de moribus German. c. 19. much less does it extend to a power of selling or lending one's wife to another, a custom among some nations, and not disapproved of by the Romans, Plut. in Catone, p. 770. Tacit. annal. 5. 1. Dio Cass. hist. l. 48. p. 384. But it consists in the right of directing a wife's actions by prudent counsel, and of defending her; and in the right of chastising an immodest one suitably to the condition and rank of both* (§21); and in divorcing her for such just causes as shall be afterwards treated of (§21). <40>

> The nature of it.

* I say, chastise suitably to the rank and condition of both parties; because, since they are one person (§19), an ignominious chastisement of a wife reflects ignominy on the husband. And because both are bound to take care of their reputation (l. 1. §153), a husband acts contrary to his duty if he chastises his wife in a manner that tends to hurt both her and his character. This imprudent discipline of husbands is severely lashed by Plutarch in his conjugal precepts, p. 139. "As some soft effeminate persons who are not able to mount their horses, teach them to stoop to them, so some husbands, who espouse rich and noble wives, are at no pains to amend themselves, but accustom their wives to submission, that they may more easily rule over them, tho' regard ought to be had in the use of the curb, as in the one case to the spirit of the horse, so in the other to the dignity of the wife." [[Plutarch, "Advice to Bride and Groom," ibid.]]

SECTION XLVI

Whether this right of the husband may be changed by pact?

But because this prerogative is only due to the husband on account of his presumed greater prudence, and of the matrimonial burdens incumbent on him (§44); since it not seldom happens that a woman of superior judgment and spirit is married to one of an inferior one, a richer to a poorer, a queen to a private man; therefore, in all these cases, the woman may stipulate the prerogative to herself.* None can deny, for we have many examples of it, that a queen may marry a prince, without giving him any power in her dominions, and likewise retain the superior power in the conjugal society; except when the consort, being heir to a kingdom, chuses to transfer the empire itself to her husband, contenting herself solely with the dignity.

SECTION XLVII

The duty of the husband in bearing the burdens of the matrimonial society.

But since ordinarily the prerogative belongs to the husband (§44), he cannot refuse the care of maintaining his wife and children, and of bearing <41> the burdens of matrimony; tho', because the children are common, and both are obliged to common care (§42), the wife ought certainly, as far as her estate goes, to bear a part of these burdens. And hence

* Thus what is related by Aristotle, Politic. 5. 11. and by Sophocles in Oedipo Colon. v. 354. of the wife's power over the husband among the Egyptians, was by pact, as Diodor. Sicul. Bibl. 1. 27. informs us. But all the questions relating to a Queen's husband are fully handled by Jo. Philip. Palthenius, in a discourse on this subject. [[Johann Philipp Palthen (*praeses*) and Samuel Palthen (*respondens*), *Dissertatio de marito reginae.*]] We have a noted instance of this in Earl Bothwell, who, when he was to be married to Mary Queen of Scotland, took an oath, "That he should claim no superior degree or pre-eminence on that account; but that he should continue to be subject to the queen as he had hitherto been." Buchanan. rer. Scot. hist. l. 16. p. 674. [[George Buchanan (1506–82), Scottish humanist scholar and author of *Rerum Scotiarum historia.*]] To all that is urged from scripture, Gen. iii. 16. 1 Cor. xi. 7. 1 Tim. ii. 11. Ephes. v. 23. Coloss. iii. 18. 1. Pet. iii. 1. Palthenius has given a full reply at great length. But these things we leave undetermined, because we proceed upon another foundation.

the origine of dowry among the Greeks and Romans, brought to husbands by wives, who were not excluded from succession to their parents.*

SECTION XLVIII

In fine, since every thing ought to be avoided that is contrary to the ends of matrimony, because education, which is no less the end of matrimony than procreation, requires a perpetual society between man and wife; hence it is plain, that the liberty of divorce, authorised by some nations, is quite repugnant to the end of matrimony. And yet because an intolerable temper and behaviour of either party no less hinder this end than divorce; and a partner cannot be blamed if he severs from him an injurious associate (§21); we think divorce is not unlawful, when either of the parties behaves themselves so that the end of matrimony cannot be obtained.† Now, that, this society being dissolved in any lawful way,

In what respect marriage is indissolvable.

---

* In several other nations, women had a portion or dowry given them at marriage, that they might not be quite cut off from all share in their parents estate, because they were otherwise excluded from succession. The same was the case among the Romans while the *lex voconia* obtained. But they used to give dowries to daughters before it took place; and after it was abolished, tho' married daughters shared the paternal and maternal estate equally with their brothers. All this matter is elegantly treated by Perizonius, in his dissertat. de lege Voconia, reprinted by us at Hal. 1722. [[Jacob Perizonius (1651–1715), professor of eloquence and history at the university of Franeker, *Dissertationum trias quarum in prima de constitutione divina super ducenda defuncti fratris uxore secunda de lege voconia feminarumque apud veteres hereditatibus tertia de variis antiquorum nummis agitur,* part 2: *De lege voconia feminarumque apud veteres hereditatibus.*]] Hence the Roman lawyers acknowledge, that the dowry was given in order to bear a part of the matrimonial expences or burdens, l. 7. pr. l. 56. §1. l. 76. fin D. de jure dot. l. 20. C. eodem.

† To these we refer not only adultery and malicious desertion, which are pronounced just causes by the divine law, Mat. v. 32. xix. 9, 1 Cor. vii. 15; but every thing that is an obstacle to the end of marriage, and renders it unattainable: We do not take upon us to determine, whether our Saviour's phrase, παρεκτὸς λόγου πορνείας, Mat. v. 32. signifies the same with what is called by Moses, Deut. xxiv. 1. *some uncleanness,* as Selden seems to think; but we are certainly persuaded, that πορνείαν and λόγον πορνείας, do not mean the same: For λόγος signifies the condition, nature or proportion of a thing (Synes. Epist. ad Joannem: τὸν αὐτὸν λόγον ἔχουσι, they are of the same nature or rank). [[Παρεκτὸς λόγου πορνείας: "except for the condition

either may make another marriage cannot be doubted, since a partner, his <42> partnership with one being dissolved, has a right to associate another partner, and thus enter into a new partnership.*

SECTION XLIX

What is to be said of imperfect marriages.

Tho' all this be required by right reason in the conjugal society, yet it is manifest that one duty hath a nearer relation to the end of matrimony, and another a more remote relation; and therefore society between a man and a woman does not cease to be marriage, if some changes are made in it by pacts; wherefore marriage is valid tho' imperfect; *i.e.* though contracted for the sake of procreation and education privately, and without any solemnity;† nor is that invalid which is called *morgenatic mar-*

---

of adultery."]] Now, this being the meaning of the word, the sense is, that no other cause of divorce is allowable, but such a one as is like to adultery, of the same nature with it, *i.e.* no less repugnant to the end of matrimony than adultery.

* [[See preceding note.]]

† To this class belongs what is called *mariage de conscience:* as also concubinacy, such as obtained among the Romans, concerning which we have said a great deal in our comment. ad legem Juliam & Papiam, l. 2. c. 4. [[Presumably in his *Elementa iuris civilis.*]] For concubine is not to be confounded with whore; and differed only in respect of dignity from a legal wife. Whence it is called *unequal marriage,* l. 3. C. de natur. lib. On the other hand, that does not deserve the name, even of an imperfect marriage, which is called by these barbarous terms *ad talacho, emancibado, casato di media carta;* and is contracted on this condition, that a man, so soon as he has children by a woman, may turn her away, or that the woman being pregnant, may desert her husband when she pleases; such the marriages of the Amazons are said to have been, tho' Arrian doubts of the truth of this report, in his expedit. of Alexander, l. 7. p. 291. See Sam. Petit. de Amazonibus, & Casp. Sagitt. Exercit. ad Justin. hist. 2. 4. [[The author is Pierre (not Samuel) Petit, *De Amazonibus dissertatio, qua an vere extiterint, necne, . . . disputatur.* The other work is Sagittarius (*praeses*) and Köpken (*respondens*), *Antiquitates Amazonias exercitatione ad Justini historici lib. 2, cap. IV.*]] And what is this indeed, but as Seneca expresses it, of benefits, 3. 6. exire matrimonii caussa, nubere divortii caussa? [["To divorce in order to marry, to marry in order to divorce." This is a not entirely accurate quotation from Seneca (the Younger), *On Benefits* 3.16 (not 3.6).2 in vol. 3 of *Moral Essays.*]] What can be more repugnant to that convenient education, which we have observed to be the end of matrimony?

*riage;** nor putative, or reputed marriage, of which Jo. Nic. Hertius hath published a curious dissertation.[3] <43> <44>

---

* [It is not unfit to explain what our Author calls, *ex lege morganatica matrimonium ad morgangabicam,* or as the writers on fiefs call it, *ad morgenaticam,* comes from the German *morgen-gab,* which signifies a morning present. The person who marries a woman in the manner here specified, or as the Germans express it, *with the left hand,* the day after his wedding makes her a present, which consists in the assignment of a certain portion of his goods to her and her future children, after his death, on which condition they have no farther pretensions. Gregory of Tours calls this *matutinale donum,* l. 9. 19. as Gronovius on Grotius observes [[Grotius, *De jure belli ac pacis,* ed. Gronovius]], who likewise refers us to Lindenberg's glossary on the Codex legum antiquarum. See Barbeyrac on Grotius, l. 2. c. 8. 8. 3.] [[Grotius, *Le droit de la guerre et de la paix,* trans. and ed. Barbeyrac.]]

3. Hertius, *Commentatio iuridica de matrimonio putativo,* originally published as a Giessen University dissertation in 1690.

Of the duties that ought to be observed in a society of parents and children.

SECTION L

Connection. By the conjunction of which we have been treating in the preceding chapter, children are procreated, who abide in society with their parents till they themselves form new families, and go from under their parents authority. For tho' children, when they come into the world, can neither expresly nor tacitely consent to this society; yet, because society may arise from presumed consent, if, by the nature of the thing, we may judge one to have consented (§16), and the condition of infants requires that they should live in society with others, (§16); there is no reason why we may not assert, that parents and children consent in the same end and means, and consequently that there is a society between parents and children (§13).

SECTION LI

The end of this society is the convenient education of children. Because infants, nay, young boys and girls, are not capable of judging how they ought to direct their actions and conduct, God, who willed their existence, is justly understood to have committed the care of such to others. And since he hath implanted not only in men, but in brutes, an ardent affection to stimulate them to this duty (§26), and men contract marriage for the sake of procreation and education, or ought to have those ends solely in their view in forming this society (§ eod.); the consequence is, that this duty is principally incumbent on the parents;

and therefore that there is no <45> other end of the society between parents and children, but convenient and proper education of children.*

SECTION LII

Education being the end of this society (§51); since it cannot be carried on without directing the actions of children, the consequence is, that parents have a right and power to direct their children's actions; they have therefore power over their children, and thus this society is *unequal* and *rectoreal.* But as the duties of every society must be deduced from its end (§14); so this parental power must be estimated by its end; and therefore it is a right or power competent to parents, to do every thing, without which the actions of children cannot be so directed, as that the end of this society may be obtained.† <46>

This end cannot be gained, unless the parents have a certain power.

SECTION LIII

Since the duty of education is incumbent upon both parents (§51), the consequence is, that this power must be common to both parents; and

It belongs to both parents.

* For tho' a man and woman may join together, not with a view to have children, but merely to satisfy their lust, yet they are not freed from this obligation, because they proposed another end to themselves. All impure conjunctions without marriage being repugnant to right reason (§34), it is no matter what end parents may really have had in their view; but we are solely to consider what end they ought to have had in view; nor is it in any one's power to renounce the preceptive law, which appoints this end of copulation (l. 1. §13).

† Hence then the origine of that power belonging to parents by the law of nature. God wills that children exist, *i.e.* that they be preserved and made happy (l. 1. §77): but they cannot be preserved and live happily without proper education (§51); and they cannot be properly educated unless their actions be directed: Therefore God wills that the actions of children be directed by those who educate children. But the right of directing the actions of children is power over children (§52): And therefore God wills that parents exercise power over their children. We therefore send Hobbes apacking, de cive, 9. 3. who derives paternal power from occupancy. Nor does Pufendorff's way, (of the law of nature, *&c.* l. 6. c. 2. §4.) satisfy us, who derives it partly from the nature of social life, and partly from the presumed consent of children. For presumed consent to this society, which we likewise acknowledge can be inferred from no other principle than that we have now laid down.

therefore, by the law of nations, this power cannot belong to the father only, as the Roman law affirms; yet, since regularly the father, as husband, has the prerogative in the conjugal society (§44), it is plain, that when parents disagree, greater regard ought to be had to the father's than to the mother's will, unless the father command something manifestly base and hurtful to his children: For to such things, as being morally impossible, neither mother nor children can be obliged.

SECTION LIV

It passes to grandfathers, grandmothers, tutors, nurses, preceptors, adepters.
Besides, because the duty of education, whence the parental power takes its rise, is sometimes undertaken, upon the death of the parents, by grandfathers and grandmothers, or other relatives, through affection; sometimes it is committed by the parents themselves to others, whom they judge more fit for the charge; sometimes a stranger desires a parent would devolve that care upon him; it therefore follows, that this power, as far as it consists in the right of directing the actions of children, is, in these cases, devolved upon *grandfathers, relations, pedagogues,* and those who *adopt** children, or take them *under their care;* and therefore all such

---

* Adoption therefore is not contrary to the law of nature, but for another reason than that upon which it is founded in the Roman law. For children being by that law under the power of the father, *i.e.* in domino juris quiritium, l. 1. D. de rei vind. Hence they inferred, that the father could alienate and sell his children, as well as the other things (mancipi) in his full possession and power. And thus adoptions were made by alienation and cession of right, as we have shewn on another occasion. Besides, men only, and not women, could adopt, except by a special indulgence from the prince to console them for the loss of their children, §10. Inst. l. 5. C. de adopt. because they could not have any person under their power. But we derive adoptions not from any dominion belonging to the father, or to both parents, but from the duty of education, and the power of directing the actions of children, necessary to that end; which duty, since sometimes it may be better performed by strangers, or at least as conveniently as by the parents themselves, there is no reason why they may not resign it to others, willing to undertake it, and thus give them their children in adoption. Nor is there any difference whether a man or a woman, a married or unmarried person adopt, because this adoption does not imitate nature, but only the duties of parents. And we have an example of this kind of adoption, not only among the Egyptians, Exod. ii. 10. but also among the Romans, among whom Lact. de mort. perseq.

persons may exercise the parental power as far as the education undertaken by them requires. <47>

SECTION LV

Since this power consists in the right of doing every thing necessary to obtain the end of the society above defined (§52); it is obvious, that parents have a right to prescribe to their children what they ought to do, and to prohibit what they ought not to do; and not only to chide and reprove the stubborn and disobedient, but to chastise them, as the circumstances of the case may require; and to use other severer methods to reduce them into good order and due obedience; provided it be done prudently, and with proper regard to age, the dignity of the family, and other circumstances.* <48>

Parents have the power of commanding, forbiding, chastising.

---

cap. 50. tells us, that Valeria Augusta, not on account of barrenness, but to console her for the loss of her children, adopted Candidianus.

* Grotius, of the rights of war and peace, 2. 5. 22. and Pufendorff of the law of nature, &c. 6. 2. 7. justly observe, that this power is greater over younger than more adult children. For since the father may do every thing that education, the end of this society, makes requisite (§52); because children of an imperfect understanding can hardly discern by themselves what is right, the very nature of the thing requires, that parents should direct their actions, and have a right to compel them to learn some useful art, as likewise to embrace the religion they themselves approve, and to chastise with the rod, or otherwise, the disobedient. But this a good father will not do to a more grown up child, who, his judgment being more ripe, ought to be induced to do what is right, rather by authority, and the weight of good arguments, than by severity and rigid command; nor ought he to force any thing upon such a child by way of command with respect to his future manner of life, against his will and inclinations. Thus, e.g. parents are right in forcing a boy against his will to attend the school; but it would be wrong to force one come to the years of discretion, to marry, or to follow a profession he does not like, &c. This we observe, in opposition to Zieglerus, who in his notes on Grotius, 2. 5. 2. thinks this distinction ought not to be admitted. [[Ziegler, In Hugonis Grotii De jure belli ac pacis libros, . . . notae.]]

SECTION LVI

Whether it
extends to the
power of life
and death?
Hence it is plain, that the end of this society does not require the power of life and death over children; unless, perhaps, in a state of nature, where parents preside over a large and diffused family as its heads; and in this case they exercise such power rather as princes and magistrates than as parents.* Whence again we infer, that the law of nature does not approve of the antient rigid power of the Romans, which was afterwards disapproved of even by them; and therefore Justinian justly affirms, §2. Inst. de patri. potest. "That no other people ever exercised such a power over children as the Romans did." <49>

SECTION LVII

Whether
parents have
the power of
selling, of
hurting delin-
quents, and of
acquiring by
their children?
Much less then have parents, by the law of nature, a right to expose their children to sale, of inflicting hurtful punishments upon them for faults, and of acquiring to themselves all that comes to their children, tho' all these things were approved of by the antient Roman laws. For none of these things is of such a nature, that the end of society cannot be obtained without it (§52). But since this power consists in directing the actions of children (§52), parents cannot be refused the right of commanding certain work from their children, suitable to their condition, and of making gain by their labor; nor of adminis-

---

* This is plain, because that power of life and death was proper to the father, and not common to both parents, and extended even to wives and widow-daughters-in-law. We have an example of the latter in Judah, Gen. xxxviii. 24. who, when he found that his Daughter-in-law Tamar had play'd the harlot, ordered her to be brought forth and burnt. Thus kings, because they are in a state of nature, exercise this power over their wives, children, and their whole family; and this power fathers in ancient times exercised, not as fathers, but as sovereigns. Thus Philip of Macedon sat as judge between his sons, Liv. 40. 8. [[Livy, *History of Rome* 40.8.]] Thus Claudius Caesar punished Valeria Messalina his adulterous wife, Sueton. in Claud. cap. 26. [[Sueto-nius, "The Deified Claudius," chap. 26 in *Suetonius,* vol. 2]] not to mention more modern examples which have been examined by others. See Barbeyrac on Pufendorff, of the law of nature and nations, 6. 2. 10.

trating what comes to their children by the favour of men, or of providence.* <50>

SECTION LVIII

We have said enough of the power of parents. As to their *duties,* they are very obvious. For they are easily deducible from the end of this society. Education is the end of this society, and therefore it is self-evident, that parents are obliged to every thing without which this end cannot be obtained, and to avoid every thing contrary to it (§24). But it is worth while to give a full view or idea of education, that thereby the duties, both of parents and children, may the more clearly and certainly appear.

The foundation of the duties of parents to their children.

SECTION LIX

The natural affection implanted in parents, inculcates, as we have already observed (§26) the obligation of parents to educate their children. Now, the love which parents owe to their children, is *a love of benevolence* (l. 1. §85), which consists in delighting to preserve and encrease, to the utmost of our power, the happiness of an inferior and more imperfect

Of education, wherein it consists.

---

* For since children themselves, while their judgment is imperfect, are subject to the direction of their parents; why may not their goods be likewise administred by them? But may this administration be gainful to them? I do not doubt of it. Whatever things children stand in need of, such as clothes, meat, lodging, the expence of education, *&c.* they have a right to demand them from their parents. They therefore do not stand in need of fruits or profits, whereas the parents often greatly want them for the support and education of their children. With what face then can children demand restitution of fruits or profits from their parents, whom they can never repay, if they would give up themselves and their all to them? Ismene says well in Sophocles, Oedip. Colon. v. 523.

> *Patrem cura: nam parentum caussa*
> *Etsi quis laborat, laborum tamen non meminisse debet.*

[[Sophocles, *Oedipus at Colonus,* in *Sophocles: Antigone; The Women of Trachis; Philoctetes; Oedipus at Colonus,* ll. 507–9 (not 523): "[S]tay here and guard our father; when one takes trouble for a parent, one must not remember that it is trouble!"]]

being (ibid.); the consequence from which is, that parents are not only bound to take care of the conservation of their children, but likewise to lay themselves out to promote their happiness to the utmost of their power. And in this does education consist, by which nothing else is understood but the care of parents to preserve their children, and to make them as perfect and happy as they can.* <51>

SECTION LX

It is the duty of parents to preserve the health, soundness, &c.

If parents be obliged to the preservation of their children (§59), the consequence is, that they are not only bound to provide for them all the necessaries of life;† *i.e.* cloaths and food, according to their condition of life, but likewise to take care of their health, and to preserve their bodies sound and intire in all their members, as much as that lies in their power; and therefore to keep them from gluttony, luxury, lasciviousness, and all the other vices which tend to enervate, weaken, or hurt their

---

* For what so great merit is there in begetting children, if care be not taken about their conservation? And what signifies it to have preserved them, if they are not so educated as to be rendered capable of true happiness? So Seneca of benefits, 3. 31. Ad bene vivendum minima est portio vivere, *&c.* [["To live well, the smallest part is to live." This exact phrase does not appear in Seneca's *On Benefits* 3.31, though another phrase with a similar meaning ("Non est bonum vivere, sed bene vivere") does: "It is not a blessing to live, but to live well" (Seneca, *Moral Essays,* vol. 3).]]

† To this class belongs chiefly suckling. For that the mother is obliged to this is evident, from the care of nature to furnish her with such plenty of milk, till the child's stomach is fit to receive and digest more solid food. Those mothers are therefore truly neglectful of their natural duty, who either for their own ease and conveniency, or for the sake of preserving their shape, delegate this care to nurses, often of little worth, if not bad women, as the heathens themselves have acknowledged, and proved by many solid arguments. See Plutarch on education, p. 3. Aul. Gell. noct. Attic. 12. 1. [[Plutarch, "The Education of Children," pp. 13–15, in *Moralia: in Fourteen Volumes,* vol. 1; Aulus Gellius, *Attic Nights,* vol. 2, pp. 353–55.]] But because necessity exeems one from the obligation of an affirmative law (l. 1. §114), mothers of a delicate constitution, or who have not milk, are not blameable if they give their child to a good nurse. But what care a mother ought to take in this matter, is elegantly described by Myia in a letter to Phyllis, apud Tom. Gale Opuscul. Mythol. Eth. & Physic. p. 750. [[Thomas Gale, *Opuscula mythologica physica et ethica.*]]

bodies; and, on this account, not rashly to leave them to themselves, or without some guardian.

SECTION LXI

To this duty are directly contrary, endeavours to bring about abortion, exposing infants, abdicating and disinheriting them without a just cause;* de-<52>nying them necessary sustenance, and other such crimes, repugnant to the end of this society. They chiefly are very blameable, nay, unworthy of the name of parents, who abandoning their children, or, by their carelesness about them, are the cause of their receiving any hurt in any of their senses, organs or members; this impiety of the parents is so much the more detestable, that the soundness of their senses, and the integrity of their members, belong not only to the preservation, but to the happiness of children.

What is contrary to this duty.

SECTION LXII

Since parents are obliged to promote the perfection and happiness of their children to the utmost of their power (§59), to which belongs the cultivation of their understandings, in order to render them capable of distinguishing true good from evil (l. 1. §146), it is certainly the duty of

The understanding of children ought to be improved.

---

* What difference is there betwixt murdering children and denying them necessary sustenance? l. 4. D. de agnos. & alend. lib. But those parents withhold necessary sustenance from their children, who abandon or desert them, or disinherit them without a cause: Nay, those laws are reprehensible which give so much indulgence to parents, as to allow them to treat their children as they please, or at least pay more regard to paternal power than to natural equity. For who can choose but blame the laws of the Tarquinians, which suffered the testament of Demaratus to hold good, "who not knowing that his daughter-in-law was pregnant, died without mentioning his grand-child in his testament; and thus the boy being born after his grandfather's decease, to no share of his estate, was on account of his poverty called Egerius." Liv. 1. 34. [[Livy, *Early History of Rome*, 72.]] And who, on the other hand, does not approve of Augustus, "who, by his decree appointed C. Tettius, an infant disinherited by his father, to inherit his father's estate by his authority, as father of his country, because the father had acted most iniquously towards his lawful son, in depriving him of his right by his father," Valer. Max. 7. 7. [[Valerius Maximus, *Memorable Doings and Sayings*, vol. 2, 175.]]

pa-<53>rents to instil early into the minds of their children the principles
of wisdom, and the knowledge of divine and human things, or to commit them to the care of proper masters to be polished and informed by
them, and to save no expence in instructing and improving them, within
their power, and agreeable to their rank. Whence we also conclude, that
parents are obliged to give due pains to find out the genius of their children, that they may choose for them a kind of life suitable to their genius,
rank, and other circumstances; and that being chosen, to exert themselves to the utmost for qualifying them to act their part on the stage of
life with applause.*

SECTION LXIII

Their will or
temper ought
to be rightly
framed.
Since the will or temper is the seat of that love by which we perceive
true good or happiness, parents do nothing, whatever care they may take
about perfecting the understanding of their children, if they neglect the
formation of their will or temper. Parents, who take not proper pains
and methods to inspire early into their minds the love of piety and virtue,
but train them up to vice, <54> if not to gross and manifest vices, yet
to cunning, avarice, ambition, luxury, and other such vices, by repre-
senting these vices to their minds under the false shew of prudence, frugality, spirit, taste, and elegance. Parents, in fine, who set a pattern of

---

* Since one and the same person often sustains several different characters, as Hertius has shewn in a dissertation on the subject [[Hertius (*praeses*) and Hasslocher
(*respondens*), *Dissertatio de uno homine, plures sustinente personas*]], education ought
to be so modelled, that children may not only be fit for the way of life chosen for
them, but likewise to act a becoming part in other characters. Hence, because children
ought to be qualified not only to be good merchants or artizans, but likewise to be
good citizens; the education of children ought to be accommodated to the state and
form of the republic to which they belong, as Aristotle has wisely observed, Polit. 5.
9. adding this reason for it, "That the best laws are of little advantage, unless the
subjects are early formed and instituted suitably to them (si leges sint populares po-
pulariter, sin oligarchicae, oligarchice), for if there be an unsuitable disposition to
the frame of government in any one of the subjects, the state will feel it."

wickedness before their children, and sadly corrupt their minds by a continued course of vitious example.* <55>

SECTION LXIV

Nothing is so flattering to youth as pleasure and ease; and therefore parents ought to take care not to educate their children too softly and delicately; not to suffer them to become languid and indolent, to dissolve in ease and laziness; not to breed them up to luxury and high living; but

Above all the mind is to be recalled from the pursuit of pleasure.

* Those are the fatal methods by which we may observe children of the best natural dispositions to be corrupted and ruined. For as none is so careless about his own reputation as to affect to shew his vices; and therefore every one endeavours to hide his crimes under some false semblance of prudence and virtue, so parents, for the most part, are not at so much pains to teach their children to live honestly and virtuously, as to teach them to deceive others by a counterfeit appearance of virtue and probity, *i.e.*

Ut Curios simulent, & bacchanalia vivant.

[[This is a slightly inaccurate quotation from Juvenal, *Satires,* Satire 2, l. 3: "[P]eople who imitate the Curii [i.e., representatives of traditional Roman virtue] but live like Bacchanals."]]

To this end are all their precepts directed, and this is the lesson their example inculcates. Insomuch that when some children, through the goodness of their natural disposition, are in the way to virtue and real honour, their excellent turn of mind is depraved gradually by the bad example of their parents. For as those who travel in a dark night, are easily misled out of their right road by false lights; so the best dispositions are easily corrupted, if bad examples are continually seducing them; especially, if their parents themselves are by their practice perpetually shewing them the inutility of all the discipline bestowed upon them. How mindful ought parents to be of that important advice of Juvenal, Sat. 14. v. 44.

Nil dictu foedum visuque haec limina tangat,
Intra quae puer est, procul hinc, procul inde puellae
Lenonum, & cantus pernoctantis parasiti.
Maxima debetur puero reverentia. Si quid
Turpe paras, nec tu pueri contemseris annos:
Sed peccaturo obsistat tibi filius infans.

[[Juvenal, *Satires,* Satire 14, lines 44–49: "Don't let any foul language or sight touch the threshold where there's a father inside. Keep away, keep well away, you pimps' girls and songs of the parasite who parties through the night! A child deserves the utmost respect. So if you're planning something disgust-

to inure them to hardship, to bear heat and cold, and to content themselves with homely fair, with whatever is at hand. For while the children
of peasants are thus bred up to work, and to homely diet, do we not see
how they surpass the youth of higher birth in health and vigour?*

SECTION LXV

And from bad
companions.

Nothing so much depraves youth as bad company; and therefore parents
ought to be watchful that their children do not associate themselves with
corrupt companions, but with their equals, and such as are well educated. For tender minds are prone to imitation,† and easily moulded into
any shape by example, but averse to admonition; and the danger of their
being corrupted is so much the greater, that they are so little capable of

---

ing, you shouldn't disregard his tender years. Rather, your baby soon should
be a deterrent when you are on the point of doing something wrong."]]

* There is an excellent epistle to this purpose from Theanus to Eubules, apud
Thom. Gale Opuscul. ethic. physic. & mytholog. p. 741. "It is not education, but a
perversion and corruption of nature, when the mind is inflamed with the love of
pleasure, and the body with lust." Nor are the precepts of Plutarch, in his excellent
treatise of education, less grave and serious.

† How propense youth is to imitation, is plain from the many instances of those,
who being bred up among the brutes, acquire their gestures, their voice and fierceness
to such a degree, that they are hardly distinguishable from them. Instances of this
sort are collected by Lambert Schaffnab. ad annum 1344. Hartknoch. de Polon lib.
I. cap. 2. p. 108. Bern. Connor. Evang. med. art. 115. p. 181. & de statu Polon. part.
I. ep. 6. p. 388. [[Hersfeld, *Lamperti Monachis Hersfeldensis opera;* Hartknoch, *De
republica Polonica libri duo;* Connor, *Evangelium medici seu medicina mystica.* The
work "de statu Polon." is presumably Hagemeier's *Iuris publici Europaei de statu Regni
Poloniae et imperii Moscovitici epistola VIII.*]] In the Leipsick Acts 1707, p. 507. we
are told of a deaf and dumb boy, who, by frequenting the church, begun to imitate
all the motions and gestures of those he saw there, in such a serious-like manner, that
the clergy could no longer doubt of his having some sense of religion: And yet, when
he afterwards had learned to speak, it could not be found out in any way, that he had
ever had any notion of religion. [[*Acta eruditorum.* This was one of the most influential learned journals published in the German territories; it appeared between 1682
and 1731.]] If such be the force of example and imitation, is it to be wondered at,
that boys receive, as it were, a new nature from the society they frequent, and are by
drinking Circe's cup transformed into beasts.

distinguishing flatterers and parasites from true friends, corrupt from good masters, or inducements to vice from wholesome precepts. <56>

SECTION LXVI

The duties of children to their parents are easily deducible from the state and right of parents, and from the end of the society we are now considering. For since parents have the right of directing the actions of their children, hence it is plain, that they ought to be regarded by their children as superior and more perfect than them; and consequently that they ought to be loved by them with a love of reverence and obedience* (l. 1. §85); whence it follows, that children ought to pay all reverence and obedience to their parents (l. 1. §86), such reverence and obedience as is due to their perfection and superiority (l. 1. §87). <57>

Children owe their parents a love of reverence and obedience.

* Hence, all the ancients have acknowledged, that next to the love due to God, is that owing to parents. So Gellius Noct. Attic. 4. 13. to prove which, he quotes Cato, Massurius Sabinus & C. Caesar. [[Gellius, *Attic Nights* 5 (not 4).13, vol. 1.]] The golden verses of Pythagoras are yet more express to this purpose.

> *Primum immortales Divos pro lege colunto*
> *Et jusjurandum: heroas, clarum genus, inde.*
> *Daemones hinc, terris mixti, sua jura ferunto.*
> *Inde parentis honos sequitor; tum sanguinis ordo.*

[["First let the immortal gods be worshipped in accordance with the law, and oaths: then the heroes, that famous race, next let spirits which are mixed with earth bring their laws, then let the honour due to a parent follow; then the order of blood." The verses are a Latin translation of the first four lines of the golden verses, which are in Greek (see Hierocles, *Commentary on the Golden Verses*).]]

In commenting upon which verses in his way, Hierocles observes, that in parents there is the image of God. And Simplicius ad Epictet. Enchirid. c. 37. p. 199. tells us, "That the more ancient Roman laws pay'd such veneration to parents, that they did not hesitate to call them (Deos) *Gods:* And out of reverence to this divine excellence, they called a father's brothers (Thios) *Divine,* to shew the high respect they thought was due by children to parents." [[Simplicius, *On Epictetus' Handbook,* vol. 2, p. 56. This is a commentary on chap. 30 of Epictetus' text.]]

SECTION LXVII

Veneration is due to parents. Because parents ought to be revered with a respect suitable to their perfection (§66), none can doubt but children are bound to prefer their parents before all others, to speak honourably to them, and of them; yea, to take care not so much as to shew disrespect by any look. And tho' it may happen, that one of the parents, or both, may not have the perfections requisite to beget veneration (l. 1. §87),* yet it is the duty of a good child to overlook these imperfections, and rather to bear injuries from them with patience, than to omit any thing which nature itself requires of children.

SECTION LXVIII

As likewise filial fear. Since parents have power or right to direct their childrens actions, and to curb and correct them, (§55), the consequence is, that parents ought not only to be loved and revered, but feared. From this mixture of love and fear arises filial fear (l. 1. §131);† and therefore we cannot choose but

---

* For even bad parents are still parents, *i.e.* they are, as Simplicius, ibidem p. 198. justly calls them, the authors of our existence next to God: And this perfection alone ought to incite us to dutifulness and reverence to our parents. Epictet. Enchirid. c. 37. says, "But he is a bad father. Have you then no union by nature but with a good father? No sure, the union is with a father, as such. Do therefore your duty to him, and do not consider what he does, but how your own conduct will be agreeable to nature." [[Epictetus, "The Manual," chap. 30 of *The Discourses as Reported by Arrian, the Manual, and Fragments,* vol. 2.]]

† What is said of the commands of magistrates by the apostles St. Peter and St. John ("Whether it is more just to obey God or you, do you yourselves judge, Acts iv. 19." "Is it better to obey God or men, Acts v. 29.") may be applied to the precepts of parents. For tho' their authority be sacred, yet that of God is more such: Nor does the paternal authority extend so far as to free their children from the laws of the supreme magistrate (§23). Hierocles, in his commentary upon the golden verses of Pythagoras reasons thus: "If any order of parents be repugnant to the divine will, what else ought they to do to whom such a collision of laws happens, but to follow the same rule that ought to be observed in other cases, where there is a competition of duties? Two honest goods or pleasures being proposed, which cannot be both enjoyed, the greater ought to be preferred to the lesser. Thus, *e.g.* it is certainly duty to obey God; but it is also duty to obey our parents. If therefore both obligations

con-<58>clude from hence, that good children will only have this filial fear of their parents; and thus they will not be so much afraid of the pain, the castigation and reprehension of their parents will give themselves, as of provoking their parents indignation against them by their vices.

SECTION LXIX

But because obedience is likewise due to parents, (§66), children cannot escape reproof and chastisement, if they do not readily and cheerfully obey their parents commands; and the morosity and severity of parents does not authorize children to withdraw their obedience. Yet, because right reason teaches us, that the greater the perfection and excellence of a being is, the greater veneration and obedience is due to that being (l. 1. §87),* the consequence is, that if parents command any thing that is base and immoral, or contrary to the divine will, and to the laws of the country, more regard is to be had to the divine will and the laws, than to the commands of parents.* <59>

As also obedience.

SECTION LXX

Moreover, since the necessity of the parents right to direct childrens actions is the sole genuine foundation of parental power (§52), none can question but that end being gained, the means must cease; and therefore the parental power does not continue till death, but expires then, when male-children are come to such maturity of years and judgment, that they are capable of directing themselves, and can make a new family, or when daughters and grand-daughters marry, and go out of their father's or grandfather's house into other families; so that the law of nature does

How parental power is dissolved.

---

concur and draw you the same way, it is a double and unexpected gain, and without controversy the greatest good. But if the divine law draw one way, and the will of parents another, in this disagreement of laws, it is best to follow the better will, and to neglect the will and command of parents in these cases, in which parents themselves do not obey God."

* [[See preceding note.]]

not approve that rigour of the old Roman law, which placed children, with their wives and children, under the father's power, till fathers or grand-fathers, of their own free accord, emancipated and dismissed them.*

SECTION LXXI

Parental power being dissolved, love ought not to cease.

But when the parental power is dissolved (§70), that love which nature hath implanted in the breasts <60> of parents towards their children ought not to cease. And therefore it is the duty of parents to delight in the welfare and happiness of their children, even after they are separated from them, and out of their family; to assist them with their counsel and their wealth to the utmost of their power, and to be no less beneficent to them than to those which are still in their family; and, in fine, to do all they can to promote their happiness: Whence it is also evident, why emancipated children ought to succeed to intestate parents as well as those who are not.†

* This flows from the paternal power, or the dominium juris Quiritium peculiar to the Romans. For time did not put an end to this dominion; nor could any one lose it without some deed of his own. Hence those imaginary sellings made use of in emancipations. For nothing appeared more consistent than that (res mancipi) things in full possession and dominion should be alienated by selling. See A. Corn. van Bynkershoek de jure occid. lib. cap. 1. p. 145. [[The work referred to concerns the right of the ancient Romans to kill and expose their children (Bynkershoek, *Curae secundae de jure occidendi et exponendi liberos apud veteres Romanos*).]] But this dominion over children, as *res mancipi,* being unknown to the law of nature (§54), this rigour we have above described, cannot belong to it.

† Wherefore, in this matter, many nations seem to have departed from natural equity, in which married daughters, having got a certain patrimony by way of dowry, were obliged to content themselves with it, and were excluded from any farther share or succession to the paternal inheritance. This law was amongst the Hebrews founded on a very solid reason, because such was the frame of that republic, that every tribe had its lot, which could not pass to any other tribe, Num. xxvii. But the Syrian custom, of which we see an instance, Gen. xxxi. 14. & seq. was not equally commendable. See a curious dissertation by Jacob Perizonius, de lege voconia, p. 119. where there are several learned observations on this subject. [[Perizonius, *Dissertationum trias.*]] Much less still can we approve of the Roman law, which excluded emancipated sons from succession to the paternal inheritance, since the Praetor had a power to soften the rigour of it, and since Justinian entirely abrogated it, Novella 1. 118. For eman-

SECTION LXXII

Hence we also conclude, that it is not in the power of parents, at their will and pleasure, to dismiss children, of whatever age, from their family, nor to retain adult children under their power so long as they please; but yet, that children are not excusable in deserting parents against their <61> will, and in refusing to submit to their authority. For as it is unjust in parents to omit any thing without which the end of this society cannot be attained (§24); so children cannot, without injustice, shake off their parents authority; because what one would not have done to himself, he ought not to do to others (l. 1. §88).

Whether it be in the power of the parents and children to dissolve the parental power at their pleasure.

SECTION LXXIII

As the love of parents ought not to be extinguished when parental power is dissolved (§71), so that love of veneration which children owe to their parents ought much less to cease with parental power; yea, since every one is bound to love his benefactor (which love is called *gratitude*) (§226); the consequence is, that children, after the parental power no longer takes place, are obliged to testify gratitude towards their parents every way; not merely by words, but to repay benefits by benefits; and therefore to undertake nothing of any moment, or that regards the honour of the family, (such as marriage) without their consent; nay, to supply them with the necessaries and conveniencies of life, if they want them. This kind of gratitude, tho' it belongs to the duties of imperfect obligation, yet it is of such a peculiar nature, that civil laws may reduce children, unmindful of their filial duties, into good order* (l. 1. §227). <62>

The obligations of children to parents after parental power is dissolved.

---

cipation ought only to dissolve parental power, and not parental love, from which we have shewn that succession to intestates ought to be derived (l. 1. §295).

* If what is told of the storks be true, that they provide for their aged parents, those brute creatures reproach children who neglect their duty to parents. "The storks (says Aelian. Hist. animal. 3. 23.) take tender care of their aged infirm parents: tho' they be commanded to do this by no laws, yet they are led to it by the goodness of their nature." [[Aelian, *De natura animalium* 3.23 (Aelian, *On the characteristics of*

SECTION LXXIV

The mutual
obligation
of tutors
and pupils.

If parents die before children have arrived at a proper age to conduct themselves, the nature of the thing requires that their education should be committed to others, who are called *tutors* or *guardians;* and therefore guardianship is nothing else, but the power of directing the actions of children, and of managing their affairs and interests in room of their parents, till the children are come to such maturity of years and judgment, as to be fit to govern themselves* (§54). From which definition we may infer, that tutors have the same power with parents, if it be not circumscribed by the civil laws within narrower bounds; and are obliged to the same fidelity, and all the same duties as parents; and, in fine, that pupils or wards are no less obliged to veneration, gratitude and obedience, than children; and that this obligation is so much the more strict, that the benefit done them is greater, when performed not in consequence of any natural tie, but from pure benevolence. <63>

---

animals, bk. 3, chap. 23, p. 183).]] But shall not reason persuade men to what nature excites the very brutes?

* How long children are to be held minors, the law of nature cannot determine, so different are the capacities, geniuses and dispositions of children, some becoming very early wise, and others continuing very long fools. But, because legislators in such cases attend to what ordinarily happens (§44), they have done well to fix a certain period to minority. But how various their determinations have been in this matter, is shewn by testimonies collected from the most ancient histories, in a dissertation of Jo. Petrus a Ludewig, de aetate legitima puberum & majorennium. [[Johann Peter von Ludewig (1668–1743), historian, philosopher, and professor of law at Halle. From 1721 he was chancellor of the University of Halle, and the relationship between Heineccius and Ludewig was not free of tension and competition. The work referred to here is his *De aetate legitima puberum et maiorvm.*]]

Concerning the duties belonging to masters and servants, and that despotical society.

SECTION LXXV

We now proceed to consider the *society of master and servants,* which is not, by nature, so necessary as the more simple societies of which we have already treated, but yet has been most frequent among mankind from the most antient times. And by it we understand a society between a master or mistress, and men or women-servants, in which the latter bind themselves to promote their master's interest by their work and labour, and the former bind themselves to maintain them; nay, sometimes to pay them a certain hire or wages. For since such is the condition of mankind, that one stands in need of another's work; and there is no reason why one may not procure to himself what he wants by another's help (l. 1. §325); the consequence of which is, that we may stipulate to ourselves the help or work of others by an intervening contract, and thus form between us and servants a despotic society, which is evidently, in its nature, unequal and rectoreal (§18).

Wherein the despotical society consists, and its origine.

SECTION LXXVI

By *master* or *mistress* we therefore understand a person who employs others to promote his interest, and obliges himself to maintain them, or over and above to pay them certain wages. *Servants* are persons who bind themselves to promote their masters interest by their labour, either for

What is a master or a mistress, and what a man or woman-servant?

their maintenance only, or for wages, together with maintenance. Now, from these definitions it is manifest, that servitude of the latter kind is mercenary, and <64> its foundation is none other than *a contract of letting and hiring;* the former is perfect servitude, and may be called *obnoxia, property;** and its foundation is dominion over the persons of servants acquired by a just title.

SECTION LXXVII

Some give themselves up to perfect servitude on account of their dullness and incapacity.

That mercenary servitude is not contrary to the law of nature none can doubt; but neither is the other servitude, since experience teaches us, that some men are naturally of so servile minds, that they are not capable to govern themselves or a family, nor to provide for themselves the necessaries of life.† But since every one ought to choose the kind of life he

---

* I use the word used by Phaedrus Fab. l. 3. praef. v. 34.

> *Servitus* obnoxia,
> *Quia, quae volebat, non audebat dicere,*
> *Adfectus proprios in fabellas transtulit.*

> [[Phaedrus, *Fabulae,* introduction to bk. 3, lines 34–35: "Slavery was hateful; because he did not dare say what he wanted, he transferred his own feelings into his fables."]]

The Greeks distinguished between servants, which were property, whom they called δούλους, and domestic or hired servants, whom they called οἰκέτας, according to Athenaeus Deipnos. 6. 19. [[Athenaeus, *The Deipnosophists,* vol. 3, sec. 267, p. 203: "But that 'domestics' may mean anyone living in the house, even if he be a free person, is generally known."]] Both kinds of servitude are very ancient. It is plain from Genesis, xi. 5. xiv. 14. xv. 3. 4. xvi. 1. & seq. that Abraham had many servants, *obnoxii,* or perfect servants, in the fourth age from the deluge. So that Jacob served Laban as a mercenary servant for many years, is well known from Genes. xxix. 15. xxx. 28. Nay, Noah makes mention of perfect servitude, Gen. ix. 25. And he condemns Chanaan to it for injuries he had done to him. But Jo. Clericus Comment. in Genes. p. 72. has justly observed, that this was rather a prediction of what was to happen a little after. [[Jean le Clerc, *Genesis sive Mosis prophetae liber primus.*]]

† This was observed by Aristotle, who says, that some men are φύσει δούλους, servants by nature, Polit. 1. 3. For tho' Pufendorff of the law of nature, &c. 3. 28. & 6. 3. 2. had reason to refute this philosopher, if his meaning were, that persons by

is fitted for, (l. 1. §147), and such persons are fit for no other kind of life, but to serve others for their maintenance, they certainly do nothing contrary to their duty, if they give themselves up perpetually to others on that condition. <65>

SECTION LXXVIII

Besides, extreme poverty, and other private or public calamities, may induce some, who are not stupid, to become servants rather than perish. For since man is obliged to preserve his life, and to avoid death and destruction (l. 1. §143), and of two imminent evils, the least ought to be chosen; it follows, that he whom providence hath placed in this situation, is not to be blamed, if, there being no other honest way of avoiding death, he give himself up in servitude.*

Some thro' extreme poverty.

---

their prudence, had a perfect right of enslaving, without any other cause, those who are stupid, as the Greeks arrogated a right to themselves over the nations they called barbarous; yet there is no absurdity in this saying, if it be understood of a servile disposition, and of a natural condition, as Dan. Heinsius thinks it ought to be, epist. ad Ge. Richterum, apud Jan. Rutgers. var. lect. 4. 3. [[Daniel Heinsius (1580–1655), Dutch scholar and professor of Latin and Greek at Leiden. Heineccius is probably referring to Jan Rutgers's *Variarum lectionum libri sex.*]] In this sense Agesilaus says, in Plutarch, apophtheg. Lacon. p. 190. that the Asiatics were bad freemen, but excellent slaves. [[Plutarch, "Sayings of Spartans," p. 333, in Plutarch, *Moralia: in Fourteen Volumes,* vol. 3. This is a statement by Callicratidas rather than Agesilaus.]]

* Thus the Egyptians gave themselves up to their king as servants, that they might not perish by famine, and held it for a favour that Pharaoh would accept of their service for their living or maintenance. Hence, having accepted of the condition of servitude, they answered Joseph, Gen. xlvii. 25. "Thou hast given us our lives, let us find favour in thy sight, and let us be servants to Pharaoh." Thus Pausanias tells us, l. 7. c. 5. "That the Thracian women, tho' freeborn, earned their bread among the Erythraei, by voluntary servitude" [[Pausanias, *Description of Greece,* vol. 3, "Achaia," chap. V, p. 197]]; not now to mention the Frisians, of whom Tacitus, Annal. 4. 72. nor the Gauls, of whom Julius Caesar de bello Gallic. 6. 13.

SECTION LXXIX

Some con-
quered in war
accept of this
condition.

Again, the fury of war much augmented the number of servants. For because all things are lawful to an enemy against an enemy, it is law-<66>ful to kill a subdued enemy (l. 1. §183). But because he who can deliver himself from danger without hurting his aggressor, or by a lesser evil, ought not rashly to proceed to killing (ibid. §181), it is certainly not unjust for a conqueror to save the vanquished, and lead them captives, that they may no longer have it in their power to hurt him; and to make servants of them, that he may not have the burden of maintaining them gratis; nor can they be blamed who choose to save their lives on these terms, rather than perish.*

SECTION LXXX

Some are born
servants.

But these kinds of perfect servitude cannot but produce the effect which one is detruded into by the very fortune of birth. For since the foundation of perfect servitude is dominion acquired by a just title (§76), and all those we have already mentioned are just titles (§76 & seq.) the consequence is, that all these servants are under the just dominion of their masters. But since out of lawful matrimony (which can hardly take place among some of those sorts of servants)† the offspring goes along

* Therefore, this society arises really from consent, tho' not voluntary, but extorted by just force (§15). For the conqueror is willing to save the conquered, but upon this condition that they become his servants; the conquered is willing to serve, that he may be saved. For if he would rather perish, what hindered him from rushing upon the conqueror's arms. Now the concurrence of two wills is consent (l. 1. §381). Wherefore, society between a master, and servants taken in war, arises from consent.

† Matrimony is a simple society between persons of different sexes, formed for the sake of procreation and education (§27). Those therefore who enter into this state, ought to have it in their power to consent to this end, and to choose it, and the means necessary to obtaining it. But the principal end, *viz.* convenient education, is not always in the power of perfect servants, but it depends wholly on the will of their master. Therefore, among some such men and women servants, there is no place for lawful matrimony. We say it cannot take place among some such, as those namely whom fortune has reduced to this condition, that their masters, after the manner of

with the mother (l. 1. §252) it is no wonder that the offspring of such women-servants undergo the same condition with the mother, as an accession to her; and therefore those kinds of servants are known to all nations, which were called by the Romans *vernae*. <67>

SECTION LXXXI

These principles being fixed, it is easy to find out the duties of masters and servants in this society, and what power masters have over their servants. For as to mercenary servants, since they are only bound by a contract of letting and hiring, (§76) the master has no other power over them, than to appoint the work to them for which they bind themselves, and to make profit by their work, and to force them to serve during the time for which they engaged: He has no right to exact any other work or service from them, but that for which they bind themselves; and much less to chastise them with great severity; tho', if the servant do not fulfil his contract, the master may not only mulct him of a part of his wages, but turn him away from him as incorrigible (§21). <68>

The power of a master over a mercenary servant.

SECTION LXXXII

As therefore it is the master's duty to fulfil his contract, and not to exact other service than was contracted for from his servant, and to maintain him as persons of that condition ought to be, and to pay him his promised wages;* so the servant is bound to reverence and obedience to his

The mutual duties of this master and servant.

---

the Romans might, descriptis per familiam ministeriis uti. But when every one has his fixed seat and abode, as among the Germans, (Tacit. de morib. Germ. c. 25.) there marriage among servants may more easily take place, as experience shews us. But tho' the proper slaves of the Germans have the *jus connubii*, liberty of marriage, yet this rule has force among them, that the birth follows the bearer, and is of the same condition with the parents, except where alternate sharing is established (l. 1. §252).

* But neither wages nor maintenance are due, if a servant, by his own fault, or by chance, is not able to perform the service he engaged to do (l. 1. §361). And therefore, tho' the humanity of those masters be very commendable, who maintain a servant while he is sick, yet what humanity enjoins cannot be exacted by perfect right. On

master as his superior; to perform his contracted service to him as his hirer, and to promote his interest with all fidelity as his partner.

SECTION LXXXIII

The power of a master over a perfect servant with respect to the disposal of him.

Perfect servants, we have said, are in dominion, (§76). But since he who hath the dominion of any thing, hath the free disposal of it (l. 1. §306); the consequence is, that a master may impose upon such a servant any work he is capable of; make all profit by him; claim him and his children as his property, and sell or alienate him and them upon any terms, unless the servant, who voluntarily delivered himself into servitude, made this condition, that he should not go out of the family, or be alienated to any other master. As to the power of life and death, none will deny that it belongs to such masters (l. 1. §308) unless either convention or law forbid it. Much less then can it be denied, <69> that such masters have a power to coerce and chastise such servants according to the exigence of the case, provided the master still bear in mind that his servant is a man, and by nature his equal* (l. 1. §177).

---

the other hand, it is most iniquitous in a master to deny a servant who has done his work, the wages due to him, or to change his wages at his pleasure, contrary to the terms of their contract, as Jacob complained that Laban had done ten times, Gen. xxxi. 7. This conduct of Laban was so displeasing to God, that he took all his wealth from him, and transferred it to Jacob, Gen. ibid. 9.

* For tho' a servant may happen to be more perfect than his master, yet it cannot be denied that the master is his servant's superior: And this diversity of perfections and states, does not alter the essence of man; so that a servant is still equally with his master, a man (l. 1. 177). That maxim of the civilians is therefore far from being humane, "That no injury can be done to a servant or slave," l. 15. §35. D. de injur. And that saying of a mistress in Juvenal is most inhumane. Sat. 6. v. 223.

> *O demens, ita servus homo est? Nil fecerit: esto*
> *Sic volo, sic jubeo, stet pro ratione voluntas.*

[[Juvenal, *Satires*, Satire 6, lines 223–24, in *Juvenal and Persius:* "You idiot! Is a slave a person? All right, let's accept that he hasn't done anything. But it's my wish and my command. Let my will be reason enough."]]

He is therefore no less excusable who hurts a servant, than he who hurts a free-man.

SECTION LXXXIV

Since to a master belongs the possession of his own, and the right of reclaiming it from every person (l. 1. §306) hence it follows, that a master may defend himself in the possession of his maid or woman-servant by any means, and reclaim his servants, whether they desert, or whether they are unjustly carried off, from any one whomsoever, with the fruits or profits, and accessions of the possession; and, in the first case, to punish the renegade according to his desert, and to take proper and effectual measures to prevent his taking the same course for the future;* unless this effect of the master's dominion be restricted by the civil laws (l. 1. §317). <70>

With respect to possession and vindication.

* Hence home-shackles, prisons, houses of correction, and other methods which necessity obliged to, or the cruelty of masters, allowing themselves all corporal power over their slaves, invented. For tho' here regard ought to be had to humanity and benevolence (§83), yet the coercive power ought not to be taken from masters, especially over servants taken in war, partly because such are upon the catch to find an opportunity of flying and returning to their own country (which is not so very blameable, as Lorarius in Plautus observes, Plaut. Captiv. 2. 1. v. 14.

> Lo. *At fugam fingitis. Sentio, quam rem agitis.*
> Cap. *Nos fugiamus? quo fugiamus?* Lo. *in patriam.*
>   Cap. *apage! haud nos id deceat,*
> *Fugitivos imitari.* Lo. *Immo, aedepol, si erit occasio, non dehortor.*)

> [[Plautus, *The Captives,* lines 208–10, in *Plautus,* vol. 1: "'Ah yes, you're planning to run for it! I see what's afoot.' 'Run—we? Where should we run to?' 'Home.' 'Get out! The idea of our acting like runaway slaves!' 'Lord! why not? I'm not saying you shouldn't, if you get the chance.'"]]

partly because they still preserve a hostile disposition, insomuch, that what Seneca says is particularly true of such servants, Ep. 47. So likewise Festus in voce: quot servi. "Totidem quemque domi hostes habere, quot servos." So many slaves at home, so many enemies at home. [[Festus, *De verborum significatu quae supersunt cum Pauli epitome.*]]

SECTION LXXXV

The duties of masters to such servants. It will not now be difficult to ascertain the mutual duties of masters and such servants. For because an *obnoxious* or perfect servant is in dominion, (§76) and therefore a master may make all the gain he can of such (§83), so that such a servant hath nothing in property; the consequence is, that the master is obliged to maintain such a servant, and this obligation does not cease, then especially, when he is not able to perform his service.* And since a servant is, with regard to nature, equal to his master (§83) it is obvious, that the master is culpable if he injuriously hurts his servant; and he is worthy of commendation, if he endeavours to reform a disobedient servant by benefits rather than by cruel methods. <71>

SECTION LXXXVI

The duties of servants to their masters. Because as many different kinds as there are of servitude, so many duties of servants there are, as correlates to the several rights of masters (l. 1. §7) hence it follows, that perfect servitude obliges a slave to every sort of work or service, to promote his master's interest to the utmost of his power, and to bear chastisement and correction, and the disposal of him and his at his master's will, with patience. That he acts contrary to his duty, if he deserts his master, or defrauds his master, by stealing, as it were, himself away from him; and that he ought rather to endeavour to

---

* A mercenary servant, besides his maintenance, receives wages (§82), so that he has something wherewithall to sustain himself, if he be disabled by sickness or accident from performing his work; wherefore, since the master is obliged to maintain such a servant only by the contract of hiring (§76), he is not perfectly bound to the alimenting of such a servant, who is not able to serve (§82). But with respect to a perfect servant or slave, the case is different: For he is not maintained for his work, but as being under his master's dominion, and having no wages, he has nothing belonging to him. Besides, charity and humanity oblige us to assist even strangers and enemies (l. 1. §219); and therefore, with what face can we deny sustenance to a sick slave, who has worn himself out in our service? Hence the Emperor Claudian gave their liberty to slaves, who were exposed in their sickness by their cruel masters, Sueton. in Claud. c. 25. l. 2. D. qui sine manum.

merit his liberty and manumission by faithful and cordial service, thus rendering himself worthy of so great a benefit.

SECTION LXXXVII

From what hath been said, we may easily understand how this society is dissolved. Mercenary servitude, depending upon a contract of letting and hiring, is dissolved in the same manner such contracts are dissolved, and more especially by the expiration of the time contracted for. Perfect servitude is principally dissolved by manumission. For since any one may derelinquish or abdicate his own (l. 1. §309), there is no doubt but a master may renounce his right to a servant, which renunciation was called by the antients *manumission*. Besides, renunciation being a kind of alienation, and seeing <72> in alienation one may except or reserve what he pleases (l. 1. §278) it is plain that manumission may likewise be granted upon any honest conditions whatsoever.*

How servitude is dissolved.

SECTION LXXXVIII

Those slaves who are manumitted by their masters are called *libertini,* and the *liberti* of the manumittor. Now, since masters, who give liberty to their slaves, confer upon them the greatest benefit they can bestow; and every one is obliged to love him who bestows favours upon him (l. 1. §226); slaves set at liberty (*liberti*) are the most ungrateful of mortals, unless they love the patrons who conferred so great a blessing upon them, and they are obliged to pay the highest veneration to them, and not only

What a freed man is, and what are his duties.

---

* Thus the old Romans at manumission stipulated to themselves certain handicraft-works, presents or gifts, l. 3. pr. l. 5. l. 7. §3. D. de oper. libert. And our ancestors, when they manumitted their slaves, reserved a right to themselves to exact from them such services as their mercenary servants, or even slaves were wont to perform to them; so that abstracting from the title and condition of the servitude, there was hardly any difference between slaves and libertines among them. And hence Tacitus de moribus Germ. says, "That their freed-men were not in a much more preferable state than their slaves." [[Tacitus, *Germania* 25.2, p. 87.]]

to perform to them cheerfully all that their masters stipulated to themselves upon giving them their liberty (§87) but likewise to be ready to render to them all other good offices in their power; or, if the power of serving them be wanting, at least to shew gratitude towards them in every manner they can* (l. 1. §228). <73>

* The ancients looked upon giving liberty to slaves as the greatest of benefits. Simo in Terence says, And. l. 1. v. 10.

> *Feci, e servo ut esses libertus mihi,*
> *Propterea, quod serviebas liberaliter:*
> *Quod habui, summum pretium persolvi tibi.*

[[Terence, *The Woman of Andros,* act 1, lines 37–40, in *Terence,* vol. 1: "You were my slave, but I gave you your freedom, because you served me with the spirit of a free man. I bestowed upon you the highest reward that was in my power."]]

For the Patron, by giving his liberty to a slave made him a *person:* and therefore, he was to the freed-man in the room of a father, who on that account assumed his patron's name, as if he were his son, Lactant. divin. Inst. 4. 3. Hence he was no less obliged than a son to provide an aliment for his patron, if he happened to be in want, l. 5. §18. l. 9. D. de agnosc. & alend. lib. And as a son, tho' the obligation to gratitude be otherwise imperfect, was forced to repay the benefits received from his father, and to maintain him; so the freed-slave was forced to do the same, and could be reduced into slavery again for pregnant ingratitude, Inst. §1. de cap. diminut. l. un. C. de ingrat. lib.

Of the complex society called a family, and the duties to be observed in it.

SECTION LXXXIX

We observed that lesser or more simple societies may coalesce or unite into larger and more *compounded* ones (§17): and of this the societies we have described afford us an example. For when these join and consent into a larger society, hence arises *a family,* which is a society compounded of the conjugal, the paternal and despotic society.* Whence the husband and wife, parents, masters and mistresses, with respect to this society, are called *fathers* and *mothers,* or *heads of a family;* the children are called *sons and daughters of the family,* and the men or women-servants are called *domestics.* <74>

What a family is.

---

* Ulpian's definition comes to the same purpose, l. 195. §2. D. de verb. signif. "We call *a family,* with its proper rights, as such, many persons subjected to one head, either by nature or by law, (ut puta patremfamilias, matremfamilias, filiumfamilias, filiamfamilias), and those who succeed into their room, as grandsons and grand-daughters, *&c.* But we take the term in a somewhat larger acceptation. For, whereas he only comprehends husband and wife, parents and children, we comprehend servants as a part of a family; as he himself a little afterwards calls them, §3. 'servitium quoque solemus vocare *familiam,*' we also reckon servants a part of the family." Besides, among the ancients *family* signified the servants, "quasi familia," as Claud. Salmas. exercit. Plin. p. 1263. has shewn. [[Saumaise (Salmasius), *Plinianae exercitationes in Caji Julii Solini Polyhistora.*]] And the parents and children were called by them *domus,* the house, as in Apuleius Apolog. p. 336. "ipse *domi* tuae rector, ipse *familiae* dominus." [[Apuleius, *Rhetorical Works* 98.7, p. 116: "In your house he and none but he is the man in charge, the one who issues orders to the staff."]] We shall therefore use the word *family,* to denote what the ancients called *domus* and *familia.*

SECTION XC

To whom the direction or government belongs in this society.

But because the larger a society is, the less practicable is it that so many members should find out necessary means for attaining the end of the society by common consent and suffrage (§18) it is evident that this society must be unequal and rectoreal; and therefore that the power of directing the rest to the end of the society, must be transferred to one of the members. Now, since the husband and father of the family has a certain authority or prerogative over the wife (§44) and his command, as father, ought to prevail over the mother's when they disagree (§53); and since he hath, as master, undoubted power over his servants of whatever sort; (§81 and 83) the power of directing the actions of the whole family must belong to the *father;* * but in such a manner however, that the mother is obliged, as sharer of his good or bad fortune, to give him all the assistance she can of every kind (§42). <75>

SECTION XCI

The end of this society in a state of nature, and in a civil state.

Now, such a family is either in a state of nature, subject to none, or it is united with other families into one state. In the first case, the end of this society is not only to acquire the things necessary to its happy subsistence, but likewise to defend itself against all invaders or enemies; and therefore they judge right, who consider such a family as a species of the lesser states or republics.† In the latter case, because every family is pro-

---

* But this is to be understood of what ordinarily or regularly happens. For that it is sometimes otherwise, we have already shown (§46). Who will deny that a queen who marries a stranger is still head of her family, and that in this case, no other part belongs to the husband but what regularly belongs to the wife, *viz.* to give all manner of assistance to his queen-wife? We have very recent examples of this.

† Thus Aristotle considers it, Polit. 3. 6. where he says, that segregate heads of families, living by themselves, are with their families as states, and defend themselves by the members of their families against all injurious invaders. Nor does Hobbes philosophize about the manner differently. Leviath. c. 20. Tho' properly indeed such a family be not a state, as Aristotle acknowledges a little after, where he says, "Yet if we accurately consider the matter, it is not properly a city or state"; yet it is very like to one, and when it grows up into a great multitude of persons, it becomes a state or

tected against the injuries of their fellow citizens or subjects by judges, and against common enemies, by the common strength of the republic, its end can be no other but the acquisition of things necessary to its more comfortable and happy subsistence.

SECTION XCII

But since the end of this domestic society, in a state of nature, is not only to acquire the necessaries to convenient and comfortable living, but likewise to defend itself against injuries (§91) the consequence is, that the father of the family has all <76> the rights necessary to attain to these ends; and therefore he may not only manage the family estate and interest as seems best to him, and allot to every one in the family his care and task, and call every one to an account for his management; but he has likewise all the rights of a prince or supreme magistrate in his family, and consequently can make laws, punish delinquents, make war and peace, and enter into treaties.*

The power of the head or father in a state of nature.

SECTION XCIII

On the other hand, since the end of a family, coalited with other families into the same state, can be no other but the acquisition of necessaries and conveniencies (§91), it is very plain that such eminent rights do not

In a civil state.

---

republic, as Plato observes in Politic. t. 2. op. edit. Serrani. [[A reference to Jean Serres' edition of Plato's works (see Plato, *Platonis opera quae extant omnia*).]]

* We have examples of this in the patriarchs Abraham, Isaac, and Jacob, who, as princes, or heads of segregate families, exercised all the rights of sovereignty. Thus Abraham, when he heard his brother Lot was taken captive, armed his trained servants born in his own house, and joined with certain confederates, and made war against the enemy, Gen. xiv. 14. The same Abraham entred into an alliance with Abimelech, Gen. xxi. 22. which was afterwards renewed by Isaac, Gen. xxvi. 26. Jacob in like manner made a covenant with Laban, Gen. xxxi. 44. and his family made war (tho' an unjust one) against Hamor and his son Shechem, Gen. xxxiv. 25. Jacob likewise gave a law to his houshold about putting away strange gods from among them, Gen. xxxv. 2. Judah, his son, condemned his daughter-in-law to be burnt, Gen. xxxviii. 24, 25. Of these facts Nicolaus Damascenus was not ignorant. Excerpt. Peiresc. p. 490. See likewise Justin. 36. 2.

belong to the heads of such families, but those only which we described (§92), without which the family cannot have a comfortable subsistence; and in this case the mother has some share; whereas the modesty and character of her sex does not permit her to partake of <77> those rights which belong to the father of a family, as the supreme magistrate of the family.

SECTION XCIV

Simple socie-
ties ought not
to be an im-
pediment to
this more
complex
society.

Moreover, since in more complex societies the interest of the more simple or lesser ought not to be opposed to that of the larger (§23), it is plain, that the conjugal, the paternal, the domestic societies ought not to be an obstacle to the end and interest of the whole united family;* and hence arise certain duties peculiar to this complex society, some of which belong to the father and mother with regard to one another; others to both, with respect to the other members of the family; others to the members of this family, with respect to the father and mother of the family; and others, in fine, to the members with relation one to another. See Wolfius de vita sociali hominum, §194.[1]

SECTION XCV

The mutual
duties of the
father and
mother of the
family towards
one another,
and their
duties to the
family.

Since the father hath the principal part or character in this society (§90); but so, that the mother is obliged to give him all possible assistance in every way (ibid.); it follows, that it belongs to the father of the family to command what he would have done, to maintain the whole family, and each member, as every one's condition requires, to coerce and punish those who do any injury or dishonour to the family, suitably to what the rights of a more simple society permit, and to support the dignity and

---

* Because, in this case, one and the same person sustains several different personages or characters, he is under so many respective obligations, and has so many respective rights correspondent to, and depending upon these different characters and relations of husband, father, and head of the family.

1. Christian Wolff, *Vernünftige Gedanken von dem gesellschaftlichen Leben der Menschen und insonderheit dem gemeinen Wesen.*

authority of the mother; and it is her duty to use her utmost care that the children and servants obey their orders;* to act in the husband's room in <78> his absence; and, in fine, to shew an example to the whole family of veneration and obedience, being sure to have so much the more authority in the family, in proportion as she studies to maintain and augment that of her husband.

SECTION XCVI

Now, if the simpler societies ought to be so managed, that they may not be a hindrance to the good of the whole family (§94), it is manifest that the father acts contrary to his duty, if he is an impediment to the mother in her care about the education of their children; and she is much less excusable, if she makes the rebellious children worse by her indulgence; and both are in the wrong, if they by their discords and jarrs, are a bad example to the children, or if they are negligent of their education and behaviour. In like manner it is evident, that a domestic society must be in a very bad state, if the children are left to the care of the servants, and are allowed to converse with them at their pleasure; or if, on the one hand, the servants give ill advice to children, and induce them to, or assist them in any crime; or if, on the other hand, the children are suffered to treat the servants rudely.† <79>

The duties of both with regard to the simpler societies.

---

* Socrates says in Xenophon. Oecon. c. 3. §15. "I think a wife who is a good partner in a family, contributes as much to its interest as the husband. For very often wealth is brought by the husband's industry into a house, and the greater part of it is at the management of the wife, which, if it be good, the family is enriched, if bad, it is ruined." [[Xenophon, *Memorabilia and Oeconomicus*, p. 389.]]

† For most servants being of the very dregs of mankind, and therefore very ill educated, it is impossible but children must be corrupted by them. We see how justly they are represented in Plautus and Terence, as often corrupting the children by flattery, and exciting them to or assisting them in very bad practices. Plutarch upon education wisely observes, "If you live with a lame person, you will insensibly learn to halt." And hence he infers, "That nothing can be more absurd and unreasonable than the very common practice, when one has many good servants, some fit for agriculture, some for navigation, some for merchandize, some for banking, others to be stewards, if he finds one slave that is idle, drunken, and unfit for every other business, to set him over his children." [[Plutarch, "The Education of Children," pp. 17–

SECTION XCVII

In a well
regulated
family all is in
good order.

Hence it is plain, that the whole matter lies in preserving good order in a family. But then are things said to be done in order, when all things are managed and done as the circumstances of each affair requires. And therefore in a family every one ought to have some business or task appointed to him, and to give a strict account of it; and each person ought to be inured to do his business, not only with due care and diligence, but also at a convenient time, and in a proper place; and, in fine, all the furniture, and every utensil ought to be kept neat, clean, and intire, and every thing ought to be found in the place appointed for it, or where it is proper and convenient it should be placed.* <80>

SECTION XCVIII

The duties of
the inferior
members of
a family.

From what hath been said of the duties of the whole *family*, it is obvious, that since all the members expect aliment from the head, each suitably to his rank (§95) every one of them is obliged to take care of the common interest of the whole body, and of that part committed to his trust in particular, to render reverence and obedience to the father and mother of the family; and, above all, to do nothing that may tend to interrupt the conjugal harmony, or to hinder the education of the children; or to

---

19 in Plutarch, *Moralia: in Fourteen Volumes,* vol. 1.]] But it is evidently much the same in effect, whether parents commit the care of their children to worthless persons, or suffer them to be familiar with them.

* All this Xenophon hath delightfully explained in his golden treatise of oeconomics, where he introduces Ischomachus discoursing with his wife about the management and oeconomy of a family. And cap. 8. she sums up all thus: That, as in a choir, in an army, or in a ship, so in a domestic society, there is a first, a second, and a last order, and that the perturbation of this order throws all into confusion, and renders the largest stock of furniture useless. In the 8. chapter she adds, "The disturbance of order seems to be like a farmer's throwing wheat, barley, and legumes, all together in a heap; and then when he wants bread, kitchen-stuff, or any other thing, he must have the trouble of separating them, and to search through the whole confused mass for what he has present need of." [[Xenophon, *Oeconomicus,* chap. VIII, pp. 429–33, in *Memorabilia and Oeconomicus.*]]

bereave the head of the profits he might justly expect from the labour, honesty, and diligence of his servants.

Remarks on This Chapter

Our Author hath treated very distinctly and fully of the duties of the simpler societies, as he very properly calls them. But because it is common in arguing about government, or the civil state, to which our author is now to proceed, especially among the defenders of absolute monarchy, to reason from the right of paternity, it will not be improper to consider domestic or family dominion in its natural causes. This will prepare the way for the consideration of civil government, or dominion in its natural causes; And it is the more necessary, because the defenders of absolute monarchy, in their reasonings to prove its *jus divinum,* from the right of paternity, or the government of families, conceal, as Mr. Harrington observes, one part of it. "For family government, says that excellent author (for it is from him, of his works p. 385. upon the foundations and superstructures of all kinds of government, I am now to transcribe) may be as necessarily popular in some cases, as monarchical in others. To shew now the nature of the monarchical family: Put the case a man has one thousand pounds a year, or thereabouts, he marries a wife, has children and servants depending upon him (at his good will) in the distribution of his estate for their livelihood. Suppose then that this estate comes to be spent or lost, where is the monarchy of this family? But if the master was no otherwise monarchical than by virtue of his estate, the foundation or balance of his empire consisted in the thousand pounds a year. That from these principles there may be also a popular family, <81> is apparent: For suppose six or ten, having each three hundred pounds a year, or so, shall agree to dwell together as one family, can any one of them pretend to be lord and master of the same, or to dispose of the estates of all the rest? or do they not agree together upon such orders, to which they consent equally to submit? But if so, then certainly must the government of this family be a government of laws or orders, and not the government of one, or of some three or four of these men. Yet the one man in the monarchical family giving laws, and the many in the popular family doing no more, it may in this sense be indifferently said, That all laws are made by men; but it is plain, where the law is made by one man, then it may be unmade by one man; so that the man is not governed by the law, but the law by the man; which amounts to the government of the men, and not of the law: whereas the law being not to be made but by the many, no man is governed by another man, but by that only which is the common interest; by which means this amounts to a government of laws, and not of men. That the politicks may not be thought an unnecessary or difficult art, if these principles be less than obvious and undeniable, even to any woman that knows house-keeping, I confess I have no more to say. But in case what has been said be to all sorts and capacities evident, *it may be referred to any one,* whether without violence, or removing of property, a popular family can be made of the monarchical, or a monarchical family of the popular. Or whether that be practicable or possible, in a nation upon the like balance or foundation in property, which is not in a family. A family being but a smaller society or nation, and a nation but a greater society or family. That which is usually answered to this point is, That the six or ten thus agreeing to make one family, must have some steward, and to make such a steward in a nation, is to make a king. But this is to imagine, that the steward of a family is not answerable to the masters of it, or to them upon whose estates (and not upon his own) he defrays the whole charge: For otherwise, this stewardship cannot amount to dominion, but must come only to the true nature of magistracy, and indeed of annual magistracy, in a commonwealth; seeing that such accounts, in the year's end at farthest, use to be calculated, and that the steward, body and estate, is answerable for the same to the proprietors or masters; who also have the undoubted right of constituting such another steward or stewards, as to them shall seem good, or of prolonging the office of the same.

"Now, where a nation is cast, by the unseen ways of providence, into a disorder of government, the duty of such particularly as are elected by the people, is not so much to regard what has been, as to provide for the supreme law, or for the safety of the people, which consists in the true art of law-giving. And the art of law-giving is of two kinds; the one (as I may say) false, and the other true. The first consists in the reduction of <82> the balance to arbitrary superstructures, which requires violence, as being contrary to nature; the other in erecting necessary superstructures, that is, such as are conformable to the balance or foundation; which being purely natural, requires that all interposition of force be removed."[2]

It is impossible to treat distinctly of family or of civil dominion, without considering it in its natural causes, or its natural generation. "The matter of all government is an estate or property. Hence, all government is founded upon an over-balance in propriety. And therefore, if one man hold the over-balance unto the whole people in propriety, his property causeth absolute monarchy: if the few hold the over-balance unto the whole people in propriety, their propriety causeth aristocracy, or mixed monarchy. If the whole people be neither over-balanced by the propriety of one, nor of a few, the propriety of the people, or of the many, causeth democracy, or popular government: The government of one against the balance is tyranny; the government of a few against the balance is oligarchy: the government of the many (or attempt of the people to govern) against the balance, is rebellion or anarchy; where the balance of propriety is equal, it causeth a state of war: To hold that government may be founded upon community, is to hold that there may be a castle in the air, or that what thing soever is as imaginable as what hath been in practice, must be as practicable as what hath been in practice. Hence it is true in general, that all government is in the direction of the balance."[3] All these truths, however much neglected by writers upon government, are of the greatest moment: They have the same relation to or connexion with theories about government, whether domestic or civil and national, whether consisting of one or many families, as the real laws of matter and motion have with theories in natural philosophy: For they are moral facts or principles upon which alone true theories in moral philosophy or politics can be built, as the other are the natural facts, laws or principles upon which alone true axioms in natural philosophy can be erected. They are all fully explained by the author already cited. And hence we may see, "That the division of a people into freemen and servants, is not constitutive, but naturally inherent in the balance. Freemen are such

2. Harrington, "The Art of Lawgiving" (1659), bk. I, "The Preface," in *The Political Works of James Harrington*, 602–3.

3. With the exception of the last sentence this is from Harrington, "The Rota or a Model of a Free State or Equal Commonwealth" (1660), in Harrington, *Political Works*, 808.

as have wherewithal to live of themselves, and servants such as have not: Nor, seeing all government is in the direction of the balance, is it possible for the superstructures of any to make more freemen than are such by the nature of the balance, or by their being able to live of themselves. All that could in this matter be done, even by Moses himself, is contained in this proviso, Lev. xxv. 29. *If thy brother that dwells by thee be grown poor, and be sold to thee, thou shalt not compel him to serve as a bond-servant, but as a hired servant, and a sojourner shall he be with thee, and shall serve thee to the year of jubilee: And then shall he depart from thee, both he and his children with him, and shall return to his own family, and to the possession of his <83> fathers shall he return.* Yet the nature of riches being considered, this division into freemen and servants, is not properly constitutive but natural." See Mr. Harrington's works, the art of lawgiving, p. 436, 437. Compare p. 248.[4] I shall only add upon this head, that the defenders of absolute monarchy can never draw any conclusions to serve their purpose, either from paternal government, or from the power of masters over their servants. For with regard to the former, what relation can be stricter than that between parents and children: There cannot be stronger obligations to subjection upon any than there are upon children: This relation and obligation is not the effect of consent, children being incapable of giving their consent, but is the effect of the necessity of nature, and in a peculiar sense, an authority or power of the author of nature's appointment: Yet let it be remembered, that our Author, and all writers on the laws of nature and nations allow, that the obligations of children do not contradict the powerful law of self-preservation and self-defence, in cases in which life, or any thing dearer than life, is concerned. But if this be true, how can one imagine, that when the ruin of the public happiness, which is as it were the life of the community, is attempted, the same law of self-defence is of no force, and ought not to be regarded? Suppose the right of dominion over men secured by an overbalance in property, and withal of divine appointment, in any con-

---

4. Harrington, "The Art of Lawgiving," bk. III, chap. 1, in Harrington, *Political Works,* 665–66. The edition Turnbull appears to be using is that edited by John Toland (*The Oceana and Other Works of James Harrington, Esq.*). The reference to p. 248, therefore, is to bk. I, chap. 1 of "The Prerogative of Popular Government" and would correspond to pp. 409–10 in Pocock's edition of Harrington's political works.

ceivable sense of these words, yet, if it be as sacred as the right of a
father, it cannot extend beyond the right of a father, which does not
extend to the destruction of the right of self-defence, or to command
immoral actions without contradiction or resistance: Or if it be more
sacred than the right of a father (could that greater sacredness be conceived) it cannot be more sacred than the law of nature, and the right
of God to exact obedience to that law, and to forbid the transgression
of it in obedience to whatever other authority, and so extend to the
demolishing of all the natural rights and duties of mankind: Power,
whatever be its title, or whatever be its foundation and security, if it be
exerced contrary to the laws of nature, contrary to the law of justice
and love, it is not *right;* it is power indeed, but guilty criminal power,
which it is, it must be a crime not to resist to the utmost of one's power,
if the law of nature, *i.e.* the law of God be immutable, universally and
indispensably obligatory upon all men.

With respect to the power of masters over servants, or slaves conquered by just war, it is likewise true that such a master is a lawful superior, and hath no equal in his family, yet hath his family, his servants,
his slaves a right to defend themselves against him, should he endeavour
to ruin or murder them; and such a master has no right to command
any thing in the smallest degree contrary to the law of nature; but every
one in his family hath a right, or more properly speaking, is obliged to
reject and resist such orders to the utmost of his power. None can have
a right to injure any one in making acquisitions of <84> property or
dominion, and none can have a right to exercise his acquired power,
property or dominion, in an injurious way to others, tho' part of their
property or dominion; because tho' dominion and property be not contrary but agreeable to the law of nature, yet the more considerable part
of the law of nature consists in limitations upon the exercise of dominion and property, or in prescribing duties to those who have dominion and property, with regard to the use and exercise of it. And (as
our Author hath often observed) where there is duty incumbent upon
any one, there is, *ipso facto,* a right vested in some other, who is the
object of that duty, to claim the fulfilment of it towards him. But we
shall have occasion to return to this subject afterwards. And it is sufficient at present to have observed, 1. The natural cause or source of
dominion. And, 2. That there are boundaries set by the law of nature

to the acquisition and exercise of dominion, which boundaries are, with respect to subjects of dominion, rights belonging to, and vested unalienably in them, by the same law which sets these limitations to power and dominion, and by setting them to it, imposes certain indispensable duties upon the possessors of power and dominion. This must be, if the law of nature is not an empty sound, the supreme law, with regard to those who have dominion, whether as fathers, masters or kings (according to this definition of a King by Grotius, de jure belli & pacis, l. 1. c. 3. "Paterfamilias latifundia possidens, & neminem alia lege in suas terras recipiens quam ut ditioni suae, qui recipiantur, se subjiciant." "A master of a family, who having large possessions, will not suffer any one to dwell in them on other terms than being subject to him.") *viz.* the greater good of their children, servants, family, or subjects. This being fixed as the fundamental law, particular duties are easily deducible from it. And this must be the supreme law, or man is subject to no law, but may exerce his power as he pleases, *i.e.* in other words, either the greater good of the whole society is the law, or strength is free from all law, and may do what it can, and there is no such thing as unlawful exercise of power. <85>

Of the origine of civil society, its constitution and qualities, or properties.

SECTION XCIX

Tho', in the societies we have described, men might have lived very comfortably; yet some reason hath prevailed upon men to form themselves
into those larger societies, which we call *states* or *republics,* and to prefer,
almost by universal consent, the civil to the natural state; there is almost
no nation so barbarous, in which we do not find some semblance of a
civil state or republic.* <86>

The civil state
has been agree-
able to almost
every nation.

* They attest the truth of this who have visited the anciently unknown countries,
northern and southern, having found in most of them either great multitudes subject
to one king, or determining matters of common concernment to them by common
consent. For what some authors have said of the Cafri, and the people inhabiting
mount Caucasus, and of certain American Islanders, (see Hert. Elem. prud. civil. 1.
1. p. 45. Becmann. geograph. 9. 8.) [[Hertius, *Elementa prudentiae civilis;* Johann
Christoph Becmann (1641–1717), German historian and Protestant theologian, author of the *Historia orbis terrarum, geographica et civilis*]] these accounts seem to be
given by persons who had not enquired very narrowly into the matter, and who
thought they saw no vestige of civil government, where they saw no palaces and
guards, nor nothing of the splendor and magnificence of a court. Petrus Kolbius,
who lived long in that corner of Africa, says of the *Cafri,* that they were divided into
seventeen provinces or nations, each of which had its own prince, whom they called
Kouqui, and that every village had its prefect, called in their language *Kralle,* who had
even the power of punishing criminals. As for public affairs, he adds, that all the
prefects met together, and consulted in a common-council, in which the prince of
the nation presided. I am afraid what Salust says of the Aborigines and Gaetuli, Catil.
cap. 6. & Jugurth. c. 18; and Strabo of the Numidians, geograph. l. 17. p. 1191. and

SECTION C

Whether it was
by indigence
of necessaries
they were
engaged to
choose a civil
state.

Tho' many, in their enquiries concerning the origine of civil society, have thought that men were compelled to it by the want of several necessaries (Plato de repub. l. 2.); yet this is the less probable; first, Because we have an account of something like civil society in Genesis iv. 17. when the world was not so populous as that there could be any want of necessaries. And next, because nothing hinders commerce from taking place where there is no civil government (§10); and, in fine, because there has been a much greater indigence of all things, since, civil government being established, luxury and wantonness began to spread and reign among mankind.* <87>

Valerius Flaccus, Argonaut. l. 4. v. 102. [[Valerius Flaccus, *Argonautica*]] of the Bebricii, Pliny of the Troglodites, hist. nat. 5. 8. and in fine, Homer of the Sicilians, that all these accounts are equally groundless. The natural state of the Sicilians is elegantly described by Homer Odyss. l. 10. v. 112.

Nec fora conciliis fervent, nec judice: tantum
Antra colunt umbrosa: altisque in montibus aedes
Quisque suos regit uxorem natosque, nec ulli
In commune vacat socias extendere curas.

[[Homer, *Odyssey* 9.112, ed. Stanford: "[Of the Cyclopes] They keep no meeting places for councils, nor for a court; they rather dwell in shady caves, their homes in the high mountains, and each man rules his own wife and children, and never calls partners in common to share his concerns."]]

* Thus we find Abraham, Isaac and Jacob, who lived sometime in a natural state, (§92), tho' they only applied themselves to husbandry, and feeding of cattle, to have lived very agreeably, and to have amassed great wealth, and to have wanted nothing, Gen. xxiv. 35. xxxiii. 11. And indeed, seeing families living separately and independently in very early times of the world, understood agriculture, and planting and dressing of vines, and were no strangers to gold and silver, and the more useful arts (Gen. xiii. 2. xxiv. 35.) what could men desire more, tho' they lived in a state of nature, if luxury were unknown, and made none of its exorbitant demands to which nature is a stranger?

SECTION CI

Again, it can hardly be imagined that elegance and politeness were the motives which induced men, in the primitive times of frugality, to prefer a civil to a natural state. For besides that, what is called *elegance,* is really vanity, and what is called *politeness of manners,* is truly but an affected complaisance and flattery (§11);* there is nothing to hinder men, in a state of nature, from improving their reason, and refining or polishing their manners. Nay, the examples of Abraham, Isaac, and Jacob, who lived by themselves with their segregate families, and had not entred into civil society, sufficiently shew us, that men, living in a state of nature, may be quite free from all barbarity, and very decent and polite.

If on the account of elegance and politeness.

SECTION CII

Equally groundless are other reasons for which men are imagined to have coalited into republics or civil states. For as to what some say of justice, <88> that civil society was formed for the sake of it, (as Hesiod. Theog. v. 87),[1] and others of interest, as if it had been done on that account, (as Aristotle, Ethic. 8. 11.)[2] and what others say, of the instigation of nature, (as the same Aristotle, l. 1. & 2.)—All these reasons, we think,

If for the security of justice.

---

* A proof of this is the mannerly polite speech of Abraham to Melchisedech, Gen. xiv. 22. and his uncommon hospitality to strangers, Gen. xviii. 2. and his conference with the sons of Heth, Gen. xxiii. 7. That Abraham had taught his servants to be most observant of decency and good manners, appears from that message carried by Eleaser to Nachor, Gen. xxiv. 22. Nor does that interview between Jacob, in his return from Mesopotamia with Esau, savour in the least of barbarity, in which they strove to outdo one another in civil words, presents, and other tokens of love and friendship. Besides, if it be true, which Joseph. antiq. Jud. 1. 9. says of Abraham, that he was skilled not only in numbers, but in astronomy; and what is said by others of skill in the interpretation of dreams being brought to great perfection in his family (Suidas Abraham. [[Suidas, *Suidae lexicon,* vol. 1, "Αβρααμ"]] & Justin. hist. 36), none can doubt but that the arts and sciences may be cultivated to a great degree of perfection in a state of nature, and therefore that there is no need of a civil state in order to gain that end.

1. Hesiod, *Theogony and Works and Days,* line 87.
2. Aristotle, *Nicomachean Ethics,* bk. 8, chap. 11, in *The Works of Aristotle,* vol. 9.

are of such a nature, that they might have contributed somewhat towards it, but could not have been the sole motives which determined men to commute a state of liberty and equality for a state of civil government and subjection.* <89>

SECTION CIII

The real cause which moved men to form large civil societies was the fear of wicked profligate men.

Wherefore, when the matter is fully and accurately considered, they appear to have hit upon the true cause, who maintain that the strength and violence of wicked men gave rise to the formation of civil states. For all men being equal and free in a state of nature (§5 and 6); but such being the temper and disposition of profligate men, that they have an insatiable lust of power and wealth; of robbing others of their possessions and rights, and bringing them under their yoke, it could not but happen that several heads of families, of this temper and genius, would unite their strength in order to subject others to them. And since a large society cannot but be unequal and rectoreal (§17), the consequence is, that such a band of robbers would choose a leader to themselves, and prescribe a certain form of government to him, according to which he was to rule

---

* For why might not the heads of segregate families have made laws, and distributed justice each in his own family, (§92)? Again, why might not the more simple societies have produced all the advantages of union, since in these every one was at liberty to acquire what he pleased, and there would be none of those tributes, taxes, imposts, upon persons or estates there, which now eat up the property and estates of subjects in civil governments? Let nature be as abhorrent of solitude, and let a state of solitude be as miserable as Pufendorff hath painted it out to be, yet we can never say, that Abraham, for example, lived in a solitary state, who besides a wife and a hand-maid, and many children by both, had such a numerous retinue of servants, that he could bring into the field three hundred and eighty servants born in his family, Gen. xiv. 13. However strong the natural propension of mankind to society may be, yet surely they were not immediately led by natural inclination to form those larger societies, in which there are many things very contrary to the natural dispositions of mankind, as Pufendorff hath shewn at great length in his 7th book, cap. 1. §4. of the law of nature, &c. It is however very certain, that in a civil state, if it be rightly constituted, justice is well administred, and all the public and private interests of mankind are wisely consulted and provided for; but those things are more properly called consequences of good civil government, than motive causes to the formation of it.

and command them; and hence the origine of civil society or political states,* which are nothing else but a multitude of people united under a common head, upon certain conditions for their mutual security, and dependent on, or subjected to no other mortal. <90>

SECTION CIV

The justest heads of families could not find any other remedy against such consociations, but to repel force by force (§9). And a few not being sufficient to accomplish that end, necessity, and the malice of wicked men, forced other men to coalesce into large bodies; the consequence from which is, that just and good heads of families were obliged, through fear of violent and wicked men, to unite their forces, and joining together under a common head on certain conditions, to form a civil society or political state† (§103); whence we infer, that there would have been no republics in a state of integrity. See Becman. meditat. pol. 11.

This obliged the innocent to unite together in order to repel force by force.

---

* This is the most natural account of the rise of civil government, if we attend to reason and the nature of things. But ancient history sets it beyond all doubt that it was so. For that is found in the sacred writings. And these records assure us, that before the deluge, not the *sons of God,* as they are called, Gen. vi. 1. but the *posterity of Cain,* built the first city, Gen. iii. 17. For tho' we should grant to the learned Jo. Clerc. comment. p. 40. [[Jean le Clerc, *Genesis sive Mosis prophetae liber primus*]] that this city consisted but of a few little cottages, set about with a mound or green hedge (which is by no means certain or indisputable) yet a society of many families, without some form of civil government, can hardly be conceived. Moreover we are told, that after the deluge Nimrod the son of Chus, being mighty in possessions or territories, founded the kingdom of Babylon, *i.e.* began to oppress others, and force them to submit themselves to his command, Gen. x. 8. Nor is any more ancient kingdom mentioned by Moses, tho' the names and transactions of several kingdoms and dynasties occur in the history of the time of Abraham, a few ages after. And who indeed can doubt that civil states were originally formed in this manner, *i.e.* by violent oppression, since this has so often happened in latter times? Hertius prud. civil. 1. 3. 4. p. 77. & seq. has shewn by instances brought from universal history, that the most potent kingdoms took their rise from oppression and robbery.

† They are not therefore in the wrong who assert that fear and force were the origine of civil society, as Bodin, de rep. 1. 6. 2. 6. [[Jean Bodin (1529/30–1596), French jurist and "absolutist"; see Bodin, *Les six livres de la République,* bk. I, chap. 6, p. 69: "La raison et lumière naturelle nous conduit à cela, de croire que la force et violence a donné source et origine aux Républiques."]] Hobbes de cive. 1. [[Hobbes,

5;[3] and that it is trifling to obtrude upon us a state of innocence as the first principle of the law of nature and nations (l. 1. §74). <91>

SECTION CV

The double
origine of
civil society.

Civil society is therefore of a two-fold origine; some were formed to oppress the innocent, and for violence; others were formed to repel force by force, and for common self-defence. The end of the former is most unjust; that of the latter just. Wherefore the former is rather *a gang of robbers* than a society; the latter is *a lawful republic.* But because things which have an unlawful beginning may be afterwards amended when the error is found out; and, on the contrary, things which had a very laudable commencement are often perverted; a band of thieves and robbers, having laid aside their oppression and violence, may become an excellent commonwealth; and a lawful republic, forsaking their humanity, may degenerate into a tribe of ruffians; yet in both the same end, *viz.* the *security* of the members is the end of consociation.*

On the Citizen 1.2, p. 24.]] nor they who say, that men formed civil societies for the sake of enjoying their properties with security, Cic. de off. 2. 21. nor those who maintain, that the imbecillity of segregate families, was the reason why men changed their natural liberty for civil government, as Grotius de jure belli & pacis, proleg. §19. & l. 1. c. 4. §7. For tho' all these opinions seem to differ in words, yet they come to the same thing in effect.

* Thus, tho' certain piratical republics in Afric were formed rather to plunder and oppress, than merely for common safety, and therefore in this respect they differed very little from bands of robbers; yet they had likewise common security for their end, as well as lawful republics have; and for that reason, they put themselves in a state of defence against all external force; and were rigid in the distribution of justice,

Ne vaga prosiliat fraenis natura remotis.

[[Horace, *Satires II,* 74: "Lest nature should spring forward when the reins are removed and go wandering."]]

This then is the common end of all civil societies; but with this difference, that the former are not very sollicitous about virtue and equity, if that end be but obtained; whereas the latter proposes that end, in order that they, as the apostle expresses it, "may lead under kings, and all in authority, quiet and peaceable lives, with all godliness and honesty," 1 Tim. 2. 2.

3. Becmann, *Meditationes politicae.*

SECTION CVI

Since the common *security* of the members is the end of all civil societies (§105); but it is from <92> the end of a society that we must judge of the means, and of the rights and duties of its members (§14); the consequence is, that they who unite into society, ought to do all, without which the common end, *viz. security,* cannot be obtained. Now, since the violence which is obstructive of public security, consists in the united force of wicked men (§103), it is necessary that others, who would secure themselves against such violence, should unite their strength; and therefore it is proper, that as many men should form themselves into a more large and compounded society, as may, with probability, be sufficient to repel, by just force, the unjust violence of injurious neighbours.*

The end of civil society is the security of its members.

SECTION CVII

A state or republic does not consist, as Nicias says in Thucydides, 7. 14.[4] and Themistocles in Justin. hist. 2. 12. in a territory, in towns, in walls, in houses, but in men; nor is it requisite to <93> constitute a civil state, that whole families, composed of persons of both sexes, be united; but it is sufficient, if many conjoin their forces and minds, so as to be able

A republic consists in a multitude of men.

---

* Hence it is an idle question, what number of persons constitutes a society? For tho' Apuleius thought fifteen freemen might constitute a republic, Apol. p. 304 [[Apuleius, "Apology," chap. 47, p. 71, in *Apuleius: Rhetorical Works*]], and others have said three tolerably numerous families might make one, Val. Max. 4. 4. 8. 4. 6. 5. yet the authors of these opinions seem not to have had common security as the end of society in their view, since that end cannot be accomplished by fifteen persons joined together; but the number ought to be increased, in proportion to that of the enemy feared. Accordingly, all history shews us, that states were very small in their beginnings, or confined within the narrow limits of a small territory. Nor were there any larger ones in their neighbourhood, to make them afraid. But so soon as large empires were formed by oppressing and swallowing up their neighbours, lesser republics united either into one larger republic, or making a confederacy, became a system of republics, that they might be able to resist their mighty and powerful neighbours, as it happened in Greece after the Persian overthrow, and in Germany after the victories of Drusus and Germanicus.

4. Thucydides, *History of the Peloponnesian War,* vol. 4, bk. 7, chap. 77, p. 159. Nicias was an Athenian general during the Peloponnesian War with Sparta.

to conquer or outwit their enemies; though it cannot be denied, that a civil state would be but of one age, if not composed of such families, but of single persons, however great its numbers might be, Florus 1. 1.*

SECTION CVIII

They must consent in the end and the means.

Since a republic consists in the union of such a number, whose united force is not unequal to that of their neighbours (§105); but there can be no <94> society without consent (§13); the consequence is, that civil states or republics are constituted by an intervening contract, whether some men voluntarily coalite into society, or whether their consent was at first extorted by violence, or whether some men acceded in either of these ways to a republic already formed; or whether, in fine, the descendants of such citizens are presumed, from their having been bred up in a society, as some time to succeed to their progenitors (§16) in it, to have consented to continue members of it.†

---

* That a republic may consist without a territory, without towns, walls, or houses, is plain from the example of the Hebrews, a most sacred republic, which wandered forty years in the deserts of Arabia, without any fixed habitation or abode, without houses or walls, till they were settled in the promised Palestine, Numb. xiv. And that a republic may consist without families, none will deny, who has considered the Papal monarchy, which hath been accurately described by Pufendorff and Thomasius. [[See Pufendorf, *Des Freyherrn von Pufendorff politische Betrachtung der geistlichen Monarchie des Stuhls zu Rom.*]] I shall not now appeal to the kingdom of the Amazons; all that is said of it having been called into doubt by many learned men. Whence it may be concluded, that it is a convenient number of men united by consent, that constitutes a republic; and that such a society does not become extinct, tho' their territory may be occupied by others, while its members survive that loss, and are in a condition to contend with their enemies. Thus the republic of Athens still subsisted, tho' Attica was entirely possessed by the Persians, while the fleet subsisted, into which Themistocles, with the whole body of the people, and every thing they could carry with them, had betaken himself, Nepos Themistoc. cap. 2. And therefore, Adimantus's speech to him was very foolish, and his answer was excellent. The former said he had no right to pretend to give law or dispence justice, having no country. The other answered, that he had both a territory and a city much larger than theirs, while he had two hundred well armed and manned ships, an invasion from which none of the Greeks could resist, Herodot. hist. l. 8. p. 305. edit. Hen. Steph. [[Herodotus, *Herodoti Halicarnassei historiae libri IX et de vita Homeri libellus.*]]

† Thus the inhabitants of Albania, and that medley of shepherds and thieves

SECTION CIX

Hence it is plain, that civil states, like other societies, are constituted or augmented either by *voluntary* consent, or by *forced* consent (§15). In the former case, the first and principal pact must be that by which all consent to constitute the same state or republic. And since every pact ought to be free, and may be made upon conditions, it is self-evident that he who does not consent, or whose terms are not agreed to, remains without that society, and is his own master.* <95>

The first pact of those who voluntarily constitute a republic.

SECTION CX

But since members of the same society must consent to the same end and means (§13), which consent cannot be expected in a great multitude, unless the society be rectoreal; therefore some governing power must be instituted, by the will of which the whole people is to be ruled (§18); and the consequence is, that this multitude ought to determine what the

Their subsequent resolution.

---

who attaching themselves to Romulus, built huts on the banks of the Tiber, from the beginning consented to form that republic. Dion. Halicar. antiq. l. i. p. 72. [[Dionysius of Halicarnassus, *Roman Antiquities,* bk. I, chaps. 9 and 10.]] Thus the Sabines acceded voluntarily to the Romans, after they had formed themselves into a commonwealth, Liv. i. 13. On the other hand, the Albans, their capital being destroyed, augmented the Roman state against their will, l. i. 29. Nor was it ever doubted of, that the posterity of Roman citizens were Roman citizens, unless they either voluntarily abandoned their country, or being exiled, were forced much against their inclination to leave it.

* This would hold, if any new republic were to be constituted at present by consent. But it happens rarely that any one stipulates for himself and his family in this manner in a republic already constituted. Yet we have an example in Ottanes of Persia, mentioned by Herodotus, hist. l. 3. p. 124. who, after the Magi, who had usurped the government were destroyed, when the Persian princes were assembled to consult together about a form of government, his opinion for a popular state not being approved, at last said: "Ye factious men, since some of us must be named king by lot, or by the election of the multitude, with the permission of the Persians, or some other way, I shall not oppose you, because I neither desire to be above you, nor will I be below any one of you. Upon this condition therefore do I give up my right of empire, that neither I, nor any of mine, ever be subject to any of you." [[Herodotus, *Histories* 3.83 (see Herodotus, *Histories,* trans. Godley, vol. 2, p. iii).]]

model of government ought to be;* and tho' they be not obliged to stand to the resolutions of the rest, who consented to the future republic, only upon condition that a certain form of government in it should be agreed to, if another form please the people (§109); yet those who entred into the first pact without any conditions, ought to submit to the plurality of suffrages. <96>

SECTION CXI

Another pact. A form of government being agreed upon, nothing remains to constitute a perfect civil society, but to nominate the person or persons a people would have to rule over them,† and to prescribe the form of government

---

* They are much mistaken who affirm there never was any such pact. The Roman history alone sufficiently overthrows that assertion. For when that rabble of Alba, and herd of shepherds and robbers, who had enriched themselves by many depredations, had agreed to coalesce into one republic, Romulus having called an assembly, or convention, asked the people what form of government they would prefer. Dionysius Halicar. has fully described the whole affair, Antiq. Rom. l. 2. p. 80. where he tells us the answer of the people, which was to this purpose. "We do not stand in need of a new form of government nor will we change that approved by our ancestors, and handed down from them to us; but we will follow their sentiment who founded our present form of government, not without great prudence, and are content with the condition we are now in. For why should we find fault with it, since we have enjoyed under kings the goods of the highest estimation among mankind, liberty and empire over others. This is our opinion concerning our form of government." [[Dionysius of Halicarnassus, *Roman Antiquities*, bk. II, chap. 4, p. 325.]]

† We find this order observed in the institution of the Roman republic, according to Dionysius Halicarn. For when the greater part of the Albans who had been inured to kingly government, had resolved to preserve that form of government, being then sollicitous to choose a king, they added: "And this honour we think is due to none so much as to you, as well on account of your virtue as your birth; but chiefly, because you have been the leader of this colony; and we have experienced in your conduct, in all your words and deeds, great prudence and valour." In like manner, a little after, when the people was divided into *curiae* and *tribes,* and a hundred fathers were chosen to compose the council or senate of the republic, the administration of the republic was so divided, that the care of sacred things, the conservation of the laws and customs, the power of judging in crimes of the higher kinds, the right of proposing to the senate, and of assembling the people, was given to the king; to the senate the right of deciding whatever was propounded to them by the king, and passing the opinion of the majority into an act or decree; and to the people under the senate

agreed upon in the former pact, to him or them; which prescription will then become, properly speaking, the *fundamental law* of the republic, (since things settled by pacts are called *laws*); and therefore it binds the governors, whether one or many, no less than the subjects; so that nothing is right that is done contrary to this primary law, or essential constitution of the society. <97>

SECTION CXII

Thus does society arise as often as a people voluntarily forms it. But so often as a people, brought under dominion by a more powerful one, coalesces into the same republic with their conquerors, the first pact is undoubtedly a consent to form one common republic with them; because, if they did not consent, they would not accept the terms offered by their conquerors, but rather perish than put themselves under such a yoke. But such a people will hardly be consulted or hearkened to with regard to the form of government, nor in the choice of rulers, but to them will be left little more than the glory of obeying.* <98>

Whether the same pacts take place when society is constituted by persons under force.

---

proposing, the right of creating magistrates, and giving the ultimate authority to laws, and of determining upon war or peace, if the king would permit. This is the fundamental law or constitution of this new government, as it is described most accurately by an author excellently versed in politics, and it lasted till the tyranny of Tarquinius. [[Dionysius of Halicarnassus, *Roman Antiquities,* bk. II, chap. 4, p. 325, and chap. 7, p. 333ff.]]

* Yet this whole matter depends upon the terms and conditions of the surrendry, which are commonly better or worse, according as the victory is more or less ambiguous. Thus, while the Sabines and the Romans disputed upon a very equal footing with regard to the event of war, they thought fit to put an end to it, by striking a league, the articles of which are recorded by Dionysius. "That Romulus and Tatius should reign at Rome with equal honour and power; that the city should preserve its name derived from the founder, and the citizens should be called Roman Citizens as before, but all should be called by the common appellation of *Quirites,* from the country of Tatius; that the right of Roman citizenship should be given to as many of the Sabines as should desire it, and that they should be admitted into tribes and curiae, with their sacred usages." Such was this treaty of union, by which the Sabines were in some respect permitted to constitute the republic. [[Dionysius of Halicarnassus, *Roman Antiquities,* bk. II, chap. 46, p. 445.]]

SECTION CXIII

So if the con-
queror forces a
new form of
government
upon the
conquered.

It sometimes happens, that a new form of government is obtruded upon a conquered people;* and the victorious people stipulates to themselves, that this new republic shall pay homage to them, as joined to their republic by an unequal covenant. In which case, the nature of the thing shews us, that the pacts we have described above (§109, 111), and the decree about a form of government, (§110), cannot take place; but the conquered people consents to all, not voluntarily, but by force.

SECTION CXIV

All the mem-
bers of a civil
state ought to
submit their
wills to the
supreme
powers in it.

But as all societies are understood to have one understanding and one will (§19); so the same must be said of a state or republic thus constituted. Now, as many associates cannot agree upon the same end and means (§17), unless that business be committed to some one, or some certain number; so in a state the same must be done.† But to do this, is the same

---

* It was the custom of the Athenians to obtrude upon those they conquered a popular state, and of the Lacedemonians to force an aristocracy upon all whom they conquered. The reasons of which are given by Xenophon, de republ. Athen. cap. 1. §14. and cap. 3. §10. tom. 3. But one is sufficient, p. 249. [[Xenophon, "Constitution of the Athenians," in Xenophon, *Scripta minora,* 474–507. This piece is now believed to be by an unknown author.]] The Athenians established, and often renewed, after it had been overturned, a popular state among the Samians. But when they were subdued by Lysander the Lacedemonian, he set up a decarchy among them in the room of a democracy. What fortunes other states in Greece underwent, according as the Athenians or Lacedemonians had the empire of the sea, is well known. And that these things could not happen without force is perspicuous to every one.

† Many cannot otherwise have the same will than by consent in the same will; or by submission of all to the same will. The first cannot be hoped for, as every one will immediately see, who hath considered the different tempers, turns, geniuses and dispositions of mankind. Hence Seneca, ep. 102. "Putas tu, posse sententiam unam esse omnium? non est unius una. Do you think all can have the same mind? no single person is of one mind." Therefore the latter way remains, which is submission to the will of one or many. For as a ship, however well manned, would perish, did not all agree to commit their safety to one pilot, skilled in navigation, who is to exert his utmost to save the ship from storms and rocky seas: so it is impossible that so many

as to submit one's will to that of another; <99> whence it is plain, that all the members of a republic ought to submit their wills to one or more; and therefore that he or they govern to whom the rest have submitted their will.

SECTION CXV

Hence it follows, that there can be no more but three regular forms of republics or civil states. For subjects must either submit their wills to *one, many,* or to the *whole multitude.* Now, when they submit their wills to the will of one physical person, hence arises *monarchy, a kingdom* or *principality.** But if to the will or decrees of many, thence arises *aristocracy.* And if to the whole people, that is, to what is decreed by the common suffrage of the whole people, then the form of government is *popular,* and called *a democracy.* <100>

Hence arise either monarchical, aristocratical or democratical states.

SECTION CXVI

But since whether one, many, or all govern, none presides over the republic by any other right but this, that the rest of the citizens have submitted their wills to such a governor or governors (§114); the consequence is, that those command unjustly; *i.e.* without right, to whom the members of a state have not submitted their will. Wherefore, if one such

To which are opposites, tyranny, oligarchy, and anarchy.

---

myriads of men who have coalesced into one large society, should escape the civil tempests to which they are continually exposed, and obtain safety and security, unless they be governed by one or more common rulers. Arrian, diss. ep. 1. observes, "That good citizens submit their wills to the law and authority of the state." [[Arrian, "Discourses of Epictetus," bk. 1, chap. 12, sect. 7; see *The Discourses as Reported by Arrian, the Manual, and Fragments,* vol. 1.]]

   * Polybius Hist. 6. 2. distinguishes between μοναρχίαν and βασιλείαν, *a monarchy* and *a kingdom.* He thus differences them: "The first, monarchy, is constituted without any art, and by the force of nature: Kingdom follows it, and takes its origine from it, then, when art comes to make emendations." [[Polybius, *The Histories,* vol. 3, bk. 6, chap. 2, sec. 4, p. 275.]] But since things, less or more polished, do not differ in species, we shall not here take notice of this difference.

person command, monarchy becomes *tyranny;* if, instead of the senate of the nobles, a few usurp the supreme command, aristocracy degenerates into *oligarchy;* and if, instead of the whole people, a certain rabble, consisting of the very dregs of the people, manage all things at their pleasure, democracy degenerates into *ochlocracy.** These vitious forms of government being very like to the regular ones, the latter easily degenerate into the former, as Polybius justly observes, and experience has abundantly confirmed. Polyb. hist. 6. 1. <101>

SECTION CXVII

What are mixed republics.

Now, since these regular forms of government may be perverted into as many opposite vitious forms (§116), it is not to be wondered at, that there are very few states to be found which have chosen any one of these three, but that many have compounded all these forms into one,† or have so

---

* This is observed by the most excellent politician Polybius, ibidem p. 629. "Therefore, there are six kinds of republics: The three we have just mentioned, which are in every body's mouth, and three nearly allied to them, the domination of one, of a few, and of the mob; some by tyranny understand monarchy, because, as we said above, this author had distinguished between monarchy and a kingdom. But he himself adds a little after, 'a kingdom, when it declines into the disease to which it is obnoxious, *viz.* a tyranny.'" [[Polybius, *The Histories,* vol. 3, bk. 6, chap. 2, sec. 4, p. 275.]] In these divisions and definitions, all the writers of morals or politics agree; and therefore, there is no need of dwelling long upon them. By whom have they not been repeated?

† Polybius pronounces this the best form of government, hist. 1. 1. p. 628. "'Tis manifest, that a republic compounded of the three forms we have mentioned, is the best." [[Polybius, *The Histories,* vol. 3, bk. 6, chap. 2, sec. 4, p. 273.]] And cap. 8. p. 638. he highly extols Lycurgus for not having founded a simple uniform republic, but for having, by mingling the good qualities of all the best republics, composed one, consisting of all of them blended together, and by that means so equally poised and balanced it, that it could not degenerate into any of the vicious forms we have mentioned, but was kept entire by various checks. [[Ibid., chap. 10, pp. 289–93.]] So Dionysius antiq. l. 2. p. 82. after having told us, that the Roman republic was constituted by Romulus much after the same manner, he adds, "This form of a republic I prefer to all others, as being equally fit for peace or war." [[Dionysius of Halicarnassus, *Roman Antiquities,* bk. 2, chap. 7, p. 333.]] I pass by several testimonies to the same purpose by Cicero apud Non. Marcell. de verb. prop. 4. 292. [[Marcellus, *Nonii Marcelli nova editio,* chap. 4, 342: "De varia significatione sermonum, per literas";

mingled two of them together, as that the one form might be a balance or check on the other. And since names are generally derived from the better or more eminent part; hence various kinds of kingdoms, aristocracies and democracies could not but arise, which it very little concerns us, whether they be called *mixt* or *irregular republics.* See Hert. element. prud. civ. 1. 2. 8. p. 2320 & seq.

SECTION CXVIII

Again, since whole societies may coalesce into a larger body (§17); hence it follows, that many republics may, each preserving its form of government <102>ment and its independency intire, make a confederacy for acting with common consent for their common preservation and safety.* Such confederated republics were the Achaian ones; and such are called *systems of republics.*

What are systems of republics.

---

a quotation from Cicero, *De republica,* arguing that the ideal state has a mixed constitution with monarchical, aristocratic, and popular elements]], by Zeno apud Laert. 7. 131. [[Diogenes Laertius, *Lives of Eminent Philosophers,* bk. 7, sec. 131, pp. 235–37]] and by Tacitus annal. 4. 33.

* Pufendorff, singulari dissertat. de systematibus civitatum, to be found in the collection of his dissert. Acad. selectae, p. 210. & seq. [[Pufendorf, *Dissertationes academicae selectiores*]] and de jure naturae & gentium, 7. 5. 16. thinks systems of societies are formed when several separate kingdoms, either by convention, or by marriage, or by succession, or by conquest, come to have one king, but in such a manner that they do not become one kingdom, but are governed each by its own fundamental laws; or by a treaty of alliance. And Hertius elem. prud. civil. is of the same opinion, 1. 12. 6. & seq. But either one kingdom is so subjected to another, that it hath no share in the common government, as anciently the kingdoms of Macedonia, Syria and Egypt were subjected to the Romans; or each retains its own constitution, as now the German empire, Hungary and Bohemia; or they coalesce in such a manner as to compose one kingdom, as now England and Scotland, Poland and Lithuania. In the first case, the conquered kingdom is reduced into a province, and does not constitute one system with the other. Nor in the second case can two kingdoms be said to have coalited into a system, since they have nothing in common, but one prince who sustains two characters. There remains therefore the third case only, in which two kingdoms, or two bodies of people uniting their will and strength for common defence, constitute one larger society, and therefore are a system of republics, according to our definition. See G. G. Titius ad Pufendorff de offic. hom. & civ.

SECTION CXIX

A monarch has a right to any title of honour.

Since *monarchy* is formed as often as all the subjects submit their will to one person (§115); the consequence is, that it is the same what title of honour he assume to himself, monarch, emperor, king, duke, or prince; and that having no superior, he may change his title, and take any other at <103> his pleasure,* tho' he cannot so easily force other kings or republics to acknowledge any new title he may take; and therefore it is more prudent for a prince, before he assumes to himself any new title or dignity, to know the sentiments of other kings and states about it, and expresly to stipulate to himself such new titles of honour.

SECTION CXX

He solely exerces all the rights of majesty.

Hence it is evident that a monarch governs all by his will; and tho' he may take counsel from persons of prudence and experience, yet their opinions are not suffrages but counsels; and that he acts at all times, and

---

* For since supreme powers live in a state of nature with regard to one another, which state is a state of liberty and equality (§4. 5. 6.) it follows, that monarch is equal to monarch, and nothing hinders any one from enjoying as much dignity in his own state as any other in his; and therefore any one may take any title to himself, to support which he finds himself equal. We have seen in our times two examples of it, to which even future ages will pay reverence, in Frederick I. King of Prussia, and Peter I. Emperor of Russia; the former of whom first took the title to himself of King, and the other of Emperor, and both of whom had these titles acknowledged to them afterwards by other Kings and Emperors. It is true Pope Clement XI. shewed his intolerable arrogance, when Frederick I. a prince worthy of immortal glory, took the title of King to himself, vainly pretending, that it depended on him alone to make Kings. But this doctrine, more becoming a Hildebrand [[Hildebrand was the original name of Pope Gregory VII (ca. 1020–85), the opponent of the emperor Henry IV in the investiture contest]] than Clement, and detested even by princes the most devoted to the Romish church, hath been sufficiently refuted by the worthy and learned chancellor of our university Jo. Petr. a Ludewig, who had formerly fully treated that controversy in several small treatises, *de auspicio regio.* Add to these a very elegant treatise by V. C. Everardus Otto, de titulo Imperatoris Russorum, inserted among his dissertat. juris publici & privati, part. 1. p. 135. [[Ludewig (*praeses*) and Lilienfeld (*respondens*), *Dissertatio iuris gentium, de auspicio regum;* Otto (1685–1756), *De titulo imperatoris Russorum.*]]

every where; so that it was justly said in the times of Hadrian the Roman em-<104>peror, "Roma est, ubi imperator est," where the Emperor is, there is Rome, Herod. hist. 1. 6. There is therefore no right of majesty which a prince may not exerce (§111); yea, a kingdom hardly deserves to be called a monarchy in which any other exerces any of the rights of majesty independently of the king.*

SECTION CXXI

But tho' a monarch governs all by his will, (§120), yet he ought not to act otherwise than the end of the state, the security of its members requires (§105); whence it follows, that the security and happiness of the people ought to be the supreme law in a monarchy; and in this does it differ from tyranny, which refers all to its own security and advantage; and which being acquired by villainous practices, cannot be retained by good methods, and therefore is very little concerned about the public welfare, provided it can sustain and preserve itself.† <105>

The difference between a monarch and a tyrant.

* For the understanding and will, like that of one moral person, ought to be one (§114). Now, if any exerces any of the rights of majesty whatsoever, independently of the king, the whole republic would not have one understanding and will. Wherefore, it would not be one republic, but a republic within a republic. And to this we may apply what Homer says, Iliad. 2. "'Tis not good that many should rule: Let there be one emperor, one king." [[Not clear to which passage in the *Iliad* this refers.]] Tho' we are not ignorant that tyrants have often abused this maxim. See Sueton. Calig. cap. 22.

† To this head belong all the tyrannical arts of which Aristotle hath treated most accurately, Polit. 5. 10. Tyrants, conscious to themselves of the public hatred, are fearful and suspicious; and therefore, being jealous of virtue, they oppress and bear it down, and cut off the heads of the more eminent and worthy, like poppies which overtop the rest: They bear hard upon the innocent, under the pretext of treason, the only crime of those who have no crime: They sow discord and animosities among their subjects: They extinguish all the light and splendor of useful literature: They prefer foreigners to natives: The latter they bereave of all dignities and riches, and reduce to the extremest misery: But how repugnant all this is to the end of civil society, and how unjust, is glaring. Polyb. hist. 2. 59. p. 202. "For the very name *Tyrant,* hath annexed to it all manner of wickedness and impiety, and includes in it all the injuriousness and criminality that is to be found amongst mankind." [[Polybius, *Histories,* vol. 1, bk. 2, chap. 59, p. 387.]]

SECTION CXXII

How the rights of majesty are exerced in aristocracy.

Again, from the definition of aristocracy, we infer, that all the rights of majesty or sovereignty belong to the whole senate or college of nobles, and cannot be exerced but by the concurring consent of the whole senate. There must therefore be a certain place where they assemble to consult about the common affairs of the state; and likewise a certain appointed time, on which the ordinary senate is held, unless some unexpected emergencies demand the calling of a senate out of the ordinary course. Besides, because the consent of many can hardly be expected but by submission (§17); the consequence is, that even in aristocracy the smaller number ought to submit to the greater number; and therefore that the voice of the plurality should determine; but in an equality of voices, nothing can be done, unless he who presides give the deciding voice, or the case be such as that there is place for the *Calculus Minervae*.* Moreover, since the vitious form of government, that is the opposite of Aristocracy is called *oligarchy* (§116), and into it does aristocracy easily degenerate (ibidem); the very nature of the thing demands that no decree be valid, unless it be made when the greater part of the senate is present, *e.g.* two thirds. <106>

* The *Calculus Minervae* is, when in an equality of condemning and absolving voices, the pannel is acquitted. For when Orestes was tried for parricide, those who condemned him being superior to his absolvers by one voice only, Minerva is said to have added one to the latter, that in an equality of suffrages, he might be absolved. And this became afterwards almost an universal law, as Euripides makes Minerva foretel it should, in Iphigen. Taur. v. 1268. [[Euripides, *Iphigenia in Tauris*, ll. 1471–72, in Euripides, *Euripides*, vol. 2: "[A]nd this shall be a law—*The equal tale of votes acquits the accused.*"]] See Boecler. dissert. singul. de calculo Minervae, and a dissertation by Henr. Cocceii de eo quod justum est circa numerum suffragiorum, & de calculo Minervae, cap. 7. where this learned author gives this natural reason for the practice, "That the first state of the person accused is changed by condemnation, and is continued by absolution; and therefore nothing is done: Wherefore, since the majority only can change a former state and introduce a new one, it follows, that in the case of equality nothing is done; and consequently, the first state of the person continues to take place, and he is absolved." [[Boecler (*praeses*) and Forer (*respondens*), *Isopsephia sive calculus Minervae;* Cocceji (*praeses*) and Meyer (*respondens*), *Disputatio juridica inauguralis . . . de calculo Minerva.*]]

SECTION CXXIII

It is the same in a democracy: For since in it whatever is decreed by the common voice of the whole people is the will of the whole republic or state (§115), it follows, that the sovereignty belongs to the people, and that they have the right to exerce all the rights of majesty. But since that cannot be done unless the people hold assemblies to consult about their affairs, it is evident, that here also a certain place and stated days must be fixed for the public assemblies; and that whatever is resolved by the plurality of peoples suffrages in tribes, in *curiae,* or singly, is valid. In fine, that a democracy may degenerate into an ochlocracy,* if the right of voting be allowed to the minority of the people, the rest being excluded or absent, is evident from the very definition of ochlocracy (§116). <107>

How in democracy.

SECTION CXXIV

But since mixed republics, as they are called, are sometimes the best, and were formed on purpose that one form might balance another, and keep it within due bounds (§107), it is plain, that all, or some of the rights of majesty, ought to be so shared in such states, either among the senators,

How in mixed republics.

---

* Then is the condition of the republic most miserable, especially if demagogues interpose their arts to stir up the people and promote faction, till one of them finds an opportunity of becoming tyrant; and the same happens that Phaedrus represents to have been the fate of Athens, Fab. 1. 2.

> *Athenae quum florerent aequis legibus:*
> *Procax libertas civitatem miscuit,*
> *Fraenumque solvit pristinum licentia.*
> *Hinc, conspiratis factionum partibus,*
> *Arcem tyrannus occupat, Pisistratus.*

> [[Phaedrus, *Fables* 1.2, lines 1–5: In the days when Athens flourished under a democracy, freedom grown rank disturbed the civic calm and licence relaxed the reins of old-time discipline. Then diverse factions formed a common plot and soon a tyrant rose and seized the citadel, Pisistratus."]]

Concerning the artifices of demagogues, see Hertius Elem. prud. civil. part. 2. §23. §24. p. 496. [[Johann Nikolaus Hertius, *Elementa prudentiae civilis.*]]

or among the people, that one order cannot determine any thing without consulting the other, and not to be so divided, that one may act either without the knowledge, or against the will of the other. For, in this case, nothing can hinder a republic from springing up within a republic.*

SECTION CXXV

How in systems of republics.

As to *systems of republics,* since they are either constituted by the coalition of two kingdoms into one under a common head (§118), or by a confederacy between several independent states (ibid.) it is plain, in the former case, that unless they <108> be distinct, perfect kingdoms, besides a common king, they ought to have a common senate, to which all the orders of both kingdoms are called proportionably to their strength. But, in the latter case, each state exercises by itself, at its own pleasure, all the immanent rights of sovereignty; and the transeunt rights, relative to their common security, ought to be exercised in a common council, composed of delegates from each, which is either perpetual or temporary; and in which all affairs concerning their common security are determined, the delegates having first consulted each his own state.†

---

* The Roman state became monstrous when it degenerated into such a condition that the mob, stirred up by the factious fury of the tribunes, made laws, condemned or absolved, and did every thing without consulting with the rest of the people; and the people neither made laws nor administred justice, nor determined concerning war or peace, without the populace. But when instead of the people a certain rabble or mob decides every thing as they please, the popular state is corrupted into an ochlocracy; and that the Roman state was then not very far from such a condition, is very evident.

† Such of old was the Amphyctionian council, of which see Boecler. dissert. de Amphyct. and Ubbo Emmo vet. Graec. Tom. 3. p. 305. [[Boecler, *Synedrion Amphyktyonikon;* Emmo, *Vetus Graecia.*]] Of this we have an example at present in the most flourishing states of Holland and Switzerland, which are described by Jos. Simlerus [[Josias Simler (1530–76), Swiss Protestant theologian and historian, author of *De Republica Helvetiorum libri duo*]], Sir Richard Temple [[Richard Temple (1711–79), English statesman]], and other learned men; so that we need not say any thing of them.

SECTION CXXVI

But because such confederacies chiefly depend upon the articles or terms of the agreement, there cannot but be a great diversity in this matter; and some will be more closely united, and others more laxly; some will have more, and some less in common. Thus some may have, by confederacy or treaty, a common treasury, a common mint, and a common armory, and others not. In fine; some may have a certain president, who is guardian of the confederacy, and takes the chair in the council and others may be confederated in a very different manner; and, in a word, neither the right of suffrage, nor the manner of contributing towards the common security, nor any of the other constitutions can be every where, or in all confederacies the same. <109>

There may be a great diversity of systems of republics.

Remarks on This Chapter

First of all, it is worth while to observe here, That tho' it be very certain that mankind may be very happy, and arrive at a considerable degree of perfection in sciences and arts, to great politeness as well as opulence, in segregate families living independently one of another, or with regard to one another, in a state of natural equality and liberty; yet, as it is beyond all doubt on the one hand, that an ill-constituted civil state is the source of the greatest misery mankind can fall into; so on the other hand, it is equally plain from the nature of things, and from experience, that there is a perfection and happiness attainable by a rightly constituted civil state, to which mankind can no otherwise attain. Now mankind may be justly said to be fitted and designed for the state of the greatest perfection attainable by them in consequence of their frame; and therefore to be designed for the civil state, by which the greatest perfection and happiness of mankind is attainable. There must be means to an attainable end; and all means cannot possibly be equally fit for attaining the same end: But any end attainable by man in consequence of his having the means for attaining to it in his power, is, properly speaking, an end within human reach, according to the laws of human nature. And it is but doing justice to the Author of nature, and but speaking of the end for which mankind is designed by the

Author of all things, in the same manner we speak of the ends for which
any mechanical structure of nature's production (as the human body,
or any other animal body) or any mechanical structure produced by
human art, (as a ship, a watch, &c.) is designed, to say that mankind
are principally designed by the Author of nature for the best end, or
the highest perfection and happiness within human reach, in consequence of man's frame and constitution, the laws of his nature, and
the means within his power. If therefore the highest perfection and
happiness within human reach be attainable, and only attainable in a
rightly constituted civil state, and if men be sufficiently impelled to,
and furnished for rightly constituting a civil state, man may be said to
be intended for a rightly constituted civil state, and all the perfection
and happiness attainable in it, or by it, in the same sense that any animal
structure, or any machine, is said to be intended for its end. Our conclusion must hold, if the premises from which it is drawn be true.

Now, that there is a very high degree of perfection and happiness
attainable by man in a rightly constituted civil state, not otherwise attainable by man, will appear from comparing civilized states one with
another, and with nations living without any order deserving the name
of civil government. But the manifold advantages of rightly constituted civil government having been fully proved by many authors, Harrington, Sydney, Locke, among the moderns, and by Plato, Aristotle,
Polybius, <110> Cicero, and others among the ancients; I shall only
add upon this head, a very remarkable saying of one ancient, with regard to the greatest happiness attainable by man. Hippodamus Thurius
Pythagor. de felicitate,[5] having described the principal ingredients of
human happiness, says,—*Quae quidem omnia contingent si quis rem-
publicam bene constitutam nanciscatur. Id quod quidem* Amaltheae *quod
dicitur cornu voco. Etenim in recta legum constitutione sunt omnia; neque
maximum naturae humanae bonum vel existere absque ea, vel comparatum
& auctum permanere possit. Nam et virtutem, & ad virtutem viam in se
continet, quandoquidem in ea partim naturae bona procreantur, partim
& mores & studia; leges optime se habent & recta ratio, pietas sanctimonia
magnopere vigent. Quamobrem qui beatus futurus & seliciter victurus est,*

---

5. Hippodamus Thurius, *Peri eudaimonias* (*De felicitate*), in Diogenes Laertius,
De vitis, dogmatis et apophthegmatis clarorum philosophorum.

eam in bene constituta republica & vivere, necesse est & mori, &c. "All
these blessings and advantages will accrue to one from a well constituted
republic. This we may justly call the horn of *Amalthea,* the horn of
plenty and felicity. For all depends upon the good orders, constitutions
and laws of a state: Nor can the greatest good of mankind be attained,
or being attained, be preserved, without right government. A well
framed government includes virtue, and the way to virtue in it: Good
orders make good men: There the goods of nature grow up as in their
proper soil; and there good manners and useful studies and employments will flourish: There the laws direct and impel into the right paths;
and there reason, virtue, piety, authority, must have their greatest splendor and vigour. Wherefore, he who would be as happy as man can be,
and would continue while he lives to be such, must live and die in a
well framed, a well constituted or balanced civil government, *&c.*"

2. But let me just observe, in the second place, that ends and means
to ends, can only be learned from nature itself by experience, and reasoning from experience. This must be equally true with regard to natural and moral ends and means. The consequence of which is, that the
political art required time, observation and experience, to bring it to
perfection, as well as natural or mechanical arts. And for this reason,
in very early times of the world, men could not be so much masters of
the science upon which the framing of government aright must depend, as to have had all the advantages and disadvantages of different
governments, all the various effects of different moral or political constitutions in their view, in framing a government: They could only learn
these natural connexions of moral things from experience. And therefore, in treating of government, two separate enquiries ought never to
be confounded; the one of which is, "what ends right reason dictates
to mankind as the ends to be proposed in constituting civil government; and what means, *i.e.* what orders and constitutions it points out
as the proper means in order to attain these good ends." And the other
is, "how in fact various governments were formed, and how, <III> being formed, they changed gradually their frame to the better or worse."
The one is a question of fact or history; and the principal advantage
reaped by history, is instruction in the natural effects of various constitutions in different situations; or the knowledge of what moral connexions and causes produce in different circumstances, and the knowl-

edge of the rise of different circumstances, from internal or external causes; which knowledge has the same relation to moral theory in moral philosophy, that the history of facts in nature, with regard to the operation of natural causes in different circumstances, has to natural theory or physics: that is, it is the only solid basis in both to build upon. For as in physics it is now agreed that we can only come to solid or real knowledge by induction from experiments; so in morals and politics it is equally true, to use the words of a great man often quoted in these remarks, "To make principles or fundamentals belongs not to men, to nations, nor to human laws. To build upon such principles or fundamentals as are apparently laid by God in the inevitable necessity or law of nature, is that which truly appertains to men, to nations, and to human laws. To make any other fundamentals, and then build upon them, is to build castles in the air."[6] The other question supposes knowledge of human affairs, and the natural operations of moral causes, learned in this way from fact, and reasoning from fact or experience; and it is properly a philosophical enquiry into what ought to be done in consequence of the natural operation of moral causes, or of the laws of human nature, known by experience, in order to frame such a civil government as would make its members as happy as men can be. And it is, when it proceeds upon facts or experiments, the most pleasant and useful of all philosophical enquiries; and that certainly, which, of all other studies, best becomes those, who, by their natural happy lot, are delivered from drudgery to their backs and bellies. Nay, may I not say, that it is the study, to which, if such do not betake themselves chiefly, they are absolutely inexcusable. For sure, if virtue and benevolence be not empty names, they must lie under the strongest, the most indispensable obligations to qualify themselves for promoting human happiness: they are bound and obliged to be tutors and guardians to mankind. And whatever other employment they may carve out to themselves, or however thoughtlessly they may waste their time, if they neglect this, they neglect the noble work providence hath put into their hands to do. A work, (a happiness should I not rather say) than which nothing can be higher, nobler, or more glorious. It is a work or employment, and a happiness of the same kind with the work, em-

6. Harrington, *Aphorisms Political*, no. 85, in *Political Works*, 773.

ployment, and happiness of the great Author of nature, the all-perfect God.

But let me observe, in the third place, that tho' our author, in speaking of the origine of civil governments, (which is a question of fact or history) hath frequently come very near the matter, especially in the scholium, where he speaks of the king-<112>dom founded by Nimrod, yet he hath not fully spoke it out: and therefore it will not be improper here to lay before the reader a series of propositions relative to that subject; *i.e.* which shew government in its natural causes, or in its natural procreation and natural variations. And these truths having a necessary connexion with what hath been already taken notice of in our remarks with regard to property, or the acquisition of dominion over things, they will be easily understood; so that there will be but little occasion to do more than just mention them. And that I shall, for the greater part, do in the very words of an excellent author, unknown to foreign writers, from whom we have already borrowed so many useful observations.[7]

1. The distribution of property, so far as it regards the nature or procreation of government, lies in the over-balance of the same. Just as a man, who has two thousand pounds a year, may have a retinue, and consequently a strength that is three times greater than he who enjoys but five hundred pounds a year. Not to speak of money at this time, (*of that we have already treated in another remark,* viz. *the remarks on chapter* 13. *l.* 1. *which the reader may turn to*) which, in small territories, may be of like effect; but to insist upon the main, which is property in land, (because to property producing empire, it is required that it should have some certain root, or root-land, which, except in land, it cannot have, being otherwise, as it were, upon the wing); to insist upon this, which is the main, the over-balance of this, as it was at first constituted, or comes insensibly to be changed into a nation, may be especially of three kinds; that is, in one, in the few, or in many. The over-balance three to one, or thereabouts, in one man against the whole people, creates absolute monarchy; as when Joseph had purchased all the lands of the Egyptians for Pharaoh. The constitution of a people

---

7. Turnbull is referring to Harrington. The following sections are a summary of Harrington's central ideas, mostly from *Oceana*.

in this, and such cases, is capable of intire servitude. *Buy us and our land for bread, and we and our land will be servants to Pharaoh,* Gen. xlvii. 19. If one man be sole landlord of a territory, or overbalance the people, for example, three parts in four, he is Grand Signior; for so the Turk is called from his property; and his empire is absolute monarchy. The overbalance of the land to the same proportion in the few against the whole people, creates aristocracy, or regulated monarchy. The constitution of a people in this, and the like cases, is (*nec totam libertatem, nec totam servitatem pati possunt, Tacit.*)[8] neither capable of intire liberty, nor of intire servitude. And hereupon Samuel says to the people of Israel, when they would have a king, "*He will take your fields, even the best of them, and give them to his servants,* 1 Sam. viii." If a few, or a nobility with the clergy be landlords, or over-balance the people to the proportion above-mentioned, it makes what is called *the Gothic balance.* (See this treated of at large by Mr. Harrington.) The overbalance of land to the same proportion in the people, or <113> where neither one nor the few over-balance the whole people, creates popular government; as in the division of the land of *Canaan* to the whole people of Israel by lot. The constitution of a people in this, and the like cases, is capable of intire freedom; nay, not capable of any other settlement; it being certain, that if a monarch, or single person, in such a state, thro' the corruption or improvidence of their councils, might carry it; yet, by the irresistible force of nature, or the reason alledged by Moses, (*I am not able to bear all this people alone, because it is too heavy for me;* Numb. xi. 14.) he could not keep it, but out of the deep waters would cry to them, whose feet he had stuck in the mire. If the whole people be landlords, or hold the lands so divided among them, that no one man, or number of men, within the compass of the few, or aristocracy over-balance them, the empire, (without the interposition of force) is a commonwealth.

2. If force be interposed in any of these three cases, it must either frame the government to the foundation, or the foundation to the government; or holding the government not according to the balance, it is not natural, but violent; and therefore, if it be at the devotion of a prince, it is tyranny; if at the devotion of a few, oligarchy; or if in the

8. Tacitus, *Histories* I.16.28.

power of the people, anarchy. Each of which confusions, the balance standing otherwise, is but of short continuance, because against the nature of the balance, which not destroyed, destroys that which opposes it. But there be certain other confusions, which being rooted in the balance, are of a longer continuance, and of worse consequence. As first, where a nobility holds half the property, or about that proportion, and the people the other half; in which case, without altering the balance, there is no remedy but the one must eat out the other; as the people did the nobility in Athens, and the nobility the people in Rome. Secondly, when a prince holds about half the dominion, and the people the other half, (which was the case of the Roman Emperors, planted partly upon their military colonies, and partly upon the senate and the people) the government becomes a very shambles both of the princes and the people. Somewhat of this nature are certain governments at this day, which are said to subsist by confusion. In this case, to fix the balance is to entail misery; but in the three former, not to fix it, is to lose the government; wherefore, it being unlawful in Turkey, that any should possess land but the Grand Signior, the balance is fixed by the law, and that empire firm. While Lacedemon held to the division of land made by Lycurgus it was immoveable, but breaking that, could therefore stand no longer.

3. Fixation of government cannot be provided for without fixing the balance of property. But fixation of the balance of property is not to be provided for but by laws. Now, the laws whereby such provision is made, are commonly called *Agrarian laws*. This kind of law fixing the balance in lands, was settled by God himself, who divided the land of Canaan to his people <114> by lots; and it is of such virtue, that wherever it has held, that government has not altered, except by consent; as in that unparallelled example of the people of Israel, when being in liberty they would needs choose a king. But without an *Agrarian,* no government, whether monarchical, aristocratical or popular, has a long lease. And as governments are of divers or contrary natures, so are such laws. Monarchy requires of the standard of property, that it be vast or great; and of *Agrarian* laws, that they hinder recess or diminution, at least in so much as is thereby entailed upon honour. But popular government requires that the standard be moderate, and that its *Agrarian* prevent accumulation. In a territory not exceeding En-

gland in revenue, if the balance be in more hands than three hundred, it is declining from monarchy; and if it be in fewer than five thousand hands, it is swerving from a commonwealth. In consequence of the same principles, wherever the balance of a government lies, there naturally is the militia of the same; and against him or them, wherein the militia is naturally lodged, there can be no negative voice. If a prince holds the over-balance, as in Turkey, in him is the militia, as the Janizaries and Timariots. If a nobility has the over-balance, the militia is in them, as among us was seen in the Barons wars, and those of York and Lancaster; and in France is seen, when any considerable part of that nobility rebelling, they are not to be reduced, but by the major part of their order adhering to the king. If the people has the over-balance, which they had in Israel, the militia is in them, as in the four hundred thousand first decreeing, and then waging war against Benjamin; where it may be enquired, what power there was on earth having a negative voice to this assembly! This always holds where there is settlement, or where a government is natural. Where there is no settlement, or where the government is unnatural, it proceeds from one of these two causes, either an imperfection in the balance, or else such a corruption in the lawgivers, whereby a government is instituted contrary to the balance. Imperfections of the balance, that is, where it is not good or downright weight, cause imperfect governments; as those of the Roman and Florentine people, and those of the Hebrew Kings and Roman Emperors, being each exceeding bloody, or at least turbulent. Government against the balance in one is tyranny, as that of the Athenian Pisistratus; in the few it is oligarchy, as that of the Roman Decemvirs; in the many, anarchy, as that under the Neapolitan Mazinello.

4. From these principles will the reader find the more remarkable changes in the Athenian, Spartan, Roman, and other states, accounted for naturally by Mr. Harrington. And from them he justly infers, that wherever, thro' causes unforeseen by human prudence, the balance comes to be intirely changed, it is the more immediately to be attributed to divine providence: And since God cannot will the cause, <115> but he must also will the necessary effect or consequence, what government soever is in the necessary direction of the balance, the same is of divine right. Wherefore, tho' of the Israelites God says, *They have set up kings, but not by me; they have made princes, and I knew it not.* Yet to the small

countries adjoining to the Assyrian empire, he says, *"Now have I given all these lands into the hands of the king of Babylon my servant.—Serve the king of Babylon and live."* The general truth here insisted upon, which history abundantly confirms, is, that the over-balance of property begets dominion, and that the balance of dominion will always follow the balance of property, be under its direction, or vary as it varies. And therefore this author says very justly (of his works, p. 70.)[9] To erect a monarchy, be it ever so new, unless like *Leviathan,* you can hang it, as the country fellow speaks, by geometry; (for what else is it to say that any other man must give up his will to the will of this one man without any other foundation?) it must stand upon old principles, that is, upon a nobility, or an army planted in a due balance of dominion. "Aut viam inveniam aut faciam,"[10] was an adage of Caesar; and there is no standing for a monarchy, unless it finds this balance, or makes it. If it finds it, the work is done to its hand; for where there is inequality of estates, there must be inequality of power; and where there is inequality of power, there can be no commonwealth. To make it, the sword, must extirpate out of dominion all other roots of power, and plant an army upon that ground. An army may be planted nationally or provincially. To plant it nationally, it must be either monarchically in part, as the Roman Beneficiarii; or monarchically in the whole, as the Turkish tenants; or aristocratically, that is, by earls and barons, as the Neustrians were planted by Turbo; or democratically, that is, by equal lots, as the Israelitish army in the land of Canaan by Joshua. In every one of these ways, there must not only be confiscations, but confiscations to such a proportion as may answer to the work intended.

5. As nothing else can fix government but an *Agrarian* suitable to its nature; so different superstructures are natural to different foundations of government. Thus, such superstructures as are natural to an absolute prince, or the sole landlord of a large territory, require for the first story of the building, that what demesnes he shall think fit to reserve being

---

9. Harrington, *The Oceana and Other Works of James Harrington, Esq.,* 70 (see *Political Works,* 198–99).

10. An adage of Julius Caesar: "Either I shall find a way or I shall make one." As Liljegren points out, this adage is probably a later invention; it has no warrant in Caesar or in any of the ancient commentators on him (*James Harrington's Oceana,* 282).

set apart, the rest be divided into horse quarters or military farms for
life, or at will, and not otherwise; and that every tenant for every hundred pounds a year so held, be, by condition of his tenure, obliged to
attend his sovereign lord in person, in arms, and at his proper cost and
charges, with one horse, so often, and so long as he shall be commanded
upon service. These, among the Turks, are called *Timariots.* The second
story requires, that these horse-quarters, or military farms, be divided
by con-<116>venient precincts or proportions into distinct provinces,
and that each province have one commander in chief of the same, at
the will and pleasure of the Grand Signior, or for three years, and no
longer. Such, among the Turks, (unless by additional honours, they be
called *Bashaws* or *Viziers*) are the *Beglerbegs.* For the third story, there
must of necessity be a mercenary army, consisting both of horse and
foot, for the guard of the prince's person, and for the guard of his
empire, by keeping the governors of provinces so divided, that they be
not suffered to lay their arms or heads together, or to hold intelligence
with one another; which mercenary army ought not to be constituted
of such as have already contracted some other interest, but to consist
of men so educated from their very childhood, as not to know that they
have any other parent or native country, than the prince and his empire.
Such, among the Turks, are the foot, called *Janizaries,* and the horse,
called *Spahys.* The prince, accommodated with a privy council, consisting of such as have been governors of provinces, is the top-stone.
This council, among the Turks, is called *the Divan,* and this prince, *the
Grand Signior.*

The superstructures proper to a regulated monarchy, or to the government of a prince, (three or four hundred of whose nobility, or of
whose nobility and clergy hold three parts in four of the territory) must
either be by personal influence, upon the balance, or by virtue of orders.
The safer way of this government is by orders; and the orders proper
to it, especially consist of an hereditary senate of the nobility, admitting
also of the clergy, and of a representative of the people, made up of
the Lord's menial servants, or such as by tenure, and for livelihood,
have immediate dependance upon them.

An aristocracy, or state of nobility, to exclude the people, must govern by a king; or to exclude a king, must govern by the people. Nor is
there, without a senate, or mixture of aristocracy, any popular govern-

ment; wherefore, tho', for discourse sake, politicians speak of pure aristocracy and pure democracy, there is no such thing as either of these in nature, art, or example: where the people are not over-balanced by one man, or by the few, they are not capable of any other superstructures of government, or of any other just and quiet settlement whatsoever, than of such only as consists of a senate as their counsellors, of themselves, or their representative, as sovereign lords, and of a magistracy answerable to the people as the distributers and executioners of the laws made by the people. And thus much is of absolute necessity to any, or every government, that is or can be properly called a commonwealth, whether it be well or ill ordered. But the necessary definition of a commonwealth any thing well ordered, is, that it is a government consisting of the senate proposing, the people resolving, and the magistracy executing. To speak of different or-<117>ders in commonwealths, would be almost endless. Some commonwealths consist of distinct sovereignties, as *Switzerland* and *Holland;* others are collected into one and the same sovereignty, as most of the rest. Again, some commonwealths have been upon rotation or courses in the representative only, as *Israel;* others in the magistracy only, as *Rome;* some in the senate and magistracy, as *Athens* and *Venice;* others in some part of the magistracy, and in others not; as *Lacedemon* in the *Ephori,* and not in the kings; and *Venice* not in the *Doge,* nor in the *procuratori,* but in all the rest. *Holland,* except in the election of states provincial (which is emergent) admits not of any rotations or courses. But there may be a commonwealth admitting of rotation throughout, as in the senate, in the representative, and in the magistracy, as that proposed by Mr. Harrington in his Oceana. Rotation, if it be perfect, is equal election by, and succession of the whole people to the magistracy by terms and vacations. Equal election may be by lot, as that of the senate of Lacedemon; or by ballot, as that of Venice, which of all others is the most equal. The ballot, as it is used in Venice, consists of a lot, whence proceeds the right of proposing, and of an unseen way of suffrage, or of resolving. From the wonderful variety of parts, and the difference of mixture (before Mr. Harrington scarce touched by any) result those admirable differences that are in the constitution and genius of popular governments; some being for defence, some for increase; some more equal, others more unequal; some turbulent and seditious, others like streams in a perpetual tranquillity. That which causes much sedition in a commonwealth is inequality, as in Rome, where the senate oppressed the people. But if a commonwealth be perfectly equal, it is void of sedition, and has attained to perfection, as being void of all internal causes of dissolution. And hence many antient moral writers, Cicero in particular, have said, that a well constituted commonwealth is immortal, *aeterna est.* An equal commonwealth is a government founded upon a balance, which is perfectly popular, being well fixed by a suitable Agrarian, and which, from the balance, through the free suffrage of the people given by the ballot, amounts, in the superstructures, to a senate debating and proposing, a representative of the people resolving, and a magistracy executing; each of these three orders being upon courses or rotation; that is, elected for certain terms injoining like intervals. And to undertake the binding of a prince from invading liberty, and yet not to introduce the whole orders necessary to popular government, is to undertake a flat contradiction, or a plain impossibility.

6. All I have further to add in this remark, designed to shew the natural generation and variation of empire is, that these principles (as Mr. Harrington has observed) were not unknown to ancient politicians, and are sufficiently confirmed by history. That they were not unknown to Moses, is plain from <118> the history given us of the orders of the commonwealth instituted by him; nor to Lycurgus, is as plain. I shall only just set down the passages Mr. Harrington quotes from Aristotle and Plutarch. The first is Aristotle, in these words: "Inequality is the source of all sedition, as when the riches of one or a few come to cause such an overbalance in dominion, as draws the commonwealth into monarchy or oligarchy; for prevention whereof the *ostracism* has been of use in divers places, as at *Argos* and *Athens.* But it were better to provide in the beginning, that there be no such disease in the commonwealth, than to come afterwards to her cure, Polit. 5. 3." The second is Plutarch, in these words: "Lycurgus judging that there ought to be no other inequality among citizens of the same commonwealth than what derives from their virtues, divided the land so equally among the Lacedemonians, that, on a day beholding the harvest of their lots lying by cocks or ricks in the field, he laughing said, that it seemed to him they were all brothers, Plutarch in Lycurg."[11] This ac-

11. This is a selective quotation from Plutarch's life of Lycurgus, chap. 8 (Plutarch, *Lives,* vol. 1, "Lycurgus," 227–29).

count of the rise, variation or fixation of empire, is abundantly confirmed by experience or history. To prove this I shall only here insert a small part of what Mr. Harrington says of several ancient republics, in order to excite the reader's curiosity to have recourse to himself, (of his works, p. 57).[12] "Israel and Lacedemon, which commonwealths have great resemblance, were each of them equal in their Agrarian, and inequal in their Rotation: especially Israel, where the Sanhedrim or senate first elected by the people, took upon them ever after to substitute their successors by ordination. And the election of the judge, suffes,[13] or dictator, was irregular, both for the occasion, the term, and the vacation of that magistracy, as you find in the book of Judges where it is often repeated, That in those days there was no King in Israel, that is, no Judge: and in the first of Samuel where Eli judged Israel forty years, and Samuel all his life. In Lacedemon, the election of the senate being by suffrage of the people, tho' for life, was not altogether so unequal, yet the hereditary right of kings, were it not for the Agrarian, had ruined her. Athens and Rome were inequal as to their Agrarian, that of Athens being infirm, and this of Rome none at all; for if it were more anciently carried, it was never observed. Whence, by the time of Tiberius Gracchus, the nobility had almost eaten the people quite out of their lands, which they held in the occupation of tenants and servants: whereupon, the remedy being too late, and too vehemently applied, that commonwealth was ruined. These also were unequal in their rotation, but in a contrary manner. Athens, in regard that the senate (chosen at once by lot, not by suffrage, and changed every year, not in part, but in the whole) consisted not of the natural aristocracy; nor sitting long enough to understand or be perfect in their office, had no sufficient autho-<119>rity to restrain the people from that perpetual turbulence in the end, which was their ruin, notwithstanding the efforts of *Nicias,* who did all a man could do to help it. But as Athens fell by the headiness of the people, so Rome fell by the ambition of the nobility, through the want of an equal rotation; which, if the people had got into the senate, and timely into the magistracy (whereof the former was always usurped by the patricians, and the latter for the most part) they had

---

12. Harrington, *The Oceana and Other Works,* 57 (*Political Works,* 184).

13. The *suffetes* ("suffes") were the supreme executive magistrates of the ancient republic of Carthage and later were considered comparable to the judges in Israel.

both carried and held their Agrarian, and that had rendered that commonwealth immoveable."

This short specimen of our Author's way of reasoning about the rise and fall, or variations of civil government, is sufficient to shew, that he reasons from natural causes in these matters, as natural philosophers do about phenomena commonly called natural ones. And indeed every thing in nature, moral or corporeal nature, must have its natural course, its natural rise, progress and variations. And as to know the one is to be a natural philosopher, so to know the other is to be a moral philosopher or politician.

Of sovereignty, and the ways of acquiring it.

SECTION CXXVII

Since those who unite into a civil state lived before that in a state of nature (§3), which is a state of equality and liberty (§5 and 6); the consequence is, that a civil state is subjected to no person or persons without it; may not be hindered or disturbed in doing any thing it judges necessary for its conservation, but may freely exerce all its rights, and cannot be forced to give an account to any of its transactions. But all those things together constitute what is called *supreme* or *absolute sovereignty* or *empire;* and therefore, in every civil state, there is supreme and absolute empire or sovereignty.* <120>

All sovereignty is supreme and absolute.

* We are now speaking of a republic properly so called, which we defined to be a multitude of people united together under a common head for their security, and independent of all others (§103). And therefore, a people conquered and brought under power by a conqueror, is not a republic, but a *province,* because subjected to others. For the same reason, a multitude of people, united indeed under a common magistracy, but subjected to a large kingdom or republic, does not properly come under the appellation of a *republic,* but of a *town-corporate:* Wherefore the civilians frequently call such towns-corporate *republics,* and thus make mention of the republic of Antioch, l. 37. D. de reb. auct. jud. possid. of the republic of the Heliopolitani, l. 4. C. qui pot. in pign. of the Tusculans, l. 38. §5. D. de legat. of the Sebastiani, l. 21. §3. D. de ann. leg. of the Arelatenses, l. 34. D. de usu & usufruct. leg. of the Sardiani, l. 24. D. de ann. legat. yet when they speak more accurately, they deny those to be absent on account of the republic, who are sent upon a commission by a city, l. 26. § ult. D. in quibus causs. mai. It is therefore of consequence how we use the word *republic.*

SECTION CXXVIII

The error of monarch-killers.

Because there is supreme empire or absolute sovereignty in every civil state or republic (§127), and citizens or subjects may have submitted their will either to one, or many, or to the whole people, (§114); the consequence is, that to whomsoever they have submitted their will, he, or they are vested with supreme power or sovereignty, and therefore they can be judged by none but God alone; and much less therefore can they be punished in any manner by the people; so that the doctrine of monarch-killers, which makes the people superior to the king or prince, and places in the former the real, and in the latter only personal majesty, is a most petulant one.* <121>

* This is the doctrine of Franc. Hotoman. Stephen Junius Brutus, (under which fictitious name some think Hub. Languetus, others think Buchanan lurked) Sidney, Althusius, Pareus, Jo. Milton, and others, of which authors see besides the observ. Halenses, 6. 1. Jo. Franc. Budd. hist. juris naturae & gentium, §52. [[Heineccius argues against the leading (Protestant) theories of resistance (the so-called Monarchomachs as set out in the following: François Hotman (1524–90), *Francogallia* (1573); Stephanus Junius Brutus, pseudonymous author of one of the most influential Huguenot writings on resistance, *Vindiciae contra tyrannos,* 1579; Algernon Sidney, *Discourses;* Johannes Althusius (1557–1638), *Politica* (1603); David Paraeus (1548–1622), German Protestant theologian, *In divinam ad Romanos S. Pauli Apostoli epistolam commentarius;* John Milton (1608–74), *A Tenure of Kings and Magistrates* (1650) and *A Defence of the People of England* (1658) (in Milton, *Political Writings*). The "observ. Halenses" are the *Observationum selectarum ad rem literariam spectantium.* The final reference is to Johannes Franz Budde's *Historia juris naturalis.*]] But the fundamental error by which they are misled into allowing power and authority over kings, lies in their making the constituent superior to the constituted; for that principle being presupposed, the people which constitutes their prince or head (111), must be superior to the prince or head constituted by them. Now this doctrine is no less absurd than it would be to say, that a servant who hath voluntarily subjected himself to a master (§78), is superior to his master, because he constituted him such. See Grotius of the rights of war and peace, 1. 3. 8. Zach. Huber. diss. l. 2. p. 124. [[Zacharias Huber (1669–1732), *Dissertationes juridicae et philologicae.* He was the son of Ulrik Huber (see note on pp. 441–42).]] Reason rather tells us, that he cannot be superior who hath subjected himself to another's will, having thus renounced his own will. And therefore, since a people does so when they unite into a republic (§128), with what front can they call themselves superior to their sovereign?

SECTION CXXIX

But since subjects have only so far subjected themselves to the will of a sovereign as their common security, the end for which they entred into the civil state, requires (§14 & 106), we must infer from hence, that they are abominable and flagitious flatterers of sovereigns, who persuade them that they may do what they please, and can do no injury to their subjects; but that their persons, lives, reputations and estates, are so absolutely dependent upon them, that subjects have no more left to them but the glory of absolute submission and obedience. From this corrupt spring flow all those pestiferous tenets, which Machiavel and Hobbes have attempted to impose upon mankind with the greatest assurance; and, together with them, all the asserters and defenders of passive-obedience in Great Britain. But who will deny that such doctrines are no less pestilential than that of *king-killing?** <122>

As likewise of the machiavelians.

---

* The tenets of Machiavel and Hobbes are well known. Nor is the controversy so warmly agitated between the authors of books intitled, *Julianus* and *Jovinianus,* and other learned men in Great Britain, less notorious. [[The debate was about the prospect of a Catholic king when James, Duke of York, was heir to the throne, and about the implications this had for the status and character of the Anglican church. More particularly, Turnbull refers to a fierce pen-fight between Samuel Johnson (1649–1703) and George Hickes (1642–1715), both Anglican clergymen. The former's *Julian the Apostate* (1682) likened James to the fourth-century emperor and thus drew a parallel between resistance to a pagan and a Catholic ruler. Hickes's answer, *Jovinian* (1683), invoked the eponymous Roman monk (d. ca. 406) who fought against fashionable asceticism by denying any inherent value in celibacy and simple living. After 1689, Hickes became a non-juring bishop, Johnson a prominent Whig pamphleteer.]] Grotius of the rights of war and peace, I. 3. 8. is thought by not a few, to have given some handle to this doctrine of passive-obedience and non-resistance. But whether a people is subdued by force, or consents voluntarily to their subjection, it is unlawful, highly criminal for a prince to injure his people, or oppress them in a hostile manner. For in the first case, the people laid aside their hostile disposition, when they surrendered or gave themselves up. And in the latter case, the prince has no power but what was transferred to him by the people, which none will say was a power to maletreat them like slaves. That passage, 1 Sam. viii. 11. gives no authority to such abuse; for whether we understand the *jus regis* there mentioned to be a narrative of fact and custom, as *jus latronis* is used, l. 5. D. ad leg. Pomp. de parricid. or of the *dominium eminens,* as the Jewish doctors interpret it, and with them Thomasius ad Huber. de jure civit. I. 2. 7. 13. p. 58. [[Thomasius, *Annotationes ad Ulrici Huberi libros tres de*

SECTION CXXX

Sovereigns
are sacred.

Since sovereigns cannot be judged by any but God, much less be punished by their people (§128); hence we conclude that sovereignty is sacred, and that Sovereigns are sacred; and therefore that sedition and rebellion are very heinous crimes. Tho' we should grant in theory, that
Sovereigns who manifest a hostile disposition against their subjects, may
be resisted as tyrants; yet this rule would be in fact of no utility, because
Sovereigns can only be judged by God, and therefore God alone can
decide whether a Sovereign truly bears a hostile mind against his subjects
or not.* <123>

---

jure civitatis; Ulrik Huber (1636–94) was a Dutch jurist at the University of Franeker,
later at Utrecht and Leiden]] or of *jus,* right, so far obligatory that it may not be
resisted, as *jus* is used by Paullus, l. 11. de just. & jure, and as V. A. Zach. Huber
explains this place, ibid. p. 237, it cannot be proved from thence, that sovereigns have
any such right as Machiavel and Hobbes, and their disciples, a *slavish race,* have dared
to attribute to them. Surely a good prince will never arrogate such power to himself,

> *Qualis apud veteres divus regnabat Ulysses,*
> *Qui nulli civi dicto factove nocebat.*
> *Scilicet hoc hominem Dis immortalibus aequat.*

> [["Among the ancients, Ulysses was such a divine king; he harmed no citizen
> in word or deed. Surely this makes a man equal to the immortal gods." The
> source of this quotation is not clear.]]

* Thomas. ad Huber. de jure civ. 1. 9. 2. 20. p. 316. hath treated largely on this
subject. The example of Henry IV. Emperor, if it be carefully attended to, will sufficiently convince any one how dangerous it is to allow the people a right of judging
of this matter. He was a most brave prince, and his only design was to recover to
himself the rights of empire and sovereignty, extorted from him in his minority. The
clergy, to whom that was imputed, were chafed; and it was easy to them to misrep-
resent and traduce a young headstrong prince, zealous of his rights, as an enemy to
the church and state, not only to the populace, but even to the princes of the empire
called secular, nay, and to Pope Gregory; and thus so to dispose things, that an excellent prince, tho' he had an army that was for the most part victorious, was strip'd
by his own son of his kingdom and all his wealth, as an enemy to the church and
state. So perilous is it to allow not only the populace, but even the nobles, to judge
of the actions of princes. [[A reference to the so-called investiture contest between
Emperor Henry IV (1050–1106) and Pope Gregory VII, which culminated in 1077.
The dispute was linked to a revolt by the German princes against the emperor.]]

SECTION CXXXI

But since every thing is not lawful to a prince (§129) the consequence is, that he cannot impose any violence or restraint upon the consciences of his subjects, nor command them to do any thing contrary to the will of God the supreme lawgiver (l. 1. §87); neither can he, without a pregnant and just reason, deprive any subject of his right, seeing subjects united into a civil state chiefly for the security of their rights (§105). Subjects therefore, in great distress, may try all methods in order to obtain their rights, and, in extreme danger, leave their native country (§21); but they may not take up arms against their prince or the republic (l. 1. §232). <131>

But yet it is not lawful to sovereigns to do whatever they please.

[I cannot go further without observing, that it is surprizing to find so distinct and clear an author, after he had laid down principles that lead, as it were, by the hand, to the true conclusion about the rights of subjects, giving and taking in such a manner upon this subject, that one cannot tell what he would be at. But Grotius, Pufendorff, and all the writers of systems of the laws of nature and nations, treat this important question in the same manner. I shall not stay here to observe, that our Author runs into the common mistake about Machiavel's doctrine; so unaccountably are that excellent politician's writings misunderstood. Our Harrington, tho' he differs from him in several points, has done justice to him, and shewn him to be a friend to liberty, and to have understood the true principles of politics better than most writers on the subject. But let me take notice, that the excellence of our constitution appears from this, that our country has produced the best treatises on government: In this matter we have left all other countries far behind. Mr. Barbeyrac, in his notes on the chapters of Grotius and Pufendorff relative to government, has done us justice in this point, and indeed in every thing. He hath set his Authors right in this matter by the help of our Sidney, Locke and others. And no where is this subject more fully and accurately handled than in an excellent treatise upon the measures of submission, published at a very seasonable time, by an inimitable defender of the rights and liberties of mankind (Dr. Hoadley Bishop of Winchester) [[Benjamin Hoadley (1676–1761), controversialist and successively bishop of Bangor (1716), Hereford (1721), Salisbury (1723), and Winchester (1734); Turnbull is referring to Hoadley's *Measures of Submission*]] whose name will be precious in our country, while the value of our constitution is known, and we preserve a just sense of the best privileges men can enjoy, or God bestow; privileges we cannot part with without the greatest of crimes, because we cannot give them up, without degrading ourselves into a state far below that for which God designed men, by making them rational and free agents. Our Author lays a mighty stress upon this maxim, That the inferior cannot call the superior to account. But is there any absurdity in our excellent Hooker's [[Richard Hooker (ca. 1554–1600), Anglican theologian]] distinction between *singulis major* and *universis minor?* [["Singulis major": "greater/more powerful than the individual citizens"; "universis minor": "less powerful than the citizenry as a whole."]] I am to return to this momentous question afterwards. But what an odd jumble is our Author's doctrine upon this article, when all he says is brought together? It amounts briefly to this: "A prince has no right to injure his subjects: It is unlawful or criminal in him to do it; and they are base flatterers who tell princes they may do what they please; but God alone can judge when they do injure their subjects; the people hath no right to judge of the matter; and if they should, in extreme misery, feel they are injured, all they, who may do every thing in that case to recover their rights, have a right to do, is to leave their dear native country." Who would have expected to have found our Author talking any where in such a manner? Let us oppose to this a few things, first from Mr. Sidney. "They who create magistracies, and give to them such nature, form and power as they think fit, do only know whether the end for which they were created be performed or not. They who give a being to the power which had none, can only judge whether it be employed to their welfare, or turned to their ruin. They do not set up one, or a few men, that they and their posterity may live in splendor and greatness; but that justice may be administred, virtue established, and provision made for the public safety. No wise man will think this can be done, if those who set themselves to overthrow the law are to be their own judges. If Caligula, Nero, Vitellius, Domitian, or Heliogabulus had been subject to no other judgment, they would have compleated the destruction of the empire. If the disputes between Durstus, Evenus III. Dardanus, and other Kings of Scotland, with the nobility and people, might have been determined by themselves, they had escaped the punishments they suffered, and ruined the nation, as they designed. Other methods were taken; they perished by their madness; better princes were brought into their places, and their successors were by their example admonished to avoid the ways that had proved fatal to them. If Edward II. of England, with Gaveston and the Spencers, Richard II. with Tresilian and Vere, had been permitted to be judges of their own cases, they who had murdered the best of the nobility would have pursued their designs to the destruction of such as remained, the enslaving of the nation, the subversion of the constitution and the establishment of a mere tyranny, in the place of a mixed monarchy. But our ancestors took better measures. They who had felt the smart of the vices and follies of their princes, knew what remedies were most fit to be applied, as well as the best time of applying them. They found the effects of extreme corruption in government, to be so desperately pernicious, that nations must necessarily suffer, unless it be corrected, and the state reduced to its first principle, or altered. Which being the case, it was as easy for them to judge whether the governor, who had introduced that corruption, should be brought to order, or removed, if he would not be reclaimed, or whether he should be suffered to ruin them and their posterity; as it is for me to judge whether I should put away my servant, if I knew he intended to poison or murder me, and had a certain facility of accomplishing his design; or whether I should continue him in my service till he had performed it. Nay, the matter is so much the more plain on the side of the nation, as the disproportion of merit between a whole people and one or a few men entrusted with the power of governing them is greater than between a private man and his servant." Discourse upon government, chap. 3. §41. The same author, chap. 3. §36. observes, "Neither are subjects bound to stay till the prince has entirely finished the chains which he is preparing for them, and has put it out of their power to oppose. 'Tis sufficient, that all the advances which he makes are manifestly tending to their oppression, that he is marching boldly on to the ruin of the state." [[Sidney, *Discourses Concerning Government*, 1704 ed., chap. 3, sec. 41, p. 399. There are some minor discrepancies between Turnbull's first quotation and the 1704 text. The second quotation (chap. 3, sec. 36) does not appear in Sidney's *Discourses* at all. Turnbull, clearly, is using Barbeyrac's note 1 on Pufendorf's *Law of Nature and Nations*, bk. 7, chap. 8, sec. 6, rather than Sidney's text as the source of these quotations.]]

The second is from Mr. Locke on government, chap. 18. §209. [[See Locke, *Two Treatises of Government*, bk. II, chap. 18, §209–10.]] It is as impossible for a governor, if he really means the good of the people, and the preservation of them and the laws together, not to make them see and feel it; as it is for the father of a family not to let his children see he loves and takes care of them (§210). How can a man any more hinder himself from believing in his own mind which way things are going, or from casting about how to save himself, than he could from believing the captain of the ship he was in was carrying him and the rest of his company to *Algiers,* when he found him always steering that course, tho' cross winds, leaks in his ship, and want of men and provisions, did often force him to turn his course another way for some time, which he steadily returned to again, as soon as the winds, weather, and other circumstances would let him. *But it will be said, this hypothesis lays a ferment for frequent rebellion. No more,* says Mr. *Locke, than any other hypothesis.* "1. For when the people are made miserable, and find themselves exposed to the ill usage of arbitrary power, cry up their governors as much as you will for *sons of Jupiter,* let them be sacred and divine, descended or authorized from heaven; give them out for whom or what you please, the same will happen. The people, generally ill-treated, and contrary to right, will be ready, upon any occasion, to ease themselves of a burden that sits heavy upon them. 2. Such revolutions happen not upon every little mismanagement in public affairs. Great mistakes in the ruling part, many wrong and inconvenient laws, and all the slips of human frailty, will be born by the people without mutiny and murmur. 3. This power in the people of providing for their safety anew by a new legislative, when their legislators have acted contrary to their trust, by invading their property, is the best fence against rebellion, and the most probable means to hinder it. For rebellion being an opposition, not to persons, but authority, which is founded only in the laws and constitutions of the government; those, whoever they be, who, by force, break through, and, by force, justify the violation of them, are truly and properly rebels." [[Ibid., chap. 19, §224–26.]] *The principle upon which all this depends is self-evident, and clearly set forth by the same author, book 2. cap. 4.* "No man can so far part with his liberty, as to give himself up wholly to an arbitrary power, to be treated absolutely as that power thinks proper: for this would be to dispose of his own life, of which he is not master. Much less has a whole people such a right, as every one of those who compose it, is intirely destitute of. The natural liberty of man is to be free from any superior power on earth, and not to be under the will or legislative authority of man, but to have only the law of nature for his rule. The liberty of man in society, is to be under no other legislative power, but that established by consent in the common-wealth; nor under the dominion of any will, or restraint of any law, but what the legislative shall exact according to the trust put in it;—as freedom of nature is to be under no other restraint but the law of nature. This freedom from absolute arbitrary power is so necessary to, and closely joined with a man's preservation, that he cannot part with it, but by what forfeits his life and preservation together." [[Ibid., chap. 3, §22, apart from the first two sentences in this quotation, which seem to be a paraphrase rather than a quotation.]]

The third is from Dr. Hoadley's measures of submission, (the defence) p. 70. [[Hoadley, *Measures of Submission,* 70]] "Supposing some should apply this doctrine, which only concerns the worst of governors to the best, and oppose good princes, under pretence that it is lawful to oppose tyrants and oppressors, this cannot affect the truth of the doctrine; nor doth the doctrine in the least justify or excuse them, but rather condemns them. Our blessed Lord hath laid down a very reasonable permission in his gospel, that husbands may put away their wives in case of adultery, and marry others; and is this ever the less reasonable, because wicked men, under the cover of this, may put away the most virtuous wives, and take others merely for the gratification of their present inclinations? Or doth this permission of our Lord's justify all pieces of wickedness that may be acted under the pretext of it? It is certainly true, that magistrates may, and ought to punish and discourage evil men, and disturbers of human society: And is this ever the less true, because some magistrates may, under the pretence of this, punish and afflict the best and most peaceable subjects? It is certainly true that a child may resist a father, if he should attempt to take away his life: And is this ever the less true, because a child may, through mistake, pretend against a good father, that he hath designs against his life, and, under that pretence, dishonour and resist him? It is agreed upon on all hands, as a good general rule, that men ought to follow the dictates of their consciences: But surely this rule is not made false; nor can it be supposed to justify a man, if he should be so void of understanding, as to be directed by his conscience to murder his parent or his prince, as a point of indispensable duty."

In this excellent treatise, all the objections against the doctrine of liberty, and all the monstrous absurdities of the opposite doctrine of passive-obedience and non-resistance are fully handled with uncommon strength and perspicuity of argumentation. But our author may be refuted in a few words from his own principles. He says expresly, (§129 in the scholium), that a prince has no right to shew a hostile disposition, or to injure even a subdued people, *Nefas est principi,* &c. Now, is not obligation the correlate of right; and have not then a people a right to demand, exact, nay, force (*i.e.* a perfect right, according to his own definition) their prince to treat them uninjuriously, that is justly. If a prince has no right to injure, he is obliged not to injure; but if he be obliged not to injure, the people whom he is obliged not to injure, hath a right to demand just treatment from him, and to keep off injuries, otherwise a prince may be under an obligation to a people, and yet the people may acquire no right by that obligation to them. If the law of nature extends to all men, it extends to those vested with power, as well as to those under power; now, as far as the law of nature extends, the law of justice and benevolence, or in one word, the law of love extends; for that is the sum and substance of the law of nature. But so far as the law of love extends, justice is of perfect obligation, and benevolence is of imperfect obligation: Princes therefore, being under the law of nature, are perfectly obliged to justice, and imperfectly obliged to benevolence. Now, since none (as our Author often says) can be under an obligation, without giving some right to some other; it is plain a prince cannot be under the perfect obligation of justice, and the imperfect obligation of benevolence, without giving the people, to whom he is perfectly or imperfectly obliged, a perfect or imperfect right, correspondent to these his different obligations to them. The people therefore must have a perfect right to justice; that is, according to our Author's definition of perfect right, they must have a just title to exact, to demand, nay, to force it. There is no avoiding this conclusion from our Author's own principles, but by saying what he denies, and never will say, "That men are only under the law of nature till they have got subjects some how or other under their power; and that then power is right, and they are no more under the law of nature." For unless this be asserted, whether a people be subdued, and, to make the best of their misfortunes, hath surrendered themselves to their conqueror as their prince; or whether a people voluntarily and freely chooses to subject themselves to one or many as their governors, it must be true that a prince is under perfect obligation to justice, in the treatment of his subjects; and consequently, that they have a perfect right to force justice from him. No misfortunes can, and far less can voluntary consent destroy or annul the law of nature. And therefore the right to justice common to all men, can neither be annulled by the superior force of arms, nor given up by voluntary consent. To say that the people, tho' they can judge of the obligations of other men to justice by the law of nature, yet cannot, or have not a right to judge of the obligations of their prince to justice by the law of nature, is either to say, that men in civil government give up not only their understandings, but their senses and feeling; or it is to say, that tho' they may still see, feel and understand injustice, yet by putting themselves under a prince, they put him in a state that exeems him from all obligation to justice, and consequently annuls their right to it; which is to say, that civil government annuls the law of nature; and which of these two is most absurd, is difficult to determine. To say the people have in civil government a perfect right to justice, and that the princes are by the law of nature perfectly obliged to render justice to their subjects; and yet that the people have in the case of unjust treatment by their governors or princes, no right left to them, but that of leaving their dear native country, is to say they have a perfect right, the exercise of which is unlawful; a perfect right which is no right at all. And to say the right of subjects to justice under civil government, is a perfect right to demand and exact justice from their governors, every way but by taking up arms, is to speak of a right not defined by our Author, or any writer on the law of nature and nations, by all of whom, either in our Author' words, or in others equivalent to them, right is divided into perfect and imperfect; and right to justice is called perfect right. So that our Author must give up his conclusions in the preceding sections, or he must say, That civil government being constituted, the right of subjects to justice from their governors, becomes, instead of a perfect right, an imperfect one, as the right to benevolence: nay, which is more, he must say, That, tho' in a state of nature a right to benevolence may become, by the law of necessity, a perfect right (as our Author hath often said it may), yet in a state of civil government, the right to justice, even in extreme necessity, is none at all. For sure that right becomes none at all, which extends no farther than to the right of tamely leaving one's native country when one cannot have justice, but is injuriously used, which is the whole of the right of subjects according to our Author, notwithstanding the full and perfect obligation of princes to justice. We may reason thus against our Author from his own concessions, his own principles. But does it indeed require any proof, that miracles from heaven cannot prove any person to have a right to exerce his power over those who are under it, whether by consent or force, in an injurious, cruel, oppressive manner? Miracles from heaven could not prove the doctrine of passive-obedience and non-resistance to be a doctrine of God. It is an immoral doctrine, which overturns the law of nature, and destroys all moral obligations. Whence could our Author, or any writer on the laws of nature, derive his conclusions, without laying down this fundamental principle, as our Author does, "That God wills the perfection and happiness of mankind, and gives them a right to make themselves happy?" But is not this principle given up, the moment it is asserted, That under civil oppression and tyranny, because it is the effect of power, submitted to for common preservation, safety and happiness (the only end of civil society) men must put up contentedly with all hardships, injuries and abuses, and no more think of any probable means to

SECTION CXXXII

Tho' these things be true of Sovereigns in general, yet it may happen, that empire is given to one with certain restrictions by pacts, and with a commissory article to this effect, that the deed shall be null, if the conditions be not fulfilled. Now, in this case, no injury is done to Sovereigns, if after they have been frequently admonished, they do not cease to invade the liberty of their subjects, and to oppress them, the Empire be taken from them. And it is evident, from the nature of pacts, if freemen hinder those from exercising rule over them, who assume it to themselves without any just title to it, or with whom they have made no pact, no transference of power, no covenant, they cannot be blamed.* <133>

What if empire be given with a commissory clause?

make themselves happy, of any probable means, should I not rather say, to rescue themselves from misery into a state somewhat congruous to the natural dignity of mankind, and to the only intention, God can be supposed, without blasphemy, to have had in view by creating them such as they are made, for religion, virtue, industry, ingenuity, social commerce, and all the goods, wisdom, benevolence, religion, virtue, good government, art and united strength can procure to human society, many of which blessings may be attained to in some degree in a state of nature, but can never be attained to in any degree under absolute slavery, or despotic, injurious, lawless tyranny.]

* Hence we see, that Brutus and the other conspirators unjustly killed Caesar:† For tho' he usurped empire in a free city, and extorted liberty from his fellow-citizens without any just cause; yet they had acquiesced in it, and renounced their liberty. And indeed since Brutus himself in Cicero, Epist. ad Brutum, 4. [[Cicero, *Epistulae ad Quintum fratrem et M. Brutum,* 4]] durst not accuse Antonius of a hostile disposition towards the republic, nor when the matter was referred to him, attack him as an enemy; with what right could he murder Caesar, whom the senate and people of Rome were so far from looking upon as an enemy, that they had rather solemnly surrendered themselves to him. Wherefore, that saying of Lucan is not agreeable to right reason, Pharsal. l. 1. v. 351.

Detrahimus dominos urbi, servire paratae.

[[Lucan, *Pharsalia* 1.351: "We are but dislodging a tyrant from a State prepared to bow the knee." Lucan, *Pharsalia,* books I–X, p. 15.]]

For if the whole city desired a master, what right had Caesar, or any other private citizen, to oppose, by a civil war, their falling under domination?

† [I do not see how this conclusion follows. But not to enter into so trite a dispute, it is sufficient to observe here, That by the confession of our Author, Grotius, Pu-

SECTION CXXXIII

Empire exerts itself in rights of majesty. What these are?

But since all empire is supreme and absolute, (§127), the consequence is, that all the rights are joined with it, without which the end of civil society, *viz.* security, cannot be obtained; all which united together constitute *majesty*, or *the rights of majesty*. Now, this security being two-fold, *internal*, by which the subjects are inwardly secured one against the other, and *external*, by which the society is defended against the arms

---

fendorff, and every writer on the law of nature, these states, kingdoms or republics, which are constituted by pact, and with what is called by the civilians *lex commissoria*, (a peremptory condition, that in case the king act otherwise, the subjects shall not be obliged) have the power of judging when their pact is satisfied, and of taking care it be fulfilled. In such states, the sovereign and the people hold their respective rights by the same express tenure or charter. But no pact being valid that is contrary to the law of nature, the law of nature really lays this restriction upon every pact about government, that the good of the people, or the governed, shall be the supreme law, and that nothing shall be imposed upon subjects repugnant to their good, as much, as if that restriction had been expresly made in the pact, by a commissory clause. All immoral things are impossible things in the language of the doctors of laws and civilians. And therefore a pact by a people, giving power to a prince to act contrary to their happiness, or to prefer whatever he may fancy to be his private interest, to their good, is a pact originally and in itself invalid. A pact by a people, giving a prince power to rule over them, otherwise than agreeably to the law of nature, that is, the law of justice and benevolence, or in one word, the law of love, and binding themselves to obey his commands, whatever they be, is a pact a people cannot make; it is an impossible pact, because an immoral one; and therefore it can never be obligatory, but to make it is a crime; and to stand to it, is to continue, nay, to increase the guilt. It is a mutual agreement between prince and people, to put the arbitrary will of a prince in the place of the law of nature, the law of God. And if such a pact can be valid, why hath our Author so often pronounced all immoral pacts invalid? But if such a pact cannot be valid, then every pact about government, and all consent to government, express, tacite, or presumed, hath, in consequence of the immutability and eternal obligation of the law of nature, this condition contained unalterably and essentially in it, "Provided the government be agreeable to the law of nature, the law of justice and benevolence." There is therefore, in all pacts about government, in all consent to government, this commissory article naturally and necessarily included, inasmuch, as it cannot be left out, but must be understood to be there by the law of nature itself, whether it be mentioned or not, its truth, existence, or obligation, being of the law of nature, and therefore universal and indispensable.]

and force of outward enemies; hence it is plain, that the rights of majesty are of two sorts; some relative to the citizens or subjects themselves, called *immanent;* and others relating to foreigners, called *transeunt.** <134>

SECTION CXXXIV

If the *internal security* of a state consist in defending the subjects against violence from one another (§133), of necessity there must be joined with sovereignty the right of making laws, and of applying these to facts or cases, which we may call *supreme jurisdiction;* as likewise the right of punishing transgressions of the laws, and of exacting *tributes* and *duties* proportionable to the exigencies of the state; the right of *constituting administrators* and *magistrates;* of regulating all that relates to sacred things, as well as to *commerce,* and the ornament of the state; and, in fine, of watching that the republic suffer no wrong or hurt.

Of the immanent rights of majesty.

* All these are confounded by several writers, who having applied themselves to the study of public law, have acted as if it had been their business, like Plautus's cooks, to mingle and confound the most distinct rights. Having read in Feud. II. §6. some things concerning regal rights usually joined with fiefs, they thought them the very same with the rights of majesty, tho' it be of great consequence whether one exercise the rights of regality as a vassal, or dependently, as it is commonly termed; or the rights of majesty as a sovereign, or independently. Besides, all the rights belonging to sovereignty, and which are exercised by it, not being recited in that place of the feudal law, they thought, that there the rights which could not be communicated to vassals without encroaching upon majesty were only treated of; and hence they called them *regalia minora,* to which they oppose *regalia majora, i.e.* in their opinion, incommunicable ones. Thus several writers have proceeded, who are solidly refuted by Thomasius ad Huber. de jur. civ. I. 3. 6. 3. p. 91. & seq. But since we are not treating here of the rights of patronage and vassalage, but of public and universal law, it is proper to caution against the above division, and to deduce the rights of majesty and their different kinds from the nature and end of civil society, *i.e.* from the fountain-head, rather than from Henningius Arnisaeus, Regn. Sixtin, and other authors of that class. [[Henning Arnisaeus (ca. 1575–1636) and Regnerus Sixtinus (1543–1617) were authors of juristic and political treatises.]]

SECTION CXXXV

What the transeunt rights of majesty.

And since those who coalited into the same republic, likewise intended their *common security* against external violence (§133); the consequence is, that from sovereignty cannot be severed the right of making *alliances* and *treaties,* sending *ambassadors,* and making *war* and *peace;* since without these rights the state could not be preserved safe and secure. For without the right of making alliances and treaties, a weaker state would often be a very inequal match for a more potent one; without the right of sending ambassadors, treaties could not be <135> made; and without the right of making war and peace, it would be impossible to repel force by force; and therefore the end of society, which is security, could not be obtained.

SECTION CXXXVI

Whether they are communicable and divisible.

Those rights of majesty flowing directly from the nature and end of sovereignty, cannot be separated from it without destroying that unity of will which is the essence of society, and rearing up a republic within a republic (§120); yet, because all, or several forms of government, are sometimes so blended together, that one may check or balance another, (§117), it may happen, that all, or the greater part of the rights of majesty may be exerced, not by one person, or by one college, but by many, or by the whole people; and in this case, there must be an assembly, in which the Sovereign exercises them according to the judgment of the different orders composing it.* <136>

* The most potent and flourishing Kingdom of Great Britain is an example of this, in which the prerogative of the King with regard to war and peace, remaining entire and unviolated, neither new laws are made, nor new taxes imposed, nor any other thing relating to the safety and glory of the nation done, but in the states of the Kingdom, called a *Parliament.* Thus likewise in Germany, nothing relating to the Empire is decreed but by the common resolution of the Emperor, Electors, Princes, and other orders of the Empire: And almost the same is now done in Poland and Sweden, with safety to the prerogatives belonging to the most august Emperor and these most potent Kings: which prerogatives are called in Germany *reservata.* Yea, some such thing takes place in particular sovereignties and republics of the German

SECTION CXXXVII

Moreover, because both the form of the government, and the governors themselves, are elected by the same people, who also prescribe fundamental laws to them (§110); hence it is evident, that none can acquire empire to himself in a civil state without the consent of the people, or contrary to its fundamental laws. But, according to these, empire may either be *elective* or *successive;* and this division extends not only to monarchies, but to aristocracies and popular governments.*

Empire is acquired either by election or by succession.

SECTION CXXXVIII

Empire is *elective,* when the people in an *interregnum* creates a Sovereign, and transfers the empire to him with his consent. But, because the people may either exerce this right themselves in a regular assembly, or give this right in perpetuity to certain persons; the consequence is, that he who is chosen by the one or the other of those who hath the right of choosing, ought to be held as Sovereign, provided he accepts of the sovereignty offered to him, and be qualified according to the fundamental laws of the state to rule and govern; and provided the election be made in the order, and with <137> the solemnities required by the public laws, or the customs of the state.†

What is just with regard to the election of a sovereign.

Empire, as is observed by Hertius de legibus consultat. & judic. in specialibus Imp. Rom. Germ. rebuspubl. [[Hertius (*praeses*) and Ehrhart (*respondens*), *Dissertatio de consultationibus, legibus et judiciis in specialibus Germaniae rebuspublicis.*]]

* Thus, when the right of governing is included in a few families, seclusive of all the rest, so that they and their descendents only have it by right of blood, aristocracy in this case is *successive.* Such are the republics of Venice, Genoa, *&c.* at this day, as is observed by Hertius, Elem. polit. 1. 10. 16. p. 212. On the other hand, if the nobles or senators be chosen, either by the people or by the college itself, then aristocracy is *elective.* See Huber. de jur. civ. 1. 8. 1. 17. p. 292. In like manner, if in a democracy the right of suffrage be given to no others but the native citizens, it is in some sort successive; but if it may be given likewise to strangers, it is in some respect elective.

† Wherefore, those are not lawful princes who are set up by a seditious mob, or an army, which hath not the right of election. What confusion and ruin was brought upon the Roman state in the latter way, we may see from the examples of Otho, Vitellius, Vespasian, Pescennius Niger, Clodius Albinus, and Septimius Severus.

SECTION CXXXIX

What is an
interregnum
in an elective
state?

Moreover, it is evident, from the definition of an elective government (§138), that in it an *interregnum* happens, that is, a state in which the republic hath no Head or Sovereign, as often as the Sovereign dies or abdicates, or is deposed by the people; unless the people, during the Sovereign's life, and with his consent, choose one who is to succeed to him; and that the designed successor hath no more power or right, during the Sovereign's life, but what is given to him by the people with his consent, or what the Sovereign himself delegates to him, either during his absence, or when he is hindered by any just cause from presiding over the state himself.* <138>

[[These were Roman emperors at times of political turmoil. Otho was briefly emperor in A.D. 69 but was replaced by Vitellius. In the same year, however, Vitellius was defeated and succeeded by Vespasian. Pescennius Niger was proclaimed Roman emperor by his troops in A.D. 193 but was defeated by Septimius Severus, who ruled as emperor from 193 until 211.]] For which reason, Plutarch in his life of Galba, p. 1053 [[Plutarch, *Lives,* vol. ii, 209]], speaking of a time, in which, as Tacitus, hist. 1. 4. says, this arcanum of empire was divulged, that a prince might be made any where else as well as at Rome, "affirms, that the Roman republic was shaken and convulsed by commotions like those of the Titans in the fable, the sovereignty being at that time bandied from one prince to another, by the avarice and licentiousness of the army, who being corrupted by bribes and largesses, drove out one Emperor by another, as we do a nail by a nail." See Petri Cunaei, orat. 9. p. 188. [[Presumably Petrus Cunaeus, *Orationes argumenti varii* (Leipzig, 1735).]] It therefore greatly concerns a civil state, in whom the elective power is lodged, to define by clear and fixed laws, the electors and the persons capable of being elected, and the form and method of choosing, that it may not suffer such violent convulsions.

* For since it is one thing to abrogate sovereignty from a sovereign, or divest him of it, and another thing to nominate a successor to him, the designed successor can have no right to take possession of the sovereignty, but when the sovereign is abrogated. Hence we may observe, that the Kings of the Romans, who are sometimes chosen in the Emperor of Germany's life, have no power unless the Emperor delegates some to them, as we know Charles V. did. [[Charles V (1500–1558) transferred power to his brother Ferdinand, who was elected Roman King on January 5, 1531; that led effectively to the division of the Habsburg monarchy. After Charles's death, Habsburg Spain was ruled by his son Philip II and Habsburg Austria by Ferdinand. The election of the future emperor during the lifetime of the present incumbent ("vivente imperatore") increased the influence of the ruling Habsburgs over the seven (after the Peace of Westphalia in 1648, eight) prince electors.]] The case is almost the same

SECTION CXL

But since an *interregnum* is a state in which the republic hath not its regular or ordinary Head or Sovereign (§139); and yet the people would not have the republic to cease, while it is consulting about the choice of a new head; the consequence is, that certain extraordinary magistrates ought to preside in the republic during that interval, by whatever name they may be called, who ought either to be elected by the suffrages of the orders in the republic at that time, or which is safer and better, be appointed by a public law before hand, making provision for the security and good order of the state on such occasions; but that their authority ceases when a Sovereign is elected, is obvious. However, since they supply the Sovereign's place for a time, it is strange to find learned men disputing whether the republic truly subsists in an interregnum, and what frame it falls into in that situation.* <139>

Whether the republic subsists in an interregnum?

---

with regard to co-adjutors, as they are called, who while the bishops or prelates live, have no other right but that of succeeding them, when their chairs come to be vacant, as they speak. See Boehmer. jur. eccles. protest. 3. 6. 23. [[Justus Henning Boehmer (1674–1749), German jurist and poet, professor of law at Halle and author of the *Jus ecclesiasticum Protestantium,* a major work on Protestant ecclesiastical law.]]

* Pufendorff, of the law of nature, *&c.* 7. 7. 7. reasons thus about this matter: "Since the intrinsic perfection of the state, and the actual existence of the sovereign power, were both owing to the latter compact between the prince and the people, it follows, that the person in whom the sovereignty properly resided being extinct, the kingdom sinks into an imperfect form, and is united only by the first antecedent pact, by which we conceive the particular members of the community to have agreed to incorporate in one society; (*of this pact we have treated* §109) not but that the primitive pact uniting the general body, is during the time of an *interregnum* considerably strengthened and assisted by the endearment of a common country, and that kind of relation or affinity which results from thence, together with this consideration, that the fortunes of most men are rooted or fixed in that particular soil, and the effects of others not easily to be transported or removed. Tho' we may with Livy, 1. 17. call a nation during an *interregnum,* a *state without government,* and, as it were, an army without a general; yet because communities at their first meeting, before the sovereignty hath been conferred either on a single man, or on a council, seem to bear the semblance of democracies; and further, since it is natural that all persons upon the decease of him, to whom they committed their guidance and safety, should take care of themselves, therefore an *interregnum* hath the appearance of a kind of temporary democracy." This is also observed by Grotius of the rights of war and peace, 1. 3. 7.

SECTION CXLI

Of succession
in kingdoms
where the
people hath
made no
settlement
with regard
to it.

Empire is *successive* when by the decree of the people a royal family is elected, one of which is always to have the supreme power, while any one of its posterity is capable of holding it by the public constitutions. When such a form of government is agreed upon, either the people determine the <140> manner of succession, or leave it undefined. In the latter case, the people is presumed to have approved of the common right of succession to intestates. But, because females are not presumed to have so much prudence as men (§44), and because a kingdom might happen to pass by a woman to a foreigner as dowry, therefore women are not admitted to succession but as subsidiaries, and failing male-heirs. In fine, since unity of will is, as were, the life and soul of a republic (§114); and this cannot be expected, if two or more have the joint administration of a monarchical kingdom, or share it between them; the consequence is, that among many equally near to the last king, the first-born is justly honoured with the prerogative (l. 1. §297).*

Hertius follows the opinion of Pufendorff, Elem. prud. civ. 1. 12. 14. and also Houtuyn. Polit. general. §100. n. 6. & seq. [[Adrian Houtuyn, *Politica contracta generalis.*]] But since for the most part an interrex is previously designed, or if not, some one or more persons are elected by the common suffrage of all the orders in the state, who for a time preside over the republic with the same power, and sometimes with larger power than the Sovereign himself is vested with; and exercise all the rights of Majesty, about things at least which do not admit of delay; there is no imaginable reason why this constitution of a state, tho' temporary, may not be called perfect, and monarchical, if this power be lodged in one hand, duarchical if in two, and aristocratical if confided to many, as it were *intercalar* princes.

* There are some who have pronounced females quite unqualified and inhabile to succeed to sovereignty, as Jo. Bodinus, but upon principles of Roman law, which do not bind free nations. And since even in the Jewish state, Deborah executed the office of a judge with great honour, and the annals of almost all nations celebrate Queens who acquired immortal glory to themselves by their prudent government and great actions; who will declare women unworthy of reigning? However, since nature hath generally given a pre-eminence to men above women, it is not absurd to say, that they ought only to be called to succession as subsidiaries. So Aristotle, Polit. 1. 3. "A man is more fit by nature to reign than a woman, unless she hath some qualities very uncommon to her sex."

SECTION CXLII

When the people hath settled and fixed the order of succession, it is plain that this rule ought to be adhered to (§III), and whether the French constitution take place, by which females are excluded; or the Castilian, which doth not exclude the women, but postpones them to the men, and runs back to the female again, in case the males, who were superior or equal to them in other respects, <141> shall happen to fail, together with their issue; (*i.e.* in the same degree of the same line, the younger males are preferred to the elder females; yet so as that no transition is made from one line to another on the bare obstacle of the sex); or whether greater regard be had to the line, or to the nearest degree of kindred; or whether there be any new or unusual method of succession fixed by the public law, that rule, whatever it be, ought to be observed as a sacred, as a fundamental constitution; whence, moreover, we conclude, that a people may give their Sovereign the power of appointing his successor, and may interpose when disputes arise about the right of succession; tho' experience teaches us, that (to use the words of Ennius) in such a difficult situation, "Non in jure manum conseri, sed mage rem ferro agi"; it is not right, but the sword that decides.*[1]

---

* Many examples are brought by Pufendorff of the law of nature, *&c.* 7. 7. 14. But the most regular way is the lineal, in which the first-born male, and his first-born male succeed, while any one of the line remains; and this line being extinct, the first-born of the next line comes in, and so on while there is any one subsisting of the first Sovereign's posterity. We know it was formerly disputed whether the first-born, tho' born before his father came to the throne, or the first-born after he began to reign, had the right of primogeniture. But since in the right of primogeniture, regard is had to the order of birth only, there is no reason why a younger brother should be preferred to his elder, merely because the court heard the former squaul in a purple cradle.

1. Actually: "Non ex iure manu consertum, sed magis ferro" (Ennius, *Annals*, bk. 8, l. 252).

SECTION CXLIII

Ordinary and
extraordinary
interregnum.

Since in elective government a single person only is chosen (§138), but in *successive* governments a royal family is elected (§141); because, in the first case, the right expires with the person elected; whereas, in the latter, it subsists while the royal family subsists; the consequence is, that in the first <142> case there is an ordinary interregnum upon the decease of the elected person; in the latter, there is an extraordinary interregnum, when the royal family is extinct; and then it falls into the power of the people to confer the regal honour upon any family they please, and to continue the same kind of government and order of succession, or to confine both within more narrow limits, as they shall think fit.*

SECTION CXLIV

How empire
is acquired
by force.

Those are the ways of acquiring empire when a people constitutes its own Sovereign; but it is often acquired by arms and force; in which case also, a conquered people, tho' forced, does yet, without all doubt, consent to that sovereignty under which they are brought; and whether the conqueror promises to govern them according to their former laws, or stipulates to himself and his successors new terms and larger power, or remits to the conquered people some things which their former princes arrogated to themselves, that rule must be the rule to their posterity.† <143>

---

* We have an example of this in the French history. See Glab. Radulph. Hist. 2. 1. and Aimon de gest. Francorum, ann. 987. "Convenientes totius regni primates Hugonem, Ducem Parisiensem, in regem ungi fecerunt." [[Glaber, *The Five Books of the Histories; The Life of St. William*, bk. 2, chap. 1, 50; Aimon de Fleury (965–1008), *Historiae Francorum libri IV*: "The leading men of the whole kingdom met and had Hugh, Duke of Paris, anointed king."]] And in Russia, when after various commotions, they chose a new royal family, from which came Alexius, John, two Peters, and Ann. For that Catharine the Empress did not succeed by right of succession, but by the last will of Peter I. every one knows.

† Hence Grotius, of the rights of war and peace, says justly, 3. 8. 1. 3. "Empire may be acquired by victory, either as it subsists in a King or Sovereign, and then it is succeeded to just as it is, and no more power is acquired; or as it subsists in the people, and then the conqueror acquires it in such a manner that he can alienate it, as the people might have done." But what he says of alienation, deserves a more accurate

SECTION CXLV

Wherefore all the ways of acquiring empire depend upon the consent of a people either voluntary, or forced and extorted either by a just or unjust cause. And therefore we think there is very little foundation for the distinction between *patrimonial* and *usufructuary empire.* For tho' Grotius first invented that distinction (of the rights of war and peace, 2. 6. 3. & 1. 3. 12.) and hath been followed in it by a numerous tribe of learned writers; yet this whole doctrine is loaded with so many difficulties, that we cannot tell what kingdoms may be called patri-<144>monial, and what usufructuary. See Thomas. ad Huber. de jur. civ. 1. 3. 2. 15. p. 69. & seq.

The division of kingdoms into patrimonial and usufructuary.

SECTION CXLVI

Grotius thinks some kingdoms are so much under the dominion of their Sovereigns, that they may be alienated by them either in their life, or in the prospect of death; and these he calls *patrimonial.* And that others

Whether this division be just?

---

inspection. We say then, that a conqueror either waged war with a King only, or with the people themselves. In the first case he succeeds to the rights of the conquered prince, and ought to change nothing in the form of government, as, *e.g.* William Prince of Orange, the War with James being ended, made no change in the British government: But in the latter case, he has a right to transact with the conquered people, and it depends on his will to reduce the conquered state into a province, as the Romans for the most part did; to impose a harder yoke upon them; or to give a specimen of his clemency, and remit some things to them. Thus Alexander, at first a most merciful conqueror, having made himself master of the Sidonian Kingdom, made no change in the form of their government, but restored it to Abdolominus, Q. Curt. 4. 1. [[Curtius, *History of Alexander,* bk. 4.1.]] The Turks, on the other hand, having conquered the Byzantine Empire, by the right of victory, imposed upon them much severer conditions, being of the opinion of Ariovistus in Caesar, de bello Gallico, "That by the right of conquest, the conqueror may command the conquered as he pleases." [[Caesar, *Gallic War,* bk. I, chap. 36, p. 55.]] In fine, Agesilaus, according to Xenophon de Agesilao Rege, cap. 1. §22. "Whatever states he subdued, he exeemed them from those things to which slaves are obliged by their masters, and only commanded those things in which freemen obey their magistrates." [[Xenophon, "Agesilaus," 71, in Xenophon, *Scripta minora.*]] But that indeed rarely happens, and much more rarely still what Justin hist. 1. 1. says of the times before Ninus, "That those who made war fought for glory, and satisfied with victory, did not affect empire."

are such, that their Sovereigns cannot alienate them, which he calls *usu-fructuary ones;* tho' Thomasius jurisprud. divin. 3. 6. 135. thinks they may be more properly called *fideicommissory* or *trusts.* But, 1. Since patrimonial things are no longer common (l. 1. §235) and therefore not public, because that supposes at least private communion (l. 1. §237), it is plain that a kingdom ceases to be a republic, and degerates into a family (§89), if it be in the dominion or patrimony of one. Besides, 2. Since all civil states are constituted, not for the sake of the Sovereign, but for common security (§105); for that reason, a kingdom cannot be patrimonial, without ceasing to be a civil state. See a dissertation of the illustrious president of this province, Jo. Gothofredi de Cocceiis, de testamentis principum, part 2. §16. & seq.*² <145>

SECTION CXLVII

The alienation of kingdoms without the consent of the people is unlawful.

Hence we think it may be justly concluded, that no Sovereign can sell, give, barter, divide, leave by last-will to any one his kingdom, or transfer it in any of those ways, one can dispose of his patrimony in his life, or in view of death to others, unless the people consent, or have given him expresly the power of alienating his sovereignty or disposing of it.†

---

* A patrimonial kingdom implies a contradiction, because a kingdom is a species of a civil state (§115); but a patrimonial kingdom is a thing under private dominion. And indeed the whole reasoning about this matter commonly runs in a circle. For, if you ask whether a prince has the right of alienating his Sovereignty or not? The answer is, That there is a great difference between patrimonial and usufructuary kingdoms. But if you insist, and enquire what is the difference between these two? they tell us, that by the former is meant a kingdom that can be alienated by its sovereign, and by the other, one that cannot: So that they have as yet given us no certain mark by which the one may be distinguished from the other. For nothing hinders why despotic kingdoms, or kingdoms acquired by war, may not be unalienable, as Huber has justly observed, de jure civ. 1. 3. 2. 18.

2. H. von Cocceji (*phrases*) and J. G. Cocceji (*respondens*), *Disputatio juridica . . . de testamentis principum.*

† Nor do the examples brought by Grotius, Pufendorff, and others, prove any thing. For tho' we read that some have divided their kingdoms, and that others have disposed of them in their last wills; yet the justice of such alienations must be determined, not from what has been done, but from the principles of right reason. And therefore the illustrious Baron de Cocceiis, gives a proper answer to all these argu-

Remarks on This Chapter

It will be easy to determine what the law of nature prescribes in other cases, if we can determine what it prescribes with respect to the exercise of the absolute empire, which is the effect of, and rooted by an over-balance in property. We have already taken notice of the natural causes of Empire, to which, if moral writers had attended, they would not have debated so much about the origine of civil government or Empire. If one man, it hath been said, be sole land-lord, or over-balance the many in property to a certain proportion, he will be sole monarch. But now, how ought such a land-lord, and absolute master, to exercise his dominion or empire? What rules does the law of nature prescribe to him? Doth it not prescribe to him these very immutable, universal laws of justice and benevolence, which have been already explained? In general, therefore, may we not answer, that such a master is under perfect obligation to exercise justice towards his subjects or servants, let them be called which you will, and under imperfect obligation to exercise beneficence towards them? But not to rest in so general an answer, the following propositions may be laid down with re-<146>gard to such empire, in consequence of what hath been said by our Author, and in the preceding remarks subjoined to him, to his two last chapters in particular. 1. It is lawful to acquire and to possess dominion; for if it be lawful to acquire property, it must be lawful to acquire all that is necessarily attendant upon property, *i.e.* the dominion which an over-balance in property will necessarily produce. 2. As an attempt to change government, without changing the over-balance of property, or to fix government without a fixation of the balance of property, is an attempt contrary to nature; so to endeavour to violate property in order to change government, is unjust force. All violation of property is unjust. 3. But he or they who hold the over-balance of property, and consequently the reins of government, are certainly obliged by the law of nature to make their dependents as happy as they can, as much *men* as they can. This must be true, or the law of love is a mere empty sound.

---

ments, when he says, de testament. principum part 2. §17. "Either these alienations had no effect, or they were done with the consent of the people, either tacite or express; or it was force that prevailed."

And therefore, 4. Tho' it cannot be pronounced unlawful for one or many, who have the over-balance in property, to hold it, no more than it is for one or many, to make use of the authority their superiority in wisdom may give them; yet it is certainly unlawful to exercise power in consequence of property in an injurious, oppressive manner over dependents, as if they were not men; as it is unlawful to make use of superior prudence, or rather cunning, in order to deceive and mislead those who pay submission and reverence to it, to their ruin or hurt. 5. It is certainly the natural right, nay, the natural duty of a people, when providence puts it in their power, by any revolution bringing property to such a balance, that an equal happy government can be constituted, to constitute such a government, and to fix and secure its duration by the only natural way of fixing and securing it. This must be their duty, if it be a people's duty to consult their best interest, or to provide for their own greatest good, and the secure continuance of happiness to their posterity. And then does providence give this opportunity, and consequently call to this duty, when by the course of things, without forcible removal, or violation of property, the people come to have the balance. And, 6. Whoever hold the over-balance of property, and by consequence the reins of empire, one or the few, he or they are under the same obligation, to constitute such orders of government as may best promote and secure the general happiness of the dependent people, that they are under to benevolence, because this is what benevolence manifestly requires at their hands. I have said the same obligation that they ly under to benevolence, because of the distinction already explained, which is admitted by all moral writers between perfect and imperfect obligation. And that it is a glorious and noble part to act, who can doubt, who hath a just idea of true glory, I had almost said, any feeling of humanity? Let it not be said that this cannot be expected of mankind. This is an unjust reproach. Our Author has, in the scholium to §144. <147> named some instances of generous princes, who made no other use of the rights, even of just conquest, but to make the conquered happy and free. And let me add some other examples from ancient history yet more heroic, as they are narrated, by an author often referred to and quoted in our remarks, with great satisfaction, with all the joy every beneficent mind must needs be touched with, by such god-like instances of generosity and public spirit. "In those ancient and heroic times (when men thought that to be necessary which was virtuous) the nobility of Athens having the people so much engaged in their debt, that there remained no other question among these, than which of those should be King, no sooner heard Solon speak, than they quitted their debts, and restored the commonwealth, which ever after held a solemn and annual feast, called the *Sisacthia* or *Recision,* in memory of that action. Nor is this example the Phoenix; for at the institution by Lycurgus, the nobility having estates (as ours here) in the lands of Laconia, upon no other consideration than the commonwealth proposed by him, threw them up to be parcelled by his Agrarian.

The Macedonians were thrice conquered by the Romans, first under the conduct of Titus Quintus Flaminius, secondly, under that of Lucius Aemilius Paulus, and thirdly, under that of Quintus Caecilius Metellus, thence called Macedonicus. For the first time Philip of Macedon, who (possest of *Acrocorinthus*) boasted no less than was true, that he had Greece in fetters, being overcome by Flaminius, had his kingdom restored to him, upon condition that he should immediately set all the cities which he held in Greece and in Asia at liberty; and that he should not make war out of Macedon but by leave of the senate of Rome, which Philip (having no other way to save any thing) agreed should be done accordingly. The Grecians being at this time assembled at the Isthmian games, where the concourse was mighty great, a crier, appointed to the office by Flaminius, was heard among them proclaiming all Greece to be free; to which the people, being amazed at so hopeless a thing, gave little credit, till they received such testimony of the truth as put it past all doubts; whereupon they immediately fell on running to the proconsul with flowers and garlands, and such violent expressions of their admiration and joy, as, if Flaminius, a young man about thirty three, had not also been very strong, he must have died of no other death than their kindness, while every one striving to touch his hand, they bore him up and down the field with an unruly throng, full of such ejaculations as these: How! is there a people in the world, that at their own charge, at their own peril, will fight for the liberty of another? Did they live at the next door to this fire? Or what kind of men are these, whose business it is to pass the seas, that the world may be governed with righteousness? The cities of Greece and Asia shake off their Iron-fetters at the voice of a crier! Was it madness to <148> imagine such a thing, and is it done? O virtue! O felicity! O fame!

In this example we have a donation of liberty to a people, by restitution to what they had formerly enjoyed, and some particular men, families or cities, according to their merit of the Romans, if not upon this, yet upon the like occasions, were gratified with *Latinity:* But Philip's share by this means did not please him; wherefore the league was broken by his son Perseus; and the Macedonians thereupon, for the second time, conquered by Aemilius Paulus, their King taken, and they some time after the victory summoned to the tribunal of the General, where remembering how little hope they ought to have of pardon, they expected some dreadful sentence: When Aemilius in the first place declared the Macedonians to be free, in the full possession of their lands, goods and laws, with right to elect annual magistrates, yielding and paying to the people of Rome one half of the tribute which they were accustomed to pay to their own Kings. This done he went on, making so skilful a division of the country, in order to the methodizing of the people, and casting them into the form of popular government, that the Macedonians, being first surprized with the virtue of the Romans, began now to alter the scene of their admiration, that a stranger should do such things for them in their own country, and with such facility, as they had never so much as once imagined to be possible. Nor was this all; for Aemilius, as if not dictating to conquered enemies, but to some well-deserving friends, gave them, in the last place, laws so suitable, and contrived with such care and prudence, that long use and experience (the only correctress of works of this nature) could never find fault in them.[3]

In this example, we have a donation of liberty to a people, that had not tasted of it before, but were now taught to use it.

But the Macedonians rebelling, at the name of a false Philip, the third time against the Romans, were by them judged incapable of *Liberty,* and reduced by Metellus to a province."

Now, with respect to incapacity of liberty, I beg leave to add a remark

---

3. The first paragraph of this quotation (pp. 462–63, above) is from Harrington, *Oceana,* 241, in Harrington, *Political Works.* For the remainder see ibid., 326–27, though there are some omissions.

from the same author. "A man may as well say, that it is unlawful for him, who has made a fair and honest purchase, to have tenants, as for a government, that has made a just progress, and enlargement of itself, to have provinces. But how a province may be justly acquired appertains to another place.[4] (*Our author treats of just war afterwards;* and this Author treats of propagation and holding at great length)—The course Rome took is best; wherefore, if you have subdued a nation that is capable of liberty, you shall make them a present of it, as did Flaminius to Greece, and Aemilius to Macedon, reserving to yourselves some part of that revenue which was legally paid to the former government, together with the right of being head of the league, which includes such levies of <149> men and money as shall be necessary for the carrying on of the public work. For if a people have, by your means, attained to freedom, they owe both to the cause and you such aid as may propagate the like fruit to the rest of the world. But whereas every nation is not capable of her liberty to this degree, lest you be put to doing and undoing of things, as the Romans were in Macedon, you shall diligently observe what nation is fit for her liberty to this degree, and what not; which is to be done by two marks: the first, if she loves the liberty of mankind; for if she has no care of the liberty of mankind, she deserves not her own. But, because in this you may be deceived by pretences, which continuing for a while specious, may afterwards vanish; the other is more certain, and that is, if she be capable of an equal Agrarian; which, that it was not observed by excellent Aemilius in his donation of liberty, and introduction of a popular state among the Macedonians, I am more than moved to believe for two reasons. The first, Because at the same time the Agrarian was odious to the Roman patricians. The second, That the *Pseudo-Philip* could afterwards so easily recover *Macedon,* which could not have happened but by the nobility, and their impatience, having great estates, to be equalled with the people: For that the people should otherwise have thrown away their liberty, is incredible."[5]

But because it will be very easy to draw a solution from the principles which have been laid down to all the questions about government; and

4. Ibid., 167.
5. Ibid., 330.

because the enquiry, what constitution of government is best, belongs not to the present subject, we shall take leave of our author here, and add no more to what he says; but in the first place, That no maxim is more false than that whatever government is best administred is best.[6] That only is good, which is, by its frame, well secured against bad men, and bad administration. 2. Nor is another maxim in politics less dangerous, which asserts that good men make good laws. It is the maxim of Demagogues. The truth is, that good laws or orders make good men. And a government ought to trust to its constitution and orders, and not to men. 3. The chief matter, the whole mystery of government is revealed to us every day (to use the words of an excellent author) by the mouths of babes, as often as they have a cake to divide; for this is their natural language, "I will divide, and you shall choose."[7] To which we may apply what Horace says of other natural instincts or directions. *Unde nisi intus monstratum?*[8] The whole secret of a well poised equal government, lies in dividing and choosing, as the same author we have so often quoted hath shewn at great length. Dividing and choosing, in the language of a commonwealth, is debating and resolving. And in order to a right division and choice, as the council dividing, should consist of the wisdom of the commonwealth, so the assembly or council choosing, should consist of the interest of the commonwealth. The wisdom of the few may be the light of mankind, <150> but the interest of the few is not the profit of mankind, nor of a commonwealth. Therefore, as the wisdom of the commonwealth is in the aristocracy, so the interest of the commonwealth is in the whole body of the people.

6. Pope, *Essay on Man,* epistle III, lines 304–5.

7. See Harrington, *Oceana,* in Harrington, *Political Works,* 172: "that such orders may be established as may, nay must, give the upper hand in all cases unto common right or interest, notwithstanding the nearness of that which sticks unto every man in private, and this in a way of equal certainty and facility, is known even unto girls, being no other than those that are of common practice with them in divers cases. For example, two of them have a cake yet undivided, which was given between them. That each of them therefore may have that which is due, 'Divide,' says the one unto the other, 'and I will choose; or let me divide and you shall choose.' If this be but once agreed upon, it is enough; for the divident dividing unequally loses, in regard that the other takes the better half, wherefore she divides equally, and so both have right."

8. Horace, *Satires II,* 1.52: "From where, unless from an internal instinct?"

And whereas this, in case the commonwealth consist of a whole nation, is too unwieldy a body to be assembled, this council is to consist of such a representative as may be equal, and so constituted as can never contract any other interest than that of the whole people. Whence it follows, 4. That government, *de facto,* may be an art, whereby some men, or some few men subject a city or nation, and rule it according to his or their private interest: which, because the laws, in such cases, are made according to the interest of a man, or of some few families, may be said to be the empire of men, and not of laws. Yet government, *de jure,* is an art, whereby a civil society of men is instituted and preserved upon the foundation of common right or interest, which is properly called by Aristotle, *an empire of laws,* and not of men.[9] The necessary definition of a government, any thing well ordered, is, that it is a government, consisting of the senate proposing, the people resolving, and the magistracy exercising. Our excellent constitution hath been judged by the most renowned politicians the very best. See our author, §116 in the scholium. But the discussion of this equally curious and important subject, belongs not to the present question.

9. Aristotle *Politics* 3.16.

Concerning the immanent rights of majesty, and the just exercise of them.

SECTION CXLVIII

The internal security of a civil state consists in external justice.

The *immanent* or *internal rights of majesty,* are rights so inseparably connected with it, that the security of the subjects cannot be attained without them (§134). Since therefore this security consists in this, that no subject may be injured by any other, and every one may have his own, or whatever he has a perfect right to demand; the consequence is, that it lies chiefly in *external justice,* by which we understand conformity of external actions to law; and therefore they are not in the wrong who contend, "That civil states were constituted for the sake of justice; or that (Velleius Pater. hist. 2. 80),[1] by giving force to laws,* and authority to <151> courts of justice, industry and religion might be encouraged, and property might be sure, and every one might enjoy with security his

1. See Velleius Paterculus, *Compendium of Roman History,* bk. 2, chap. 89 (not 80), p. 237.

* For tho' none can deny, that internal justice, or a constant disposition to injure no person, but to render to every one his own, be a more noble degree of virtue; yet that such virtue is not to be expected from so many men as coalesce into the same civil state, will not be controverted. It will therefore be sufficient, so to hold men to their duties by laws, that they shall conform their external actions to laws, and not refuse to any one what he hath a perfect right to demand, or do any thing contrary to justice and equity. Yet it becomes good rulers to take all proper methods, by the right education and discipline of their subjects, to make internal justice or virtue to flourish among them. "It is the duty of prudent magistrates, (says Isocrates in Ar-

own lawful acquisitions": And therefore they justly assert that a civil state cannot subsist, unless that justice prevail in it, by which subjects are kept to their duty, Aristot. polit. 1. 2.

SECTION CXLIX

Because external justice, necessary to the security of a civil state, consists in the conformity of external actions to law (§148), the consequence is, that it is the office of the supreme powers to arm a state with laws; and therefore they must have the right and power of law-making, and of executing the laws, and consequently of adjusting the laws to the end, form, and interest of the republic.* They have therefore power and right to add to them, take from them, abrogate or change them, as the good of the state may require; which power is expressed by the Roman lawyers in a stile <152> accommodated to the nature of the Roman government, by *rogare, obrogare, derogare, abrogare, surrogare,* Ulpian fragm. 1. 3.[2]

To sovereignty therefore belongs a legislative power.

---

eopag. p. 27.) not to multiply laws, but to endeavour to render their subjects sincere lovers of justice. For it is not laws and edicts, but good education that will make a state truly happy. Men who are not rightly formed will dare to despise the best laws; but those who are well educated, are led by their inward disposition to approve good laws." [[A paraphrase rather than a quotation from Isocrates, "Areopagiticus," secs. 40–42, pp. 129–31, in Isocrates, *Isocrates,* vol. 1.]]

* Because there is this difference between natural and civil law, that the former hath for its object good and bad actions, internal as well as external; the latter respects indifferent and external actions, as far as the safety of a people or state requires the regulation of them (lib. 1. §18.); it is therefore impossible that the laws of all states should be uniform. Whence it is very difficult to determine which state hath the best laws; and Herodotus says very justly (apud Stobaeum serm. 21. p. 180.), "If one should lay before a people laws of all sorts, and bid them choose the best, every one would approve of the laws of his own state; every people thinks their own laws the best." And indeed the laws which are best with regard to one state, because of its end and form of government, may not be proper for another state; but, on the contrary, what is very advantageous to one may be very hurtful to another.

2. Ulpian, "The Rules of Ulpian" (3), p. 223, in Justinian, *The Civil Law,* vol. 1.

SECTION CL

What civil law is, and what is its object?

Since there ought to be one understanding and one will in a state (§114), which thus happens, when all the members have the same end in view, and choosing the same means, regulate all their actions by the same rule; an agreement that cannot be expected, considering the diversity of human dispositions, otherwise than by the submission of all the members of a state to the will of its rulers (§114); hence it follows, that the supreme power ought to make the rule known to which he would have them to conform their external actions, which are in themselves indifferent. Now, this can only be done by prescribing laws to them; and therefore civil laws are commands of the supreme power in a state concerning the regulation of external, indifferent actions for the good and honour of the state; whence it is evident, that this legislative <153> power cannot extend to the subversion of divine laws (l. 1. §17).

SECTION CLI

What power or authority the supreme magistracy hath with regard to divine laws.

We say, that civil laws consist in the adjustment of the external indifferent actions of subjects to the honour and interest of the state (§150). For tho' it be often necessary that magistrates repeat some divine positive as well as natural laws, and extend and interpret them;* give actions and civil remedies against transgressors of them; and threaten punishments

---

* It is true, God hath commanded that nothing be added to or taken from the divine law, Deut. iv. 2. But the former ought certainly to be understood of superstitious rites contrary to the divine law, or of will-worship, to which the Jews were so propense. But this is no reason why the civil legislative may not extend a divine prohibition to cases not expresly included in it, that thus the divine law be more strictly fenced and guarded. The Hebrew doctors call this a mound to law, by which men are kept at a greater distance from the violations of it, and the first steps towards transgression are guarded against. See upon this subject Schickard, jur. reg. cap. 5. theor. 18. p. 391. and Carpz in his notes on that place, and Jo. Selden, de uxor. Heb. 1. 2. [[Wilhelm Schickard (1592–1635), German mathematician and orientalist, professor of Hebrew and Aramaic at the University of Tübingen, author of *Jus regium Hebraeorum.* The 1674 edition includes the notes by Carpzov referred to in the text.]]

to those who shall dare to violate laws established by God himself; yet it is plain, from the nature of the thing, that then these laws do not owe their original obligation to the will of the civil magistrate, but that he then only exerts himself, as guardian of the divine laws, to make their authority sacred in the state.

SECTION CLII

Because civil laws are commands of the chief magistrate concerning the regulation of external indifferent actions for the good and honour of the state (§150); but such is the nature of mankind, that internal obligation alone is not sufficient to influence them (l. 1. §8); nay, civil laws cannot <154> produce internal obligation (l. 1. §7); the consequence is, that all civil laws must be enforced by some penal *sanction;* and therefore a perfect law consists of two parts, *the preceptive part,* and the *penal sanction:* But rewards are not due by a republic to those who obey its laws; unless something be not promiscuously enjoined to all the subjects, but it be proper that some should be excited by a particular condition to do something extraordinary for the public good.*

The constituent parts of a law.

---

* This it is proper to observe in opposition to Cumberland of the laws of nature, proleg. c. 14. & cap. 5. §40. where he asserts the promise of rewards to be no less necessary to maintaining the authority of laws than the commination of punishments. [[Richard Cumberland, *A Treatise of the Laws of Nature*, 260 and 587–88. Cumberland (1631–1718) was bishop of Peterborough and a political theorist. His treatise on the laws of nature (*De legibus naturae*) first appeared in 1672.]] But a legislator does not owe rewards to those who do what it would be criminal in them not to do, but to those only who do any thing extraordinary for the common good (lib. 1. §99). Hence in vain does he expect a reward, who does not commit murder or adultery, or theft, since he who perpetrates any such crime is worthy of punishment. But one hath a right to claim a reward, if the legislator having preferred a recompence, he is thereby excited to carry provisions to ships, to furnish arms at his own expence, or to do any such like good service to the public, to which all and every one are not obliged. And in this appears the wonderful goodness of God, that whereas he hath a right to threaten punishments to the transgressors of his laws, without promising rewards to the obedient, he profers recompences, recompences even to a thousand generations, to them who obey his will, Exod. xx. 6.

SECTION CLIII

Penal sanc-
tion is either
definite or
indefinite.

Seeing by punishment is understood an evil effect of the transgression of a law (l. 1. §99), which evil effect may consist not only in a certain evil of suffering, but likewise in the nullity of the act done in disobedience to a law; yea, in both: For this reason, a law which both pronounces an act contrary to it null, and renders a transgressor liable <155> to some evil of suffering, is called by the Civilians *a perfect law;* and other laws are called *imperfect,* or *less than perfect,* Ulpianus fragment. 1. 1.[3] Moreover, because an illicit action may be either determinate or indeterminate, and may be varied by a great diversity of circumstances (l. 1. §100), the consequence is, that punishment may be *definite* or *indefinite* and *arbitrary.*

SECTION CLIV

Judiciary
power likewise
belongs to the
supreme
magistrate.

Because laws would be ineffectual, were they not applied to facts; *i.e.* unless enquiry were made into the agreement or disagreement of actions with laws (l. 1. §95); it follows, that there must be some person, in a civil state, who hath the power of judging of the imputation of actions; which power, is nothing else but a power of judging of the actions of others (l. 1. §97); whence it is plain, that *judiciary power* is necessary in a republic. Now, because between equals neither magistracy nor punishment can take place (§6), this judiciary power in a republic must belong to the superior; *i.e.* to the supreme power in it;* and therefore it is one of the internal rights of majesty (§134).

---

* Indeed a father of a family may administer justice in a natural state to his segregate family, as we have already observed (§92). But in a republic that cannot be done, but so far as the laws permit the head of a family to do it (§93). Judiciary power therefore in civil states, belongs to the supreme magistracy, which is chiefly constituted for this very end, according to the ancients, Hesiod. Theog. v. 88.

> *Hac una reges sapienti lege creantur,*
> *Dicere jus populis, injustaque tollere facta.*

[[Hesiod, *Theogony,* line 88: "Kings are created by this one, just law, to pronounce justice to the people and to remove unjust deeds."]]

3. Ulpian, "The Rules of Ulpian" (1), p. 223, in Justinian, *The Civil Law,* vol. 1.

SECTION CLV

But it being the office of a judge to apply laws to facts or actions, and actions contrary to law being either detrimental to the republic itself, or to <156> private persons; it follows from hence, that all judgments are either *private* or *civil, public* or *criminal;* the former of which consist in determining suits or controversies; the latter in punishing bad actions, Cic. pro Caecin. c. 2. And tho' a prince cannot be blamed, if he delegates the judiciary power to prudent and good men, skilled in the laws (l. 1. §101), and so constitute magistrates and judges every where; yet there ought always to be access to the supreme power for those who think themselves oppressed by an unjust decree of the judges; and therefore, the ultimate determination of doubtful causes belongs to the Sovereign of a state.*

What it is, and how it ought to be exerced.

SECTION CLVI

Because it belongs to a judge to apply laws to facts, and to determine whether an action be imputable to a person or not (l. 1. §95); but to impute an action, is to declare whether the effect assigned by a law to a certain action takes place or not (l. 1. §99); hence it follows, that the Sovereign, who has the supreme judiciary power, has also the power *of inflicting punishments.* And be-<157>cause it cannot be denied, that he who hath the power of making laws, must also have the power not only of taking away a part of a law, or of making some exception to it,

As also the power of punishing.

---

* Therefore, it belongs in monarchical states to Kings and Princes; in aristocracies to the college of nobles; and in democracies, the right of appeal is to the people; nor ought any tribunal rashly to be established from which there is no appeal: This the Romans could not long brook under their Kings and Dictators, l. 1. 26. 2. 8. 3. 55. 10. 9. But because the right of appealing may be not a little abused, it is not to be wondered at, that various remedies have been invented to restrain it within due bounds. Such are, the power of determining without appeal lodged in some magistrates, a certain sum being defined by the law above which appeal may be made, an oath of calumny, a certain sum of money to be deposited by the appellant in case he should be cast, and the like; which, whether they be expedient or not, is rather a question of civil prudence than of natural jurisprudence.

but even of abrogating a law (§149); much less can it be refused, that he hath the power of exeeming a delinquent for just reasons from a law, so as to give him a remission from the punishment due by it.*

SECTION CLVII

Hence again we conclude, that there is no right of punishing among equals,† and that neither one's integrity of life, nor another's confirmed inveterate habit of sinning, gives an equal any right of punishing; and therefore, that the nature of punishment is not fully pointed out by Grotius's definition of it, who says, "It is an evil of suffering inflicted for an

* The stoics denied this. Their maxim is known to every one: "Sapientem non dare veniam, nec ignoscere," Diogenes Laert. 7. 123. Senec. de clement. 2. 6. 7. [["The wise man does not grant pardon nor forgive" (see Diogenes Laertius, *Lives,* bk. 7, sec. 123); Seneca, *De clementia,* bk. 2, chaps. 6–7, in Seneca, *Moral Essays,* vol. 1).]] But if the most just God forgives sins without violating his essential justice, why may not a supreme magistrate, who hath the power of making penal laws, cancel these laws; and why therefore may he not pardon a criminal? But we have said *for just causes:* For as laws ought not to be enacted but for grave and important reasons, so neither ought any indulgence to any one to be granted without just and good reasons. But what if the punishment be appointed by a divine law? If it can be made appear that there is such a penal law, we scruple not to affirm, that no Sovereign hath power to change such a law, or to dispense with it (lib. 1. §17). But whether there be any such law, hath been much disputed among the learned, and is yet undetermined. See Thomasius dissert. de jure adgrat. princip. circa poenam homicid. [[Thomasius (*praeses*) and Clusener (*respondens*), *Dissertatio inauguralis juridica, de jure aggratiandi principis Evangelici in causis homicidii.*]]

† For we are speaking here of *civil punishment,* properly so called, and appointed by law, and not of *conventional,* to which one of his own accord subjects himself; nor of that revenge by which one deprives another of certain benefits on account of his crimes, renounces his friendship and acquaintance, *&c.* nor of these natural evils, such as diseases, pains, infamy, *&c.* which one brings upon himself by his wicked practices. Again, there is a great difference between punishing and that right of *chastising* which the laws give to parents, and sometimes to a husband, and to a master. For *chastisements* are applied at pleasure by way of discipline: But *punishment,* properly so called, is inflicted by the prescription or appointment of a law, in the way of jurisdiction. Whence it is self-evident, that an equal cannot punish an equal; but he alone can punish who hath the right of making laws, and of applying them to facts: Which since the supreme magistrate alone hath the power of doing (§151 and 154), he alone therefore hath the power of punishing. It is then a very singular opinion of Grotius (of the rights of war and peace, 2. 20. 3. 1.) to say, "That nature sufficiently

evil of doing." Nor by Becmann's, "who defines it to be pain inflicted for a crime." The evil of suffering inflicted by the sufferer, is not punishment, but revenge; and if it be inflicted by a third person, who is not a superior, it <158> is injury. But that neither of these ought to be permitted in a civil state, is plain from hence, that the judiciary power in it belongs only to the supreme magistrate, and those to whom he hath delegated and intrusted it (§154, 155). <159>

SECTION CLVIII

Nor will it be difficult to determine what is the end of punishment from the very reason which makes it requisite. For since punishment, properly so called, took its rise upon the introduction of civil government (§6), and the right of inflicting it, is one of the immanent rights of civil majesty (§134); the end of which is nothing else but the security of subjects; the consequence is, that the same must be the end of punishments. But because subjects are rendered secure, by reducing them in such manner, that they shall no more be disposed to transgress, or that they shall no longer have it in their power; *i.e.* either by amending them, or by taking the power from them of offending for the future; hence it is evident, that the former is the end of punishments, which are inflicted without taking away the criminal's life; and that the latter is the end of capital punishment, "punishment joined with the loss of life," as Justinian

What are the ends of punishments.

---

shews it to be most proper that punishments should be inflicted by a superior; but that it cannot be demonstrated, that it is necessary, unless the word *superior* be taken in such a sense as to signify, that he who does a bad action, does thereby, as it were, detrude himself out of the rank of men, into that of the brutes subjected to men." As if moral superiority or pre-eminence could give any mortal the right of punishing, and superiority of empire were not necessary. See Thomasius, jurisp. divin. 3. 7. 31. Wherefore, if an offender is punished by the person injured, it is not punishment, but revenge; and if he is punished by a third person, it is an injury. But that both these are prohibited in a civil state, Grotius does not deny. And therefore *Sanio* in Terence reasons much better, Adelph. 2. 1. v. 34. "I am a pimp, I confess: the bane of youth: a perjured villain: a common nuisance and pest: but I have done you no injury." [[Terence, "The Brothers," act 2, lines 188–89, in Terence, *Terence,* vol. 2, 271.]]

speaks, §2. Instit. de pub. jud.* And because sufficient provision would not be made for the security of the state, if those only who had offended should cease to transgress, and the like transgressions may still be apprehended from others; it is obvious, that by the same punishments, as by examples, others ought to be admonished of the danger of transgressing; and therefore the guilty ought to be punished publickly, unless some weightier reason forbid it. <160>

SECTION CLIX

Whether a delinquent be obliged to suffer punishment?

These principles being fixed, it is very perspicuous, whether there be any obligation upon a delinquent to suffer punishment. For since he who lives in a civil state, is obliged to all, without which its end, *i.e.* the public security, cannot be obtained or expected (§106), undoubtedly a delinquent is obliged to suffer the punishment defined by the law, tho' not to punish himself, and therefore not voluntarily to offer himself to cruel sufferings:† no injury is done to one who suffers condign punishment,

---

* Hence it appears, that to human punishments, the end, of which some speak so much, does not belong, *viz.* the expiation of guilt, and the satisfaction due to divine justice: For neither can we absolve those from cruelty, like that of Phalaris, who punish delinquents for no other end but to torment them. Nor could the suffering of a guilty person make any satisfaction to the infinite divine justice, had it not been satisfied by another satisfaction truly infinite. But they who talk in this manner do not consider the origine of punishments, which is nothing else but the necessity of them to the security of a civil state; and seem at the same time not to attend to the distinction between human and divine justice, and between civil punishments and those eternal ones which abide sinners in the life to come.

† Yea, because punishment is an evil of suffering, from which nature is abhorrent, what one is willing to undergo would not be a punishment. Quintilian Declam. 11. says, "He is mistaken who measures the atrocity of torments by their names: Nothing is a punishment but what is unwillingly undergone. We suffer no pain but by impatience, and it is fear that alone can make a thing appear cruel or terrible. Will any one call that a punishment to one, to which one runs, and which he calls for? Drag condemned malefactors whither they are unwilling to go." [[Quintilian, "XI: The Case of the Rich Man Accused of Treason," 142, in *The Major Declamations Ascribed to Quintilian,* 137–44.]] It is a barbarous custom to force men to lay violent hands on themselves, to rip up their bowels, or to take poison, or to choose any other way of death. For we are not obliged to be ourselves the instruments of the punishment we are obliged patiently to submit to.

being convicted of a crime; nor is it lawful to any one to resist the supreme power, when it inflicts the punishment appointed by law. <161>

SECTION CLX

Now, from the end of punishments (§158), we infer, that they ought to be adjusted to the end of the republic, and therefore to be of such a nature as is most proper for its internal security. Whence it follows, that the supreme power is obliged to punish such crimes as disturb the security of the state, or hinder the subjects from living conveniently and tranquilly. But it is not necessary to punish vitious acts which rest in the mind, nor yet such minute faults as every man is liable to; nor the omission of the offices of humanity, unless these crimes become, by their prevalence, dangerous, or disgraceful to the state, and therefore necessity oblige to restrain even them.*

If all crimes ought to be punished, and what crimes ought to be punished.

SECTION CLXI

It is abundantly plain, from the very definition of punishments (l. 1. §99), that they only ought to be punished who have committed any evil action; not their heirs or their families,† or sureties, who bound them-

Who are to be punished.

---

* Thus we find in matters of treason, the very thought or knowledge of it in some states is punished; and in some nations inhospitality is punished: We have given some examples of this, (lib. 1. §216). And we shall now add, that the ancient Germans commanded humanity to strangers by laws, with penalties annexed to them. There are such sanctions in the *Lex Burgund.* 33. 1. *Capitular.* 1. 75. in which a pecuniary mulct is ordered against those who shut their house or the market-place against a stranger. The Goths ordered by a law the houses of those to be burnt who had three times refused access to travellers, Joan. Mag. hist. Goth. 4. 1. See Element. juris Germ. 1. 18. §420. [[*Burgundian Code*, 38.1. *Capitularia Regum Francorum*. Johannes Magnus, *Gothorum Sueonumque historia*. The last reference is to Heineccius's own *Elementa iuris Germanici*.]]

† The Persians were so barbarous, of which cruelty, see Barn. Brisson. de regno Persic. 2. 227. p. 591. [[Brisson, *De regio Persarum principatu libri tres*.]] We have some traces of it in Daniel, vi. 24. and Esther ix. 14. And that this barbarity still prevails very universally in the eastern nations, hath been observed by those who have described their manners with the greatest accuracy. But as this usage is absolutely re-

selves to punishment for others, contrary to right and justice (l. 1. §146). But since whole societies constitute one moral person (§19), and therefore are bound by the same laws prescribed to the rest (§23), it is obvious, <162> that communities and societies may be punished, tho' humanity itself pleads for the mitigation of the punishment, that the innocent may not suffer equally with the guilty; and that those who transgressed by mistake, or thro' weakness of judgment, may not feel the same severity with those who were the stirrers up and ringleaders in such tumults. And in punishing large bodies, corporations or communities, that the remedy may not be worse than the disease, care ought to be taken that fear may affect all, and punishment may reach but to few.

SECTION CLXII

The principles upon which the quantity of punishment is determined.

What kind of, and how great punishments ought to be inflicted, is plain from the nature and end of punishment. For since the end of punishment consists in the security of the subjects (§158), the consequence is, that punishment ought to be sufficient to impress fear, and to restrain and coerce evil dispositions. But such being the nature of mankind, that any evil concupiscence, which hath once got possession of the heart, cannot be restrained, but by setting before men a greater evil or good, (l. 1. §52); hence we have reason to conclude, <163> that a penal sanction will not impress sufficient fear, unless men judge it a greater evil to undergo the threatened punishment, than to omit the crime forbidden under that penalty, and be deprived of the pleasure or profit they expect from it.*

---

pugnant to right reason, so it is not possible by any prudence to prevent the falling of punishment inflicted upon parents, indirectly, at least, upon their children, especially when their estates are confiscated by law. And this consideration hath moved more humane legislators very rarely to use this punishment, and not but in case of treason, to confiscate all the goods, that as much as it was possible for them to do, they might prevent punishment from extending so much as indirectly to the children of the punished.

* The punishment of injuries by the laws of the twelve tables, furnishes us with an example. For it struck so little terror into wicked rich men, that they rather took pleasure in committing insults, which could cost them but a very trifling fine. The

SECTION CLXIII

From these principles we further conclude, that the security of the civil state does not admit of the punishment of retaliation, or like for like.* Nor is the rule about proportion between the crime and the punishment a just one, unless it be understood, not so much of the actions them-

Conclusions from hence.

---

whole matter is related at great length by Aulus Gellius Noct. Attic. 20. 1. who tells us there, "That the fine for an injury or insult being a very few pence, that hardly any one was so poor, as that he could be restrained by it from indulging his arrogance and insolence. And therefore Labeo in his commentary on the twelve tables, did not approve of this law. He mentions one L. Neratius, a person of remarkable pride and insolence, whose great joy it was to give a freeman a blow on the face with his fist, and who went about diverting himself in this outrageous manner, attended with his servant, who carried a purse to count down the fine of five pence, appointed by law for the offence to every one he cuffed. For which reason, the Praetors afterwards abolished this law, and published an edict, in which they constituted themselves repairers of estimable injuries." [[Gellius, *Attic Nights,* bk. 20, chap. 1.13, pp. 411–13.]] So far then was such a slight penalty from checking, that it rather provoked and encouraged insolence and injuriousness.

   * God himself seems to have approved this law, Exod. xxi. 23. Levit. xxiv. 50. Deut. xix. 19. That law of the Decemviri is also well known, "Si membrum rupsit, ni cum eo pacit, talio esto." apud Gell. Noct. Attic. 20. 1. [[Gellius, *Attic Nights,* bk. 20, chap. 1: "If one has broken another's limb, there shall be retaliation, unless a compromise be made."]] But as the Jewish Rabbis themselves so interpret the divine law, that such injuries might have been expiated by money consistently with it: So Caecilius denies that ever this law took place among the Romans, apud Gell. ibid. And they are perhaps proverbs indicating, that he is not injured by one who suffers the same from another, he himself did to him, tho' perhaps the same thing may not occasion equal suffering to both. See Jo. Clericus ad Exod. xxi. 22. In which sense Pythagoras said punishment was compensation, or equal suffering. However that may be, that the law of like for like hath not always place, may be proved from these considerations. 1. That sometimes such a punishment would scarcely deserve the name of punishment, *e.g.* if I should be ordered to take as much money from one as he had taken from me, in the highway; or if a man of no rank give a blow to a magistrate, should be struck himself by the magistrate. 2. Sometimes it cannot be done, *i.e.* the one cannot be made to suffer as much as the other, *e.g.* if a person with one eye should beat out another's two eyes. 3. Sometimes equality cannot be so observed but that the delinquent must suffer more than the person injured. Thus, *e.g.* I know an instance of one run through the body by a night-walker in such a manner, that his intestines not being touched he soon recovered. But could all the physicians in the world, with their united skill, thus run a sword through one without doing him more mischief?

selves, as of the disposition to perpetrate them. Besides, since some crimes are more noxious to the public than others, and some tend more than others to its dishonour, it is easy to find a reason why an action, which is more hurtful to the public security, is fenced against <164> by more severe and awful punishment, and punishment is augmented when crimes become more frequent.

SECTION CLXIV

In appointing punishments regard ought to be had to all circumstances.

But, as in the imputation of other human actions, so likewise in the imputation of crimes, all circumstances ought to be attended to; for one circumstance often changes the whole affair (l. 1. §100). And therefore it may happen, that one ought to be more severely punished than another for the <165> same crime; and in defining punishments, regard ought to be had not only to the person of the delinquent, but likewise to the person injured, and also to the object, the effect, the place, the time, and like circumstances.*

* Thus, with respect to the delinquent, he deserves a greater punishment whom kindred, prudence, age, dignity ought to have kept back from a crime, than a stranger, an ignorant unthinking person, one under no special obligation, a boy or stripling, one of the lower rank of mankind (l. 1. §113). A robust person will require a severer corporal punishment than one of a weakly delicate constitution; and if a pecuniary mulct is to be inflicted, more ought to be laid upon a rich *Neratius,* than upon a poor man. In like manner, if an injury be done to a magistrate, or to a person of dignity, who will deny that it ought to be more heavily punished than an affront to one of the vulgar and dregs of mankind? Besides, if it be a crime to seize the goods of a private person to make gain of them; how much greater a crime must it be to rob the public, or to commit sacrilege? Thus we find a soldier's deserting from his post in an encampment is more severely punished than one's running away from winter-quarters, on account of the more dangerous consequences of the former. And in like manner, all equal judges pronounce an injury done in church, or during divine worship, more heinous than one done in a private place, and at another time. So that the public sense does not approve the doctrine of the Stoics, concerning the equality of all crimes, Cic. Paradox. 3. Diogen. Laert. 7. 120. against which we find Horace reasoning thus:

> *Non vincet ratio hoc, tantumdem ut peccet, idemque,*
> *Qui teneros caules alieni infregerit horti,*
> *Et qui nocturnus divûm sacra legerit. Adsit*

SECTION CLXV

Nor ought it to be forgot, that since all punishments are not intended to cut off the flagitious delinquent; but they are often only intended to reform <166> him, and make him more regular and circumspect for the future (§158); care ought therefore to be taken, that all who suffer for their faults be not marked with ignominy; because they would thus be no longer useful members in the republic, and could scarcely gain their living by any honest art or employment.

Punishments inflicted to amend persons, ought not to be ignominious.

SECTION CLXVI

To the internal rights of majesty belongs the power of exacting *tributes* and *taxes* from subjects, and of applying their goods to public uses when necessity so requires; which last is called *eminent dominion.* * For all being in the power of a Sovereign, without which the end of a republic, *viz.* internal and external security, cannot be obtained (§133); which cannot

A Sovereign hath the power of laying on taxes and imposts, and hath a certain eminent dominion.

Regula, peccatis quae poenas irroget aequas:
Ne scutica dignum horribili sectere flagello.
Horat. Serm. 1. 3. v. 115.

[[Horace, *Satires I,* 3.115: "Nor will reason prove this, that the sin is one and the same, for one who cuts the young cabbages from someone else's garden and for one who steals the sacred objects of the gods by night. Let there be a rule to assign fair penalties to offences, to avoid flaying with the terrible scourge what only deserves the strap."]]

* We confess that this term is not very apposite to express the thing, the ideas of empire and dominion being very different, and because the former and not the latter belongs to Sovereigns. Wherefore, what Grotius (of the rights of war and peace) first termed *dominium eminens;* Seneca of benefits, 7. 4. has more properly called *potestas.* "Ad reges, potestas omnium, ad singulos proprietas pertinet." [["[E]verything belongs to the king, and yet property, to which the king lays claim by his universal right" (Seneca, *Moral Essays,* vol. 3, 465).]] See V. A. Corn. van Bynkersh. Quest. jur. publ. 2. 15. p. 290. [[Bynkershoek, *Quaestionum juris publici libri duo,* vol. 1, 290.]] And hence certain lawyers of Wirtemberg have contended against Jo. Fr. Hornius [[Johann Friedrich Horn (ca. 1629–65), German jurist]], that this supreme right is not to be derived from dominion, but from sovereignty. (See Guil. Leyseri collectio scriptorum eristicorum pro imperio contra dominium eminens.) [[Wilhelm Leyser (1592–

be obtained without contributions from the subjects for bearing the necessary charges of the republic, and unless the Sovereign may sometimes apply the goods of subjects for public uses; the consequence of this is, that Sovereigns must have a right to exact contributions from subjects, and likewise a right of exercing an eminent dominion. <167>

SECTION CLXVII

What this right is in the ordinary state of a republic.
Now, since a Sovereign hath this right (§166), it is obvious, that to him belongs the protection and guardianship of private properties;* that when the exigencies of the state require it, they may be ready, and in a condition to answer the necessities of the republic; and therefore he has a right of making laws concerning the right use of property, and concerning alienations and conveyances (l. 1. §317); as likewise of settling commerce by treaties, and of restricting it according as the interest of the republic may require; of regulating import and export, promoting manufactures and arts, making sumptuary laws; and, in one word, of doing every thing to make the state thriving and opulent, and sufficient to defend and maintain itself in a flourishing condition.

1649), *Dissertatio pro imperio contra dominium eminens.*]] But this debate being about words, while all are agreed that a Sovereign hath the right of applying the goods of subjects to public uses, when necessity requires it, there is no reason for exploding a received phrase.

* Upon this depends the right of Sovereigns to give tutors and curators to minors, to persons labouring under any disease which incapacitates for business, to mad persons, to prodigals, to women, *&c.* and of prescribing rules to such administrators, calling them to an account, and removing them from their trust, if they are unfaithful. See Plato de legibus, l. 11. where he says, that pupils are under the care and guardianship, not of private persons, but of the public, and are one of its most sacred charges. Hence the Germans, from the most ancient times, claimed from their Emperors a certain supreme guardianship or tutorage, of which I treated long ago in a dissertation de suprema principum & magistratuum tutela. [[Heineccius (*praeses*) and Russel (*respondens*), *De suprema principum magistratuumque tutela dissertatio iuridica inauguralis.*]]

SECTION CLXVIII

Such is the right of sovereignty in the ordinary state of a republic. But because it is in an extraordinary state of the republic that eminent dominion takes place (§166), the consequence is, that a Sovereign has the right, in time of war, to make en-<168>campments upon the fields of private persons, and to make necessary fortifications and public works upon them, l. 9. C. de oper. public. to bring in corn and other necessaries by foraging; to make new highways through the lands of subjects when the old ones fail, l. 14. §1. D. quemadm. serv. amitt. throw down houses in the suburbs when Hannibal is at the gates, and such other like things.

And what in an extraordinary state.

SECTION CLXIX

But since this right only takes place in urgent *necessity* (§166), and since that is necessary, without which the public good, *the supreme law in every state* (§24), or liberty, property and security, cannot be maintained and preserved; hence we may justly infer, that this right may not only take place when the extreme necessity of a republic requires it, but even as often as it is truly requisite to the public utility; especially since utility often becomes necessity (V. A. Corn. van Bynkersh. ibid. p. 292).[4] But this right scarcely takes place, when it is merely the private interest of the Sovereign that demands it, if any one's just right is taken from him by it; much less, when it is not his real utility but pleasure that is the motive. And, in fine, of such a nature is this eminent dominion, that a good prince will easily submit to fixing bounds to it, and will use it very modestly (Bynkersh. ibid.).* <169>

When this eminent dominion justly takes place.

4. Bynkershoek, *Quaestionum juris publici libri duo,* vol. 1, p. 292.
* We have added these limitations, because without them this right would degenerate into the highest injuriousness. Hence God *was exceeding wroth* with King Achab, when he would have violently extorted Naboth's vineyard from him, because contiguous to his palace, that he might make a Kitchen-garden of it, 1 Kings xxi. 2. For such a demand proceeded rather from the wantonness and voluptuousness of a wicked King, than from real utility. The Roman senate refused an action to the Praetors against M. Licinius Crassus, when they would have carried an aqueduct thro' his

SECTION CLXX

How they
ought to
exerce it.

Since equity teaches us that the common burdens of the republic ought to be supported at the common charge (§166), the consequence of this is, that one subject ought not to be loaded more than another; and therefore, that compensation ought to be made to him who must part with any thing for the public utility out of the treasury or the public coffer.* And if that cannot be done immediately, they who are thus deprived of any part of their property have a right to exact it, unless they build contrary to law, and such an edifice, or whatever kind of work it is, be destroyed, the public utility so requiring. For, in this case, so far are they from having a right to demand refunding the value, that they are liable to the penalty appointed by the laws. V. A. Corn. van Bynkersh. ibid. p. 297. <170>

---

ground, because they said it was rather a matter of pleasure and ornament than of public utility, Liv. 40. 51. Thus the case is represented by Marc. Zuer. Boxhorn. Disquisit. polit. casu 31. [[Boxhorn, *Disquisitiones politicae.*]] Yet Bynkersh, hath produced a charter by William Prince of Orange, in which he gives power to the magistracy of Leyden, of taking possession of the court-yards of private persons, paying them the price, even though it was not otherwise necessary, but for the ornament of the Academic buildings, and the pleasure of the students: upon which, however, he adds this remark, "Such a right I would not use, nor did the Roman senate use it in the case of Crassus; nor did even Augustus use it, of whom Sueton tells us, Aug. c. 56. 'That the Roman Forum was made narrow by him, because he would not take the neighbouring houses from their proprietors.'" [[Bynkershoek, *Quaestionum juris publici libri duo,* vol. 1, p. 295.]]

* This is acknowledged by Grotius of the rights of war and peace, 2. 14. 7. by Pufendorff of the law of nature and nations, 8. 5. 7. by Huber de jure civitatis, 1. 3. 6. 44. and by all who have treated at any length of this dominion; among whom Bynkersh. ibid. deserves the first place, who has shewn that the Romans followed this maxim, from Tacitus Annal. 1. 75. and l. 9. cod. de oper. pub. And undoubtedly the same principle of equity takes place here, upon which the Rhodian law concerning goods thrown over board, was founded, Paulus l. 1. D. ad leg. Rhod. *viz.* That what is given up for all should be made up by the contribution of all.

SECTION CLXXI

Besides, from the same definition it is plain that this right can only be exercised upon the goods of subjects, and not upon the goods of foreigners who are not enemies. Wherefore those princes are hardly excusable, who lay their hands upon the goods and merchandize of nations in friendship with them, force them to lend them money, or seize their ships to transport troops or provisions. But such pressing, as it is called, is frequent, and defended under this colour, that foreign ships, found in the harbours of a prince, are subject to him;* and it is practised by a received custom among nations and empires.

Whether it can be extended to the goods of foreigners not enemies.

SECTION CLXXII

So much for the *eminent dominion* or *transcendental propriety.* As to *taxes* and *imposts,* it is the interest of a republic to be strong in money on a dou-<171>ble account. First, in order to support its Sovereign suitably to his dignity. And secondly, that money, the nerves of all business, may not be wanting either in time of war or peace; and therefore in republics there are usually two public coffers, one of which is intended for the suitable maintenance and support of the Sovereign, and is called *the exchequer;* the other for the public use, which is called *the treasury.* † That

What is the exchequer and treasury.

* Since the Greeks returning from the expedition of Cyrus, could not so much as use this colour, what they did is so much the less excusable, tho' Grotius does not seem to condemn it (of the rights of war and peace, 2. 2. 10). By Xenophon's advice, as he himself tells us, de expedit. Cyr. 5. 1. 6. they, "having the most pressing occasion for shipping, seized such as passed by, but so that the cargo was preserved untouched for the owners, and to the seamen they not only gave provisions, but paid them the freight." [[See Xenophon, *Anabasis,* vol. 2, bk. 5, chap. 1, 10–12.]] This indeed had been excusable on account of necessity, had it been a public expedition. But we cannot see how this right could in any way belong to a handful of soldiers, who had engaged in an expedition with Cyrus without the consent of their several states, an expedition more memorable by its greatness than its justice.

† It is right to distinguish these two, tho' not unfrequently in monarchies princes take all to themselves in such a rapacious manner, that there is in fact no difference between the two. Dion. Cassius, hist. 53. p. 506. tells us, That Augustus had both

both of these should be well filled, is greatly the interest of every civil state.

SECTION CLXXIII

What hath been contrived for enriching the treasury.

Since the money destined for the support of a Sovereign is brought into the (*fiscus*) or *exchequer,* (§172), some nations have thought fit not only to assign to their Sovereigns certain lands and territories, out of the revenues of which their dignity is to be supported, which are now called *demesnes* of the crown, or *crown-lands;* but likewise certain customs, duties, tollages, or taxes; and all things within the territory of the republic not under dominion (l. I. §243 & seq.); which latter way of enriching the king's treasury hath been the more readily agreed upon in all nations,* that it is done with the least cost to particulars. <172>

---

money and soldiers at his absolute command; and he adds, "And tho' in words he distinguished between his own money and the public treasury, yet in fact he made use of both at his pleasure." [[Cassius, *Roman History,* bk. 53, chap. 22, p. 251.]] But here we are not enquiring what is done, but what ought to be done: and therefore, it is proper to distinguish between these two public coffers, as is carefully done even in aristocracies and other republics.

* The nations of German origine chiefly, of whom Grotius of the rights of war and peace, lib. 2. c. 8. §5. says, "The people of Germany consulting about making some allowances to their Princes and Kings to support their dignities, thought it proper to begin with such things as might be given without damage to any one, such are those which no person could lay particular claim to, which I find that the Egyptians also practised. For there the King's Intendant, whom they called ἴδιον λόγον, seized on all such things to the use of the crown." But what Grotius says here of the Egyptians, as from Strabo, whom he quotes in the margin, Geog. l. 17. p. 1148. edit. noviss. does not relate to the Egyptians, but to the Romans, after they had reduced that country to the form of a province. [[Presumably the "editio novissima" of Strabo's work is the *Rerum geographicarum libri XVII,* published in Amsterdam in 1707.]] The office which Strabo calls ἴδιος λόγος, was the same as the *Digest* calls *Procurator Caesaris,* or *Rationalis.* What Strabo says is this, "There is another officer called ἴδιος λόγος [[a kind of "special agent" of Caesar (see Strabo, *Geography,* vol. 8, bk. XVII, chap. 1.12, p. 51)]] whose business it was to demand such things as had no master, and consequently ought to fall to Caesar." This is justly observed by Casaubon on this passage of Strabo.

SECTION CLXXIV

Since therefore the demains of a Sovereign are intended for the maintenance of his dignity ($173), it is plain that they cannot be alienated, and therefore may be reclaimed by a successor singular or universal, if they are alienated; nor does it make any difference whether they are alienated in part or in whole, since of what is not ours we cannot alienate the smallest part, as Grotius justly observes (of the rights of war and peace, 2. 6. 11.) where he remarks, that such alienations made with the consent of the people are valid,* and the fruits of this demain or patrimony of the crown are to be distinguished from the patrimony itself. <173>

His rights over his demenial goods.

SECTION CLXXV

Moreover, because things having no master have been assigned to Sovereigns ($173), it is not difficult to find a reason why the crown every where pretends to a right to all those things which are by the Roman law pronounced either common or public, as the seas which wash their territory, rivers, large forests, and therefore the rights of fishing and hunting; as also the right of digging for minerals and metals, and of taking possession of vacated goods, and of gems or precious stones cast out by

The right of a Sovereign over things which have no master.

---

* Whether the people originally consented, or afterwards ratified the alienation, of which innumerable instances hath happened in Germany. For the ancient Emperors being so very profuse in giving away their demains, especially to the church, that at present hardly any of them remain; none will say, that the Emperor can now reclaim them, since these alienations have been confirmed long ago by the orders of the Empire; yea, tho' the Emperor usually promises to recover the rights and revenues of the Empire, Capitul. Caroli 6. art. 10. yet this is understood by the interpreters of the public law of Germany, to mean so far as it can be done consistently with the public laws. [[This refers to the so-called electoral capitulation of Charles VI, Holy Roman Emperor from 1711 to 1740. The electoral capitulation contained the concessions the emperor elect made to the Holy Roman Empire's electoral princes in return for their votes (see Charles VI, *Capitulatio Caroli VI*).]] And the Emperors and Kings, who were sollicitous about this recovery, had very bad success, such as Henry V. Rudolph I. Albert I. and others. See Schweder dissert. de domanio imperii. [[Schweder (*praeses*) and Pregitzer (*respondens*), *Dissertatio inauguralis de Domanio S. Romani.*]]

the sea, alluvions, new islands, deserted channels, and, in some places, trove-treasure, and vagabonds and bastards; tho' all these things differ according to the different usages of nations, as Huber has justly observed, de jur. civ. 2. 4. 4. 48. p. 468.* <174>

* The disputes about the dominion of the sea between Grotius and Selden, Rob. Jonston, Petr. Bapt. Burgus, Guil. Welwood, Jo. Isaac Pontanus, Theod. Graswinckelius, and more lately between Pufendorff, Huber, Jac. Gothofredus, Jo. Hen. Boeclerus, Corn. van Bynkershoek, and Christ. Thomasius, and others, are known; nor need we enter into the controversy. [[These works are Grotius's *Free Sea* (1609); Selden, *Mare clausum* (1635), written around 1618; Robert Johnson, *Nova Brittannia* (1609); Borgo (Burgus), *De dominio serenissimae Genuensis reipublicae in Mari Ligustico libri II* (1641); Welwood, "Of the Community and Propriety of the Seas" (1613), in Grotius, *Free Sea;* Pontanus, *Discussionum historicarum libri duo* (1637); and Graswinckel, *Maris liberi vindiciae* (1652), which was directed against Borgo's treatise. Pufendorf, Huber, and Thomasius did not publish separate treatises on the freedom of the seas, though they referred to this question in their more general juristic works. The jurist Jacques Godefroy (Jacobus Gothofredus, 1587–1652) published *De imperio maris deque iure naufragii colligendi* (1637). The work by Boecler (1611–72) presumably is a university dissertation for which he acted as *praeses,* with the title *Minos maris dominus* (1656); Bynkershoek published *De dominio maris dissertatio* (1703). It is not clear who "Rob. Jonston" is.]] We are of opinion, that as none can doubt that the sea is under the dominion of none, so it cannot be questioned but it may be occupied, and falls to the occupant, (lib. 1 §241); especially since that hath been long ago done, and is still, as experience teaches us. But because things of exhaustless use are not occupied, nor is it lawful to exclude others from the use of them by occupancy, (lib. 1. §235), some things in the sea being of exhaustible use, such as the larger kinds of fishes, pearls, tolls, and such other emoluments; and other things being of inexhaustible use, as navigation; others may be excluded from the former, but not from the latter. Much more then have they who have certain territories beyond sea, a right to exclude all others from navigation to them, whether with a view to occupancy or for commerce, unless it be otherwise provided by treaties and pacts; since it depends upon the will of every nation, to permit or not permit commerce with foreigners to its subjects. But navigation to other territories not belonging to us, for the sake of commerce, is as unjustly denied by us as the use of a public road, unless this navigation be hindered by pacts and treaties. This is our opinion about this celebrated question. Nor need we be very anxious about it, since this matter is rather decided by force than by words and arguments; so true is what Horace says, Carm. 1. 3. v. 21.

> *Necquidquam Deus abscidit*
> *Prudens Oceano dissociabiles*
> *Terras, si tamen impiae*
> *Non tangenda rates transiliunt vada.*
> *Audax omnia perpeti*
> *Gens humana ruit per vetitum nefas.*

SECTION CLXXVI

Since it is the interest of the republic that the exchequer should be as rich as possible (§172), it is not strange that other advantages and means of gain are given to it; especially the right of coining money, mulcts, and contreband goods, and the right of seizing* all unlawful acquisitions, and other such, which are commonly, tho' not so justly, called *the regalia minora* (§133). But here the customs of nations are different, according as kingdoms allow more or less to Sovereigns, or they have arrogated more or less to themselves by long use. <175>

Other laws of the Exchequer.

SECTION CLXXVII

As for the public treasury, it is chiefly filled by taxes and duties, unless there be so much public land that the republic can be preserved by its revenues. For since (§172) republics can do nothing without money, either in war or peace (Tacit. hist. 4. 74), and, there not being a sufficient quantity of public land, that can be no otherwise got than from the subjects; the consequence is, that the chief magistrate can impose tributes and taxes upon the subjects, either with or without the consent of the different orders of people in the state, according to the different forms of government; and that they may lay them upon persons, lands, merchandize imported and exported, consumable commodities, manufactures and commerce, as is most convenient, provided regard be had to the condition of the people and the quality of things,* and subjects

The treasury is enriched by taxes and duties.

[[Horace, *Odes* 1.3.21ff. in *Odes and Epodes:* "All to no avail did God deliberately separate countries by the divisive ocean if, in spite of that, impious boats go skipping over the seas that were meant to remain inviolate."]]

* This appeared most equal to Serv. Tullius King of the Romans, and by that means he was very popular, Dion. Halicar. antiq. Rom. lib. 4. p. 215. He declared he would not suffer the poor to be over-loaded with taxes, and to be obliged to contract debt; and therefore, that he would rather make a valuation (*census*) of the estates of his subjects, and make every one contribute according to his fortune, as used to be done in well constituted and regulated states. "For (said he) I reckon it just that he who has large possessions should contribute largely, and that little should be exacted from those who have but little." [[Dionysius of Halicarnassus, *Roman Antiquities,* vol. 2, bk. IV, chap. 9.7, p. 297.]]

be not so oppressed, that they, like slaves, do not acquire to themselves, but to their Sovereign.

SECTION CLXXVIII

What is just with regard to it.

But if in levying taxes, regard ought to be had to every one's faculties, and the subjects ought not to be oppressed with burdens (§177), it is manifest that what is above the power of the subjects, ought not to be exacted from them; nor ought they in <176> times of peace to be so spunged, that they can be able to contribute nothing in case of danger: Besides, this contributed money ought not to be collected with too much rigidity, and it ought to be honestly and faithfully managed, and employed for the purposes to which it is destinated, or which the very end of the contribution requires. This is evident from the nature of the thing.

SECTION CLXXIX

The right of the Sovereign to constitute magistrates and ministers.

Moreover, another of the internal rights of majesty, is to constitute *ministers* and *magistrates* (§134). By *ministers* we understand those who govern a part of the republic entrusted to them in the name of the Sovereign: By *magistrates,* who manage a part committed to them in their own name, but dependently on the Sovereign. Since therefore ministers act in the name of the Sovereign, and magistrates dependently on him, the consequence is, that the Sovereign has the sole right of nominating them, unless he hath granted to others the right of choosing and presenting, or to a community the right of election: that they are under particular obligation to him, and are bound to render account to him, and may be justly degraded from their dignity by him, if they do not acquit themselves well in their charge; nay, may be punished, if they be guilty of knavery, or any gross misdemeanor, as the demerit of their crime requires.* <177>

---

* But an unfraudulent counsel or design, disappointed by the event, is not punishable, since none can be obliged to answer for the event of things. Nor does he deserve punishment who executes the commands of his prince or country, if it be

SECTION CLXXX

As a part of the public concerns is entrusted to ministers as well as magistrates (§179), it therefore is the duty of a prince to know his men well, and to take care to choose none but such as are proper for the trust; and it is the duty of subjects, on the other hand, not to ambition trusts to which they are not equal; and much more is it so, not to brigue for them, or to use bribery, largesses, and other vile arts to procure them, or to buy them, unless it appear to the Sovereign to be for the interest of the republic that such offices should be matter of commerce. Moreover, it is self-evident that every minister and magistrate is obliged to all diligence and fidelity, and to regard the happiness of the state as his chief, his supreme law; and much more is this obligation incumbent upon a first and chief minister, upon whose shoulders the Sovereign hath laid the chief burden of the government.* <178>

The duties of Sovereigns and their ministry, and of magistrates.

---

not contrary to justice and morality. See V. A. Corn. van Bynkersh. Quaest. jur. publ. 2. 2. p. 196. & seq. [[Bynkershoek, *Quaestionum juris publici libri duo*, vol. 1, p. 196.]] It was therefore a barbarous custom of the Carthaginians to punish their best Generals, if their designs missed of success. Nor is that custom of the Turks and other eastern nations less detestable, who measuring a counsel by the event, condemn those whose designs prove successless. For this is not only contrary to justice, but to prudence. "If any one," says that excellent writer, "desire advice in difficult affairs; there are many who are capable of giving it; but none will answer for the event; and if you require this, none will assist you with their counsel, no, not one."

* Such are usually called (*ministrissimi*) chief ministers; and concerning these, two questions are commonly asked; first, whether it be for the interest of a state to entrust the care of the whole state to one: And secondly, whether it can be lawfully done. The first is a question of civil prudence or expediency, upon which it is worth while to read Hert. Elem. prud. civil. 1. 10. 11. Guil. Schroeter and Jac. Thomas their dissertations on this subject. [[Jacob Thomasius (*praeses*) and Georg Heinrich Groer (*respondens*), *De ministrissimo*. Wilhelm Schroeter's (d. 1689) treatise on chief ministers continued to appear in several editions in the early eighteenth century, including one in 1737 (*Fürstliche Schatz- und Rent-Kammer*).]] The latter may be easily answered by any who have considered with any attention the principles of the law of nations. For since we may delegate to another what we do not think ourselves sufficient to manage, why may not princes likewise delegate their office to others, especially when age, the weight of government, and other just reasons induce to it: And if it be not unjust to put a Kingdom under tutorage, while the King is not of an age to take the reins of government into his own hands, why should it be deemed unjust for a King

SECTION CLXXXI

The right in sacred things belonging to Sovereigns.

One of the chief immanent rights of Sovereigns is the right relative to religion, sacred things, or the church, by which we understand a society formed on account of religion. Now, since (§23) all communities and societies of the simpler kind ought to be so subordinated, that they may do nothing contrary to the interest of the larger society; the consequence is, that a church ought to be subordinate to the republic; and therefore, that the chief magistrate has the right of directing its affairs and concerns.* This may be proved from this consideration, that a republic ought to have one will (§114), which could not be the case, if the church in a state were not subject to the chief magistrate, but constituted by itself a free and independent community, not subject to the chief magistrate. Besides, that since all the rights belong to majesty, without which the security of the subjects cannot be obtained (§133); and experience has abundantly shewn us how much the internal and external security

---

to commit it to a minister? However, a prince would act most unjustly, if he should devolve the care of the public upon a first minister, merely that he might pursue his pleasure, and not be troubled with it, since he ought to use him as a minister, and not transfer the government absolutely to him. The Persians seem to have been sensible of this, when they called ministers *the eyes and ears of the King,* Xenophon Cyrop. 8. 2. 7. p. 483. of which Brisson. de regno Persic. has discoursed at large, lib. 1. §190. p. 264.

* Therefore this right belongs to a Sovereign as Sovereign, and not as Bishop, as some have said, who have been solidly refuted by Hen. Boehmer. dissert. de jure Episcop. princip. evangel. [[Boehmer (*praeses*) and de Becquer (*respondens*), *Doctrina de jure episcopali principum evangelicorum.*]] And therefore that distinction of Constantine the great (in Eusebius vita Constant. mag. 4. 24) between the oversight of things without the church and within the church, is without any foundation. [[Eusebius of Caesarea (260–339), author of the *Vita Constantini* (*Life of Constantine*).]] Nor do they come nearer to the truth, who attribute this right about sacred things to a Sovereign, as the primary member of the church; or they who derive it from compact; the first of which opinions is defended by Jaeger. de jure suprem. potest. circa sacra, cap. 3. p. 74. & seq. [[Jäger, *De concordia imperii* [*et*] *sacerdotii sive de jure potestatum supremarum circa sacra.*]] For it being a right of majesty or sovereignty, a Sovereign wants no other title to the exercise of it but his sovereignty; whence the Roman lawyers have pronounced long ago, "Jus publicum etiam in sacris & sacerdotibus consistere," [["That public law also extends to sacred affairs and priests," trans. T. A.]] l. 1. §2. D. de inst. & jur.

of subjects hath been disturbed under the pretext of religion; who then can deny that a Sovereign has the right of so directing religious affairs that the republic may suffer no detriment? <179>

SECTION CLXXXII

Religion, on the account of which men coalesce into the particular society called *a church* (§181), consists chiefly of two things. The first is a just idea of God (l. 1. §127). The last is perfect love to God (ibid. §130). Now, from hence it is evident, that with regard to the former a Sovereign can have no power, since the understanding cannot be forced (l. 1. §129);* and therefore his right ought not to be stretched to a right of imposing new articles of faith upon his subjects, and proscribing former ones; (*i.e.* of imposing a yoke upon their consciences); tho' it be incumbent upon him to take care, that his subjects be instructed in the doctrines he judges to be agreeable to reason and revelation; and that these doctrines be rendered subservient to promote piety and virtue, instead of feuds and divisions, to the equal detriment of the church and state. <180>

Whether it extends to articles of faith?

---

* The doctrine of Hobbes and others is therefore monstrous, which subjects the consciences of subjects to a Sovereign (§129). [[Heineccius's harsh criticism of Hobbes is unfounded, since Hobbes clearly makes the distinction between conscience (*foro interno*) and external actions (*foro externo*); cf. Hobbes, *On the Citizen,* 3.27, p. 54, and Hobbes, *Leviathan,* chap. 16, p. 110. See also *Leviathan,* chap. 46, p. 471: "There is another Errour in [. . .] Civill Philosophy [. . .] to extend the power of the Law, which is the Rule for Actions only, to the very Thoughts, and Consciences of men."]] For not to insist upon what was just now said, that the understanding cannot be forced; and that a Sovereign can no more command it to believe or not believe, than he can command the eye not to see what it sees; what horrible butchery would these principles occasion, if a Nero or a Domitian, possessed of sovereignty, should take it into his head that the Pagan or Mahometan religion was better for society than the Christian, or to forge a new one? Nay, who does not see, that this doctrine, despising the true, the sole end of religion, perverts it into an engine of tyranny.

SECTION CLXXXIII

What with regard to the internal worship of God? As for divine worship, we said before it is either *internal* or *external.* Now, the *internal* is of such a nature, that the obligation to it is obviously deducible from principles of right reason (l. 1. §130); and therefore, no mortal hath power to change it, (l. 1. §17); and consequently, a Sovereign can neither abrogate nor alter it; tho' all men being obliged to promote the glory of God to the utmost of their power (l. 1. §128); a prince must be obliged, and have the right to take care that his subjects be duly instructed in the internal worship of God; to use proper methods to reform the impious, and bring them to a just sense of the reverence they owe to the Supreme Being; *i.e.* by reasoning and argumentation; and to guard his state against the spreading either of atheism or superstition, by such fences as the nature of religion and persuasion admits.

SECTION CLXXXIV

What with regard to external worship? *External* worship consists partly in external actions flowing from love, fear, and trust in God (l. 1. §135), partly in arbitrary indifferent actions (ibid. §138). With regard to the former, the same rule takes place as with respect to internal worship; and therefore, with regard to it, a good prince will arrogate no power to himself, besides that of endeavouring to the utmost to promote it by due methods.* The latter are neither prescribed nor dis-<181>approved by reason (l. 1. §138); and therefore they are subject to the direction of a Sovereign; and he hath all the right and power with regard to them, which is neither repugnant to reason nor revelation.

---

* Hence it is plain, that the supreme magistrate has no right to hinder any one from praising God with hymns, and offering prayers to him, or performing other such religious actions; but he hath a right to prescribe the order and manner in which these actions ought to be publickly performed. Therefore, the command of Darius, that none should dare to petition either God or man during thirty days, was most absurd, Dan. iv. 7. But the care of David and other pious Kings, to order the worship of God in such a manner, that the people might neither want hymns to sing to God, nor be ignorant of the most serious and decent way of singing them, was most reasonable.

SECTION CLXXXV

Since all direction with regard to the arbitrary acts of external worship, which is neither repugnant to reason nor revelation, belongs to sovereignty, (§184); the consequence is, that the chief magistrate hath the right of reforming and of abolishing abuses truly such, so far as the public laws or pacts permit; the right of making and amending ecclesiastical laws; the care of ecclesiastical goods or possessions, and of applying them to their proper uses; the right of jurisdiction over all persons, causes, and things ecclesiastical; and of conveening and directing synods and councils;* and finally, the right of permitting meetings of dissenters; or of not tolerating them, but obliging them to leave the kingdom, when important reasons require such severity. <182>

The chief articles of the power of a Sovereign about sacred things?

SECTION CLXXXVI

Schools and *academies* are seminaries to the church and to the state; nurseries for ministers, magistrates and good citizens, as well as for divines, their end being to instruct the youth in all useful arts and sciences necessary to qualify them for the various offices of life, and the several different stations in which they may be placed, or professions they may

The right or power of the chief magistrate about schools or academies.

---

* They are called for various reasons; as to confirm doctrines called into doubt by new decrees and creeds, and to consult about indifferent rites; and in fine, to settle matters relating to discipline. Synods of the first kind are contrary to the nature and genius of religion; first, because that is not always true, which appears to be such to the greater number; and in matters of opinion and belief, 'tis not the plurality of votes but the weight of arguments that ought to preponderate and determine. Next, because these decrees of councils are obtruded upon the members of a church by way of laws, with public authority, whereas laws cannot be given to the understanding. Besides, it often happens, that one part of the judges usurps power over the rest, and thus the wounds of the church are not so likely to be healed as to be festered; which is so confirmed by experience, that Gregory Nazianzenus, ep. 55. ad Procopium, says, "That he never expected any good from councils, and that they generally rather exasperated than cured any evil." [[Gregory of Nazianzus (ca. 330–ca. 389), Greek saint and theologian.]] The other synods may be sometimes of use to the church; but only when the church has no legislative power without the direction and authority of the supreme magistrate.

choose, as well as to form their manners to virtue and probity, and decency of conduct. For which reason, it is the duty of the supreme power in a state to establish such schools, and to adorn them with good laws and constitutions, and with learned and well qualified professors or masters; to take care that no hurtful doctrines be taught in them, that discipline be kept upon a good footing; and, above all, that turbulent genius's do not sow divisions and contentions in them;* so as to render them like the school of Megara in ancient times, οὐ σχολήν, ἄλλα χολὴν; "Not a school, but a seat of choler and scufling," Diogenes Laert. 6. 24. <183>

SECTION CLXXXVII

The right of the chief magistrate with respect to commerce.

The other right of magistracy which remains to be considered, is what regards commerce (§134). For since mankind, far less a republic, cannot subsist without commerce (l. 1. §325), the governors of a civil state ought to take care to promote and maintain it, and to direct it into a right and proper channel. And therefore they have all the rights relative to it, without which these ends cannot be obtained (§133); the consequence of which is, that they can make laws concerning traffic, manufactures, export and import, payment of bills and debts, and about money or coin; give privileges to traders, stipulate security to foreign commerce by

---

* The mischief scholastic wars do to youth, and to useful learning, cannot be expressed. They are frequently occasioned by stupid sluggish men, to whom the learning and industry of others in their proper business is an eye-sore. For the more learned men are, the further they are removed from a spirit of contention. And the scufle is carried on with calumnies, libels, and fraudulent arts, by which they hope to bear down their enemy, or render him suspected by his auditors. And hence it comes about, that the hours which ought to be devoted to the education and instruction of youth, are consumed in writing controversial pamphlets, and that the students, tho' not capable of judging of the dispute, and unacquainted with the true nature and rise of it, are divided into factions; so, that from words it not seldom comes to blows. But how prejudicial such feuds must be to the most flourishing universities, is very manifest.

treaties, and defend it by arms; grant immunities and rights to larger societies of merchants; and, in general, do every thing necessary to support and promote trade, consistent with pacts and treaties made with other princes or states.* <184>

* This whole subject is well illustrated by two dissertations: one by Jo. Fridr. L. B. Bachovius ab Echt dissert. de eo quod justum est circa commercia inter gentes, Jenae 1730. [[Bachovius, i.e., Johann Friedrich Freiherr Bachoff von Echt (1643–1726), German jurist and civil servant (1680, Geheimrat) at the court of Sachsen-Gotha (Bachoff von Echt, *De eo quod Iustum est*).]] Another by Jo. Jac. Mascovius de foederibus commerciorum, Lip. 1735. [[Johann Jacob Mascov (1689–1761), German jurist and historian, *Ratsherr* (councillor) in Leipzig; see Mascov (*praeses*) and Plessen (*respondens*), *De foederibus commerciorum.*]] To which, if we add the writings pro and con with regard to the disputes between the Dutch and the Imperial Netherlands, about the Ostend Company, we shall not need to look further into this subject. See Refutation des argumens avancés de la part de Mrs. les Directeurs de Compagnies d' orient & d' occident des provinces-unies, contre la liberté du commerce des habitans des Pais-bas, Hague 1723, and Jo. Barbeyrac Defense du droit de la compagnie Hollandoise des Indes orientales, contre les nouvelles pretensions des habitans des Pais-bas Autrichiens. [[Macneny, *Réfutation des argumens avancés de la part de MM les directeurs des Compagnies d'Orient et d'Occident des Provinces-Unies contre la liberté du commerce des habiters des Pays-Bas;* Barbeyrac, *Defense du droit de la Compagnie Hollandoise des Indes Orientales contre les nouvelles prétensions des habitans des Pays-Bas Autrichiens.*]]

Concerning the transeunt rights of Sovereignty.

SECTION CLXXXVIII

It is lawful to make war.

Because all empire is supreme and absolute, (§127), it follows, that different empires or civil states are independent, and subject to no common authority on earth (§ eodem). But such states are in a state of nature, and therefore in a state of natural equality and liberty (§5 & seq). And because in such a state the injured have no defence or protection but in themselves, and therefore in it every one has a right to repel violence and injury, and to extort by force what is due to him by perfect right (§9), it is abundantly evident, that every civil state or republic has the right of making war.* <185>

* This might be proved by other arguments. For nature hath not only endued men, but even brute animals with a principle of self-defence; and hath furnished the latter with certain arms to protect themselves.

> *Ut, quo quisque valet suspectos terreat; utque*
> *Imperet hoc natura potens, sic collige mecum.*
> *Dente lupus; cornu taurus petit. Unde, nisi intus*
> *Monstratum?*   Horat. Serm. 2. 1. v. 50.

[[Horace, *Satires II*, 1.50–53: "How everyone, using the weapon in which he is strong, terrifies those he fears, and how powerful nature commands that this should be so, you must infer, along with me, in this way: the wolf attacks with its fangs, the bull with its horn; from where did this come, except from an internal instinct?"]]

Many testimonies of the ancients to this purpose are collected by Grotius, of the

SECTION CLXXXIX

By *war* we understand a state in which free and independent men or   What is war.
nations, living in a state of nature, contend in prosecution of their rights
by force or stratagem, while they retain that intention.* From which
definition, it is plain that war does not consist in the act itself of contending, but in a hostile state, and in the fixed purpose of contending;
and therefore truce does not belong to a state of peace, but to a state of
war; and, on the other hand, the quarrels and tumults, the private or
public violences of men who are not their own masters, but subjected
to civil government, do not come under the definition of war. <186>

---

rights of war and peace, 1. 2. 1. 4. Again, since private persons living in society have
the right of self-defence, when they cannot have recourse to public protection (lib.
1. §181), much more must it be allowable to a free people to defend themselves, since
in a state of nature there is no common magistrate to judge between the injurer and
the injured, and to defend against violence (ibid. §183). The ancient fathers of the
church have brought several arguments from the sacred writings against the right of
war, as Tertullian de idolol. cap. 18. & de corona milit. cap. 11. [[Tertullian, *De idololatria,* ed. Waszink and van Winden; Tertullian, *De corona militis,* in Tertullian,
Tertulliani libri tres.]] Origen adv. Cels. l. 8. p. 425. [[Origen, *Adversus Celsum,* in
part 2 of his *Opera quae quidem extant omnia.*]] Erasmus in milite Christiano, &
Adagiorum Chil. 4. Cent. 1. adag. 1. and likewise the Anabaptists, of whom Arnold.
in Hist. eccles. & haeret. part. 2. l. 16. cap. 21. n. 24. [[Erasmus, *Enchiridion militis
Christiani;* Erasmus, *Adages* iv.i. 1, vol. 35, of *Collected Works of Erasmus;* Arnold,
Unpartheyische Kirchen- und Ketzer-Historie.]] But these objections have been sufficiently answered by Grotius in his masterly way (ibid. §5. & seq.) and by Huber de
jur. civ. 3. 4. 4. 6. & seq.
* Thus we think it proper to define war, tho' it be otherwise defined by others.
According to Cicero (off. 1. 11.) all contention by force is war. But Grotius (of the
rights of war and peace, 1. 1. 2. 1.) observing, that not the act but the state is properly
denominated war, amends this definition, by calling war a state of contention by
force, as such. Yet because this definition agrees as well to tumults, or private and
public violence, as to war, the definition of Albericus Gentilis (of the rights of war,
1. 2.) is rather preferable. [[Albericus Gentilis (1552–1608), Italian jurist considered to
be the founder of the theory of international law. Grotius drew extensively on his
main work, *De jure belli.*]] He defines it to be a just contention by public arms. But
the best of all, is the definition given by V. A. Corn. van Bynkersh. Quaest. juris
publ. 1. 1. which we follow.

SECTION CXC

To whom the right of war belongs, and in what it consists.

Since war is made by free nations, and men who live in a state of nature (§189), the consequence is, that in the latter case the right of war belongs to all promiscuously, as being all equal (§5 & 9); but in the former to the supreme power only (§135); and therefore it is the right of the Sovereign to levy or hire troops,* to build fortresses and fortify towns; to raise money for the maintenance of an army, to make provision of arms, war-like stores, ammunition, and other necessaries for war; to build, man, and store ships, to declare war, wage war against an enemy, and thus expose soldiers to the greatest danger, and make laws relative to military discipline and exercise, and such like things. For the end of this right being the external security of the state (§135): because the chief magistrate of a state must have all the rights, without which that end cannot be obtained (§133); every one may easily see that the right of war must make one of them. <187>

* It is well known, that there are three kinds of armies: one when every subject bears arms for his country, as in the Grecian republics of old, and among the Romans during their freedom, and as at present in Switzerland: another is mercenary, when soldiers, even foreigners, are listed for money; which kind of army Augustus, by the advice of Maecenas, preferred for certain reasons to the other, Dion. Cass. hist. lib. 52. p. 482. and which is at present preferred by all monarchs, who are not secure of the hearts of their people: another is confederate, when republics by alliance, or in consequence of due homage, are bound to furnish a certain quota of forces; such were the auxiliaries furnished by the Latins to the Romans: of which kind of armies see a curious dissertation by Herm. Conringius. [[Hermann Conring (1606–81), German philosopher at the University of Helmstedt and councillor and doctor to the Swedish queen Christina. Conring held views similar to those of Machiavelli on the uselessness of mercenary armies. Heineccius here is probably referring to Conring (*praeses*) and Koch (*respondens*), *Discursus politicus de militia lecta, mercenaria et sociali.*]] Concerning hired or mercenary troops, it hath been often questioned, whether it be lawful for a prince to keep up such amidst his well-affected subjects. Upon which question, see V. A. Corn. van Bynkershoek, Quaest. jur. publ. 1. 22.

SECTION CXCI

From the same definition of war, it is evident that an inferior magistrate, or the governor of a certain province or fortress, cannot make war; tho' that such may defend the towns or provinces under their command and government against any aggressor whatsoever, on a sudden attack, even without a special order, none can doubt; nay, because a province may be so remote, that its governor cannot inform the Sovereign of its imminent danger speedily enough to receive proper instructions, in this case certainly, if the right of making war be given to the governor by a general mandate, there can be no doubt of his right to make war without particular order from his superiors.* <188>

Whether an inferior magistrate may make war?

SECTION CXCII

Moreover, from this definition we learn that single combats are unlawful, unless undertaken by the command of the supreme powers;† and therefore Grotius's distinction between *private* and *public* war hath no foun-

Whether private persons have the right of war?

---

* Hence the war of Cn. Manlius [[Gnaeus Manlius, Roman proconsul in 187 B.C.]] against the Gallo-Graeci was unjust. And for this reason, he was refused a triumph, Liv. 38. 45. "because, says he, he did it without any reason, and without the authority of the senate, or the command of the people, which none ever had dared to do." And it is known that the senate were not far from giving up Julius Caesar to the Germans, for having made war against them without the command of the people, Sueton. Jul. Caes. cap. 24. But the governors sent by the Spanish, Portuguese, Dutch, &c. into American provinces, have commonly such full power of making war and peace, that the news of the victory are often the first news of the war.

† For such kind of single combats were a sort of representative war, used among the ancients, when they chose persons out of each army to decide the fate of the war by a single combat, agreeing that the party which had success in it, should have the right of victory or conquest. Ancient annals are full of such examples. Many of them are gathered together by Grotius, (of the rights, &c. 3. 20. 43. & seq.) who, however, pronounces such combats unlawful, because no person is master of his life and members. But sure, if a Sovereign may expose whole armies to an enemy, he may expose one or a few persons. Whether this practice be agreeable to civil prudence, is another question. Of that there is reason to doubt, because thus the whole republic is submitted to one chance, nor can they afterwards try their fortune with the remains of their strength, as the Albans felt to their sad experience, Dionys. Halicar. antiq. lib. 3.

dation, nor does it quadrate with the definition of war. Much less can that be called war which is carried on by citizens against one another, and is commonly called *a civil war.* Again, the state of violence and enmity, which pirates and robbers are in with all mankind, as it were, is not a state of war, but of robbery and plunder; and therefore such persons have not the rights of war, but ought to be punished as disturbers of the public security.

SECTION CXCIII

The justifying causes of war.

Since war is carried on by free nations (§189) in prosecution of their rights, the consequence is, that there are only two *just causes of war:* One is, when a foreign people injures another people, or attempts to rob them of their liberty, wealth, or <189> life: the other is, when one people denies another their perfect right.* The first is a just cause of *defensive* war, the last of *offensive;* and therefore the third, first mentioned by Grotius (of the rights of war and peace, 2. 1. 2. 1.) *viz.* the punishment of crimes,

---

* Nor does the reason assigned by Grotius prove any thing else, ibid. n. 1. "As many sources as there are of judicial actions, so many causes may there be of war. For where the methods of justice cease, war begins. Now in the law there are actions for injuries not yet done, or for those already committed. For the first, when securities are demanded against a person that has threatened an injury, or for the indemnifying of a loss that is apprehended, and other things included in the decrees of the superior judge, which prohibited any violence. For the second, that reparation may be made, or punishment inflicted; two sources of obligation, which Plato has judiciously distinguished. As for reparation, it belongs to what is or was properly our own, from whence real and some personal actions do arise; or to what is properly our due, either by contract, by default, or by law; to which also we may refer those things which are said to be due by a sort of contract, or a sort of default, from which kind all other personal actions are derived. The punishment of the injury produces indictments and public judgments." [[Grotius, *Rights of War and Peace,* bk. II, chap. 1, 2.1.]] So far Grotius. But as we cannot reason from a state of nature to a civil state; so no more can we reason from a civil state to a state of nature. One nation hurts another, either by its default, or does not hurt any other, *e.g.* if it worships idols, or eats human flesh. In the first case, the injured people attacks the delinquent people with a just and lawful war, not a punitive but a defensive war. In the last case, there is absolutely no right to make war, because none but a superior can punish a delinquent.

is not to be admitted as a just cause of war; the rather, that it is certain an equal cannot be punished by an equal; and therefore one nation cannot be punished by another (§157). <190>

SECTION CXCIV

As the denial of perfect right only is a just cause of war (§193), hence it follows, that it is not allowable to have recourse to arms for the refusal of an imperfect right (§9); and therefore these are not just causes of war; as, for instance, if one refuses passage to an army, or denies access to a people in quest of a new habitation, will not grant the liberty of commerce to a people at their desire, or furnish money, provision or shelter, to those who are carrying on war, unless these things be due by an antecedent treaty, or be demanded in extreme necessity, or be of such a kind, that they may be granted without any detriment* (§9 & seq.). For then a refusal of such things becomes an injury, and is therefore a most just cause of defensive war (§193).

Whether war be just on the account of refusing to render imperfect right?

SECTION CXCV

But it being sometimes the same whether we ourselves are immediately injured, or we are so thro' the side of another; and, in like manner the same, whether perfect right be denied to us or to others, whom we are obliged, either by treaties, or on our own account, to assist; hence we may justly conclude, that war may be engaged in for allies and confederates; yea, and for neigh-<191>bours, if it be very certain that we must suffer by their ruin. For who will blame one for hastening to extinguish

If war may be waged for others?

---

* That rarely happens. For either there is danger from the army that demands liberty to pass, or from the enemy, who may take it amiss that passage was granted. But if the passage be absolutely without danger, and so necessary that there is no other way for them who ask it to take, he does an injury who refuses such passage. And to this cause we may refer the war waged by the Israelites at God's command, Num. xxi. 21, 22. But the Idumeans were not touched for the same reason, Num. xx. 21. either because that passage was not so safe, or not so necessary, there being another way to Kadesh.

fire near to his own house? Who does not consent to the truth of the antient saying, "Your interest is at stake, if your neighbour's house be on fire"? However, since we cannot make war even for ourselves without a just cause (§193), much less will a war be just and vindicable, if we engage in the behalf of others for injustifiable reasons.

SECTION CXCVI

Mere colours do not justify war.

But tho' these just causes be easily distinguishable from the mere pretexts often used by those who make war most unjustly; yet men, who regard nothing but their own interest, often lay more stress on the latter than the former. However, it is plain, that if these causes we have mentioned be the only justifiable causes of war (§193), war must be very unjust, if made merely because opportunity, and the weak, defenceless state of another nation invites to it, or purely to gain some great advantage, and to extend one's empire, for the glory of martial achievements, or from religious enmity, without any other just cause.* <192>

* And I know not but the cruel wars carried on in the middle ages against the Mahometans by Christians, must be referred to this class: as likewise those which the Spaniards dared to undertake against the Americans, a nation not inured to war, and that had never done any injury to the Europeans. The former were not coloured over with any other pretext, but that the Holy-land, Jerusalem chiefly, were possessed by aliens from the Christian church, and that it was the interest of Christians thus to promote and propagate their religion. The latter with this only pretext, that the Americans were impious idolaters, or rather worshippers of demons. But since Christianity does not permit of propagation by force; and neither reason nor revelation allows places which appear sacred to certain men, to be therefore claimed by arms and violence; and since besides all this, all wars in order to punish are unlawful (§193), these wars must needs be pronounced most unjust. Wherefore, Herm. Conringius ad Lampad. p. 242. says very justly, "Tho' many things were done in them which deserve the praise of zeal and courage; yet, if we may speak the truth, all these expeditions were owing to the weakness, imprudence, and superstition of the Kings and Princes of that age." [[Conring, "Discursus ad Lampadium posterior ex manuscripto editus," in Conring, *Opera*, vol. 2, pp. 238–461.]] See likewise Jo. Franc. Buddeus, exercitat. de expeditionibus cruciatis, §5. & seq. [[Budde (*praeses*) and Greulinck (*respondens*), *De expeditionibus cruciatis dissertatio politica.*]] As to the opinion of the Spaniards, about a right to punish the Mexicans for their crimes against nature, which Grotius defends (of the rights of war and peace, 2. 20. 40. & seq.) it is given up even by the Spanish doctors themselves, Victoria, relat. 1. de Indes. n. 40. Vasquius controver. illust. 1. 25. Azorius, Molina, and others. [[Vitoria, *Relectio de Indis;* Vazquez, *Illus-*

SECTION CXCVII

Many nations have thought that war, so soon as resolved upon, ought
to be solemnly declared; and hence the known distinction between *solemn* or *just, less solemn,* or *unjust* war. The former, in the opinion of
most writers, is that which is undertaken by one who hath the right to
make war with a previous solemn denunciation. The latter, that which
is undertaken by one who hath not the right of war, and is not previously
declared. But tho' we grant that this is become almost an universally
received rule, and victory is generally thought more glorious, when it is
obtained by a war that was previously declared by a manifesto, or by
heralds, or with other solemn rites; yet, because rites and solemnities are
arbitrary, and such customs do not constitute a part of the law of nations
(l. I. §22); * we think there is no difference as to legal effect between war
declared and *not declared;* and therefore, that this division is of very little
moment.* <193>

The distinc-
tion between
solemn and
less solemn
war is of
little use.

SECTION CXCVIII

But right reason clearly teaches us, that recourse ought not to be had
immediately to arms; but then only, when a people hath shewn a hostile
disposition against us (l. I. §183). But seeing he shews a hostile disposition

The causes of
war ought to
be manifest.

---

trium controversiarum, aliarumque usu frequentium libri sex. Luis de Molina (1535–
1600) was a Spanish Jesuit theologian, as was Juan Azor (1535–1603).]]

* Grotius of the rights of war and peace, and Alberic. Gentilis of the rights of
war, lay great stress on this distinction, who are followed in this matter by Pufendorff,
Huber and others, for a double reason. First, because by such an appeal or declaration,
it is made evident, that we cannot otherwise obtain what is due to us. And secondly,
because thus it appears that the war is made by the consent of the whole body in both
nations. But these reasons only prove, that a previous declaration of war is of use and
laudable, not that it is necessary to make a war just, because both these facts may be
evidenced by other means, besides a solemn declaration. Wherefore, Dio. Chrysostom. Orat. ad Nicomed. asserts with reason, and agreeably to the principles of the
laws of nations, "Several wars are undertaken without denunciation." [[Dio Chrysostom, "The Thirty-eighth Discourse: To the Nicomedians, on Concord with the
Nicaeans," p. 67, in Dio Chrysostom, *Dio Chrysostom,* vol. 4, pp. 48–93.]] But this
subject hath been exhausted by Thomasius ad Huber. de jur. civ. 3. 4. 4. 27. and by
V. A. Corn. van Bynker. Quaest. jur. publici, I. 2. p. 5. & seq. who hath there likewise
treated of the most modern European customs.

against us, who obstinately rejects all equal terms and conditions of peace (§ eodem); hence we justly infer, that before we take violent methods, what is due, or we think is due to us, ought to be demanded, and the dispute ought to be clearly stated with the arguments on both sides, and all means ought to be tried to prevent war;* which being done, he certainly takes up arms justly, who, having proposed good and adequate reasons, cannot obtain from his enemy any reasonable satisfaction. <194>

SECTION CXCIX

What is lawful against an enemy. Seeing princes and free nations make war in order to vindicate their rights (§193), the consequence is, that every thing is lawful against an enemy, without which these rights cannot be obtained. But they cannot be obtained but by reducing the enemy to such a state, as that he either cannot, or will not any longer shew a hostile disposition: and therefore every one has a right to use force or stratagem against an enemy, and to

---

* Three means are particularly recommended by Grotius, of the rights of war and peace, 2. 23. 7. and Pufendorff of the law of nature and nations, 5. 13. 3. and 8. 6. 3. an interview or friendly conference, reference to arbitrators, and lot. But as for the last, besides that it can rarely have place but when a thing is to be divided, princes and states seldom choose to submit their fortunes to chance. The other methods are received in all civilized nations, and are most agreeable to right reason; for no wise man will take a dangerous way to obtain what he may have without force (lib. 1. §181), so true is what the soldier in Terence says, tho' upon a ridiculous occasion,

> Omnia prius experiri, quam armis, sapientem decet.
> Qui scis, an, quae jubeam, sine vi faciat?

> [[Terence, *The Eunuch*, lines 789–90: "The wise man should try everything before resorting to arms. For all you know, she will do what I tell her without force" (see *Terence*, vol. 1).]]

For this end are these public writings called *Manifestos* and *Declarations,* tho' the former are more commonly published at the very point of striking the blow, rather to declare and justify the war, than with a view to decline and prevent it. See Jo. Henr. Boecler. exercitat. de clarig. & manifestis. [[Boecler (*praeses*) and Barnekow (*respondens*), *Dissertatio de clarigatione et manifestis.*]]

employ all means against his person or effects, by which he can be weak-ened, without regard even to the offices of humanity, which then cease (l. 1. §208); nay, we cannot call it absolutely unjust to make use of poison or assassines, tho' such practices are with reason said to be repugnant to the manners of more civilized nations, and to what is called (*ratio belli*) the humanity of war.* <195>

* Grotius (of the rights of war and peace, 3. 4. 15. and 18.) is of a different opinion. But actions, because they are more glorious, and shew more greatness of mind, are not for that reason so obligatory, that it is unjust not to do them. Poison is not used by more civilized nations; but the Turks and Tartars poison their darts and arrows. We may therefore call them less humane on that score, but not unjust, because every thing is lawful against an enemy. Thus we may justly refer to the class of greatness of mind, what the Roman consuls are said to have wrote to Pyrrhus, "We do not choose to fight by bribery or by fraud," Gell. Noct. Attic. 3. 8. But we cannot call Ehud unjust for killing Eglon, Jud. iv. 20; nor Jael for driving a nail into the temples of Sisera, Jud. iv. 21. or Judith for cutting off Holofernes's head, if the story be true. Besides, the manners of nations, who pretend to greater politeness than others, often degenerate into vile dissimulation; of which see Bynker. Quaest. jur. publ. 1. 3. p. 17. [[Bynkershoek, *Quaestionum juris publici libri duo*, vol. 1, 17–18.]] "To such a height did flattery rise in the preceding age, and is it at present, that princes do not lay it aside even in war. For now it is common for enemies most politely to wish one another all prosperity, and to exchange compliments of condolence. So do the letters of the States General to the King of England run, 10th July, 16th September, and 26th November 1666, and those of the King of England to the States General, 4th August and 4th October 1666, tho' they were then preparing for destroying one the other, yet the states wrote, that the offices of friendship might take place amidst the rights of war, July 10. ep. 1666. So the King of France, tho' he was in war with the King of England in the year 1666, sent an envoy to condole him upon the burning of London. It is indeed glorious to exercise humanity, clemency, and other virtues of a great mind in war, but it is silly and absurd to use such unmeaning unsincere words. For what is it but to use deceitful false words, to regret the burning of a city one would willingly have set fire to?" Are not these rare specimens of humanity? Shall we then pronounce C. Popilius Laenas [[Roman consul in 172 B.C.]] more unjust than those princes and states, who being saluted by Antiochus [[king of Syria]], declared he would not return his salute till they were friends; and refused the King's hand when he stretched it out to him? Polyb. Excerpt. legat. cap. 92. [[probably Polybius, *Ex libris Polybii Megapolitani selecta de legationibus*]] Liv. 45. 12. These are harsher methods, but not unjust, yea much more decent than hostile adulations and false compliments.

SECTION CC

Whether it be lawful to deceive an enemy by pacts and treaties?

But since it is against an enemy only that it is lawful to use force or stratagem (§199), the consequence is, that it is not lawful to use either against those with whom we are in treaty; because then we pledge our faith to them not as an enemy, but as a people treating with us.* Whence it is evi-<196>dent, that they are guilty of abominable perfidiousness, who break a short or long truce before it is expired; tho' it be very true that both parties may exert defensive acts during that time, Pufendorff of the law of nature and nations, 8. 7. 10. Nor is their treachery less abominable, who basely violate the articles of surrendery, pacts concerning the conveyance of provisions, or the redemption of prisoners, foolishly pretending to justify themselves by this pretext, that all is lawful against an enemy.

SECTION CCI

What is lawful against others not enemies.

From the same principle we conclude, that none may use the rights of war against such as are in peace and friendship with them, under the pretext that an enemy may seize their castles and fortresses, or harbours, and make advantage of them against us; nor is it lawful to seize or hurt enemies or their ships in the territory, or within the ports of a people in peace with us, unless that people designedly gives reception to our enemy, because such violence is injurious to the people with whom we are in peace, whose territory or ports are entred by force. See V. A. Corn. van Bynkershoek. quest. <197> jur. publ. 1. 8. On the other hand, there

---

* Agesilaus in Plutarch, p. 600, well distinguishes between an allowable stratagem and perfidy. There is there recorded an excellent saying of his: "To break the faith of a treaty is to contemn the Gods: but to outwit an enemy is a laudable, and withal a saving method." [[Plutarch, "Agesilaus," in Plutarch, *Lives,* vol. 5, p. 23.]] But what if an enemy had formerly proved treacherous and false? May we not then render like for like? I think not. For tho' the perfidy of one of the contracting parties exempts the other from his obligation (l. 1. §413), yet this is to be understood of the same bilateral pact, the conditions of which are not fulfilled by one of the parties. But if we make a new pact with one who had not stood to his former, we are deemed to have passed over his former perfidy, and are therefore bound to fulfil our new contract.

is no reason why we may not hinder such a people from conveying arms, men, provisions, or any such things to our enemy, and hold such things for contreband;* (Bynkers. ibidem, cap. 9. & seq.) tho' equity requires that we should not promiscuously condemn the goods belonging to our friends with those belonging to our enemies. (Bynkers. 1. 12. & seq.). See likewise our dissertation de navibus ob mercium illicitarum vecturam condemnatis.[1]

SECTION CCII

We have observed, that the persons and estates of enemies may be spoiled or taken ($199); whence it is plain, that it depends on the will and pleasure of an enemy to lead persons taken in war captive into servitude, or which is now the prevailing custom in European nations, to detain them till they are exchanged or ransomed. The effects of enemies, moveable or immoveable, corporeal or incorporeal, fall to the conqueror; moveable, so soon as they are brought within the conqueror's station; immoveable, and other things, from the moment they are occupied, tho' the possession of them be not secure, till peace being concluded, treaties about them are transacted. But that moveable things, as well as persons and territories, being retaken, or recovering their antient liberty, have the right of postliminy, none can call into doubt.† <198>

How acquisitions may be made by war.

* This is granted by Grotius, l. 3. cap. 17. §3. but with a restriction. "It is the duty," says he, "of those that are not engaged in a war, to sit still and do nothing that may strengthen him that prosecutes an ill cause, or to hinder the motions of him that hath justice on his side." But because a neutral party ought not to take upon them, as it were, to sit as judges, and determine upon which side justice lies, but, on the contrary, to take no part in the matter, as Livy observes, 35. 48; hence it is evident, that there is no place for this restriction. See V. A. Corn. van Bynkersh. Quaest. jur. publ. 1. 9. p. 69.

† Here many questions occur in Grotius, 3. 5. & seq. Pufend. 8. 6. 20, as how things taken in war are acquired? whether incorporeal things and actions, &c? But since all these things depend rather upon the customs of nations than the laws of nations, and many of them may be easily decided from the principles already explained, we shall not insist upon them. All these are handled by V. A. Corn. van Bynkershoek Quaest. jur. public. l. 1. cap. 4. & seq. in a masterly manner.

1. Heineccius (*praeses*) and Kessler (*respondens*), *De navibus ob mercium illicitarum vecturam commissis.*

SECTION CCIII

What reprisals are.

From the definition of war it is plain, that if there is no controversy between nations and states themselves, when we lay hands upon persons or effects belonging to another republic in peace with us, on the account of justice refused to any of our society, this cannot be called *war,* but is making *reprisals.** But since this may very probably give rise to a war, it ought not to be done by any private person, but with the approbation of the Sovereign; and it ought to be carried no farther, than to make satisfaction to our member to whom justice was refused. <199>

SECTION CCIV

How empire is acquired over the conquered.

But since in a state of nature the right of defence lasts while an enemy shews a hostile disposition (l. 1. §183), which he cannot be said to have laid aside, who is not willing to return into friendship, but repels all reasonable conditions of peace, (ibidem) no injustice certainly is done to the conquered, if we prosecute our right till they are fully subdued, and we have obtained compleat empire over them; and we may constitute this empire as we judge proper, and exercise it, till peace being concluded, some articles are agreed upon with relation to it; or the nation

---

* This right, since ever it hath been practised, hath been called *Reprisals.* The ancients not being acquainted with it, there is no word in the Latin language that properly expresses it, (Corn. van Bynkersh. ibidem. 1. 24). Grotius derives this right from the right of taking pawn, competent to every person (of the rights of war and peace, 3. 2. 7. 3.); and so likewise Bodinus de republica, 1. 10. [[Bodin, *De republica libri sex.* This was Bodin's own translation of his *Les six livres de la République.*]] But this opinion is refuted by Hertius ad Pufendorff, 8. 6. 13 [[Pufendorf, *Acht Bücher vom Natur- und Völkerrecht*]]; and before him by Ziegler de jure majestatis, 1. 34. 8. [[Ziegler, *De juribus majestatis*]] where he asserts, §32. that this right proceeds rather from the rights of war. And certainly, if a republic may justly vindicate by war an injury done to it and its members (l. 1. §245), it may likewise lay its hands on the goods of others, for an injury done to any one of its subjects, unless the greater and not the less may be allowable.

not being totally overthrown, and no treaty being yet made, recovers its antient liberty, or is bravely rescued by their former Sovereign.* <200>

SECTION CCV

Another right of majesty, which may be reckoned among the external or transeunt ones, is that *of making treaties* among free nations about things belonging to the utility of both, or any of them. From which definition it is plain, that some of them are *equal,* in which the condition of both parties are equal; others are *unequal,* in which both parties have not the same rights granted to them, but one has better, and the other worse conditions; which, as examples shew us, may be either with regard to the conditions to be fulfilled, or to the manner of performing them.†

What a treaty is, equal or unequal.

---

* And then in both these cases, it is most equal that recovered towns, cities, provinces, nations, should have the right of postliminy (§202), and thus recover their former rights, if their falling into the enemy's hands was not by their own fault, or even if it be not very clear, that they could have made a longer or stronger opposition to the enemy. Hence, when the French Garisons having left the country, a dispute arose between the states of Utrecht and Friezeland about the right of precedency, upon pretext that the former had given themselves up without resistance, yet the province of Utrecht recovered its former place and state, Huber. Prelect. ad Dig. l. 49. tit. 15. §9. But the case would be quite different, if a city or province, which, unmindful of their faith to their Sovereign, had wilfully deserted and gone over to the enemy, should afterwards be recovered by war. For such would be justly deemed unworthy of this benefit, and therefore it is in the conqueror's power and right to reduce them into any condition he pleases. Such examples did the Romans make of the Brutii, Lucani and Campani, who deserted to Hannibal; of Capua chiefly, which city was so far from having its ancient rights restored to it, that it was deprived of its municipal privileges, its right of magistracy, and its territories, and reduced into the form of a province, Liv. 26. 16. & seq.

† Thus one of the confederate parties being stronger, engages to furnish the other not so powerful, a certain pecuniary subsidy, or a certain quota of ships, troops, or marines, and stipulates little or nothing to itself. In this case the treaty or alliance is unequal, in respect of the things to be done. But it is often provided by treaties, that one republic shall be bound to pay homage to another; not to undertake war without another's consent; not to keep a fleet; to pay an annual tribute; to make use of no iron or iron-smiths, except for agriculture, 1 Sam. xiii. 19, 20. which Pliny, hist. nat. 34. 14. says was done in the first treaty of Porsena with the Roman people. All these are unequal treaties with respect to the manner of doing, since the one makes itself the other's client by this manner of treating.

SECTION CCVI

Treaties are ei-
ther matters of
simple general
friendship, or
which oblige
to something
in particular.

Because free nations can contract about things relating either to the utility of either or of both, (§205), it follows, that those good offices which are owing by natural obligation, may be stipulated to themselves by free nations or states; and these are called *leagues of friendship.** And other things may be stipulated, to which there was no prior <201> obligation; which treaties we call *treaties of particular obligation.* The first are not unnecessary, because there is no other way of securing another's performance to us of the duties of humanity, but by pacts (l. 1. §386). And it often happens, that war puts an end to all the duties of humanity (§199), and therefore it is absolutely necessary that friendship should be renewed by pacts and covenants.

SECTION CCVII

Some treaties
are made in
time of peace.

A thing may be useful to a state either in peace or war, and therefore some treaties relate to *peace,* and others to *war;* but it being the interest of a state, that peace be rendered as durable and stable as possible, and

---

* To these treaties Grotius (of the rights of war and peace, 2. 15. 5. 3.) refers leagues which provide for the entertainment of strangers, and the freedom of commerce on both sides, as agreeable to the law of nature. But since the law of hospitality comprehends many good offices, which are not perfectly due by the law of nature alone (of which Jo. Schilterus has treated very accurately) [[Schilter, *De jure hospitii*]], and since the permission of commerce with foreigners depends upon the will of the supreme powers in every state (§187), such leagues can hardly in any case be referred to those, by which one nation stipulates to itself from another nothing more than is due by the law of nature. As to leagues of commerce, that there is not so much difficulty about any others as about them, is proved by Jo. Jac. Mascou. dissert. de foeder. commerc. §6. [[Mascov (*praeses*) and Plessen (*respondens*), *De foederibus commerciorum*]] by an example from Jac. Basnag's Hist. Belg. tom. 1. p. 51. and 439. [[Basnage, *Annales des Provinces-Unies.*]] And the Athenians, Smyrnians, and other republics, struck medals to be monuments of such treaties, as the same author has shewn from Ezek. Spanheim. de usu & praestantia numismatum, diss. 3. p. 143. & dissert. 13. n. 4. as likewise in his Orbe Rom. cap. 4. [[Spanheim, *Dissertationes de praestantia et usu numismatum antiquorum;* Spanheim, *Orbis Romanus*]] and from Vaillant de numis imp. Graec. p. 221. [[Vaillant, *Numismata imperatorum.*]] But who ever thought a simple league of mere friendship worthy of being commemorated by such monuments?

as profitable to its subjects as may be, we may refer to the first end, treaties
by which certain guarantees engage their faith, that the ar-<202>ticles
of peace shall be faithfully observed, and promise assistance to the injured party;* as likewise treaties about building new fortifications, or for
admitting and keeping garisons in certain fortified places, for defending
frontiers, commonly called *barrier-treaties;* for not sheltering fugitive
soldiers or subjects; or not giving reception to enemies, *&c.* to the latter
of the above mentioned ends we may refer treaties of commerce.

SECTION CCVIII

But in time of war various treaties are made by free nations with *friends*
and *enemies.* With the former, treaties are made sometimes about joining
their forces against a common enemy, which are <203> called *offensive*
and *defensive treaties;* sometimes about free passage through a territory,
and furnishing provisions; and sometimes about not interposing in the
war, which last are called *treaties of neutrality.* With the latter, treaties

*Some treaties
are made in
times of war.*

---

* Upon these treaties it is worth while to consult Ulr. Obrecht. diss. de sponsore
pacis, the seventh of his Academic dissertations, and Henr. Cocceii de guarantia pacis,
Franckfort 1702. [[Ulrich Obrecht (1646–1701), German jurist and historian, professor of history and eloquence in Strasbourg; see Obrecht (*praeses*) and Stauffer
(*respondens*), *Sponsor pacis sive de garantia dissertatio.* Cocceji (*praeses*) and Stephani
(*respondens*), *Disputatio juris gentium publici de guarantia pacis.*]] The principal question that is moved on this subject is, whether the guarantees of a peace be obliged in
general to enter into a war-alliance with the injured party, for any breach of peace
whatsoever? But Pufendorff (of the law of nature and nations, 8. 8. 7.) has justly
denied that the guarantees are bound to send aids in any war that takes its rise from
other reasons than the violation of the articles of peace of which they are guarantees.
For as it would be absurd for a creditor to demand a debt from a surety, contracted
by the principal debtor after the suretiship; so it would be no less unjust for a prince
or a state to demand that a guarantee should take up arms in his defence, if the war
takes its rise from some new cause. For a guarantee is only bound, when the peace
of which he was surety is broken. But peace (as Grotius has well observed, 3. 20. 27.
& seq.) is broken, if any thing be done contrary to what is included in every treaty
of peace, or may be inferred from the very nature of peace in general, or to the express
articles of a particular peace. And the matter is clear enough in general theory; yet
when the question comes to be, whether a particular deed be a violation of a certain
treaty of peace; it is not so easily determined, as very recent examples abundantly
prove.

are made, sometimes about paying tributes, sometimes about giving up certain towns, sometimes about the redemption or exchange of prisoners, which are called *Cartels*. (Of these Hertius has expresly handled in his diss. de lytro) and sometimes about a truce of hours, days, or months,* and other like matters.

SECTION CCIX

Some are personal, and others are real. Besides, that interest, for which treaties are made, either respects the person of the Sovereign only, or the state itself. For which reason, some treaties are *personal,* and others *real;* and the former expire with the persons; the latter continue after both the contracting Sovereigns are extinct. Now, from these definitions it is plain, that all treaties for the conservation of a prince or his family are personal, and those relating to the utility of a state itself are real.† And to this division may all those of Pufendorff (of the law of nature and nations, 8. 9. 6.) be most conveniently referred. <204>

* Here it is usually asked, when that time commences? Grotius 3. 21. 5. insists that the day from which the measure of the time is to commence, is not included within that measure or compass of time: but he is solidly refuted by Pufendorff of the law of nature and nations, 8. 7. 8. And therefore, if for instance, it should be agreed that there shall be a truce from the first of July to the first of September, both these days are included; and in like manner, if from the first of June for thirty days, the first day of June is the first day of the truce, and the thirtieth day is the last day of it, so that the day after it is lawful to take arms.

† This question arose when the Romans changed their regal government. For the Sabines having contracted with their Kings, upon the change of the government they declared war against the Romans, pretending that the Roman people, in a popular state, had no right to the advantage of treaties made with their Kings, Dionys. Halicarn. Antiq. l. 5. p. 307. In the year from the foundation of Rome 267, the Hernici had recourse to the same plea, denying that they had ever made any treaty with the people of Rome, and asserting that their treaty made with Tarquin had ceased, because he being dethroned had died in exile, Dionys. Hal. 8. p. 530. But both these nations having made a treaty upon their being conquered by the Roman arms (See Dionys. ib. l. 4. p. 252. & seq.) it is indisputable that they had not contracted with Tarquin only, but with the Roman state, and therefore their treaties continued obligatory even after his expulsion.

SECTION CCX

What is advantageous to a state is likewise advantageous to its allies and confederates; and therefore we may consult not only our own interest, but that of our allies likewise, in treaties; and that either by mentioning them in general, or specially and particularly. And here it is plain from the nature of the thing, that in the last case, the treaty cannot be extended to any others but those mentioned in the articles. But in the first case, it extends to all our allies at the time the treaty was made; but not to such allies as joined themselves to us afterwards;* because pacts cannot be extended to comprehend things not thought of when they were entered into (lib. 1. §393). <205>

Whether treaties may include, or be beneficial to allies?

SECTION CCXI

Moreover, because a league is a convention between free nations or states, it is plain (§205), that none can make leagues but those who have a commission to do it, either expresly, tacitly or presumptively. And therefore, what ministers of a Sovereign have promised without a commission from him, if it be not afterwards ratified, comes under the denomination of *sponsion,* and not of *league.* Now, hence it is evident that a republic is not bound to ratify a pact made without their order; but it is certain, on the other hand, that a minister who contracts with a state is obliged

What may be done by sponsion?

---

* This question really happened when Hannibal besieged Saguntum. For the Romans complained that Hannibal had unjustly attacked them, because the Carthaginians were bound by their treaty with the Romans not to annoy their allies. The Carthaginians insisted, on the other hand, that the Saguntini were not comprehended in their treaty, because they were not allies to the Romans at the time it was made, Polyb. hist. 3. 29. Liv. 21. 19. But tho' both these authors take the part of the Romans, I do not hesitate to say with Grotius, 2. 16. 13. that this treaty could not hinder the Carthaginians from making war against the Saguntines, and yet the Romans had a right to make new allies, and to defend them against the Carthaginians. For the Romans had not in the treaty made any provision for their future allies, and could not oblige the Carthaginians to understand as comprehended in the treaty things not thought of in making it; nor did the Carthaginians stipulate to themselves from the Romans, that they should make no new allies; and therefore they had no right to object against their defending their new allies.

to make satisfaction to that state, which by the fecial law of the Romans, consisted in giving him up naked with his hands tied behind his back.* And it is no less certain, that the exception against a treaty for want of a commission to the minister, is for the most part a cavil, seeing a republic who gives the command of an army or province to a minister with full powers, is justly deemed to have given him all the power, without which an army or province, nay, the republic itself, cannot be secure. <206>

SECTION CCXII

If it be lawful to make treaties with infidels.

Because treaties are made by free nations (§205), it is plain that it makes no difference, whether a people profess the same religion we do, or one which we look upon as impious and abominable: for as a private person may lawfully contract or bargain with one of a different religion; so neither a republic nor its rulers ought to be blamed if they make useful treaties for their people with infidels; and that revelation hath made no alteration with respect to this natural truth, Grotius has fully demonstrated (of the rights of war and peace, 2. 15. 9. & seq.).† <207>

---

* There are two remarkable instances of this in the Roman history, the *Sponsio Caudina & Numantina,* Liv. 9. 8. & seq. and 55. 15. The Romans would not stand to the treaty by which Posthumius Coss. and the other Generals had extricated the army at the Furculae Caudinae, nor to that of Hostilius Mancinus with the Numantines, pretending that both were done without their orders. But who can doubt but Generals, when an army is in danger, have all the power necessary to deliver them from it, and which the safety of the army and the state requires. Such sponsions ought therefore either to have been confirmed, or things ought to have returned to the posture they were in before the sponsions, if the Romans had not been more ingenious in devising cavils, than faithful in observing their treaties. See Christ. Thomasius and G. Beyerus de sponsionibus Numantina & Caud. [[Thomasius (*praeses*) and Ryssel (*respondens*), *Dissertatio juris publici ad l. 4. de captiv. & l. ult. de legation;* Thomasius (*praeses*) and Brix von und zu Montzel (*respondens*), *De sponsione Romanorum Caudina.* There does not appear to be a dissertation by the jurist Georg Beyer (1665–1714) on this subject.]]

† Thus before the Mosaic law was given, Abraham and Isaac made a covenant with Abimelech, and Jacob with Laban, who most certainly worshipped idols, Gen. xxi. 22. xxvi. 26. xxxi. 44. And after the law of Moses was given, we know David and Solomon made leagues with Hierom King of the Tyrians, 2 Sam. v. 11. 1 Kings v. 12. We likewise read in the sacred records, of the alliances of Abraham with Escol and

SECTION CCXIII

Moreover, since treaties are conventions (§205); the consequence is, that all we have said above of pacts, takes place likewise in treaties. So that nothing ought to be held more sacred than treaties, nor nothing more detestable than the perfidiousness of treaty-breakers. Yet because no society is obliged to prefer another's interest to its own (§22), a republic cannot be obliged by an alliance or treaty to assist another, if its own condition doth not permit; as, *e.g.* if it be overwhelmed in war, or be in any imminent danger;* nor is a republic ever obliged to engage in an unjust war for its allies.

Duties with respect to treaties.

SECTION CCXIV

So far have we treated of leagues in general, the noblest of which undoubtedly is that pact by which an end is put to war among free nations, commonly called *a treaty of peace*. But peace being the ordinary state of a republic, and, as it were, its natural state; and war being its extraordinary and preternatural state, it is evident, that Sovereigns are obliged to maintain peace, and to restore it, if it be interrupted; and consequently that these are savage wars, which are carried on, not with a view to peace, which is *better than a thousand million of triumphs*. <208>

The right of Sovereigns with regard to peace.

Aner, Gen. xiv. 13. of David with Achish King of the Philistines, 1 Sam. xxvii. 2. & seq. and with Toi King of Hemath, 2 Sam. viii. 10. of Asa with Benhadad, 1 Kings xv. 18. & seq. The objections brought from Scripture are answered by Grotius.

* But this is to be understood, not of pretended but real danger. For that false pretexts are used by Sovereigns, as well as by private persons, is daily complained. And the excuses and delays of friends are elegantly represented by Aesop in the fable of the Lark in Aulus Gellius Noct. Attic. 2. 29. who there advises every one to place his chief dependence on himself, and not on his friends or allies, who often promise mountains of gold, and do nothing. This is likewise the counsel of Ennius in his Satires, preserved to us by the same Gellius.

> *Hoc erit tibi argumentum, semper in promtu situm:*
> *Ne quid exspectes amicos, quod tute agere possis.*

> [[From the *Satires* of the Roman poet Ennius, quoted in Gellius, *Attic Nights,* bk. II, chap. xxix, 20: "This adage ever have in readiness; Ask not of friends what you yourself can do."]]

SECTION CCXV

What a treaty
of peace is.

By *a treaty of peace* we understand a convention between free nations involved in war, by which their quarrels are accommodated by way of transaction. From which definition it is plain, that peace, in its own nature, ought to be perpetual; and therefore, if it be made for a certain time only, however long, it is not properly peace, but a truce;* because the quarrel which engaged the nations in war is thus not ended, but the design of disputing it by arms still subsists; which state, as we observed, is a state of war, and not of peace, (§189).

SECTION CCXVI

If the
exception of
inequality
be valid.

Peace being made by way of transaction (§215), the consequence is, that it may be made giving, retaining, or promising something; and therefore, that equality in its articles is not requisite; nor can either of the parties justly complain of being wronged, however enormous the wrong may be; since the conqueror may impose any terms, and the conquered may prefer any terms never so hard to perishing.† <209>

* And yet such truces not unfrequently are called *peace,* because not only all hostile acts cease, but even a state of war ceases, as if the contending parties had laid aside their hostile intentions. Thus we are told by historians, that the Lacedemonians made peace for fifty years; the Romans for a hundred years, Justin. hist. 3. 7. Livy. 1. 15. Sozom. hist. eccles. 9. 4. [[Sozomenos (fifth century A.D.), Greek ecclesiastical historian (see Sozomenos, *Historia ecclesiastica*).]] And we have more recent examples of such truces between Spain and Portugal, Sweden and Denmark, England and Scotland, Venice and the Turks, who seldom make peace with Christians, but for a limited period of time. See Pufendorff 8. 7. 4. & ibidem Hertius, p. 1249.

† Provided it be evident, from the articles of the peace, that the conquered submitted to these terms. For if by malitious cavil, invidious interpretation, or by open force, harder terms are obtruded on the conquered than they consented to, they have just reason to complain that they are injured. Thus Q. Fabius Labeo egregiously cavilled, when Antiochus having promised to deliver up to him the half of his navy, he ordered all his ships to be cut in two, and thus ruined his whole fleet, Valer. Maxim. 7. 3. which piece of false cunning he had perhaps learned from the Campani, who, as Polyaenus Stratag. 6. 15. [[Polyaenus, *Stratagems of War*]] tells us, had thus destroyed the arms of their enemies, one half of which was to be surrendered to them by treaty. And how detestable was the open force with which the Galli Senones in-

SECTION CCXVII

Much less can an exception of fear or force be opposed to a treaty of peace; for this exception never takes place when one has a right to force another (l. 1. §108). But war is as just a way of forcing among independent free nations, as the authority of a judge in a civil state (§9); nor is it to any purpose to say that the war was unjust, and therefore that the victor used unjust violence in extorting hard conditions from the conquered. For besides, that neither of the parties engaged in war hath a right to make himself judge in his own cause, and determine concerning the justice of the war, the conquered, by transacting with the conqueror, remits that injury, and consents to the amnesty included in all such treaties.* <210>

Nor the exception of force or fear.

------

sulted the Romans, with whom, tho' conquered by them, they had transacted, obliging themselves to pay them a thousand pound weight of gold, when they not only brought false weights, but put a sword into the scale with the gold, saying insolently, *vae victis esse* [["Alas for the conquered"]], Liv. 5. 48.

* And hence we may see what ought to be answered to Pufendorff, who maintains against Grotius, that this exception takes place. See Grotius l. 2. cap. 17. §20. & ib. 3. cap. 18. §11. and Pufendorff of the law of nature and nations, 8. 8. 1. For these are two very different things, *viz.* to oppose an exception of fear, and to renew the war because the conquering party had taken occasion to do something contrary to the articles of peace. In the latter case we readily grant there is a just reason for war (§117); but we deny that the first is valid. But these two are not sufficiently distinguished by Pufendorff, as is plain from the example he brings. Polyb. hist. 3. 30. asks whether the Carthaginians had just reasons for their declaring the second punic war against the Romans? And he thinks they had, on this account, that the opportunity the Carthaginians took to revenge themselves, was of the same kind with that the Romans had taken to injure them; which is the same as if he had said, that the Carthaginians might justly plead the exception of fear, because, while they were embroiled in troubles and confusions at home, the Romans had forced them to give up Sardinia, and extorted a vast sum of money from them. But tho' in the articles of peace between the Romans and the Carthaginians, nothing was transacted concerning Sardinia, yet the Romans acted unjustly, and contrary to their treaty of peace, in taking advantage of the confusions the Carthaginians were involved in at home, to make themselves masters of Sardinia, as Polybius himself acknowledges, 1. 88. And therefore the Carthaginians did not object an exception of fear against the treaty of peace which put a period to the first punic war, but they complained that this treaty was broken by the Romans, by their taking occasion from their distress to force them to give up Sardinia.

SECTION CCXVIII

If peace ought to be kept with rebellious subjects? Grotius 3. 19. 6. and Pufendorff of the law of nature and nations, 8. 8. 2. ask whether a commonwealth or government is obliged to observe a treaty of peace made with rebellious subjects? And they justly affirm it ought, against Boxhornius, instit. polit. 1. 14. 19.[2] and Lipsius. For peace is made by way of transaction (§215); but he who transacts with one who had injured him, is deemed to have remitted the injury done to him. And therefore Sovereigns, by making a treaty of peace with rebellious subjects, give an indemnity to them for their rebellion; and thus this peace cannot be broken without injustice, unless for a new cause; except it was not valid from the beginning, either on <211> account of some fraud on the part of the rebels, or of the state of the prince who made the treaty.*

SECTION CCXIX

The obligations of the contractors, mediators, and sponsors. Besides, as other treaties, so those of peace ought to be (§213) most religiously observed; and therefore the time within which articles ought to be fulfilled, must be strictly observed, and delays cannot be easily excused. See Grotius 3. 20. 25. It is likewise evident to every one, that *mediators,* who undertake the office of making peace, and *guarantees,* who answer, as it were, for the contractors, are obliged, by pact, to the con-

---

* Thus in the year 1488, the people of Bruges having invited Maximilian I. to their city, forced him by an unparalleled treachery to a very shameful pact with them: But so far was the Emperor Frederick, from ratifying it, that in a convention of the nobles at Mechlin, it was decreed that Maximilian was not bound by these promises, Jo. Joach. Muller Reichs-tags-Theatr. in Maximilian I. act. 1. cap. 8. [[Müller, *Des Heiligen Römischen Reichs, Teutscher Nation, Reichs Tags Theatrum, wie selbiges, unter Keyser Maximilians I.* Maximilian I was king of Germany and later Holy Roman Emperor from 1493 to 1519.]] And surely the people having by knavery and unjust force made a prisoner of the King till he should promise whatever they were pleased to demand of him; such an extorted promise was no more binding upon him than the promise a robber on the highway forces from one.

2. Boxhorn, *Institutionum politicarum libri tres.*

tracting parties;* because, having undertaken the business, they oblige themselves to whatever it requires. Whence we conclude, that it is the duty of mediators not to favour one party more than another, but to judge impartially of the cause on both sides, and to persuade each to what is most equal and advantageous; and the duty of guarantees to use their utmost endeavours that the articles of the treaty be fulfilled on both sides, and to assist the injured party by their advice and aids, and with forces, if promised. < 212 >

SECTION CCXX

Sovereigns having the right of making leagues and peace with enemies (§135), which cannot be done without employing agents or messengers; the consequence is, that they are allowed to have the right of sending ambassadors. Now, since he who receives another's ambassadors, by that very deed is deemed to promise them a safe admission and exit (l. 1. §391); the consequence is, that ambassadors ought to be held sacred amongst enemies, and not only as exeemed from the jurisdiction of him to whom they are sent (of which V. A. Corn. van Bynkersh. hath admirably dis-

The right of sending ambassadors, and their sacredness.

---

* The same is to be said of hostages, *i.e.* persons pledged for the faith of a state, whether they voluntarily offered themselves, or they were given up as such by the supreme power in a state. Grotius of the rights of war and peace, 3. 4. 14. In the former case they are bound by their own consent; in the latter, by the convention between their sovereign and the other state with whom the peace is made. Whence it is plain, 1. That hostages may not fly. Nor, 2. a republic receive them by the right of postliminy. Therefore, when Cloelia being a hostage, fled, Porsena demanded that the hostage might be sent back, threatening to hold the treaty as broken if it was not, and the Romans acted justly in delivering back this pledge of their treaty. 3. That hostages ought not to be treated as slaves, or even as prisoners of war. And therefore, 4. That their estates cannot be confiscated as persons incapable of testating, tho' this was the old rigid Roman law, l. 31. D. de jure fisci. 5. That their obligation expires with their persons; and therefore, that when one hostage dies, ransom only is due for the other. 6. But if the treaty of peace be broken, the hostages may be kept in chains, and spoiled of their liberty and effects, tho' it be very hard, to kill them, if the treaty be violated without any fault of theirs. But of all this see Grotius of the rights of war and peace, 3. 20. 52. & seq. Pufendorff of the law of nature and nations, 8. 8. 6. and Schilter. opusculum singulare de jure obsidum. [[Schilter, *De jure et statu obsidum dissertatio juridica.*]]

coursed in his treatise *de foro legatorum*);[3] but as having the right of saying, writing, and acting whatever they are ordered by their constituent republics or Sovereigns, to speak, write, <213> or do, provided they shew no hostile disposition against the state to which they are sent.*

SECTION CCXXI

Different customs of nations with regard to ambassadors.

Other matters relating to ambassadors, which are treated of at great length by Marselarius, Wicquefort,[4] and others, may either be easily deduced from the preceding principles, or belong to the customs of nations, and not to the laws of nature and nations; such as the jurisdiction of an ambassador over his own family, his rights with regard to the exercise of his religion in his family, his immunities, his right of giving protection, and the solemnities of his reception, entry, and taking leave; his titles and honours, and the forms of audience; and the different orders and degrees of ambassadors, their titles of honour, precedency, and many other such like questions; as likewise concerning what is become now universal usage, the inviolability of trumpeters, drummers, and heralds (as among the Greeks of old) of whom Homer often makes mention (Odyss. 10. v. 59. & 102. & 19. v. 294. and Iliad 10. v. 14. & 178). But upon these matters it does not concern us to dwell. <214>

---

* If there are evident proofs of this hostile disposition, neither a prince nor a republic is obliged to receive an ambassador, and may command him to get out of their territories, as is usually done when war begins to rekindle between two states, the treaty of peace being broken: For we are not obliged to admit an enemy into our bosom or house, and therefore not his minister or commissioner.

3. Bynkershoek, *De foro legatorum tam in causa civili, quam criminali liber singularis.*

4. Fredericus de Marselaer (1584–1650), author of the treatise *Legatus libri duo.* Abraham van Wicquefort (1598–1682), author of a treatise on ambassadors (*L'ambassadeur et ses fonctions*) published in French, German, and English editions in the early eighteenth century.

ᖇᖇ CHAPTER X ᖇᖇ

Of the duties of subjects.

SECTION CCXXII

Hitherto we have treated of the rights of the supreme magistrate both within and without his dominions. Let us now enquire into the *duties of subjects;* but all of them may be so easily deduced from the rights of Sovereigns as correlates to them, (l. 1. §7), that we shall quickly dispatch them. For as subjects may be considered either as members or parts of the state entrusted to them, or as their subjects, their *duties* are either *general* or *special;* the former of which arise from the common obligation they lie under to the sovereign power; the latter, from their particular stations in the state.

The duties of subjects special and general.

SECTION CCXXIII

Their *general duties* are either owing to the state itself, or to the supreme power in it, or to their fellow subjects and citizens. But since the whole state is one society, and every member of a society is bound to adjust his actions to the common end of the society (§21); it follows, that nothing ought to be dearer or more sacred to a subject than the security and public welfare of his state; that he ought to prefer its good to his life and all the advantages of life,* and to promote it by every just and honest method. <215>

The general duties towards the state.

---

* And this is that obligation to one's country, which some ancients carried to such a height, that they said, it comprehended in it all the other branches of benevolence,

523

SECTION CCXXIV

Towards the supreme power.

Again, because the life of a *republic* consists, as it were, in this, that all the subjects submit their <216> wills to the will of the supreme power (§114); the consequence is, that subjects are obliged to pay to the supreme magistrate, as to their superior, a love of veneration and obedience* (l. 1. §86). And since they are likewise bound by pact, it is evident

---

and that none ought to hesitate about sacrificing his life for his country, when its good called for it at his hands. Cicero in his offices, 1. 17. 3. 23. The ancient saying, "Dulce est pro patria mori," is in every one's mouth. But Jo. Clericus, in his examination of this maxim, Ars Critica, 2. 2. 5. 16. says, "Men rarely know what they mean by the word *country*. And in reality," says he, "what was it an Athenian or a Roman called his country? If by it was understood the soil of Italy or Attica, there is no more reason why it should be a more glorious thing to die for it, than to die for that of Africa or Asia. For the soil in which one is born no more belongs to him, than the soil upon which he may live conveniently: It is therefore foolish to prefer dying in a country lying to the east or west, to living in another that lies to the south or north. If by it was understood the inhabitants, what were the Athenian and Roman republics but societies of robbers, if we look narrowly into the matter? And therefore, he who died for them was a robber, and sacrificed his vile life for a band of thieves." [[Jean le Clerc, *Ars critica*, part 2, sec. 2, chap. 5.16, pp. 428–29.]] But all this is very empty stuff, of which we may justly say,

> *Nil intra est oleam, nil extra est in nuce duri.*
>
> [[Horace, *Epistles* 2.1.31, in *Satires, Epistles, and Ars Poetica:* "The olive has no hardness within, the nut has none without."]]

For by one's country is meant not a spot of ground, nor yet a set of men among whom there may be many knaves and fools, but that civil constitution which connects our happiness and safety with that of the whole state: And certainly, it is better to die than to see that society dissolved, upon which our liberty, dignity, and all our happiness depends. The prophet Jeremiah philosophizes in a very different manner from Mr. le Clerc; Jeremiah xxix. 7. "And seek the peace of the city, whither I have caused you to be carried away captive, and pray unto the Lord for it, for in the peace thereof you shall have peace." Might not these captives have said, Why should we be more concerned about this soil than any other? Why should we pray for so many robbers, idolaters, for so many impure and wicked persons, with which this city of Babylon is filled? But God does not command them to be concerned about the Babylonian soil, nor its inhabitants, but about the republic, upon the safety of which their safety depended. "In the peace thereof shall ye have peace."

* And that not only internal but external, which consists in giving them certain titles, and paying them certain honours, according to the custom of the state. Thus,

that they are bound to fidelity, and that it is incumbent upon them not to be factious, and thus disturb the state by their feuds and animosities, but to pay allegiance to their rulers, and not to hurt them by word or deed, but to hold them sacred, and to render dutiful obedience to all their laws and orders.

SECTION CCXXV

Besides, it being the duty of fellow subjects to live together, as the common end of their society requires; they are certainly obliged to love one another, to live peaceably together, and not only to render justice one to another, but likewise to be more humane towards one another than to strangers. In fine, not to be invidious, or calumniators; not to envy those whom either birth, the benevolence of the prince, or merit has raised to greater dignities;* those who excel in any virtue, or those to whom providence hath been more favourable <217> with respect to their outward circumstances or fortunes.

Towards fellow subjects.

---

among the Persians the subjects were obliged to call their Kings Βασιλέας Βασιλέων, and to salute them with this acclamation *vivas aeternum,* and other such like. Of other titles of honour and gestures of respect, many have treated, as Becman Notitia dignitatum, diss. 6. [[Becmann, *Notitia dignitatum illustrium civilium, sacrarum, equestrium.*]] But tho' Sovereigns may justly require certain titles and ceremonies of honour and respect from their subjects; yet there is no reason why strangers should be forced to pay them, as the ambassadors of other princes or republics, who do their duty if they render reverence to a foreign prince according to the received manner and custom of their own nation. See Corn. Nep. Conon, cap. 3. [[Nepos, "Conon," chap. 3, p. 105, in Cornelius Nepos, *Cornelius Nepos.*]]

* This is the vice to which democracies are exceeding liable; for such governments can neither bear with vices, nor brook more eminent virtues. Hence that horrible decree of the Ephesini, on account of which Heraclitus pronounced them all worthy of dying in the prime of life. "Let none of our citizens excel others in merit; if he does, let him live elsewhere and with others." (Diogenes Laert. 9. 2.) How many eminent men suffered at Athens by their ostracism is well known. See Corn. Nep. Themistocles, cap. 8. Aristides cap. 1. Cimon. cap. 3. and Sigonius de Republ. Atheniensium. 2. 4. [[Sigonius, *De republica Atheniensium libri IV,* in Jacobus Gronovius, *Thesaurus Graecarum antiquitatum,* vol. 5 of *Attici imperii amplitudinem ac mutationes.*]]

SECTION CCXXVI

The founda-
tion of the
special duties
of subjects.

All the *special* duties of subjects flow from the ends of the particular station of each in the republic; and therefore they are all obliged to do, every one, what the end of his station requires; and not to do any thing that is repugnant to its end; and moreover, not to desire any offices for which they are not equal. From which few rules, one may easily perceive what must be the duties of generals, counsellors, ambassadors, treasurers, magistrates, judges, ministers of the church, professors and doctors in universities, soldiers, &c.*

SECTION CCXXVII

One ceases to
be a subject,
the republic
being
destroyed.

Moreover, the general duties of subjects oblige as long as they continue subjects; the special, only so long as they continue in the stations to which their respective duties belong. But one ceases to be a subject several ways. For a republic consists of a number of men (§107), whom we call *a people;* whence it follows, that the people being extinct or < 218 > dispersed (which may happen by an earthquake, war, inundations, and other public calamities) a few surviving persons cease to be subjects, unless they maintain their state till they grow again to a sufficient number of people.† But one does not cease to be a subject, if a people, being conquered in war, accedes as a province to another state, because he then

---

* It is not therefore necessary to speak more fully of the special duties belonging to every station. Of those Pufendorff of the duties of a man and a citizen, 2. 18. 7. has treated at large, and may be consulted.

† A few so surviving, Grotius, 2. 9. 4. thinks, may, as private persons, seize the dominion or property of the things which the whole people formerly possessed, but not the empire. But so long as the surviving persons have a mind to have a common supreme magistrate, and to submit themselves to his will for their common internal and external security, why does not the republic remain? Thus did the Athenian republic remain, when the people were reduced to the greatest extremity, insomuch, that all fit to bear arms being destroyed, they gave the right of citizenship to strangers, freedom to slaves, indemnity to condemned persons, and after all, that medley was scarcely able to maintain their liberty, Just. Hist. 5. 6.

becomes the subject of another state; nor if the form of the republic be changed, because a people does not then cease to be the same.

SECTION CCXXVIII

But because the people remains the same, tho' the form of their government be changed (§227); the consequence is, that the real treaties made by a people with other states (§209), and the public pacts made with private persons, while the former government remained unaltered, still subsist; and therefore the obligations of the people still are valid, tho' their form of government be changed. But that subjects are not bound by the deeds of those who unjustly usurped the government, or did any thing contrary to their fundamental laws,* is certain, for this reason, that they never consented to their power or empire. <219>

Not when the form of government is altered.

SECTION CCXXIX

Moreover, from the same principle (§226), we conclude, that one does not cease to be a citizen or subject, if one state is divided into many, or many coalesce into one system; tho' it may happen, in the former case, that one is no more a subject of the same, but of another state. If a republic or state resolve to send a colony, it is of great moment of what kind that colony is. For some may go out of a larger country to constitute

What if the empire be divided, and a colony sent.

---

* Thus the Athenians, when they had got rid of the thirty tyrants, made a law that all their acts and judgments, private or public, should be null, Demost. in Timocrat. p. 782. [[Demosthenes, "Against Timocrates," chap. 56, p. 409, in *Demosthenes.*]] The Emperor Honorius made a like constitution with relation to the deeds of the tyrant Heraclianus, l. 13. C. Theod. de infirm. quae sub tyrann. But here prudence and moderation are requisite, 1. If the obligation arise from something that hath been profitable to the people, and turned to their advantage. 2. If one chosen by the people holds the sovereignty for some time by mistake, l. 3. D. de off. praet. upon which law there is a most learned dissertation by Jac. Gothofredus, *De electione magistratus inhabilis.* [[Jacques Godefroy (Jacobus Gothofredus), 1587–1652, author of *De electione magistratus inhabilis seu incapacis per errorem facta.*]] 3. If one's government was originally just, and he afterwards degenerates into a tyrant, to which case I refer l. 2. & 3. C. Theod. eodem, where Constantine the Great justly confirms all the lawful deeds and rescripts of Licinius.

a republic that shall not be obliged to any thing with regard to its *metropolis,* but homage; and others, so as still to remain a part of their mother-country.* Now, it is plain, that the former case is the same as when an empire is divided; and in the latter there is no alteration with respect to the first obligation of the subjects who make the colony. <220>

SECTION CCXXX

If by changing habitation. Again, since one is a subject, in regard that he constitutes with others one republic, or with regard to a republic into which he willingly enters (§108); it follows from thence, that one ceases to be a citizen, so soon as he willingly removes with that design from his native country, and joins himself to another state, settling there his fortune and family, unless the public laws forbid subjects to remove, as among the citizens of Argos, of whom Ovid says, Metam. l. 15. v. 28.

* Such colonies the ancient Greeks used to send. Whence in Thucydides, l. 1. p. 25. the Corcyraeans say, "They are not sent into colonies on these terms that they may be slaves, but that they may be equal to those who still remain in their native country." To which the Corinthians answer, "We did not plant a colony of them to be affronted and despised by them, but that we might still remain their masters, and have homage paid by them to us. For the other colonies love and respect us." [[Thucydides, *History of the Peloponnesian War,* vol. 1, bk. I, chap. 34, p. 61.]] Therefore, it was the only duty of those colonies to pay respect to their mother country, and to testify that respect by some solemnities, as the same Thucydides speaks, p. 18. ibidem, adding (as his scholiast explains it) that these honours chiefly consisted, in giving, at the public sacrifices, when they distributed the entrails, the first share to the citizens of the metropolis. Hen. Valesius not. ad Excerpta Peiresc. p. 7. has largely treated of the other honours rendered in colonies to the subjects of their ancient mother-country. [[Henri de Valois (Valerius) (1603–76), French scholar and editor of *Polybii, Diodori Siculi, Nicolai Damasceni, Dionysii Halicar., . . . excerpta;* a reference to de Valois' edition of manuscripts acquired by his countryman Nicolas-Claude Fabri de Peiresc (1580–1673).]] But the customs amongst the Romans were different: For their colonies received their laws and institutions from the Romans, and did not make them themselves. See Gellius Noct. Attic. 17. Yet the Albanian colony was their own masters from the first, and not only did not pay any homage to their primitive country, but scrupled not to bring it under subjection to them; for which Metius Fufetius reproaches them in Dionys. Halicarn. Antiq. Rom. l. 3. p. 143.

Prohibent discedere leges,
Poenaque mors posita est patriam mutare volenti.[1]

or that liberty be indulged only with regard to a part of one's effects, which is the custom in several European nations. That they change their seat, but not their obligation to their country, who desert to an enemy, is manifest; and therefore, when they can be brought back, they are justly punished. <221>

SECTION CCXXXI

In fine, because those who are members of any society, and do not conform to its laws, may be severed from the society by the other members
(§21); the same right certainly belongs to members of a civil state; and
therefore, bad subjects may very justly be exiled; and this being done,
they certainly cease to be subjects. But this is not the case with respect
to those who, tho' sent out of a country, still possess estates in it, or to
those who are transported to a certain place subject to the country, there
to lead a disagreeable life, or perform some task by way of punishment.
In general, I should think, that those who are deprived, for any crime,
of the right of citizenship, are deprived of the privileges of subjects, but
are not thereby freed from their obligation to their country, so far at least,
as that they may molest it, or, imitating Coriolanus, take up arms against
their countrymen, Liv. 2. 35. <222>

*If by banish-
ment.*

1. Ovid, *Metamorphoses* 15, line 28, vol. 2: "[H]is country's laws prohibited his departure. The punishment of death was appointed to the man who should desire to change his fatherland."

A

SUPPLEMENT

Concerning the Duties of

SUBJECTS *and* MAGISTRATES.

We have had little occasion to differ, very considerably at least, from our Author, except in one important question, about the measures of submission to the supreme power; and as little occasion to add to him, except with relation to the natural causes of government, and their necessary operations and effects; *a consideration of great moment in moral and political philosophy, which hath however been overlooked, not by our Author only, but by Grotius and Pufendorff, and all the moral-system writers I have seen.*

These few things excepted, which we have endeavoured to supply in our remarks, our Author will be found, having had the advantage of coming after several excellent writers, to have given a very full compend of the laws of nature and nations, in which, they are deduced by a most methodical chain of reasoning, from a few simple and plain principles, and they are applied to as many proper cases as is requisite to initiate any attentive intelligent reader into this science, and enable him to decide, by his own judgment, any questions that may occur in life concerning justice and equity, between subject and subject, in whatever relations, natural or adventitious, as parent, husband, master, &c. between subject and magistrate; or finally, between <223> separate and independent states. Now, upon a review of what our Author hath done, every one, I

531

think, must perceive that the science of morals may be divided into two parts. The first of which is more general, and very easy and plain, consisting of a few axioms, and certain obvious conclusions from them, with relation to the general conduct of our life and actions. The second consists in finding out from these more general rules, what equity requires in various more complicated cases. And here, as in all other sciences, for the same reason, the deduction must be longer or shorter, according as the conclusions lie nearer to, or more remote from the first fundamental truths in the science. There is no science in which the first axioms or principles are more evident than that of morality. Thus, for example, the only principle our Author, or any other moral writer requires, or has occasion for, in order to demonstrate all the social duties of mankind, is, "That it is just to hurt or injure no person, and to render to every one his own, or his due; or in other words, That it is just and equal to do to others, as we would have them to do to us." The reasonableness of this principle is self-evident; and there is no case, however complex, relating to social conduct, wherein the reasonable part one ought to act may not be inferred from this principle. Certain general rules of conduct obviously arise from this principle. And the resolution of particular cases consisting of many circumstances by it, only appears difficult till one hath been a little practised in attending to circumstances, and separating, weighing, and balancing them. Here indeed study is requisite, as in other sciences, where the first principles are likewise very simple; and many truths are easily deducible from them, but others lie more remote, and require a longer train of argumentation: But yet it may be averred, that the remotest truths, and the most complex <224> cases in morals, are not so difficult to be resolved, or do not lie so distant from their first principles, as the higher truths in most other sciences. And therefore, it is justly said by moralists, that the science of morality is more level to every capacity than any other science; tho' certainly a thorough acquaintance with it requires a good deal of close thought and attention, and considerable practice in the examination of examples or cases. This, I think, every one, who hath read our author with any degree of attention, will readily acknowledge, whatever he may have thought, while he viewed this science at a greater distance. But, in order to give a short view of the extent of this science, and distinguish what is more easy and obvious in it from what is more complex and difficult, let us first consider an excellent summary given us by Cicero of the general laws or obligations of nature; and then let us cast our eye on what he says upon the design of civil law, which is to settle the rules of equity in more complex or compounded cases. We find him discoursing thus of the general laws of nature. "The law of nature," says he, "does not consist in opinion merely, neither is the sense of its obligation wholly formed by education and art; but it is from nature: we are led, directed, and impelled to fulfil its obvious dictates by certain dispositions cogenial with us: we feel its force, so soon as objects proper to excite and stir certain affections deeply inlaid into the frame of our minds, are presented to us. Nature thus leads us to religion, to piety, to gratitude, to resentment of injustice, to esteem and veneration, to veracity and candour. Religion consists in reverence toward some superior divine nature, and concern to approve ourselves to that Being, by whom we and all things subsist. Piety directs us to the love of our country, our parents, and of all who are endeared to us by natural ties of blood. Gratitude teaches us to main-<225>tain a kindly resentment of good offices, and to love, honour, and reward our benefactors. Resentment of injustice impels us to ward against and punish all injuries to ourselves, or to others who ought to be dear to us; and in general, to repel all iniquity and violence. Reverence is naturally excited in us by grave and wise old age, by eminence in virtue, or worth and dignity. Veracity consists in fulfilling our engagements, and acting consistently with what we promise, profess or undertake." Cicero de inventione rhetorica, l. 2. n. 22. & n. 54.[1] where he adds excellent definitions of prudence, justice, magnanimity, patience, temperance, modesty, perseverance, and all the virtues which make men good and great.

This is Cicero's succinct abridgment of the more general laws of nature: And he calls them laws of nature, because the obligation to them is founded in human nature; the happiness of mankind consists in the observance of them; and mankind are pointed and prompted to fulfil them by natural dispositions or principles in their minds. Insomuch that

---

1. Cicero, *De inventione* 2.22.66 and 2.54.163–64.

the idea of a supreme Governor of the universe cannot be presented to our minds, without exciting religious veneration and love in them; nor can the idea of our parents, our relatives by blood, or of our country, be set before us, and we not feel certain kindly affections stir within our breasts, which are very properly called, in a peculiar sense, natural affections; nor the idea of a generous benefactor, and our hearts not burn with gratitude towards him; nor the idea of injustice to ourselves, or even to others, and we not be filled with indignation and resentment; nor the idea of great wisdom, virtue and integrity, and we not be affected with esteem and reverence towards such characters; nor finally, the idea of consistency, faithfulness and candour, and we not admire and approve the beautiful image; and own such conduct to be truly <226> laudable and becoming. We are naturally affected by the several objects that have been mentioned in the manner described: And it is easy to perceive, that the private happiness of every individual, and the common happiness of our kind, which we cannot reflect upon without feeling a very high satisfaction in it, and a very strong tendency to promote it, are inseparably connected with the practice of those virtues. They are therefore, in every sense, of natural obligation. This, I take to be a just paraphrase upon what Cicero says in the passages above referred to, and to be sufficient to shew the strength and evidence of the more general rules of morality.

Now Cicero, agreeably to this account of human nature, and of the primary laws and obligations arising from it, thus defines the end of civil society (to which nature likewise strongly excites and impels us) and of its laws. (Topic ad Tribatium, n. 2.) "The end of civil society, and civil laws, (says he) is security of property, and equal treatment to the members of the same state, in consequence of just constitutions, formed and guarded by mutual consent."[2] And how elegantly doth he elsewhere enlarge upon the advantages of good civil laws, which secure the members of a state against all violence and injustice, and all feuds, animosities and quarrels, in the peaceable unmolested possession and use, each of his own honest acquisitions, (Orat. pro Caecinna, n. 26). "—A remarkable

---

2. Cicero, *Topica* 2.9, in Cicero, *De inventione*.

thing indeed, and worthy of your attention and remembrance, ye protectors of civil rights, on this very account. For what is the end of civil law? Is it not a security for our properties and rights, which cannot be biassed by affection, bended by force, nor corrupted by money; and which, tho' not totally violated, yet if but deserted in the smallest degree, or if negligently observed, we are neither sure of inheriting what our fathers may leave to us, nor of making our children our heirs? For what signifies it, to <227> have houses or lands left us by a father, if our possession be precarious and uncertain? Let an estate be yours by the fullest right, yet how can you be sure of keeping it, if this right be not sufficiently fortified, if it be not protected by civil and public law against the covetousness of the more powerful? What avails it, I say, to have an estate, if the laws relating to confines, marches, possession, use, the rights of water, passage, &c. may be changed or disturbed on any account? Believe me, many greater advantages redound to us from good laws, and the conservation of justice, than from those who leave us an inheritance. A piece of land may be left me by any one, but my secure possession and use of it depend upon the inviolability of the civil laws. My patrimony is left me by my father, but the usucapion of this estate, which puts an end to all sollicitude, and secures against all vexatious suits, is not left me by my father, but by the laws. My estate, with the rights of water, air, passage, light, &c. is left me by my father, but my security for the undisturbed possession of these rights, is an inheritance I owe to the laws. Wherefore, we ought to be no less concerned about this public patrimony, the good laws and constitutions handed down to us from our ancestors, than about our private estates; not only because these are secured to us by the laws, but because tho' one may lose his estate without hurt to any other person but himself, yet right cannot be violated without the greatest detriment and injury to the whole state, &c."[3]

Here Cicero briefly runs through some of the principal points which ought to be settled by civil laws, agreeably to natural equity, for the encouragement of honest virtuous industry, and in order to exclude all injustice, violence and molestation; such as, succession by testament,

---

3. Cicero, *Pro Caecina,* chap. 26, in Cicero, *Pro lege Manilia.*

and to intestates, possession, use, usufruct, perfect or im-<228>perfect
dominion, services, contracts, &c. And it is the rules of equity with regard to these and such like matters, which it is the business of the moral
science to deduce from certain and evident principles, for the direction
of society in fixing and determining its laws. And therefore, to be a master of the moral science, it is not enough to know the first axioms of it,
and its more general and obvious rules; but one must be capable of following them thro' all their remotest consequences, in these and other
such complicated cases, so as to be able to judge of civil laws by them.
And surely, however close attention and long reasoning this more difficult part of morality may require, it does not require long reasoning
to prove, that this is the most proper study of those whose birth and
fortunes furnish them with time and means for improving themselves
to serve their country in the highest stations of life. Who doth not at
first sight perceive that this is the character every man of birth ought to
aim at, and that his education ought to be adapted to qualify him for
attaining to, even that glorious one which Cicero (ibidem) gives of C.
Aquilius? "Wherefore, let me aver it, that the authority of the person I
have just mentioned, can never weigh too much with you. Aquilius,
whose singular prudence the people of Rome hath so often proved, not
in deceiving, but in rightly advising them, and who never severed equity
from civil law. Aquilius, whose extraordinary judgment, application and
fidelity, have been so long devoted to the service of the public, and have
been on many occasions so ready and powerful a stay to it. One so just
and good, that he seems to have been formed for giving counsel and
administring justice, rather by nature than by discipline: One so wise
and knowing, that he seems by his study of the laws to have acquired
not merely knowledge, but likewise virtue and probity: One, in fine,
whose understanding is <229> so clear and accurate, and his integrity
so habitual and impervertible, that whatever ye draw from this fountain,
ye perceive, ye feel to be pure and unadulterated."[4] For such excellent
qualities shall the memory of a *Talbot* be ever dear and precious: And
hence the manifold advantages we daily receive under the upright and

4. Ibid., 27.77.

prudent guardianship of a *York*.[5] And all our youth, who have the noble ambition to be equally useful, and equally loved and honoured, must pursue their paths, and add to the same incorruptible integrity, the same thorough knowledge of natural equity, and of our excellent constitution and laws.* It is in order to contribute my mite to as-<230>sist them in this glorious pursuit, that I have given them this admirable abridgement of the laws of nature and nations in English, with some necessary supplements. For every science hath its elements, which, if they be well understood and carefully laid up, not in the memory but in the judgment, the science itself may be said to be mastered, it being then very easy to make progress in it. Let me only suggest here, that it will still be necessary, after having well digested this small system, to read Grotius,

---

* Because this study is generally supposed to belong only to those who are to follow the law as a profession, and not to make a necessary part of liberal education, I can't choose but insert here the account that is given us of ancient education in the schools at Apollonia, to which Augustus was sent by Julius, and Maecenas by his parents. See Dion. lib. 45. p. 307. [[Dio Cassius, *Dio's Roman History,* vol. IV, bk. 45, p. 413]] and Velleius Paterculus, l. 2. cap. 59. with Boecler's note upon these words,—"Apolloniam cum in studia miserat." (edit. Petri Burmanni.) [[See Velleius Paterculus, *Compendium of Roman History,* bk. 2, chap. 59. The edition Turnbull is using appears to be *C. Velleii Paterculi quae supersunt ex historiae Romanae voluminibus duobus* (1719).]] First, it is observed, that Julius took care to have Octavius instructed in all the arts of government, and in every thing requisite to qualify him for a suitable behaviour in the exalted station for which he had designed him. Then the several particular parts of his education are mentioned, such as the languages, rhetoric, military exercises, and which was chief, morals and politics, τὰ πολιτικὰ καὶ τὰ ἀρχικὰ; and in all these useful arts it is said the youth were instructed diligently, accurately and practically, τὸ ἀκριζῶς, τὸ ἐρρωμενως, τὸ ισχυρως. Boecler refers to Lipsius, l. 1. polit. c. 10. where there are several observations on this subject. [[*Politicorum sive civilis doctrinae libri sex.*]] And how indeed can that but be a principal part in the education of young men, whose birth and fortune call them to the higher stations of life? What good purpose can their education serve if this be neglected? Or what is principal, if that be not, which is absolutely necessary to qualify them for their principal duties, and for the noble employments by which alone they can acquire glory to themselves, or do good to their country? Is the art of ruling, law-giving, or of discharging any important office in the state, the only one that requires no preparation for it, no previous study or practice?

5. Charles Talbot, first baron Talbot of Hensol (1685–1737), lord chancellor from 1734; Philip Yorke, first earl of Hardwicke (1690–1764), succeeded Talbot as lord chancellor in 1737.

and together with him his best commentator Pufendorff,* and several other authors, the treatises of Bynkershoek so often commended by our Author in particular; and after having read these excellent writers, it will not be improper often to return to our Author, and review him as a good compend of them all. And to add no more on the utility of this study, as without some acquaintance with the principles of moral philosophy, it is impossible to reap more than mere amusement by reading history; so when one hath once taken in a clear view of the more important truths in morality and politics, it will be equally easy, pleasant and advantageous for him to apply these truths, as a measure or standard, to the facts or cases he meets with in history, to private or public actions, and their springs or motives, and to the laws, constitutions and policies of different states: And it would not certainly be an improper way of studying our laws, first to get well <231> acquainted with the laws of nature (large commentaries upon which are generally at the same time commentaries upon the Roman laws, the examples being commonly taken from thence), and then to go over the same laws of nature again in order, and to enquire into our laws under each head, and try them by the laws of nature, as the Roman laws are commonly canvassed by the maxims of natural equity, in treatises upon universal law.

But tho' I could not take my leave of our author without saying these few things about the nature and use of the science to which his treatise is so good an introduction; yet the design of this supplement is chiefly to treat a little more fully than he hath done of the duties of subjects and magistrates; and here I shall only cut off some things, and add a few others to what is to be found in the learned Barbeyrac's notes upon the tenth and following sections in the eighth chapter of the seventh book of Pufendorff of the law of nature and nations.

The duties of subjects are either general or particular. The first arise

---

* I have said his best commentator; because he is constantly examining Grotius's reasonings and determinations, and very rarely differs from him. And they ought to be read together, which may be easily done, Barbeyrac in his notes upon Grotius having all along mentioned the chapters in Pufendorff where each question in Grotius is handled.

from the common obligation they are under, as submitting to the same government. The others result from the different employments and particular offices with which each subject is honoured or entrusted. 1. The general duties of subjects respect their behaviour either towards the governors of state, the whole body of the people, or their fellow subjects. 1. As to the governors, every one ought to shew them the respect, fidelity and obedience which their character demands. So that subjects ought not to be factious or seditious, but to be attached to the interest of their prince, and to respect and honour him. This is certainly just. But then, in order to this, a prince must deserve love and honour. For tho' power may force submission, 'tis merit only that can create respect, give authority, or beget love. The <232> command to honour a king must be understood as the command to honour any other person must be understood; not as a command to honour him whether he deserves it or not; for that would be an absurd command; a command to prostitute honour and respect. 'Tis good princes alone that can be honoured, because they alone deserve it, or have the great and amiable qualities that can excite esteem. We ought even to have a veneration for the memory of good princes; but for those who have not been such, behold the judicious reflections of Montagne.

"Among those laws," says he, "which relate to the dead, I take that to be the best, by which the actions of princes are to be examined and searched into after their decease. What justice could not inflict upon their persons while they were alive, and equal to, if not above the laws, is but reasonable should be executed upon their reputation when they are dead, for the benefit of their successors. This is a custom of singular advantage to those nations where it is observed, and by all good princes as much to be desired, who have reason to complain that the memories of the tyrannical and wicked should be treated with the same honours and respects as theirs. We owe indeed subjection and obedience to all our kings alike, for that respects their office; but as to esteem as well as affection, those are only owing to their virtue. Should it therefore be granted, that we are to be very patient under unworthy princes while they hold the rod over us? Yet, the relation between prince and subject being once ended, there is no reason why we should deny to our own liberty, and common justice, the publishing of our wrongs.—Livy, with abundance of truth, says, that the language of men educated in a court was always full of vanity and ostentation, and that the characters they give of their princes are seldom <233> true. And tho' perhaps some may condemn the boldness of those two soldiers, one of whom being asked by Nero, why he did not love him? answered him plainly to his face, I loved thee whilst thou wast worthy of it; but since thou art become a parricide, an incendiary, a waterman, a player, and a coachman, I hate thee as thou dost deserve: And the other being asked, why he should attempt to kill him? as warmly replied, Because I could think of no other remedy against thy perpetual mischiefs. Yet who, in his right senses, will blame the public and universal testimonies that were given of him after his death, and will be to all posterity, both of him, and of all other wicked princes like him in his tyrannies and wicked deportment? I am scandalized, I own, that in so sacred a government as that of the Lacedemonians, there should be mixed so hypocritical a ceremony at the interment of their kings, where all the confederates and neighbours, all sorts of degrees of men and women, as well as their slaves, cut and slashed their foreheads in token of sorrow, and repeated in their cries and lamentations, that that king (let him be as wicked as the devil) was the best that ever they had; by this means prostituting to his quality, the praises which only belong to merit, and that which is properly due to supreme merit, tho' lodged in the lowest and most inferior subjects, Essay, l. 1. cap. 3.[6]

2. With respect to the whole body of the people, it is the duty of every good subject to prefer the good of the public to every other motive or advantage whatsoever, chearfully to sacrifice his fortune and life, and all that he values in the world, for the preservation and happiness of the state. Union is generally recommended to subjects as their duty. It is said, that union will make a people flourish, and dissention will ruin any people. <234> But there must be care taken to have a just notion of the meaning of those words. An union serviceable to a state, is what designs the universal good of those who live in it. For if, *e.g.* in a monarchical state, where the power of the Sovereign is limited by the laws, the prin-

6. See Montaigne, *Essays,* vol. 1, bk. I, chap. 3, pp. 26–27.

cipal subjects of the state should willingly, or by force, consent to submit all the laws to the prince's pleasure, such an union would not be advantageous to it in any respect. It would change a society of free people into a company of miserable slaves. The ready compliance of the Chinese to obey their king blindly, does but strengthen his tyranny, and add to their misery. But it is asserted, that the general obedience of the Chinese is of service to preserve the peace of their country, and that they enjoy by it all the advantages which the strictest union can procure. They must mean all the advantages that can be possessed in slavery. But sure there is not a free-man but had rather see the most frequent commotions than suffer an eternal slavery. Moreover, it is false to affirm that there are no intestine wars under such a form of government. The most enslaved people will, in time, grow weary of an exorbitant tyranny, and upon the first opportunity shew that the desire of liberty cannot be quite stifled in the souls of men born to freedom. This happens among the Chinese and Turks. The union of those who govern an aristocratical state would be useless, if it did not preserve the observation of the laws, and the universal good of the commonwealth. This we may understand from the history of the thirty tyrants of Athens and the Decemviri of Rome. The union of those men served only to crush the people, and make them miserable; because their principal design was to gratify their passions, without having the least respect to the public good. Union may be also considered with regard to the people, who, when the <235> state is happy, and well administred, ought to esteem themselves happy, and to obey chearfully. Now, to keep the people in so firm an union, it is requisite that not only they may be the better for it, but also that they should be sensible of their own happiness. In general, the agreement and union both of governors and people, ought to tend to the public good: from whence it follows, that whatsoever has not such a design is injurious, and ought rather to be termed a conspiracy than an union; since the name of a virtue cannot with reason be attributed to a thing which injures and ruins a society. Public spirit is the motive that ought to lead and govern subjects. And then is one truly public-spirited, when nothing is dearer to him than the liberty and happiness of his country. Yet we must here observe, that the engagement of every particular person does in some measure depend upon the performing of what the rest are obliged to do, as well as himself, for the public good. For indeed the public good is only the consequence of the united forces and services of many conducing to the same end. If then in a state it is become customary for the generality openly to prefer their own private interest to that of the public, a good subject will not, in that case, be to blame in the least, in not caring to expose his person or his fortune by a zeal impotent and useless to his country.

Lastly, the duty of a subject towards his fellow subjects, is to live with them in a peaceable and friendly manner; to be good humoured and complaisant to them in the affairs of human life, and to give mankind no uneasiness by peevish, morose, and obstinate temper; and, in short, not to envy or oppose the happiness or advantages of any one.

2. The particular duties of subjects are annexed to certain employments, the discharge of which <236> influences, in some measure, either the whole government, or only one part of it. Now, there is one general maxim with regard to them all, and that is, that no one aspire to any public employment, or even presume to accept of it, when he knows himself not duly qualified for it. What consciences must those men have, who not only accept of, but brigue for places they are absolutely unqualified for; as for example, a seat in the supreme judicatures of a nation! A trust which requires, besides great virtue, great knowledge and wisdom; a thorough acquaintance with the constitution and laws of a state, and the interests of the people. And yet (as Socrates observed very truly) the manner of the world is quite otherwise. For tho' no body undertakes to exercise a trade, to which he has not been educated, and served a long apprenticeship; and how mean and mechanical soever the calling be, several years are bestowed upon the learning of it; yet, in the case of public administrations, which is, of all other professions, the most intricate and difficult (so absurd, so wretchedly careless are we) that every body is admitted, every body thinks himself abundantly qualified to undertake them. Those commissions are made compliments and things of course, without any consideration of mens abilities, or regarding at all whether they know any thing of the matter; as if a man's quality, or the having an estate in the country, could inform his understanding, or secure his

integrity, or render him capable of discerning between right and wrong, and a competent judge of his poorer (but perhaps much honester and wiser) neighbours. See *Charron sur la sagesse.*[7] To buy public offices, or procure them by bribery, or to give it a softer name, largesses, is still more infamous and abominable, the most sordid, and the most villainous way of trading in the world. For it is plain, he that *buys in the piece, must make himself whole* <237> *again by selling out in parcels.* Besides, this way of procuring public trusts corrupts a people, and renders them mercenary and venal, and fit to be sold. And a dishonest, corrupt people, neither deserves to be free, nor can they long preserve themselves from being bound with the fetters, their vile prostitution of honour and conscience to sordid gain demerits. Let me only add upon this head, that to a free people, who have the right of making their laws, and laying on their own taxes by their representatives, it may be justly said, as it was to the people of Israel of old, *That their evil is of themselves; whatever they suffer, they have themselves to blame for it;* and consequently, the guilt of it lies upon themselves. A horrid, inexpiable guilt, of which the greatest misery that a nation can fall into, is but the just punishment, for which no commiseration is due to them who brought it upon themselves; but to their unhappy posterity, who must curse them, if they are not quite insensible of the value of the liberty and happiness their ancestors basely gave up, and the deplorable condition they are depressed into by the corruption and venality of those who gave them birth, *i.e.* till slavery, as long continued slavery never fails to do, detrudes them into a state not far removed above that of the brutes. But we must be a little more particular with regard to the duties belonging to employments.

1. Ministers of state, or privy counsellors, ought, with the greatest application, to study, and perfectly to know the affairs and interests of the state in all the parts of government, and to propose faithfully, and in the most proper manner, whatever appears to them to be advantageous to the public, without being influenced by either affection, passion, or any sinister views. The public good ought to be the only design of all their advice and endeavours, and not the advancement of their own pri-

7. Pierre Charron, *De la sagesse.*

vate fortunes, and the promoting their <238> own power and greatness. Nor must they ever, by vile and nauseous flattery, countenance or encourage the criminal inclinations of the prince. 1. They ought, first of all, to be men of virtue and good principles. 2. Persons of great abilities, well acquainted with politics, and particularly well versed in the constitution, laws and interests of the nation. 3. Persons tried before, who have come off with honour and success in other trusts; men practised in business, and accustomed to difficulties. For hardships and adversities are the most improving lessons. "Fortune," says Mithridates in Salust, "in the room of many advantages she has torn from me, has given me the faculty of advice and persuasion."[8] Men, at least of ripe years, to give them steadiness, experience, and consideration; for it is one of the many unhappinesses attending youth, that persons then are easily imposed upon. 4. And finally, they ought to be men of openness, freedom and courage in all their behaviour when they are consulted with; who will use their utmost care that all their proposals be for the honour and advantage of their prince and their country; and when once they have secured this point, that the advice is good, will lay aside all flattery and disguise; detest and despise all equivocations and reservations, and craftiness of expression, by which they may seem to aim at ingratiating themselves, or to contrive that what they say may be acceptable to their master: The very reverse of those men whom Tacitus describes, "Who accommodate their language as they see occasion, and *do not so properly discourse with the prince, as with his present inclinations and circumstances.*"[9]

2. The clergy, as being the public ministers of religion, ought to discharge their duty and function with the utmost gravity and application; should teach no doctrine, nor advance any opinion in religion, which does not appear to them to be sincerely true; and should be themselves a shining <239> example by their own conduct of those instructions which they deliver to the people. "Never did a covetous preacher make his hearers liberal. Never did a voluptuous clergyman persuade any one to abstain from pleasures, or to use them with moderation; at least, when

8. Sallust, "Letter of Mithridates," sec. 4, 433, in Sallust, *Sallust.*
9. It is not clear which work by Tacitus Turnbull is referring to here.

those persons were discovered to be what they really are."[10] Their bad
example will do abundantly more mischief than their best sermons can
do good; for example is more powerful than precept.

3. Magistrates, and all other officers of justice ought to be of easy
access to every body; protect the common people against the oppressions
of the more powerful; be as forward in doing justice, and that with the
same impartiality to the mean and poor as to the great and rich; not spin
out a cause to an unnecessary length; never suffer themselves to be corrupted by bribes and sollicitations; examine thoroughly into the matter
before them; and then determine it without passion or prejudice; regardless of every thing while they are doing their duty. Tho' it be an
excellent qualification in a magistrate, to temper justice with prudence,
and severity with gentleness and forbearance; yet it must be confessed
to be much more for the common advantage, to have such magistrates
as incline to the excess of rigour, than those who are disposed to mildness
and easiness and compassion. For even God himself, who highly rec-
ommends, and so strictly enjoins all those humane and tender dispositions on other occasions, yet positively forbids a judge to be moved with
pity. The strict and harsh magistrate is the better restraint, the stronger
curb.

From the duties of inferior magistrates, let us pass to those of the
supreme magistrate. And how happy is that post which every minute
furnishes opportunities of doing good to thousands! But, on the other
hand, how dangerous is that station which every moment exposes to the
injuring of millions! The <240> good which princes do, reaches even
to the most distant ages; as the evils that they occasion are multiplied
from generation to generation to the latest posterity. If the care of a
single family be so burdensom, if a man has enough to do to answer for
himself, what a weight, what a load is the charge of a whole Kingdom.
Isocrates calls a Kingdom the greatest of human affairs, and such as requires more than ordinary degrees of prudence and foresight.[11] And Cy-

10. The source of this quotation is not clear.
11. See Isocrates, "To Nicocles," secs. 4–6, in *Isocrates,* vol. 1.

rus well observes, that he who is above all the rest in honour and authority, should be so in goodness too.[12]

A prince and his court, as experience teaches us, is the standard of
manners as well as of fashions. For nothing is truer than what Pliny says
(Paneg. C. 45. n. 6.) "Nec tam imperio nobis opus, quam exemplo, &
mitius jubetur exemplo." "We do not want precepts so much as patterns,
and example is the softest and least invidious way of commanding."[13]
The virtues requisite to a prince, and of which he ought to be the best
pattern, are, 1. Piety, which is the foundation of all virtues: a solid and
reasonable piety, free from hypocrisy, superstition and bigotry. 2. The
love of justice and equity. For the chief design a prince was made for, is
to take care that every man has his right. *And this obliges him to study not
only that part of human learning, which qualifies those famous civilians,
that are fit to be legislators themselves, who go up to that justice which at
first regulated human society, who exactly knew what liberty nature has left
us in civil government, and what freedom the necessity of states takes from
private people, for the good of the public: But that part of the law too, which
respects the rights, and descends to the affairs of particular persons.* 3. A
prince must above all things accustom himself to moderate his desires.
The philosopher Arrian, de exped. Alex. says, "That it is easy to see from
the example of Alexander, that whatever fine actions a man performs to
out-<241>ward appearance, it signifies nothing to true happiness, if one
does not at the same time know how to rule and moderate himself."[14]
4. Valour is requisite to a prince, but then it must be managed with
prudence. 5. And above all, a prince ought to shine in goodness and
clemency. 'Tis by no other means, but by the sole good-will of the people
that he can do his business; and no other qualities but humanity, truth
and fidelity, can attract their goodwill. *Nihil est tam populare quam bo-*

---

12. Again, the exact source of this is not clear, though it may be a reference to
Xenophon, *Cyropaedia,* vol. 1, bk. II, chap. ii, 20.

13. Pliny, *Panegyricus* 45.6, in Pliny, *Letters and Panegyricus,* vol. 2. The phrase "&
mitius jubetur exemplo" is missing in the Loeb edition.

14. Arrian, *The Campaigns of Alexander the Great.* It is not clear which specific
passage Turnbull is referring to here, but Arrian repeatedly criticized Alexander for
his immoderate ambition.

nitas, says Cicero; nothing is so popular as goodness, Orat. pro Ligar. cap. 12.[15] A prince who does not reign in the hearts of his people, does not reign over the better part of his subjects. Their minds are not obedient or submitted to him. 'Tis love only that can produce cordial obedience. Cicero gives us this enumeration of the virtues of a prince, *Orat. pro rege Deiotar.* cap. 9. *"Fortem esse, justum, severum, gravem, magnanimum, largum, beneficum, liberalem; hae sunt regiae laudes."*[16] And to fortitude, justice, gravity, temperance, magnanimity, liberality, beneficence, which are allowed to be virtues necessary to make a prince great and glorious, he adds another, which he says is generally thought to be a private virtue only, *viz.* frugality. *"Sed praecipue singularis & admiranda. frugalitas, etsi hoc verbo, scio, reges non laudari solere. Ut volet, quisquam accipiat: ego tamen frugalitatem, id est, modestiam & temperantiam, virtutem maximam esse judico."*[17] Cicero tells us, de legibus, l. 3. c. 3. "That the good of the public ought to be the sole rule and motive of a prince's conduct, *salus populi suprema lex esto."*[18] And an excellent author said (Marcus Antonin. l. 4. c. 42.)[19] "A prince ought always to have these two maxims in view; To do for the good of mankind all that the condition of a legislator and a king requires of him. And the other, To change his resolution, whenever men skilled in such matters give him better advice. But still the change must be made from <242> the motives of justice, and the public interest, and never for his own pleasure, his own advantage, or his own particular glory."

---

15. Cicero, *Pro Ligario* 12.37, p. 493, in Cicero, *The Speeches.*

16. "Bravery, justice, earnestness, dignity, magnanimity, liberality, kindliness, generosity—these are the qualities we commend in a king." Cicero, *Pro rege Deiotaro* 9.26, p. 525, in Cicero, *Pro T. Annio Milone, . . . Pro rege Deiotaro.*

17. Ibid. "[I]n nothing is he more remarkable and more admirable than in his sobriety; although I know that kings are not commonly praised in such terms. . . . Everyone is free to put what construction he pleases upon my words; none the less I pronounce sobriety, by which I mean moderation and temperance, to be the highest of virtues."

18. Cicero, *De legibus* 3.3.8 (see Cicero. *De re publica; De legibus*).

19. Presumably a reference to Marcus Aurelius's *Meditations,* though in that case the book and chapter number are incorrect and it is not clear which passage Turnbull had in mind.

The truth of it is, that the very interest of the Sovereign requires that he should direct all his actions to the public good.

Qui sceptra duro saevus imperio regit;
Timet timentes; metus in auctorem redit.

Seneca in Oedip. v. 705.[20]

The following quotation from Mr. de Cambrai[21] will serve to explain and illustrate this sentence. "Where the sovereign command is most absolute, these princes are least powerful. They take and ruin every thing, and are the sole possessors of the whole state; but there the state languishes, the country is uncultivated, and almost desert, the towns every day decay and grow thin, and trade is quite lost. The king, who can never be such by himself, but must be such with regard to his people, undoes himself by degrees, by insensibly undoing his subjects, to whom he owes both his riches and his power; his kingdom is drained of money and men, and the loss of the latter is the greatest, and the most irreparable of losses. His arbitrary power makes as many slaves as he has subjects; they all seem to adore him; and all tremble at the least motion of his eye. But see what will be the consequences upon the least revolution; this monstrous power, raised to too excessive an height, cannot long endure; it wants supplies from the hearts of the people; it has wearied out, and exasperated the several ranks of men in the state, and forces all the members of that body to sigh with equal ardour for a change: and at the first blow, the idol is pulled down, and trampled under foot. Contempt, hatred, fear, resentment, jealousy; in a word, all the passions combine together against so injurious and detestable a power. The king, who in the days <243> of his vain prosperity, could not find one person that durst tell him the truth, shall not find one in his adversity that will vouchsafe to excuse or defend him."[22] All writers on this subject take notice of the danger of flattery to which kings, and sons of kings, are so much

---

20. "One who wields the sceptre with tyrannical harshness / fears those who fear him; terror rebounds on its author." Seneca, *Oedipus,* line 705, in Seneca, *Tragedies.*

21. François Fénelon, bishop of Cambrai (1651–1715).

22. Fénelon, *Telemachus,* bk. 10, pp. 170–71.

exposed. And on this occasion a famous saying of Carneades is commonly quoted, "That sons of princes, and other great and wealthy men, learn no art but that of horsemanship well, because their horses cannot flatter them."[23] But there is an excellent book upon the education of a prince, lately translated into our language from the French, in which all the qualities, virtues and duties of a prince are admirably described.[24] And therefore, I shall add no more upon this subject, but the short account Cicero gives us of Plato's doctrine concerning the business and duty of supreme magistrates, and one most beautiful passage from Cicero himself concerning empire, founded not in love, but fear. The first is in his first book of offices, chapter 25. "Rulers, or those who design to be partakers in the government, should be sure to remember those two precepts of Plato. First, To make the safety and interest of their citizens the great aim and design of all their thoughts and endeavours, without ever considering their own personal advantage. And secondly, so to take care of the republic, as not to serve the interest of any one party, to the prejudice or neglecting of all the rest. For the government of a state is much like the office of a guardian or trustee, which should always be managed for the good of the public, and not of the persons to whom it is entrusted; and those men, who, whilst they take care of one, neglect or disregard another part of the citizens, do but occasion sedition and discord, the most destructive things in the world to a state. From this root have sprung many grievous dissentions among the Athenians, and not only tumults, but even deadly civil wars in our <244> own republic. Things, which one who deserves to hold the reins of the government, will detest; and will give himself so to the service of the public, as to aim at no riches or power for himself; and will so take care of the whole commonwealth, as not to pass over any part of it."[25] The other is in the second book, chapter 7. "It is well observed by Ennius, *Whom men fear, they hate; and whom they hate, they wish out of the world.* But that no

---

23. This is quoted in Plutarch, "How to Tell a Flatterer from a Friend," chap. 16, sec. 58, in *Moralia: in Fourteen Volumes,* vol. 1.

24. Presumably a reference to Fénelon's *Telemachus.*

25. Cicero, *De officiis* 1.25.85–86.

force of power or greatness whatever can bear up long against the stream of public hate, if it were not sufficiently known before, was of late made appear by an instance of our own. And not the violent death of that tyrant only, who by force of arms oppressed the city (which now most obeys him, when taken out of the world) but the like untimely ends of most other tyrants, who have generally been attended with the same ill fate, are a manifest token that the hatred of the people is able to ruin the most absolute power. *For obedience, proceeding from fear, cannot possibly be lasting; whereas that which is the effect of love, will be faithful for ever."*[26] <245>

26. Ibid., 2.7.23.

A

DISCOURSE

UPON THE

NATURE *and* ORIGINE

OF

MORAL *and* CIVIL LAWS.

By *GEORGE TURNBULL,* L. L. D.

LONDON:
Printed in the Year MDCCXL.

A

DISCOURSE

Upon the NATURE and ORIGINE of

MORAL *and* CIVIL LAWS, *&c.*

It will be acknowledged that subjects of importance deserve to be set in various lights. Let us therefore endeavour to set the first principles of the science of laws in a light, which, if not altogether new, yet may perhaps prove more satisfactory to several understandings, than that in which they are more commonly represented. One great thing to be avoided in the first steps of a science, is dispute about words. And we think that it will contribute not a little to this good effect in the science we now propose to explain the first foundations of in the clearest manner we can, if, for some time, we only make use of terms well known to those who are in the least acquainted with natural philosophy, in the very sense they are used in that science.

SECTION I

Natural Philosophy is defined to be the science of the laws, according to which nature operates in producing its effects, and to which human art must conform in order to produce certain effects. And the settled methods, according to which nature works, and human arts must work, in order to produce certain effects, are called *laws of nature.* <248> An example or two will shew the truth and justness of these definitions. That part of natural philosophy, which is properly called *mechanics,* consists

What is called a law of nature by natural philosophers.

553

in shewing the laws of motion, and what it is in particular that constitutes the quantity of motion in a body, and in deducing from thence certain rules to be observed by human art in the contrivance of machines, in order to give them a certain useful force. And this connexion in nature is found to be the principle of mechanics, or the rule according to which machines for raising weights, or overcoming obstacles, must be constructed, *viz.* That the moment of a body being its quantity of matter inducted into its velocity, any other body, however short of another in quantity of matter, will be rendered equal to it in moment, by adding to the less heavy body, just as much more in velocity as it wants of the heavier in quantity of matter. For this plain reason, that because if a body have a quantity of matter, as four, and a velocity as two, its force of motion or moment will be four multiplied by two; *i.e.* eight; and if another body have a quantity of matter, as two, and a velocity, as four, its force or moment will likewise be as two multiplied by four; that is, as eight; *i.e.* the two will be equal in moment. This principle is therefore called *the law of mechanic powers,* or *the law of nature,* with respect to quantity of motion. And upon this principle are balances, levers, cranes, pullies, wedges, screws, and inclined planes constructed. And he who attempts to assist mankind in raising weights, or overcoming obstacles, upon any other principle besides this, attempts to make new laws in nature, and his aim will prove absurd and lost labour. In the same manner, optics is a science which shews the laws observed by nature in the reflexion and refraxion of light, and points out the way of assisting vision, and attaining to certain other optical ends, as magnifying, diminishing, or <249> multiplying objects, &c. And the laws observed by nature in reflecting and refracting light, are the laws of this human art; the laws according to which it must work to answer these purposes.

SECTION II

What is called a law in moral philosophy.
Now, in the same sense, that in these, and other parts of natural philosophy, certain settled methods, according to which nature operates, are laws to human arts; in the same sense must any other connexions in nature be laws to other human arts, or laws to other human actions, if

they are the established means or orders, according to which certain other ends can only be attained by us. If therefore there are any other ends distinct from those called *natural ends,* or *the ends of mechanical arts;* which, to distinguish them from the latter, may properly be called *moral ends;* the established connexions in nature with regard to the attainment of these latter ends, will be, properly speaking, the connexions which constitute means to moral ends; and the science of these means and ends will be properly called *moral philosophy.* And this philosophy will naturally divide itself into the same parts as natural philosophy does; *i.e.* into the part which investigates the connexions or laws of nature, and reduces effects into them; and the part which shews how certain ends may be attained by human art or action, in consequence of the settled laws of nature; the first of which is justly denominated a *theoretical,* and the other a *practical science.* So that as there are two parts in natural philosophy, one of which rests in the explication of phaenomena, by reducing them into laws of nature already found out by induction from experiments; and the other of which directs human labour in pursuing ends for the conveniency or ornament of life; in like manner, there are two parts of moral philosophy, one of which is employed in investigating <250> by experiments the laws according to which phaenomena of the moral kind are produced, and in reducing other phaenomena into these laws so ascertained; and the other consists in deducing rules for human conduct in the pursuit of certain moral ends from the established connexions and laws of nature relative to them.

It cannot be said, that we here take it for granted, without any proof, that there are *moral* ends and means; for in the sense we have hitherto used *moral,* we have taken nothing for granted, but that there are certain phaenomena or certain ends and means, which are distinct from those commonly called *natural, physical,* or *mechanical.* And hardly will it be called into question, that there are phaenomena, and means and ends, which do not fall within the definition of those which are the object of natural philosophy. Who will deny that there are phaenomena, means and ends relative to our understanding and temper; relative to progress in knowledge, to the acquisition of habits, to constitution of civil society, and many other such like effects, which do not all belong to what

What is meant by moral ends and means.

is properly called *natural philosophy?* In short, none will say that the regulation of our affections and actions, in order to promote our own happiness, or the common happiness of mankind, is not an end quite distinct from that proposed in physics. And this being granted, we have gained all we plead for at present, which is, that if there be other ends, for attaining to which there are established means by nature, besides those considered in natural philosophy, such as the regulation of our inward affections, &c; these may be called *moral ends,* to distinguish them from the objects of natural philosophy. And by whatever name they are called, they are a very proper subject of enquiry for man. For it must be granted in general, to be a very proper sub-<251>ject of human study, to enquire into all the good ends within human power, and into the established means, in order to the attainment of them. And all such establishments or connexions in nature, are, with regard to men, principles or laws, according to which they must act, if they would attain to certain ends; no end, of whatever kind, being otherwise attainable by us, than as it is the effect of certain means, or as there are certain laws constituting a certain order of operation, according to which it may be attained. All such connexions are therefore in the same sense laws of nature; and do no otherwise differ from one another, but as their respective distinct ends, physical and moral, differ. Let not, however, what hath been said be understood as if the laws of nature, with regard to the attainments of moral ends, had not a title to be called *moral laws* in another peculiar sense, which cannot belong to any other laws of nature. For we shall by and by see that they have. But if what hath been said be true, whatever other titles the laws of nature relative to moral ends, may, or may not deserve, it is certain that these laws highly merit our attention. And the following general conclusion, with regard to us, must, in consequence of what hath been premised, be incontrovertible.

SECTION III

The frame and constitution of man is a natural law to him.

That the frame and constitution of man, and the connexions of things relative to him and his actions; *i.e.* in one word, the natural consequences of human affections and actions within and without man, are a natural law to man. They limit, fix or settle the effects of his behaviour and conduct; they shew what are the different results of different manners of acting; and so determine what must be done to get certain goods, and what must be done, or not done, to avoid certain evils. <252> And man can no more alter these connexions of things, than he can alter the connexions upon which mechanical arts depend.

Now hence it follows, 1. That it is necessary for man to enquire into these connexions of things upon which his good or evil, his enjoyment or suffering, his happiness or misery depend, in order to attain to any goods. And, 2. That it is necessary for him to regulate his actions according to these connexions, in order to attain to any goods. And therefore these two may be called the primary laws of our nature: *viz.* the necessity we are in of knowing the connexions relative to our happiness and misery, and the necessity we are in of acting conformably to these connexions, in order to have pleasure and avoid pain. We may, if we will, call the necessary determination of every being capable of distinguishing pain from pleasure to pursue the one and avoid the other, the first law of nature. But it is more properly a determination essential to and inseparable from every reflecting being, and that which constitutes the necessity of its attending to the connexions of things relative to its happiness and misery, than a law or rule relative to the means of its happiness. The two first things therefore that offer themselves to our consideration with regard to beings capable of attaining to any goods, or of bringing any evils on themselves by their actions, are the necessity of understanding the connexions established by nature with regard to the effects or consequences of their actions, and the necessity of regulating their actions according to these fixed connexions.

SECTION IV

Now that all connexions of nature, of whatever kind, whether those respecting matter and motion, and mechanical powers and arts, or those respecting the consequences of our affections and actions, can only be learned from experience, by attention to the <253> effects of different methods of operation, is too evident to be insisted upon. And therefore

Whence this law is learned, and whence it comes.

we shall only add upon this head, that as when speaking of the laws of nature, which are the object of natural philosophy, tho' they are shortly called laws of matter and motion; yet by them is really meant constitutions and connexions established and taking place in consequence of the will of the Author of nature: so the moment we have found out any connexions relative to happiness or misery with regard to human affections and actions, we have found certain constitutions or connexions relative to them, established and taking place by virtue of the will and appointment of the Author of nature; so that tho', speaking shortly, we call them natural laws, or moral laws of nature, yet in reality by them must be meant rules, laws or connexions of the Author of nature. For this must be true in general, that certain setled and fixed orders and connexions of things can only take place by virtue of the will of some mind sufficient to give them subsistence and efficiency. Laws, whether in physics or in morals, can only mean certain appointments by the will of the mind who gave being to the world, and by whom it subsists. If by laws the appointments of some supreme Being be not meant, they are words without any meaning. So that we may henceforth indifferently say, either the connexions of things relative to man, the laws of nature relative to moral ends attainable by man, or the law and will of the Author of nature with regard to the consequences and effects of human conduct. This we may certainly do without begging any thing in morality which we have not proved, since natural philosophers use or may use these phrases promiscuously; and we as yet only desire to be allowed to use those phrases in the same sense they are used by natural philosophers, when they speak of means and ends, or connexions in nature, according to which effects are produced, <254> and human arts must operate in order to be successful.

May we not now therefore go on to enquire, if we can find out any of the more important connexions in nature relative to our good or happiness, which are the laws of our nature, or the laws of the Author of nature with regard to our conduct, that may be called moral laws, or laws relative to moral ends.

SECTION V

In order to this, it is plain we must enquire what affections belong to our nature. For nothing can be more evident, than that without particular affections no object could give us more pleasure than another, or to speak more properly, nothing could give us pleasure or pain: And the happiness of any one particular nature can only be the happiness or good of that particular nature. The happiness of an insect, for example, can only make an insect happy: Another nature, that is, a nature consisting of other affections, will require other objects to make it happy; that is, objects adjusted to the gratification of its particular affections. These things are very evident: For tho' after having experienced several particular pains and pleasures, we can form to ourselves a general idea of happiness, and a general idea of misery, which ideas will excite a general desire of happiness, yet there is no such thing in nature as general gratification to general desire of happiness. Every pleasure is a particular pleasure; a particular gratification to some particular affection. We may be properly said to desire happiness in general; but every gratification we meet with, is a gratification to some one particular appetite or affection in our nature. As our eyes are said to be so formed as to receive pleasure from colours; but yet it is always some particular colour or mixture of colours that gives us that pleasure we call pleasure <255> arising from colours; so it is with regard to all other pleasures. We may class pleasures under different general names, and say very intelligibly, we would have pleasure of such a sort; but in order to have our longing satisfied, some particular object must be applied to satisfy it: Or we may say more generally, we would have pleasure without fixing so much as upon a general class of pleasures, as pleasures of sight, of hearing, of smell, &c. But still it must be some particular object, suited to some particular affection, or particular sense of pleasure in our nature, that satisfies us in this undetermined longing or restlessness of the mind. In fine, however much philosophers talk of a general desire of happiness, and of our being actuated by this desire, which is properly called *self-love,* in all our pursuits; yet it is particular objects, adjusted to certain particular affections in our nature, that constitute our happiness. And it

Every being is constituted capable of a particular happiness, by the particular affections belonging to its nature.

is only by gratifying some one of these particular affections that we can have pleasure. Nor is it less evident that all our particular affections rest each in its object. "The very nature of affection (says an excellent writer)[1] consists in tending towards, and resting on its objects as an end. We do indeed often in common language say, that things are loved, desired, esteemed, not for themselves, but for somewhat further, somewhat out of and beyond them; yet in these cases, whoever will attend, will see that these things are not in reality the objects of the affections, *i.e.* are not loved, desired, esteemed, but the somewhat further out of and beyond them. If we have no affections which rest in what are called their objects, then what is called affection, love, desire, hope, in human nature, is only an uneasiness in being at rest, an unquiet disposition to action, progress and pursuit, without end or meaning. But if there be any such thing as delight in the company of one person rather than of another, whether in the <256> way of friendship, or mirth and entertainment, it is all one, if it be without respect to fortune, honour, or increasing our stores of knowledge, or any thing beyond the present time; here is an instance, of an affection absolutely resting in its object as its end, and being gratified in the same way as the appetite of hunger is satisfied with food. Yet nothing is more common than to hear it asked, what advantage a man hath in such a course, suppose of study, particular friendships, or in any other; nothing, I say is more common, than to hear such a question put, in a way which supposes no gain, advantage, or interest, but as a means to somewhat further: And if so, then there is no such thing at all as a real interest, gain or advantage. This is the same absurdity with respect to life, as an infinite series of effects without a cause is in speculation. The gain, advantage or interest consists in the delight itself arising from such a faculty's having its object: Neither is there any such thing as happiness or enjoyment but what arises from hence. The pleasures of hope and of reflexion are not exceptions. The former being only this happiness anticipated, the latter the same happiness enjoyed over again after its time. Self-love, or a general desire of happiness, is inseparable from all

1. Joseph Butler, sermon XIII, "Upon the Love of God," 259, in Butler, *Fifteen Sermons Preached at the Rolls Chapel*.

sensible creatures, who can reflect upon themselves, and their own interest or happiness, so as to make that interest an object to their minds. But self-love does not constitute this or that to be our interest or good; but our interest or good being constituted by nature, and supposed, self-love only puts upon gaining, or making use of those objects which are by nature adapted to afford us satisfaction. Happiness or satisfaction consists only in the enjoyment of those objects, which are by nature suited to our several particular appetites, passions and affections. And there is therefore a distinction between the cool principle of self-love, or general desire of our own happiness, as one part of <257> our nature, and one principle of action, and the particular affections towards particular objects as another part of our nature, and another principle of action, without which there could be absolutely no such thing at all as happiness or enjoyment of any kind whatsoever." From all which it follows, 1. That it is absurd to speak of self-love as engrossing the whole of our nature, and making the sole principle of action. And, 2. That in order to know what we ought to pursue, or what happiness we are capable of, it is absolutely necessary to know our particular affections which constitute our capacities of enjoyment or happiness, and the objects adapted by nature to them.

But why we have insisted so long on this observation, will appear when we come to mention several of our particular affections and their objects.

SECTION VI

Now, if we attend to ourselves, we shall find that we have affections of various kinds. 1. Affections to several sensible objects, adapted by nature to give us pleasure, which may be called *sensitive appetites,* some of which are absolutely necessary to put us upon pursuits requisite to our sustenance, or the support and preservation of our bodily frame, such as hunger and thirst, *&c:* and others which are not so necessary to that end, but are given us to be capacities of enjoyment, such as the pleasures we receive from light and colours by the eyes, and from sounds by the ear, *&c.* About these affections there is no dispute. 2. But these are not the

The particular affections belonging to human nature.

only affections belonging to our nature. We have other affections which are called *intellectual:* such as, a capacity of receiving pleasure by the discernment of the relations of ideas or things by our understanding or reason, properly called the perception of truth, or knowledge; a taste or sense of beauty, which may be defined to be that agreeable percep-<258>tion which objects that have uniformity amidst variety or regularity and unity of design, are adapted to afford us, *&c.* And, 3. Besides these there is yet another class of affections, which may be justly called *social.* Inclination to union and society, delight in the happiness of others, compassion toward the distressed or suffering, resentment against injustice or wrong, love of esteem or good reputation, desire of power to help and assist others, gratitude to benefactors, desire of friendship, and several other such like, which have some things in our fellow creatures for their objects. I do not pretend that this is a full enumeration of all the particular affections belonging to human nature. Some others shall be mentioned afterwards. But I am apt to think the principal affections constituting our nature, or our capacities of gratification and enjoyment, will be found to be reducible into one of these three classes. And let me observe with regard to them, before we go further, 1. That the greater part of these affections rest in some external object, and may therefore properly be said to have something without ourselves for their object, towards which they tend. As hunger hath food for its object, so hath the love of arts, arts for its object, and the love of reputation, reputation for its object; and as none of these objects is more or less external than another, and none of these affections is more or less distinct from self-love, or the general desire of happiness, than another; so benevolence, or delight in the good of another, hath an object which is neither more nor less external than the objects of those other above-named affections; and is an affection which is neither more nor less distinct from self-love than these other affections. And therefore all the grave perplexity with which moral writings have been tortured with respect to the interestedness and disinterestedness of certain affections, might as well have been objected against any other affections as against <259> those, the reality of which it hath been thought sufficient to explode, to say, that if they are allowed to take place in our frame, then would there be a disinterested principle of action in the nature of a being, which like every sensible being, can only be moved by self-love, or regard to itself, which is absurd. It is sufficient to evince the impertinence and absurdity of this jangling, to shew that by the same argument it may be proved, that we have no affections which tend towards and rest in external objects. And yet it is certain, that had we not particular affections towards external objects, there could absolutely be no such thing as happiness at all, or enjoyment of any kind. If by saying that all our affections must be interested, and that none of them can be disinterested, be meant that they are our own affections, and that the gratifications they afford us are gratifications to ourselves, our own pleasures, or our own perceptions, then are all our affections in that sense equally interested; they are all equally our own, for they are all equally felt by ourselves. But if by saying none of our affections are or can be disinterested, be meant, that none of our affections can tend towards, or rest in an external object: This is to say, not merely that the good of others cannot be the object of any affection in our nature; but to say that nothing without us can be the object of our desire, whether animate or inanimate, which none will assert. This I mention, because all the arguments brought by certain philosophers against a principle of benevolence in our nature, turn upon an imagined contrariety between such a principle and self-love, as a principle of action. But, 2. It is in the gratifications of these particular affections in our nature, that the greater part of the enjoyments of which we are made capable by nature consists. And therefore, if we would know the laws or connexions of nature with regard to our happiness, we must know the establish-<260>ed laws or connexions of nature with regard to these affections, and the objects adapted to them. That is, we must know in what manner and to what degree they give pleasure to us; what are the consequences of indulging any one of them too little or too much; the several tones and proportions nature hath prescribed to them, by fixing the boundaries of pain and pleasure; their relations one to another; their agreements or disagreements; their jarrings and interferings, or coalitions and mixtures; and, in one word, as many of their effects and consequences in different circumstances of action, as we can observe, in order to know how to regulate them, so as to have the greatest

pleasure and the least pain we can. The rules of our conduct, in order
to have happiness, can only be deduced from the laws or rules, according
to which, in consequence of the frame and constitution of our minds,
and the relations we stand in to external objects, our particular affections
operate, or are operated upon by objects, or by one another.

SECTION VII

It is the busi-
ness of reason
to know the
nature of our
affections, their
objects, and
the manner and
consequences
of their vari-
ous operations.

Now, it is the business of our reason to find out these rules or laws of
nature, and the rules of conduct which they indicate or point out to us.
Reason is as plainly given us for this purpose, as our eyes are given us for
seeing. It is the eye of the mind which is to look out for us in order to
direct our paths, *i.e.* to discover what we ought to pursue, and what we
ought to avoid. It must be given us for this purpose. And if we do not
exercise it to this purpose, it is of no use to us. It cannot be owned to
be implanted in us, without owning that it is the intention of nature
that it should be exercised by us as our guide and director. Nor is there
indeed any other way by which beings can be guided, who have reason
to discover how they ought to regulate their affections and actions, that
<261> is, how their happiness requires that they should regulate them,
besides their reason. Their nature admits of no other guidance. For in
this does the difference consist between them and other beings, which
have no reflecting or guiding principle, but are led by mere impulse toward an end, without foresight, intention or choice, that they have the
direction of themselves; and being endued with a principle of observation and reflexion, are left to its guidance. Beings without reason are
directed, or rather driven by particular affections excited in their minds
to pursuits, which can in no sense be called their pursuits, but are properly the pursuits of the principle by which their affections are excited in
them. But beings who have a reflecting and guiding principle in them,
are so constituted that they may and must guide themselves; and therefore their particular affections must necessarily be considered as subjected by their frame to their guiding principle as such. Their directing
principle must be considered as the superior and chief principle in them,
and that to which the direction, the rule, command or guidance of all

their particular affections, is committed by nature. And indeed, if we attend to our own minds, we shall find, 1. That our reason claims a superiority to itself, and talks to us (if I may so speak) with the authority of a law-giver or ruler. It often, whether we will or will not, takes to itself the power and authority of a judge, a censor, and pronounces sentence upon our conduct. And, 2. We are so framed that our greatest inward satisfaction depends upon the approbation of our reason, or our consciousness of our acting by its direction, and in conformity to its rules. Nothing gives us so much torment as the consciousness of despised and contradicted reason: and no pleasure is equal to that the mind feels when reason approves its conduct. The approbation with which a mind, conscious of its habitually giving the autho-<262>rity due to its guiding principle in the government of its affections and actions, applauds itself, is sincere and abiding satisfaction. So are we made: And therefore,

The first law of nature with regard to our conduct, is to maintain reason in our mind as our governing principle over all our affections and pursuits. It was said before (§3), that we are under a necessity of knowing the connexions relative to our happiness, in order to conform our conduct to them, and under a necessity of conforming our conduct to them in order to be happy. And we have just now seen what that principle is which is given us by nature, both to discover the connexions relative to our happiness, and to conform our conduct to them. Whence it follows, that according to our frame, we can neither be sure of avoiding evil, nor attaining to good, unless reason be our steady ruler; which implies two things. 1. That we be at due pains to know the connexions relative to our happiness, and to lay up this knowledge in our minds, in order to have counsel at hand upon every emergency: in order not to be surprized, and to have our directory to seek, when occasion calls upon us immediately to determine and act. And, 2. To accustom our particular affections to submit to, and receive their commands from our reason; not to sally forth at random upon every invitation offered to them by objects, but to await the decision of our reason, and to obey it. The first is the hability or sufficiency of reason to direct. The other is its actual command. And that reason may be very well informed, and consequently very well qualified to direct us, and yet not be actually our ruler and

The first law of nature with regard to our conduct, is to maintain reason in our mind as our guiding principle.

commander, but a slave to our headstrong passions, is too evident to experience to be denied. Nor is any one who hath ever given any attention to his own mind, a stranger to the only way in which rea-<263>son can become our habitual ruler and guide, and our affections become habitually subject to its government, which is the habitual accustomance or inurance of our appetites, affections and passions, to receive their orders from our reason, or the habitual upholding of our reason in the exercise of directing all our pursuits. And indeed to what purpose can the knowledge qualifying reason to direct our affections serve, but to upbraid us, if reason be not actually our habitual director; if our passions are quite tumultuous and undisciplined, and reason hath no power over them, to restrain, direct, or govern them? This therefore is the first law of nature pointed out by our constitution, and the necessity of nature, even to set up and maintain our reason as our governing or directing principle. Till this be done we are not masters of ourselves; and however well any one's affections may happen to operate, in consequence of a particular happiness of constitution, or in consequence of his necessary submission to others upon whom he depends, none can have a title to the character of rational, but in proportion as his own reason is his director and ruler; in proportion as his passions are submitted to reason, and he acts in obedience to its authority. But this rational temper may be called by different names, as it is considered in different views. It is prudence, as it discerns the connexions relative to our happiness, and the rules of our conduct resulting from thence. It is virtue or strength of mind, as it enables one to hold his passions in due discipline and subjection, and to act as prudence directs. It is self-love, as it is firm and steady adherence to the rules of happiness. It is self-command, as it is empire over ourselves, dominion over our affections and actions, all our choices and pursuits. And it is health or soundness of mind, as thus all our affections and appetites are in their regular, na-<264>tural and proper order, *i.e.* duly submitted to the principle to which the authority of guiding them is due. It is indeed the whole of virtue, human excellence or duty, as this empire being once obtained, all must go right; every affection will be duly obedient to the principle that ought to govern; and thus the mind will be conscious to itself of inward order and harmony, and of being in the state it ought to be in: for no other general definition of human excellence or duty can be given, but acting conformably to reason. But still it remains to be enquired what general rules for our conduct reason discovers to us.

SECTION VIII

We may however observe, before we go farther, 1. That unless the mind be early rendered of a temper for thinking and enquiring about the proper rules of conduct, it will not set itself to find them out, but will give up the reins to its affections, and be tossed to and fro by them in a most desultory irregular manner; and the longer this unthinking way of living takes place, the more difficult will it be to recover the mind from the tyranny of its passions, and to establish reason into its due authority and command over them. And therefore the great end of education ought to be to produce the love and patience of thinking; to establish the deliberative disposition and temper, or the habit of consulting reason, and weighing things maturely before one chooses and determines. This is the chief end of education. And if one be not obliged to wise education for this happy temper of mind, it seldom happens that one ever attains to it, till he is awakened and roused to think, by some great suffering brought upon himself, by his not having exercised his reason, but suffered his passions and appetites to drive him whithersoever they listed. The reason is, that by repeated acts, habits are formed, <265> which it is exceeding difficult to undo, and which cannot be undone but by the strong opposition of reason. And therefore, if the habit of ruling ourselves by reason, be not early formed in us by right education, the habit of indulging every passion and appetite that assails us, and of living without exercising our reason, must soon become too fixed, settled and inveterate to be easily conquered. It is fit, highly fit, nay absolutely necessary for us, that the law of habits should take place in our constitution. Yet this must be the effect of it, that unless great care be taken, by proper education and discipline, early to form the reflecting and considering habit, in young minds, which is to establish the government of reason in them, it must be extremely difficult for us ever to become reasonable

It ought to be the end of education to produce the patience of thinking, or the government of reason.

creatures, or to attain to self-command, and to establish our reason as our ruler and guide, in the room of appetite, humour and passion. Mr. Locke hath made admirable observations on this subject, in his excellent treatise of education.[2]

When this temper is formed, happiness and duty are easily discovered.

But, 2. When the love and patience of thinking are once attained, and the sedate, deliberative temper is fairly established, it is then very easy to find out the proper rules of action, or what is the most eligible course of life and behaviour, and how the affections ought to be governed. The affections then range themselves, as it were, spontaneously into good order. The understanding is then clear and undisturbed, and duty is easily discerned. Whatever difficulty reason may find in establishing its authority, it is no sooner fixed and settled in the mind, as the ruling and commanding principle, than the rules which ought to be observed in conduct are immediately discovered. True happiness is then immediately felt to consist chiefly in the very consciousness of this temper, in the consciousness of reason's having this sway within us. And when this is looked upon to be the chief part of <266> happiness, the chief part of our happiness is then something dependent upon ourselves, which nothing can deprive us of, while reason presides and rules in our breast. A source of inward consolation, far superior to all other enjoyments, and which is as steady as all other things are uncertain, is thus discovered. And the mind, which hath once fixed upon this as its main good, will be proof against all the most specious appearances of pleasures, till their pretentions have been examined, and their consistency with this chief principle of happiness hath been duly considered; and will therefore be a calm and impartial judge of what pleasures it may allow itself, and of what it ought not to give indulgence to. But if the mind be calm and unbiassed, and resolved to act the part that shall appear wisest and best upon due attention to the laws of nature fixing the connexions relative to our happiness, the whole difficulty is over. Till then it is not capable of judging; but when that point is gained, it is very easy to judge right. In every case, not to judge, but to be fit to judge, is the difficult part. The first thing therefore that our frame and consti-

2. Locke, *Some Thoughts Concerning Education,* pp. 142–43.

tution points out to us as the law of our conduct, is to take care to establish reason in our mind, as the ruler, without consulting which we will not allow our passions to indulge themselves, and the dictates of which we are resolved steadily to obey, that we may always enjoy that delightful consciousness of having been guided by our reason, which is by our make the greatest of all enjoyments. But to this education ought, and must contribute; otherwise the establishment of this excellent temper, in proportion to the prevalence of which one is more or less a reasonable being, must be a very difficult, a very hard task; and to assist in conquering the contrary habit, distress and suffering will be necessary. And why should we not look upon the evils that are brought upon ourselves by thoughtlessness, <267> folly, or, in one word, by not governing ourselves by reason, to be intended chiefly for this very end; even to awaken, rouze, and excite us to think, by making us feel the necessity of exercising our reason, and obeying it, instead of indulging every appetite that assails us, without considering the consequences of living in such an irrational manner! For this is self-evident, that were not agents placed in a state where certain manners of acting produce good, and others evil, there would in such a state be no place for choice and agency; for prudence and imprudence; nor consequently, for reason and self-approbation. And therefore to the existence of the highest rank of created beings, it is necessary that certain methods of acting be attended with evil consequences. For tho' we may, by adding more and more to our own active powers, conceive various species of created agents above us, till we rise in our contemplation to the Supreme Being, in whom all perfections meet, and are united in their highest degree; yet we can conceive no order of beings above mere passive ones, without conceiving them to be disposers of their own actions by their reason, understanding and choice: And as for more or less, *i.e.* a larger or lesser sphere of activity, here the known rule takes place, *That more and less do not alter the species.* If any one should ask what the proper method of education is in order to produce the reasonable thinking temper? it is sufficient to answer here, that the chief business is to accustom youth early to examine the associations of ideas in their minds, and to consider whether these associations be founded in, and agreeable to nature, or not; which ought to be the unintermitted exercise during life of every one who would maintain the empire of his reason. But because this would lead me into a digression, or rather into a subject, for which we have not yet sufficiently prepared the way, we shall only refer those who ask this question <268> to the above mentioned treatise of Mr. Locke, and go on to take notice of some particular laws of our conduct, pointed out to us by the make of the human mind, and the circumstances in which we are placed by the Author of nature.

SECTION IX

The first particular law which appears to those who consider the nature and circumstances of mankind is the law of industry.

The pleasures we are capable of, are gratifications to our particular affections, the principal of which have been named (§6); for hardly can any enjoyment we are susceptible of, be specified, which is not a gratification of one or other of these outward or inward faculties or senses of pleasure. Our pleasures may therefore be divided into two classes; the goods of the body, and the goods of the mind. For all our affections, all our senses of pleasure, either have some sensitive, or some intellectual and moral gratification for their objects. Gratification to our eyes, our ears, our touch, and our other organs of sense, are bodily gratifications. Gratifications to our discernment of truth, and our delight in it; to our taste of beauty and harmony and delight in it; to our public sense, or our delight in the happiness of others, &c. are gratifications to capacities, senses of pleasure, or affections, which, to distinguish them from those afforded by corporeal objects to our sensitive organs, may be called *intellectual* or *moral,* or *goods of the mind.* But however the goods or pleasures we are capable of be divided or classed, this is certain, with regard to them all, that they are made to be the purchase of our activity or industry to have them; they do not drop into the mouth (if we may so speak) of the sluggard; but we must exert ourselves to attain to them. As we cannot otherwise have the pleasures of sense, or the goods of the body; so no more can we, without industry and application, have the pleasures of knowledge, refined taste, benevolence, &c. And hence that antient observation concern-<269>ing the government or frame of the world with respect to man; θεοι τἀγαθα τοὶς πονοις πολοῦνται. *God or nature sells all to industry.*[3] This truth is so plain to daily experience, that we need not stay to prove it. But from this general law of nature arises a law to us, *viz.* the law of industry; or the necessity of our activity, application or industry, in order to attain to any goods. And if we will reflect a little upon our minds, we shall find, that as no goods can be attained by us, but by exerting ourselves actively to have them; so activity or exercise is necessary to our happiness in another sense, *i.e.* immediately, or in itself. The mind of man is made for exercise, exercise is its natural pleasure. It is of a restless temper, and must be employed. If it is not, it preys upon, and consumes itself. Nor is exercise less necessary to the health, soundness, vigour, and agreeable feeling of the body, than employment is to the strength, agility, soundness, and pleasant state of the mind. We need not insist long to prove this; for daily experience shews, that as it happens among mankind, that whilst some are by necessity confined to labour, others are provided with abundance of things by the industry and labour of others; so if, among the superior and easy sort, who are thus relieved from bodily drudgery, there be not something of fit and proper employment raised in the room of what is wanting in common labour; if, instead of an application to any sort of work, such as hath an useful end in society (as letters, sciences, arts, husbandry, public affairs, &c.) there be a thorough neglect of all study or employment, a settled idleness, supineness and inactivity; this does of necessity occasion a most uneasy, as well as disorderly state of mind; a total dissolution of its natural vigour, which ends in peevishness, discontent, and sickly nauseating at life, and all its enjoyments. So necessary is some employment to the mind, that to supply exercise to <270> it, many strange amusements and unaccountable occupations for time, thought, and passion have been invented by those, whom fortune hath rescued from drudgery to their backs and bellies, but good education hath not

3. "The Gods sell good things in exchange for toil": Turnbull's Greek appears not to be accurate, but this is probably a phrase attributed to Epicharmus by Xenophon in his *Memorabilia* 2.1.20. Xenophon, *Memorabilia and Oeconomicus*. We are very grateful to Dr. Antony Hatzistavrou for identifying the probable source of this quotation.

directed into proper pursuits and employments, which are their only security against utter discontent with themselves, and every thing about them, amidst the greatest abundance. Such strange occupations are their sole relief. But they are such only as they are some exercise to the mind, and prevent that languishing, fretting and nauseating, which total supineness and ease produces. And how feeble a security they are against the misery, which employment more suited to a mind capable of higher pursuits would absolutely prevent, is plain from the many bitter, sickly, discontented moments the men of pleasure, as they are absurdly called, cannot, by all their amusements, escape, compared with the equable contentedness of an honest daily labourer, conscious of the usefulness of his toil; not to mention the sedate, uniform satisfaction and cheerfulness of one, who having qualified himself for it, divides (as Scipio is said to have done) his time between elegant studies and public services to his country. The mind of man must have exercise and employment. Exercise itself is agreeable, and it is absolutely necessary to relief from the greatest of uneasinesses. And no goods can be attained without application and industry. If one would preserve his health and relish for sensitive pleasures, he must exercise his body. And if he would have the pleasures of knowledge, of refined imagination and good taste, the pleasures of power and authority, or the pleasures of benevolence and doing good, he must be diligent in the culture of his moral powers, and be ever intent upon some truly useful pursuit. If these ends do not employ him, he must either find other pursuits for himself, or he will be exceedingly unhappy. But <271> what other pursuits can one devise to himself besides those of which he can say any thing better, than that they employ his mind, and keep time from hanging upon his hands, as the phrase is, or, more properly speaking, murder it? Can he name any other besides those that bear any congruity to the more noble and distinguishing powers and affections of the human mind? or that he can depend upon for steady and uncloying satisfaction? any other that can be re-enjoyed by reflection? any other that will stand a cool and serious review and examination?

But that I may not be thought to proceed too fast in my conclusions, and to have determined concerning the comparative value of pursuits too hastily, all I desire to have concluded at present, is, that according to the constitution of the human mind, and in consequence of the natural state of things, no goods, no enjoyments can be procured by us without application and industry, and that we are made to be busied and employed for exercise, or to be engaged in some pursuit. The greatest abundance of outward things, tho' it relieves from certain toils, to which the necessities of life subject others; yet it does not, it cannot make one happy, if, in the room of the pursuits from which it delivers him, he do not find out some other satisfactory pursuit or employment for himself. Under this necessity hath nature laid us; nay, properly speaking, this necessity constitutes our dignity above inactive, or merely passive creatures, as free agents. For it is implied in the very notion of agency. One cannot otherwise be an agent, than as he is made to procure his happiness to himself by the active application of his powers in the pursuit of goods within his reach, if laboured for according to the way nature hath fixed and chalked out for attaining to them. And as the pleasure of considering goods as one's own acquisition, is a pleasure that a being must be so framed to have; so <272> this is a very high satisfaction, and an excellent natural reward to industry. How insipid are the satisfactions in which this is not an ingredient, in comparison of those which one owes to his own skill, prudence and industry, and in which he therefore triumphs as his own purchase, his own conquest, the product of his own abilities and virtues! 'Tis only beings so framed as that they must work out their own happiness, who can be capable of self-approbation. And who doth not feel the difference with which one reflects on the goods which are not of his own procurance to himself, such as beauty and the advantages of birth, for instance, and those accomplishments which he can vindicate to himself as his own proper purchase? And where self-approbation can take place, there only can good desert, with regard to others, take place; or can there be any foundation for praise and esteem from others, without which, how dull and insipid would life be? This is the general voice of mankind.

> *Ergo ut miremur te, non tua, primum aliquid da*
> *Quod possim titulis incidere praeter honores*
> *Quos illis damus, & dedimus, quibus omnia debes.*[4]

4. "So if I'm to be impressed by you and not your heritage, offer me something

Thus far then are we advanced in finding out the connexions or laws of nature with regard to our happiness. We are made to work out our own happiness by our industry; we are made for activity and exercise. But how ought our industry to be directed, in consequence of what hath been observed concerning the presidence which reason ought to have in our minds (§8)? Must not the objects of our industry be chosen by reason, and all our exercises directed by it, in order to our having the satisfaction of reflecting upon our exercise as conformable to reason; and that it may be agreeable to the connexions of nature relative to our happiness; and so prove neither vain nor hurtful but turn to good account, and not produce repentance and suf-<273>fering for having mistaken our end, and misapplied our labour and diligence; but contentment with ourselves for having acted with prudence, by the direction of reason for an approveable end, and in the proper manner for attaining that end. This therefore is one characteristic of our proper happiness, that it consists in a course of industry to attain ends which reason approves, under the direction and guidance of reason, as to the use of means.

SECTION X

The second particular law that appears from the consideration of human nature, and the circumstances in which mankind are placed, is the law of sociality. But another special characteristic of our proper pursuits, in consequence of our frame, and the connexions of nature relative to our happiness, will immediately appear, if we reflect how strictly mankind are bound together; by how many close ties and dependencies they are cemented; ties arising from mutual wants, and ties arising from certain affections common to mankind, exactly corresponding to their mutual wants. First of all, it is evident, that we can attain to no goods of whatever kind, external or internal, by our single industry, or without social assistances. Nothing can be more manifest than this. 2. Nor is it less evident, that there is no enjoyment, of which mankind are capable, which does not, as our excellent poet very happily expresses it, *Some may lean and hearken*

---

personal, something I can inscribe in your record of achievement, apart from those titles which we gave and (continue to give) to those men to whom you owe everything" (Juvenal, *Juvenal and Persius,* Satire 8, lines 68–70).

to our kind.[5] If we separate communication and participation from all our pleasures of whatever kind, we really abstract from them the main ingredient that gives them relish. Take all of the social kind away from sensitive gratifications, and what remains but mere allay to some raging appetite, mere relief from pain? And as for all our other pleasures, what are they but participation, or communicating and sharing with our fellow creatures? Such is the joy of relieving the distressed, or of promoting the happiness of the deserving. <274> Such is a sense of merited esteem; such is gratitude to a benefactor; such is creating dependence upon us, &c. And as for knowledge, however pleasant it is in itself, yet is it not doubly agreeable, when considered as qualifying us to be useful, and as procuring us authority and regard? In short, the chief article in all our pleasures, in consequence of our make, consists in mutually giving and receiving; it is of a social kind. And we are formed, and placed as we are, that there might be variety of exercise to our social affections. Nature hath so framed us, that our chief happiness must be sought from communication and participation with others; and so placed us, that all such dependencies might arise as were necessary to gratify our social appetites and affections. This will more fully appear afterwards, when we come to consider some of the principal dependencies by which mankind are united and cemented together; which, tho' they be objected against by narrow thinkers,[6] will be found to be in reality so many proofs of nature's kind care about us; or to make proper provision for the exercises, from which alone our social happiness, or gratification to our social affections can arise, since it must consist in mutual giving and receiving, which cannot take place but where there are mutual dependencies. Mean time, let it only be observed, 1. That such is the constitution of things with respect to mankind, that no man can attain to any considerable share of the goods either of the body or of the mind by his single endeavours;

5. "Some may lean and hearken to our kind." Turnbull uses a similar phrase in his *Observations upon Liberal Education,* 99.

6. Presumably Turnbull has Thomas Hobbes in mind, since he denied that a natural sense of benevolence would allow for man's security and happiness. See *Leviathan,* chap. 13.

but he must, in order to that, engage many others to help and assist him: nay, such is the constitution of things, that no man can subsist in any convenient, not to say comfortable degree or manner, without receiving many services and good offices from others. Mankind are therefore, by the necessity of nature, obliged to seek mutual assistances from one another, to unite together, and to com-<275>municate their industry. But, 2. Mankind are so framed, that this union and communication is in itself as agreeable as it is necessary. Our best enjoyments are acts of social communication. Assisting, relieving, herding, concerting, confederating, and such like social dealings, are all of them in themselves most pleasing and agreeable exercises. So that there is something in them that rewards them, and invites to them independently of their necessity to our having any of the conveniencies or comforts of life. Need I stay to prove this to any one who hath ever felt any of the generous emotions and workings of the soul? or to any one who can reflect upon his having at any time done a good office? For nothing is more certain, than that it is only acts of compassion, humanity, friendship, gratitude, benevolence, that afford any considerable satisfaction to the mind upon reflexion; or that it is the generous mind alone that can reiterate its actions in its reflexion, memory, or conscience, (let it be called what you will) with thorough delight; and thus feast most agreeably upon them after they are past. Indeed so social is our make, that the highest entertainment even the poetic art or ingenious fictions can give us, is by exciting generous benevolent emotions in our minds, and deeply interesting us in the affairs of others. For of the satisfaction we receive in this way, which we so readily own to be preferable to any mere sensitive enjoyment, no other account can be given but this; *"Homo sum, & nihil humanum a me alienum puto."*[7] Whatever concerns man, tenderly interests every man in it, in consequence of the human make. We are therefore formed by nature for social exercises; for the pursuit of public good; for offices of benevolence or charity, and for uniting together in the interchange of various acts of kindness and sociality.

7. "I'm human, and I regard no human business as other people's": Terence, *The Self-tormentor* (*Heauton timoroumenos*), act 1, scene 1, line 77, in *Terence,* vol. 1.

And thus there appears another character of the happiness and the employment or industry we are <276> intended for by nature: It is industry beneficial to mankind, for which we are framed and intended: Industry proper to make human life as comfortable and agreeable as it can be rendered. For this is the industry or employment, which, in consequence of our social make, gives us the greatest pleasure. And this industry alone can give a satisfying account of itself to our reason. For this also is found to be true by experience, that no sooner is the idea of industry beneficial to mankind, or of activity to relieve mankind from as many pains, and to give them as much pleasure as we can; no sooner is this idea presented to our reflexion, than our mind is necessarily determined to approve of it, and pronounce it the best part, nay the only commendable, worthy part one can act. And therefore we have now attained to a very distinguishing characteristic of the pleasures we ought to pursue, *i.e.* of those which are made by nature of the highest, the most uncloying, satisfactory and durable relish to us, *viz.* exercises of our abilities or powers, which tend to promote the public good. If it is said that there is no reasoning in all this deduction, but simply appeal to experience: let me ask how we can prove any quality, affection or power to belong to us, or any sensation to be pleasant, but from experience? What are all the conclusions of natural philosophers, but inductions from experience, the experience of our senses? And is outward experience a proper proof of matters of outward experience; and inward experience not a proper proof of matters of inward experience? If it is objected, that experience proves that some men have high pleasure in acts of cruelty and malice: to this I answer, the gradual degeneracy of the mind into savageness and malignity, can be accounted for from the laws according to which social affections, and a moral or public sense are impaired and corrupted. But that any degree of this state of mind <277> cannot be happiness, is plain, since where there is a total apostacy, an absolute degeneracy from all candour, equity and trust, sociableness or friendship, there is none who will not acknowledge the absolute misery of such a temper of mind. For sure here, as in other distempers, the calamity must of necessity keep pace and hold proportion with the disease, the corruption. It is impossible that it can be complete misery, to be absolutely immoral and inhumane, and not be proportionable misery or ill, to be so in any however so small a degree. And indeed, tho' there were no considerable ill in any single exercise of inhumanity and unsociality, yet it must be contrary to interest, as it necessarily tends, in consequence of the structure of our minds, that is, the dependence of our affections, and the law of habits, to bring on the habitual temper, which is so readily owned by every one to be consummate misery, and to render incapable of any enjoyment, even amidst the most luxurious circumstances of sensitive gratification. But having insisted very fully on this subject in another treatise;[8] and chiefly, because it is impossible to set the sociability of our nature in a clearer and stronger light than my Lord Shaftsbury has done, in his *Essay on virtue,*[9] I shall only add, that if it be really true (as I think he has demonstrated) that, in consequence of the constitution of the human mind, and of the connexions relative to our happiness, the affections which work towards public good do likewise work towards the greatest good of every individual, then are we by a necessity of nature under obligation to be social, humane, and well affectioned towards our kind: And consequently, sociality is a law of nature to us. For this being the case, in it hath nature, whose constitutions we cannot alter, placed our chief happiness. But this general truth will be yet more evident, when we consider the particular dependencies by which mankind are strictly linked and tied together. <278>

SECTION XI

The natural and necessary dependence of mankind, points out to us the order in which our social affections ought to operate.

Which we now proceed to point out, that we may shew the particular order in which nature at once impels and obliges us to exercise and gratify our social affections. Nature may, as we have already seen, be very properly said to oblige, or lay us under a necessity of regulating our affections and actions in the way that the constitution of our mind, and the circumstances in which we are placed, make necessary to our happiness. And nature may be said to impel us to exert our affections in the way in

---

8. Turnbull, *Principles of Moral Philosophy.*
9. Shaftesbury, *An Enquiry Concerning Virtue or Merit* [1699], in Shaftesbury, *Characteristics of Men, Manners, Opinions, Times.*

which they naturally tend to work or exert themselves. And if we attend to our affections, and the order in which they naturally tend to operate or exert themselves, we will find that it is that very order which our constitution and circumstances make necessary to our well being and happiness; so exactly are our constitution and our circumstances adapted the one to the other. It is plain that social affections could not have their proper exercises, except where many mutual dependencies take place; because giving and receiving, or communication, can not take place but where there are mutual wants. Now, our mutual wants and dependencies must be wants and dependencies either with respect to the goods of the body, or the goods of the mind. For all our goods, as hath been observed (§9), are reducible into these two classes: Wherefore, mutual wants and dependencies in these respects, are necessary to the exercises of our social affections, or to our social enjoyments. Take away from mankind all the exercises of social affection, and we reduce them into a state of mere indolence and inactivity, and leave nothing in human life to employ men agreeably, or actuate them warmly or strongly: We take away all that gives the highest relish to life, all its most touching and interesting exercises and employments. But if we take away the objects of af-<279>fections or exercises, we to all intents and purposes destroy the affections themselves; for it is to all intents and purposes the same, whether they do not take place in a constitution, or taking place, have not objects to call them forth into action and employ them. The differences therefore which obtain among mankind, in consequence of the different talents, genius's and temperatures of mind, or of different circumstances, necessarily occasioning different operations, various degrees and turns of the same powers and affections, do indeed serve to cement and unite mankind together, and to produce a constitution of things, in which alone our social affections can have various proper exercises; a constitution of things, in which alone various social enjoyments can take place. And therefore, with regard to us,

All nature's diff'rence keeps all nature's peace.[10]

10. Pope, *An Essay on Man,* epistle IV, 56.

Several of
these depen-
dencies, and
the affections
corresponding
to them
explained.

This will be evident, if we but consider what the affections and employments are which give us social enjoyment. For how can benevolence,
love of power, compassion, charity, gratitude, or any other affection,
which hath the qualities, conditions, and actions of others for their objects, take place but where wants are supplied, dependence is created,
happiness is given; or where beings can mutually gratify one another in
various manners, by mutually adding to one another's happiness and
enjoyment, or alleviating one another's pains? But it will still be more
evident, when we consider the dependencies which actually obtain
among mankind, and the affections in human nature, corresponding to
these dependencies. Now, 1. In general, to the very support of our bodies,
many labours are necessary, and consequently, various communications
of labour: nor are various united labours less necessary to our having the
pleasures which arise from knowledge, and the improvements of the
understanding and ima-<280>gination. These two facts are too evident
to stand in need of any proof. And in order to our having enjoyments
of both these kinds by united labours, mankind are endued with various
talents, various genius's and turns of mind. Some are fitted for one kind
of labour and employment, and some for another. Every one stands in
need of many, and every one is peculiarly adapted by nature to assist the
rest in some particular way. It is in order to promote a general commerce
among mankind, that through the whole globe, the habitation of mankind, every climate, every country, produces something peculiar to it,
which is necessary to the greater convenience, or at least to the greater
comfort and ornament of the inhabitants in every other. So in every
country, throughout all mankind in general, there prevails a division of
talents, genius's and abilities, which makes every one necessary in a particular way to the general good, or at least renders every one capable of
contributing something towards general happiness, by the application
of his talents in their proper way, or to the end for which they are peculiarly adapted. And indeed in the narrowest view we can take of human happiness, that is, even when we confine it to our bodily subsistence, to eating, drinking, protection against the injuries of weather, and
such other conveniencies, which will be readily acknowledged not to be
all that mankind are qualified to have and enjoy, even tho' we should

quite abstract from the higher pursuits of understanding and imagination, in the improvements of arts and sciences, from every thing that comes under the notion of ornament, elegancy or grandeur; yet even in this confined view, many labours, various industry is necessary. And consequently, men are laid by a necessity of nature under obligation mutually to engage one another, to unite their labours, and communicate their industry for one another's subsistence. But as men would <281> have but very little pleasure in labour, and the communications of their industry which are necessary to their subsistence, were not exercise, as hath been observed (§9), naturally agreeable to men, and were we not so constituted as to have immediate pleasure in social communication, in every social exercise; so men, as we are constituted, cannot engage one another in mutual assistance, but by shewing each his willingness to assist the rest, and his sincere cordial regard to the well-being and interest of the whole body. Every one, in order to be liked and regarded by others, must at least put on the shew of liking and regarding others; for one would otherwise be looked upon as a common enemy, and as such be abandoned, nay, hated and persecuted by all men. And let me just observe here, in opposition to those who assert that there is not really any benevolence or regard to the interests of others in human nature, but that it is self-love which assumes the affected appearance of it, in order to deceive, well knowing the necessity of seeming to love others, in order to be assisted by them, as our necessities require.[11] Let me observe, that were there not generally prevailing among mankind a real principle of sociality and benevolence, this imposition, this counterfeit regard to others, would not be able to answer its end. Were all men utterly devoid of any such principle, and were the appearance of sociality every where counterfeited, the false appearance would nowhere take; it would nowhere be believed, and nothing like trust, or harmony and union could prevail among mankind, but they would live in continual jealousies and

11. Turnbull is again criticizing Hobbes and Mandeville. See, for example, Hobbes, *Leviathan,* chap. 13; Mandeville, "A Search into the Nature of Society," in *The Fable of the Bees,* vol. I, 344, and Mandeville, "Dialogue between Horatio, Cleomenes, and Fulvia," in *The Fable of the Bees,* vol. II, 132.

suspicions. So that of necessity it must be owned, that there is in the generality of mankind naturally a real principle of sociality and benevolence. This is plain from the necessary effect of one's being discovered to have acted under a mask of benevolence and honest regard to others; for in that case, hardly can any power or <282> strength such a person may have acquired, protect him against just resentment. Such a one must indeed be strongly defended to secure himself against the condign vengeance of mankind. And whatever his power may be, in consequence of his wrath and guards, or armies attached to him by his wealth, hanging upon him by the teeth (to use the phrase of a very great author),[12] yet he cannot avoid being hated by all the rest, and he cannot be loved even by them who are thus tied to him: And consequently, it is no wonder, that every one of this character, and in this situation with regard to mankind, in consequence of his known character, hath ever been found most compleatly miserable; tormented by galling fears, suspicions and jealousies. There never was a tyrant who was not in this terrible condition, as Cicero observes, Offices, book 2.[13]

Dependencies and correspondent affections considered.

Mankind then are not only under a necessity by nature of being social, but they are actually provided with affections which make them such, as well as with the various talents necessary to a variety of industry, and communication of industry. So that thus far nature obliges and impels to the same course of life, *viz.* a course of social industry and communication, a course of honest and cordial interchanges of mutual assistances and services. 2. But besides this general dependence diffused throughout the whole species, there are dependencies of another kind

---

12. "Hanging upon him by the teeth." This phrase is derived from James Harrington's *Oceana:* "To begin with riches, in regard that men are hung upon these, not of choice as upon the other [that is, authority], but of necessity and by the teeth: for as much as he who wanteth bread is his servant that will feed him, if a man thus feed an whole people, they are under his empire," Harrington, *Political Works,* 163. Harrington distinguishes between "authority" and "power." The former is based on "prudence, or the reputation of prudence." Contrary to Hobbes, however, Harrington believes that this authority is insufficient as a basis of political power, which must rest on "riches," in particular land ownership. See the discussion in Fukuda, *Sovereignty and the Sword.*

13. Cicero, *De officiis* 2.7.23–26.

among mankind, to which likewise there are correspondent affections in human nature, that without such dependencies would not have exercise or employment. The Author of nature hath spread over mankind a natural aristocracy, which appears in every assembly of mankind. Some are superior in understanding to the greater part, in every casual or designed meeting of men, consisting of suppose ten, twenty, or any other number. And what is the natural effect of this, in consequence of the hu-<283>man frame? Superiority in wisdom, by fitting to give proper counsel in matters of common concernment, naturally produces esteem, veneration, submission, and gratitude in those who feel the benefit of their superior wisdom, or to whom it serves as a light to direct them; that is, it gives authority to the men of superior wisdom; and it excites cordial dependence and confidence upon them in the breasts of those who reap the advantages of it. And thus those who excel in wisdom, have the pleasure of having authority and respect paid to them. And those who receive counsel and direction from them, have the pleasure of being instructed by them, and the sincere satisfaction which arises from gratitude and affection to benefactors, which is naturally so strong, that it is hard to say who are happiest, those who give, or those who receive. This we may observe, from the pleasure with which youth receive information from a prudent affectionate teacher: and in general, from the warm and zealous affection with which persons obliged attach themselves to a wise and generous patron, follow his directions: and espouse his interest.

> Condition, circumstance is not the thing:
> Bliss is the same, in subject or in king,
> In who obtain defence, or who defend,
> In him who is, or him who finds a friend.
>
> Essay on man.[14]

But let it be observed, that this is only the case while those of superior parts shew a sincere regard in their counsels and directions to the general good; and do not attempt to deceive those who depend upon them into

14. Pope, *An Essay on Man*, epistle IV, 57–60.

hurtful measures, with a selfish narrow view. For so soon as that is perceived, veneration is changed into contempt and hatred. And thus the superior in parts deprives himself of one chief reward of superior prudence, which is, the authority, leading and dependence it would other-<284>wise give him. History is full of instances, which are so many clear proofs of this. The Roman history in particular, in the language of which republic, as an excellent author hath observed, the influence of superiority in wisdom united with benevolence, was called *auctoritas patrum;* and the veneration paid by the people to it was called *verecundia plebis.*[15] There is in every man naturally a desire of power. It indeed enlarges and becomes stronger, in proportion as the mind enlarges and opens. But it is so strong, even in the meanest, that unless they depend, or hang upon others by the teeth, they may be led, but they will not be driven. If nature had not implanted in all men a desire of power, and a strong sensibility to wrong and injury, the veneration which superiority in parts naturally inspires, would have rendered the generality of mankind, who stand in need of leading and direction, too submissive, too tame and humble. But notwithstanding the natural aristocracy diffused over mankind, yet such is the general temper of mankind, that not only superiority in parts, without benevolence, will not gain respect and submission, but even a stricter and closer dependence will hardly be able to keep men in subjection when power over them is abused, if it can by any means be shaken off. 3. And this leads me to take notice of another kind of dependence among mankind; a dependence necessarily resulting from inequality in property. I need not stay to prove that earth, the habitation of men, being given by nature to be possessed and appropriated by the industry of the first occupants, the world could no sooner be tolerably well peopled, but in every district there would be inequality of property. I need not stay to prove how this would naturally happen in consequence of the manner in which mankind is propagated by successive generations, the natural aristocracy among mankind, which <285> hath been mentioned, and other causes; nor to shew what revolutions in property, commerce, not

---

15. *Auctoritas patrum* is the "authority of the fathers," *verecundia plebis* the "reverence of the people." See Harrington, "The Prerogative of Popular Government," bk. I, chap. v., p. 416, in *Political Works.*

to mention force, will naturally be ever bringing about, where the balance of property is not fixed by civil laws and constitutions; far less need I stay to prove that an over-balance of property will produce power or dominion proportional to it. These things have been sufficiently explained by the most ingenious Harrington.[16] All that it belongs to our present purpose to observe with relation to it, is, that as inferiorities and superiorities, with regard to the good of the body as well as of the mind, are necessary to social communication; necessary to make mankind mutually dependent, or to lay a foundation for mutual giving and receiving; so, with respect to external dependencies, or hanging by the teeth, that must necessarily take place among mankind in consequence of unequal property, men are furnished by nature with all the affections such dependencies require, in order to render them a means of agreeable union and coherence, or to found upon them very various social commerce. For, 1. Men have a principle of benevolence to excite them to take delight in doing good, and in being serviceable to one another. And, 2. They have a sensibility to oppression and injustice, which impels them to ward against injury, and resent it with great vehemence. Wherefore, as without some sort of dependencies there could be no such thing as social commerce; so mankind could not be better provided by nature than they are for reaping all the advantages of mutual dependencies, and for securing themselves against all the inconveniencies that can arise from mutual dependency. And as reciprocal dependence lays mankind under a necessity of social communication; so the natural affections with which men are endued, point out to us the manner in which social communication ought to be carried on. For benevolence <286> naturally produces love and gratitude. But no one can be so powerful as not to want assistance in many respects; and the indignation against injury, and aversion to slavery or absolute subjection, natural to mankind, will render power very ineffectual to true happiness without benevolence. Since that alone can excite love, affection, trust, or esteem; and he who knows himself to be hated and despised, must be very unhappy amidst the greatest

16. Harrington argued that political power depended on the distribution of wealth, especially landed property. See note 12, p. 583.

affluence of outward enjoyments, as well as very unsecure of long possessing them. Thus therefore nature hath made the exercises of benevolence, good-will, compassion, generosity, gratitude, fidelity, integrity and friendship, to be, in every respect, the happiness of mankind, and the happiness of every individual. And therefore, of the mutual wants and dependencies among mankind, which some look upon as an objection against the good government of the world, it may justly be said,

> *To these we owe true friendship, love sincere,*
> *Each home-felt joy which life inherits here.*

Essay on man.[17]

But this will yet more clearly appear, when we consider, 4. The necessary dependence of children upon their parents, in consequence of the manner in which nature hath appointed the propagation of mankind, and the affections which nature hath implanted in men, in order to direct and impel them to the care of their infant-offspring, and to the propagation of mankind in the way necessary to the general happiness of mankind. It is evident, that proper care cannot be taken of infants, as they come into the world in a most helpless condition, unless their parents unite together in concern about bringing them up to a state capable of doing for themselves. Neither their bodies nor their minds can otherwise be taken <287> due care of. Now, in order to excite us to this care, nature hath implanted in us several strong affections, all centering in it as their end; so that a great part of human happiness, a great part of our most agreeable employments, really consists in parental cares, and filial returns to such cares. There is not only a strong mutual sympathy between the sexes, founded in, and supported by many mutual wants and ties. But mankind have a strong natural inclination to continue themselves in a new race, which they may look upon as their own; to which a regular union between the sexes, in such a manner, that love and fidelity may be most securely depended upon, is evidently necessary. And no sooner are children born to parents in such a way, that there is no doubt of their being the offspring of faithful embraces, than a warm

17. Pope, *Essay on Man,* epistle II, 255–56.

love springs up in their minds towards this progeny, which is considerably increased by our sense of their absolute dependence upon our care, and soon receives an additional warmth from the gratitude, love and attachment to us, which they very early discover, and which become firmer, by becoming more rational, in proportion to the care parents take of what is principal in relation to their childrens happiness, the formation of their minds. Desire to be a parent, and the head of a family, is an affection that early sprouts up in every mind, and hath betimes a great share in all our pursuits. And when the marital and parental ties are once formed, then nature points our views more immediately towards our offspring and family, as the most proper object of our care. And this is evidently the manner in which benevolence should operate in order to the general happiness of mankind. Thus nature makes certain persons nearer and dearer to one another, and by so doing ascertains or appropriates to every one certain more immediate objects of his concern and affection; and, at the same <288> time, instead of severing or dividing mankind by this means into so many separate bodies, with separate interests, binds mankind together by so many more ties. For every one, who hath a warm attachment to the welfare of many endeared to him by special bonds and affections, must feel a stronger obligation, than those who are strangers to such motives, to gain the love of mankind, without which his own power to do good to such would be of very little consequence, however great it might be with it. There is this remarkable difference between the instinct of brutes, that impels them to the care of their offspring, and the natural affections of mankind.

> *Not man alone, but all that roam the wood,*
> *Or wing the sky, or roll along the flood;*
> *Each loves itself, but not itself alone,*
> *Each sex desires alike, till two are one;*
> *Nor ends the pleasure with the fierce embrace,*
> *They love themselves a third time in their race.*
> *Thus beast and bird their common charge attend,*
> *The mothers nurse it, and the sires defend;*
> *The young dismiss'd to wander earth or air,*
> *There stops the instinct, and there ends the care.*

> *The link dissolves, each seeks a fresh embrace,*
> *Another love succeeds another race.*
> A longer care man's helpless kind demands,
> That longer care contracts more lasting bands;
> *Reflexion, reason, still the ties improve,*
> *At once extend the interest and the love.*
> *With choice we fix, with sympathy we burn,*
> *Each virtue in each passion takes its turn;*
> *And still new needs, new helps, new habits rise,*
> *That graft benevolence on charities.*
>
> Essay on man.[18]

Now nature, by thus ordering the propagation of mankind, and enduing us with corresponding affections as parents and as children, assigns to eve-<289>ry one a more immediate and particular task or care; the faithful discharge of which by each in his sphere, would make human life all peace, love and harmony. Our general benevolence hath thus a particular biass, which points it into its proper road, or into its first cares and principal employments. Were mankind to be propagated as they are, and we not endued with the affections which are really implanted in us by nature, to how many bad chances, with regard to their education more especially, would mankind be exposed in their infant-state? And, on the other hand, if we had not those natural affections in us which tend to regular propagation, in order to have certain children, and to due care of our thus certain offspring; would not we want many sincere pleasures, many warm, interesting, delightful cares? Would it not our general benevolence want a strong source for nourishing and supporting it? And would not be left too vague and undetermined by nature? But being constituted as we are, our benevolence is properly directed, and properly invigorated; and nature hath given us affections to impel us to what necessity obliges us; with affections which makes every one feel immediate satisfaction in that regular exertion of benevolence, which the interest of all in general requires. Thus, while every man touches us as such, certain particulars strongly call upon our special attention; and we have

18. Ibid., III, 119–38.

each a particular province assigned to us by the natural tendency of our affections, the faithful discharge of which is contributing a very great share towards the public good. And this determination of our mind to particular exercises of benevolence, is so far from stinting and confining benevolence, or from having a natural tendency to degenerate into a narrow *clannish* disposition, that it naturally produces a fellow-feeling with all other parents and their cares, *i.e.* with all mankind; and renders the mind in general much <290> more tender and sympathizing than it can be without frequently feeling such kindly emotions. For this plain reason, that humanity and benevolence, like all other affections, grow stronger and stronger by exercise; or, in other words, repeated exercises form a general temper correspondent to them.

We have now therefore found that nature lays us under the necessity of social communication, and impels us to it by strong affections; and lays us under the necessity of social communication in a certain order, to which it likewise prompts and impels us by very strong affections, giving particular determinations to our benevolence, or assigning a nearer, a more immediate province to it. And hitherto certainly we have found our nature to be very well constituted, even in that respect against which the greatest objections have been made (*viz.* differences or inequalities among mankind): and hitherto also we have found the obligations arising from our constitution, and the connexions of things relative to our happiness, to be very obvious. They stare every one, who considers human nature with any attention, so to speak, in the face.

SECTION XII

But we will still perceive another security in our constitution against the degeneracy of family attachments into too narrow, confined, and partial benevolence, when we consider another determination in our nature, excellently adapted to check not only self-love, but partial affection of whatever sort, whether towards relatives by blood or friends; and admirably adapted to the circumstances of human life in general; which is the sympathy and pity distress immediately excites in the human breast, violently interesting us in the miseries of others. An embodied

Other affections in the human mind explained.

state must necessarily be liable to various calamities, in consequence of
the very laws of matter and motion, which make the best, the most or-
<291>derly, convenient and beautiful system, as our mundan system is
well known to natural philosophers to be. And nature hath, by wise and
kind care, implanted in the human heart a principle of compassion,
which is admirably well adjusted to such a condition. For by this we are
impelled to sympathize with the afflicted, and to run without delay to
their relief. And how much doth even sympathy itself alleviate pain and
suffering! Such is the nature of compassion, that it considers or attends
to no more but distress, is immediately excited, and directly pushes to
give the relief which the calamity calls for, without counting kindred,
or so much as asking who the sufferer is; and gives indeed no small pain,
when help is not in our power. Now, surely nature could not have more
clearly pointed out to us the order in which our benevolence ought to
work, than by determining it to receive such an impression, such a tendency from distress. It is true, this affection may be too strong to answer
its end, as it plainly is, when it quite overpowers and enfeebles one. And
by pains taken to harden the heart, it may, on the other hand, become
very weak, nay, be almost quite erased out of the mind. But have we not
reason to guide all our affections to their proper end, obedience to which
is, as hath been observed, our first duty or obligation by the laws of our
nature? And what can be more evident to a considering person, than that
the end of this passion is to knit mankind together, and to give them a
fellow-feeling with one another, that they might thus be kept from injuring one another, and be prompted to assist one another in the calamities and distresses to which all men in common are obnoxious? Or who
will say, that tho' there be a mixture of pain in this affection, yet it is
not, notwithstanding, so agreeable an emotion of the mind, that the
pleasures arising from the exercises of it, make a counterbalance to the
bodily evils resulting <292> from the necessity of nature sufficient to
vindicate providence, when we reflect at the same time upon the many
other goods arising from the same excellent laws which make these evils
necessary? That the exercise of compassion is a high satisfaction, the
tragic art, the principal charm of which lies in violently moving and
agitating our pity, is a sufficient proof. And indeed, by the consent of

all mankind, a breast quite devoid of compassion, is pronounced inhuman; *i.e.* unfit for human life; a stranger to the best feelings, the most agreeable and becoming emotions of the human heart. The reason is, because such are in fact found to be equally strangers to natural affections, to friendship, to a sense of honour, and consequently to all the richest sources of human delight; the richest sources of human delight for these affections being removed, what remains but the palate, and a few other organs of sense, in the whole list of human means or capacities of gratification? But wherever compassion prevails, there nature hath given a particular determination to our benevolence, the use of which to mankind in general is very evident; there nature hath made a connexion with regard to public and private happiness that merits our attention; there nature hath given a sense, a capacity of pleasure, that deserves our care and keeping: it cannot be impaired or corrupted, without sadly diminishing the provision nature hath made for our enjoyment, for the happiness of every individual, as well as the common happiness of our kind. Every road that nature hath made to true happiness, is a law of nature to us. And therefore, if natural affections belong to us, or if compassion belongs to us, they are, in this sense, laws of nature to man, that they indicate to us a certain course of affection and action, which nature hath made to be one considerable source of enjoyment to us. For can happiness be found but where nature hath placed it? <293> Can we change and alter the natures of things at our pleasure, and make any thing painful or agreeable as we will? If we cannot, we must take nature's paths, and seek happiness where nature has laid it. But nature hath placed it in industry, benevolence, natural affection, compassion, and the presidence of reason. These are the chief sources from which we must draw it. We can no more alter these connexions than we can change the laws of motion and gravity. They are therefore laws to us in the same sense, that the laws of motion are laws to human arts for the attainment of their ends.

But the human mind is a very complicated structure: It is composed not of one, but many principles of action, all of which are sources of very considerable enjoyment, and at the same time mutual checks or poises one to another, in order to point and lead us into, and keep us in the course of behaviour, which is at once the interest of every individual,

Other affections adapted to our dependencies and necessities explained.

and of the whole species. Several such have been already mentioned, and there are yet two others, the use of which in our frame well deserve our attention. 1. The first is a principle of resentment. By this we mean not merely sudden anger, which is nothing else but the necessary operation of self-defence, or sensibility to danger and hurt, and hath hurt as such for its object; for this is common to man with all sensible creatures: But we understand that indignation which injury or wrong, as such, necessarily excites in our mind, which supposes a sense of injustice or injury, and can only take place in minds capable of distinguishing equity and iniquity. In this do these two principles, which are often confounded together, in treating of the human affections, differ, that one hath suffering for its object and motive cause, the other that suffering only which is apprehended to be injurious. It is opposition, sudden hurt, violence, which naturally <294> excites sudden or momentary anger; reflexion on the real demerit or fault of him who offers that violence, or is the cause of that opposition or hurt, is not necessary to occasion this mere sensation or feeling. It is mere instinct, as merely so, as the disposition to shut our eyes upon the apprehension of something falling into them, and no more necessarily implies any degree of reason. For it works in infants, in the lower species of animals, and (not seldom) in men towards them, in none of which instances this passion can be imagined to be the effect of reason, or any thing but mere instinct or sensation. And no doubt the reason and end for which man was made thus liable to this passion, was to qualify and arm him to prevent (or perhaps chiefly) to resist and defeat sudden violence, considered merely as such, and without regard to the fault of him who is the author of it.

But resentment, which on account of what it hath in common with sudden anger, may be called deliberate anger, is not naturally excited by mere harm, but in order to move it, harm must be apprehended as injurious or wrong. "This is so much (says an excellent author) understood by mankind, that a person would be reckoned quite distracted, who should coolly resent an harm, which had not to himself the appearance of injury or wrong."[19] Now that the reason and end for which this prin-

---

19. Butler, Sermon VIII, "Upon Resentment," *Fifteen Sermons,* 145. There are minor discrepancies between the original text and Turnbull's quotation.

ciple is implanted in us by nature, is to fill us with indignation against injury, and to excite us to resist, defeat and punish it, is evident; for this is the end to which it naturally tends. And therefore, with regard to it, it is plain, that it is in its nature a social affection: it is a fellow-feeling which each individual hath in behalf of the whole species. For tho' injury to ourselves must affect us more intimately than injury done to others, in consequence of the nearer sensibility to one's self, which is inseparable from the constitution of every sensible being; yet we find that <295> the way in which injuries to others affect us, is exactly the same in kind. To be convinced of this, we need only attend to the manner in which a feigned story of baseness and villainy works up this passion in us. And such being the nature of this passion, it is far from being any defect or fault in our constitution, or from being in the least degree a-kin to malice: It is, on the contrary, so connected with a sense of moral good and evil, or of virtue and vice, that it could not take place without it; and may be properly said to be resentment or indignation against vice and wickedness. Far less still can this affection in our constitution be reckoned of a pernicious tendency, when we consider it as united in our frame with the other affections we have already mentioned, as compassion in particular; for as it is counter-balanced by them, and intended to co-operate with them, it can be designed for no other end but to make the resistance and opposition to vice which vice demerits, and not to give pain for the sake of tormenting others. For our compassion being moved by the suffering of another as such, and our resentment being only excited by wrong as such, we are thus by nature equally furnished for repelling injuries, and for commiserating innocent sufferers. Reason hath thus, as it were, two handles to guide us by, whether in repelling injuries, or in pitying sufferers, by each of which the other is kept within due bounds. Compassion is of use to moderate resentment, and resentment to hinder compassion from misplacing its tenderness upon the undeserving and vicious, to the prejudice of innocence and merit. So social then is our frame, that there is no passion in our nature which delights immediately in misery as such. But, on the contrary, misery always excites compassion, unless when it is apprehended as the just desert of injury. And so far is resentment generally from being too strong in human nature, that however eagerly it may desire and pur-<296>sue the punishment of injustice, yet the punishment, which is the end of the passion, is no sooner gained, than commonly it gives way to compassion to such a degree, that it requires keeping the injustice of the sufferer very fully and strongly in our view, not to succumb entirely to pity. 2. But I have chiefly mentioned this principle in our nature here, as it, together with what I am now to take notice of, *viz.* the love of fame and power, renders mankind capable of several great actions. For if we examine narrowly into what it is that impels the human mind to dangerous and bold atchievements, and gives heroic spirits such high delight in pursuits seemingly so opposite to self-love, we will find that these are the sources in our nature, from whence the delight in them, and the motives to them principally flow; I say, principally flow, because no doubt a moral sense of beauty in actions (of which afterwards) hath no small share in true heroism; and religious principles, as they are of a very proper nature to promote true fortitude, patience and courage, so they have often produced the greatest actions, the bravest heroes.

Whence the hazardous enterprizes with which the history of all ages and countries is filled, that strike us with such admiration and amazement? To what do historians ascribe them? And to what source does every reader chiefly refer them in his own mind? Is it not to the love of power or empire, and the love of fame? Now surely, if these be the main incentives to atchievements, in which life and all its advantages are so boldly risked; we may justly conclude, that the love of power and fame may arrive to a very great pitch of vigour and force in the human mind. And such indeed are the circumstances of several most renowned actions in history, that so much of the motives to them must needs be ascribed to these sources, as makes it very proper in an analysis of the human <297> affections, to give particular attention to the love of fame and power, and the ends for which they are implanted in us by nature. Now, into whatever extravagancies the love of fame and power may run; (as what passion in our nature may not be perverted, and so degenerate into something very wild, foolish and hurtful) yet they are implanted in us for very useful purposes. Let us consider the two separately. 1. The love of fame. Is it not a passion that takes its rise from sociability, and that strongly cements us to the interests of our kind? For what is it at bottom but regard to the esteem and love of mankind? Can we love mankind

without desiring to be respected, esteemed and honoured by them? or
can we like actions which tend to gain us the love of mankind, without
liking the love they tend to gain? Love of fame is inseparable from sociality; and true honour consisting in the merited real esteem of mankind, is a noble aim; not a mean or mercenary view, but a truly generous
and laudable motive. Nay, so nearly allied is this praise-worthy ambition
to virtue, that he who despises fame will soon forsake the paths which
lead to it. And therefore Cicero justly says, *Vult plane virtus honorem nec
est virtutis alia merces.*[20] 2. As for the love of power. It is absolutely necessary to beings made for progress in perfection, and to extend and enlarge their faculties. For what else is it at bottom, but desire to expand
and enlarge ourselves, to dilate and widen our sphere of activity? Without this impulse, without being made to receive high delight from the
consciousness of our growing and advancing in perfection, in knowledge, in authority, in power to serve others, and promote their interests,
how listless and inactive would our minds be? And how listless indeed,
sluggish and inactive are the minds, where the love of encreasing all their
powers, the desire of being as independent of others, and as sufficient
to themselves as they can <298> be, does not prevail in some degree!
3. And in a life subject to evils of various sorts, to many natural calamities, and many greater moral ones, arising from the perverted, corrupt
affections of men, how necessary are both these principles to fortify our
minds with patience and courage, and to qualify us to oppose and defeat these evils? Where these passions do not obtain in a great degree,
how easy a conquest are a people to every proud usurper or tyrant;
how tamely and submissively do they yield their necks to the yoke of
arbitrary power? But as useful as these noble principles are in our
nature, and as great a share as they have in the great actions which
chiefly render the history of human life capable of attracting or detaining our attention, yet all must not be ascribed to them. For that
just resentment against injury, just indignation against oppression, tyranny and despotic insolence, often kindle the heroe's breast with a gen-

20. "Virtue clearly desires honour, and has no other reward." Cicero *De re publica,*
III, xxviii, 40.

erous ardour to destroy and root out these enemies of mankind, and make him rush intrepidly into the thickest dangers to rescue his fellow-creatures, his country, from slavery and misery;—that this passion is often the patriot's chief motive in his most perilous and brave enterprizes, almost the only thing he hath in his view to animate and invigorate him, might be proved by many shining instances from history. But all that it belongs to our present purpose to observe is, that none of these passions are inconsistent with a social principle, but on the contrary take their rise from it: it is the only root from which they can spring: Nor are these affections weakened or perverted by any other means than those which equally weaken or pervert every other generous or great affection in our minds. Thus, the same long subjection to arbitrary power, which almost quite effaces all ideas of liberty, all greatness, boldness and freedom of mind, is it not likewise observed to render them, who have been long inured to it, sluggish, indolent, ungenerous, revengeful, and rather nearer to the <299> temper of monkeys or buffoons in all respects, than to the spirit and temper of men? However these principles or dispositions may be corrupted, they are to us, as they naturally stand in our frame, sources of very noble pleasures, and motives to very great and laudable activity. We cannot suppose them removed out of our constitution, without reducing mankind to a very low and contemptible creature, in comparison of what it is the natural tendency of these affections to render us, as they are united in our frame with benevolence, compassion, and natural affections to our parents and offspring. They cannot be taken from us, without cutting off from mankind all capacity of the greater pursuits that now adorn and bless human life. Nor can they indeed be objected against in our frame, when they are thus considered. And when the Author of nature is blamed by any philosopher for having implanted them in our frame, they are represented by such as making the only principles of action in our minds; and are thus disjoined from other principles in us, with which they are naturally united, and consequently intended by nature to co-operate. But certainly, in order to judge of a constitution, we must consider all its parts as they mutually respect one another, and by these mutual respects make a whole. Thus we judge of all other constitutions or structures, natural or artificial. And thus likewise ought we to judge of the fabric of the human mind.

SECTION XIII

Now, having thus analized the human mind into the chief principles, dispositions or affections of which it is compounded; what follows, but that, this mind so constituted is a law to itself; or that it, and the connexions relative to it, which have likewise been explained as we proceeded in this resolution of the human mind into its component parts, make to man the laws and rules of his ac-<300>tions? Thus laws of conduct are constituted to man for the government of his affections, in order to the attainment of happiness in the same manner that the laws of matter and motion constitute rules to human arts for the attainment of their ends. In the same sense that it is necessary for man to act consonantly to the properties of air and water, in order to gain certain purposes, such as raising water, &c. in the same sense are the connexions relative to our affections, laws or rules to us, how to regulate and direct them, in order to avoid certain evils and to obtain certain goods. We have not in this enquiry meddled with a question, the manner of handling which hath greatly perplexed the science of morality, *viz.* the freedom of human will: For this evident reason, that it neither more nor less concerns morals, than it does an enquiry into the connexions of nature, whence the rules in mechanical arts must be deduced. This is manifest. Because, if man be not at all master of his actions, it must be as much in vain to direct him how to act in any one way, as how to direct him in any other. Directions and counsels, or exhortations, can only be of use with respect to things in human power. But if directions, counsels, or exhortations, with regard to industry in cultivating mechanical arts for the benefit or ornament of human life, can be of any use to man, then must man be acknowledged to be master of almost all the powers, faculties and affections to which any other counsels, directions or exhortations can be addressed. For then must he be master of getting knowledge, if he will; master of applying himself to study and labour; he must be capable of being moved by representations of what the interests of society require, and of making that the end of his pursuits; master of despising toil and hardships in that view; and master of aiming at fame and honour, by doing some laudable service to mankind in that way. But if he be so far master of his af-<301>fections and actions, which

Recapitulation.

Why we do not here enter into the dispute about liberty and necessity.

affections and actions is he not master of in the same sense? Indeed all the grave sophistry about liberty and necessity, with which moral enquiries have been so sadly embarrassed, to the great obstruction of true and useful knowledge, might as well be prefixed to a system of physics as of morals. For if they prove any thing at all, they prove that mankind ought to fold their arms, and let things go as they will. If they prove, or are designed to prove this, are not rules about sowing in seed-time in order to reap in harvest, rules about building ships, or any other machines, as idle as rules about the government of the affections? And if they are not designed to prove this, what are they intended for? For till this is proved to be a necessary consequence of God's foreknowledge, or of our being influenced by motives, or of whatever other truth from which necessity is thought to follow,—till this be proved, what is called *necessity,* cannot be contrary to what is called *liberty, viz.* our having certain things in our power, or our being the disposers or masters of our actions. In fine, whatever proves any thing repugnant to our liberty, must prove that we are not at all masters of doing, or not doing as we will in any case; that we have no power, no dominion, no sphere of activity; or, in one word, that we are not agents: and this being proved, mechanical arts, which are rules to certain actions, or rules for our attaining certain ends, are just as much affected by it, as the science of morals, which is a system of rules to certain other actions, or for our attaining certain other ends. The arguments brought against human liberty, were never said only to prove that necessity extends merely a certain length, and no further. Nor can it be said; for if they prove any thing at all, they must prove universal necessity. And if they do indeed prove universal necessity, then human action in every sense is absurd, and <302> consequently all rules to human actions of any sort or kind are equally absurd; or by the universal necessity they are said to prove, and brought to prove, is meant a necessity with which human agency is very consistent; which will be to say, that they are brought to prove, and do prove that we are not agents in a sense that is however very compatible with our being agents. Surely the controversy about liberty and necessity must be of very little moment, nay, a very idle, impertinent logomachy, if any asserters of necessity think that the necessity they plead for is absolutely consistent with our being masters of our actions, our having a sphere of power which we are capable of using well or abusing, as we please. For never was liberty understood to mean more than dominion and power, and accountableness, in consequence of our being disposers of our actions. And so in this case their necessity is our liberty. But if they really mean an universal necessity, absolutely repugnant to our agency, *i.e.* to our having the disposal of our actions, which renders rules and directions about actions absurd, as proceeding upon a false supposition; then are those, who treat of gaining certain natural ends by certain actions adjusted to natural connexions, as much concerned in the controversy as moralists, when they treat of attaining certain other ends by actions adjusted to other natural connexions. And for this reason, we may dismiss it as a question which does not particularly concern our subject; but every subject equally, which supposes man to be an agent.

And therefore, to go on with our conclusion, we say, that the connexions which we have found to be fixed by nature, relative to our happiness, are laws of nature to our conduct in the same sense that the connexions in nature, relative to certain physical ends, are laws with regard to certain physical arts. They are laws we cannot alter, but to which we must conform, in order to attain our greatest <303> happiness, our best enjoyments, or greatest goods. And they are laws appointed by the Author of nature to our conduct. For all established connexions in nature must mean connexions appointed and upheld, or subsisting by virtue of the will of the Author of nature, who gave being to all things, and to all orders and connexions of things (§3). Now, all this being true, it follows, that man is in the same sense made for prudence and self-government; for industry; for acting with reason, and agreeably to its dictates; for benevolence, or the pursuit of public good; for paternal cares and filial gratitude; for indignation against injury and oppression, and for compassion towards our suffering or distressed fellow-creatures; it follows, I say, that we are made for these ends in the same sense that the eye is made to see, the ear to hear, that a certain structure is made for flying, and another for swiming and living in water, or that bodies are made to gravitate in proportion to their quantities of matter, or are to be considered as having that property in human arts. The Author of

The conclusion from the whole preceding reasoning.

nature, who hath made the one kind of connexions, hath likewise made and fixed the other. And if the preceding account of human nature, or of our internal principles and dispositions, and the connexions relative to them be true, to say man is not made for the exercises above-mentioned, to which we may now certainly give the name of virtues, without taking any thing in morals for granted, is to say, a being endued with a governing principle, by which it is intended he should govern himself, is not intended to be so governed; which is to assert, that a governing principle is not, in its nature and end, a governing principle: it is to say, a being endued with a governing principle, the use and end of which is to give him self-command, or the mastership of his affections, is not made to be master of his affections by his governing principle; which is to assert, that he hath a principle which hath an end and <304> use which it hath not: It is to say, that a being who hath social affections, and a principle of benevolence, determined, or adapted to receive different kindly impressions from different objects, is not intended to have these social, affectionate, generous impressions, nor to exercise these affections; but has them for no end at all, or for a quite opposite and contrary end. In fine, let any man consider these virtues, and compare them with the make of the human mind, and all our internal principles and dispositions, and then say that man is made for imprudence, folly, wilfulness, and precipitancy; to be tossed to and fro by tumultuous contradictory affections, without any order or government; and to be cruel, tyrannical, abusive, oppressive, uncompassionate, quite unsocial. Let him say what reason he can give for affirming that the eye is made to enjoy the light, the ear to receive pleasure from music; or, in one word, what reason he can give for saying any thing natural or artificial is made for an end, that will not equally oblige him to say, man is framed, made and intended for rational government of his affections, for benevolence, and the other virtues which have been named. If he says, whatever affections men may have, man is made to pursue his pleasure, let him shew how men can have pleasure but from the gratifications of particular affections; and let him shew that the affections we have named are not belonging to human nature, or that they are not belonging to it as sources of pleasure and enjoyment. In fine, let him shew what other enjoyments human nature is provided for which are superior to the presidence of reason, affections disciplined by reason, and exerting themselves in the order of benevolence that hath been described. We reason from fact or experiment; and what we have maintained, can only be refuted by shewing our analysis of the human mind not to be fact. For if the resolution of the human mind <305> that hath been given be just, our conclusion stands upon the same bottom with all the reasonings in natural philosophy concerning the structures, properties, laws, and final causes of things. The only thing that can be objected against this deduction of the ends for which men are made and intended, is, that men are in fact very irregular; that the affections of mankind are generally very tumultuous and undisciplined, and there is much malignity, ill humour, envy and hatred amongst them; and that the love of power and fame do not generally lead men to benevolent, but rather to mischievous actions. But let mankind be represented as villainous as they have ever been said to be, by any philosopher or politician; or, if you will, more black and deformed than any hath ever yet called them, it will not shake or weaken our reasoning. For though that be not true, but, on the contrary, a very false charge, yet we can sufficiently account for the vilest corruptions that ever have, or ever can take place among mankind, very consistently with the preceding analysis of human nature, and the deduction of our duties; *i.e.* our natural ends, from that analysis. 1. First of all, there is no other conceivable way of furnishing or qualifying any agent for pursuing the virtues above-named, but by giving them the affections above described, and reason to conduct them. There is no way of qualifying one for doing all under the direction of reason, but by giving him faculties to be guided by reason, and reason to guide them. There is no other way of qualifying one for benevolence, but by giving him a benevolent disposition, and so disposing him, as that he may feel great pleasure in its exercises. Let the objectors against human nature point out what else could be done. Let them name what is wanting to make us rational and benevolent in our behaviour, that nature hath not done for us. If <306> they say reason is too weak in human nature, or does not grow up fast enough to do us great service as a guide, this leads to the second thing to be considered on this head. 2. Which is, that reason must grow and

Objection why there is so little virtue, so much vice among mankind.

improve by culture. It can only become strong by exercise and improvement. It can only become so powerful as to be habitually our fixed and settled guide and ruler, by repeated acts. For thus alone can any habits be wrought in us; thus alone can any affections, dispositions, principles, or powers and faculties of action in us become habits; *i.e.* become strong and prevalent. Repeated exercise is the sole way of acquiring habits. It is therefore the sole way of perfecting reason, or any faculty or principle in our constitution; and what other way can we conceive, by which it is better to attain to perfection of any kind than by industry, diligence, and repeated acts? But if this be a necessary or fit law of our nature, in order to our attainment to perfection, that habits should be formed by repeated exercise, and only be so formed; must not the effect of this be, that bad and hurtful habits will be contracted by repeated bad exercises, and that false or wrong associations of ideas will be very powerful, very difficult to be disjoined or undone? Must not the effect of it be, that if bad habits are suffered to grow up to a great degree of strength in our minds by bad education, or through carelessness about our education, and reason is not early accustomed to rule and govern in young minds, that rational dominion over the affections will be very difficultly acquired; the sensitive appetites will be exceeding riotous; and every passion that has been often called forth, or incited to indulge itself by tempting shews of pleasure, will become imperious, headstrong, and unruly? For it must be remembered, that we are not merely intellectual beings, but that we have senses and corporeal appetites, <307> which will necessarily become, in consequence of the law of habits, too strong for reason and benevolence to govern, if they are not early accustomed to the government and discipline of reason. And it must likewise be remembered, that our opinions of goods must regulate our affections; and therefore, if false ideas have been imbibed early, and have long passed unexamined, uncontroverted in the mind, these wrong associations of ideas, and false judgments of things, will be very hard to overcome; it will be extremely difficult to eradicate or correct them. But what is all this, but, in one word, a long habit of acting without reason, or of despising reason, instead of inuring our ideas, fancies, opinions, and appetites, to receive their direction from our reason, and to act under its presidence and government. And therefore, in speaking of our being made to consult reason, and act under its conduct and guidance, we took notice of the necessity of right education, in order to establish reason early into our governing principle (§8). But having elsewhere* discoursed at great length of the power of habits, and the way in which they are formed, and of the chief sources of corrupt affections amongst mankind, it is sufficient to take notice here in general, that there are almost no vices among mankind which could take place amongst them, were we not endued by nature with the best affections; affections necessary to make us social, benevolent, great and good. They are corruptions or misguidances of them. Every hurtful affection is a very good one perverted. Accordingly Mr. Locke hath shewn us in his excellent *treatise on education*,[21] how easily all the vices may be early engendered, nay, brought to a very great height of obstinacy by bad example and wrong methods of education; but he hath, at the same time, shewn us how all the vir-<308>tues may be yet more easily formed in tender minds. And indeed there is no character in human life however enormous, that shews any affection naturally belonging to us, which is not of the greatest use, however hurtful its wrong turns, degeneracies, perversions or corruptions may be. Nor is there any other cause of degeneracy and corruption but bad habit, or not accustoming ourselves to exert our reason, and to act under its direction; which, how nature could have better furnished us for doing, than by giving us reason capable of high improvements; or have better impelled us to do, than by making us to see from examples, and feel from our own experience, as it does, the dismal effects of not acting rationally, the sad consequences of not consulting, or not obeying our reason, and of rashly giving way to every passion or appetite that circumstances may tempt into hurtful indulgences to specious semblance of pleasure, is inconceivable.

> *Nature well known, no miracles remain,*
> *Comets are regular, and* Clodio *plain.*
> Pope's Ethic. Ep. to Lord Cobham.[22]

---

* Principles of moral philosophy.
21. Locke, *Thoughts Concerning Education*, 127–34.
22. Pope, *An Epistle to the Right Honourable Richard Lord Viscount Cobham*, 11.

For howsoever odd, whimsical, or foolish the ruling passion in any heart may be, it is some passion necessary to excellent enjoyments and gratifications, that is become so odd, fantastical, or unreasonable. If it is any sensual appetite that is the ruler, and triumphs over all other affections of whatever kind, intellectual or social, will it follow from hence, that we ought not to have had senses, or to have been capable of sensitive pleasure? If it is the lust of power that has got the ascendant over benevolence in any one, to such a degree, that it is become his maxim; *Si violandum est jus, regnandi gratia violandum est; aliis rebus pietatem colas.*

> *If ever we break the ties of right,*
> *'Tis when a kingdom is the glorious prize:*
> *In other things be strictly just.*[23] <309>

Which is almost as great a height of villainy as it can arrive at. Yet ought the desire of power to have had no place in our frame, or is it of no use in it? Or finally, because the desire of getting riches to support a vain and extravagant way of living, if not severely checked, gradually corrupts the honestest minds, and at last engages them in pursuits, which some time before they could not think of without abhorrence; are for this reason all desire of property and power, of preeminence and honour, or even of elegance and grandeur, passions, absolutely condemnable in themselves, and to which human nature ought to have been an utter stranger? What we learn from *Salust, Sueton,* and other Authors, is by no means improbable, *viz.* That *Julius Caesar* had never attempted to destroy the liberties of his country, had he been able to have paid the debts which he had contracted by his excessive prodigality; and that abundance of people sided either with him or *Pompey,* only because they wanted wherewithal to supply their luxury, and were in hopes of getting by the civil wars, enough to support and maintain their former pride and greatness. But does it follow from hence, that all taste of elegance, all desire of glory, all love of power and wealth, are absolutely pernicious,

---

23. Cicero, *De officiis* 3.21.82. The passage is a Latin translation from Euripides' play *Phoenician Women*, lines 524–25, in *Euripides,* vol. 5.

and that they ought to have no place in our frame, or that we ought to have been made totally incapable of forming any ideas or affections that could ever degenerate into such perverse opinions and lusts? How much more just and truly philosophical is this reasoning in our excellent poet concerning human passions.

> *Envy, to which th' ignoble mind's a slave,*
> *Is emulation in the learned and brave:*
> *Lust, thro' some certain strainers well refin'd,*
> *Is gentle love, and charms all womankind.*
> *Nor virtue, male and female can we name,*
> *But what will grow on pride, or grow on shame.* <310>
> *Thus nature gives us (let it check our pride)*
> *The virtue nearest to our vice ally'd;*
> *Reason, the biass turns to good from ill,*
> *And* Nero *reigns a* Titus, *if he will.*
> *The fiery soul abhorr'd in* Cataline,
> *In* Decius *charms, in* Curtius *is divine.*
> *The same ambition can destroy, or save,*
> *And makes a patriot, as it makes a knave.*

Essay on Man.[24]

Nature, in order to make a necessary diversity of tempers among mankind, must either have made some particular affection originally stronger in one breast, and another in another; or have so ordered the situations of mankind, that the same original affections should of necessity take various turns in consequence of different circumstances calling forth more frequently, some one and some another affection, equally natural to all men. But what follows from hence, but that there is a vice, or a hurtful turn, into which every affection is in peculiar danger of degenerating, as is well known to poets, who describe characters, and place them in various circumstances of actions? Sure it does not follow that any of the affections implanted in the human mind by nature, ought to be wanting. Take them away, and the vices or diseases to which they are

24. Pope, *An Essay on Man,* epistle II, 191–202.

incident, will likewise be removed: But so will the perfections or virtues to which they may rise and be improved by due culture, likewise be sent apacking. And to what a low size will men be thus reduced? Tho' it be reason that forms the virtues, yet our affections are the principles or materials that are formed into virtues by reason. Reason would indeed have nothing to guide, nothing to work upon, if we were not endued with all the affections, from the misguidances of which the most hurtful disturbances of human life proceed. <311>

Man is made for virtue and virtuous happiness. Now what is the result of this, but that man is excellently furnished by nature for attaining, by the due discipline of the affections implanted in him, to prudence, to self-command, to benevolence, to fortitude, and to all that is called virtue; and that this is the end for which he is so made and framed, in the same sense that any thing is said to be made for the end to which its frame and constitution is well adapted; that this is his happiness, his perfection, the ultimate scope and design of his frame and all the laws relative to it, in any sense of end, scope or design.

SECTION XIV

Another proof of this, from the moral sense natural to us. 'Tis true, we are not merely intellectual beings; we have senses and sensitive appetites, as well as moral capacities and social affections (§6): But it hath appeared, that we are made to govern all our appetites and affections by our reason; that our sensitive appetites ought to be under its command, and not to be allowed to obscure it, far less to triumph over it, and trample it under foot; and that our sensitive appetites are so far from engrossing or making the whole of our constitution, that we have other affections, the regular exercises of which, under the presidence and direction of reason, are our highest and noblest enjoyments. This hath been fully proved. And therefore, let it be now observed, that kind nature hath not only placed our happiness in the virtuous exercises which have been described, but hath so constituted and framed us, that the ideas of the presidence of reason, and of benevolence, can no sooner be presented to our minds than we must necessarily assent to and approve those two general rules of life, "That reason ought to hold the reins of government in our minds." And, "That benevolence, or regard to public good, ought to be the reigning affection in them." None can reflect upon these two rules without per-<312>ceiving their fitness, and that immediately without making any calculations about their consequences. And therefore we may justly say with an excellent author (Domat in his *treatise of laws*) "That the first principles of morality or laws, have a character of truth, which touches and persuades more than that of the principles of other human sciences; that whereas the principles of other sciences, and the particular truths which depend upon them, are only the objects of the mind, and not of the heart, and that they do not even enter into the minds of all persons; the first principles of morals or laws, and the particular rules essential to these principles, have a character of truth which every body is capable of knowing, and which affects the mind and the heart alike. The whole man is penetrated by them, and more strongly convinced of them, than of the truths of all the other human sciences."[25] Or with another admirable moralist (Hutcheson in his *Enquiry, &c.*) "The Author of nature has much better furnished us for virtuous conduct, than many philosophers seem to imagine, or at least are willing to grant, by almost as quick and powerful instructions as we have for the preservation of our bodies. He has given us strong affections to be the springs of each virtuous action, and made virtue a lovely form, that we might easily distinguish it from its contrary, and be made happy by the pursuit of it. As the Author of nature has determined us to receive by our outward senses, pleasant or disagreeable ideas of objects, according as they are useful or hurtful to our bodies, and to receive from uniform objects the pleasures of beauty and harmony, to excite us to the pursuit of knowledge, and to reward us for it; in the same manner, he has given us a moral sense to direct our actions, and to give us still nobler pleasures; so that while we are only intending the good of others, we undesignedly promote our own greatest private good."[26] But having else-

Of our moral sense.

---

25. Jean Domat (1625–96), *Les loix civiles dans leur ordre naturel.* Turnbull quotes (with near accuracy) from the English translation: *The Civil Law in Its Natural Order: Together with the Publick Law,* page ii (in both eds.).

26. Francis Hutcheson, *An Inquiry into the Original of Our Ideas of Beauty and Virtue* (London, 1725; 3rd ed. 1729; 4th ed. 1738), pp. 9 and 99. Turnbull spliced

where <313> handled this subject at great length,[27] it will be sufficient to remark here, 1. That in consequence of the sense of beauty in outward forms, and of the sense of beauty in affections, actions and characters, with which the human mind is endued, all the pleasures which man is intended by nature to pursue, may properly be comprized under the general notion of order or beauty: For they have all this general or common character, that they proceed from well disciplined and regulated affections, and they all tend to produce order within and without the mind. What is the presidence of reason, but reason maintaining order and harmony; and what do the regular exercises of benevolence which have been described produce, but inward and outward harmony? What makes the pleasure of contemplation and knowledge, besides the views of regularity, order and harmony? What is it that charms the imagination in any of the imitative arts? Or what hath what is called *good taste* for its object and scope, besides order and harmony in composition? And how gross and contemptible are all the pleasures of sense, when we abstract from them all elegance, all symmetry, proportion and order? Man therefore, may in general be said to be framed by nature to pursue order and harmony. And this is indeed the pursuit of the Author of nature himself, universal order and harmony, or, which is the same, universal good. But, 2. As the presidence of reason over all our appetites and affections, and the prevalence of benevolence in our temper, cannot be considered by us without being perceived, or rather felt to be our most reasonable and becoming part, nor the opposite character be reflected upon, without being disapproved and condemned by us; so we cannot consider the Author of nature, without immediately perceiving, that he deserves our highest adoration and love; and that benevolence, and the rational government of our affections, can alone render us like him, or recom-<314>mend us to his favour, upon whom all our interests depend. We must of necessity own an universal cause, by which all things are made, and are upheld in being and governed. And our moral sense of

By this moral sense we are led to conceive the virtues above described as commanded by God the Author of nature.

---

together two separate passages and also inserted a few words of his own. He used either the third or the fourth edition.

27. In his *Principles of Moral Philosophy* of 1740.

what is the best, the most perfect disposition of mind, naturally leads us at once to ascribe perfect reason and benevolence to the first cause of all things, our Creator: And to apprehend it, 1. "To be his will, that we should act a rational and benevolent part in all our conduct." And, 2. "That according to the constitution of things in his universal government, such conduct must be the only road to true happiness in the sum of things; so that whatever difficulties and trials may be necessary to the first state of rational agents, for their improvement in moral perfection, yet upon the whole, sincere virtue shall make happy, and confirmed vice shall render miserable." These truths are obvious necessary consequences, from the idea of an all-perfect Maker and Governor of the universe. But these truths being fixed, then are we under obligation to benevolence and rational government, in this strict and proper sense of obligation, "That the Author and Governor of the Universe, our Lord and Creator, wills or commands us to exert our reason, as the Governor of our affections, and to pursue in all our conduct the good of our kind." The virtues for which we have found man to be furnished and intended, do, when considered in this light, take the character of laws in a sense applicable to them only, *i.e.* of universal unalterable commands laid upon us by the Author of nature, the Sovereign disposer of all our interests. The connexions observed by nature in the production of physical effects, are very properly called laws of matter and motion, or laws by which the Author of nature has willed that matter should operate, or more properly be operated upon; and they are of necessity laws to human arts, since human art cannot accomplish any end but by acting in conformity to <315> them. But the connexions relative to our moral powers, our reason, our social affections, and the subordinacy of all our appetites and affections to reason, in consequence of which certain rules must be observed by us in order to private and public happiness, are not only laws to us in this respect, that we can only attain to our best enjoyments by acting conformably to them; they are also laws to us in this sense, that acting conformably to them is agreeable to our Creator; and it is his will that we should conform our conduct to them. So that they are not merely moral laws, as they are laws of nature respecting moral ends; but they are moral laws in this respect, that they are rules for the conduct of our

And consequently to be enjoined by moral laws properly so called.

life and manners, which cannot be transgressed or departed from without incurring guilt in the sight of God, without offending against his will and authority, and rendering ourselves obnoxious to all the consequences of his regard to virtue or moral perfection, and his disapprobation or detestation of vice. They are rules which he hath necessarily determined our minds to approve, and to conceive as his commands, as often as we consider them, and take a view of the perfections which must belong to the Divine Mind. And therefore, they are laws that come up to this definition of a law, *viz.* "The will of a superior who hath a just title to command, and sufficient power to enforce conformity to his commands." And indeed it is when prudence, temperance, fortitude, benevolence, and all the other virtues are considered in this light, that they alone can have their full force. For in this light only are they fully and perfectly considered; or till we conceive of them in this view, we have not an adequate notion of all the obligations to conform our practice to them, which essentially belong to them. It will be readily acknowledged, that two motives must needs have more force than one. But this is not all: No view that can be ta-<316>ken of the virtues above described, can have so much power to influence mankind as the conception of them under the notion of the divine will or law, not commanding arbitrarily or without reason, but for the good of rational agents; since what is thus apprehended or considered, must work upon us in various manners; excite our emulation to be like the most perfect of Beings, and agreeable to him; stir up our gratitude to engage us to act the part he approves and commands; influence our hope with high expectations of great advantages from his love and favour; and raise our fear of offending him to a due pitch of reverence towards his authority.

Regard to the divine law is religion. Now, regard to virtue, influenced by these considerations, is properly called religion. And that man is made for religion, as well as for virtue, is evident, since we cannot reason at all about the nature of things, without being led to apprehend a first Supreme Cause: nor can we represent to ourselves the perfections of an eternal all-sufficient Mind, the Creator and Governor of the Universe, without being filled with the highest veneration towards him, and his will with relation to our conduct. And meditation upon the divine perfections, is in reality the noblest source of delight to the human mind, and an exercise that hath the sweetest, the benignest influence upon the temper. But not to insist at present upon the pleasures which a just sense of God and divine providence afford to the mind; if the being of a God be owned, it must certainly be true, that we are under religious obligation to that rational government of our affections, and to the benevolence, for which we have been found to be so excellently furnished and fitted by nature, *i.e.* under obligation to this conduct, in order to approve ourselves to God; under obligation to it, as the conduct he commands, and will reward. And this being true, this conduct is our duty. And in every sense are we obliged to be virtuous. We <317> shall therefore only add, 1. That the sacred writings give us a very just view of the whole of our duties, arising from our nature, and our relation to our Creator, the Author and Ruler of the universe, when they are reduced there into two commandments, the first of which is to love God, and the other to love mankind; or when it is there asserted that love is the fulfilment of the law of God. And there is no other law which commands every one to love himself, because no one can love himself better than by keeping the law which enjoins love to God and love to our fellow-creatures. Self-love is not so properly a law, as it is a principle inseparable from all beings capable of that reflection, without which they would be incapable of governing their actions, distinguishing rules for their conduct, or pursuing ends. And for this reason the sacred writings do not mention self-love as a law; but they suppose this general desire of happiness as a principle necessarily inherent in us, which is to be directed by reason, *i.e.* by such rules or laws as reason is able to discover, by due attention to the relations and connexions of things. And these rules it justly reduces sometimes to two, the love of God, and the love of mankind; and sometimes to one general law, *love*. 2. Yet it may very justly be said, that the whole of our duty consists in well regulated self-love, or in the pursuit of our true happiness. For our greatest happiness consists, by our constitution, in such government of our affections by reason as hath been described, in the exercises of devotion towards God, and the approbation of our moral sense or conscience. As our duties cannot be inferred but from the internal principles of action implanted by the Author of nature in our minds, and the connexions relative to them; so indeed no commands repugnant to our internal principle, and the connexions relative to them, repugnant to what the <318> Author of nature hath placed our happiness and perfection in, can come from the Author of nature. Now, the two great commands which revelation tells us are the whole of human duty, the whole of religion and virtue, love to God, and love to mankind, are the very laws which our constitution prescribes, or makes necessary to be observed by us in all our conduct, in order to attain to the greatest happiness our nature is capable of. They are indicated or pointed out to us by nature with so much clearness, that we may see plainly, that if any man is ignorant of them, it is only because he does not know himself, or does not reflect upon the frame of his mind, and turn his eyes inward to consider the internal principles of action with which he is endued; and therefore nothing is more astonishing than the blindness that hinders any one from seeing them. 3. Tho' many disputes have been raised about the meaning of, as, in the divine commandment, *to love our neighbour as ourself,*[28] by those who like jangling; yet it plainly means the same with that other precept, *to do as we would be done by;* the equity of which is so plain, that it hath been acknowledged in all ages and countries of the world as a most perfect summary of all the duties we can owe one to another, and to be a directory, which cannot be applied in any case, without immediately perceiving, or rather feeling what we ought to do. This Grotius, Puffendorf, and Barbeyrac, have fully proved. 4. These two commands have a most strict and intimate alliance. One cannot love God without loving mankind; nor love mankind, and having an idea of an infinitely good supreme Being, the Creator of all things, and the common Father of mankind, not love this all-perfect Being. And the best security men can have for their living together in harmony and love, is from the prevalence of true religion, or of a just notion of a supreme Being, and due regard to <319> his will and authority, among them. It is, in its nature or tendency, the strongest bond of society. And from experience, or the history of mankind, there is reason to say with Cicero, "I know not, but that upon taking away religion and piety, all faith and

The harmony of this account of our nature and duties with the scripture doctrine.

28. For the *golden rule,* see Matthew 7:12 and Luke 6:31.

society of human kind, and even the most excellent of virtues, justice, would soon leave the world."[29]

Upon the whole therefore, when we proceed from considering the constitution of the human mind, and the connexions and relations of things respecting man, to the contemplation of the supreme Author of mankind and of these connexions, and of the whole frame of things, we have good ground to conclude, with the same antient, in a passage of his books *de republica,* preserved to us by Lactantius. "There is indeed a law agreeable to nature, and founded in it, which is no other than right reason, made known to all men, constant and immutable, that calls us to duty by commands, and deters us from fraud and villany by threats; neither are its commands and threats in vain to the good, tho' they may make but little impression upon the wicked and corrupt. This law we can neither disannul nor diminish; nor is it possible that it should be totally reversed; the senate or the people cannot free us from its authority. Nor do we need any explainer of it besides our own consciences. It will not be different at Rome and at Athens, now or hereafter, but will eternally and unchangeably bind all persons in all places; God himself, the universal Master and King, being its Founder and Author. 'Tis He who is the Establisher, the Enactor, the Interpreter of this law; which, whosoever refuses to obey, shall be afraid to look into his own mind, or converse with himself, because he contemns and vilifies his nature; and shall thus undergo the severest penalties, tho' he should escape every thing else which falls under our common name and notion <320> of punishment."[30] And thus I am naturally led to consider the origine and design of civil laws.

29. "Atque haud scio an pietate adversus deos sublata fides etiam et societas generis humani et una excellentissima virtus iustitia tollatur" (Cicero, *De natura deorum,* I, 4).

30. This is from Cicero's *De re publica* (see Cicero, *De re publica,* xxii, 33). Until a major part was found in 1819, this work of Cicero was known only in the form of few and brief quotations, especially by patristic authors such as Lactantius.

SECTION XV

These two laws are the foundation of civil laws. Now, we may be very short on this head. For, having found what are the laws and rules men must observe, in order to attain to the greatest perfection and happiness their nature is capable of, it is plain, that the rules and laws they ought to observe, or agree to observe, when they unite together in certain civil or political bodies for the promotion of their common happiness, can be no other than those very laws of nature which have been delineated. And it is very easy to trace the civil laws in well regulated states into the principles above explained as their foundations. The laws of a civil or political state may be divided into these three classes; the laws relating to the private property, quiet and happiness of persons; the laws relating to religion; and those which concern the public order of the government. The first comprehends the laws which regulate covenants or contracts of all kinds, the security of property, alienation and prescription, regular propagation and education, guardianships, successions, testaments, and other matters of the like nature. Now, all these laws are, or ought to be nothing else in their spirit, but the order of that love which we reciprocally owe to one another. Thus the spirit and substance of all the laws, with regard to engagements or covenants, consists in forbidding all infidelity, treachery, double dealing, deceit and knavery, and all other ways of doing hurt and wrong. Thus the regular propagation and education of mankind, or the natural order in which our benevolence ought to exert itself, are the foundation of all the laws relating to marriage, and to parental and filial duties, and to unlawful conjunctions. The same is likewise the foundation of the laws relative to successions. For the order of successions is <321> founded on the necessity of continuing and transmitting the state of society from one generation to another; which is done, by making certain persons to succeed in the place of those who die, and enter upon their rights and offices, their relations and engagements, which are capable of passing to posterity. Good laws of this kind have their foundation on the order in which our benevolence ought to exert itself in parents to children, and reciprocally in children to parents; and on that perfect security of property which is necessary to encourage industry; for men are spurred to industry, not merely by regard to themselves, but by regard to their posterity; and would be very indifferent about making acquisitions, were they not sure of disposing of them as they please, and of transmitting them after they are gone to those they love best, and are most nearly interested in. Many other laws have their foundation in the same principles, and are merely intended to secure the perpetuity of property, such as the regulations about prescription; or to render contracts of various sorts about labour and property equally free and certain. Sumptuary laws have their foundation likewise in the care that parents ought to have of making and leaving suitable provisions to their children; and, in general, in the necessity of promoting industry, and discouraging that idleness, effeminacy and debauchery, which is known to be the source of so many direful ills, and the greatest bane of mankind; the very reverse of all that renders human society either great or happy.

The laws of religion, under which we may comprehend all regulations with regard to education, the main design of which is to tincture the mind early with just notions of God and of human duties, and to form good habits and dispositions; as well as regulations about public worship: these have their foundation in the strict alliance between religion and virtue, in the chief duty of pa-<322>rents towards their children, and in the general interest of society, which is universal virtue.

The public laws are those which fix or regulate the order of making, and of executing laws for the general good. And what these ought to be, must likewise be determined from the nature of mankind, and of that happiness which they are made and intended for by nature. Men may very properly be said to be intended for that civil state, in which, it is plain, from experience, the happiness for which mankind are formed by nature, may be best attained. And the orders of such a civil state must be deduced from the lines of them, as a great author expresses it, which appear in human nature. *It is according to them,* says he, *that this building must be limned.* But we are not now to enter into this curious and important enquiry. All we would take notice of, with regard to the civil laws, which it is the design of civil society to make and execute, is, 1. That in all well-regulated states, the sum and substance of what is called its civil laws, are really laws of natural and universal obligation. Whatever hath the force of civil law in civil courts, derives that force from civil authority. Yet the chief part of civil law is really natural law. What belongs particularly to the civil law, may be reduced, as Pufendorff observes, to these two heads: To certain forms prescribed, and certain methods to be observed in civil affairs, either in transferring rights, or else in laying obligations upon persons, which shall be looked upon to be valid in the civil courts; and to the several ways how a man is to prosecute his rights in the same courts.[31] So that if we give the law of nature all that belongs to it, and take away from the Civilians what they have hitherto promiscuously treated of, we shall bring the civil law to a much narrower compass than it at first sight appears to be. In all commonwealths the natural law supplies the defects of the civil. <323> And in all commonwealths natural law ought to be the substance of the civil law; and the regulations it adds about things which the law of nature prescribes only in a general and indefinite manner, ought to be conformable to the spirit and scope of the law of nature. For which reason, Hobbes calls the law of nature *the unwritten civil law;*[32] and the constitutions of particular commonwealths, justly adapted to the public good, (which, as Cicero says, ought to be the end of all laws, and is the best comment upon, and interpretation of them)[33] are properly called, by some authors, *appendages* to the law of nature. 2. But all the laws of nature have not the force of civil laws allowed them in commonwealths; but such only, upon the observation of which the common quiet of mankind intirely depends; as well because the controversies about the violation of them would be very perplexed and intricate, as to prevent the multiplication of litigious suits; and also, that the good and virtuous might not be deprived of the most valuable part of their character, the doing well out of reverence to their Creator, and sincere love to mankind, without regard to the fears

31. See Pufendorf, *Of the Law of Nature,* VIII.I.I.

32. "Civill, and Naturall Law are not different kinds, but different parts of Law; whereof one part being written, is called Civill, the other unwritten, Naturall" (Thomas Hobbes, *Leviathan,* chap. 26).

33. Perhaps a reference to Cicero's statement in *De legibus* that "the well-being of the people should be the supreme law" ("salus populi suprema lex esto"); see Cicero, *De legibus,* III, iii, 8, in *De re publica; De legibus.*

of human penalties. For this they must necessarily lose, when there is no distinction made whether a man doth well out of love to virtue, or out of fear of punishment. 3. Civil laws are justly said to respect external actions only, whereas moral laws principally regard the habit of the mind, because civil punishments can only be applied against what appears. Yet it is an antient and true observation, that the best and most useful laws, and which are approved of by all such as are subject to them, are of no use, unless subjects be trained up and educated in a manner of living conformable to them. *Plato* says, that to lay the foundations of a good government, we must first begin by the education of children, and must make them as virtuous as possible; as an experienced <324> gardiner employs his care about the young and tender plants, and then goes on to others.[34]

> *Quid leges sine moribus*
> *Vanae proficiunt.* Hor. l. 3. Od. 24.[35]

Isocrates (in Areopagit.) tells us, "The Athenians did not believe that virtue derived so much advantage and assistance in its growth from good statutes as from custom and practice. The greatest part of men must, said they, of necessity frame their minds according to those patterns by which they were first taught and instructed; but a numerous and accurate establishment of laws, is really a sign of the ill condition of the commonwealth, edicts and ordinances being then heap'd upon one another, when governments find themselves obliged to endeavour the restraining of vice, as it were by banks and mounds. That it became wise magistrates, not to fill the public places with proclamations and decrees, but to take care that the subjects should have the love of justice and honesty firmly rooted in their minds. That not the orders of the senate or people, but good and generous education was the thing which made a government happy: Inasmuch as men would venture to break through the nicest ex-

---

34. The importance of children's education for the political community was a central theme in Plato's *Republic*. See in particular the passages from 376d.

35. "What use are laws, vain as they are without morals?" Horace, *Odes,* 3.24.35–36, in *Odes and Epodes.*

actness of political constitutions, if they had not been bred up under a strict obedience to them. Whereas those who had been formed to virtue by a regular and constant discipline, were the only persons who by their just conformity could make good laws obtain a good effect. The principal design of the Athenians, when they made these reflexions, was not how they might punish disorders, but how they might find a way of making the people to be willing not to do any thing that might deserve punishment. This last view seemed to them worthy of themselves and their employment. But as for the other, or an exact <325> application to punish people, they thought it a business proper only for an enemy. And therefore they took care of all the subjects in general, but particularly of the youth."[36]

Thus I have endeavoured to deduce the laws of nature, and the end of civil society and its laws, by an analysis of the human mind, from our internal principles and dispositions. For the virtue or excellence of any being can be nothing else but its nature brought to the perfection of which it is capable. And therefore, the virtue, excellence, or happiness of a being must be deduced from its constitution and situation. *Virtus enim in cujusque rei natura supremum est & perfectio.—Tum oculi, in oculi natura, supremum & perfectio; tum hominis in hominis natura supremum & perfectio.—Hominis virtus est hominis naturae perfectio, nam & equi virtus est ea, quae naturam ejus ad supremum perducit.*" Timaeus Locrus de anima mundi, & Metopus Pythagoreus de virtute.[37] So Cicero de legibus, l. 1. n. 15. & de finibus passim.

FINIS.

---

36. Isocrates, *Areopagiticus,* 182–83, in Isocrates, *Opera omnia,* vol. II, 174–91.

37. This quote is in fact from Hippodamus Thurius, *Peri eudaimonias:* "For virtue is the highest level and the perfection in the nature of everything. The highest level and the perfection of the eye is in the nature of the eye. The highest level and the perfection in a man is in the nature of a man." In Gale, *Opuscula mythologica, physica et ethica,* 660. It is also used by Turnbull in his *Principles of Moral Philosophy,* vol. I, 185.

BIBLIOGRAPHY

The bibliography identifies the works referred to in Heineccius's text and in Turnbull's notes and additions, including editions used in the present editors' annotations. It also lists any other sources that were originally published before 1800 and are referred to in the new introduction.

Primary Sources

Acta eruditorum. 50 vols. Leipzig, 1682–1731.

Aelian (Claudius Aelianus). *Historical Miscellany.* Edited and translated by N. G. Wilson. Loeb Classical Library. Cambridge, Mass.: Harvard University Press, 1997.

————. *On the Characteristics of Animals.* Translated by A. L. Scholfield. Loeb Classical Library. London: Heinemann, 1959.

Africanus, Iohannes Leo. *Africae descriptio IX lib. absoluta.* Leyden, 1632.

Agathias. *De bello Gothorum et aliis peregrinis historiis, per Christophorum Persona Romanum priorem Sa[n]ctae Balbinae e Graeco in Latinum traductus.* Rome, 1516.

Aischines. *Aeschinis Socratici dialogi III. De novo recensuit, vertit et animadversionibus suis auxit Petreus Horreus.* Leeuwarden, 1718.

Alberti, Valentin. *Compendium juris naturae, orthodoxae theologiae conformatum et in duas partes distributum.* Leipzig, 1678.

Althusius, Johannes. *Politica* [1603]. Edited and translated by F. S. Carney. Indianapolis: Liberty Fund, 1995.

Ambrose. *De officiis.* Edited with an introduction, translation, and commentary by Ivor J. Davidson. Oxford: Oxford University Press, 2001.

Amyraldus, Moses. *De jure dei in creaturas dissertatio.* In *Dissertationes theologicae sex, quarum quatuor . . . antehac editae, nunc revisae prodeunt; duae . . . ad superiores additae sunt.* Saumur, 1660.

Andala, Ruardus ab. *Syntagma theologico-physico-metaphysicum, complectens Compendium theologiae naturalis.* Franeker, 1711.

Apollinaris Sidonius (Caius Sollius Apollinaris Sidonius). *Poems and Letters.* 2 vols. Translated and edited by W. B. Anderson. Loeb Classical Library. London: Heinemann, 1936–65.

Apuleius, Lucius. *Apulei Apologia sive pro se de magia liber.* Introduction and commentary by H. E. Butler. Oxford: Clarendon Press, 1914.

———. *Apuleius' Golden Ass or The Metamorphosis, and Other Philosophical Writings viz. On the God of Socrates & On the Philosophy of Plato.* Translated by Thomas Taylor. Frome, Somerset, U.K.: Prometheus Trust, 1997.

———. *Apuleius: Rhetorical Works.* Translated and annotated by Stephen Harrison, John Hilton, and Vincent Hunink. Edited by Stephen Harrison. Oxford: Oxford University Press, 2001.

Aristides, Publius Aelius. *The Complete Works.* 2 vols. Translated by C. A. Behr. Leiden: Brill, 1981–86.

Aristophanes. *Wasps.* Edited by D. M. MacDowell. Oxford: Clarendon Press, 1971.

Aristotle. *The Metaphysics.* Translated with an introduction by Hugh Lawson-Tancred. London: Penguin Books, 1998.

———. *Politics.* Translated and edited by E. Barker. Oxford: Clarendon Press, 1961.

———. *The Works of Aristotle Translated into English.* Vol. IX: *Ethica Nicomachea, Magna Moralia, Ethica Eudemia.* Translated by W. D. Ross, St. George Stock, and J. Solomon. Oxford: Clarendon Press, 1915.

Arnold, Gottfried. *Unpartheyische Kirchen- und Ketzer-Historie.* Frankfurt am Main, 1700.

Arrian (Flavius Arrianus). *The Campaigns of Alexander the Great.* Translated by Aubrey de Selincourt. Revised, with a new introduction and notes by J. R. Hamilton. Harmondsworth, U.K.: Penguin Books, 1971.

Athenaeus. *The Deipnosophists.* 7 vols. Translated by Charles Burton Gulick. Loeb Classical Library. London: Heinemann, 1927–41.

Augustine of Hippo. *On Free Choice of the Will.* Edited and translated by Thomas Williams. Indianapolis: Hackett, 1993.

Babrius and Phaedrus. *Babrius and Phaedrus.* Translated and edited by B. E. Perry. Loeb Classical Library. Cambridge, Mass.: Harvard University Press, 1965.

Bachoff von Echt, Johann Friedrich. *De eo quod Iustum est circa commercia inter gentes ac praecipue de origine et Iustitia societatum istarum mercatori-arum maiorum, quae Octroyirte Compagnien adpellari solent.* Jena, 1730.

Baluze, Etienne, ed., *Capitularia regum Francorum.* 2 vols. Paris, 1677.

Barbeyrac, Jean. *Defense du droit de la Compagnie Hollandoise des Indes Or-ientales contre les nouvelles prétensions des habitans des Pays-Bas Autrichiens, et les raisons ou objections des Avocats de la Compagnie d'Ostende.* The Hague, 1725.

————. "Preface du Traducteur." In Hugo Grotius, *Le Droit de la guerre et de la paix.* 2 vols. Amsterdam, 1724.

Basnage, Jacques. *Annales des Provinces-Unies, depuis les négociations pour la paix de Munster avec la description historique de leur gouvernement.* The Hague, 1726.

Bayle, Pierre. *Dictionnaire historique et critique.* 4 vols. 5th ed. Amsterdam, 1740.

Becmann, Johann Christoph. *Historia orbis terrarum, geographica et civilis: de variis negotiis nostri potissimum et superioris seculi, aliisve rebus selectioribus.* Frankfurt and Leipzig, 1707.

————. *Meditationes politicae, iisdemque continuandis & illustrandis addita politica parallela, XXIV dissertationibus academicis antehac exposuit Joh. Christoph Becmanus.* 4th ed. Frankfurt an der Oder, 1693.

————. *Notitia dignitatum illustrium civilium, sacrarum, equestrium: XVI. dissertationibus academicis.* Frankfurt and Leipzig, 1685.

Beger, Lorenz (Daphnaeus Arcuarius). *Daphnaei Arcuarii Kurtze, doch unpartheiisch- und gewissenhafte Betrachtung des in dem Natur- und Gött-lichen Recht gegründeten heyligen Ehstandes.* N.p., 1679.

Beza, Theodore. *Jesu Christi Domini Nostri Novum Testamentum, sive Novum Foedus, cujus Graeco contextui rependent interpretationes duae: una vetus, altera Theodori Bezae.* Cambridge, 1642.

————. *Tractatio de polygamia, in qua et Ochini Apostatae pro polygamia, et Montanistarum ac aliorum adversus repetitas nuptias argumenta refutantur.* Daventer, 1651.

Bodin, Jean. *De republica libri sex, Latine ab auctore reddita.* 5th ed. Frankfurt am Main, 1609.

————. *Les six livres de la Republique.* Paris, 1583.

Bodinus, Heinrich (*praeses*) and Otto Henricus Becker (*respondens*). *Jus mundi seu vindiciae juris naturae.* Rinteln, 1690.

Boecler, Johann Heinrich. *In Hugonis Grotii Ius belli et pacis, ad illustrissimum baronem Boineburgium commentatio.* Strasburg, 1663–64.

————. *Synedrion Amphyktyonikon*. Strasburg, 1657.

Boecler, Johann Heinrich (*praeses*) and Christian Barnekow (*respondens*). *Dissertatio de clarigatione et manifestis, ut appellantur, quam supremo belli pacisque arbitro annuente*. Strasburg, 1648.

Boecler, Johann Heinrich (*praeses*) and Johann Andreas Forer (*respondens*). *Isopsephia sive calculus Minervae*. Strasburg, 1654.

Boecler, Johann Heinrich (*praeses*) and Karl Sigismund von Kronegk (*respondens*). *Minos maris dominus*. Strasburg, 1656.

Boehmer, Justus Henning. *Jus ecclesiasticum Protestantium, usum hodiernum iuris canonici iuxta seriem decretalium ostendens et ipsis rerum argumentis illustrans*. 5 vols. Halle, 1717–37.

Boehmer, Justus Henning (*praeses*) and Joannes Christianus de Becquer (*respondens*). *Doctrina de jure episcopali principum evangelicorum* [1712]. Halle, 1724.

Borgo, Pietro Battista. *De dominio serenissimae Genuensis reipublicae in Mari Ligustico libri II*. Rome, 1641.

Bourgogne, Nicolas de. *Ad consuetudines Flandriae aliarumque gentium tractatus controversiarum*. Arnhem, 1670.

Boxhorn, Marcus. *Disquisitiones politicae, id est, sexaginta casus politici ex omni historia selecti*. Erfurt, 1664.

————. *Institutionum politicarum libri tres: in captiva sua et quaestiones distincti, quibus Reipublicae constitutio &c. diversae formae, rectaque ejusdem administratio, succincte & nervosè demonstratur*. Königsberg, 1678.

————, ed. *Historiae Augustae scriptores Latini minores*. Leyden, 1632.

Brisson, Barnarbé. *De regio Persarum principatu libri tres, post Frid. Sylburgii editionem*. Strasburg, 1710.

Brunsmann, Johann. *Monogamia victrix: sive Orthodoxa Ecclesiae Christianae sententia, de unis duntaxat eodem tempore concessis Christiano nuptiis, a criminationibus vindicata*. Frankfurt, 1678.

Brutus, Stephanus Junius. *Vindiciae contra tyrannos, or, Concerning the Legitimate Power of a Prince over the People, and of the People over a Prince*. Edited and translated by George Barnett. Cambridge: Cambridge University Press, 1994.

Buchanan, George. *Rerum Scotiarum historia*. Edinburgh, 1582.

Budde, Johann Franz. *Historia juris naturalis*. Halle, 1718.

————. *Institutiones theologiae moralis, variis observationibus illustratae*. Leipzig, 1712.

————. *Introductio ad historiam philosophiae ebraeorum*. Halle, 1702.

————. *Theses theologicae de atheismo et superstitione variis observationibus illustratae et in usum recitationum academicarum editae.* Jena, 1717.

Budde, Johann Franz (*praeses*) and J. H. Greulinck (*respondens*). *De expeditionibus cruciatis dissertatio politica.* Halle, 1694.

The Burgundian Code. Translated by Katherine Fischer Drew. Philadelphia: University of Pennsylvania Press, 1972.

Butler, Joseph. *Fifteen Sermons Preached at the Rolls Chapel.* London, 1726.

Bynaeus, Antonius. *De calceis Hebraeorum libri duo.* Dordrecht, 1682.

Bynkershoek, Cornelius van, *Curae secundae de jure occidendi et exponendi liberos apud veteres Romanos.* In Gerard Noodt, *Julius Paulus, sive de partus expositione et nece apud veteres.* 3rd ed. Amsterdam, 1710.

————. *De dominio maris dissertatio* [1703]. Photographic reproduction of 2nd ed. of 1744. Translated by Ralph van Deman Magoffin. New York: Oceana, 1923.

————. *De foro legatorum tam in causa civili, quam criminali liber singularis.* Leyden, 1721.

————. *Observationum iuris Romani libri quatuor.* Leyden, 1710.

————. *Quaestionum juris publici libri duo, quorum primus de rebus bellicis, secundus de rebus varii argumenti* [1737]. 2 vols. Translated by Tenney Frank. Oxford: Clarendon Press, 1930.

Caesar, Gaius Julius, *The Civil War,* books 1–3. 2 vols. Edited and translated by J. M. Carter. Warminster, U.K.: Aris & Phillips, 1991–93.

————. *The Gallic War.* Translated by H. J. Edwards. Loeb Classical Library. London: Heinemann, 1952.

Capitularia Regum Francorum. 2 vols. Edited by E. Baluze. Paris, 1677.

Casaubon, Isaac. *Auli Persii Flacci Satirarum liber, cum ejus vita, vetere scholiaste et Isaaci Casauboni notis et commentario libro illustravit, una cum ejusdem Persiana Horatii imitatione.* Editio novissima. Leyden, 1695.

Cassius, Dio. *Dio's Roman History.* 9 vols. English translation by Earnest Cary based on the version of Herbert Baldwin Foster. New York: Macmillan, 1914–27.

Charles VI (Holy Roman Emperor). *Capitulatio Caroli VI. Electi Romanorum Imperator semper Augusti.* The Hague, 1713.

Charron, Pierre. *De la sagesse.* Bourdeaux, 1601.

Chrysostom, Dio. *Dio Chrysostom.* 5 vols. Translated by J. W Cohoon and H. Lamar Crosby. Loeb Classical Library. London: Heinemann, 1932–51.

Chrysostom, John. *Homilies on the Epistles of Paul to the Corinthians.* Edited by T. W. Chambers. Grand Rapids, Mich.: Eerdmans, 1956.

Cicero, Marcus Tullius. *Cato major de senectute.* Edited with introduction and commentary by J. G. F. Powell. Cambridge: Cambridge University Press, 1988.

———. *Defence Speeches.* Translated by D. H. Berry. Oxford: Oxford University Press, 2000.

———. *De finibus bonorum et malorum.* 2nd ed. Translated by H. W. Rackham. Loeb Classical Library. London: Heinemann, 1951.

———. *De inventione; De optimo genere oratorum; Topica.* English translation by H. M. Hubbell. Loeb Classical Library. London: Heinemann, 1993.

———. *De natura deorum, academica.* Edited and translated by H. W. Rackham. London: Heinemann, 1951.

———. *De officiis.* Translated by Walter Miller. Loeb Classical Library. London: Heinemann, 1951.

———. *De re publica; De legibus.* Translated by C. W. Keyes. Loeb Classical Library. Cambridge, Mass.: Harvard University Press, 1977.

———. *Epistulae ad Atticum.* Edited by L. C. Purser. Vol. 3 of *M. Tulli Ciceronis epistulae.* Oxford: Clarendon Press, 1958–62.

———. *Epistulae ad familiares.* Edited by L. C. Purser. Vol. 1 of *M. Tulli Ciceronis epistulae.* Oxford: Clarendon Press, 1979.

———. *Epistulae ad Quintum fratrem et M. Brutum.* Edited by D. R. Shackleton Bailey. Cambridge: Cambridge University Press, 1980.

———. *On Academic Scepticism.* Translated and edited by Charles Brittain. Indianapolis: Hackett Publishing, 2006.

———. *Paradoxa Stoicorum.* Introduction and notes by A. G. Lee. London: Macmillan, 1953.

———. *Pro lege Manilia; Pro Caecina; Pro Cluentio; Pro Rabirio Perduellionis.* Translated by H. Grose Hodge. Loeb Classical Library. Cambridge, Mass.: Harvard University Press, 1990.

———. *Pro Publio Quinctio; Pro Sexto Roscio Amerino; Pro Quinto Roscio comoedo; De lege agraria 1, 2, 3.* Translated by J. H. Freese. Loeb Classical Library. Cambridge, Mass.: Harvard University Press, 1967.

———. *Pro T. Annio Milone; In L. Calpurnium Pisonem; Pro. M. Aemilio Scauro; Pro M. Fonteio; Pro C. Rabirio Postumo; Pro M. Marcello; Pro Q. Ligario; Pro Rege Deiotaro.* Translated by N. H. Watts. Loeb Classical Library. London: Heinemann, 1953.

———. *The Speeches, with an English Translation.* Translated by J. H. Freese. Loeb Classical Library. London: Heinemann, 1956.

———. *Tusculan Disputations.* Translated by J. E. King. Loeb Classical Library. London: Heinemann, 1927.

Claudian (Claudius Claudianus). *Claudii Claudiani poetae praegloriosissimo quae exstant.* Edited and with a commentary by Caspar Barth. Frankfurt, 1650.

———. *Panegyricus de sexto consulatu Honorii Augusti* (*Panegyric on the Sixth Consulship of Honorius Augustus*). Edited by M. J. Dewar. Oxford: Clarendon Press, 1996.

Clement of Alexandria. *Clement of Alexandria.* Translated by G. W. Butterworth. London: Heinemann, 1919.

———. *Les Stromates* (*Stromateis*). *Stromate V.* 2 vols. Edited by Alain de Boulluec, translated into French by Pierre Voulet. Paris: Éditions du Cerf, 1981.

———. *Die Teppiche* (*Stromateis*). Translated into German by Franz Overbeck, edited and with an introduction by Carl Albrecht Bernoulli and Ludwig Früchtel. Basel: B. Schwabe, 1936.

Clerc, Jean le (Johannes Clericus). *Ars critica.* 3 vols. Leipzig, 1713.

———. *Genesis sive Mosis prophetae liber primus: ex translatione Joannis Clerici, cum ejusdem paraphrasi perpetua, commentario philologico, dissertationibus criticis quinque, et tabulis chronologicis. Editio nova auctior et emendatior.* Tübingen, 1733.

———. *Mosis prophetae libri quatuor: Exodus, Leviticus, Numeri, et Deuteronomium; cum ejusdem paraphrasi perpetua, commentario philologico.* Tübingen, 1733.

Cocceji, Heinrich von (*praeses*) and Johannes Gothofredus Cocceji (*respondens*). *Disputatio juridica inauguralis de testamentis principum.* Frankfurt an der Oder, 1699.

Cocceji, Heinrich von, and Samuel von Cocceji. *Dissertatio de principio iuris naturae unico, vero & adequato.* Frankfurt an der Oder, 1699.

Cocceji, Heinrich von (*praeses*) and Franciscus Meyer (*respondens*). *Disputatio juridica inauguralis, de eo, quod justum est circa numerum suffragiorum, ubi de calculo Minervae.* Frankfurt an der Oder, 1705.

Cocceji, Heinrich von (*praeses*) and Daniel de Stephani (*respondens*). *Disputatio juris gentium publici de guarantia pacis.* Frankfurt an der Oder, 1702.

Cocceji, Heinrich von (*praeses*) and Otto Philipp Zaunschliffer (*respondens*). *Discursus juridicus inauguralis de eo quod fit ipso jure.* Heidelberg, 1678.

Coke, Edward. *The First Part of the Institutes of the Laws of England, or A Commentary upon Littleton.* 13th ed. London, 1788.

Connan, François. *Commentariorum juris civilis libri X.* Naples, 1724.

Connor, Bernard. *Evangelium medici seu medicina mystica; de suspensis naturae legibus sive de miraculis.* 4th ed. Jena, 1724.

Conradi, Franz Karl. *De pacto fiduciae: exercitatio II.* Helmstedt, 1733.

Conring, Hermann, *Opera.* 6 vols. Edited by Johann Wilhelm Goebbel. Braunschweig, 1730.

Conring, Hermann (*praeses*) and Joachim Christian Koch (*respondens*). *Discursus politicus de militia lecta, mercenaria et sociali.* Helmstedt, 1663.

Cujas, Jacques (Jacobus Cujacius). *Iustiniani . . . Institutionum sive elementorum . . . libri IV emendatissime ex editione Jacobi Cujacii* [1576]. Leyden 1719.

———. *Opera omnia, in decem tomos distributa . . . Editio nova emendatior . . . cura Caroli Annibalis Fabroti.* Paris, 1658.

Cumberland, Richard. *De legibus naturae: disquisitio philosophica.* London, 1672.

———. *A Treatise of the Law of Nature.* Edited by Jon Parkin. Indianapolis: Liberty Fund, 2005.

Cunaeus, Petrus. *Orationes argumenti varii.* Leipzig, 1735.

Curtius Rufus, Quintus. *Alexander Magnus.* 2 vols. Edited by Johannes Freinshemius. Strasburg, 1639–40.

———. *History of Alexander.* 2 vols. Translated by J. C. Rolfe. Loeb Classical Library. London: Heinemann, 1946.

Cuspinianus, Johannes. *De Caesaribus atque Imperatoribus Romanorum . . . opus.* Frankfurt, 1601.

Delphinus, Hieronymus. *Eunuchi conjugium = Capaunen-Heyrath: hoc est scripta et judicia varia de conjugio inter Eunuchum et Virginem Juvenculam anno MDCLXI. contracto. Editio novissima summa fide emendata.* Jena, 1737.

Demosthenes. *Demosthenes.* Vol. 3. Translated by J. H. Vince. Loeb Classical Library. London: Heinemann, 1935.

Dietherr, Christoph Ludwig. *Orbis novus literatorum, praeprimis jurisconsultorum, detectus, sive continuatio thesauri practici Besoldiani.* Nuremberg, 1699.

Diodorus Siculus. *The Bibliotheca historica of Diodorus Siculus.* Vol. I: *The Text.* Translated by John Skelton. Edited by F. M. Salter and H. L. R. Edwards [1956]. London: Published for the Early English Text Society by the Oxford University Press, 1968.

Diogenes Laertius. *De vitis et dogmatis et apophtegmatis clarorum philosophorum*. Geneva, 1616.

———. *Lives of Eminent Philosophers*. 2 vols. Translation by R. D. Hicks. London: Heinemann, 1925.

Dionysius of Halicarnassus. *The Roman Antiquities of Dionysius of Halicarnassus*. 7 vols. Translated by Earnest Cary. Loeb Classical Library. London: Heinemann, 1937–50.

Domat, Jean. *The Civil Law in Its Natural Order: Together with the Publick Law*. 2 vols. Translated by William Strahan. London, 1722.

———. *Les loix civiles dans leur ordre naturel*. Paris, 1695.

Doneau, Hugues (Hugo Donellus). *Commentariorum juris civilis libri viginti octo in quibus jus civile universum singulari artificio atque doctrina explicatur. Scipio Gentilis recensuit, editit, posteriores etiam libros supplevit.* Frankfurt, 1626.

Emmo, Ubbo. *Vetus Graecia, opus distinctum in tomos tres*. Leyden, 1699.

Empiricus, Sextus. *Outlines of Scepticism (Pyrroneioi hypotyposeis)*. Translated by Julia Annas and Jonathan Barnes. Cambridge: Cambridge University Press, 1994.

Ennius, Quintus. *Annals*. Edited by O. Skutsch. Oxford: Clarendon Press, 1985.

Epictetus. *The Discourses and Manual*. 2 vols. Translated by P. E. Matheson. Oxford: Clarendon Press, 1916.

———. *The Discourses as Reported by Arrian, the Manual, and Fragments*. 2 vols. Translated by W. A. Oldfather. Loeb Classical Library. London: Heinemann, 1926–28.

Epiphanius. *The Panarion of St. Epiphanius, Bishop of Salamis: Selected Passages*. Translated by Philip R. Amidon. New York: Oxford University Press, 1990.

Erasmus, Desiderius. *Adages*. 6 vols. In *Collected Works of Erasmus*, vols. 31–36. Toronto: University of Toronto Press, 1982–2006.

———. *Enchiridion militis Christiani: An English version*. Edited by Anne M. O'Donnell. Oxford: Published for the Early English Text Society by Oxford University Press, 1981.

———. *Opera omnia emendatiora et auctiora*. Edited by Jean le Clerc. 10 vols. [1703]. Hildesheim: Olms, 2001.

Euripides. *Euripides.* 4 vols. Translated by A. S. Way. Loeb Classical Library. London: Heinemann, 1930–35.

———. *Euripides.* Vol. 1: *Cyclops, Alcestis, Medea.* Edited and translated by David Kovacs. Loeb Clasical Library. Cambridge, Mass.: Harvard University Press, 2001.

———. *Euripides.* Vol. 5: *Helen, Phoenician Women, Orestes.* Edited and translated by David Kovacs. Loeb Classical Library. Cambridge, Mass.: Harvard University Press, 2002.

———. *Hippolytus.* Edited by W. S. Barrett. Oxford: Clarendon Press, 1964.

———. *Iphigenia in Aulis.* Edited by S. MacEwen and T. A. Tarkow. Bryn Mawr, Pa.: Thomas Library, Bryn Mawr College, 1988.

———. *Iphigenia in Tauris.* Translated and edited by M. J. Cropp. Warminster, U.K.: Aris & Phillips, 2000.

———. *Medea.* Edited by A. Elliott. [London]: Oxford University Press, 1969.

———. *Orestes.* Edited and translated by M. L. West. Warminster, U.K.: Aris & Phillips, 1987.

Eusebius. *Life of Constantine.* Introduction, translation, and commentary by Averil Cameron and Stuart G. Hall. Oxford: Clarendon Press, 1999.

———. *Praeparationis evangelicae libri XV.* 5 vols. Translated and edited by E. H. Gifford. Oxford: E Typographeo Academico, 1903.

Fabricius, J. A. *Abriss einer allgemeinen Historie der Gelehrsamkeit.* Leipzig, 1754.

Feder, K. A., ed. *Excerpta e Polybio, Diodoro, Dionysio Halicarnassensi atque Nicolao Damasceno.* 5 vols. Darmstadt: Leske, 1848–50.

Fénelon, François de Salignac de La Mothe-. *Explication des maximes des saints sur la vie intérieure.* Paris, 1698.

———. *Telemachus, Son of Ulysses.* Translated and edited by Patrick Riley. Cambridge: Cambridge University Press, 1994.

Festus, Sextus Pompeius. *De verborum significatu quae supersunt cum Pauli epitome.* Edited by W. M. Lindsay. Reprint of 1913 edition. Stuttgart: Teubner, 1997.

Flaccus, Valerius. *Argonautica.* English translation by J. H. Mozley. Cambridge, Mass.: Harvard University Press, 1998.

Flacius Illyricus, Matthias. *De translatione imperii Romani ad Germanos.* Basileae, 1566.

Fleury, Aimon de. *Historiae Francorum libri IV.* In Marquard Freher, ed., *Corpus Francicae historiae veteris et sincerae.* Hanover, Germany, 1613.

Florus, Lucius Annaeus. *Epitome of Roman History.* Loeb Classical Library. Translated by E. S. Forster. Cambridge, Mass.: Harvard University Press, 1984.

Fragmenta philosophorum Graecorum, vol. 1. Edited by F. W. A. Mullach. Reprint of 1860 ed. Aalen: Scientia, 1968.

Gale, Thomas, ed. *Opuscula mythologica, physica et ethica.* Amsterdam, 1688.

Garnett, George, ed. *Vindiciae contra tyrannos, or, Concerning the Legitimate Power of a Prince over the People, and of the People over a Prince.* Cambridge: Cambridge University Press, 1994.

Gellius, Aulus. *Attic Nights (Noctes Atticae).* 3 vols. Translated by J. C. Rolfe. Loeb Classical Library. London: Heinemann, 1948–54.

Gentili, Alberico. *De jure belli* [1588]. Edited by C. Phillipson; translated by J. C. Rolfe. Oxford: Clarendon Press, 1933.

Gentili, Scipione. *In L. Apuleii philosophi & aduocati Romani Apologiam, qua se ipse defendit Publico de Magia iudicio commentarius.* Hanau, 1607.

———. *Originum ad Pandectas liber singularis.* In *Parergorum ad Pandectas libri duo.* Frankfurt, 1588.

Gerhard, Johann. *Loci theologici.* 9 vols. Jena, 1610–22.

———. *Locorum theologicorum cum pro adstruenda veritate, tum pro destruenda quorumvis contradicentium falsitate per theses nervose, solide & copiosè explicatorum Tomus VII: In quo continentur capita: 28. De conjugio, caelibatu & cognatis materiis.* Vol. 7 of *Loci theologici.* Jena, 1620.

Gesenius, Friedrich. *Christiani Vigilis Germani ad Sincerum Warenbergium Suecum Epistula seu Dissertatio super polygamia simultanea, in qua primaevum conjugii institutum de non nisi una uxore simul habenda . . . miscuerit.* Germanopoli, 1673.

Glaber, Rodulfus. *The Five Books of the Histories; The Life of St. William.* Edited by Neithard Bulst and John France, translated by John France and Paul Reynolds. Oxford: Clarendon Press, 1989.

Godefroy, Jacques (Jacobus Gothofredus). *De electione magistratus inhabilis seu incapacis per errorem facta: dissertatio ad L. Barbarius Philippus III. D. de officio praetorum.* Helmstedt, 1732.

———. *De imperio maris deque iure naufragii colligendi.* Geneva, 1637.

Goes, Willem, and Nicolas Rigault, eds. *Rei agrariae auctores legesque variae.* Amsterdam, 1674.

Goldast, Melchior, and Christoph Senckenberg. *Rerum Alamannicarum scriptores aliquot vetusti.* 3rd ed. Frankfurt and Leipzig, 1730.

Graswinckel, Theodorus. *Maris liberi vindiciae.* The Hague, 1652.

Gronovius, Jacobus. *Thesaurus Graecarum Antiquitatum.* Vol. 5, *Attici imperii amplitudinem ac mutationes, ut et Lacedaemonis complexum.* Leyden, 1699.

Gronovius, Johann Friedrich. *Observationum libri III.* Leyden, 1662.

Grotius, Hugo. *De aequitate, indulgentia, et facilitate liber singularis.* In Hugo Grotius, *De jure belli ac pacis libri tres.* Amsterdam, 1720.

―――. *De jure belli ac pacis libri tres, in quibus jus naturae & gentium, item juris publici praecipua explicantur.* Edited by J. F. Gronovius. The Hague, 1680.

―――. *Le droit de la guerre et de la paix.* 2 vols. Translated and edited by Jean Barbeyrac. Amsterdam, 1724.

―――. *The Free Sea* [1609]. Edited by David Armitage. Indianapolis: Liberty Fund, 2004.

―――. *The Rights of War and Peace.* Edited by Richard Tuck. 3 vols. Indianapolis: Liberty Fund, 2005.

Gundling, Nicolaus Hieronymus. *Gundlingiana darinnen allerhand zur Jurisprudenz, Philosophie, Historie, Critic, Literatur und übrigen Gelehrsamkeit gehörige Sachen abgehandelt werden.* Halle, 1717.

Gundling, Nicolaus Hieronymus (*praeses*) and Johann Heinrich Benz (*respondens*). *Dissertatio iuridica, qua doctrina vulgaris maiorem a feminis, quam a viris, requirens castitatem.* Halle, 1717.

Hagemeier, Joachim. *Juris publici Europaei de statu Regni Poloniae et imperii Moscovitici epistola VIII. ad Illustrissimum Dominum Anthonium, Comitem Aldenburgensem.* Frankfurt am Main, 1680.

Harrington, James. *James Harrington's Oceana.* Edited by S. B. Liljegren. Heidelberg: C. Winter, 1924.

―――. *The Oceana and Other Works of James Harrington, Esq; Collected, Methodiz'd, and Review'd, with an Exact Account of His Life Prefix'd, by John Toland.* London, 1737.

―――. *The Political Works of James Harrington.* Edited and with an introduction by J. G. A. Pocock. Cambridge: Cambridge University Press, 1970.

Hartknoch, Christoph. *De republica Polonica libri duo: quorum prior historiae Polonicae memorabiliora; posterior autem ius publicum reipublicae Polonicae, Lithuanicae provinciarumque annexarum comprehendit.* 3rd ed. Leipzig, 1698.

Hauteserre, Antoine Dadin de. *De fictionibus juris tractatus quinque.* 2 vols. Paris, 1659–79.

Heineccius, J. C. G. *De vita, fatis et scriptis Jo. Gottlieb Heineccii iurisconsulti.* In vol. I of *Opera omnia.* 8 vols. Geneva, 1744–49.

Heineccius, Johann Gottlieb. *Elementa iuris civilis secundum ordinem Institutionum.* Giessen, 1727.

———. *Elementa iuris civilis secundum ordinem Pandectarum, commoda auditoribus methodo adornata.* Amsterdam, 1728.

———. *Elementa iuris Germanici tum veteris tum hodierni. Editio nova auctior et emendatior.* 2 vols. Halle, 1736–37.

———. *Elementa philosophiae rationalis et moralis.* Frankfurt an der Oder, 1728.

Heineccius, Johann Gottlieb (*praeses*) and Johann Gunther (*respondens*). *De testamentifactione iure Germanico arctis limitibus passim circumscripta: dissertatio iuridica inauguralis.* Halle, 1734.

Heineccius, Johann Gottlieb (*praeses*) and Frederic Kessler (*respondens*). *De navibus ob mercium illicitarum vecturam commissis: dissertatio iuridica.* Halle, 1721.

Heineccius, Johann Gottlieb (*praeses*) and Johann Matthias Egelgraser (*respondens*). *De reductione monetae ad iustum pretium dissertatio iuridica.* Halle, 1737.

Heineccius, Johann Gottlieb (*praeses*) and Christian Eberhard Russel (*respondens*). *De suprema principum magistratuumque tutela dissertatio iuridica inauguralis.* Frankfurt an der Oder, 1730.

Heliodorus, *An Ethiopian Romance.* Translated with an introduction by Moses Hadas. Philadelphia: University of Pennsylvania Press, 1999.

Herodotus. *Herodoti Halicarnassei historiae libri IX et de vita Homeri libellus; . . . utraque ab Henrico Stephano recognita.* Frankfurt, 1620.

———. *Histories.* 4 vols. Translation by A. D. Godley. Loeb Classical Library. London: Heinemann, 1921–31.

———. *Histories.* Translated by Aubrey de Selincourt; revised with introductory matter and notes by John Marincola. London: Penguin, 1996.

Hersfeld, Lambert. *Lamperti Monachis Hersfeldensis opera.* Reprint of 1894 edition. Hannover: Hahn, 1956.

Hertius, Johann Nikolaus. *Commentatio iuridica de matrimonio putativo.* Giessen, 1727.

———. *Elementa prudentiae civilis.* Frankfurt, 1703.

Hertius, Johann Nikolaus (*praeses*) and W. L. Ehrhart (*respondens*). *Dissertatio de consultationibus, legibus et judiciis in specialibus Germaniae rebus-*

publicis = *Von Land-Tägen, Gesetzen und Gerichten besonderer Republiquen in Teutschland* [1686]. Halle, 1736.

Hertius, Johann Nikolaus (*praeses*) and Johann Hartmuth Gärtner (*respondens*). *Disquisitio juridica, de obligatione alium daturum facturumve.* Giessen, 1693.

Hertius, Johann Nikolaus (*praeses*) and Johannes David Gilfeld (*respondens*). *De societate facto contracta.* Giessen, 1695.

Hertius, Johann Nikolaus (*praeses*) and Georg Heinrich Hasslocher (*respondens*). *Dissertatio de uno homine, plures sustinente personas.* Giessen, 1691.

Hertius, Johann Nikolaus (*praeses*) and J. C. Viselius (*respondens*). *De Lytro von Rantzion.* Giessen, 1686.

Hesiod. *Theogony and Works and Days.* Translated and edited by M. L. West. Oxford: Oxford University Press, 1988.

———. *Works and Days.* Edited by R. Hamilton, E. G. Rainis, and R. L. Ruttenberg. Bryn Mawr, Pa.: Thomas Library, Bryn Mawr College, 1988.

Hickes, George. *Jovian. Or, An Answer to Julian the Apostate.* London, 1683.

Hierocles. *Commentary on the Golden Verses of the Pythagoreans.* In *Hierocles of Alexander.* Edited by Hermann S. Schibli. Oxford: Oxford University Press, 2002.

Hieronymus. *Opera.* 11 vols. Verona, 1734–42.

Hippodamus Thurius. *Peri eudaimonias* (*De felicitate*). In Diogenes Laertius, *De vitis, dogmatis et apophthegmatis clarorum philosophorum.* Geneva, 1616.

Hirtius, Aulus. *Caii Iulii Caesaris de bellis gallico et civili Pompeiano: nec non A. Hirtii aliorumque de bellis alexandrino, africano, et hispaniensi commentarii.* Leyden and Rotterdam, 1737.

Hoadley, Benjamin. *The Measures of Submission to the Civil Magistrate Consider'd: In a Defense of the Doctrine Deliver'd in a Sermon Preach'd . . . Sept. 29. 1705. The fourth edition.* London, 1710.

Hobbes, Thomas. *Leviathan.* Edited by Richard Tuck. Cambridge: Cambridge University Press, 1992.

———. *On the Citizen* (*De cive*). Translated by Michael Silverthorne, edited by Michael Silverthorne and Richard Tuck. Cambridge: Cambridge University Press, 1998.

Hochstetter, Andreas Adam. *Collegium Pufendorfianum, super libris duobus de officio hominis et civis, anno MDCC. In academia Tubingensi XII. exercitationibus institutum.* Tübingen, 1710.

Homer. *The Iliad of Homer.* Translated by Alexander Pope. 6 vols. London, 1715–20.

———. The Iliad. 2 vols. Translated by A. T. Murray. Loeb Classical Library. London: Heinemann, 1924–25.

———. *The Odyssey.* Translated by Alexander Pope. 5 vols. London, 1725–26.

———. *Odyssey.* Edited by W. B. Stanford. London: Bristol Classical Press, 1996.

Horace (Quintus Horatius Flaccus). *Odes and Epodes.* Edited and translated by Niall Rudd. Loeb Classical Library. Cambridge, Mass.: Harvard University Press, 2004.

———. *Satires I.* Edited by P. M. Brown. Warminster, U.K.: Aris & Phillips, 1993.

———. *Satires II.* Edited by F. Muecke. Warminster, U.K.: Aris & Phillips, 1993.

———. *Satires, Epistles, and Ars Poetica.* Translated by H. Rushton Fairclough, Loeb Classical Library. London: Heinemann, 1947.

Hotman, François. *Francogallia* [1573]. Edited by R. Gisey and J. H. M. Salomon. Cambridge: Cambridge University Press, 1972.

Houtuyn, Adrian. *Politica contracta generalis.* The Hague, 1681.

Huber, Ulrik. *De jure civitatis libri tres.* Franeker, 1672.

———. *Praelectionum juris civilis tomi III: Secundum Institutiones et Digesta Justiniani.* Leipzig, 1735.

Huber, Zacharias. *Dissertationes juridicae et philologicae, quibus explicantur ac observationibus humanioribus illustrantur selecta controversiarum et legum capita.* 2 vols. Franeker, 1703–6.

Huet, Pierre-Daniel. *Alnetanae quaestiones de concordia rationis et fidei.* Leipzig, 1692.

———. *Origeniana.* Cologne, 1685.

Hutcheson, Francis. *An Inquiry into the Original of Our Ideas of Beauty and Virtue.* London, 1725.

———. *An Inquiry into the Original of Our Ideas of Beauty and Virtue.* 3rd edition. London, 1729.

———. *An Inquiry into the Original of Our Ideas of Beauty and Virtue.* 4th edition. London, 1738.

———. *An Inquiry into the Original of Our Ideas of Beauty and Virtue.* Revised ed. Edited by Wolfgang Leidhold. Indianapolis: Liberty Fund, 2008.

————. *A Short Introduction to Moral Philosophy.* Glasgow, 1747.

Iamblichus. *Iamblichus on the Mysteries of the Egyptians, Chaldeans, and Assyrians; and, Life of Pythagoras.* Translated by Thomas Taylor. Frome, 1999.

Isidore. *Isidori Hispalensis Episcopi Etymologiarum sive originum libri XX.* 2 vols. Edited by W. M. Lindsay. Oxford: Clarendon Press, 1966.

Isocrates. *Isocrates.* 3 vols. Translated by George Norlin and Larue van Hook. Loeb Classical Library. London: Heinemann, 1928–45.

————. *Isocratis epistola ad Archidamum Lacedaemoniorum regem in omnibus Isocrateis editionibus ad hoc usque tempus desiderata cum interpretatione gemina et notis quibusdam edita studio et opera Io. Davidis Koeleri.* Wittenberg, 1706.

————. *Opera omnia.* Edited by V. G. Mandelaras. Munich and Leipzig: K. G. Saur, 2003.

Jägero, Johann Wolfgang. *De concordia imperii [et] sacerdotii sive de jure potestatum supremarum circa sacra.* Tübingen, 1711.

Johnson, Robert. *Nova Britannia* [1609]. Amsterdam and New York: Da Capo Press, 1969.

Johnson, Samuel. *Julian the Apostate.* London, 1682.

Josephus, Flavius. *Judean Antiquities 1–4.* Translated and with a commentary by Louis H. Feldman. Leiden: Brill, 2000.

Justinian. *The Civil Law.* 17 vols. Translated and edited by S. P. Scott. Union, N.J.: Lawbook Exchange, 2001.

————. *The Digest of Justinian.* Translated and edited by T. Mommsen, Paul Krueger, and Alan Watson. Philadelphia: University of Pennsylavania Press, 1985.

————. *Imp. Caes. Iustiniani P. P. Augusti institutionum quatuor, nova interpretatio et methodus Theodori Marcilii.* Paris, 1612.

Justinus, Marcus Junianus. *Epitome of the Philippic History of Pompeius Trogus.* Translated by J. C. Yardley, with introduction and commentary by Waldemar Heckel. Oxford: Clarendon Press, 1997.

————. *Justini Historiae Philipicae: cum versione Anglica, . . . or, The History of Justin.* Translation by John Clarke. London, 1742.

Juvenal. *Juvenal and Persius.* Edited and translated by S. M. Braund. Loeb Classical Library. Cambridge, Mass.: Harvard University Press, 2004.

Kant, Immanuel. *Groundwork of the Metaphysics of Morals* [1785]. In *Immanuel Kant, Practical Philosophy.* Edited by M. J. Gregor. Cambridge: Cambridge University Press, 1996.

Koehler, Heinrich. *Exercitationes juris naturalis, eiusque cumprimis cogentis methodo systematica propositi.* 2nd ed. Jena, 1732.

———. *Juris socialis et gentium ad ius naturale revocati specimina VII.* Jena, 1735.

Lactantius. *De mortibus persecutorum.* Edited and translated by J. L. Creed. Oxford: Clarendon Press, 1984.

———. *The Divine Institutes, Books I–VII.* Translated by Sister Mary Francis McDonald. Washington, D.C.: Catholic University of America Press, 1964.

Lancelotti, Johannes Paulus. *Institutiones juris canonici: cum notis variorum praecipue arcana dominationis papalis, episcopalis, et clericalis in ecclesia Romana detegentibus. In usum auditorii Thomasiani.* Edited by Christian Thomasius. Halle, 1715–17.

Leibniz, Gottfried Wilhelm. *Codex iuris gentium diplomaticus.* 2 vols. Hanover, 1693–1700.

———. *Ephemerides Hanoveranae.* Hanover, 1700.

———. *Nova methodus discendae docendaeque jurisprudentiae.* Frankfurt am Main, 1667.

Leyser, Augustin, *Meditationes ad Pandectas.* 10 vols. Leipzig, 1717–47.

Leyser, Wilhelm. *Dissertatio pro imperio contra dominium eminens: Acc., quae circa hanc matereiam antehac inter autorem et Johannem Fridericum Hormium agitata fuere.* Wittenberg, 1673.

Limborch, Philipp. *Theologia Christiana.* Amsterdam, 1686.

Lipsius, Justus. *Manuductio ad stoicam philosophiam libri tres.* Antwerp, 1604.

———. *Politicorum sive civilis doctrinae libri sex.* Antwerp, 1589.

Livy (Titus Livius). *The Early History of Rome.* Translated by Aubrey de Selincourt, edited by R. M. Ogilvie and S. P. Oakley. London: Penguin, 2002.

———. *History of Rome.* 5 vols. Edited by P. G. Walsh. Warminster, U.K.: Aris & Phillips, 1991–96.

Locke, John. *Some Thoughts Concerning Education.* Edited by J. W. and J. S. Yolton. Oxford: Clarendon Press, 1989.

———. *Two Treatises of Government.* Edited by Peter Laslett. Cambridge: Cambridge University Press, 1988.

Lucan (Marcus Annaeus Lucanus). *Pharsalia (The Civil War), Books I–X.* Translated by J. D. Duff. Loeb Classical Library. London: Heinemann, 1928.

Lucian, *Demonactis philosophi vita ex Lutiano Latine conversa a Christophoro Hegendorphino.* Hagenau, 1535.

Lucretius (Titus Lucretius Carus). *De rerum natura (On the Nature of Things).* Translated by W. H. D. Rouse. Loeb Classical Library. Cambridge, Mass.: Harvard University Press, 1992.

Ludewig, Johann Peter von. *De aetate legitima puberum et maiorum, Vom Mannbarem und mündigem alter, Caesaris; regum; principum; clientum; subditorum; idque Europae universae, praesertim Germaniae.* Halle, 1725.

Ludewig, Johann Peter von (*praeses*) and Christian Krimpff (*respondens*). *De differentiis iuris Romani & Germanici in donationibus et, Barbari adnexus, acceptatione.* Halle, 1721.

Ludewig, Johann Peter von (*praeses*) and Johann Ludwig Stoesser von Lilienfeld (*respondens*). *Dissertatio iuris gentium, de auspicio regum* [1701]. Halle, 1736.

Ludovici, Jacob Friedrich. *Delineatio historiae juris divini naturalis et positivi universalis.* Halle, 1701.

Lydius, Jacobus. *Dissertatio philologico-theologica de juramento opus posthumum.* In Jacobus Lydius, *Jacobi Lydii syntagma sacrum de re militari, nec non de iure iurando dissertatio philologica.* Dordrecht, 1698.

Lyser, Johann. *Alethophili Germani discursus inter polygamum et monogamum de polygamia: prodit jam Latine, cum cautione, praefatione, et notis marginalibus Christiani Vigilis, hujus epistola ad Warenbergium subnexus.* N.p., 1673.

———. *Sinceri Wahrenbergs Kurtzes Gespräch von der Polygami.* In Balthasar Mentzer, *Kurtzes Bedencken über eines von sich selbst also genannten Sinceri Wahrenbergs Kurtzes Gespräch von der Polygami.* Frankfurt am Main, 1672.

Lysias. *Lysias.* English translation by W. R. M. Lamb. Loeb Classical Library. London: Heinemann, 1930.

———. *Orationes.* Edited by Charles Hude. Oxford: Clarendon Press, 1990.

Macneny, Marc. *Réfutation des argumens avancés de la part de MM les directeurs des Compagnies d'Orient et d'Occident des Provinces-Unies contre la liberté du commerce des habiters des Pays-Bas, sujets de S. May. Impérials.* The Hague, 1723.

Macrobius. *Commentary on the Dream of Scipio.* Translated and edited by William Harris Stahl. New York: Columbia University Press, 1966.

———. *Saturnalia.* Translated by Percival Vaughan Davies. New York: Columbia University Press, 1969.

Magius, Hieronymus. *Variarum lectionum seu miscellaneorum libri III.* N.p., 1564.

Magnus, Johannes. *Gothorum Sueonumque historia.* Basel, 1617.

Maimonides, Moses. *Constitutiones de jurejurando ex R[abbi] Mosis Maimonidis Opere . . . Latine redditae, variisque notis illustratae a Justo Christophoro Dithmaro.* Leyden, 1706.

Mandeville, Bernard. *The Fable of the Bees.* Edited by F. B. Kaye. Indianapolis: Liberty Fund, 1988.

Marcellinus, Ammianus. *Ammianus Marcellinus.* English translation by John C. Rolfe. 3 vols. Loeb Classical Library. Cambridge, Mass.: Harvard University Press, 2000.

Marcellus, Nonius. *Nonii Marcelli nova editio.* Sedan, 1614.

Marcus Aurelius (Marcus Aelius Aurelius Antoninus). *The Meditations of the Emperor Marcus Antoninus.* 2 vols. Edited, with a translation and commentary, by A. S. L. Farquharson. Oxford: Clarendon Press, 1944.

Marianus Scotus. *Chronicorum libri tres.* Edited by Burckhard Gotthelf Struvius. Regensburg, 1726.

Marselaer, Fredericus de. *Legatus libri duo.* Antwerp, 1626.

Martial (Marcus Valerius Martialis). *Epigrams.* Translation by D. R. Shackleton Bailey. Loeb Classical Library. Cambridge, Mass.: Harvard University Press, 1993.

Mascov, Gottfried. *Exercitatio inauguralis de sectis Sabinianorum et Proculianorum in jure civili.* Altdorf, 1724.

Mascov, Johann Jacob (*praeses*) and Christian Siegfried von Plessen (*respondens*). *De foederibus commerciorum.* Leipzig, 1735.

Maximus of Tyre. *Dissertationes.* Edited by M. B. Trapp. Stuttgart: Teubner, 1994.

———. *The Philosophical Orations.* Translated, with an introduction and notes, by M. B. Trapp. New York: Oxford University Press, 1997.

Ménage, Gilles. *Iuris civilis amoenitates.* Paris, 1664.

Mérille, Edmond. *E. Merillii ad libros II. quaestionum Callistrati: . . . commentarius.* Basileae, 1741–44.

———. *Observationum libri VIII . . . nova editio ab innumeris, gravibusque mendis, quibus Parisiensis inquinata prodierat, emaculata.* Naples, 1720.

Meteren, Emanuel van. *Historien der Nederlanden en haar naburen oorlogen tot het jaar 1612.* Amsterdam, 1663.

Meyer, Johann. *Pyrrhonii und Orthophili Unterredung von der im nechsten*

Jahr unter dem Nahmen Daphnaei Arcuarii ans Liecht gekommenen Betrachtung des . . . Ehestandes. Hamburg, 1680.

Milton, John. *Political Writings.* Edited by Martin Dzelzainis. Cambridge: Cambridge University Press, 1991.

Montaigne, Michel de. *Essays.* 3 vols. Translated by John Florio; introduction by L. C. Harmer. London, 1980.

Montesquieu, C. L. de Secondat, baron de. *Persian Letters.* Translated by John Ozell. Reprint of the 1722 edition, with an introduction by William Graves. New York: Garland, 1972.

———. *The Spirit of the Laws.* Edited by A. M. Cohler et al. Cambridge: Cambridge University Press, 1989.

Mornac, Antoine. *Observationes in 24 priores libros digestorum, ad usum fori gallici.* Paris, 1721.

Müller, Johann Joachim. *Des Heiligen Römischen Reichs, Teutscher Nation, Reichs Tags Theatrum, wie selbiges, unter Keyser Maximilians I: allerhöchsten Regierung gestanden und was auf selbigen in Geist- und Weltlichen Reichs-Händeln berahtschlaget, tractiret und geschlossen worden.* 2 vols. Jena, 1718–19.

Müller, Johann Sebastian. *Des chur- und fürstlichen Hauses Sachsen, Ernestin- und Albertinischer Linien, Annales, von Anno 1400 bis 1700.* Weimar, 1701.

Nepos, Cornelius. *Cornelius Nepos.* Translated by J. C. Rolfe. Loeb Classical Library. Cambridge, Mass.: Harvard University Press, 1984.

Noodt, Gerard. *De foenore et usuris libri tres.* Leyden, 1735.

———. *Opera omnia ab ipso recognita.* Cologne, 1732.

Obrecht, Ulrich (*praeses*) and Johann Ferdinand Stauffer (*respondens*). *Sponsor pacis sive de garantia dissertatio.* Strasburg, 1675.

Observationum selectarum ad rem literariam spectantium tomi I–X. 10 vols. Halle: Officina Libraria Rengeriana, 1700–1705.

Origen. *Opera quae quidem extant omnia.* Edited by Johannes Jacobus Grynaeus. Basel, 1571.

Otto, Everhard. *Ad Fl. Iustiniani PP. Aug. Institutionum, sive elementorum libros IV, notae criticae et commentarius.* Utrecht, 1729.

———. *De titulo imperatoris Russorum.* Halle, 1724.

Otto of Freising. *Chronica; sive Historia de duabus civitatibus.* Edited by A. Hofmeister. Hanover: Hahn, 1912.

Ovid (Publius Ovidius Naso). *Amores; Medicamini faciei femineae; Ars amatoria; Remedia amoris.* Edited by E. J. Kenney. Oxford: Clarendon Press, 1995.

————. *Metamorphoses.* 2 vols. Translated by F. J. Miller. Loeb Classical Library. Cambridge, Mass.: Harvard University Press, 1976–77.

Palthen, Johann Philipp (*praeses*) and Samuel Palthen (*respondens*). *Dissertatio de marito reginae.* Greifswald, 1707.

Paraeus, David. *In divinam ad Romanos S. Pauli Apostoli epistolam commentarius.* Frankfurt am Main, 1608.

Pascal, Blaise. *Ludovicii Montaltii litterae provinciales de morali & politia Jesuitarum disciplina. Accedit Samuelis Rachelii examen probabilitatis Jesuiticae novorumque casuistarum.* Helmstedt, 1664.

Paterculus, Velleius. *Compendium of Roman History.* Translated by Frederick W. Shipley. Loeb Classical Library. London: Heinemann, 1924.

————. *C. Velleii Paterculi quae supersunt ex historiae Romanae voluminibus duobus: cum integris scholiis, notis, variis lectionibus, et animadversionibus doctorum. Curante Petro Burmanno.* Leyden, 1719.

Pausanias. *Description of Greece.* 5 vols. Loeb Classical Library. London: Heinemann, 1918–35.

Perizonius, Jacob. *Dissertatio de aere gravi: ut et responsio ad epistolas Andr. Morellii V. C. de variis familiarum Romanarum nummis ex Ursino & aliis.* Leyden, 1713.

————. *Dissertationum trias quarum in prima de constitutione divina super ducenda defuncti fratris uxore secunda de lege voconia feminarumque apud veteres hereditatibus tertia de variis antiquorum nummis agitur.* Halle, 1722.

Persius. *The Satires of Persius.* Edited by G. Lee and W. Barr. Liverpool: Cairns, 1987.

Petit, Pierre. *De Amazonibus dissertatio, qua an vere extiterint, necne, . . . disputatur.* Amsterdam, 1687.

Petronius Arbiter. *Petronius and the Apocolocyntosis of Seneca.* Translated by M. Heseltine. Loeb Classical Library. London: Heinemann, 1961.

————. *Satyricon.* Translated and edited by Sarah Ruden. Indianapolis: Hackett, 2000.

Philostratus. *Philostratorum quae supersunt omnia . . . recensuit notis perpetuis illustravit versionem totam fere novam fecit Gottfridus Olearius.* Leipzig, 1709.

Placcius, Vincenz. *Theatrum anonymorum et pseudonymorum, ex symbolis & collatione virorum per Europam doctissimorum et celeberrimorum.* Hamburg, 1708.

Plato. *The Laws of Plato.* Translated and edited by Thomas L. Pangle. Chicago: University of Chicago Press, 1988.

————. *Platonis opera quae extant omnia.* 3 vols. Notes by Jean Serres. Geneva, 1578.

————. *The Republic.* 2 vols. Translated by Paul Shorey. Cambridge, Mass.: Harvard University Press, 1999–2000.

Plautus (Titus Maccius Plautus). *Plautus.* Translated by P. Nixon. Vol. 1: *Amphitryon, The Comedy of Asses, The Pot of Gold, The Two Bacchises, The Captives.* Loeb Classical Library. London: Heinemann, 1928.

————. *Plautus.* Translated by P. Nixon. Vol. 3: *The Merchant, The Braggart Warrior, The Haunted House, The Persian.* Loeb Classical Library. London: Heinemann, 1930.

————. *Plautus.* Translated by P. Nixon. Vol. 4: *The Little Carthaginian, Pseudolus, The Rope.* Loeb Classical Library. London: Heinemann, 1932.

————. *Plautus.* Translated by P. Nixon. Vol. 5: *Stichus, Three Bob Day, Truculentus, The Tale of a Travelling Bag, Fragments.* Loeb Classical Library. London: Heinemann, 1938.

Pliny the Elder (Caius Plinius Secundus). *Natural History.* Vol. 1. Loeb Classical Library. London: Heinemann, 1938.

Pliny the Younger (Caius Plinius Caecilius Secundus). *Letters and Panegyricus.* Translated by Betty Radice. 2 vols. Loeb Classical Library. Cambridge, Mass.: Harvard University Press, 2000–2004.

Plutarch. *The Greek Questions of Plutarch.* Translated and with a commentary by W. F. Halliday. Oxford: Clarendon Press, 1928.

————. *Moralia: in Fourteen Volumes.* Translated by F. C. Babbitt. Vol. 1. Loeb Classical Library. London: Heinemann, 1927.

————. *Moralia: in Fourteen Volumes.* Translated by F. C. Babbitt. Vol. 2. Loeb Classical Library. London: Heinemann, 1928.

————. *Moralia: in Fourteen Volumes.* Translated by F. C. Babbitt. Vol. 3. Loeb Classical Library. London: Heinemann, 1931.

————. *Moralia: in Fifteen Volumes.* Translated by P. H. de Lacy and B. Einarson. Vol. 7. Loeb Classical Library. London: Heinemann, 1959.

————. *Moralia: in Seventeen Volumes.* Translated by H. Cherniss. Vol. 13, part 2. Loeb Classical Library. Cambridge, Mass.: Harvard University Press, 1976.

————. *Plutarch's Lives.* Translated by Bernadotte Perrin. Vol. 1: *Theseus and Romulus, Lycurgus and Numa, Solon and Publicola.* Loeb Classical Library. Cambridge, Mass.: Harvard University Press, 1998.

————. *Plutarch's Lives.* Translated by Bernadotte Perrin. Vol. 2: *Themis-*

tocles and Camillus, Aristides and Cato Major, Cimon and Lucullus. Loeb Classical Library. London: Heinemann, 1968.

―――. *Plutarch's Lives.* Translated by Bernadotte Perrin. Vol. 5: *Agesilaus and Pompey, Pelopidas and Marcellus.* Loeb Classical Library. London: Heinemann, 1914.

―――. *Plutarch's Lives.* Translated by Bernadotte Perrin. Vol. 10: *Agis and Cleomenes, Tiberius and Caius Gracchus, Philopoemen and Titus Flaminius.* Loeb Classical Library. London: Heinemann, 1919.

―――. *Plutarch's Lives.* Translated by Bernadotte Perrin. Vol. 11: *Aratus and Artaxerxes, Galba and Otho.* Loeb Classical Library. London: Heinemann, 1914.

Polyaenus. *Stratagems of War.* 2 vols. Edited and translated by Peter Krentz. Chicago: Ares, 1994.

Polybius. *Ex libris Polybii Megapolitani selecta de legationibus.* Antwerp, 1582.

―――. *The Histories.* 6 vols. Translated by W. R. Paton. London: Heinemann, 1922–27.

Pomponius Mela. *De situ orbis libri tres, cum notis variorum, cura et studio Abrah. Gronovii.* Leyden, 1722.

Pontanus, Johann Isaac. *Discussionum historicarum libri duo; praecipue quatenus et quodam mare liberum vel non liberum clausumque accipiendum dispicitur expenditurque.* Harderwijk, 1637.

―――. *Rerum Danicarum historia, libris X unoque tomo ad domum usque Oldenburgicam deducta.* Amsterdam, 1631.

Pope, Alexander. *An Epistle to the Right Honourable Richard Lord Viscount Cobham.* London, 1733.

―――. *An Essay on Man.* Edited by Maynard Mack. London, 1950.

Pseudo-Iustinus. *Cohortatio ad Graecos; De monarchia; Oratio ad Graecos.* Edited by Miroslav Marcovich. Berlin: W. de Gruyter, 1990.

Pufendorf, Samuel von. *Acht Bücher vom Natur- und Völkerrecht. Mit des weitberühmten JCti. Johann Nicolai Hertii, Johann Barbeyrac und anderer hoch-gelehrten Männer ausserlesenen Anmerckungen erläutert und in die teutsche Sprache übersetzet* [reprint of 1711 edition]. 2 vols. Hildesheim: Olms, 2001.

―――. *De jure naturae et gentium libri octo.* Lund, 1672.

―――. *Des Freyherrn von Pufendorff politische Betrachtung der geistlichen Monarchie des Stuhls zu Rom: mit Anmerckungen; zum Gebrauch des Thomasischen Auditorii.* Edited and with a preface by Christian Thomasius. Halle, 1714.

————. *Dissertationes academicae selectiores.* Upsala, 1677.

————. *Of the Law of Nature and Nations.* Translated by Basil Kennet, with notes by Jean Barbeyrac. 3rd ed. London, 1717.

————. *On the Duty of Man and Citizen.* Edited by J. Tully. Cambridge: Cambridge University Press, 1991.

————. *Specimen controversiarum circa jus naturali ipsi nuper motarum.* In Pufendorf, *Eris Scandica,* 193–238. Frankfurt am Main, 1686.

Quintilian (Marcus Fabius Quintilianus). *Declamationes minores.* Edited by D. R. Shackleton Bailey. Stuttgart: Teubner, 1989.

————. *Declamationes quae supersunt CXLV.* Edited by Constantin Ritter. Reprint of 1874 ed. Stuttgart: Teubner, 1965.

————. *The Institutio oratoria of Quintilian.* Translated by H. E. Butler. 4 vols. Loeb Classical Library. London: Heinemann, 1922.

————. *The Lesser Declamations.* 2 vols. Edited and translated by D. R. Shackleton Bailey. Loeb Classical Library. Cambridge, Mass.: Harvard University Press, 2006.

————. *The Major Declamations Ascribed to Quintilian.* Translated by L. A. Sussman. Frankfurt am Main: P. Lang, 1987.

Rachel, Samuel. *Examen probabilitatis Jesuiticae novorumque casuistarum.* In Blaise Pascal, *Ludovicii Montaltii litterae provinciales de morali & politia Jesuitarum disciplina. Accedit Samuelis Rachelii examen probabilitatis Jesuiticae novorumque casuistarum.* Helmstedt, 1664.

Radevicus. *De rebus gestis Friderici I. Romanorum Imperatoris, continuatae ad Ottonem historiae, libri duo.* In Christianus Urstisius, *Germaniae historicorum illustrium.* Frankfurt am Main, 1670.

Rathlef, E. L. *Geschichte jetzlebender Gelehrten, Johan Barbeirak.* Vol. 1. Zelle, 1740.

Reid, Thomas. *Practical Ethics.* Edited by Knud Haakonssen. Princeton: Princeton University Press, 1990.

Repgow, Eike von. *The Saxon Mirror: A Sachenspiegel of the Fourteenth Century.* Translated by Maria Dobozy. Philadelphia: University of Pennsylvania Press, 1999.

Ricaut, Paul. *The History of the Present State of the Ottoman Empire, Containing the Maxims of the Turkish Polity, the Most Material Points of the Mahometan Religion, Their Sects and Heresies, Their Convents and Religious Votaries; Their Military Discipline, with an Exact Computation of Their Forces Both by Sea and Land.* London, 1686.

Roo, Gerardus de. *Annales rerum belli domique ab Austriacis Habsburgicae gentis principibus a Rudolpho I usque ad Carolum V gestarum.* 2nd ed. Halle, 1709.

Rutgers, Jan. *Variarum lectionum libri sex ad Gustavum II. Suecorum &c. regem.* Leyden, 1618.

Sagittarius, Caspar (*praeses*) and Jonathan Köpken (*respondens*). *Antiquitates Amazonias exercitatione ad Justini historici lib. 2, cap. IV.* Jena, 1685.

Sallust (Gaius Sallustius Crispus). *Sallust.* Translated by J. C. Rolfe. Loeb Classical Library. London: Heinemann, 1921.

Salvianus. *De gubernatione Dei, et de iusto praesentique eius iudicio libri VIII.* Venice, 1689.

Saumaise, Claude (Claudius Salmasius). *De usuris liber.* Leyden, 1638.

———. *Disquisitio de mutuo, qua probatur non esse alienationem.* Leyden, 1645.

———. *Plinianae exercitationes in Caji Julii Solini Polyhistora: item Caji Julii Solini Polyhistor ex veteribus libris emendatus.* Paris, 1629.

Scheffer, Johannes. *De natura et constitutione philosophiae italicae, seu, Pythagoricae liber singularis.* Uppsala, 1664.

Schickard, Wilhelm. *Jus regium Hebraeorum, e tenebris Rabbinicis erutum, et luci donatum: Cum animadversionibus & notis Jo. Benedicti Carpzovi.* Leipzig, 1674.

Schilter, Johann. *De jure et statu obsidum dissertatio juridica.* Naumburg, 1664.

———. *De jure hospitii apud veteres.* Helmstedt, 1677.

———. *Exercitationes theoretico-practicae ad L libros Pandectarum.* 4 vols. Jena and Helmstedt, 1680–84.

Schoock, Martin. *Exercitationes variae, de diversis materiis.* Utrecht, 1663.

Schroeter, Wilhelm. *Fürstliche Schatz- und Rent-Kammer. Nebst seinem Tractat vom Goldmachen, wie auch vom Ministrissimo oder Ober-Staats-Bedienten.* Leipzig and Königsberg, 1737.

Schütz, Johann Jakob, and Wolfgang Adam Lauterbach. *Thesaurus juris civilis, sive succincta explanatio Compendii Digestorum Schützio-Lauterbachiani.* Lemgo, 1717.

Schweder, Gabriel (*praeses*) and Johann Eberhard Pregitzer (*respondens*). *Dissertatio inauguralis de Domanio S. Romani.* Tübingen, 1703.

Seckendorff, Veit Ludwig von. *Commentarius historicus et apologeticus de Lutheranismo.* 2 vols. Frankfurt, 1688–89.

Selden, John. *De jure naturali et gentium juxta disciplinam Ebraeorum.* Strasbourg, 1665.

————. *De synedriis & praefecturis juridicis veterum Ebraeorum: libri tres.* Amsterdam, 1679.

————. *Mare clausum.* London, 1635.

————. *Uxor Ebraica: seu de nuptiis et divortiis ex jure civili, id est, divino & talmudico, veterum Ebraeorum, libri tres; Ejusdem de successionibus ad leges Ebraeorum in bona defunctorum liber singularis. In pontificatum libri duo. Editio nova.* Frankfurt an der Oder, 1695.

Seneca the Elder (Lucius, or Marcus, Annaeus Seneca). *Declamations.* 2 vols. Translated by M. Winterbottom. Loeb Classical Library. Cambridge, Mass.: Harvard University Press, 1974.

Seneca the Younger (Lucius Annaeus Seneca). *Ad Lucilium epistulae morales.* 3 vols. Translated by Richard Gummere. Loeb Classical Library. London: Heinemann, 1917–25.

————. *Apocolocyntosis.* Translated by W. H. D. Rouse. In *Petronius and Apocolocyntosis of Seneca.* Loeb Classical Library. London: Heinemann, 1961.

————. *Hippolytus.* Translated by F. J. Miller. Loeb Classical Library. Cambridge, Mass.: Harvard University Press, 1960.

————. *Moral Essays.* 3 vols. Translated by J. W. Basore. Loeb Classical Library. London: Heinemann, 1932–58.

————. *Tragedies II: Oedipus, Agamemnon, Thyestes, Hercules on Oeta, Octavia.* Edited and translated by J. G. Fitch. Loeb Classical Library. Cambridge, Mass.: Harvard University Press, 2004.

————. *Tragoediae incertorum auctorum: Hercules Oetaeus, Octavia.* Edited by O. Zwierlein. Oxford: Clarendon Press, 1995.

Servius. *Servii Grammatici qui feruntur in Vergilii carmina commentarii.* 2 vols. Edited by G. Thilo. Reprint of 1881 Leipzig edition. Hildesheim: Olms, 1986.

Shaftesbury, Anthony Ashley Cooper, third earl of. *Characteristics of Men, Manners, Opinions, Times.* Edited by L. E. Klein. Cambridge: Cambridge University Press, 1999.

Sharrock, Robert. ῾Υπόθεσις ἐθική *de officiis secundum naturae jus, seu De moribus ad rationis normam conformandis doctrina.* Oxford, 1660.

Sidney, Algernon. *Discourses Concerning Government.* 2nd ed. London, 1704.

————. *Discourses Concerning Government.* Edited by T. G. West. Indianapolis: Liberty Fund, 1996.

Sidonius, Apollinaris. *See* Apollinaris Sidonius.

Sigonius, Carolus. *De republica Atheniensium libri IV.* In Jacobus Gronovius,

Attici imperii amplitudinem ac mutationes, ut et Lacedaemonis complexum. Leyden, 1699.

Simler, Josias. *De Republica Helvetiorum libri duo.* N.p., 1576.

Simplicius, *On Epictetus' Handbook (Commentarius in Enchiridion Epicteti).* Translated by Charles Brittain and Tad Brennan. 2 vols. London: Duckworth, 2002.

Sophocles. *Antigone.* Edited by Mark Griffith. Cambridge: Cambridge University Press, 1999.

———. *Oedipus at Colonus.* Edited and translated by F. Storr. Loeb Classical Library. Cambridge, Mass.: Harvard University Press, 1988.

———. *Sophocles: Antigone, The Women of Trachis, Philoctetes, Oedipus at Colonus.* Edited and translated by Hugh Lloyd-Jones. Loeb Classical Library. Cambridge, Mass.: Harvard University Press, 1994.

Sozomenos, *Historia ecclesiastica.* Edited and translated into German by Günther Christian Hansen. Turnhout: Brepols, 2004.

Spanheim, Ezechiel. *Dissertationes de praestantia et usu numismatum antiquorum.* 2 vols. Edited by Isaac Verbuurg. Amsterdam, 1717.

———. *Orbis Romanus, seu ad constitutionem Antonini imperatoris, de qua Ulpianus Leg. XVII digestis de statu hominum exercitationes duae: cum figuris numismatum.* With a preface by Johann Gottlieb Heineccius. Halle and Leipzig, 1728.

Statius, Publius Papinius. *Silvae.* Edited and translated by D. R. Shackleton Bailey. Cambridge, Mass.: Harvard University Press, 2003.

———. *Thebaid.* 2 vols. Translated by D. R. Shackleton Bailey. Cambridge, Mass.: Harvard University Press, 2003.

Stobaeus, Johannes. *Anthologium.* 5 vols. Edited by C. Wachsmuth and O. Hense. Reprint of 1884–1923 edition. Berlin: Weidmann, 1974.

Strabo. *Geography.* 8 vols. English translation by Horace Leonard Jones. Cambridge, Mass.: Harvard University Press, 1997–2001.

———. *Rerum geographicarum libri XVII.* Edited by Theodor Janssonius. Amsterdam, 1707.

Strada, Famianus. *De bello belgico decas prima.* Amsterdam, 1700.

Strauchius, Johannes. *Amoenitatum juris canonici semestria duo . . . Editio novissima correctior et locupletior.* Jena, 1718.

Suetonius. *Suetonius.* 2 vols. Translated by J. C. Rolfe. London: Heinemann, 1928–30.

Suidas. *Suidae Lexicon.* 5 vols. Edited by A. Adler. Leipzig: Teubner, 1928–38.

Surenhuys, Willem. *Mischna sive totius Hebraeorum juris, rituum, antiqui-tatum, ac legum systema. Cum clarissimorum Rabbinorum Maimonides et Bartenorae commentariis integris.* 6 vols. Amsterdam, 1698–1703.

Sykes, Arthur Ashley. *The Principles and Connexion of Natural and Revealed Religion Distinctly Considered.* London, 1740.

Tabor, Johann Otto (*praeses*) and Hermann Hopfener (*respondens*). *De servitutibus realibus: dissertatio juridica.* Strasburg, 1647.

Tacitus, Gaius Cornelius. *The Annals of Tacitus.* 2 vols. Edited by H. Furneaux. Oxford: Clarendon Press, 1884–91.

———. *Germania.* Translated and with an introduction and commentary by J. B. Rives. Oxford: Clarendon Press, 1999.

———. *The Histories.* Translated by W. H. Fyfe, revised and edited by D. S. Levene. Oxford: Oxford University Press, 1999.

———. *Tacitus.* Vol. 1: *Agricola, Germania, Dialogus.* Translated by M. Hutton and W. Peterson; revised by R. M. Ogilvie, E. H. Warmington, and M. Winterbottom. London: Heinemann, 1970.

Terence (Publius Terentius Afer). *Terence.* 2 vols. Edited and translated by John Barsby. Loeb Classical Library. Cambridge, Mass.: Harvard University Press, 2001.

Tertullian. *De idololatria.* Critical text, translation, and commentary by J. H. Waszink and J. C. M. van Winden. Partly based on a manuscript left behind by P. G. van der Nat. Leiden: E. J. Brill, 1987.

———. *Tertulliani libri tres: De spectaculis, De idololatria, et De corona militis.* With English notes, an introduction, and indexes. Edited by G. Currey. London: John W. Parker, 1854.

———. *Treatises on Penance.* Translated and annotated by W. P. Le Saint. Wesminster, Md.: Newman Press, 1959.

Themistius. *Orationes quae supersunt.* 3 vols. Edited by H. Schenkl, G. Downey, and A. F. Norman. Leipzig: Teubner, 1965–74.

Theodoretus. *Ecclesiasticae historiae libri quinque.* Edited by Henri de Valois and Thomas Gaisford. Oxford: E Typographeo Academico, 1854.

Theophrastus. *Theophrastus: Characters. Herodas: Mimes. Sophron and Other Mime Fragments.* Edited and translated by J. Rusten and I. C. Cunningham. Loeb Classical Library. Cambridge, Mass.: Harvard University Press, 2002.

Thietmar von Merseburg. *Ottonian Germany: The Chronicon of Thietmar of Merseburg.* Translated and annotated by David A. Warner. Manchester: Manchester University Press, 2001.

Thomasius, Christian. *Annotationes ad Ulrici Huberi libros tres de jure civitatis.* Halle, 1708.

————. *Einleitung zur Sittenlehre.* Halle, 1692.

————. *Fundamenta juris naturae et gentium* [1705]. Reprint of 1718 edition. Aalen: Scientia, 1979.

————. *Institutiones jurisprudentiae divinae* [1688]. Reprint of 1720 edition. Aalen: Scientia, 1994.

————. *Notae ad singulos institutionum et pandectarum titulos varias juris Romani antiquitates imprimis usum eorum hodiernum in foris Germaniae ostendentes.* Halle, 1713.

————. *Summarischer Entwurf der Grundlehren, die einem Studioso Juris zu wissen und auf den Universitäten zu lehren nötig sind.* Halle, 1699.

Thomasius, Christian (*praeses*) and Carl Heinrich Brix von und zu Montzel (*respondens*). *De sponsione Romanorum Caudina.* Leipzig, 1684.

Thomasius, Christian (*praeses*) and Bernhard Friedrich Buhle (*respondens*). *Dissertatio juridica de fundamentorum definiendi causas matrimoniales hactenus receptorum insufficientia.* Halle, 1698.

Thomasius, Christian (*praeses*) and Rembert Clusener (*respondens*). *Dissertatio inauguralis juridica, de jure aggratiandi principis Evangelici in causis homicidii* [1707]. Halle, 1714.

Thomasius, Christian (*praeses*) and Phillip Reinhold Hecht (*respondens*). *Dissertatio inauguralis juridica de pretio affectionis in res fungibiles non cadente.* Halle, 1701.

Thomasius, Christian (*praeses*) and Andreas Georg Hofmann (*respondens*). *Dissertatio juridica de perpetuitate debitorum pecuniariorum.* Halle, 1706.

Thomasius, Christian (*praeses*) and Johannes Jacobus von Ryssel (*respondens*). *Dissertatio juris publici ad l. 4. de captiv. & l. ult. de legation. De sponsione Romanorum Numantina.* Leipzig, 1688.

Thomasius, Jacob (*praeses*) and Georg Heinrich Groer (*respondens*). *De ministrissimo.* Leipzig, 1668.

Thucydides. *History of the Peloponnesian War.* 4 vols. Translated by Charles Forster Smith. London: Heinemann, 1928–35.

Titius, Gottlieb Gerhard. *Observationes in Samuelis L. B. de Pufendorfii De officio hominis et civis juxta legem naturalem libros duos.* Leipzig, 1703.

Toland, John. *Christianity Not Mysterious.* London, 1696.

Tulp, Nicolaus. *Observationes medicae.* 5th ed. Leyden, 1716.

Turmair, Johannes. *Johannes Turmair's genannt Aventinus Sämmtliche Werke.* 6 vols. Munich: Kaiser, 1881–1908.

Turnbull, George. *Obervations upon Liberal Education* [1742]. Edited by Terrence O. Moore. Indianapolis: Liberty Fund, 2003.

―――. *The Principles of Moral and Christian Philosophy* [1740]. 2 vols. Edited by Alexander Broadie. Indianapolis: Liberty Fund, 2005.

―――. *A Treatise on Ancient Painting.* London, 1740.

[Ulpian]. *Institutionum et regularum iuris romani syntagma: exhibens Gai et Iustiniani Institutionum synopsin, Ulpiani librum singularem regularum, Pauli Senteniarum libros quinque, tabulas systema institutionum iuris Romani illustrantes, praemissis Duodecim tabularum fragmentis. Edidit et brevi annotatione instruxit Rudolphus Gneist.* Leipzig: Teubner, 1880.

Urbicus, Aggenus. *De limitibus agrorum libro duo.* In Willem Goes and Nicolas Rigault, eds., *Rei agrariae auctores legesque variae.* Amsterdam, 1674.

Vaillant, Johannes. *Numismata imperatorum, Augustarum et Caesarum, a populis, Romanae ditionis, Graecè loquentibus, ex omni modulo percussa: . . . Editio altera.* Amsterdam, 1700.

Valerius Maximus. *Memorable Doings and Sayings.* Edited and translated by D. R. Shackleton Bailey. Loeb Classical Library. Cambridge, Mass.: Harvard University Press, 2000.

Valois, Henri de, ed. *Polybii, Diodori Siculi, Nicolai Damasceni, Dionysii Halicar., Appiani Alexand., Dionis et Ioannis Antiocheni excerpta.* Paris, 1634.

Varro, Marcus Terentius. *On Farming. M. Terenti Varronis Rerum rusticarum libri tres.* Translated and edited by Lloyd Storr-Best. London: G. Bell and Sons, 1912.

―――. *On the Latin Language (De lingua Latina).* 2 vols. Cambridge, Mass.: Harvard University Press, 1938.

Vazquez, Fernando. *Illustrium controversiarum, aliarumque usu frequentium libri sex: in duas partes divisi, et plurimis mendis sedulo expurgati.* Frankfurt, 1668.

Vega, Garcilaso de la. *Royal Commentaries of the Incas and General History of Peru.* Preface by H. V. Livermore. Austin: University of Texas Press, 1966.

Virgil (Publius Vergilius Maro). *Virgil.* 2 vols. Translated by H. Rushton Fairclough. Loeb Classical Library. London: Heinemann, 1916–18.

Vitoria, Francisco de. *Relectio de Indis.* Critical edition by L. Pereña, translated into Italian by A. Lamacchia. Bari: Levante, 1996.

Vitruvius. *Ten Books on Architecture*. Translated by Ingrid D. Rowland, with commentary and illustrations by Thomas Noble Howe. New York: Cambridge University Press, 1999.

Wachter, Johann Georg. *Glossarium Germanicum: continens origines et antiquitates linguae Germanicae hodiernae*. Leipzig, 1727.

Wehner, Paul Matthias. *Practicarum iuris observationum selectarum liber singularis*. Strasburg, 1701.

Wicquefort, Abraham van. *L'Ambassadeur et ses fonctions*. 2 vols. Edited by C. van Bynkershoek. Amsterdam, 1730.

Wolff, Christian. *Jus naturae methodo scientifica pertractatum*. 8 vols. Frankfurt/Leipzig/Halle, 1740–48.

———. *Philosophia moralis sive ethica, methodo scientifica pertractata*. 5 vols. Halle, 1750–53.

———. *Theologia naturalis methodo scientifica pertractata*. 2 vols. Frankfurt and Leipzig, 1736–37.

———. *Vernünftige Gedanken von dem gesellschaftlichen Leben der Menschen und insonderheit dem gemeinen Wesen*. Reprint of 1721 Halle edition. Frankfurt am Main: Athenäum, 1971.

———. *Von den Absichten der natürlichen Dinge*. Edited by Hans Werner Arndt [1726]. Hildesheim: Olms, 1980.

Xenophon. *Anabasis*. Translated by C. L. Brownson, revised by John Dillery. Loeb Classical Library. Cambridge, Mass.: Harvard University Press, 2001.

———. *Cyropaedia*. 2 vols. Translated by W. Miller. Loeb Classical Library. London: Heinemann, 1914–25.

———. *De Cyri institutione libri octo*. Edited by Thomas Hutchinson. Oxford, 1727.

———. *Memorabilia and Oeconomicus*. English translation by E. C. Marchant. Loeb Classical Library. London: Heinemann, 1923.

———. *Scripta minora. Pseudo-Xenophon. Constitution of the Athenians*. Translated and edited by E. C. Marchant and G. W. Bowersock. Loeb Classical Library. London: Heinemann, 1971.

Ziegler, Caspar. *De juribus majestatis: tractatus academicus; in quo pleraque omnia, quae de potestate et juribus principis disputari solent, strictim exponuntur*. Wittenberg, 1710.

———. *In Hugonis Grotii De jure belli ac pacis libros, quibus naturae & gentium jus explicavit, notae et animadversiones subitariae*. Wittenberg, 1666.

Secondary Literature

This section includes all secondary literature cited in the editors' introduction and in the editors' notes on the original text.

Ahnert, Thomas. "Enthusiasm and Enlightenment: Faith and Philosophy in the Thought of Christian Thomasius." *Modern Intellectual History* 2 (2005): 153–77.

———. "Pleasure, Pain, and Punishment in the Early Enlightenment: German and Scottish Debates." *Jahrbuch für Recht und Ethik* 12 (2004): 173–87.

———. *Religion and the Origins of the German Enlightenment: Faith and the Reform of Learning in the Thought of Christian Thomasius.* Rochester, N.Y.: University of Rochester Press, 2006.

Bergfeld, Christoph. "Johann Gottlieb Heineccius und die Grundlagen seines Natur- und Völkerrechts." In Johann Gottlieb Heineccius, *Grundlagen des Natur- und Völkerrechts,* 507–32. Translated by Peter Mortzfeld and edited by Christoph Bergfeld. Frankfurt am Main: Insel, 1994.

Dufour, Alfred. "Die école romande du droit naturel—ihre deutschen Wurzeln." In *Humanismus und Naturrecht in Brandenburg-Preussen,* 133–43. Edited by H. Thieme. Berlin: De Gruyter, 1979.

Fukuda, Arihiro. *Sovereignty and the Sword: Harrington, Hobbes, and Mixed Government in the English Civil Wars.* Oxford: Clarendon Press, 1997.

Haakonssen, Knud. *Natural Law and Moral Philosophy: From Grotius to the Scottish Enlightenment.* New York: Cambridge University Press, 1996.

Hochstrasser, Tim. "Conscience and Reason: The Natural Law Theory of Jean Barbeyrac." *Historical Journal* 36 (1993): 289–308.

———. *Natural Law Theories in the Early Enlightenment.* Cambridge: Cambridge University Press, 2000.

Liljegren, S. B. *James Harrington's Oceana.* Heidelberg: C. Winter, 1924.

Luig, Klaus. "Gli elementa iuris civilis di J. G. Heineccius come modello per le 'Institutiones de derecho romano' de Andrés Bello." In *Andrés Bello y el derecho latinoamericano,* 259–74. Caracas: La Casa de Bello, 1981.

———. "Zur Verbreitung des Naturrechts in Europa." *Tijdschrift voor Rechtsgeschiedenis* 60 (1972): 539–57.

Norton, David Fate. "George Turnbull and the Furniture of the Mind." *Journal of the History of Ideas* 35 (1975): 701–16.

Othmer, Sieglinde. *Berlin und die Verbreitung des Naturrechts in Europa:*

Kultur- und sozialgeschichtliche Studien zu Jean Barbeyracs Pufendorf-Übersetzungen und eine Analyse seiner Leserschaft. Berlin: De Gruyter, 1970.

Pocock, J. G. A. "Enthusiasm: The Anti-Self of Enlightenment." In *Enthusiasm and Enlightenment in Europe, 1650–1850,* 7–28. Edited by A. J. La Vopa and L. Klein. San Marino, Calif.: Huntington Library, 1998.

Reibstein, Ernst. "Johann Gottlieb Heineccius als Kritiker des grotianischen Systems." *Zeitschrift für öffentliches Recht und Völkerrecht* 24 (1964): 236–64.

Schröder, Peter. "Natural Law and Enlightenment in Comparative Perspective: Differences and Similarities between the French and the Scottish Case." In *Early Modern Natural Law Theories: Contexts and Strategies in the Early Enlightenment,* 297–317. Edited by Tim Hochstrasser and Peter Schröder. Dordrecht: Kluwer Academic Publishers, 2003.

Stewart, M. A. "George Turnbull and Educational Reform." In *Aberdeen and the Enlightenment,* 95–103. Edited by J. J. Carter and J. H. Pittock. Aberdeen: Aberdeen University Press, 1987.

Sullivan, J. P. *The Satyricon of Petronius: A Literary Study.* Bloomington: Indiana University Press, 1968.

Tuck, Richard. *Natural Rights Theories: Their Origin and Development.* Cambridge: Cambridge University Press, 1979.

———. *The Rights of War and Peace: Political Thought and the International Order from Grotius to Kant.* Oxford: Oxford University Press, 1999.

INDEX

This book is set in Adobe Garamond, a modern adaptation by
Robert Slimbach of the typeface originally cut around 1540 by the
French typographer and printer Claude Garamond. The Garamond
face, with its small lowercase height and restrained contrast between
thick and thin strokes, is a classic "old-style" face and has long been
one of the most influential and widely used typefaces.

Printed on paper that is acid-free and meets the requirements of
the American National Standard for Permanence of Paper for
Printed Library Materials, z39.48-1992. ∞

Book design by Louise OFarrell
Gainesville, Florida
Typography by Apex Publishing, LLC
Madison, Wisconsin
Printed and bound by Worzalla Publishing Company
Stevens Point, Wisconsin